Time Out
San Francisco

Penguin Books

PENGUIN BOOKS

Published by the Penguin Group
Penguin Books Ltd, 27 Wrights Lane, London W8 5TZ, England
Penguin Books USA Inc., 375 Hudson Street, New York, New York 10014, USA
Penguin Books Australia Ltd, Ringwood, Victoria, Australia
Penguin Books Canada Ltd, 10 Alcorn Avenue, Toronto, Ontario, Canada M4V 3B2
Penguin Books (NZ) Ltd, 182-190 Wairau Road, Auckland 10, New Zealand

Penguin Books Ltd, Registered Offices: Harmondsworth, Middlesex, England

First published 1996
Second edition 1998
10 9 8 7 6 5 4 3 2 1

Copyright © Time Out Group Ltd, 1996, 1998
All rights reserved

Colour reprographics by Precise Litho, 34-35 Great Sutton Street, London EC1
Mono reprographics, printed and bound by William Clowes Ltd, Beccles, Suffolk NR34 9QE

Edited and designed by

Time Out Magazine Limited
Universal House
251 Tottenham Court Road
London W1P 0AB
Tel: 0171 813 3000
Fax: 0171 813 6001
E-mail guides@timeout.co.uk
http://www.timeout.co.uk

Editorial

Managing Editor Peter Fiennes
Editor Caroline Taverne
Consultant Editor Colin Berry
Copy Editor Cath Phillips
Researcher Kath Stanton
Indexer Dorothy Frame

Design

Art Director John Oakey
Art Editor Paul Tansley
Designer Mandy Martin
Design assistant Wayne Davies
Picture Editor Catherine Hardcastle
Picture Researcher Michaela Freeman

Advertising

Group Advertisement Director Lesley Gill
Sales Director Mark Phillips
Advertisement Sales (San Francisco) Media Corps

Administration

Publisher Tony Elliott
Managing Director Mike Hardwick
Financial Director Kevin Ellis
Marketing Director Gillian Auld
Production Manager Mark Lamond
Accountant Catherine Bowen

Features in this guide were written and researched by:

Introduction Colin Berry. **History** Colin Berry, Elgy Gillespie. **San Francisco Today** Colin Berry. **Architecture** Colin Berry, Elgy Gillespie. **Literary San Francisco** Colin Berry, Andrew Moss. **San Francisco by Season** Colin Berry, Brad Wieners. **Sightseeing** Colin Berry, Elgy Gillespie, James Pretlove (Urban Stairmaster), Larry Smith (Crusin' the Castro). **Museums & Galleries** Colin Berry, Marty Olmstead. **SF by Neighbourhood** Colin Berry, Shirley Fong-Torres, Ricardo Sandoval, Tessa Souter, Brad Wieners. **Accommodation** Erika Lenkert, Matthew Poole. **Restaurants & Cafés** Colin Berry, Pamela Raley, Ellen Towell. **Bars** Colin Berry, Jennie Ruggles. **Shopping & Services** Susan Lydon, Victoria Maitland-Lewis. **Children** Colin Berry, Elgy Gillespie. **Film** Colin Berry, Robin Stevens. **Gay & Lesbian San Francisco** Sara Miles, Steven Sassaman, Robin Stevens. **Media**, **Music**, **Nightlife** Colin Berry, Larry Smith & Christine Triano (Supper Clubs), Brad Wieners. **Sport & Fitness** Colin Berry, Brad Wieners. **Theatre & Dance** Colin Berry, Robin Stevens. **Trips Out of Town** Victoria Maitland-Lewis, Marty Olmstead. **Directory** Colin Berry, Erika Lenkert, Matthew Poole.

The editors would like to thank Kristin Brown at the San Francisco Convention & Visitors Bureau and Nick Rider.

Map on pages 276-277 by Reineck & Reineck; **maps on pages 278-289** by Mapworld, 71 Blandy Road, Henley-on-Thames, Oxon RG9 1QB; **map on page 290** by JS Graphics, 17 Beadles Lane, Old Oxted, Surrey RH8 9JG.

Photography by Jon Perugia except for: pages 4, 6, 8, 12, 13, 14, 15, 26, 27, 28, 29, 31, 33, 35, 36, 37 **Corbis**; pages 7, 10 **Hulton Getty**; page 9 **AKG London**; page 19 clockwise from top left **Mondino, Warner Bros, Frank Masi/Hollywood Pictures, Authenticolor, Pictorial Press**; pages 20, 78, 176 **Barry J Holmes**; page 70 (top) and page 71 (bottom, right) **San Francisco Art Commission**; page 213 **Jed Jacobsohn/Allsport**; page 247 **Gary Cralle/Image Bank**; page 178 **Warner-Pathe**; pictures on pages 61, 71, 199, 224, 225 were supplied by the featured establishments.

The following photos on pages 70-71 have been reproduced by kind permission of the artists: 'One Tree', 'Extinct', 'Sea Change'.

Contents

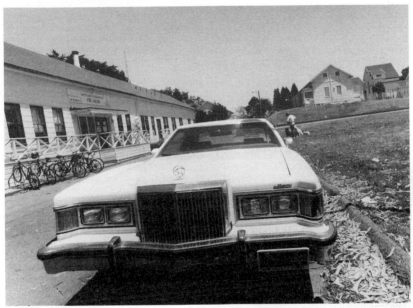

About the Guide

The *Time Out San Francisco Guide* is one of an expanding series of city guides that also includes London, Paris, Amsterdam, Rome, Prague, New York, Los Angeles and Miami. Our hard-working team of resident writers has striven to provide you with all the information you'll need to take on one of America's most exciting and culturally diverse cities. The guide has been completely revised for this second edition, so that we can offer the most up-to-date advice on which sights to see (and which to avoid), where to eat, drink, shop, stay and play in San Francisco. We have also included 'out of town' round-ups for the whole of the Bay Area.

CHECKED AND CORRECT

Above all, we've tried to make this book as useful as possible. Addresses, telephone numbers, transport details, opening times, admission prices and credit card details are all included in our listings. And, as far as possible, we've given details of facilities, services and events, all checked and correct at the time we went to press. But owners and managers can change their arrangements at any time. Before you go out of your way, it's always best to telephone and check opening times, dates of exhibitions, and other details.

ADDRESSES

Apart from the area around Twin Peaks and the outer neighbourhoods, most of San Francisco is laid out on a grid plan, with Market Street bisecting it into north and south segments from the Embarcadero to the Castro. Each block increases its numbering by 100, but we have included cross streets in all our addresses, so you can find your way about more easily. We've also included a fully-indexed colour street map, as well as a map of the Bay Area and the city's transport network at the back of this guide.

Streets have both names and numbers; it's important not to confuse the numerical avenues (to the west) with the streets (which start at the Embarcadero, in the east). It is also worth noting that in the US, what is called the ground floor of a building in the UK, is the first floor, which makes the first floor the second, and so on.

PRICES

The prices we've supplied should be treated as guidelines, not gospel. Fluctuating exchange rates and inflation can cause prices, in shops and restaurants particularly, to change rapidly. If prices vary wildly from those we've quoted, ask

whether there's a good reason. If not, go elsewhere. Then please write and let us know. We aim to give the best and most up-to-date advice, so we always want to know if you've been badly treated or overcharged.

CREDIT CARDS

The following abbreviations have been used for credit cards: **AmEx**: American Express; **DC**: Diners' Club; **JCB**: Japanese credit cards; **MC**: Mastercard (Access); **V**: Visa (Barclaycard). Virtually all shops, restaurants and attractions will accept dollar travellers' cheques issued by a major financial institution (such as American Express).

TELEPHONE NUMBERS

There are three area codes that serve the Bay Area: 415 for San Francisco and Marin County, 510 for Berkeley, Oakland and the East Bay, and 650 for the peninsula cities. All telephone numbers printed in this guide take the 415 code, unless otherwise stated. Numbers preceded by 1-800 can be called free of charge from within the US.

RIGHT TO REPLY

It should be stressed that the information we give is impartial. No organisation has been included in this guide because its owner or manager has advertised in our publications. We hope you enjoy the *Time Out San Francisco Guide*, but we'd also like to know if you don't. We welcome tips for places that you think we should include in future editions and take notice of your criticism of our choices. There's a reader's reply card at the back of this book.

There's an on-line version of this guide, together with weekly events listing for San Francisco and other cities, at http://www.timeout.co.uk.

Introduction

Concealed behind verdant hills or shrouded in a scrim of fog, San Francisco comes as a surprise to the first-time visitor. As you approach it from any direction – emerging from the tunnels before the Golden Gate Bridge from the north and Bay Bridge from the east, rounding the curves on Highways 101 or 1 from the south – the city seems to play hide-and-seek, offering coy glimpses of itself and finally appearing in view quite suddenly – a shimmering, silvery grid perched precariously at the tip of the dark Bay. It has always been that way: the playful, spirited black sheep of American destinations, San Francisco has cultivated a reputation as a city of surprises, a metropolis offering myriad contrasts, incredible plenitude and startling diversity.

San Francisco's native Ohlone forebears understood this, living in harmony with the bountiful land for thousands of years; so did the explorers, trappers, prospectors and immigrants, arriving in succession to exploit the region, understanding that the so-called 'Barbary Coast' was both frisky and risky – a place where anything could happen. Through its twentieth century history as the epicentre for devastating earthquakes and fires, literary and musical movements (from Beat poetry to American punk rock and acid jazz) and wellspring for political and social thought, San Francisco has prided itself on being the place where one can count on finding something different … on being surprised.

This is a city of blaring contrasts and contradictions: one where July and August are chilly, grey and damp while September and October are sunny, hot and dry; one where a district of incredible curved hills butts against a flat and featureless neighbour, where an Irish pub, Russian church and Chinese restaurant can share a single city block; where countless economic, ethnic, architectural, topographical and social extremes peacefully coexist. It's a city where Korean grandmothers gossip in front of murals depicting Latin and Central American history in the Mission, where camera-laden mid-western tourists share their Muni seats with tattooed lesbians and gay men in full leather regalia. Where else would the anachronistic clang of a cable car be overheard on the cell phone conversations of well-suited business people than from downtown San Francisco?

Such diversity and history of tolerance doesn't make for a laid-back city, however. The area is a region of constant change – from the daily advances in digital technology emanating from South Park's 'multimedia gulch' to major banking and commercial decisions unfolding in the Financial District. In the creative realms, the city's Museum of Modern Art, Center for the Arts and hundreds of independent galleries constantly push the envelope of modern design; likewise, the freshest sounds in jazz and rock spill from the doors of its nightclubs. And everyone agrees that some of the finest food, wine and coffee in all the world can be found in San Francisco.

Such a passion for innovation is borne though the city's combination of vibrant history and natural appeal to the restless and adventurous – to those in society who are dissatisfied with the status quo. Perhaps it's the region's geography – literally balanced, as the Ohlone once said, 'on the brink of the world' – that draws those who don't quite fit into 'normal' society: like the city itself, those who come to San Francisco prefer to live on the edge.

Trace the demographics of any particular neighbourhood and you'll find a history of challenge and change. The Mission's slow transformation, for example, from a district of Irish to German, Italian and Latin to – most recently – Asian residents marks but one shift. There are as many other variations as there are neighbourhoods. The Castro is coming to terms with the possibilities of gay life after the Aids epidemic; Bernal Heights is contemplating its pending collar-change from blue to white; as becomes grows more expensive to live in the inner neighbourhoods, the Richmond and Sunset districts are enjoying new commercial opportunities. And South of Market continues to amaze the rest of the city with the success of its artistic, economic and gastronomic ventures. As always, the city is in a state of transformation.

Whether arriving for the first time or returning to San Francisco, the visitor should take comfort in the fact that those who have chosen to live in the city take none of this change for granted: they love the city just as much as you do (or will), and make it part of their everyday existence to enjoy its riches. Whether discovering a dusty volume high on a shelf in a favourite bookshop, enjoying the spine-tingling notes of a saxophone solo in a smoky blues club or spending a beautiful autumn evening traversing a leafy stairway, residents count on the city to reveal something special, something unexpected. They know San Francisco will always reward them with a surprise.
Colin Berry

Welcome to New York.

Now get out.

In Context

Key Events

The Ohlone Age

10,000 BC The Ohlone and Miwok – or 'Costanoan' – Indians begin to settle the Bay Area.

In Search of Eldorado

1542 Juan Cabrillo sails up the California coastline.
1579 Francis Drake lands north of San Francisco Bay, claiming the land he finds for Elizabeth I as New Albion.
1769 Gaspar de Pórtola and Father Junípero Serra lead an expedition overland of 300 men to establish a mission at San Diego. An advance party is sent to scout out the coast and become the first white men to see San Francisco Bay.
1775 The *San Carlos* is the first ship to sail into the Bay.
1776 On 4 July, 13 American colonies declare their independence from Great Britain. In the autumn, a Spanish Presidio is founded near Fort Point and Father Junípero establishes the Mission Dolores to convert the Ohlone to Christianity.

Frontiersmen & Trappers

1821 Mexico declares its independence from Spain and annexes California.
1828 Fur trapper Jedediah Smith becomes the first white man to reach California across the Sierra Nevada range.
1835 William Richardson founds 'Yerba Buena'.
1846 The 'Bear Flag Revolt' against Mexican dominion.
1847 Yerba Buena is renamed San Francisco. It has 800 inhabitants.
1848 US-Mexican treaty confirms American dominion over California.

Gold!

1848 Gold discovered in the low Sierras near Sacramento.
1849 The Gold Rush swells the city's population from 800 to 25,000 in less than a year. On Christmas Eve a huge fire levels the tent city.
1850 California becomes the 31st State of the Union. But lawlessness still rules in San Francisco.
1851 Vigilantes hang four men in Portsmouth Square.
1859 The Comstock Lode is discovered in western

Nevada, triggering the Silver Rush.
1861 Civil War breaks out between the Union and the Confederacy in the US. Being so far west, California remains largely untouched by hostilities.
1868 University of California is established at Berkeley.
1869 The Central Pacific Railroad reaches San Francisco.
1873 Andrew Hallidie builds the first cable cars.

The Great Quake Strikes

1906 The Great Earthquake strikes and the fire that follows razes the city.

Building Bridges

1913 The Los Angeles aqueduct opens.
1915 San Francisco celebrates the opening of the Panama Canal with the Panama-Pacific Exposition.
1932 San Francisco Opera House opens.
1934 On 'Bloody Thursday', police open fire on striking longshoremen, leaving two dead, and prompting a three-day general strike that brings the Bay Area to a standstill.
1936 The Bay Bridge is completed.
1937 The Golden Gate Bridge is completed.
1941 The Japanese attack Pearl Harbour and America enters World War II.
1945 Fifty nations meet at San Francisco Opera House to sign the United Nations Charter.

From the Beats to the Present

1955 Allen Ginsberg reads *Howl* at the Six Gallery, with other members of the Beat Generation cheering him on. The first Disneyland opens in California.
1961 UC Berkeley students stage a sit-in protest against a HUAC meeting at City Hall.
1964 Student sit-ins and mass arrests grow as the Civil Rights, Free Speech and anti-Vietnam War movements gain momentum. John Steinbeck receives the Nobel Prize for literature.
1967 The Human Be-in, organised by Ginsberg, marks the start of San Francisco's Summer of Love. The San Francisco sound is defined by groups like Jefferson Airplane (*pictured*) and the Grateful Dead.
1968 Seventeen year-old Bobby Hutton is killed in a Black Panther shoot-out with Oakland police.
1972 The Bay Area Rapid Transit (BART) system opens.
1978 Gay supervisor Harvey Milk and Mayor George Moscone are killed by former supervisor Dan White. Dianne Feinstein becomes Mayor.
1981 First cases of AIDS are recorded.
1989 An earthquake measuring 7.1 on the Richter scale strikes San Francisco.
1992 Fire sweeps through the Oakland hills killing dozens and destroying 3,000 homes.
1995 San Francisco 49ers win their fifth Super Bowl.
1995 Jerry Garcia, icon of the Grateful Dead, dies. Willie Brown Jr becomes the city's first African-American mayor.
1996 Engineers announce the Bay Bridge needs a $1.3 billion seismic retrofit. Voters approve a $255 million baseball park in the China Basin neighbourhood.
1997 Herb Caen, longtime columnist for the *Chronicle*, dies at 80.

History

From colonisation to counter-cultural revolution.

The Ohlone Age

San Francisco Bay began to take shape through the melting of the last glacial ice sheet a couple of millennia ago. The swelling waters of the Sacramento River and successive earthquakes created what we now call Northern California, giving it roughly the outline it has today. Forty-three prominent hills jostle around two sandy peninsulas that almost meet at either end of the Golden Gate, like a forefinger and thumb crooked around towards each other, and this natural bay protects three islands – Alcatraz, Angel and Yerba Buena.

DANCING ON THE BRINK OF THE WORLD

Until the eighteenth century, the sand-swept, fault-striped peninsulas and surrounding area had scarcely changed in thousands of years. After the Ice Age had scooped out the deep gouge of the Bay and dappled the marshes with reeds and the hilly banks with meadows, the area came to sustain more than 10,000 Northern Californian Indians of different tribes, collectively known as the Costanoans – or 'coast-dwellers' – as they were later dubbed by the Spanish.

The people who inhabited the site of the future San Francisco were the Ohlone. They apparently lived in harmony both with their Miwok neighbours and the land, which provided them with such rich pickings of game, fish, shellfish, fruit and nuts that they were scarcely forced to develop an agriculture. On the contrary, they were able to survive with little effort in a land of 'inexpressible fertility' in the words of a later French explorer.

Protected by the Bay's seeming inaccessibility, the Ohlone and their neighbours lived a successful hunter-gatherer existence – 'dancing on the brink of the world,' so an Ohlone song went – until their disastrous introduction to 'civilisation' with the arrival of Spanish missionaries. Up to this moment, their rare contacts with Europeans had been friendly. In fact, visiting Europeans had been impressed by the welcome the Costanoans afforded them. But the Spanish brought with them the dubious gifts of God, hard labour in the fields and diseases like smallpox, which would all but annihilate the tribes in a matter of 200 years.

The destruction of their culture has been largely ignored because the Ohlone and other tribes had no tradition of recording their history, orally or otherwise. Indeed, in Ohlone culture it was considered impolite to mention the past, the dead or your ancestors. Malcolm Margolin's *The Ohlone Way* is an attempt to trace the lost culture of Northern Californian Indians; today the only surviving traces of the Costanoans feature in the records of their colonisers and destroyers.

In Search of El Dorado

Looking at the Golden Gate Bridge today, it's hard to imagine how anyone could miss the mile-wide opening into a bay that was twice as large back then as it is now. The Bay and its Indians were hidden from view by 'stynkinge fogges' (as Drake later complained) and a lush green island.

COLONISING CALIFORNIA

A series of Spanish missions sent up the coast by Hernán Cortés, notorious conqueror of Mexico and the Aztecs, never got as far as Upper California. In 1542, under the flag of Cortés' successor Antonio de Mendoza, Portuguese Juan Cabrillo became the first European to visit the area. The Spanish named their new-found land El Dorado, after a mythical island in an ancient book, and hoped they would find gold here as they had done further south. Yet, though he passed it both on his way north and back again, Cabrillo failed to discover the Bay's large natural harbour.

An Englishman got even closer, yet still managed to miss it. In 1579, during a foraging and spoiling mission in the name of the Virgin Queen Elizabeth, the then-unknighted Francis Drake landed in Miwok Indian territory just north of the Bay. With one ship, the *Golden Hind*, and a crew in dire need of rest and recreation, he put in for a six-week berth somewhere along the Marin coastline, probably near Point Reyes. Long before the Pilgrims landed at Plymouth Rock or the English settled Cupid's Cove at Newfoundland, Drake claimed California for Queen Elizabeth I, naming it 'Nova Albion' or 'New Britain'.

It would take another 190 years for a white man to set eyes on the Bay. Spurred on by the pressure of British colonial ambitions in America, the Spanish sent northbound missions to stake out their own territories, intent upon converting the 'bestias' and claiming land for the Spanish crown. In 1769, the 'Sacred Expedition' of Gaspar de Pórtola, a Spanish aristocrat who would become the first governor of California, and the Franciscan priest Father Junípero Serra, set off with 300 men

Two views of Kit Carson (1809-1868): scout, frontiersman and trapper.

on a gruelling march across the Mexican desert to establish a mission at San Diego. The expedition then worked its way north to Monterey, to claim it for Spain, building missions and baptising the Indians as they went. During the expedition, an advance party discovered the unexpectedly wide bay 100 miles further up the coast, but since the expedition's brief was only to claim Monterey, the party returned to San Diego.

It was not until August 1775 that the *San Carlos*, the Spanish supply vessel under command of Juan Manuel de Ayala, docked inside the Bay. Meanwhile, a mission under Juan Bautista de Anza and Father Pedro Font set off to establish a safer land route to what would eventually become San Francisco.

MISSION ACCOMPLISHED

Roughly concurrent with the signing of the American Declaration of Independence, a Spanish military presidio, or garrison, was begun near Fort Point to strengthen Spain's western claims. It was completed on 17 September 1776. The Mission San Francisco de Asis, named after the holy order operating in Upper California, but popularly known as Mission Dolores, was established by Father Junípero Serra on 9 October 1776.

Father Serra's Mission was catastrophic for the Ohlone and their fellow tribes. Intrigued by the curious ways of the strangers , the 'bestias' were easily led into harsh servitude at the Mission, where their numbers were savagely reduced by illness and hard labour in the fields.

Frontiersmen & Trappers

Just as elsewhere in Latin America, the combination of favouritism, authoritarianism and religious fervour helped sow seeds of resentment and resistance in all the territories colonised by Spain. The country's hold on its American empires first began to crumble in Mexico, which declared itself a republic in 1821. The Mexican annexation of California in the same year opened up the area to foreign settlers, among them American pioneers like fur trapper Jedediah Smith, who in 1828 became the first white American to reach California over the Sierra Nevada mountain range. His feat might have been the more impressive, but the sedate arrival, by whaler ship, of an Englishman had a more lasting impact. Captain William Richardson, who built the first dwelling on the site of the future San Francisco in 1835, is credited with giving San Francisco its first name: Yerba Buena, named after the sweet mint the Spanish used to make tea.

That same year the United States tried unsuccessfully to buy the whole Bay Area from the Mexicans, but in the long run they got California for free: the Texan declaration of independence, and its consequent annexation by the United States triggered the Mexican-American war in June 1846. The resulting Guadalupe-Hidalgo Treaty of 1848 officially granted the Union all the land from Texas to California, and the Rio Grande to Oregon. But before the treaty could be nailed down, a few American hotheads decided to 'liberate' the territory from Mexico themselves.

THE BEAR FLAG REVOLT

The short-lived Mexican rule of California coincided with the era of idealistic frontiersmen like Captain John Fremont and Kit Carson. In June 1846, Fremont convinced a motley crew to take over the abandoned Presidio to the north of the Yerba Buena in Sonoma, proclaiming his new state The Bear Flag Republic after the ragged bear flag he raised over Sonoma's adobe square (the design was eventually adopted as California's state flag). Fremont also christened the mouth of San Francisco Bay the 'Golden Gate', after Istanbul's Golden Horn, insisting it would some day become glorious. A few weeks after the Bear Flaggers annexed Sonoma, the US Navy captured Yerba Buena's Presidio without a struggle, and the whole of California became US territory.

At this point, the infant Yerba Buena was just a sleepy trading post of 800 people. On 30 January 1847, the newly appointed mayor, Lieutenant Washington A Bartlett, officially renamed it 'San Francisco'. Unbeknown to its residents, the tiny settlement was about to change beyond all recognition: something gold was glittering in the hills...

Gold!

In the early 1840s, the Swiss-born John Sutter was running New Helvetia, a large ranch, as though it were his own dukedom. With the consent of the Mexican Governor of California, he encouraged American citizens to settle the land. One of his homesteaders was James Marshall, who built a sawmill for his landlord at Coloma, near Sacramento. Returning from the Bear Flaggers' adventure, Marshall discovered gold in the sawmill's water. Sutter and Marshall attempted to keep their findings secret, but word got out. Once the news hit town, 'boosters' – the San Francisco equivalent of town criers – and newspapermen quickly spread it around the world. The 1849 Gold Rush was on.

CALIFORNIA OR BUST

The news of riches brought drifters and fortune-seekers to California. Some sailed around Cape Horn in windjammers, sloops and steamships, some trekked across Panama, others crossed prairies from the east in covered wagons. Their fever was fanned by people like Sam Brannan, whose *California Star* newspaper told of men extracting fortunes within an hour, and who marched down Market Street with a jar of gold dust, shouting: 'Gold! Gold!', but many potential prospectors never made it. By land, the journey meant months of exposure to blizzards, mountains, deserts and hostile Indians; by sea, they faced disease, starvation or brutal weather.

Those who made it became known as Forty-Niners. The port town they arrived in was one

without structure, government, or even a distinct name – to many it was still 'Yerba Buena'. They found hardship more than gold: on their way through San Francisco to the mines, predatory merchants fleeced them; when they returned, broke, they were left to grub mean existences from the city streets, seeking refuge in brothels, gambling dens and bars. Within a year of the Sutter discovery, 100,000 men had passed through the city, swelling the tiny community into a giant, muddy campsite. A huge fire levelled the settlement on Christmas Eve in 1849, but a new camp quickly rose up to take its place. The population leapt from 800 to 25,000, with a transient population four times as large.

DUCKS, HOUNDS AND HOODLUMS

San Francisco at the time of the Gold Rush was not a place for the faint-hearted. Lawlessness and arson ruled. Writers Mark Twain and Bret Harte, and, later, visitors Robert Louis Stevenson, Oscar Wilde and Anthony Trollope all reported on its exciting, if lurid reputation, describing an anarchic boom town where guns, violence, gambling and prostitution were commonplace.

The opening of the post office marked the city's first optimistic stab at improving communications with the rest of the continent and the world. John White Geary, appointed postmaster by President James Knox Polk, rented a room at the corner of Montgomery and Washington Streets, where he marked out a series of squares for each letter of the alphabet and began filing letters. This crude set-up

Panning for gold in the low Sierras.

was the first postal system for San Francisco's 10,000 residents. In April 1850 – the year California became the Union's 31st state – San Francisco's city charter was approved and the city elected Geary its first mayor. In order to furnish the city with proper streets, Geary established a council, which later bought the brig *Euphemia* and turned it into San Francisco's first jail. It proved a sound investment.

The council's first concern was to impose law and order on San Francisco's massive squatter town. Vicious hoodlums controlled certain districts: the Ducks, led by Australian convicts, lived at a spot known as Sydney Town. Together with New York toughs the Hounds, they roamed Telegraph Hill, raping and pillaging among the more orderly community of Chilean merchants who occupied 'Little Chile'. Eventually, their outrages incurred the wrath of right-minded citizens who decided to take the law into their own hands. Whipped into a fury by rabble-rousing newspaperman Sam Brannan, vigilantes lynched their first victim, John Jenkins, at a Portsmouth Square 'necktie party' in June 1851. They strung up three more thieves during the following weeks by way of warning to the other Ducks and Hounds – who cut out for the Sierras.

Though their frontier justice temporarily curbed the area's excesses, Mayor Geary viewed the vigilantes as part of the problem, not the solution; his crusade against lawlessness was hardly helped when the riverbed gold started running dry. By 1853, boom had turned to bust, and the resulting depression set a cyclical pattern oft-repeated through the city's history. By the mid-1860s, San Francisco was bankrupt.

NOBS AND SNOBS

But then came the Silver Rush. Henry Comstock's 1859 discovery of a rich blue vein of silver (the 'Comstock Lode') in western Nevada triggered a second invasion by fortune-seekers. This time,

The view from Telegraph Hill in the 1860s.

though, the ore's nature demanded more elaborate methods of extraction, with high yields going to a small number of companies and tycoons rather than individual prospectors. Before the supply had been exhausted, silver barons had made enough money to transform San Francisco, establishing a quarter of *nouveaux riches* mansions atop Nob Hill. By 1870, the city was no longer just a town of seething brothels.

If the nobs on the hill took the moral and geographical high ground, those on the waterfront at the bottom of Telegraph Hill were busy legitimising their reputation as occupants of the 'Barbary Coast'. Naïve newcomers and drunken sailors were viewed as fair game by the gamblers and hoods waiting to 'shanghai' them (like 'hoodlum,' 'shanghai' is a San Francisco expression), as were immigrant girls who found themselves trapped into a life of prostitution or slavery. At one low point, the female population numbered just 22; the mere sight of a woman could reduce the city's roughnecks to a state of silent awe. Many a brothel madam made fortune enough to buy her way onto Nob Hill.

WIND FROM THE EAST

The seed of San Francisco's present-day multiculturalism were sown in this period, when a deluge of immigrants providing food, goods and services poured in from all over the world. French immigrants vying with Italians for the 'best bread' vote in North Beach started baking sourdough. A young German garment maker named Levi Strauss used rivets to strengthen the jeans he made for miners. In Chinatown, the Tong family controlled the opium dens and other rackets; another Chinese immigrant, Wah Lee, opened the city's first laundry.

Chinatown later expanded with the coming of the transcontinental railroad, which employed thousands of Chinese labourers at criminally low pay rates. Ironically, despite their usefulness as a cheap source of labour, the Chinese became the targets of racist anti-immigrant activity. Proscriptive anti-Chinese legislation would persist until 1938.

Entertainment was always high on the agenda for San Franciscans. In 1853, the city boasted five theatres and some 600 saloons and taverns serving 42,000 customers. Citizens downed seven bottles of champagne for every bottle swallowed in Boston. When Lola Montez, entertainer to European monarchs and thieves, arrived on a paddle-steamer from Panama in 1853, her 'Spider Dance' became an instant hit at the American Theater.

COME WEST, YOUNG MAN

San Francisco's relative isolation from the rest of the continent meant the city was hardly affected by the Civil War that devastated the South in the early 1860s. The rest of the country seemed remote;

Chinatown began to expand with the arrival of the transcontinental railroad.

sometimes mail took six months to arrive. Communications were slowly improving, however. Telegraph wires were gradually being strung across the continent, and where the telegraph poles ran out, the Pony Express would pick up messages, relaying up to 75 despatch riders across the West to the Pacific Coast. But by the mid-1860s, the telegraph had all but rendered the Pony Express obsolete, and its *coup de grâce* was provided by the coming of the transcontinental railroad.

The completion of the Central Pacific Railroad in 1869 was the signal for runaway consumption in the city. The biggest spenders were the 'Big Four', the mighty millionaires who were the powerful and influential principal investors behind the Central Pacific – Charles Crocker, Collis P Huntington, Mark Hopkins and Leland Stanford. Their eagerness to impress the West with their flamboyantly successful business practices manifested itself in the mansions they built on Nob Hill.

The Big Four were highly adept at making money for themselves and their favoured partners. They were brutally competitive, too. By 1871, 121 businessmen controlled $146 million, according to one newspaper – but others got in on their act. Four legendary Irishmen – James Flood, William O'Brien, James Fair and John W Mackay – were rough-hewn miners and barmen who'd chipped their fortunes from the silver Comstock Lode. The Bonanza Kings, as they were known, also had money enough to buy their way onto Nob Hill.

A Scottish-Irish banker, Billy Ralston, opened the Bank of California on Sansome Street in 1864. Partnered by a Prussian engineer called Adolph Sutro (later famous for the first Cliff House and the Sutro Baths), the industrialist was determined to extract every last ounce of silver from Sun Mountain. Unfortunately, the precious ore ran out

before he and Sutro had recouped their investment, and Ralston's bank collapsed. Smiling to the last in an effort to calm his investors, Ralston was later found drowned. He left behind the luxurious Palace Hotel and a lasting contribution towards the development of the symbol of San Francisco's new civic pride – Golden Gate Park. Ralston's company provided the water for designer William Hammon Hall's audacious project, which ultimately transformed the sand dunes of the 'Outside Lands' into 1,013 magnificent acres of trees, plants, flowers and lakes.

The Great Quake Strikes

The city continued to grow, and by 1900 its population had reached more than a third of a million, making it the ninth largest city in the Union. But on 18 April 1906, shortly after 5am, dogs began howling and horses whinnying – noises, along with glasses tinkling and windows rattling, that marked the few tense and unnerving seconds before an earthquake.

WHOSE FAULT?

The quake hit: a rending in the tectonic plates 25 miles (40 kilometres) beneath the ocean bed that triggered the shifting of billions of tons of rock, generating more energy than all the explosives used in World War II. The rip snaked inland, tearing a gash now known as the San Andreas Fault down the coastline. Cliffs appeared from nowhere, cracks yawned, ancient redwoods toppled and the dome of the 29 year-old City Hall collapsed like a soufflé. Streets began to undulate and church bells pealed crazily. A second tremor struck, ripping the walls out of buildings. A ghastly pause followed, then people ran into the streets, some in nightgowns or pyjamas, or less.

A Union Pacific construction train, taken the year before the railroad was completed.

Tragically, one of the earthquake's many victims was a man the city badly needed just then: Fire Chief Dennis Sullivan, who was not long back from fighting a cannery fire when the earthquake struck. He was found in the rubble of the firehouse and died some days later. The fire brigade seemed lost without him. The second tremor had destroyed the city alarms and disrupted the water pipes feeding the fire hydrants, leaving the famous firefighters of the West absolutely helpless.

The fire that followed compounded the disaster of the earthquake. It spread until Mayor Eugene Schmitz and General Frederick Funston were forced to carry out a desperate plan to blow up the houses along Van Ness Avenue to create a fire-break. The mansions belonged to rich folk that any politician would be loathe to alienate; in this instance, however, necessity spoke louder than money.

RISING FROM THE ASHES

The earthquake and 74-hour inferno was initially thought to have accounted for some 700 dead, though military records now reveal that the figure probably ran into several thousand. Those suspected of looting were shot dead in the chaos that followed the quake and fire. Three-quarters of a million people were left homeless and 3,000 acres of buildings were destroyed. On the third day the wind changed direction and brought rain, and by 21 April the fire was out.

Yet even before the ashes had time to cool, the citizens set about rebuilding their city, and within 10 years San Francisco had risen from the ashes. Some claimed that in the rush to rebuild, city planners passed up the chance to replace its street grid system with a more sensible one that followed the natural contours of the area. But there's no doubt that San Francisco was reborn as a cleaner, more attractive city and one that, within three years of the fire, could boast half of the United States' concrete and steel buildings. Such statistical pride was not out of keeping with the 'boosterism' that accelerated its post-gold rush growth from tiny settlement to the large, anarchic and exciting city now ready to meet the twentieth century head on.

Building Bridges

The San Franciscans set about rebuilding their city with a vengeance. The most potent symbol of their restored civic pride was the new City Hall, whose construction secured an $8 million city bond. By the time it was completed in 1915, City Hall rose some 16 feet (5 metres) higher than its model – the Capitol building in Washington DC.

Between 1913 and 1915, two new waterways opened, which proved crucial to California's economic vitality. In 1913, the Los Angeles aqueduct was completed, beginning the transformation of a sleepy cowtown into the urban sprawl of modern LA. In 1915, the Panama Canal's opening considerably shortened shipping times between the Atlantic and Pacific coasts; San Francisco celebrated this achievement by hosting the Panama-Pacific Exposition.

Not even the outbreak of World War I in Europe could dampen the city's spirits. On the contrary, the war provided a boost to California's mining and manufacturing industries. But, as elsewhere in America, the good times were quickly swallowed up in the world depression signalled by the Wall Street Crash of 1929.

BLOODY THURSDAY

The Depression brought to an end the economic well-being of the 1920s. It hit San Francisco port especially badly – three-quarters of the workforce was laid off. On 9 May 1934, under the leadership of Harry Bridges, the International Longshoremen's Association declared a coast-wide strike. Other unions, including the powerful Teamsters, came out in sympathy, shutting down work in the Bay for three months. A crew of black-leg workers managed to break the picket on 5 July – Bloody Thursday – but with disastrous results. As violence escalated, police opened fire, killing two strikers and wounding 30. A general strike was called for 14 July, when 150,000 people stopped work and brought San Francisco to a standstill for three days, but it fizzled out when its leaders couldn't agree on how to end the stalemate. But the action wasn't completely futile: the longshoremen won a wage increase and more control in the hiring halls.

BRIDGING THE BAY

Despite this black chapter in the city's labour relations, San Francisco managed an extraordinary amount of construction. In 1932, the San Francisco Opera House was completed; in 1933, the island of Alcatraz was transferred from the army to the Federal Bureau of Prisons, which set about building a high-security lock-up for 'incorrigible' convicts.

The decade's two other landmark constructions were the San Francisco-Oakland Bay and Golden Gate bridges. The former, completed in 1936, constituted two back-to-back suspension bridges connected by a tunnel though Yerba Buena Island. Six months after the Bay Bridge was finished, the russet-orange Golden Gate Bridge began to rise from the Bay with its revolutionary, gusset-ribbed suspension design. The bridges' impact on ferry traffic that had served the city and its suburbs so well was devastating, and commuter trains also suffered – at least until the completion of the Bay Area Rapid Transit (BART) subway system in 1972.

To celebrate the new era ushered in by the opening of bridges, the city hosted another fair in 1939,

Merry Prankster and Beat saint, Neal Cassady.

on landfill off Yerba Buena Island. The Treasure Island Golden Gate International Exposition was described as a 'Pageant of the Pacific'; those who went were dubbed the Thirty-Niners by local wits. It was to be San Francisco's last big celebration for a while: in 1941 the Japanese attacked Pearl Harbour and America entered into World War II.

THE FORTUNES OF WAR

World War II changed the city almost as much as the Gold Rush or the Great Quake. More than a million-and-a-half men and thousands of tons of material were shipped out to the Pacific from the Presidio, Travis Air Force Base and Treasure Island. Between 1941 and 1945, almost the entire Pacific war effort passed under the Golden Gate. Oakland's shipyard workers worked overtime, and the massed ranks of troops and some half-million wartime civilian workers flooding San Francisco turned the city into a milling party town hell-bent on sending its boys into battle with smiles on their faces.

Towards the end of the war in Europe, in April 1945, representatives of 50 nations met at the San Francisco Opera House to draft the United Nations Charter. It was eventually signed on 26 June 1945 and formally ratified in October at the General Organisation of the United Nations in London. Many people felt – and still do – that San Francisco was the ideal location for the UN headquarters, but the British and French thought it was too far to travel, and – much to the city's disappointment – the headquarters moved to New York.

From the Beats to the Present

Just as San Francisco during the war was characterised by mass troop mobilisation, the immediate post-war period was coloured by the return of the demobilised GIs. One was poet Lawrence Ferlinghetti, who, while studying at the Sorbonne on a GI scholarship in the early 1950s, discovered Penguin paperbacks and was inspired to open his tiny wedge-shaped bookshop at 261 Columbus Avenue. Called City Lights, it became a mecca for the bohemians later dubbed the Beat Generation, many of whose works he published in the City Lights Pocket Poets series.

BEAT BUT NOT BEATEN

The Beat Generation, so named by novelist Jack Kerouac, reflected the angst and ambition of a post-war generation attempting to escape both the shadow of the Bomb and the rampant consumerism of ultra-conformist 1950s America. In Kerouac's definition, Beat could stand for beatific or being beat – exhausted. The condition is best explained in his novel *On the Road*, which charts the coast-to-coast odysseys of San Francisco-based Beat saint Neal Cassady (thinly disguised as Dean Moriarty), poet Allen Ginsberg and Kerouac himself (named Sal Paradise).

'The emergence of the Beat Generation made North Beach the literary centre of San Francisco – and it nurtured a new vision that would spread far beyond its bounds,' reflected poet Lawrence Ferlinghetti, 40 years on. 'The Beats prefigured the New Left evolution and the impulse for change that swept eastward from San Francisco.' The attention of the world might have been on the beret-clad artists and poets populating North Beach cafés (*see chapter* **Literary San Francisco**), but an event 500 miles (800 kilometres) south was perhaps more truly reflective of mainstream America: Disney's first theme park, Disneyland, opened in Anaheim in 1955.

SUMMER OF LOVE AND HAIGHT

Kerouac, Ginsberg and mass media exposure established the Bay Area as a centre for the burgeoning counter-culture, renewing American suspicions that San Francisco was the fruit and nut capital of the US. Their fears were about to be confirmed by the hippie explosion of the 1960s.

The Beats and the hippies might have shared a love of marijuana and a common distaste for 'the system', but the Beats sometimes mocked their juniors as part-time bohemians. For his part, Kerouac – by now an embittered alcoholic – abhorred what he perceived as the hippies' anti-Americanism. His distaste for these new bohemians was shared by John Steinbeck, winner of the Nobel Prize for Literature in 1964, who shied away from the recognition he was receiving in the streets.

Where the Beats were never interested in political action, the newer generation were prepared to embrace it full on. A sit-in protest against a closed session of the House of Representatives Un-American Activities Committee at the City Hall in 1961 drew ranks of protesters from San Francisco State University and Berkeley's University of California. It quickly degenerated into a riot, establishing a pattern of protest and police response to come. In the following years, the civil rights movement and America's involvement in the Vietnam War added urgency to the voices of dissent; Berkeley students were at the forefront of protests on campuses around the country. By the mid-1960s, the counter-culture was split between the politically conscious students behind the Free Speech movement and the hippies who'd chosen to opt out of the system altogether.

The spreading popularity of LSD, boosted in San Francisco by such events as the Human Be-in organised by Allen Ginsberg in 1967, and the Acid Tests overseen by Owsley Stanley and the Grateful Dead, drew an estimated 8,000 hippies from across America. Some 5,000 of them stayed, occupying the cheap Victorian houses round the Haight-Ashbury district (later dubbed 'the Hashbury') not far from Golden Gate Park. The combination of San Francisco's *laissez-faire* attitude, sun, drugs and the acid-induced psychedelic music explosion produced the famous Summer of Love that year. By 1968, however, the spread of hard drugs, notably heroin, had taken the shine off the hippie movement.

BLACK PANTHERS & THE PUBLISHER'S DAUGHTER

The politics were getting harder, too. Members of the Black Panther movement, a radical black organisation founded across the Bay in Oakland by Huey Newton and Bobby Seale, asked themselves why they should ship out to Vietnam and shoot Southeast Asians when the real enemy was at home. Around Oakland, the Panthers took to exercising the American right to bear arms; gunfights inevitably followed. In April 1968, Panther leader Eldridge Cleaver was wounded and 17 year-old Bobby Hutton was killed in a shoot-out with Oakland police. By the early 1970s, the Black Panther movement had petered out, its leaders either dead, imprisoned or, like Cleaver, on the run. The 1997 release of Panther Geronimo Pratt may herald a re-examination of some of the Panthers' alleged crimes.

The kidnapping of the Hearst newspaper empire's heir Patty by the tiny radical outfit the Symbionese Liberation Army in 1974 was perhaps the point where the 1960s revolution turned to deadly farce. Hearst was eventually captured, along with the SLA, after apparently being brainwashed into joining their cause.

Despite the violence that characterised the student and anti-war protests, black radicalism and failed revolutions, the enduring memory of 1960s' San Francisco is as the host city to the Summer of Love. The psychedelic blasts of the Grateful Dead, Big Brother and the Holding Company, Janis

The candle-lit vigil held outside City Hall after the murder of Mayor Moscone and Harvey Milk.

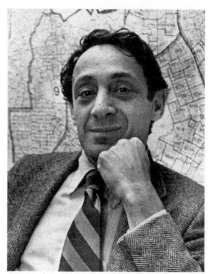

Harvey Milk, shortly after his election.

Governor of California in the early 1970s.

Joplin, Country Joe and the Fish, Jefferson Airplane and Quicksilver Messenger Service defined both the San Francisco sound and counter-cultural attitude. Jann Wenner founded *Rolling Stone* magazine in 1967 to explain and advance the cause, and later document its growth into a multi-million dollar mass entertainment industry, helping to invent New Journalism in the process.

THE KILLING OF HARVEY MILK

San Francisco's radical baton was taken up in the 1970s by the Gay Liberation Movement. Local activists insisted that gay traditions had always existed in San Francisco, first among the Ohlone Indians, and later during the 1849 Gold Rush, when women in the West were scarcer than gold. Early homophile groups like the Daughters of Bilitis, the Mattachine Society and the Society for Individual Rights (SIR) had paved the way for more radical political movements in the 1970s. In 1977, gay activists made successful forays into mainstream politics. SIR's Jim Foster became the first openly gay delegate at a Democratic Convention; Harvey Milk was elected onto the city's Board of Supervisors.

Then, on 28 November 1978, Dan White, a former supervisor, entered City Hall and shot and killed Milk and Mayor George Moscone. White was a former policeman from an Irish Catholic working-class background, who had run for supervisor as an angry, young, blue-collar populist – and won. But he suffered poor mental health and had to resign under the strain of office. He quickly changed his mind and asked Mayor Moscone to reinstate him. But Milk, who held the deciding vote, persuaded the Mayor not to let the unstable White back in – with catastrophic consequences. White turned himself in after the killings. In the subsequent poorly prosecuted court case, the jury returned two verdicts of voluntary manslaughter and White was sentenced to seven years.

As the killings had stunned San Francisco, so the verdict outraged its gay populace. Gays responded by storming City Hall and hurling rocks through its windows. The disturbance escalated into a full-blown battle, known as the White Night Riot. White's sentence prompted a journalist to wonder jokingly why the jury had not posthumously convicted the slain Milk of 'unlawful interference with a bullet fired from the gun of a former police officer'. White committed suicide not long after his release from prison.

THE AIDS CURSE

Gay life and politics changed radically and irrevocably with the onset of the HIV virus which tore the gay community apart and initially caused controversy when the bath houses – symbol of gay liberation and promiscuity – were closed in panic over the disease's spread. Gay radicals branded activist Randy Shilts a 'fascist Nazi, traitor and homophobe' when he ran a story in the *San Francisco Chronicle* criticising bath house owners who refused to post safe sex warnings.

To date, there have been nearly 17,000 Aids-related deaths in San Francisco. Though levelling

HIV numbers and the dangerous misperception that the epidemic is ebbing have endangered fundraising efforts of late, the city remains home to the most efficient volunteer activists in the country. Caretakers have taken charge of housing, food and legal problems for many thousands of people diagnosed as HIV-positive. Hospices, support agencies, hotlines, pet services – San Francisco cares deeply about its HIV-positive patients. And as those living with HIV are living longer, the city continues to need more resources and money to assist them.

STRIKE TWO

Because of its location on the San Andreas Fault, San Francisco has always lived in expectation of a major earthquake to rival the 1906 disaster. One came in October 1989, while Oakland was playing the San Francisco Giants during the Baseball World Series. The Loma Prieta earthquake (named after the ridge of mountains at its epicentre) hit 7.1 on the Richter Scale in the middle of the play-offs. A section of the West Oakland Freeway collapsed, crushing drivers beneath the concrete and arousing fears that hundreds more had been killed. The Marina district and Bay Bridge were hit hard, but in the final count, damage was relatively slight and the number of deaths was less than 70, though nearly 4,000 people were injured. Far worse than the damage itself, from the survivors' point of view, was the incompetence of the city's rebuilding programme,

which compared unfavourably with the clean-up following the LA earthquake of 1987.

TOWARDS 2000

As it approaches the new millennium, San Francisco suffers the same social problems that blight many major US cities in the wake of the economic and welfare cutbacks exercised by President Ronald Reagan's administration in the 1980s. Homelessness is particularly severe in the city. More than 12,000 destitute men and women overwhelm the 44 under-funded downtown agencies set up to help them. Roughly a fifth of these are former institutional inmates, homeless since Reagan – when Governor of California – emptied the mental hospitals. Others have drink problems or are drug users, but some are simply those who fell behind with the rent.

On a more positive note, the city remains a magnet for the world's economic migrants dreaming of a better life. With an Asian community that makes up one-fifth of its population, San Francisco is set to remain the US's most Asian city at the turn of the century, and the Hispanic community is almost as large. Immigrants from Russia and Eastern Europe pour in at the rate of 1,000 or more each month, and Americans, too, continue to flock to the city where it's still possible to reinvent yourself. Multicultural San Francisco continues to function as a crucible for new trends and influences as it looks forward to a new century of 'dancing on the brink of the world'.

An apartment block in the Marina district, brought to its knees by the 1989 earthquake.

San Francisco Today

Part big city, part small town, San Francisco maintains its lure as the black sheep of American destinations.

At the end of the twentieth century, San Francisco represents an odd set of contradictions – savvy and urbane in many ways, naïve and unpolished in others.

Liberal politics remain at the heart of City Hall, with each mayor wrestling to establish his or her own legacy. Art Agnos, who succeeded popular Dianne Feinstein in 1987, found himself saddled with the task of restoring the city's lustre and confidence in the wake of the 1989 quake. Though it's not clear that anyone could have done the job satisfactorily, voters lost confidence in him and Agnos only lasted for one term. Former police chief Frank Jordan served as mayor from 1992 to 1995 and is best remembered as the moderate conservative who did little of anything during his term. He did fire his own police chief, Dick Hongisto, in the wake of the 1992 Rodney King riots for stealing copies of the *Bay Times* after the weekly published an unflattering photo collage of the chief. Jordan lost his 1995 re-election bid to Willie Brown Jr, a local politico squeezed from his machiavellian post as Speaker of the California State Assembly by recently repealed laws limiting terms in office.

HERE COMES DA MAYOR

Though his methods smack of old-school politics based on influence and favouritism, Mayor Brown (nicknamed 'Da Mayor') is, to his credit, seems able to inspire coalitions within the city to get things done. He has bullied Muni into relative reliability and made a start on addressing the city's homeless problem. He's a loud-mouthed advocate for students, workers and gays and has been lobbying for San Francisco to host the summer Olympic Games in 2008. As an African-American politician, Brown has given minorities a strong voice in local government, and counts on black voters to support his ideas. He's audacious, obnoxious, irritating – and outlandishly well-dressed. Brown is also a seasoned palm-presser who can wheel and deal when he needs to: a regular in Washington DC, he campaigned for a 1997 nationwide mayors' council that proved a public-relations coup for the city.

GRIDLOCK

But he's governing a metropolis with problems typical of the modern age, and high on the list of concerns is that of traffic. It took nearly ten years to dismantle the freeways crippled by the 1989 Loma Prieta earthquake, the physical results of which are spectacular: a two-mile pedestrian promenade along the Embarcadero is no longer crowded by the greyed perimeter of the highway. Those on foot can enjoy unobstructed views of the Bay, Bay Bridge and Berkeley in one direction and a sweeping vista of the Financial District in the other. Hayes Valley, a neighbourhood once shadowy with concrete overpasses, is now drenched in sunlight (on those rare non-foggy days) and packed with upmarket new shops.

For drivers, however, the missing freeways mean that traffic on and off the still-existing viaducts is painfully impacted. A simple hop across town now constitutes a frustrating hour stuck in stop-and-go traffic. Once on the grid, anyone behind the wheel in San Francisco is daunted by street and lane closures, road construction, double-parked delivery trucks and the all-too-frequent red light runner. Finding a parking space can be as frustrating. The Board of Supervisors and Da Mayor remain at odds over the fate of the existing Central Freeway, but it seems unlikely that anything will prove a quick panacea to the city's gridlock problems.

TO BUILD OR NOT TO BUILD?

Sports stadiums are another problematic subject. For years San Franciscans regularly rejected proposals for a new baseball arena, until 1996 when Brown threw his weight behind a $255 million, 42,000-seat ballpark proposed for China Basin. Despite warnings about earthquakes, wind and the omnipresent lack of parking, voters approved the site, which is scheduled to open in 2000. Brown was evidently warming up for his big battle however, one that found him allied with San Francisco 49ers owner Eddie DeBartolo and a development company with a plan for converting the ageing 3Com (Candlestick) Park football field into a new $525 million mall, restaurant, shopping and sports complex.

Martini hour at Skylark. The city plans to celebrate the millennium with a decadent party.

Muni's latest addition, the historic trolley line F-Market, made up of 1930s streetcars.

Amid accusations of election fraud and influence peddling, the controversial measure was passed by a hairline margin in 1997, backed by a coalition of Brown's supporters who believe their neighbourhoods – Hunter's Point and Bay View – stand to profit from jobs created by the stadium's construction. Results from the divisive proposal (in which pro-development forces outspent opponents by 20 to 1) won't be evident for a few years; the new arena itself won't open until after the millennium. Many residents, however, feel that pro sports teams in San Francisco should earn their own keep, and that the city's coffers would be better spent on more pressing problems.

URBAN AILMENTS

And there are plenty. Other concerns within the city include the fate of the Bay Bridge, whose retrofitting – the ubiquitous term for making a construction earthquake-safe – threatens to cost as much as building a new structure altogether. New designs have been drawn up. The MH de Young museum also faces an uncertain future, since the building needs a new parking structure and a seismic upgrade in order to fulfil insurance requirements for its blockbuster exhibitions. Plans are under way to move the de Young from its present location in Golden Gate Park.

The Aids epidemic continues apace, and though new drug treatments mean patients are living longer, they also require additional funding at a time when charities – including the San Francisco Aids Foundation and Project Open Hand – are facing budget cuts. For local non profit-making outfits, money has become harder to get, at a time when the (misinformed) word on the street is that the Aids crisis is over.

Homelessness too remains a serious problem. High housing costs, illicit drug and alcohol abuse, the implosion of traditional family structures, the demise, two decades ago, of the state's mental health institutions under governor Ronald Reagan, not to mention the city's spirit of tolerance and mild climate – all contribute to the increasing problem.

Various remedies have been mooted: the conversion of the Presidio from military to civilian use has spurred some to advocate recommissioning the 1,400-acre site as a fresh starting place for low-income families and the homeless. Others suggest utilising Treasure Island (also returning to civilian management) for public housing. But these ideas clash with conservationists angrily advocating the return of prime National Park land to its original use; solve this problem within existing city space, they say. To date, these issues remain unresolved.

BOOM TOWN

But don't think for a minute that 'The City', as it's known, doesn't have the wherewithal to counter many of its concerns. Like much of the rest of the country, San Francisco is currently enjoying economic salad days – an amazing contradiction when one considers its estimated 14,000 homeless residents. Nonetheless, banking and computer industries remain strong, real estate is at a premium and service industries gain the influx of consumer spending. Tourism – the city's number one business – brings in millions of dollars a day; conventions are scheduled far into the next century. Clothing retailers such as Levi Strauss, Esprit and The Gap oversee their highly successful trade from headquarters in San Francisco.

Landlords are salivating over a record-low five per cent vacancy rate, leasing vacated flats and studios at astronomical rates. For their part, newcomers to the city are compromising their budgets and neighbourhood choices, signing leases where they can find them during a housing crunch that shows only gradual signs of ease. A 1993 study placed San Francisco as the top-ranked metropolitan area in the nation for per capita personal income. Most of its residents are well-educated and wealthy – sometimes too visibly so in the face of homelessness and outlying neighbourhood poverty.

Like the boom times during the Gold Rush of 1849, however, San Francisco is a place that knows how to enjoy itself, a proud city that wears its chequered past and controversial image like a badge of honour. Thousands move to the city every month to start bands or businesses, to go to school, to come out of the closet, to follow a dream or lead a tiny revolution. Many are lured by the city's arts: the Opera House is sporting a new facelift that will render it as swanky as Symphony Hall across the street; the new Main Library is a showpiece of 1990s architecture and hospitable public space. SFMOMA continues to dazzle, as do the verdant Yerba Buena Gardens across the street. The Palace of the Legion of Honor has greatly expanded its museum space with four additional galleries; the Asian Art Museum will re-open in 2001 in the recommissioned space of the old Main Library.

BACK TO THE FUTURE

What will happen next for San Francisco? Barring a civic coup d'état, voters will probably re-elect Mayor Brown for a second term in 1999. The housing shortage will drive away some of the homeless and discourage a major wave of newcomers. Traffic will continue to worsen, perhaps until another freeway project – or a substantive Muni overhaul – relieves the congestion. Other fiscal fights are destined to be

San Francisco players past and present (clockwise from top): North Beach regulars Tom Waits, Robin Williams and Nicholas Cage; Marilyn Monroe, who married Joe DiMaggio at City Hall; the late Jerry Garcia; and Mark Twain, who chronicled the city during the gold rush years.

fought. Yet people will still flock to the city for the reasons they always have: for its diversity, its open-mindedness, its potential for riches, its great food; for the whiff of the Barbary Coast that still hovers in the air. The city is set to celebrate the millennium the best way it knows how – with a decadent party.

San Francisco likes to think of itself as a big city, a metropolitan centre in a league with New York, Paris or London. In some ways, it is: its arts programmes are sophisticated, its restaurants world-famous, its populace diverse. But in many ways the 46 square-mile city is still too intimate to compete as a metropolis. San Francisco is more like a mighty small town, with all the accompanying perks and pleasures. Tiny, relatively safe neighbourhoods, familiar faces, bartenders and shop-keepers and bankers who recognise you on sight – all undermine San Francisco's cold urbaneness in the best possible way, affecting its future as a place that, after 15 decades, remains unique. Perhaps that's why so many people choose to stay.

The Costanoans were correct in assessing the sheltering peninsula that became San Francisco as a place of unparalleled bounty and dynamic natural beauty. It's fitting that centuries before a white settler ever dreamed of the region, it already had a reputation as a place to dance, a community balanced perpetually on the brink. Of its future, only two things about the city are certain: that its fortunes are cyclical and that sometime soon, literally and metaphorically, the ground beneath it will shake again.

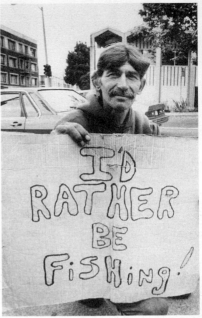

The city has an estimated 14,000 homeless.

San Francisco by numbers

759,300 official city population

6.5 million population of the nine Bay Area counties

207,469 estimated gay and lesbian population of the city

54 per cent workforce with college or professional degrees

14,000 estimated homeless population

46,38 square miles area of San Francisco

15,609.2 number of San Franciscans per square mile (extrapolated) making the city the second densest in the US after New York City

29.5 miles of shoreline

16 million approximate number of visitors each year

34 million number of passengers a year at San Francisco International Airport

30,575 number of hotel rooms

$150 million annual economic impact of the arts industry in San Francisco

9 per cent workforce in arts-related jobs

127 number of city-owned outdoor monuments, sculptures and statues

3,566 number of eating establishments

8.8 miles of cable car track

1,200,000 total annual visitors to Alcatraz

14,000 number of Victorian houses

8,981ft total length of Golden Gate Bridge, including approaches

5,000 gallons of paint used annually to paint the Bridge (the official colour is International Orange)

22 number of earthquakes over magnitude 6.0 in the Bay Area over last 160 years (an average of one every seven years)

67 per cent possibility of the Bay Area experiencing an earthquake of 6.7 before 2020

Architecture

Tracing the history of the city's skyline, from trade-mark 'Victorians' to the latest civic constructions.

Pastel-painted Victorians, cheek-by-jowl with the towers of the Financial District.

Rather than being a handicap, San Francisco's spectacular topography – a series of dramatic hills, each steep enough to lean against, framed by the Bay's surrounding waterscape – poses challenges that draw architects to it and inspires some of their best designs.

Since they erected its first buildings, San Francisco's citizens have fought to save the city from sand dunes, fires, earthquakes and the visually banal – and they struggle on with mixed results. Twenty years ago, they voted $25 million to beautify Market Street, which now boasts palm trees and restored Muni trolley tracks. The recently completed Embarcadero Promenade continues the Market Street motif with additional stripes of glass brick and Muni tracks – though current plans remain unclear as to which line will run down them. By and large, San Francisco's resolute avoidance of 'Manhattanisation' – the unwillingness to build concrete boxes a mile high – is helped by the threat of earthquakes and the success of conservation lobbies.

EARLY ARCHITECTURE

The Ohlone Indians, the first inhabitants of the Bay Area, left no permanent structures. The early European settlement of Yerba Buena, however, is represented by the simplicity of the thick adobe walls and painted hammer beams found in the **Mission Dolores** (Dolores Street, at 16th Street). Founded in 1776, the chapel sits north of a cemetery of Indian and outlaw graves that mingle with those of the city's first Irish and Hispanic mayors. It is the oldest building in San Francisco and was one of 21 missions built in California by the Spanish. Only two others, at Carmel and Monterey, rival it for authentic atmosphere. Together with a portion of the original walls of the Officers' Club in the Presidio, Mission Dolores is the only remaining piece of colonial architecture to have outlived the city's steep progress from hamlet to metropolis.

The town inhabited by the 'Forty-Niners' or 'Argonauts', as the Gold Rush immigrants were called, suffered a series of repeated fires. Tiny **Portsmouth Square** (in present-day Chinatown)

The **Jackson Square Historical District**, *overlooked by the* **Transamerica Pyramid**.

marked the heart of the early outpost, but was razed by successive fires; the surrounding streets all perished in the fire that followed the 1906 earthquake. The best examples of buildings surviving from the Gold Rush era are preserved in nearby **Jackson Square Historical District** (best viewed on Jackson between Montgomery and Sansome Streets) and are now used as design showrooms, law offices and antique shops.

THE PAINTED LADIES

A sudden burst of nineteenth-century prosperity and an *arriviste* urge to spend, spend, spend quickly filled San Francisco's once-empty sloping streets with what have become its trade-mark Victorian terraced houses. Built by middle-class tradesmen in the Mission and Lower Haight districts and by rich merchants in Presidio Heights and around Alamo Square, these famous 'Painted Ladies' provide the most distinctive architectural face of San Francisco. One of the city's most familiar views is of the row of six painted Victorians along **Steiner Street** on the east side of Alamo Square between Hayes and Grove Streets in the Lower Haight; although these are sparkling examples, over 14,000 equally charming versions of the city's architectural vernacular rival them in ornamentation.

Though all are built of wooden frames decorated with mass-produced ornamentation, four distinct styles of Victorian can be found in San Francisco. The earliest Gothic Revival houses have pointed arches over their windows and are often painted white, rather than the bright colours

of the later styles. The Lower Haight, notably Grove Street near Webster Street, contains versions of the later Italianate style, with its tall cornices, neo-classical elements and add-on porches. Perfect examples can be found at **1900 Sacramento Street** (near Lafayette Park) and at the 1876 **Lilienthal-Pratt House**, at 1818 California Street.

The Italianate style was succeeded by the Stick-Eastlake style, characterised by square bay windows framed by angular, carved, redwood ornamentation. Perhaps the most common among Victorian houses left in the city, the 'Sticks' are named after London furniture designer Charles Eastlake. A shining Stick glory is the over-the-top extravaganza standing at **1057 Steiner Street**, at the corner of Golden Gate Avenue.

With its turrets, towers and curvaceous corner bay windows, the so-called Queen Anne style is amply demonstrated by the **Wormser-Coleman House** in Pacific Heights (1834 California Street, at Franklin Street). Fans of this last and more ornate of the Victorian styles will find no more extravagant example than the **Haas-Lilienthal House** (2007 Franklin Street, near Washington Street), built in 1886 by Bavarian grocer William Haas. He treated himself to a home with 28 rooms and 6 bathrooms – one of which features a bidet, a Victorian Gothic shower head and a gas jet used for heating curling tongs. The house has been turned into a museum and is one of the few Victorians open to the public (noon-4pm Wed, 11am-5pm Sun). Phone 441 3004 for more information.

You can also visit the **Octagon House** at 2645 Gough Street, near Union Street (441 7512; open noon-3pm on second Sun and second and fourth Thur of each month except Jan). Built in 1861, when the latest craze dictated that an eight-sided building was better for one's health, the house is one of just two octagon-shaped buildings left in the city. Furnished in early colonial style with Chippendale and Hepplewhite furniture, the upper floors have been restored to their original state with a central staircase leading to a domed skylight.

HOTELS & MANSIONS

Another example of the ostentation that was part and parcel of San Francisco's booming late nineteenth-century lifestyle can be seen at the **Sheraton Palace Hotel** (at Market and New Montgomery Streets), where everyone from Rudyard Kipling to visiting royalty stayed. Opened in 1875, it epitomised local entrepreneur Billy Ralston's dreams – and his inability to resist Italian marble and solid gold dinner services, still on display in the lobby. San Franciscans mourned the original building after it burned down in the Great Fire of 1906, but the city rebuilt it, glassing in the atrium for elegant dining and adding fashionable Art Deco murals in the bar. Painstakingly and splendidly restored, the Sheraton remains a wonderful time-tunnel to the past, combining echoes of Old Vienna and a Prohibition Era speakeasy.

Engineer Adolph Sutro was Ralston's friend and equal in ambition, buying a sandy wasteland at the very western edge of San Francisco in 1881 for his elaborate **Sutro Baths** (now in ruins) and the elegant **Cliff House**. Freshly annexed and civilised by the new Golden Gate Park, Sutro's property provided the city with the most elaborate baths in the western world. Much in need of repair by the 1960s and badly burned in a fire, the baths were sold to developers for high-rise apartments that were never built. For its part, the adjoining Cliff House was twice burned to the ground; the eight-storey 'castle' that was destroyed in 1907 was rebuilt in an unremarkable style, and is now open to the public as an equally unremarkable bar and restaurant. It does offers spectacular views of Seal Rocks and the Pacific Ocean, however, and houses a Camera Obscura and Musée Mécanique, which contains a collection of vintage mechanical games.

San Francisco's 'Big Four' businessmen – Mark Hopkins, Leland Stanford, Collis P Huntington and Charles Crocker – also added their mark to the burgeoning city in the late nineteenth century. Their mining investments funded railroads and public transport, banks and businesses, and their baronial mansions on Nob Hill, victims of the 1906 fire, now mark the sites for some of the city's best luxury hotels. These include the **Mark Hopkins Inter-Continental Hotel** (1 Nob Hill, at California and Mason Streets) and the **Stouffer Stanford Court Hotel** (905 California Street). The Crocker Mansion, a Queen Anne pile built in 1888, filled half the block now occupied by **Grace Cathedral** (between Taylor, Jones, California and Sacramento Streets); it too was lost in the fire following the 1906 quake. One surviving house that has not been turned into a hotel is the **Spreckels Mansion** (2080 Washington Street), an impressive Beaux Arts building occupying an entire block, built in 1912 for sugar baron Adolph Spreckels and now owned by best-selling novelist Danielle Steel.

ODDITIES & HOMAGES

The city has more than its share of architectural curiosities, among them the **Columbarium** (1 Loraine Court, off Anza Street, open 10am-1pm daily). Built in 1898, this tubby neo-classical temple houses the ashes of thousands of San Franciscans and is decorated with Portuguese mosaic tiling and elaborate urns in imaginatively bedecked niches – a china football and photo of Candlestick Stadium fill one, doll's furniture another. Another eccentricity is the **Vedanta Temple** (2963 Webster Street), where oriental promise meets occidental vulgarity. Built in 1905 for the Vedanta Society, its bizarre mix of architectural styles includes a Russian Orthodox onion-shaped dome, a Hindu cupola, castle-like crenellations and Moorish arches. It is open to the public for Friday night services only.

When the growing city began to burst at the peninsular seams, a ferry network evolved to carry passengers to and from the Bay Area cities. In 1896, the Embarcadero **Ferry Building** was built, the clock-tower inspired by Seville Cathedral's Moorish campanile, and it became the heart of the city's commuter network.

AFTER THE 1906 EARTHQUAKE

After the earthquake, a passion for engineering spurred an interest in Chicago architect Daniel Burnham's City Beautiful project. This proposed a heroic new Civic Center planted below a terraced Telegraph Hill, enlaced with tree-lined boulevards that traced the city's contours. The plan was the result of Burnham's two-year consultations with leading city architects Bernard Maybeck and Willis Polk and a direct contrast to the city's impractical grid street pattern – but it never came to fruition.

Under Mayor 'Sunny Jim' Rolph, the main thrust of the 1915 $8.5 million **Civic Center** complex came from public contests, many won by Arthur Brown, architect of the mighty-domed **City Hall** (200 Polk Street, at Van Ness Avenue). Other Civic Center buildings erected at this time include the former **Main Library** (Larkin Street at McAllister Street), the **War Memorial Opera House** (301 Van Ness Avenue) and the **Bill Graham Civic Auditorium** (99 Grove Street). All reflected the imperial style named after the Ecole des Beaux Arts in Paris and sometimes described as French Renaissance or Classical Baroque. The buildings were distinguished by their grandiose proportions and ornamentation, theatrical halls and stairways.

It was largely Rolph's idea to host the huge Panama-Pacific Exposition in 1915, for which he commissioned Bernard Maybeck to build the romantic Tower of Jewels, the **Palace of Fine Arts** and its myriad pavilions. Originally made of wood and plaster, the Palace (3601 Lyon Street, on the eastern edge of the Presidio) is the only building to survive the Exposition, having been rebuilt in reinforced concrete in the 1960s. At around the same time, Arts and Crafts architect Julia Morgan was at work on much of the East Bay, and on the extravagant Hearst Castle, home of San Francisco newspaper magnate William Randolph Hearst, located 322 kilometres (200 miles) down the coast at San Simeon.

Passionate rebuilding continued in the Bay Area during the Depression, resulting in the **Bay Bridge** (1936), **Golden Gate Bridge** (1937) and a slew of Works Project Administration buildings such as the **Coit Tower** on Telegraph Hill and **Alcatraz** island prison. The WPA – introduced as part of President Franklin Delano Roosevelt's New Deal job-creation scheme – had a hand in everything from murals by Mexican artist Diego Rivera to the organisation of community archives. The best examples of projects from this period include the 1932 **Herbst Theater** with its murals by Frank Brangwyn (inside the Veteran's Building at 401 Van Ness Avenue), the 1930 **Pacific Coast Stock Exchange** with its Rivera mural (301 Pine Street) and the **Rincon Annex Post Office Building** (now part of the Rincon Center on Spear Street). The last is a wonderful example of steel-trimmed marble, built in 1940; the entire building, including Anton Refregier's murals of Californian history, was a WPA project.

The only Frank Lloyd Wright building in the city is the red brick, oval-entranced **Circle Gallery** (140 Maiden Lane, off Union Square). A prototype of the Guggenheim in New York and designed in 1948, it is now a private gallery.

RECENT ARCHITECTURE

St Mary's Cathedral (1111 Gough Street), designed by Pietro Belluschi, with its 61 metre (200 foot) high concrete structure supporting a cross shaped, stained-glass ceiling, is a 1970s symbol of anti-quake defiance. So is the 260 metre (853 foot) high **Transamerica Pyramid** (600 Montgomery Street), built in 1972. One of the best-known buildings in San Francisco, the Transamerica's $34 million seismic-proofed structure boasts internal suspension to protect it against tremors. Successfully, it would seem: the 48 storeys and 65 metre (212 foot) spire did not suffer in the 1989 quake. At first unpopular, the tower now has few detractors and features prominently in

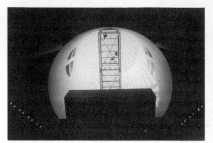

The **San Francisco Museum of Modern Art**.

the *Beach Blanket Babylon* revue – a sure sign of civic affection.

Along with John Portman's spectacularly glassy **Hyatt Regency Hotel** in the Embarcadero Center and the post-modern 'jukebox' **Marriott Hotel** (55 Fourth Street), which opened on the day the 1989 earthquake struck, a preponderance of suspended glass panels has dominated the architecture of buildings erected in the late 1980s and early 1990s. Exceptions include the still-under-construction **Moscone Convention Center** and the nearby brick-trimmed **San Francisco Museum of Modern Art** (both part of the $87 million Yerba Buena arts complex), the latter by Swiss architect Mario Botta.

The **New Main Library** (on Larkin and Fulton Streets), designed by Cathy Simon of architects Pei Cobb Freed, is a discreet marriage of Beaux Arts and new form. One side links the building to the more contemporary Marshall Plaza while the other, with grandiose, grey-corniced, neo-classical columns, echoes the old Main Library to the north. The interior is just as theatrical, centred around a five-storey atrium beneath a 15 metre (50 foot) domed skylight designed to let natural light filter throughout the building.

The new site for the **Asian Art Museum** (Larkin and Fulton Streets), which will occupy the former library space when it reopens in 1999, is to be similarly light-centric. Architect Gae Aulenti's dramatic plan features a skylit piazza encircling the grand staircase and loggia of the historic Beaux Arts building, originally opened to the public in 1917. The lobby opens on to a bright courtyard and a cantilevered stairway, enclosed in glass, climbs along one wall.

With optimistic projects continuing to alter her skyline, as well as the pre-millennial re-opening of Civic Center gems including the Asian and City Hall, San Francisco can once again lay claim to architecture as dramatic as her topography.

The **Columbarium**: *elaborate final resting place of thousands of San Franciscans.*
See page 23.

Literary San Francisco

The literary history of a city where Jack London was born, Mark Twain met Tom Sawyer in a bar, the Beat movement came into being and cyberauthors flourish.

Novelist and prospector, Bret Harte.

Perhaps it's the hills that rise and fall like the plot of a good story or the fog that seems to foreshadow mystery, but San Francisco has always drawn writers to its streets – poets, novelists and essayists who eke out their living by spinning words. In the mid-1800s, Mark Twain and Bret Harte came to report the weirdness during the Gold Rush; a hundred years later, Tom Wolfe arrived to write about hippies, remembering them in his *Electric Kool-Aid Acid Test*. From Dashiell Hammett and Jack London to Alice B Toklas, William Saroyan, Danielle Steel and Anne Rice – some of the country's best-known writers have called the city home. And while a few big names anchor the city on the literary map, a number of lesser-known authors are intent on guaranteeing the city's future as a storytellers' haven.

FROM TOM SAWYER TO MCTEAGUE

Journalist and budding fiction writer **Mark Twain** worked in the city in the 1860s, constructing his literary persona and leaving for New York once *The Celebrated Jumping Frog of Calaveras County* hit the big time in 1867. Like most San Francisco writers, Twain came to create himself and went East when he was ready. Legend has it he took the name Tom Sawyer from a man who owned a bar on Montgomery Street. Twain, **Bret Harte** and **Ambrose Bierce** built on a foundation of journalistic irony and muckraking that gave the West an independent literary culture in the 1860s and 1870s – something that didn't happen again in the city until after World War II.

Robert Louis Stevenson arrived in 1879 in pursuit of the strong-willed (but already married) Fanny Osbourne. He lived at 868 Bush Street while Osbourne was in Oakland awaiting her divorce. Stevenson eventually collapsed from tuberculosis and she scooped him up. He wrote about San Francisco in *The Wrecker*, and about their Napa Valley honeymoon in *The Silverado Squatters*. Stevenson's house is in Saint Helena (the Silverado Museum at Library Lane, St Helena, Napa County; 1-707 963 3757), and the Stevenson State Park is nearby.

Jack London, one of San Francisco's few native sons to make it as a writer, was born at Third and Brannan Streets, the illegitimate son of a wandering astrologer and a medium. He survived all manner of child labour and after a stop in Berkeley, headed north for the Yukon gold rush. He is the Bay Area's only world-class novelist and the first great American writer of proletarian origins. London became famous with *The Call of the Wild* and *The Sea Wolf* and spent his later years in Wolf House in Glen Ellen in the Sonoma Valley, north of San Francisco. The rebuilt Wolf House is worth a visit, if only to get a chilling sense of the connection between turn-of-the-century US Nietzscheanism and Nazi philosophy. The Jack London Museum, Wolf House and the writer's

Dead Beat

We still get people coming in all the time, looking for his work,' says a personable employee at City Lights bookstore, standing on a knee-high ladder to stock copies of *Howl* in the shop's poetry section. 'They're why we're in business. If it wasn't for him and for his friends, we'd have closed years ago.'

Though Allen Ginsberg was no native son of the city, his work as part of the larger Beat movement remains inextricably woven into the fabric of San Francisco's literary history. Ginsberg moved to the city in 1954, where he met the wizened anarchist poet Kenneth Rexroth. Rexroth encouraged him to drop formal poetic forms and meters and write to please himself. Ginsberg's subsequent experimentation with various forms – Kerouac's firecracker prose, William Carlos William's extended triadic verse, even the bebop forms the jazz musicians of the day were proffering – made for him a poetic niche unlike any of his predecessors. Though it languished in Ginsberg's journals for some years, upon first performance, *Howl* became an instant hit, a guttural scream of fragmentary, jarring and horrific modern imagery. *America, A Supermarket in California* and dozens of others followed.

With the subsequent waning of the Beats' popularity, Ginsberg remained active at the heart of the creative arts, collaborating with such diverse artists as The Clash, the Kronos Quartet and playwright/director Gus Van Sant. His recognisable monotone spiced the mix of various musical and spoken-word performances. Dividing his time between San Francisco and New York, Ginsberg also founded a poetry institute in Boulder, Colorado. True to his political leanings, he railed against various causes throughout his life, from the ideologies espoused by First Lady Nancy Reagan to the religious fundamentalist agenda forwarded by the Christian Coalition. Ginsberg's life was dedicated to howling.

And yet no creative genius can live forever: in April 1997, Ginsberg died of a heart attack that followed on the heels of the revelation that he had terminal cancer. His San Francisco funeral service, held at the Temple Emanu-El (though Ginsberg had converted to Buddhism decades

earlier) was attended by many who'd heard his iconoclastic work at the Six Galley 40 years ago. Lawrence Ferlinghetti, Michael McClure, Nobel prize-winner Gary Snyder, Diane Di Prima, US Poet-Laureate Robert Hass – the walls rang with the sound of poetry and fond remembrance. Ferlinghetti's *Allen Ginsberg Dying* closed with the lines: 'Here by the sea/in San Francisco/where the waves weep/They make a sibilant sound/a sibylline sound/Allen/they whisper/Allen'. In all, 2,000 attended the funeral. 'He would have loved it,' smiled McClure.

Back at City Lights, the clerk stacks the last spines into place. 'Most people buy a copy of *On the Road* or *Howl*, even if they already have one,' he explains. 'It's important to them to buy it here, to get it at the source.' Long after the Beats' creative tide has ebbed, Ginsberg's words ring through the heads of his friends and fans in San Francisco.

grave are all in the Jack London State Historic Park in Glen Ellen (1-707 938 5216).

Like London, **Gertrude Stein** was raised in Oakland. Her partner **Alice B Toklas**, on the other hand, was born on O'Farrell Street and raised at 2300 California among the Jewish haute bourgeoisie. Toklas wrote about it – and about the 1906 earthquake – in her autobiography *What is Remembered*. 'My father was apparently asleep,' Toklas wrote of the quake. 'Do get up, I said to him. The city is on fire. That, said he with his usual calm, will give us a black eye in the

Beat literarti Jack Kerouac (left) and Ken Kesey.

East.' Jack London wrote a much more dramatic account of the quake for the *Argonaut*. Both remembrances are published in the excellent collection *San Francisco Stories*, edited by John Miller (Chronicle Books, 1990).

Frank Norris, Jack London's contemporary, represents the left-wing version of the turn-of-the-century mixture of romanticism and naturalism. Norris was one of the first American disciples of Zola and a forerunner of the progressive era. His most famous novel, *The Octopus*, is about the railroad barons; *McTeague*, set on Polk Gulch where Norris grew up, was made into Eric von Stroheim's silent movie *Greed*.

THE CITY OF SAM SPADE

Dashiell Hammett came to San Francisco in 1921, at the tail end of his career as a Pinkerton operative. Beginning in 1923, Hammett published eleven of his 'Continental Op' stories in *Black Mask*, stories set in the city and written while the tubercular Hammett was living at 620 Eddy Street. In 1926 he went to work for the Albert Samuels jewellery company at 985 Market (the Samuels clock is still standing). Shortly after-

wards he was found collapsed in a pool of blood. He went on full disability pay, shipped his family to the countryside and became a full-time writer. Living at 891 Post Street, he wrote the sequence of novels that established the crime novel as *the* American genre, including *Red Harvest* and *The Dain Curse* (1929), *The Maltese Falcon* (1930) and *The Glass Key* (1931).

The Maltese Falcon sent Hammett to Hollywood, where he wrote *The Thin Man* and a string of disagreeable movie sequels; he was saved from drinking himself to death by the onset of World War II. Blacklisted in the 1950s as a Communist, Hammett was jailed for refusing to testify during the McCarthy trials and disappeared from public life until Lillian Helman rehabilitated him.

America is still uncomfortable with Hammett, which may be why his commemorative plaque (on Burrit Street, off Bush Street) acknowledges Sam Spade, not his creator. 'On approximately this spot,' it reads, 'Miles Archer, partner of Sam Spade, was done in by Brigid O'Shaughnessy'. The plaque's author, Warren Hinkle (a San Francisco journalist famous for bankrupting magazines), published a Dashiell Hammett issue of his *City* magazine in 1975. It lists every known Hammett and Sam Spade location and is required reading for enthusiasts. Hammett's and Spade's intertwined journeys are also detailed in Don Herron's *Literary Guide to San Francisco* (City Lights, 1985). John's Grill (63 Ellis Street, at Market; 986 0069) which appeared in *The Maltese Falcon*, is another shrine for Hammett fans.

THE BEAT GENERATION

Jack Kerouac came to the city in 1947, at the end of the cross-country trip that was to make him famous a decade later with the publication of *On the Road*. Because Neal Cassady was in San Francisco, the city became the western terminus of Kerouac's restless cross-country swings. He cut the original teletype-roll manuscript of *On the Road* into paragraphs in Cassady's flat on Russian Hill in 1952. *San Francisco Blues* was written in the Cameo Hotel in what was then skid row on Third Street. *The Subterraneans*, written in 1953, is set in North Beach – actually a New York story transposed to protect the characters. The old Third Street that served as Kerouac's spiritual home was bulldozed to make way for the Moscone Center.

Another novel, *The Dharma Bums*, chronicles the impact of the Beat movement on the West Coast. It also vividly reports the poetry reading of 13 October 1955 at the old Six Gallery on Fillmore Street, when **Allen Ginsberg** read the first part of his famous poem *Howl*, with Kerouac and the 150-strong crowd shouting 'Go! Go! Go!'. That night, other notable poets **Philip Whalen**, surrealist **Philip Lamantia**, **Michael McClure** and **Gary Snyder** were also introduced to the wildly enthusiastic audience by literary guru **Kenneth Rexroth**, the leading figure of post-World War II literary San Francisco. An irascible literary pacifist and Orientalist whose salon at 250 Scott Street was the centre of the post-war poetry renaissance, Rexroth's main contribution to San Francisco literary history – much to his own disgust – became his role as godfather to the Beats.

Ginsberg himself had come to San Francisco to (in his own words) 'find the Whitman self-reliance to indulge a celebration of self'. Here he came to terms with his homosexuality, met his lover Peter Orlovsky, moved into the Hotel Wentley and began writing a poem that would turn into *Howl*. The central image of the poem is the Moloch-face of the Drake Hotel on Powell Street as observed by Ginsberg high on peyote. There is a fine picture of Ginsberg (and of the Moloch-faced hotel) in **Lawrence Ferlinghetti** and Nancy Peters' *Literary San Francisco* (City Lights, 1980). Lawrence Ferlinghetti, owner of the City Lights bookshop, later wrote to Ginsberg: 'I greet you at the beginning of a great career. Where's the manuscript?' *Howl*'s subsequent obscenity charges and the resulting trial catapulted the Beats to public attention and opened the way for the breakdown of the American obscenity laws in the 1960s.

The Beat scene was centred around North Beach – the Coexistence Bagel Store at Grant Avenue and Green Street, the Cellar on Green, the

Lawrence Ferlinghetti (back, left) oversees a controversial sale at his City Lights bookstore.

Coffee Gallery and the Place on Upper Grant (home of the 'blabbermouth nights', predecessors of today's poetry slams). Gino and Carlo's bar still stands at 548 Green Street (at Columbus Avenue; 421 0896). Vesuvio's Café (255 Columbus Avenue, at Broadway; 362 3370) is where Kerouac drank away his chance of meeting Henry Miller. The bar is located across Jack Kerouac Alley from City Lights, the scene's epicentre and still the best literary bookshop in San Francisco. 'So here comes Snyder with a bottle of wine,' Kerouac wrote, 'and here comes Whalen, and here comes what's-his-name... Rexroth and everybody... and we had the Poetry Renaissance of San Francisco.'

FROM THE HASHBURY TO BARBARY LANE

Compared to North Beach, the Haight-Ashbury scene doesn't seem to have left much of a literary monument – though this is perhaps because (to quote **Tom Wolfe**) if you can remember it, you weren't really there. **Ken Kesey** and the reborn **Neal Cassady** began their trips festivals at the Longshoreman's Hall on Fisherman's Wharf, and the scene moved through the Avalon Ballroom on Polk Street and the Fillmore on Geary, to the Haight itself. Wolfe's *Electric Kool-Aid Acid Test* is the best account of the literary and psychological voyage, along with **Emmet Grogan**'s memoir of the Diggers, *Ringolevio*. Kesey and **Robert Stone**, who was part of the scene and wrote about the psychic fallout of the era in *Dog Soldiers*, were both products of **Wallace Stegner**'s writing programme at Stanford. Stegner, a long-respected Western writer of an older school, must have been horrified to see what his literary progeny made of themselves.

The Castro hasn't produced its literary testament yet either, perhaps because the epidemic that

Bay Area author Amy Tan.

The cast from the televised 'Tales of the City'.

brought the excesses of the Castro of the early 1980s to a crashing halt is still rampant. Before his death, **Randy Shilts** produced a stirring (if somewhat melodramatic) account of the coming of AIDS in *And The Band Played On*, a treatise on gays and lesbians in the US military, and also wrote the biography of Harvey Milk. **Frances Fitzgerald** gives a cooler view in *Cities on a Hill*. **Armistead Maupin's** charming and dippy 'Tales of the City' series is in fact set in Macondray Lane on Russian Hill, not particularly a gay venue.

The literary tradition remains strong in San Francisco, however, as writers continue to settle in and write about the city. Readings and author signings are still a popular SF pastime, and the advent of zine publishing has delivered a crop of nouveau publishers to the city. The Bay Area of the 1990s enjoys a strong multicultural feminist presence, and authors including **Amy Tan** (whose *Joy Luck Club* is set in Chinatown), **Alice Walker** (who wrote *The Color Purple* from her Alamo Square Victorian), **Dorothy Allison** (who won a National Book Award for her coming-of-age novel, *Bastard Out of Carolina*), **Isabel Allende**, **Terry McMillan** and **Anne Lamott** all regularly sell out the city's auditoriums for their reading and speaking engagements. In addition, a generation of new writers are carving their names on the literary tree trunks: novelists **Molly Giles** and **Ethan Canin** and cyberauthors **Po Bronson** and **Martha Baer** seem to be leading the pack. For a book list containing details of these and other titles relating to San Francisco, *see page 266* **Further Reading**.

San Francisco by Season

From the sock fights of the St Stupid's Day Parade, to the bun fights of the Gilroy Garlic Festival, the Bay Area calendar is never empty.

Seasons in San Francisco, at least in terms of climate, can seem to come and go in the space of a week, or even within the week. Spring and autumn are best; during the summer, two or three hot days will be punished by a chilling fog. In mid-January, when everyone's spirits are low from constant rain, a week of brilliant sunshine will suddenly find the beaches packed with pasty locals. Then the sun will just as abruptly disappear and the grey will seem infinite. Tourists shivering in T-shirts are a never-ending source of amusement for locals: San Francisco may be in California, but it has a climate all its own, so pack layers accordingly.

Rain or shine, San Francisco remains a city that knows how to throw a civic party and, along with the national holidays, there's almost always some kind of celebration hitting the streets.

Dates of events listed below are approximate. For the most up-to-date information on events, consult the **San Francisco Visitor Information Center** (391 2000) or check local arts and daily newspapers.

National Holidays

New Year's Day (1 Jan); **Martin Luther King Jr Day** (3rd Mon, Jan); **President's Day** (3rd Mon, Feb); **Memorial Day** (last Mon, May); **Independence Day** (4 July); **Labor Day** (1st Mon, Sept); **Columbus Day** (2nd Mon, Oct); **Veteran's Day** (11 Nov); **Thanksgiving Day** (4th Thur, Nov); **Christmas Day** (25 Dec).

Spring

St Patrick's Day
Information (1-510 339 1116). Parade goes from Fifth and Market Streets to the Embarcadero Center. BART Powell Street/Muni Metro F, J, K, L, M, N/bus 5, 9, 14, 26, 27, 31. **Date** Sunday before 17 March.
Like everywhere in the world where St Patrick's Day is celebrated, this is a long day filled with shamrocks, parades and booze. Most Irish pubs celebrate long into the night.

Tulip Mania
Information (981 7437). Pier 39, Embarcadero. Bus 12, 32, 42/cable car Powell-Hyde or Powell-Mason. **Date** March.
To get the feeling that spring has really sprung, go to Pier 39 and gaze at the 35,000 tulips planted for this annual flower festival.

St Stupid's Day Parade
From Transamerica Pyramid, on Washington and Montgomery Streets. Bus 1, 15, 41. **Date** 1 April.
On April Fools' Day for the past 19 years, Bishop Joey of the First Church of the Last Laugh has led the St Stupid's Day Parade, a zany, parodic assembly that snakes through San Francisco's Financial District. The parade concludes on the steps of the Pacific Stock Exchange, where sermons are given and everyone removes a sock for the 'Pacific Sock Exchange'. It should come as no surprise to learn that many go home sockless, as the exchange generally degenerates into a sock fight. The starting point may not be the same each year; check the *Bay Guardian* near the time.

Cherry Blossom Festival
Information (563 2313). Japan Center, Geary Boulevard, between Fillmore and Laguna Streets. Bus 2, 3, 4, 22, 38. **Date** early April.

Japantown's Cherry Blossom Festival.

Held over two weekends in April, this is a celebration of traditional Japanese arts and crafts, including a parade, dance, drumming and martial arts performances.

San Francisco International Film Festival

Information (931 3456/929 5000). Kabuki 8 Cinema at Post and Fillmore Streets, and other cinemas around town. Bus (to Kabuki) 2, 3, 4, 22, 38. **Date** mid April-early May.

Featuring two weeks of events, the San Francisco Film Festival may not be the largest, but it definitely screens enough films to make a run at being the world's most eclectic cinematic experience. It is particularly strong on independent documentaries and Third World films rarely shown at other US festivals. Book in advance if you can.

Cinco de Mayo

Information (826 1401). Civic Center Plaza. BART Civic Center/Muni Metro F, J, K, L, M, N/bus 5, 19, 26, 42, 47. **Date** Sunday before 5 May.

Many San Franciscans join the city's Mexican population in a weekend of parades, fireworks and music celebrating General Ignacio Zaragoza's defeat of the French army at Puebla in 1862.

Candlelight March for Aids

Information (863 4676). Begins at Castro and Market Streets and finishes at United Nations Plaza in Civic Center. Muni Metro F/bus 8, 24, 33, 35. **Date** mid-May.

San Francisco's Aids Candlelight Memorial and Mobilization begins with a solemn parade from the Castro to Civic Center, then continues with an evening of speakers, awards and remembrances.

Bay to Breakers Foot Race

Information (808 5000 ext 2222). Starts at corner of Howard and Spear Streets. BART Embarcadero/Muni Metro J, K, L, M, N/bus 1, 2, 6, 7, 9, 14, 21, 31, 66, 71. **Date** third Sunday in May.

The *San Francisco Examiner* and a host of other sponsors encourage 100,000 or more athletes, weekend warriors, jogwalkers, joggers-for-a-day and just plain freaks to run to Ocean Beach. The course is about 12km (7.6 miles), a perfect length since most can make it without much training. Famous for its costumes, nudity (there's always a few running free and bouncy), and the occasional beer jock, who runs alongside his keg in a shopping cart. Don't try to cross the city north-to-south on Bay to Breakers day.

Carnaval

Information (826 1401). Mission Street, from 24th to 16th Streets. BART 16th, 24th Streets/bus 12, 14, 22, 49, 53. **Date** Memorial Day weekend.

Carnaval gets better every year: the South American festival features a dazzling parade, excellent cuisine and music that will get even the most staid souls up and dancing. If you like steel drum bands, samba and sangria, catch this party that transforms the Mission into Rio de Janeiro once a year.

North Beach Festival

Information (403 0666/www.sfnorthbeach.com). Grant Avenue, Green Street, Washington Square. Bus 15, 30, 41, 83/cable car Powell-Mason. **Date** mid-June.

North Beach's fair is heavy on art, homemade crafts and great Italian food. Not as crowded as some of the street fests, and loaded with old world music.

Haight Street Fair

Information (661 8025). Haight Street, between Masonic and Stanyan Streets. Muni Metro N/bus 6, 7, 43, 66, 71. **Date** early June.

Then again, there's the Haight Street Fair, a sardine-fest with over 200 booths of food, a pair of stages and plenty

of folks tripping on real and imaginary acid. Strictly for the courageous thrill-seeker, especially if you get there late in the day when the crowd is thickest and the hallucinogens are wearing off. A walk – er, squeeze – on the wild side.

Lesbian and Gay Freedom Day Parade and Celebration

Information (864 3733/www.sf.pride.org). Market Street, between Embarcadero and Eighth Street. Phone for venues and information. **Date** third or fourth weekend in June.

One of the most famous and popular of San Francisco's celebrations, the gay parade (held on Sunday) and the great party that follows it (in front of the appropriately named Ferry Building) is just as outlandish as you've always heard. Local pols share the route with drag queens, leather daddies, Harley-riding dykes, transvestites in platform heels and gay marching bands. It's the wildest, friendliest parade you'll ever witness. Bring plenty of camera film and an open mind, and remember: for all its entertainment value, the event is also about countless numbers of private lives going public with their desire.

Summer

Making Waves Festival

Information (431 9962). Throughout the city. **Date** 21 June.

The celebration is in its formative years, but you'll find 20 or more free stages of music performed throughout the city, from backyard bands to well-known artists. Making Waves is a local, neo-pagan extension of World Music Day. The longest day of the year closes with a drum circle in Justin Herman Plaza.

Fourth of July

Information (777 7120/from June 777 8498). On the Bay, between Aquatic Park and Pier 39. **Date** from 1pm, 4 July.

On Independence Day, even San Francisco admits that it is part of the US, with live entertainment, food, shows for children and so on, culminating in spectacular firework displays shortly after dark.

Jazz and All That Art on Fillmore

Information (346 9162). Fillmore Street, between Jackson and Post Streets. Bus 1, 2, 3, 4, 12, 22, 24, 38. **Date** early July.

With a long history of great jazz, the Fillmore pays tribute to its legacy with a street fair that mixes the usual crafts and handiwork with lots of original art and live music. Over 300 artists show their wares, and local foodsters purvey their goods along with a satisfying selection of wine and beer.

Stern Grove Festival

Information (252 6252). 19th Avenue and Sloat Boulevard. Muni Metro K, M/bus 17, 23, 28. **Date** mid June-late August.

A series of free concerts set in an idyllic grove of eucalyptus trees, this amphitheatrical tradition is a pleasant summer reprieve – as long as the fog doesn't roll in. Bring a picnic lunch, something to lie or sit on and an extra sweater. Parking is a problem, so use public transport.

Mime Troupe in the Park

Information (285 1717). First show held at Dolores Park, at 18th and Dolores Streets. Muni Metro J/bus 33. **Date** early July-early September.

For more than 30 years, the San Francisco Mime Troupe has developed and performed free shows in the parks of San Francisco during the summer. Between the wit of the Mime Troupe, the sun, the grass, the dogs and the views of the city, the festival goes a long way toward restoring one's sanity.

Weather watch

While southern California languishes in summer sun, San Franciscans are often bundled up in sweaters, damp, chilly and surrounded by the familiar foggy 'marine layer'. Yet when some of its northern counterparts are freezing in late autumn or early spring, the city is often basking in radiant stretches of clear, warm days that locals refer to as 'earthquake weather'. The rainy season generally lasts only about a month, from March to early April, yet it has been known to snow in February. The only thing consistent about San Francisco's weather is that cold or hot, it's windy most of the time. Most of the year, the city has more in common climatically with Australia's west coast than with the rest of North America. What makes San Francisco's weather so unique?

Part of the explanation comes from San Francisco's geography, located as it is at the north end of a peninsula and surrounded on three sides by cold water – the Pacific on one side, San Francisco Bay on two. If you've dipped a toe into the coastal tides you'll know how chilly they are, due to the Gulf Stream which traverses the west coast from the Arctic to the Equator. Add to this combination steady prevailing winds, buffeting the coastal range that runs parallel to the Northern California coastline, blowing chilly air off the water and across the maze of city hills.

In the summer, the wide, hot Central Valley (the agricultural region spanning the coastal ranges and the Sierras on California's eastern border) creates pressure differences that draw fog off the Pacific and over the city itself. Afternoon and evening winds exacerbate the condition, shooting fog across the city and across the Bay to Berkeley and Oakland, catching many a tourist in shorts and T-shirt, shivering in the cable car queue or on deck of a ferry.

Even on the foggiest days, however, the San Franciscan visitor can generally find temperate regions: the further south and east you go in the city, the more likely you are to find sun. The **Mission** district is famously warmer than other neighbourhoods, as is **Bernal Heights** (though the wind is formidable), **South Park**, **SoMa** and **South Beach**. The beer gardens in **China Basin** are nearly always hot enough to warrant cooling off with a pint. By the time you get to **3Com Park** in the **Bay View** district, however, the point is lost: the sports stadium – voters recently approved a new one to be built around the turn of the century – is notoriously cold and brutally windy.

The solution is to dress in layers, peeling them off when the sun shows and pulling them back on again when the wind starts whipping. Often a cold afternoon will be followed by a gorgeous, warm night; a chilly, grey beach will might clear by noon. Temperatures rarely rise above 21°C (70°F) or fall below 40°F (5°C). And don't forget that the wind blows away the smog – one of the main reasons you'll have a terrific view of the city anywhere you look. For daily weather information, phone the National Weather Service Forecast Office on **364 7974**.

The annual Columbus Day Parade: an autumnal national holiday.

Comedy Celebration Day

Information (777 7120). Sharon Meadow, Golden Gate Park. Muni Metro N/bus 5, 6, 7, 21, 33, 43, 71. **Date** mid-late August.

There's no better way to round out the summer than lying on a blanket in the park, drinking, eating and laughing hour after hour with local and national stand-up comedians. The event, formerly known as Comedy in the Park, has been moved from the Music Concourse to the more comfortable Sharon Meadow. Watch out for cameos by famous figures from San Francisco's comedy history.

Absolut A La Carte, A La Park

Information (383 9378). JFK and Kezar Drives, Golden Gate Park. Muni Metro J/bus 6, 7, 21, 33, 66. **Date** 11am-6pm, Labor Day weekend. **Tickets** $8.50.

At this huge outdoor food fair, you can sample an impressive array of cuisine from over 40 restaurants in the San Francisco and Bay Area in just three days. With all the Californian wine that pours, plan to take a bus or cab home.

Autumn

San Francisco Shakespeare Festival

Information (422 2222/recorded information 422 2221). Golden Gate Park. Muni Metro N/bus 5, 6, 21, 33, 66, 71. **Date** September.

The Bard knows no chronological or geographical limits, especially in northern California. No less than five theatre companies produce Shakespeare plays during the summer, but the one closest to home (and free) is the San Francisco Shakespeare Festival, performed on outdoor stages in Golden Gate Park at weekends throughout September.

Cycle Messenger World Championships

Information (626 2692). Downtown San Francisco. **Date** early September.

Stunt riding, speed contests and load-carrying races mark this competition dedicated to the hard-pedalling souls who keep San Francisco's businesses afloat. Besides the friendly rivalries, you'll also find art displays, bike repair booths and lots of great haircuts, tattoos and piercings. Since most messengers are in a band, there's also usually some live music to accompany the races. Check the press for locations.

Festival de las Americas

Information (826 1401). 24th Street, between Mission and Hampshire Streets. BART 24th Street/bus 12, 14, 26, 27, 48, 49, 67. **Date** around 15 September.

The Mission district can't go more than a few weeks without some kind of fiesta and at the Festival de las Americas (formerly the Mexican Day of Independence), many of the newest *Norteamericanas* celebrate the nation of their birth. There's music and parades, dancing and food.

San Francisco Blues Festival

Information (826 6837/www.sfblues.com). Great Meadow, Fort Mason Center, at Marina Boulevard and Laguna Street. Bus 28. **Date** third or fourth weekend in September. **Tickets** *advance* $20 per day; $35 two days; *on the door* $25 per day; free under-6s.

Traditionally kicking off at noon on a Friday, this weekend-long festival blurs into one eternal afternoon, exposing blues fans to the elements and set after set of broken-hearted chords. Wear your shades and bring a blanket and a cooler full of refreshments. Tickets are available in advance from Wherehouse (951 8612) and Tower Records (885 0500).

Folsom Street Fair

Information (861 3247). Folsom and Harrison Streets, between Seventh and 12th Streets. Muni Metro J, K, L, M, N/bus 12, 14, 16, 27, 42. **Date** 11am-6pm, last Sunday in September.

The Queen Mother of leather street fairs, the Folsom Fair – like Chinese New Year, the late Herb Caen and the Golden Gate Bridge – is a San Francisco institution. Parental discretion is advised. *See also chapter* **Gay & Lesbian San Francisco**.

Dave Brubeck in concert at the San Francisco Jazz Festival.

Solo Mio Festival

Information (626 6422). The Cowell, Bayfront, Young Performers Theaters, Fort Mason Center, Buchanan Street and Marina Boulevard. Bus 19, 28, 30, 47, 49. **Date** mid September to mid October. **Tickets** $10-$25 from City Box Office (392 4400) or BASS Tickets (1-510 762 2277).

Although a form that can attract egocentric hacks, performance art lives up to its name at the Solo Mio Festival, devoted to one-person shows. Started in 1989, the festival already has a rich history of infamous past performances from Karen Finley, Spalding Gray and John Waters.

Artists' Open Studios

Information (861 9838). Phone for venues. **Date** October.

Local Bay Area artists invite the public to visit their studios every weekend during October. A free map and the Directory of San Francisco Artists ($12.95) are available from bookshops; a map is also published in the *Sunday Examiner & Chronicle* on the last Sunday in September. Bring your chequebook.

Reggae in the Park

Information (383 9378). Sharon Meadow, Golden Gate Park. Muni Metro N/bus 5, 6, 7, 21, 33, 43, 44, 66, 71. **Date** early October. **Tickets** $12-$20.

You'll hear it from blocks away, and smell the ganja long before you get there: RITP is quickly becoming one of the city's best-attended music festivals, primarily because it seems to happen during some of the best autumn weather. The two-day event attracts artists from all over the world.

Fleet Week

Information (395 3928/981 7437). Pier 39, Embarcadero. Bus 32. **Date** Columbus Day weekend.

Frightening local pets and setting off car alarms in the Marina district, the US Navy's Blue Angels tear up the heavens in a *Top Gun* display of speed, daring and taxpayer abuse (though to watch them fly *beneath* the Golden Gate Bridge is an undeniable thrill). If you prefer your fleet aqueous, you can take free tours of various US and foreign ships.

San Francisco Jazz Festival

Information (398 5655/outside California 1-800 627 5277/www.sfjazzfest.org). Phone for venues. **Date** third and fourth weeks in October. **Tickets** $3-$50 from City Box Office (392 4400) or BASS Tickets (1-510 762 2277).

Growing every year, the San Francisco Jazz Festival attracts some of the biggest names in jazz.

Hallowe'en

Check the local press near the time for details. **Date** 31 October.

It used to be that Hallowe'en meant joining the claustrophobic fray in the Castro, where outlandish costumes, cameras and cops were *de rigeur*. But the scene became infiltrated with obstreperous out-of-towners, so the SFPD banned assembly there. The Castro is still crowded with drag queens (and half-naked pagans celebrating Samhain) on the hallowed night, but the city has yet to adopt an official locale for its favourite transformative holiday. Keep an eye on the local papers to see whether the masked masses are convening in Civic Center, the Embarcadero or elsewhere. And don't forget to shop for your get-up early.

Día de los Muertos

Information (826 8009). Evening procession starts from Mission Cultural Center, 2868 Mission Street, between 24th and 25th Streets. BART 24th Street/bus 14, 48, 49, 67. **Date** 2 November.

A celebration of Mexican Hallowe'en – the Day of the Dead – a traditional holiday for welcoming the departed spirits with a feast and a night-time procession.

Harvey Milk March

Information (647 5421). Begins at 572 Castro Street, between 18th and 19th Streets and proceeds to United Nations Plaza in Civic Center. Muni Metro F/bus 8, 24, 33, 35. **Date** 27 November.

November 27 marks the anniversary of the assassination of Supervisor Harvey Milk, the first openly gay elected politician in the city's history. Milk, along with then-mayor George Moscone, was murdered in 1978; the Harvey Milk Lesbian/Gay/Bisexual Democratic Club organises this annual candlelit march in honour of the two men, and to underscore the continuing need for gay rights.

Winter

San Francisco Bay Area Book Festival

Information (908 2833). Concourse Exhibition Center, Eighth and Brannan Streets. Bus 19, 27, 42. **Date** November. **Admission** $2 adults; free under-17s.
The biggest book fair of the year occurs in the picturesque Exhibition Center, with acres of retail sales, remainders and new release racks from big-name houses and independent publishers alike. One of the best-kept secrets in the city, the Book Fair draws up-and-coming authors to its readings. A great place to shop for the looming holidays.

Christmas Tree Lighting Ceremonies

Pier 39 (981 8030). Bus 42. **Date** noon-6pm, Saturday before Thanksgiving.
Ghirardelli Square (775 5500). Bus 19. **Date** around 6pm, day after Thanksgiving.
Fell and Stanyan Streets (831 2700). Bus 6, 7, 33, 66, 71. **Date** around 5.30pm, second week of December.
Your chance to get into the Thanksgiving and Christmas spirit. Check the local press for precise information near the date.

Run to the Far Side

Information (564 0532). Golden Gate Park. Bus 5, 7, 21, 33, 66, 71. **Date** weekend after Thanksgiving.
A 5km (3 mile) walk and 10km (6 mile) run through Golden Gate Park, where participants dress as their favourite characters from Gary Larson's cartoons. Money is raised for the California Academy of Science and runners get a free T-shirt and free museum entry for limited period.

Martin Luther King Jr Birthday Celebration

Information (771 6300). Start of parade varies; ends with rally at Yerba Buena Gardens, Fourth and Mission Streets. BART Powell Street/Muni Metro F, J, K, L, M, N/

bus 14, 26 30, 45. **Date** Monday after 15 January (King's birthday).
In honour of the great civil rights leader, the US takes a day off and holds birthday parades.

Tet Festival

Information (885 2743). Larkin Street, between Eddy and O'Farrell Streets. Bus 19, 31, 38. **Date** January-February (phone for exact date).
San Francisco has a sizeable population of Vietnamese-Americans and at Vietnamese New Year they transform the Civic Center and Tenderloin areas with a multi-cultural festival, joined by hundreds of Cambodian, Latino and African-American San Franciscans.

Chinese New Year

Information (982 3000). Parade starts from Market Street, at Steuart Street, through Union Square. BART Montgomery Street/Muni Metro F, J, K, L, M, N/bus 2, 3, 4, 9, 30, 45, 71, 76. **Date** January, February or March (phone for exact date).
With a huge parade through Chinatown, beauty pageants, drumming, martial-arts displays, mountains of food and endless strings of fireworks, Chinese New Year turns San Francisco jubilant and upside-down. If you're in town, don't miss it.

Jubilant celebrations for Chinese New Year.

Out of town

Festival at the Lake

Information (1-510 286 1061). Lake Merritt, Oakland. BART Lake Merritt. **Date** June or October.
Held over a long weekend, Oakland's Festival at the Lake is the city's largest annual shindig, with food stalls, arts and crafts, water sports and several stages with bands. In recent years it has been held in either June or October: ring the information line to find out which.

Gilroy Garlic Festival

Information (1-408 842 1625). South of San Jose on US 101. **Date** last full weekend in July. **Admission** $10; $4 concessions.
This food and wine fest features the fruit of Gilroy – the lowly garlic clove, made into every edible concoction you can imagine. Over 100 craft booths, puppetry, magicians, singing and live music round out the event. You'll come home smelling like the Stinking Rose, San Francisco's garlic restaurant (781 7673).

Burning Man

Burning Man, PO Box 420572, San Francisco, CA 94142-0572 (985 7471/www. burningman.com). Near Black Rock Desert, Nevada. **Date** Labor Day weekend. **Tickets** advance $65 available via mail-order and the Internet; at the gate $75.
Hundreds of San Franciscans ride in convoy out to Nevada for a long weekend of bizarre fun. A camp forms for parties, fashion shows, neo-pagan rituals, live music, pirate radio stations, drive-by shooting ranges and just about any game you'd care to invent. The climax is the immolation of a 12m (40ft) figure, laced with neon and packed with explosives. After it collapses in flames, circle dances begin. Originally a ceremony held with a few friends, Burning Man in recent years grown huge; for some, it has replaced Christmas as the main ritual of the year. Get your tickets well in advance.

Time Out

Film
Guide

Edited by John Pym

Annually updated, the *Time Out* Film Guide is a comprehensive A-Z of films from every area of world cinema and has stronger international coverage than any other film guide.

Each entry includes full details of director, cast, running time, release date and reviews from the *Time Out* magazine critics. There are also indexes covering films by country, genre, subject, director and actor. So if you want to get the lowdown on a film, pick up the latest edition of the *Time Out* Film Guide - available in a bookshop near you.

'Without doubt, the "bible" for film buffs.'
British Film and TV Academy News

Sightseeing

Sightseeing

Our round-up of the essential sights of the city, both on and off the beaten track.

San Francisco's geographical restrictions – the Pacific Ocean on one side and the Bay on two more – mean that the city is squeezed into a relatively small area, a blessing for the visitor keen to explore its sights. Tramping the city's streets is the best way to experience it, but if the shockingly steep hills become too much, you can always turn to the efficient public transport system and hop on a bus or cable car. Listed below are some of the major attractions; for more detailed information on where to explore off the beaten track, *see chapter* **San Francisco by Neighbourhood**.

Islands & Bridges

Alcatraz Island

Blue & Gold ferry half-hourly departures from Pier 41, Embarcadero (tickets 705 5555/recorded information 773 1188). Bus 32, 42/cable car Powell-Mason. **Open** *ticket phoneline 7am-8pm daily; Pier 41 box office 8am-6pm daily.* **Departures** *summer 9.30am-4.15pm daily; winter 9.30am-2.15pm daily.* **Return tickets** *with audio tour* $11; $5.75-$7.75 *concessions; without audio tour* $7.75; $4.50-$6 *concessions.* **Credit** AmEx, Disc, MC, V.

Don't miss

The Japanese Tea Garden p54: serenity amidst the manicured walks.
Alamo Square p42: get your snap of postcard row.
A ferry ride on the Bay pp41-42: to a spooky prison or a sunny promontory.
Golden Gate Bridge p42: the city's ubiquitous symbol.
Baker Beach p55: for a stunning view of the Pacific, Marin Headlands and Golden Gate Bridge.
SFMOMA p53: one of the city's architectural gems.

Alcatraz means 'pelican' in Spanish, after the birds that nest there, but to Al Capone, Machine Gun Kelly and Robert 'the Birdman' Stroud, the tiny island was 'the Rock'. The first lighthouse on the West Coast was built here in 1854; Alcatraz first became a prison in the 1870s. It housed quarantined soldiers after the Spanish-American War, then prisoners from city jails that crumbled after the 1906 earthquake. Now the

The slopes of **Alamo Square**, *flanked by picturesque Victorians. See page 42.*

craggy outcrop lures 4,000 willing visitors a day – well over a million each year – and is San Francisco's single biggest tourist attraction. Every November, Native Americans land to commemorate their 1969 occupation with an Un-thanksgiving ceremony, and Hollywood still favours it as a place to shoot motion pictures – though 1996's The Rock was consummately more forgettable than Clint Eastwood's 1979 Escape From Alcatraz. The island also boasts one of the only deep-pitched foghorns left in the Bay Area. Admission includes a walking tour of the facility, with audio narration by former inmates. Visit the semi-derelict concrete cell blocks where incorrigible lifers were sent between 1934 and 1963, after which the cost of supporting an island jail without its own water supply forced its closure. Book your visit far in advance and come prepared for crowds and chilly weather.

Angel Island

San Francisco Bay, off Tiburon (546 2628). Blue & Gold ferry from Pier 41, Embarcadero. Bus 32, 42/cable car Powell-Mason. **Return tickets** $10; $5.50-$9 concessions.
If you're seeking a forested getaway that's close to the city, a ramble and bicycle ride around this rocky island – the largest in the Bay – is only a 20-minute ferry ride away. Boats arrive at Ayala Cove, where you can rent bikes and claim a picnic table. The 8km (five mile) Perimeter Trail brings you to the deserted Camp Reynolds, with its picturesque Civil War barracks – the only remaining garrison of its type. The top of Mount Livermore (238m/781ft) affords a great view. Now part of the Golden Gate Park Recreation Area, Angel Island has served as a quarantine station (the West Coast's answer to Ellis Island between 1910 and 1940) and a prisoner of war camp for Italians and Germans during World War II. Today, ghostly barracks lurk among the volleyball courts on the island, and the shouts of playing children are never out of earshot. The visitors centre at Ayala Cove offers 20-minute video tours, and a bus takes you across the island to Quarry Beach – a sheltered, sandy, sunbathing strip popular with kayakers. The island also offers nine 'environmental' campsites (with running water, pit toilets and barbecues, but no showers) with stunning views of the Bay and city skyline; call Destinet on 1-800 444 7275 for reservations.

Bay Bridge

Linking the East Bay and Oakland with downtown, near Rincon Annex. Bus 32, 42 to the bridge/AC Transit bus F, O, N across the bridge. **Map J3**
Distinguished as the longest high-level steel bridge in the world (13.52km/8.5 miles), the two-part San Francisco-Oakland Bay Bridge marks the city's most dramatic entrance by highway. Designed by Charles H Purcell and opened in 1936, the bridge and its piers are bigger than the highest pyramid and built of more concrete than New York's Empire State Building. Its two levels and five lanes of traffic tunnel through **Yerba Buena Island**, where tourists stop off for the spectacular views of the West Bay section. **Treasure Island**, at the halfway point, marks the site of the 1939 World Fair held to celebrate the bridge's completion; the site later served as a naval base. Treasure Island Museum (*see chapter* **Children**), currently undergoing renovation, relives the building of the bridges and the island's military history. For a brief moment in October 1989, the Bay Bridge became more famous than the Golden Gate Bridge when part of the upper storey collapsed during the Loma Prieta quake. Since then, engineers have advocated rebuilding the eastern span: the city is currently inching bureaucratically towards a more suitable design.

Golden Gate Bridge

Linking the Toll Plaza near the Presidio with Marin County. Bus 28, 29, 76 to the bridge/Golden Gate Transit bus 10, 20, 30, 50, 60, 70, 80, 90 across the bridge. **Map A1**
Luminous symbol of San Francisco and star of countless films, the Golden Gate Bridge remains the city's ultimate icon. Taking its name from the mile-wide span of bay christened by Captain John Fremont in the 1840s, the Golden Gate took 13 years to plan, five to build and had claimed 11 lives by its completion in 1937. It incorporates 129,000km (80,000 miles) of cable into its 27,572 pencil-thick strands. The span is continuously repainted with rust-proof paint (5,000 gallons of 'International Orange' each year), rendering it fiery at sunset and surreally suspended when foggy. Walk across it for the best views of how the unique metal gussets allow flexibility in high winds. When the city threw a party to celebrate the bridge's 50th anniversary in 1987, a third of its population came – and the construction bowed visibly. Over 1,000 people have jumped from the bridge in suicide attempts, a statistic the police try not to publicise. A film on its construction can be seen at Fort Point, located beneath the south tower (556 1693; 11.30am, 3.30pm Wed-Sun).

Alamo Square

Bounded by Steiner, Scott, Hayes and Fulton Streets. Bus 5, 21, 24. **Map E5**
Alamo Square affords the most photographed view of the city, thanks to the six picture-perfect restored Victorian houses ('postcard row') that flank its eastern side. The windy square also incorporates a tennis court, picnic area and children's playground. Similar attractions and other fine views can be found to the north at **Alta Plaza Park** in Pacific Heights (also on Steiner, between Jackson and Clay Streets), and at **Lafayette Park** (on Gough at Sacramento Street). All these leafy havens are patronised by dog owners, children, joggers and pensioners sunning themselves.

Jackson Square

Bounded by Washington, Kearny and Sansome Streets and Pacific Avenue. Bus 12, 15, 30, 41, 42, 83. **Map H3**
All that remains of the once-notorious Barbary Coast is this renovated block, built on foundations made from the hulls of ships abandoned during the Gold Rush. In its heyday during the 1860s, 'terrific' Pacific Avenue harboured brothels and bars where young girls were reputedly spirited into white slavery and boys force-fed drink until they passed out – only to wake up on board ship as reluctant sailors. Much of the area perished in the 1906 Great Fire, but today it's lined with turn-of-the-century red brick offices lovingly restored and a distinct collection of antiques, furniture and bookshops.

Lombard Street

Between Hyde and Leavenworth Streets. Cable car Powell-Hyde. **Map F2**
San Francisco's 'crookedest street' snakes steeply down the edge of Russian Hill from Hyde Street, packing nine hairpin bends into one brick-paved and landscaped block. In the summer, tourists queue up for the thrill of driving down its hazardous 27 per cent gradient at 5mph – arrive early or late to avoid them and their cameras. For more on the surrounding streets of Russian Hill, and Telegraph Hill at the far end of Lombard Street, *see chapter* **San Francisco by Neighbourhood**. For further thrills, try negotiating the steepest street in the city: Filbert Street descends at a whopping 31.5 per cent gradient between Hyde and Leavenworth.

Nob Hill

Bounded by Bush, Larkin and Stockton Streets and Pacific Avenue. Bus 1, 27/cable car Powell-Hyde, Powell-Mason or California. **Map H3**
A short but incredibly steep walk (or cable car ride) up from Union Square, Nob Hill stands 103m (338ft) above the Bay. It wasn't until after the opening of the cable car line in the 1870s that its steep slopes began to attract wealthy residents,

Civic symbol: the **Golden Gate Bridge**. *See page 42.*

namely the 'Big Four' Boom Era spenders – Charles Crocker, Leland Stanford, Mark Hopkins and Collis P Huntington. Their palatial mansions perished in the fire that razed the city after the 1906 earthquake. Sole survivor was the mansion built for James C Flood in 1886, which was remodelled, and is now home to the exclusive 'gentlemen's' Pacific-Union Club. The grand residences were replaced by what are now the city's most élite hotels. They include the **Fairmont**, with its plush marble lobby and infamous ersatz-islander Tonga Room, complete with simulated tropical rainstorm; the **Huntington Hotel** with its Big Four bar; and the **Mark Hopkins Inter-Continental**, where the Top of the Mark bar offers fabulous views over the city. **Grace Cathedral** was built (starting in 1928) on the site of the former Crocker mansion. Local lore has it that Nob Hill is the safest place to stand in an earthquake.

Twin Peaks

Twin Peaks Boulevard, off Portola Drive, between Glenview Drive and Woodside Avenue. Bus 37, 48, 52.
The crackerbox apartments in the foreground are ugly and the climate may be windy, cold and foggy, but if you've hired a car, it's worth the gamble driving to the top of Twin Peaks for the city view. Ohlone legend stated that these paired mountains are actually twin daughters of an Indian chief, frozen for ever by the Great Spirit. On a clear day you'll get an unobstructed view of Market Street, the Financial District, Civic Center, the Mission, Bay Bridge and the East Bay cities of Oakland and Berkeley. To the north you'll see ugly Sutro Tower and catch a glimpse of the Golden Gate Bridge. Though you're only 270m (900ft) above the street grid, you'll feel as though you're flying.

Union Square

Bounded by Geary, Powell, Stockton and Post Streets. Bus 2, 3, 4, 30, 38, 45, 76/cable car Powell-Hyde or Powell-Mason. **Map G3/4**
The small square surrounded by plush shops and grand hotels takes its name from the pro-Union rallies held here on the eve of the Civil War. Though it's a little bedraggled, the square stands at the heart of the downtown district's hotels and upmarket shopping – from Tiffany and Hermès to Cartier and Georgiou – and so is usually packed with tourists. Palm trees shelter the buskers, mime artists, street musicians and a determined army of panhandlers who congregate here. Kerbside flower stalls add a Parisian touch; double-decker buses emulate those of London. On the Stockton Street side, the **TIX Bay Area** booth (433 7827) proffers half-price theatre tickets. At the centre of the square stands the **Dewey Monument**, a 30m (97ft) Corinthian column that commemorates the 1898 US naval victory at Manila during the Spanish-American war. After the Great Quake, the square became a tent refuge for the VIPs who had been staying in the nearby hotels. There are plans afoot to redesign the square – suggestions have included a landscaped urban mall or a new underground home for the displaced de Young museum – though none are definite yet.

Washington Square

On Columbus Avenue, at Union Street. Bus 15, 30, 39, 41. **Map G2**
Anchored by the Romanesque church of **Sts Peter and Paul**, this grassy park marks the heart of North Beach, San Francisco's oldest Italian community. North Beach was home to the raucous Beat poets, jazz musicians and free sex advocates who put down roots in the 1950s. Now, with Chinatown only a block away, tai chi practitioners and Chinese grandmothers mix in the park with young parents and kids, elderly gents chatting in Italian, poets hurrying from one café to another, and lawyers and accountants who've moved into the increasingly gentrified neighbourhood. The 1879 statue in the centre is of Benjamin Franklin, donated by a prohibitionist who wanted to offer water to thirsty citizens to keep their minds off booze. For the true flavour of the city's cultural, epicurean and artistic history, grab a cappuccino at **Mario's Bohemian Cigar Store** *(see chapter* **Restaurants & Cafés***)* and pay a visit to any of a number of public art fairs that fill the park during summer weekends.

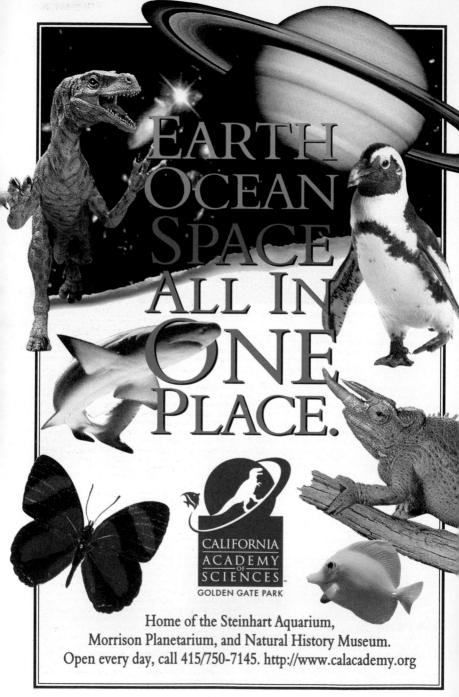

Civic Symbols

Balmy Alley

Off 24th Street, between Treat and Harrison Streets.
BART 24th Street/bus 12, 48, 67. **Castro/Mission**
Map Z2

The Mission district is famous for the hundreds of exuberant, brilliantly coloured murals that decorate everything from restaurants, banks and buildings to garage doors. Subjects range from Carnival to the building of the BART system, covering the political and social preoccupations of this working-class neighbourhood once populated by Italian, German and Irish residents. It's home to thousands of Hispanic families (who began emigrating from Central America in the 1960s) as well as Asian immigrants from Vietnam, Cambodia and Laos. While Balmy Alley was once a showplace for some of the city's best and freshest murals, it's beginning to suffer from neglect – and from home-owners who resent the constant flow of pedestrian traffic that the urban gallery brings. Some works have been replaced by iron fencing, others painted over. Still, there's plenty to see, and you shouldn't miss this crucial tableaux of San Francisco's artistic and political history. For tours of the Mission murals, *see p60* **Tours**; *see also chapters* **San Francisco by Neighbourhood** *and* **Museums & Galleries**.

Cable Cars

(Route information 673 6864). **Open** 6.30am-12.30am daily.

If the cable cars are a legendary part of the city, so is the hassle of getting a ticket to board one at the downtown Powell Street terminus. Scotsman Andrew Hallidie's quaint invention was originally intended to take passengers to the top of Nob Hill, but the story about how he got the idea – after watching a hapless horse-drawn vehicle being dragged backwards down the steep hill – is probably apocryphal. As it happened, he owned the patent on a wire cable grip developed by his father and wanted a market for it. His invention was first tested along five steep blocks of Clay Street in 1873. An amusing photograph of this maiden voyage can be seen at the **Cable Car Barn Museum** (*see chapter* **Museums & Galleries**), where you can also view the engines and wheels that operate the cables in operation. Out of the original 30, only three cable car lines survive: the Powell-Mason, Powell-Hyde and California lines. The California-Van Ness line is the least crowded, while the tourist-jammed Powell-Hyde line to Fisherman's Wharf affords the best views. Be wary of the close-passing traffic when jumping on and off. *See also p254* **Directory**.

Chinatown Gateway

Grant Avenue, at Bush Street. Bus 2, 3, 4, 15, 30, 45, 76.
Map G3

The ornate, three-arched gateway that marks the southern entrance to Chinatown was a gift from Taiwan in 1970. The design of the Dragons' Gate, as it's known, is based on the ceremonial entrances traditional in Chinese villages, and its three, green-tiled roofs are topped by various good-luck symbols, including two dragons and two large carp. The gateway leads onto Grant Avenue, Chinatown's main – and usually most tourist-thronged – thoroughfare. For more information on what to see in Chinatown, *see chapter* **San Francisco by Neighbourhood**. For details of Chinatown walking tours, *see page 60*.

City Hall

200 Polk Street, at Van Ness Avenue (554 4000).
Bus 5, 42, 47, 49. **Map F4/5**

Currently being retrofitted to protect it against earthquake damage, City Hall was originally built in 1915 under the auspices of Mayor 'Sunny Jim' Rolph to replace the one that collapsed during the 1906 quake. Designed by architect Arthur Brown in the Beaux Arts style, at a cost of $3.5

Lombard Street. *See page 42.*

million, it boasts a huge dome modelled on St Peter's in Rome and higher than the Capitol's in Washington DC by 4.9m (16ft). The centrepiece of the Civic Center complex, it was here that Dan White assassinated Mayor George Moscone and gay Supervisor Harvey Milk in 1978, and later marked the scene of the violent 'White Night Riot' after White was found guilty only of manslaughter (*see chapter* **History**). In recent years, the plaza around City Hall has been the subject of a battle between the Mayor and the homeless who have set up encampments only to be roused by police. City Hall is scheduled to re-open to visitors in January 1999.

Coit Tower

Telegraph Hill (362 0808). Bus 39. **Open** 10am-6.30pm daily. **Admission** (elevator) $3; $1-$2 concessions.
Map G2

Shaped like the nozzle of a fire hose, this 64m- (210ft-) high concrete tower, built by City Hall architect Arthur Brown in 1933, was a gift to the city from Lillie Hitchcock Coit. Coit, who was a fun-loving crossdresser, was snatched as a child from a blaze by a fireman and subsequently became a lifelong fan of fire fighters; when she died in 1929, she left San Francisco $118,000 to build a monument to them. Before you take the lift to the top, spend some time inspecting the murals inside the base of the column, artworks supervised by Diego Rivera for the WPA (Works Project Administration) set up by Roosevelt to create employment during the Depression. The Socialist Realist images of muscle-bound Californian workers were deemed subversive at the time of their completion in 1934; a hammer and sickle were erased from one, and nervous authorities delayed the tower's opening. **Telegraph Hill**, on which Coit Tower stands, marked the site of the West Coast's first telegraph, which tapped out bulletins of ships arriving from across the Pacific.

CONNECTING YOU FROM HART TO SEOUL.

© 1997 AT&T

 AND 1 800 **CALL ATT**® GETS YOU
FROM THE U.S. TO THE WORLD.

It's all within your reach.

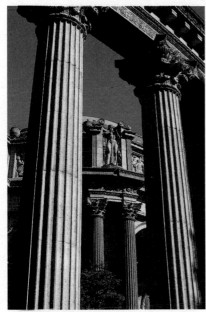

The **Palace of Fine Arts**.

Palace of Fine Arts

3601 Lyon Street, between Jefferson and Bay Streets (563 6504). Bus 28, 30, 43, 76. **Map C2**

The only surviving piece of finery left from the 1915 Panama-Pacific Exposition, the Palace was the centrepiece of a mile-long swathe of temporary buildings that stretched as far as Fort Mason and included an astonishing, multi-coloured, 132m- (432ft-) high Tower of Jewels. Builder Bernard Maybeck's *pièce de résistance* – his ode to the 'mortality of grandeur' – is a neo-classical domed rotunda supported by a curved colonnade topped with friezes and statues of weeping women, and is one of the most atmospheric spots in the city. Its lifespan was intended to be short, and the original plaster structure was mortal indeed. It was expensively replaced by a permanent concrete version in the 1960s, finished in time for the 1969 opening of the famous **Exploratorium**, a hands-on science museum which lies behind the Palace (*see chapter* **Museums & Galleries**). The Palace is flanked by a lagoon full of lily pads, ducks and swans, set in a small park at the foot of the pastel-painted Marina district.

San Francisco Main Library

Corner of Larkin and Grove Streets (557 4400). BART Civic Center/Muni Metro F, J, K, L, M, N/bus 5, 6, 7, 9, 19, 21, 66, 71. **Open** 10am-6pm Mon; 9am-8pm Tue-Thur; 11am-5pm Fri; 9am-5pm Sat; noon-5pm Sun. **Admission** free; $25 3-month visitor's card to check out books. **Map F/G4/5**

San Francisco's Main Library re-opened in 1996 in a gorgeous seven-storey building that combines the Beaux Arts style favoured by its compatriots in Civic Center with a healthy dash of modernism. Enter from the Larkin Street side and descend the stairway into the atrium-like lobby, where vaulted floors rise in tiers above you. At this first level, you can investigate the video, audio book and compact disk

sections or find the Deaf Services Center. A library for the blind and print-handicapped is on the second floor; the African, Filipino, Chinese and International sections are on the third. Upper levels include a business and technology centre on the fourth, a huge magazine and newspaper hub on the fifth, and an unparalleled San Francisco History room on the sixth. This top floor also offers a Skylight Art Gallery and a roof garden and terrace – don't miss either one. The café in the basement serves mediocre, expensive food; it's good only in a pinch. Though the library has been criticised since it opened for lack of resources and an unreliable reshelving system, it's nonetheless a remarkable resource.

Transamerica Pyramid

600 Montgomery Street, between Clay and Washington Streets (983 4100). Bus 1, 15, 41, 42. **Open** 8.30am-4.30pm Mon-Fri. **Map H3**

William Pereira's 260m (853ft) building – the tallest in San Francisco – provoked public outrage when it opened in 1972, but has since become an accepted (if not particularly loved) element of the city skyline. Built to be earthquake-proof, the exterior of San Francisco's most recognisable building is covered with panels that move laterally and sits on giant rollers that allow it to rock safely; something must work, because the building wasn't damaged by the 1989 Loma Prieta quake. Sadly, the observation area on the 27th floor, about halfway up, is no longer open to the public.

Churches & Cathedrals

Glide Memorial United Methodist Church

330 Ellis Street, at Taylor Street (771 6300). BART Powell Street/Muni Metro F, J, K, L, M, N/bus 27, 31, 38. **Map G4**

Glide's Sunday morning services at 9am and 11am are a San Francisco institution: multi-cultural and liberationist, packed with worshippers of every age and race (although increasingly white and middle-class), drawn by the exuberance of the gospel choir and the exhortations to do good. Minister Cecil Williams, whose roots go back to the early days of the civil rights movement, is a major player in the city's left-of-centre politics and anti-poverty efforts. Glide spearheads major drug treatment initiatives, runs self-help programmes for people who are HIV-positive and staffs a soup kitchen for the homeless.

Grace Cathedral

1100 California Street, at Taylor Street (749 6300). Bus 1, 27/cable car California. **Open** 7am-6pm daily. **Map G3**

With a façade modelled on Notre Dame in Paris, a gorgeous rose window, gilded bronze doors made from casts of the Doors of Paradise in Florence's Baptistry and a magnificent organ, the city's Episcopalian cathedral is a mock-Gothic extravaganza. Midnight mass here, intoned by the celebrated boys' choir, is a Christmas ritual. Sung eucharist is heavily attended too, and there's always plenty of action in between – from concerts, weddings and funerals to appeals by visiting dignitaries. The cathedral stands on what was once the site of Charles Crocker's family mansion on Nob Hill: he donated the land after his house burned to the ground in the 1906 fire. Grace took 54 years to build and sports a recent $13.3 million retrofit.

Mission Dolores

Dolores Street, at 16th Street (621 8203). BART 16th Street/Muni Metro F, J, K, L, M/bus 22. **Open** *summer* 9am-4.30pm daily; *winter* 9am-4pm daily. **Admission** $2; $1 concessions. **Map E6**

Small wonder that the cool, dim interior of the Mission San Francisco de Asisi looks authentic. The oldest standing structure in the city, its 4ft-thick adobe walls have withstood

Beaux Arts with a dash of modernism: the new **San Francisco Main Library.** *See page 47.*

the test of time (and earthquakes). Dedicated on 2 August 1791, Mission Dolores was the sixth of 21 Franciscan missions built by Spanish settlers, and was named for the nearby Laguna de los Dolores (Lake of Our Lady of Sorrows). Now it's attached to a basilica (rebuilt in 1918) where most of the religious services take place, including the traditional midnight mass at Christmas. There's a tiny museum and a flower-filled cemetery containing the remains of the city's first mayor as well as Spanish settlers, and the mass grave of thousands of Indians who died in their service.

Old St Mary's Cathedral

660 California Street, at Grant Avenue (288 3800). Bus 1, 15, 30, 45/cable car California. **Open** 7am-7pm Mon-Fri; 10am-7pm Sat; 7.30am-5pm Sun. **Map G3**
When the city's first-ever Catholic cathedral was built in 1854, it represented the most solid structure yet built on the West Coast and, although its bell and altars melted, it did survive the 1906 earthquake and fire. Constructed of granite imported from China, the church offered the city's first English language school for the Chinese community. The clock tower reads 'Son, observe the time and fly from evil' – probably a reference to what was at the time the particularly seedy neighbourhood in which it was built.

St Mary's Cathedral

1111 Gough Street, at Geary Boulevard (567 2020). Bus 2, 3, 4, 38. **Open** 6.45am-4.30pm Mon-Fri; 6.45am-6.30pm Sat; 7.15am-4.45pm Sun. **Map F4**
The city's newest Catholic cathedral (designed by Pietro Belluschi and finished in 1971) is a huge, white, concrete structure that resembles a washing machine (some say a food mixer) and dominates the skyline for miles around. Even its soaring, 61m- (200ft-) high, stained glass windows look dated, although the interior is light, plain and simple. These days, the church, which seats 2,500, is popular for large funerals and tour groups whose buses line the street outside. Local legend has it that Belluschi took some flak for the fact that on some sunny days, the perfect silhouette of a female breast appears on the cathedral's side.

Waterfront & Wharf

Aquatic Park

Between Hyde Street and Van Ness Avenue. Bus 19, 30, 32, 42/cable car Powell-Hyde. **Map F1**
The shores of Aquatic Park offers one of the best strolls in the city, providing a panorama of the Golden Gate Bridge, Alcatraz, windsurfers, sailing boats, wildly coloured kites and dogs catching Frisbees. Along the Municipal Pier, Vietnamese fishermen try their luck; historic ships are moored at Hyde Pier, to the east, including the *Eureka*, an 1890 steam-powered ferry. It's here that the 2.17km (32 mile) Golden Gate Promenade begins, continuing along the Bay past the defunct gun emplacements of **Fort Mason** to Crissy Field, where open-air concerts are held, and the **Golden Gate Bridge**. The entire waterfront (as far west as Ocean Beach) was incorporated into the Golden Gate National Recreation Area in 1972, when authorities barred the tourist kitsch of Fisherman's Wharf that interrupts this, the world's largest urban park. Only hardy regulars from the nearby Dolphin Club, wearing matching Speedos, risk a plunge into the choppy sea.

The Embarcadero

Between Pier 41 and China Basin. BART Embarcadero/bus 32, 42. **Map F1-J4**
Once obscured by a glum freeway overpass, San Francisco's most spectacular promenade has been refurbished, dotted with public art, fortified with historical markers and benches and framed with palm trees. At its centre is the stately Ferry Building, which divides even-numbered piers (to the south) from odd (to the north). Before the opening of the bridges in the 1930s, 50 million ferry passengers used the Embarcadero annually – now less than two million embark for the Marin suburbs of Sausalito, Tiburon and Larkspur or sunny East Bay communities like Alameda and Vallejo. Opposite the Ferry Building stands Justin Herman Plaza and a walk-through water sculpture by French-Canadian artist Armand Vaillancourt. Justin Herman is the rallying

point for most big demonstrations from anti-war to pro-choice, and the centre of an ebullient farmers' market every Saturday morning. A section of the Embarcadero has been christened 'Herb Caen Boulevard...' in honour of the Chronicle's longtime daily columnist, who died in 1997 (*see chapter* **Media**). He attended the renaming ceremony before he died, and there's a statue of him next to the Ferry Building. The clock on the Ferry Building's tower – an 1894 replica of Seville cathedral's campanile – stopped at the precise minute the 1906 and 1989 earthquakes struck, but, although the building's spire leaned precariously, on neither occasion did it fall.

Fisherman's Wharf

Jefferson and Beach Streets, between Kearny and Hyde Streets. Bus 15, 30, 32, 39, 42/cable car Powell-Hyde or Powell-Mason. **Map F1**

San Francisco's port was once the soul of the city, but as the shipping and fishing business moved on the Wharf was converted into a garish and tacky tourist site, amusing only to those with a taste for kitsch or the macabre. The magic of its history survives only in the wee small hours when the few fishermen still working unload their catch for buyers from the city's gourmet restaurants. The **Maritime Museum** (556 3002) on Beach Street, at the foot of Polk Street, remains one of the only buildings to remember that past. Among the offered 'amusements' are **Ripley's Believe It Or Not! Museum** (175 Jefferson Street; 771 6188), with its two-headed calf and nasty photos of people doing nasty things; the **Wax Museum** (145 Jefferson Street; 1-800 439 4305), which displays more than 300 life-size figures, including various US presidents, members of the British royal family, Elvis Presley and William Shakespeare; and countless restaurants, cafés and souvenir shops. The World War II *Pampanito* submarine is docked at Pier 45 and worth a tour. Further to the west (at 2801 Leavenworth Street), **The Cannery** – once a Del Monte vegetable canning factory and now a renovated shopping centre – and **Ghirardelli Square** (900 North Point Street, between Polk and Larkin Streets) – a collection of carefully restored red-brick buildings that once belonged to the celebrated chocolate-makers – comprise a series of (marginally) more up-market shops and restaurants.

Fort Point

Marine Drive (556 1693). Bus 28, 29. **Open** 10am-5pm Wed-Sun. **Admission** free. **Map A1**

A spectacular brick fortress with a melodramatic setting beneath the southern edge of the Golden Gate Bridge, Fort Point resembles a vast outdoor stage crying out for some good open-air theatre. Interestingly, the performances here are historic re-enactments of the Civil War, performed by and for children. The fort was built between 1853 and 1861 to protect the city from a sea attack (that never came), and its 126 cannons remained idle until the fort was closed in 1900. The four-storey vaulted building houses a giant ten-inch Rodman gun as well as various military exhibitions; guided tours are available. The pier is famous as the spot where Kim Novak's character attempts suicide in *Vertigo.*

The Arts & Sciences

For more museums, including the Asian Art Museum, *see chapter* **Museums & Galleries**.

California Academy of Sciences

See chapter **Museums & Galleries** *for listings.*

Located in Golden Gate Park, opposite the de Young museum, this is the oldest scientific institution in the western US. It houses the fabulous **Steinhart Aquarium** (*see chapter* **Children**), the Morrison Planetarium and laserium as well as some wonderful natural history displays and an earthquake exhibition.

The **Embarcadero***. See page 49.*

California Palace of the Legion of Honor

See chapter **Museums & Galleries** *for listings.*

Spectacularly placed on a promontory overlooking the Golden Gate Bridge, just north of Land's End, the Palace of the Legion of Honor is architect George Applegarth's homage to the Palais de la Légion d'Honneur in Paris. Built in the 1920s, it was donated to the city as a memorial to California's World War I dead. The museum originally only displayed French works of art, but today lesser paintings by Fra Angelico, Titian, El Greco, Rubens, Rembrandt, Renoir, Degas, Monet and Cézanne are on view. New galleries – opened after a three-year retrofitting of the building following the 1989 quake – offer viewers more opportunities to glimpse the museum's permanent collection. Of these, the **Rodin Collection** is the finest outside the Musée Rodin in Paris, and includes a cast of 'Le Penseur', and fine works by Camille Claudel, while the vast **Achenbach Foundation** is devoted to works of graphic art. Outside, the surrounding Lincoln Park houses an 18-hole golf course. Just north of the Palace's parking lot, is the haunting **Jewish Holocaust Memorial** sculpted by George Segal.

Fort Mason Center

Marina Boulevard (entrance at Buchanan Street) (441 5706). Bus 28. **Map E1**

Home to cultural organisations such as the Magic Theater (which has premiered several Sam Shepard plays), the Cowell and Hearst performance theaters, various eateries, shops, galleries and several small museums, Fort Mason is a waterfront complex of reconditioned military buildings that served as a command post for the US Army in the 1850s. To the city's benefit, Fort Mason was converted to peaceful use in 1972, and now forms part of the Golden Gate National Recreation Area. Among the museums on site is the delightful **Mexican Museum**, which exhibits Mexican art and

Trusted by the world to send money in minutes.

Track what remains of the city's fishing fleet down at **Fisherman's Wharf**. *See page 51.*

sells handcrafted jewellery and embroidery; the **African-American Historical & Cultural Society Museum**; the **Museo Italo-Americano**; and the **San Francisco Craft and Folk Art Museum**, which features exhibitions covering anything from book binding to furniture. The Book Bay Bookstore (771 1076), run by Friends of the San Francisco Public Library, sells second-hand books for a mere 25¢. Fort Mason also houses one of the city's favourite restaurants, Greens (*see chapter* **Restaurants & Cafés**), which serves gourmet vegetarian meals in a spectacular dining room overlooking the Marina and Golden Gate Bridge. *See also chapters* **Museums & Galleries** *and* **Theatre & Dance**.

San Francisco Museum of Modern Art

See chapter **Museums & Galleries** *for listings.*
A symbol of the city's growing status as a centre for modern culture, SFMOMA is fast becoming another local icon. Red brick dominated by a huge cylindrical skylight and trimmed with a stunning play of black and white striped stone, the museum is America's first design by Swiss architect Mario Botta. It stands as the centrepiece of the **Yerba Buena Gardens** complex, which also contains a theatre, a convention centre, acres of gardens and other exhibition halls and galleries with a penchant for showing edge-cutting local artists. Since it opened in 1995, SFMOMA has attracted huge crowds lured by its collection of abstract, expressionist and post-modern artists (from Wassily Kandisky to Sigmar Polke). Especially strong is the photography collection and the Cultural Center's programme of contemporary music.

War Memorial Opera House

See chapter **Music** *for listings.*
San Francisco has been an opera buffs' paradise since the 1850s, and has never had any trouble in attracting world-class performers. Enrico Caruso gave a triumphant performance here the night before the 1906 earthquake and then fled the next day. In 1923, Gaetono Merola founded the San Francisco Opera and in 1932 the company moved into its permanent home, a Beaux Arts gem designed by Arthur Brown and dedicated to solders who fought in World War I. It was here in

June 1945 that 51 nations signed the United Nations charter and gave birth to the UN. The Opera House recently underwent major retrofitting and renovation – an $86.5 million task that included everything from newly gilded trim on the doors and walls to re-upholstered seats, new curtains and a 66,000-watt chandelier. To the north of the Opera House is the **Veteran's Building**, constructed at the same time, which formerly housed the Museum of Modern Art.

Gardens & Parks

See also page 42 **Hills, Streets & Squares;** *for Golden Gate Park see page 54.*

The Presidio

Main entrances at Lombard Street (at Lyon Street), Presidio Boulevard (at Broadway), Arguello Boulevard (at Jackson Street), Lincoln Boulevard (at 25th Avenue) and Golden Gate Bridge Toll Plaza (561 4323). Bus 3, 29, 43. **Map A1-C3**

Golden Gate Park's **Japanese Tea Garden.**

Covering 1,590 acres of fabulous bayside views and rolling green hills by the Golden Gate Bridge, the Presidio was a military outpost from 1776, when Captain Juan Bautista de Anza planted the Spanish flag here. It became a US army outpost, which it remained until 1993, when the 18km (11 miles) of hiking trails, 22.5km (14 miles) of bike routes and five kilometres (three miles) of beaches became part of the Golden Gate National Recreation Area. Among the 500-odd buildings, from Civil War mansions to simple barracks dating from the 1890s, is the old-fashioned **Presidio Museum** (Lincoln Boulevard at Funston Avenue; 561 4323). Built in 1864, it is based in the old station hospital and serves as a repository of documents and artifacts from the city's military and political past. It is open from noon to 4pm, Wednesday to Sunday.

The Presidio's recent return to civilian management finds its future use in question: current opinion vacillates between returning the land to natural uses, reclaiming part of the vacated housing for the homeless or favouring takeover by prestigious social and cultural bodies – Mikhail Gorbachev has rented the Coast Guard Lifesaving Station for his Peace Foundation. Commercial developers clamour for its more than $2 billion in prime real estate, and the seven-member trust recently appointed by President Clinton to run the Presidio must try to make it financially self-sufficient to avoid major development. Don't miss the long Lovers' Walk that runs parallel to Presidio Boulevard just north of the Broadway gate – it marks the original path from the Presidio to the (then much smaller) city.

Golden Gate Park

One of the world's largest urban green havens – its 1,013 acres range from the Haight to the Pacific – Golden Gate Park forms an oasis of lakes, landscaped vistas, flower beds, meadows, trails and forest, much of it seemingly completely removed from the city.

In 1871, landscape architect William Hammond Hall took up the challenge of turning a barren stretch of sand dunes into a park respecting the land's natural contours. A million trees were planted over the years under the tutelage of gardener John McLaren and, as the park's fame spread, horticulturists from all over the world sent in seeds and cuttings. The result is a treat: a Japanese tea garden, a Chinese pavilion,

an arboretum, an antique carousel and a Dutch windmill are but a scattering of the treasures found in the park. The **Conservatory of Flowers** (currently closed after suffering storm damage in 1996), at the park's eastern edge on John F Kennedy Drive, is modelled on London's Palm House in Kew Gardens; at the opposite end, the **Beach Chalet** is a brewpub and art gallery displaying some of the city's finest reconditioned murals. There are also two museums – the **California Academy of Sciences** (*see page 51*) and the **de Young Museum** – stables and trails for horses and a pasture for a herd of American buffalo, lakes for boating, miles of bike trails and swooping concrete paths for rollerbladers.

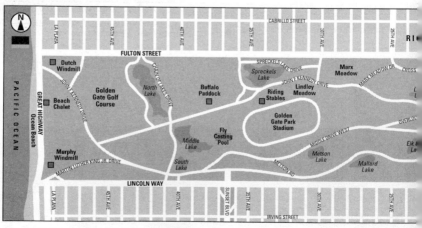

Beaches

Because of cold currents and rare Great White shark sightings, it's mostly the wetsuited few who enjoy beach culture (in the southern Californian sense) in San Francisco, paddling into the chilly waves to boogie-board, surf or occasionally snorkel and dive. Yet to the south and north of the city, along Hwy 1 (SR 1), runs a glorious string of beaches, each a protected pearl guarded by conservationists and sinfully underused. To the north are several with nudist corners, including Kirby Cove, Black Sand, Red Rock, Bonita, Bolinas, Rodeo and Muir beaches. To the south unfold endless miles of ravishing sands, including Devil's Slide (recently reopened after storm damage), Gray Whale Cove, continuing past San Gregorio and Pomponio to Bonny Doon, Santa Cruz and Monterey.

In the city there are three great beaches, all of which are accessible by public transport:

Baker Beach

To the south-west of the Golden Gate Bridge. Bus 1, 29.
Running for almost a mile along the craggy shoreline, Baker Beach is the former hiding place of a huge cannon, camouflaged

Over the years, the park has hosted everything from encampments for earthquake victims and the homeless to rock concerts, performances of Shakespeare and opera, the annual Bay to Breakers running race, a funeral for Grateful Dead icon Jerry Garcia attended by 10,000 fans, and food festivals serving up every imaginable type of cuisine. There are days' worth of activities to be discovered in this magnificent reserve. *See also chapters* **History**, **Children** *and* **Museums & Galleries**.

Between Fulton and Stanyan Streets, Lincoln Way and the Great Highway. Muni Metro N/bus 5, 7, 18, 21, 28, 29, 33, 44, 66, 71. **Open** dawn to dusk daily.

The park's Aids memorial.

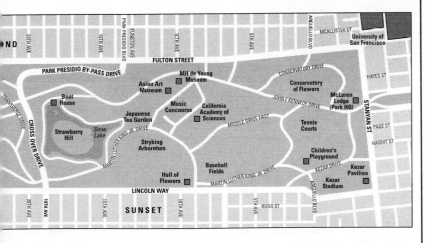

here by the army in 1905 to protect the bay, although it never saw active service. A replica of the original 95,000-pounder has been installed for the curious. Picnic tables, sunbathing and fishing are the real lure now, since cold water, occasional water pollution and strong currents deter swimmers. A northern section of the beach (towards the Golden Gate Bridge) is predominantly gay and nudist, and recommended only for those really keen to connect with nature. To the south lie the backs of expensive Sea Cliff homes that sit perched above the water.

Part of the fun of Baker Beach is getting there. If you're driving from the north, take Lincoln Boulevard through the Presidio to Bowley Street; from the south, take 25th Avenue to Lincoln Boulevard. You can also cycle or walk the Coastal Trail from Golden Gate Bridge, flanked by the Presidio and providing some breathtaking views of the coastline.

James D Phelan Beach (China Beach)

Seacliff Avenue. Bus 18, 29.
Slotted between Baker Beach and Lincoln Park in the exclusive Sea Cliff neighbourhood is the beautifully sheltered and windproof China Beach, which took its nickname from the settlement of Chinese fisherman who camped here in the last century. It's the nicest of all the beaches, and local residents would prefer to keep it for themselves. Public demand prevails, however, and it's still open to all. Despite the free sundeck, showers and changing rooms, the beach remains uncrowded. Pacific Heights nannies, students and unmolested sunbathers call this their own, with plenty of parking and a pleasant hike down to the sand. China is also a popular spot for barbecues and weddings.

Ocean Beach

Great Highway. Muni Metro N/bus 18, 31, 38.
The city's biggest beach is a five kilometre (three mile) sandy strip along the Pacific coast at the end of the fog-bound Sunset district, where people stroll, walk dogs, paddle and have illicit midnight revels. It's also a haven for homeless (when the weather is nice) and the local pagan community, and several times a year hosts local surfing competitions. If nature had its way, the beach would advance up as far as Twin Peaks, but it is prevented by a large wall (added in the 1920s) that runs parallel to the Great Highway. A cycle path passes along Ocean Beach as far as Sloat Avenue and San Francisco Zoo, from where you can stroll to Fort Funston ('Fort Fun') and to Mussel Rocks, headquarters of hanggliders and windsurfers. However, the currents are strong, especially at Point Lobos, where a number of experienced surfers drown every year, and swimming is not advised.

Views

With its plummeting hills and Bay vistas, the city offers an abundance of amazing views. One of the most clichéd is from the 19th-floor bar of the Mark Hopkins Hotel on Nob Hill, where the **Top of the Mark** offers a panorama of the night sky (*see chapter* **Bars**). One of the best cheap thrills to be had downtown is a ride in one of the great glass elevators of the **Westin St Francis Hotel** (335 Powell Street, at Union Square). Framed like a vanity mirror with light bulbs, the lifts shoot up the outside of the hotel's tower, providing stunning views and a rollercoaster adrenaline rush.

Another popular panorama is from the slopes of **Twin Peaks** (bus 37 takes you to the top), which overlook the Castro and Cole Valley at the start of the often fog-bound Sunset district in the west. Further north and to the west of the Castro is a much better scramble onto a rocky outcrop called **Tank Hill** (bus 33, 37), where you'll find an old water tank and an exhilarating vista that puts you in mind of Batman's view of Gotham City (and indeed, it's not a good idea to go at night).

Ocean Beach: *not recommended for swimming, but great for strolling.*

Communion in B-flat

The throb of a rhythm section spilling from the modest storefront – wedged between a grocer's and a used kitchen appliance shop – sounds strangely out of place on a sunny Sunday morning. But one step through the colourful tiled doorway delivers you not into a smoky all-hours club or a stuffy chapel but into St John's African Orthodox Church, where you'll discover an incense-scented sanctuary, its floor shaking with live music. Here, in a realm where religiousness is a state of mind and music is the only sacred text, the seemingly disparate worlds of hard bop and Christian worship proudly co-exist.

Located within walking distance of Golden Gate Park and the Haight-Ashbury, St John's is dedicated to preserving the musical and spiritual philosophies of its patron saint, the late saxophonist John William Coltrane. Part art gallery and part living shrine, the church features, alongside traditional icons and images of the Orthodoxy, portraits of Coltrane, beautifully painted in gold leaf, with fire leaping from his saxophone.

At St John's, it's best to leave preconceptions of 'church music' outside: the house of worship is the only one in the country where its reverend and founder, Bishop Franzo FW King, plays a mean soprano sax as part of his liturgy, and where parishioners wear protective earplugs as part of their Sunday best. St Johns' service features stirring organ, piano, electric bass and drums as well as numerous saxophones and various percussion instruments. As the room rocks to noisy renditions of 'Africa' and 'Lonnie's Lament', half the members are playing and the other half swaying to the music. The resulting tohubohu is a choreographed exercise in good will and deep spirituality, a glorious testimony to the power of Coltrane's music.

St John's is a friendly place where bleary-eyed Deadheads and unshaven jazz aficionados join impeccably dressed African-American families, where an ecumenical collar appears above a Miles Davis T-shirt. You'll be asked to chip in during the passing of the basket, so come with a few dollars to hand. The parishioners come and go throughout the service, eating, chatting and laughing. But like the crowd at a warehouse club on a weekend night, those gathered at St John's have come first and foremost for Coltrane's music, which – like a healthy dose of old-time religion – will always have a place in this world.

St John's African Orthodox Church

351 Divisadero Street, between Oak and Page Streets (621 4054). Bus 6, 7, 24, 66, 71. **Services** 6pm Wed; 10am, 10.30am, 11.45am Sun. **Map E5**

During the day, take the lift to the top of the **Coit Tower** on Telegraph Hill (bus 39) for another favourite view, where you can see piers and jetties poking out into the Bay. Descend the hill by the secluded trail to the east, down the Filbert Steps (*see pages 58-59*), with its flower bedecked paths and earthquake cottages, and past the eccentric Julius Castle restaurant perched at the crest of Montgomery Street.

Stroll along the **Golden Gate Promenade** (bus 19, 22, 28, 30), past the Marina Green and Crissy Field from Aquatic Park for more Bay- and bridge-scapes, and continue round the coastal path in the **Presidio** (bus 28, 29) for more of the same. **Fort Point** (bus 28, 29) provides an underside view of the Golden Gate Bridge. Further to the west, the **Cliff House** (bus 18, 31, 38), across Point Lobos Avenue from **Sutro Heights Park**, is another tourist-packed spot, but nonetheless a good one for gazing out over the Seal Rocks at sunset.

South along the coast past the San Francisco Zoo is **Fort Funston** (bus 18), a promontory which makes a handy jumping-off point for hang-gliders, surfers and other foolhardy types. You can

gaze out to sea with them, or lie on the sand underneath staring up at them.

The **Marin Headlands**, just north of the Golden Gate Bridge off US 101 (bus 28, 76 and all Golden Gate Transit buses), provides another much-loved perspective. The usual stop for tourists is Vista Point, just across the bridge. Another option is to cross under the highway to the Marin Headlands, and then take the winding, windswept road that climbs past gun emplacements to any of a number of parking areas, then look east over the city.

Finally, nothing beats the view you get of the Financial District – by day or night – when you enter the city via the top deck of the **San Francisco-Oakland Bay Bridge**.

Tours

San Francisco offers visitors an astonishing variety of customised tours – from boat or bus trips to tours on foot with a literary, artistic or culinary bent. There are excursions that cover specific

Urban stairmaster

Many of them overgrown with foliage and often unmarked, San Francisco's stairways provide a network of some of the city's most untravelled paths and unspoiled views, both broad and intimate. Nearly 400 different stairways connect the city's 42 hills, treacherous topography that not even a Roman army would have joined with a road. If you don't spend much time on foot, you could visit the city without even noticing their existence – but once you discover one hidden stairway, uncovering others becomes compulsive. Park your car and lace up your favourite pair of all-terrain climbers, and discover another side of San Francisco.

Novice stairway spotters should look for the yellow diamond-shaped signs on hilly routes that say 'Not a Through Street' and assume that a staircase lies beyond. You won't walk many before you become a stairway snob. Soon you'll be discriminating between those that are just a small set of stairs ending a street (such as you'll find descending the seven steps at the corner of Clifford Terrace and Roosevelt Way in Twin Peaks), those that are just pavements with stairs in them (Filbert Street, between Leavenworth and Hyde Streets, on Russian Hill) and those that offer architect-designed steps, breathtaking views and arum lilies growing in the adjacent flower beds (Vallejo Street, between Jones and Mason Streets, and several stairways on Russian Hill).

On a hot day you can seek out a stairway shaded from the sun's rays beneath a canopy of Monterey pines (Baker Street, between Broadway and Green Street, in Pacific Heights). Don't get too carried away with the view if you're descending this particular staircase, however, since halfway down some joker changed the pitch of the stairs. It may be one of the best views in the city, but it isn't good enough to be your last.

The best stairways are those that replace road or pavement altogether. Moving into the houses that line them must be quite a feat, though they're so beautiful you can't imagine anyone wanting to move out again. Just such a stairway street is leafy Macondray Lane (off Leavenworth Street, between Union and Green Streets), inspiration for Armistead Maupin's Barbary Lane and miraculously secluded. Idiosyncratic houses line one side, through which you can catch tantalising glimpses of the Bay beyond. As with many of the better stairways, the signpost is hard to spot (look for the imprint of the name in the concrete of the kerb).

For a long graceful descent, start at Jones and Vallejo Streets and walk east (uphill) for a block, admiring the collision of architecture here at the peak of Nob Hill. Take the stairs to the right of the overlook (made famous in a scene during the 1978 remake of *Invasion of the Body Snatchers*) and, winding past landscaped backyards and friendly cats, descend slowly to Coolbrith Park a block down. Continue down another long block of stairs, enjoying the view of the Bay Bridge, the piers and Treasure Island, until you reach Mason Street – where you'll find the Mason Street cable car line at the periphery of Chinatown and North Beach.

Stairway-walking is not for the faint-hearted or cardiac-challenged. But for those who persevere, there is usually a parapet or seat at the top to rest on while admiring the city view (something you don't get on the machines at your local gym). Try the climb along Broadway between Taylor and Jones Streets, where you can rest on a bench and take in the view of the Bay Bridge with the Transamerica Pyramid and the Financial District spread out below. At the Pemberton stairway in Twin Peaks, a seat is perfectly positioned for the waverers in your party – at the bottom.

---

areas, such as Chinatown, the Mission, the Castro or North Beach; and those that focus on themes – the architecture, film locations, views or crime scenes, whether real (the Patty Hearst bank robbery) or fictitious (the murder of Miles Archer, Sam Spade's partner in *The Maltese Falcon*).

A rough selection of what's on offer appears below; for more suggestions, visit the Visitor's Information Center, at the corner of Market and Powell Streets under Hallidie Plaza (*see page 251* **Directory**), or consult the pink Datebook section of the Sunday *San Francisco Chronicle and Examiner*.

Walking Tours

For details of **Cruisin' the Castro**, *see page 61*.

Architectural Tours

Heritage Tours, Foundation for San Francisco's Architectural Heritage (441 3004). **Tickets** $5; $3 concessions. *Victorian Home Walks (252 9485).* **Tickets** $20.
Heritage runs two tours, exploring Pacific Heights (on Sundays), long the preserve of the city's wealthiest residents, and the Yerba Buena area of the SoMa district (on the first Saturday of the month); phone for timings and meeting places. Jay Gifford of Victorian Home Walks conducts daily, laid-back, custom-designed, 2½-hour tours of the city's Victorian architecture; meet at Union Square at 11am.

For more detailed guidance, consult Adah Bakalinsky's exhaustive (and exhausting) *Stairway Walks in San Francisco* ($10.95), which offers 27 graded and tested stairway walks.

Near Pacific Heights

Culebra Terrace
Chestnut Street, between Larkin and Polk Streets. Bus 19/cable car Powell-Hyde. **Map F2**
A climb shaded by Monterey pines, which offers a great view of the Golden Gate Bridge.

Lyon Street Steps
Between Green Street and Broadway. Bus 3, 24, 43. **Map D3**
Begin at Green Street, where you'll climb the edge of the Presidio into Pacific Heights. Great views of Alcatraz, the Palace of Fine Arts and the Golden Gate Bridge. At the top you're just a stone's throw from the entrance to the Presidio.

Macondray Lane
Leavenworth and Jones Streets, between Union and Green Streets. Bus 41, 45/cable car Powell-Hyde. **Map F2**
A great climb for *Tales of the City* nostalgia and leafy views from Russian Hill.

Vallejo Street
Between Jones and Taylor Streets. Bus 41, 45/cable car Powell-Mason. **Map G2**
More views, with houses and steps designed by Willis Polk (1867-1924). Don't miss 1045 Vallejo, the top floor of which was remodelled by Polk to allow views in all directions. Laura Ingalls Wilder stayed with her daughter Rose at No. 1019 in 1915.

Near Twin Peaks

Ord Court
Off Levant Street, between States and Lower Stairway Terrace Streets. Bus 33, 37.
A shady, intimate walk in the heart of Buena Vista overlooking the Upper Haight. More cats than people will be visible on your descent.

Pemberton Place
Between Clayton Street and Crown Terrace. Bus 33, 37.
This pulse-pounder affords stunning views of the city from Twin Peaks.

Sanchez Street
Between Liberty and 21st Streets. Muni Metro J/bus 24, 35. **Castro/Mission Map X2**
Descend the wide stairway in Dolores Heights, the hilly region of the Mission district. With views of downtown and sloping Dolores Park, this climb is one of the best in the city.

23rd Street Urban Hike
Begin at Diamond Street. Bus 24, 53, 48. **Castro/Mission Map X2**
Climb west (towards Eureka, streets are alphabetical). At Grand View, take the pedestrian overpass across Portola, then follow the series of stairways that climb to the base of Twin Peaks. A trail to the right will lead you to the top of the southernmost peak, a full 278m (910ft) above the city's skyline. Pack a camera.

Chinatown
All About Chinatown Tours (982 8839).
Tickets $25; $10 under-17s.
Wok Wiz Chinatown Tours & Cooking Co (1-800 281 9255).
Tickets $25 walk only; $37 with lunch.
Glorious Food Culinary Tours (441 5637).
Tickets $35 with lunch.
Each of the many tours of the 24-block enclave offers a varied menu of stops both historical and culinary. Led by television chef and writer Shirley Fong-Torres, the Wok Wiz tour covers historical alleyways, Chinese herbalists and groceries, dim sum restaurants and fortune cookie factories, among other things. Glorious Food also offers a North Beach tour ($30; $50 combined with Chinatown tour).

Dashiell Hammett Walking Tour
Tour details 1-510 287 9540. Starts from San Francisco Main Library, at Larkin and Grove Streets. Muni Metro F, J, K, L, M, N/bus 5, 19, 21, 26, 47, 49.
Time *May-Aug* noon Sat. **Tickets** $10.
Follow writer-guide Don Herron around the Tenderloin in the footsteps of his hero, Dashiell Hammett. The tour starts at the Main Library: look for the guy in the hat and trenchcoat. As Herron's four-hour tour proves, it's hard not to trip over Hammett's ghost; if you don't fancy Wild Turkey, pork chops or the Reading Room at the Main Library, check the placard near the Stockton Tunnel which reads 'On approximately this spot, Miles Archer, partner of Sam Spade, was done in by Brigid Shaughnessy'. Or visit Spade's apartment at 811 Post Street, where Sam clamped his teeth together and said to Brigid, 'I won't play the sap

for you'. Finish your tour at Hammett's regular restaurant, John's Grill at 63 Ellis Street. *See also chapter* **Literary San Francisco**.

Golden Gate Park

Friends of Recreation and Parks (recorded information 263 0991).
Free walking tours (May-Oct) of the 1,013-acre green giant, led by the Friends of Recreation and Parks, take in all the major points such as the Strybing Arboretum and Botanical Gardens, the museums and the Conservatory of Flowers, as well as more flora and fauna and additional history.

The Haight-Ashbury

Flower Power Haight-Ashbury Tours (221 8442). **Tickets** $15.
This two-hour walk relives the Summer of Love some three decades later, with pointers to the history and locations of the Haight's most famous subcultural movement. See where the Grateful Dead shacked up, where Janis Joplin died and where hippies and the 1960s will live forever.

Mural Tours

Precita Eyes Mural Arts Center Tours (information 285 2287). **Tickets** $4-$30.
Choose among half a dozen different public art tours made available by Precita Eyes, the experts with 15 years' experience in local mural painting and preservation. Led by volunteers, the most popular tour is a Mission mural walk that includes over 75 works of art in an eight-block stroll, including those on and around 24th Street and on both sides of Balmy Alley. Other tours are given on bikes, aboard a Mexican bus (with refreshments), and in various groups. Tours in Spanish are also available. For more on San Francisco murals and public art, *see chapter* **Museums and Galleries**.

Neighbourhood Walks

The City Guides, Friends of the San Francisco Public Library, Main Library, San Francisco, CA 94102 (information 557 4266).
Voluntary guides steer visitors around town, shedding light on some unusual corners of the city. Most popular are their tours of North Beach, Victorian San Francisco, Pacific Heights, the Mission and Japantown; others cover the Beaux Arts Buildings and City Hall, Chinatown, Cityscapes and Roof Gardens. All tours are free and extra ones are organised from May to October; for a brochure, send an SAE to the above address. *See also chapter* **San Francisco by Neighbourhood**.

By Public Transport

Pick the right routes, allow plenty of time and you can explore the city for the price of a Muni ticket. Here are some of our favourites:

J-Church Muni Metro

The J starts at the Embarcadero, heads underground along Market Street and then turns south at Church Street. You can jump off to explore the Mission district or continue overground through Dolores Heights and Noe Valley.

L-Taraval Muni Metro

If you're heading for San Francisco Zoo or Ocean Beach, take the L. It runs underground as far as West Portal station and then heads west along Taraval Street towards the sea.

Bus 29

This north-south bus route starts in the Presidio on Lombard Street and takes you across Golden Gate Park near Stow Lake, through the Sunset district to the shores of Lake Merced. Enjoy views of the Golden Gate Bridge and the ocean en route.

Bus 38

The 38 takes you via Union Square and much of downtown before travelling east along Geary Boulevard, through the Western Addition and Richmond, ending up at Lincoln Park, near the Cliff House and the ocean.

Other Tours

49-Mile Scenic Drive

The city's basic driving tour, signposted by blue-and-white seagull markers, is a good one, designed to take tourists through the most scenic or historic parts of the city. The Visitor's Information Center (*see page 251* **Directory**) provides a map of the tour, which will lead you to all the city's standard attractions. If this is your first visit to San Francisco, the 49-Mile Drive is worth taking.

Bus Tours

Gray Line (558 7300); Golden City Tours (692 3044); Golden Gate Tours (788 5775); Super Sightseeing Tours (362 7808).
Gray Line offers six bus tours daily that pick up passengers at central hotels; its Cable Car Tours send motorised cable cars from Union Square to Fisherman's Wharf, or to the Golden Gate Bridge, the Presidio and Japantown. Among the many other tour companies is Golden City Tours, which runs an enjoyable series of three-hour city tours, half-day trips out of town or Bay cruises; the company will pick up tourists from the airport or airport hotels. The city tours cost around $25 for adults and are usually half-price for children.

Cycling Tours

The San Francisco Department of Parking and Traffic (585 2453).
The SFDPT recently designated a grid of major bicycle routes that criss-cross the city. Although they're not organised tours per se, the routes will give you a particular view on the city – and improve your quads at the same time. *See page 258* **Directory** for more details; *see chapter* **Sport & Fitness** for bike hire.

Seaplane Tours

San Francisco Seaplane Tours (332 4843/www.seaplane.com). **Tickets** Golden Gate Tour $89; $59 children.
Fly the old-fashioned way on a seven-seater de Havilland seaplane, taking off from the water just outside Pier 39 for a 30-minute trip over the Bay, the Golden Gate Bridge and downtown. There are also flights from Sausalito.

Out of Town

For a tour of the beauty spots outside the city, try the **Great Pacific Tour**, which offers trips in the Bay Area and Wine Country (626 4499). For more information on exploring the countryside beyond the bounds of the city (*below*), *see chapter* **Trips Out of Town**.

Cruisin' the Castro

So you're in SF and the friend you've come to visit has to work all day. You've got some time to kill and no plans for lunch, and are pretty sure someone is going to get hurt if you see another sourdough chowder bowl. Indeed, it's high time to spend a few hours in the Castro with one of the City's true characters, Trevor Hailey, creator of a home-grown walking tour, 'Cruisin' the Castro.'

While others are at the mercy of more manicured tours, for four hours Hailey leads the gathered into ground zero of the gay mecca of the world. 'I wanted to do this tour because the Castro offers a very large part of the history of a major part of San Francisco that doesn't get the recognition it deserves,' she explains.

Although the tour covers only a few blocks of San Francisco, these streets are cobbled by a history of sexual freedom and the story of America's best-known gay community. But the tour doesn't just cover the birth of a hot bar scene (or the neighbourhood of the first openly gay elected official): Hailey's stories vividly describe the development of one of America's great cities.

As the Castro awakens and the tour begins, Hailey seems to know nearly every one of its inhabitants – the young and restless, hipsters, old-timers, merchants and friends. Decked out in a white sweatshirt covered with gay pride flags, some seriously stylish lavender pants and a pair of can't-miss rainbow earrings, she sure looks like the Mayor of Castro Street. After 15 minutes in the company of the lady with the famously husky voice, there's no doubt that she's the right person for the job.

Appropriately enough, the day begins at Harvey Milk Plaza on the corner of Market and Castro (the spot dedicated to Hailey's friend,

assassinated in 1978). Over the course of the next few hours the tour encounters the people, places and things that make the Castro tick, beginning with the community's origins in North Beach, emigration to Polk Street and its present home in the Castro.

The guide points out historic landmarks (like the Castro movie theatre) and hidden treasures (the best chocolateria in town), offering homespun anecdotes to spots like Milk's former camera store-cum-campaign headquarters, now inhabited by Skin Zone, a cosmetic shop from which a continuous stream of soap bubbles floats out onto the street.

Whether explaining the transformation of San Francisco from the Barbary Coast Gold Rush years into a wild centre of alternative culture, the ubiquitous San Francisco bandanna (worn during the Gold Rush days at all-male square dances to signify the male/female roles) or why so many of the bars are either glass-fronted or open-air (a backlash to the days of windowless bars, designed for discretion during a bygone era of gay prohibition), Hailey is a history book on legs. Between a quick pitstop at the kitsch Barbra Streisand museum and the emotional finale at the Names Project, Hailey also slips in helpful tips, like where a single girl can go to find another on a Tuesday night.

'Cities, just like people, have personalities,' says Hailey. 'I used to think that history 'was', now I know that history 'is' – and being gay or lesbian in the Castro is to be a part of an incredible time in history.'

Cruisin' the Castro
375 Lexington Street, San Francisco, CA 94110 (550 8110). **Tour** 10am-2pm Tue-Sat. **Admission** $35 including brunch. Booking essential.

Museums & Galleries

From high art to cultural kitsch.

The changing museum scene in San Francisco is as dynamic as some of the art you'll find within. The **San Francisco Museum of Modern Art** (SFMOMA) opened with a flourish in 1995, sporting dramatic architecture and a commitment to current worldwide art movements, and still feels incredibly new. The re-opening of the **California Palace of the Legion of Honor**, which had been closed for three years for renovation and seismic upgrading, re-awakened the city's interest in a regal, conservative setting housing (among other draws) the best Rodin collection outside Paris.

Yet, even as SFMOMA and the Palace of the Legion of Honor are thronged with new crowds, the **MH de Young Memorial** and **Asian Art Museums**, both located in Golden Gate Park, find themselves facing uncertain futures. The Asian is slated to move to the space vacated by the old Main Library in Civic Center, a move that is proving complicated and prolonged. And word is just out that the de Young, built for the California Midwinter International Exposition in 1894, must vacate its park locale for one with better parking facilities and upgraded earthquake safety measures.

Despite such difficulties, the only real complaint a museum-goer might have is that San Francisco's civic galleries are relatively conservative, especially for a city that prides itself on provocative culture. Perhaps it's the old money that pours into these institutions; perhaps it's that, in this day and age, all arts facilities are toeing the line since funding is slim. But such a discrepancy has put the city's commercial art scene in the spotlight once again. Curators and collectors have gravitated to San Francisco and the ripple effects are likely to be long-lasting. Considering the city's small size – only 46 square miles – a plethora of private art galleries await the art-lover. In general, the older, more mainstream galleries are located downtown, north of Market Street. Head for SoMa, the Mission or into Hayes Valley for the cutting-edge stuff.

Bay Area figurative art continues to flourish and local artists like Wayne Thiebaud have withstood the ravages of time and economics. By most accounts, however, the booming art scene of the early 1980s has faded to a dull roar, and the overpricing of collectable art has been corrected. Relatively few established galleries failed during the economic downturn, but several gallery owners have cited the effect of the state of the poor Japanese economy on California's artistic community. Nonetheless, the Californian art market has remained more stable than that in other major US cities such as New York and Los Angeles.

You can pick up a copy of the *San Francisco Gallery Guide* at any of the art galleries listed below – it contains a map and the addresses of dozens of places to visit in the city. For museums of special interest to kids, including the Museum of the City of San Francisco, *see chapter* **Children**.

Don't miss

Ansel Adams Center for Photography
All the big names in photography.
Asian Art Museum
The biggest collection in the Western world.
California Palace of the Legion of Honor
San Francisco's prettiest museum.
Refusalon
Some of the most interesting 'peripheral' art in town.
Exploratorium
Who said science was boring?
SFMOMA
For the building, if not for the collection.
Virginia Breier
The high priestess of American crafts.
Yerba Buena Gardens
Gorgeous urban garden with several indoor galleries.

Museums

Major Museums

Asian Art Museum
Music Concourse, Golden Gate Park (668 8921/ www. asianart.org). Muni Metro N/bus 5, 21, 44, 71.
Open 9.30am-5pm Wed-Sun; 9.30am-8.45pm first Wed of

George Segal's 'Jewish Holocaust Memorial' lies just outside the **California Palace of the Legion of Honor.** *See page 64.*

the month. **Admission** $7; $4-$5 concessions; free first Wed of the month. **Credit** MC, V. **Map B5**

Adjacent to the MH de Young Memorial Museum (*see below*), the Asian makes the most of San Francisco's enviable position on the Pacific Rim. The Avery Brundage Collection here is considered the biggest and best of its kind in the Western world, so large that only a fraction of its holdings is on display at any given time. These exhibits put European history in perspective: some Chinese pieces date from 70 centuries ago. There are jade pieces, bronzes, ceramics, fans, albums, scrolls – all in the first-floor galleries devoted to Chinese and Korean art. Works from 40 other countries, including India, Tibet, South East Asia, Japan and Middle Eastern nations, are displayed upstairs. Plans to relocate the museum to the Civic Center building vacated by the Main Library continue; the move won't happen for a few years yet. Admission includes entry to the de Young.

California Academy of Sciences

Music Concourse, Golden Gate Park (recorded information 750 7145/Morrison Planetarium 750 7141/ www.calacademy.org). **Muni Metro N/bus 5, 21, 44, 71.** **Open** *summer* 9am-6pm daily; *winter* 10am-5pm daily. **Admission** $8.50; $2-$5.50 concessions; *Planetarium* $2.50; $1.75 concessions. **Credit** AmEx, MC, V. **Map B6**
This science museum, which faces the de Young, is a perennial favourite for locals as well as out-of-towners. More than 1.5 million visitors come here each year to see the displays mounted by the oldest scientific institution in the western US. The big attraction is the **Steinhart Aquarium** (*see chapter* **Children**), but there's much more, including a simulated earthquake exhibit that recreates the seismic lurches of the 1906 and 1989 temblors and a brilliant display of the flora and fauna of California's numerous climates and varied terrain. The Academy also has a permanent exhibition of works by 'Far Side' cartoonist/science freak Gary Larson. Also within the complex is the **Morrison Planetarium**, presenting educational and amusing sky shows as well as laser light and music spectaculars.

California Palace of the Legion of Honor

Lincoln Park, Legion of Honor Drive, at 34th Avenue and Clement Street (750 3600/www.thinker.org). **Bus 18, 38.** **Open** 9.30am-5pm Tue-Sun. **Admission** $7; $4-$5 concessions; free second Wed of the month. **Credit** AmEx, MC, V.
San Francisco's prettiest museum, founded by a well-known city name, Alma de Bretteville Spreckels, re-opened in the autumn of 1995 after a three-year hiatus for renovation (including seismic upgrades) and interior expansion. Located in a wooded spot near the Pacific, the Legion's historic neoclassical façade has not been altered. A cast of Rodin's 'Le Penseur' still dominates the entrance, which has now been enhanced by a glass pyramid. The Legion's famous collections include more than 87,000 paintings, sculptures, decorative arts, works on paper, tapestries and other objects, spanning 4,000 years. The entrance level is dedicated to the permanent collection; an expanded garden level houses temporary exhibition galleries, as well as the **Achenbach Foundation for Graphic Arts** and the **Bowles Porcelain Gallery** and study centre. The Fine Arts Museums of San Francisco has redistributed its holdings, concentrating the art of the Americas at the de Young, and the European and ancient art collections here. An added bonus: your ticket stub to the Palace gets you into the de Young on the same day.

Center for the Arts at Yerba Buena Gardens

701 Mission Street, at Third Street (978 2787/ www.yerbabuenaarts.org). **BART Powell Street/Muni Metro F, J, K, L, M, N/bus 15, 30, 45, 76. Open** 11am-6pm Tue-Sun; 11am-8pm first Thur of the month.

Admission $5; $3 concessions; free first Thur of the month. **Credit** AmEx, DC, MC, V. **Map H4**
Lurking in the shadow of the gorgeous SFMOMA (*see p65*) across the street, the ambitious Yerba Buena Gardens project overcame controversy, criticism and three decades of intra-city bickering and now provides one of the most appreciated greenswards in the city. The centrepiece is the Center for the Arts, which includes galleries, a 96-seat theatre for film and video, the Forum for performances and a café. First-time visitors may find the hunt for the exhibition galleries a confusing one: they're housed in a futuristic-looking building designed by top Japanese architect Fumihiko Maki. In lieu of a permanent collection, the centre serves as an outlet for new artists (or even unlikely ones, such as prisoners at San Quentin) working in a variety of media. The gardens outside provide a great setting for lunch.

Exploratorium

3601 Lyon Street, between Jefferson and Bay Streets (563 7337/recorded information 561 0360/Tactile Dome 561 0362/www.exploratorium.edu). **Bus 22, 28, 29, 30, 43, 76. Open** *summer* 10am-6pm Tue-Sun; 10am-9.30pm Wed; *winter* 10am-5pm Tue-Sun; 10am-9. 30pm Wed. **Admission** $9; $2.50-$7 concessions; free first Wed of the month. **Credit** MC, V. **Map C2**
Conceived by physicist Frank Oppenheimer and opened in 1969, the Exploratorium reveals the secrets of heat, light, electricity, electronics, temperature, touch, vision, waves, patterns, motion, language and colour through clever, mostly hands-on exhibits. While much of the space resembles a post-space age video arcade, there are also more passive displays. A series of charts on the history of language, for example, traces hundreds of languages according to their family trees, while simple exhibits impart theories on balance, perspective and other concepts that kids often grasp quicker than adults. There's also a library where you can search for explanations the old-fashioned way. The Exploratorium offers a smorgasbord of seminars and weekends devoted to such offbeat topics as bubble blowing. To a background cacophony of blinking lights, whizzing machines and 'oohs' and 'ahhs', you can grab a decent bite at the Angel's Café right on the spot, or pick up an espresso or Spanish *churros* as you go along. There's also a great gift shop filled with scientific toys and educational baubles. The series of artist-in-residence exhibits are not to be missed.

MH de Young Memorial Museum

Music Concourse, Golden Gate Park (750 3600/ www.thinker.org). **Muni Metro N/bus 5, 21, 44, 71.** **Open** 9.30am-5pm Wed-Sun; 9.30am-8.45pm first Wed of the month. **Admission** $7; $4-$5 concessions; free first Wed of the month. **Credit** MC, V. **Map B5**
The recent re-organisation of the Fine Arts Museums of San Francisco has tightened the focus both here and at the California Palace of the Legion of Honor (*see above*). Now the de Young, as it's known, houses the art of the Americas. The collections, which date from colonial times to the present, include sculpture, paintings, textiles and decorative arts. American masters such as Thomas Eakins, John Singer Sargent and George Caleb Bingham are represented, as well as works by contemporary Bay Area artists. Because of damage sustained in the 1989 quake, the de Young (named after the local family that launched the *San Francisco Chronicle*) will eventually relocate within the city; insurance concerns have meant that major exhibitions scheduled for here will be moved to the Palace of the Legion of Honor. But the relocation won't happen for several years, and the de Young remains a showpiece for Western treasures meanwhile. The indoor/outdoor café has decent food; the gift shop is excellent. Admission includes entry to the adjacent Asian Arts Museum and your ticket stub will get you into the Palace of the Legion of Honor on the same day.

San Francisco Museum of Modern Art

*151 Third Street, between Mission and Howard Streets
(357 4000/www.sfmoma.org). BART Montgomery/
Muni Metro F, J, K, L, M, N.* **Open** 11am-6pm Mon, Tue,
Fri-Sun; 11am-9pm Thur. **Admission** $8; $4-$5
concessions; free first Tue of the month. **Credit** (café and
bookstore only) AmEx, MC, V. **Map H4**
This 20,925sq m (225,000sq ft) edifice, designed by Swiss
architect Mario Botta, looms above Yerba Buena Gardens,
and is the second-largest structure in the US devoted to modern art. SFMOMA opened with a flourish in 1995, culling
enthusiastic approval (as much for its modernist design as
for any improvement over its predecessor). Four floors of
galleries rise from a stark and stunning black marble lobby,
an awe-inspiring and neck-craning reception area that holds
a great café and splendid bookstore. The permanent collection of over 15,000 works includes some 4,700 paintings,
sculptures and works on paper, 9,000 photographs, and a
growing collection of works related to the media arts. Its
range of exhibits are formidable – Katharina Fritsch,
Dorothea Lange, Matisse, Diebenkorn, Klee; you're likely to
encounter just about anyone, though not in any numbers –
and its resources wide and inventive. Bay Area artists seem
to make their way into nearly every line-up. As in the old
quarters, a lot of stair climbing is required (there are lifts,
but they're slow) to reach the fifth-floor galleries. Once you've
reached the top, however, don't miss the spectacular catwalk
just beneath a giant skylight – though it's not recommended
for those suffering from vertigo.

Specialist Museums

African-American Historical &
Cultural Society Museum

*Building C, Fort Mason Center, at Buchanan Street and
Marina Boulevard (441 0640). Bus 28.*
Open noon-5pm Wed-Sun; noon-7pm first Wed of the
month. **Admission** $2; $1 concessions; free first Wed of
the month. **Credit** AmEx, MC, V. **Map E1**
One of two facilities managed by the society (the other, with
a library and listening room for historical tapes, is on Fulton
Street), this museum/gallery features a permanent collection
and changing exhibitions. Its archival materials relate to
African-American life and culture from the nineteenth century to the present day, including photos and related items
that shed light on little known aspects of American history,
while the gallery's emphasis is on new and master artists of
African descent. The gift shop sells African and African-
American arts and crafts.

Cable Car Barn Museum

*1201 Mason Street, at Washington Street (474 1887/
www.sfcablecar.com). Bus 1, 12, 83/cable car Powell-
Mason or Powell-Hyde.* **Open** *summer* 10am-6pm daily;
winter 10am-5pm daily. **Admission** free. **Map G3**
The single sound most often associated with San Francisco
is the clanging bells of the cable cars, the city's mobile landmarks. Supposedly inspired by a disastrous carriage crash,
Scotsman Andrew Hallidie introduced cable cars to this hilly
town more than 120 years ago. The best way to study them
is, of course, to take a ride on one of the three lines that operate nowadays. The second best way is to tour the Cable Car
Barn, where an underground excavation area allows visitors
to see the system in operation and to understand how the
cables, wheels and engines keep everything moving. You'll
learn about emergency procedures, bell-ringing competitions, and workmanship. Vintage cable cars, associated
artifacts and a short film round out the exhibits.

Cartoon Art Museum

*814 Mission Street, between Fourth and Fifth Streets
(227 8666/recorded information 546 3922). BART
Powell Street/Muni Metro F, J, K, L, M, N/bus 6, 7, 14,*

Out of town

Bay Model Visitors Center

*2100 Bridgeway Avenue, Sausalito (332 3871/
www.spn. usace.army.mil/bmvc/). Golden Gate
Transit bus 10/ferry from Pier 41.*
Open *Apr-Sep* 9am-4pm Tue-Fri; 10am-6pm Sat,
Sun; *Oct-Mar* 9am-4pm Tue-Sat.
Admission free.
A 15-acre model of the Bay established by the US
Army Corps of Engineers shows how navigation,
recreation and ecology all interact in this complex
water system. Best of all, walkways are strung all over
so that visitors can, figuratively at least, walk on
water. When the model is in operation, a lunar day is
simulated in under 15 minutes, complete with tidal
action. Hands-on exhibits include video games and an
introduction to indigenous birds and fish, and there
are videos on the Corps' work in hydro-electric power,
flood control and construction.

Oakland Museum of California

*1000 Oak Street, at 10th Street, Oakland (1-510
238 3401/www.museumca.org). BART Lake
Merritt.* **Open** 10am-5pm Wed-Sat; noon-7pm Sun.
Admission $5; $3 concessions; free 4-7pm Sun.
No credit cards.
The only museum in California devoted exclusively
to the art, history and environment of the state, the
Oakland Museum was established in 1969. The
Gallery of California Art displays paintings, sculpture, prints, illustrations, photos and decorative arts
by Californian artists, or by artists addressing related themes and subjects. Exhibited in some 2,790sq m
(30,000sq ft) of space, the collection includes sketches
by early explorers; genre pictures from the Gold Rush;
massive panoramic landscapes; Bay Area figurative,
pop and funk works. The Natural Sciences displays
are devoted to the variegated Californian landscape
and the Cowell Hall of California History has furniture, machines, tools, costumes, craftwork, clothing,
decorations and vehicles prominent in the state's
development.

Berkeley Art Museum &
Pacific Film Archives

*2626 Bancroft Way and 2625 Durant Avenue,
between Bowditch and College Streets (1-510 642
0808/www. bampfa.berkeley.edu). BART Berkeley.*
Open 11am-5pm Wed, Fri-Sun; 11am-9pm Thur.
Admission $6; $4 concessions; free 11am-noon,
5-9pm Thur. **No credit cards**.
Modernist printer Hans Hofmann provided the impe-
tus for an art museum on the UC Berkeley campus.
Opened in 1970, the dramatic exhibition space is
arranged in terraces enabling visitors to see the works
from various vantage points. The collection's strength
is in twentieth century painting, sculpture, photography and conceptual art, as well as Asian art. Ten
galleries and a bookstore occupy the upper level,
while the Sculpture Garden and café share the lower
level with the Pacific Film Archives, one of the country's most comprehensive academic film programmes.
The PFA screens some 650 films and videos a year,
and has a collection of 7,000 titles, including Soviet,
US avant-garde and Japanese cinema, among other
genres (*see also chapter* **Film**).

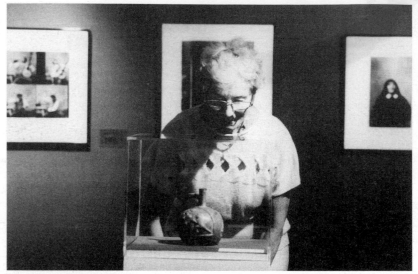

*The excellent **Mexican Museum**, soon to be rehoused. See page 67.*

15, 26, 27, 30, 45, 66, 71, 76/cable car Powell-Hyde or Powell-Mason. **Admission** $4; $2-$3 concessions. **Open** 11am-5pmWed-Fri; 10am-5pm Sat; 1-5pm Sun. **Credit** MC, V. **Map G4**

A treat for artists and 'toonphiles, the Cartoon Art Museum consists of four rooms of exceedingly well-arranged exhibits. The sources are myriad – individual artists, sketchbooks, comic books, *The New Yorker* – and add up to an informative lesson on this original art form for its artistic, cultural and historic merits. Exhibitions cover artists from Edward Gorey to Hanna-Barbera. Currently the only museum west of the Mississippi dedicated to the preservation, collection and exhibition of original cartoon art, the 558sq m (6,000sq ft) space also includes a children's museum, an interactive CD-ROM gallery and a nifty gift shop with books, cards and related comic-ery.

Chinese Historical Society Museum

650 Commercial Street, between Montgomery and Kearny Streets (391 1188/www.channelA.com). Bus 1, 15/cable car California. **Open** 10am-4pm Tue-Fri; 11am-3pm Sat. **Admission** free. **Map H3**

Bilingual displays at this subterranean space trace the presence and contributions of the Chinese in California, from the frontier years to the Gold Rush, the building of the railroads

Open studios

For four weekends during October each year, more than 600 San Francisco artists open their studios to the public between 11am and 6pm. *See chapter* **San Francisco by Season** *for more information.*

(which would have taken another 100 years were it not for low-paid Chinese labour) and the days of opium dens on the Barbary Coast. Lovingly kept displays include a small Chinese Buddhist altar dating from 1880; a 4m (14ft) Californian sampan for fishing, and a Chinese dragon head made in 1911 for use in ceremonies and parades, one of the first to incorporate electric lights. Like the Wells Fargo museum (*see below*), this stop is a must for unravelling California's complex tapestry of history.

Jewish Museum of San Francisco

121 Steuart Street, between Mission and Howard Streets (543 8880). BART Embarcadero/Muni Metro F, J, K, L, M, N/bus 1, 2, 7, 9, 14, 21, 31, 32, 66, 71. **Open** noon-6pm Mon-Wed; noon-8pm Thur; 11am-6pm Sun. **Admission** $5; $2.50 concessions; free first Mon of the month. **Credit** MC, V. **Map J3**

One of the most diverse cities in the country, ethnically as well as religiously, San Francisco now has its own museum devoted to linking the Jewish community with the community at large, through exhibitions and educational programmes. More a gallery than a stodgy exhibit hall, the 12 year-old Jewish Museum shows works by established artists and students, many of which are political or controversial in nature.

Levi Strauss Museum

250 Valencia Street, between 14th Street and Duboce Avenue (565 9159). Bus 26. **Open** *tours only* 9am, 11am, 1.30pm Tue, Wed. **Admission** free. **Map F6**

Of all the inventions emanating from the West Coast, perhaps the most ubiquitous is blue jeans. The history of this all-American icon is displayed at this museum, housed in a 1906 commercial Victorian building. Trace the birth of jeans during the Gold Rush, when a German immigrant named Levi Strauss fashioned a pair of trousers from the heavyweight canvas normally used for gold miners' tents, and follow it to the present day, where middle America – and the world – has made them indispensable. The walking tour includes a video and a visit to the factory's cutting and sewing rooms. Book in advance.

Getting to grips with the addictive **Musée Mécanique**.

Mexican Museum

Building D, Fort Mason Center, at Buchanan Street and Marina Boulevard (441 0404). Bus 28.
Open noon-5pm Wed-Fri; 11am-5pm Sat, Sun; noon-7pm first Wed of the month. **Admission** $3; $2 concessions; free first Wed of the month. **Credit** (shop only) AmEx, MC, V. **Map E1**
As we go to press, the first museum in the US dedicated to the work of Mexican and other Latino artists is still awaiting its relocation to a new building in SoMa. But the Fort Mason site, cramped though it is, is excellent. Over the years, the curators have acquired some 9,000 objects reflecting a spectrum of Mexican art ranging from traditional to experimental, decorative to functional, ancient to contemporary. The museum curates shows on Mexican surrealism and also mounts travelling exhibits, including a major Frida Kahlo retrospective and superb spraycan artists' workshop. There is also a sizeable gift shop.

Musée Mécanique

Cliff House, 1090 Point Lobos Avenue, at the Great Highway (386 1170). Bus 18, 38. **Open** *summer* 10am-8pm daily; *winter* 11am-7pm daily.
Admission free.
Pack a pocketful of quarters and visit this wonderful cliffside museum – actually an arcade housing a few dozen old-fashioned mechanical gizmos ranging from Laughing Sal to fortune-telling machines. Best of all is the Unbelievable Mechanical Farm, with 150 moving objects and figures. Check out the Camera Obscura next door, a replica of Leonardo da Vinci's invention which 'films' the world outside and projects it onto a giant parabolic screen.

Museo Italo-Americano

Building C, Fort Mason Center, at Buchanan Street and Marina Boulevard (673 2200/www.well.com/~museo). Bus 28. **Open** noon-5pm Wed-Sun; noon-7pm first Wed of the month. **Admission** $2; $1 concessions; free under-12s; free first Wed of the month. **Credit** MC, V.
Map E1

One of three ethnic museums housed in unprepossessing quarters in the Fort Mason complex (the others are the African-American and Mexican Museums; *see above*), the Museo Italo-Americano functions as a gallery and community centre, offering classes in Italian language, art, architecture and related subjects. Along with a few historical exhibits, the museum shows works by Italian and Italian-American artists. It, too, has a nice little gift shop.

National Maritime Museum

Jefferson Street, at Polk Street (556 2904/www.maritime. org). Bus 30, 42/cable car Powell-Hyde. **Open** 10am-5pm daily. **Admission** free. **Map F1**
Located in a classic 1930s building that looks like a ship, the National Maritime Museum documents maritime history with the aid of photographs and ship models, including miniatures of passenger liners and US Navy ships. It's a little dated, but still offers interactive exhibits that children will enjoy and enough sea lore to fill a few hours. The museum is a just across the street from Ghirardelli Square shopping centre (*see chapter* **Shopping & Services**).

San Francisco Performing Arts Library & Museum

399 Grove Street, at Gough Street (255 4800/ www. sfpalm.org). Bus 21, 42, 47, 49. **Open** 1-7pm Wed; 10am-4pm Thur, Fri; noon-4pm Sat. **Admission** free.
Map F5
With exhibitions relating to the performing arts, be it a puppet show or an opera, this museum is worth a visit if you're in the Civic Center neighbourhood. Of most interest to fine arts scholars is the prodigious amount of resource material: thousands of books on design, fashion, music, theatre, opera and other art forms augment a focus on local arts groups.

Tattoo Museum

841 Columbus Avenue, at Greenwich Street (775 4991). Bus 15, 30/cable car Powell-Mason. **Open** noon-9pm Mon-Thur, Sun; noon-10pm Fri, Sat. **Admission** free.
Map G2

The revival of the art of tattooing in the Western world supposedly occurred after the English privateer William Dampier returned from the South Pacific to shock and titillate London with the sight of Giolo, a native 'painted prince'. Trust quirky San Francisco to have a museum dedicated to it. Master tattoo artist Lyle Tuttle has gathered what may be the world's largest assortment of skin art paraphernalia – designs, newspaper articles, photographs and even old equipment such as a set of hand needles. If you like what you see, you can get one yourself: Tuttle is one of the best in the world (*see chapter* **Shopping & Services**).

Wells Fargo History Room

420 Montgomery Street, at California Street (396 2619). Bus 1, 15, 41/cable car California. **Open** 9am-5pm Mon-Fri. **Admission** free. **Map H3**

The bright red stagecoach in the front window at the spacious ground-floor Wells Fargo museum would have held as many as 18 people, although it's difficult to imagine them all fitting in. The coach and other exhibits managed by the Wells Fargo bank, one of California's original lenders, overshadow the displays that seek to tout the bank itself. Pony Express memorabilia and a first-rate relief map illustrate the routes and the risks run by the banks in the old days before Federal Express came to the rescue. In one corner, an old telegraph machine lets visitors try their hand at tapping out a message. Most impressive is the elaborate leather, brass and iron harness once used to control a 'six-up' stage coach. In all, the museum paints an expansive and exciting picture of the Old West.

Galleries

Campbell-Thiebaud

645 Chestnut Street, at Columbus Avenue (441 8680). Bus 30/cable car Powell-Mason. **Open** 11am-5pm Tue-Fri; noon-4pm Sat. **No credit cards. Map G2**

Located on a quiet residential street in North Beach, this gallery marks a joint venture between Charles Campbell, long-time owner, and Paul Thiebaud, son of acclaimed local artist Wayne Thiebaud. Some of the latter's paintings hang in the two-storey gallery, along with work by many other Bay Area figurative artists. Most of the names on display are well-known: Frank Auerbach, Robert Kulicke, Fairfield Porter, Willem de Kooning, August Gay, Bay Area painter and sculptor Manuel Neri, and painter Frank Lobdell, who taught at the San Francisco Art Institute and Stanford.

Capp Street Project

525 Second Street, between Bryant and Brannan Streets (495 7101). Bus 15, 32, 42. **Open** noon-6pm Tue-Sat. **No credit cards. Map J4**

One of the more progressive spaces in town. The non-profit Capp Street Project mounts site-specific installations, and also offers a three-month residency programme whereby artists can live and work on large-scale installation pieces for the gallery. Admission is free but donations are welcome.

Don Soker Gallery

251 Post Street, between Grant Avenue and Stockton Street (291 0966). BART Montgomery Street/

Some of the 'peripheral' art on show at **Refusalon.** *See page 69.*

Muni Metro F, J, K, L, M, N/bus 2, 3, 4, 30, 45, 76.
Open 11am-5pm Tue-Sat. **Credit** MC, V. **Map G3**
Don Soker specialises in minimalist, abstract work, which means a lot of works on paper. The gallery also has etchings by Theodora Varnay-Jones, who recently studied in Japan, and works by other local artists such as Peter Boyer, Susan Parker, Roland Castellon (ex-curator of SFMOMA) and Yutaka Yoshinaga.

Dorothy Weiss

256 Sutter Street, between Grant Avenue and Kearny Street (397 3611). Bus 2, 3, 4, 30, 45, 76. **Open** 11am-5pm Tue-Sat. **No credit cards. Map H3**
This upper-floor gallery can be described simply: dynamic contemporary ceramics.

Gallery Paule Anglim

14 Geary Street, between Grant Avenue and Kearny Street (433 2710). BART Montgomery Street/Muni Metro F, J, K, L, M, N/bus 2, 3, 4, 15, 30, 38, 45, 76. **Open** 11am-5.30pm Tue-Sat. **No credit cards. Map H3**
Situated between the chic shopping streets of Union Square and the alternative spaces south of Market Street, this gallery is on the cusp in more ways than one. Paule Anglim is known for exhibiting Bay Area and international artists – both established as well as cutting-edge – in a variety of media. Two young sculptors discovered by the gallery, Melissa Pokorny and Michelle Rollman, are now being shown in minor museums. Some of the displays are controversial, but this gallery is one of only three in the city to claim membership of the prestigious Art Dealers Association of America (the others being John Berggruen and Fraenkel; *see below*).

Galeria de la Raza

2857 24th Street, at Bryant Street (826 8009). Bus 27, 48. **Open** noon-6pm Tue-Sat. **Credit** AmEx, MC, V. **Castro/Mission Map Z2**
An unpretentious corner shopfront in the Mission district is the setting for up to six exhibitions a year of Latin American artists new to the US. Galeria de la Raza devotes all its space and time to artists from Mexico, El Salvador and other Latin American countries. La Raza's adjacent shop, Studio 24, sells handcrafts, books and children's toys from these same countries. Donations are welcome.

John Berggruen Gallery

228 Grant Avenue, between Post and Sutter Streets (781 4629). BART Montgomery Street/Muni Metro F, J, K, L, M, N/bus 2, 3, 4, 76. **Open** 9.30am-5.30pm Mon-Fri; 10.30am-5pm Sat. **Credit** MC, V. **Map G/H3**
For over 25 years, this blue-chip gallery's openings have been a routine stop for socialites as well as collectors of more modest means. Occupying three floors in a narrow Grant Avenue building in the heart of the gallery district, John Berggruen is known for showing major artists; recent acquisitions include work by Henri Matisse, Alberto Giacometti, Nathan Oliveira, Mark Tansey, William Bailey, painter and ceramist Squeak Carnwath and Saul Steinberg.

Limn Company

292 Townsend Street, at Fourth Street (977 1300). Bus 30, 32, 42, 45. **Open** 1-5.30pm Tue-Sat. **Credit** AmEx, MC, V. **Map H5**
In a new, larger location, this cross between a gallery and a showroom represents artists and craftspeople creating one-of-a-kind furniture items in various special exhibits. Its roster has included Brian Russell, known for tables and candelabra utilising forged steel or copper; Stephen Tiffany, who creates (appropriately enough) mostly lighting fixtures; Alan Sklansky, who makes cabinetry, bookcases and chairs in wood and metal; and Michael Albrecht, famous for his maplewood armoires in a contemporary design. Call for a current schedule.

Meyerovich Gallery

251 Post Street, between Grant Avenue and Stockton Street (421 7171). BART Montgomery Street/Muni Metro F, J, K, L, M, N/bus 2, 3, 4, 30, 45, 76. **Open** 9.30am-6pm Mon-Fri; 10am-5pm Sat. **Credit** AmEx, MC, V. **Map G3**
Although it has been several years since Grisha Bruskin's painting 'Fundamental Lexicon' sold for nearly half a million dollars at the Sotheby auction in Moscow, ripples of excitement are still being felt at this elegant little gallery, which has been representing him for some time. The Russian-Jewish painter-turned-sculptor moved from the edge of respectability to the pinnacle of fame. The gallery also has works by Chagall, Keith Haring, David Hockney, Roy Lichtenstein, Matisse, Miró, Picasso, Frank Stella and Andy Warhol.

New Langton Arts

1246 Folsom Street, between Eighth and Ninth Streets (626 5416). Bus 12, 19, 27, 42. **Open** noon-5pm Wed-Sat. **No credit cards. Map G5**
In the forefront of the alternative art scene, this second-floor loft is as unprepossessing as some of its SoMa neighbours, at least from the outside. The choice of exhibitions is eclectic, to say the least, but the gallery is best known for its installations and performance pieces. It hosts an annual autumn showcase, the Bay Area Awards show, presenting top regional talent in literature, media arts, music, performance and the visual arts. As the National Endowment for the Arts' (NEA) regional grant-making site for northern California, it also acts as an unofficial cultural centre for many different artists. Call to check the schedule of shows.

Olga Dollar Gallery

Second floor, 210 Post Street, at Grant Avenue (398 2297). BART Montgomery/Muni Metro F, J, K, L, M, N/bus 2, 3, 4, 76. **Open** 10.30am-5.30pm Tue-Sat. **Credit** MC, V. **Map G3**
Formerly the Allport Gallery and known for its prints, the Dollar has shifted emphasis to contemporary and emerging Californian artists – the stranger the better. If hyper-realism appeals to you, this is the place to look for it. Also here are works by Troy Dalton, Stephen Braun, Patricia Ancona and Seiji Kunishima as well as two young female artists, Francesca Sundsten and Chicako Okada.

Refusalon

20 Hawthorne Street, between Second and Third Streets (546 0158). Bus 9, 12, 38. **Open** noon-6pm Tue-Sat; noon-8pm first Thur of the month. **Credit** MC, V. **Map H4**
Though its artists might not yet be household names, Charles Linder's charming, austere gallery – recently relocated into the shadow of SFMOMA – houses some of the most interesting art in the city. Specialising in 'peripheral' works, Refusalon has hosted shows by Eric Saks, Patrick Tierney, Pip Culbert and her sons Rae and Clay, and edge-surfers like Gay Outlaw. Watch for Refusalon's group shows, which often include works by Linder himself.

San Francisco Art Institute Galleries

800 Chestnut Street, at Jones Street (749 4564). Bus 30/ cable car Powell-Hyde. **Open** 9am-8pm daily. **No credit cards. Map F2**
Three galleries are on display at the Art Institute: in one you have the rare chance to see an original Diego Rivera mural; in the next, a solid collection of contemporary art; and in the third, work by the talented students at the school is on display (and on sale). The Art Institute may seem a detour from the cluster of galleries downtown and south of Market Street, but a trip here is worth it. Take the Powell-Hyde cable car to Chestnut Street and walk two blocks to Jones, where you get one of the most breathtaking views of San Francisco.

The writing on the wall

One of the first characteristics the newcomer to San Francisco is certain to notice is the city's predilection for public art. It's everywhere: in hotel lobbies, bus shelters (and sometimes on the buses themselves), on street corners and public plazas, tucked away in hard-to-find places visible only to those who know where and when to look for it.

Of all art forms, the mural seems to be most popular. **Coit Tower** features the work of some 25 muralists from the 1930s, including John Langley Howard and Diego Rivera, covering over 1,220 metres (4,000 feet) of wall space. You'll find more work by Rivera inside the **Pacific Coast Stock Exchange** (301 Pine Street) and at **City College** (50 Phelan Avenue); a dazzling Rivera mural (*opposite, middle)* is also on view at the **San Francisco Art Institute** (800 Chestnut Street).

Preservationists have recently restored murals by the French painter Lucien Labaudt

(*opposite, bottom*) inside the **Beach Chalet** at Ocean Beach, at the city's western edge. You can view the public works on the main floor and get a great meal upstairs (*see chapter* **Restaurants & Cafés**). The Mission district is particularly rich in murals: if you want an informed approach, the **Precita Eyes Mural Art Center** (348 Precita Avenue; 285 2287) conducts tours of the colourful works found around the working-class district (*see also chapters* **Sightseeing** *and* **San Francisco by Neighbour-hood**). Guides will take you down **Balmy Alley** (between 24th and 25th Streets) and past **St Peter's Church** (24th and Florida Streets), encountering over 70 murals in the course of the tour.

But many works do more than provide visual stimulus for the public patron: in the Marina district, the **Wave Organ** lies east of the St Francis Yacht Club off Marina Boulevard, at the farthest tip of the yacht harbour jetty.

Constructed, by Peter Richards and George Gonzales, of stones from a demolished cemetery, the sculpture encloses partially-submerged vertical pipes 'played' at random by the motion of the Bay's waves. This surreal rock outcropping, accessible only by foot or boat, is a perfect place to enjoy a magnificent view of Fort Mason and the sounds of the sea's primal symphony.

Several works by sculptor Douglas Hollis create ambient sounds by design: the **Rain Column**, a four-storey waterfall inside the art-fortified **Rincon Center** (101 Spear Street, at Mission Street) adds a pleasant natural hiss to what would be a noisy brick food court. His **Aolian Harp**, an acoustic, wind-driven lyre, sings from above the entrance of the wonderful **Exploratorium** (*see page 64*); a whistling **Wind Gate** faces 3Com (Candlestick) Park in the **Candlestick Point National Recreation Area** at the city's southeastern edge (*see chapter* **Sport & Fitness**).

The **San Francisco Art Commission** (25 Van Ness Avenue, suite 240; 252 2590) publishes a brochure that includes many of these works and describes several walking tours, particularly along the waterfront and south of Market Street. Many works have been set in what might seem unlikely places – a jail, a children's recreation centre in an at-risk neighbourhood and in a mental health institution. Another established locale for public art is the **San Francisco International Airport**, where changing art exhibits are on display in all the terminals.

Some art isn't so tidily commissioned, however. If you're riding the Muni Metro line through the **N-Judah Tunnel** that connects the Lower Haight with Cole Valley, look out of the train windows for the city's best spray can art. Graffiti artists careful to avoid police and trespassing charges have turned the space into a mile-long, eye-popping gallery of urban murals. Local writers, including **Neon**, **Giant** and **Amaze**, have ongoing pieces in here, along with **Reminisce**'s well-known horse paintings. An occasional work by **Twist** still remains – though his work can now be seen in the permanent collection at **SFMOMA** (*see page 65*). Though it's illegal, some people enter

the tunnel on foot at Duboce Park after the trains stop (usually after 11pm), to get a better look.

Local muralist **Rigo** has appropriated the visual urban screech of the graffiti writers into his own style: he paints billboard-sized works that mimic traffic signs (*above and opposite*), tweaking them to reflect environmental or social messages. A recent work, **One Tree** (Tenth and Bryant Streets) points directly at the lone cypress in the shadow of a freeway on-ramp; yellow-and-black **Extinct** (Fifth and Folsom Streets) points warningly to the air above a petrol station. As you traverse the city by public transport, auto or on foot, keep an eye out for this artist's clever and controversial portfolio.

Finally, don't miss the open-air displays of public works to be found in and around the **Embarcadero**. North or south from the Ferry Building, you'll find commissioned art ranging from the post-apocalyptic **Villencourt Fountain** to Mark di Suvero's bright red, wind-driven sextant **Sea Change** (*opposite*), a short stroll away in front of **Pier 40**. Along the way, historical signposts outline the story of the city's early settlers and industry. At night the length of the Embarcadero is lit with a glowing trail of glass and brick.

The **Ansel Adams Center for Photography**.

Virginia Breier
3091 Sacramento Street, at Baker Street (929 7173).
Bus 1, 3. **Open** 11am-6pm Mon-Sat. **Credit** MC, V.
Map D3
Always a pleasure to visit, this gallery specialises in sculpture, wall hangings, furniture and other three-dimensional pieces that defy categorisation. Metal sculptures by William Allen reflect his background as a professional zoologist; his overscale insects, for instance, feature incredible anatomical detail. Patricia Sannit, Paul di Pasqua, Stan Peterson and many other artists represented here have day jobs as professors in northern California, but this is no one-size-fits-all collection. How do you categorise a massive wall installation comprised of dozens of neon fish that can be set to flash by computer? No wonder a local rag recently dubbed Breier the 'high priestess of American crafts'.

Vorpal Gallery
393 Grove Street, near Gough Street (397 9200). Bus 21,
42, 47, 49. **Open** 11am-6pm Tue-Sat. **Credit** MC, V.
Map F5
Located in a turn-of-the-century building replete with high ceilings, hardwood floors and white brick walls, Vorpal bills itself as an eclectic gallery. Among the better-known contemporary artists here is Yoyo Hamaguchi, but Latin American artists also have a presence and the gallery carries prints by Escher, Picasso, Rembrandt and the Belgian pre-Expressionist James Ensor. Vorpal mounts half a dozen special exhibitions each year.

Photography Galleries

Ansel Adams Center for Photography
250 Fourth Street, between Folsom and Howard
Streets (495 7000). Bus 12, 30, 45, 76. **Open** 11am-
5pm Tue-Sun; 11am-8pm first Thur of the month.
Admission $5; $2-$3 concessions. **Credit** AmEx, MC, V.
Map H4

In 1989, 22 years after Ansel Adams founded the Friends of Photography with other prominent photographers, the group relocated headquarters from Carmel to the area around Yerba Buena Gardens. Of the centre's five galleries, one is devoted to exploring and preserving Adams' photographic legacy; the rest showcase contemporary and historical photography, such as the Nagasaki exhibition held on the 50th anniversary of its bombing. Students of photography should take a look at the outstanding bookshop.

Fraenkel Gallery
49 Geary Street, at Kearny Street (981 2661). BART
Montgomery Street/Muni Metro F, J, K, L, M, N/bus 5,
6, 7, 15, 21, 30, 31, 38, 45, 71. **Open** 10.30am 5.30pm
Tue-Fri; 11am-5pm Sat. **No credit cards**. **Map H3**
Walking around the exhibition rooms at the Fraenkel Gallery – housed in a building packed with commercial galleries – one starts to wonder if there is any major twentieth-century photographer not on view. As it turns out, there are a few gaps in the collection, but photographers represented include Robert Mapplethorpe, Henri Cartier-Bresson, Irving Penn, Diane Arbus, Helen Levitt, Garry Winogrand, Richard Misrach, Edward Weston, Walker Evans, Paul Strand, Alfred Stieglitz, Edward Steichen and Chuck Gibson, as well as Carleton E Watkins and Edward Muybridge. Phew.

Shapiro Gallery
250 Sutter Street, between Grant Avenue and Kearny
Street (398 6655). BART Montgomery Street/
Muni Metro F, J, K, L, M, N/bus 2, 3, 4, 15, 30, 45, 76.
Open 11am-5.30pm Tue-Fri; 11am-5pm Sat. **Credit** MC, V.
Map H3
A relatively small gallery, Shapiro is devoted exclusively to twentieth-century photography. The gallery represents Steven Brock, Kenro Izu, Margaretta Mitchell, George Tice, Masao Yamamoto and others; works by Ruth Bernhard, Margaret Bourke-White, Henri Cartier-Bresson, Imogen Cunningham and Edward Weston are also available.

SF by Neighbourhood

Such a mix would be exhausting if it were not for the fact that San Francisco is relatively small, enabling you to explore the neighbourhoods on foot, by car or using public transport, with relative ease. And don't think for a minute that each neighbourhood doesn't have a broad mix of architecture, resources and residents: the city is not so much a melting pot as a presentation of flavourful individual dishes. More information on many of the places and sights mentioned here can be found elsewhere in the guide, particularly in chapters **Sightseeing, Museums & Galleries, Bars, Nightlife** and **Restaurants & Cafés**.

Downtown

San Francisco's most diverse region offers everything from the plush shops and chic boutiques of Union Square to the funky cool of a Tenderloin nightclub, as well as the spectacular architecture found in both the Civic Center and Financial District sectors.

Around Union Square

Bordered by Market Street from (roughly) Second to Fifth Streets and north as far as Pine, San Francisco's downtown is a bustling hub where smartly dressed salespeople and businessmen on their lunch-hour mix with gawking tourists, homeless people engaging in creative panhandling and blue-collar workers waiting for a bus. The region marks the city's most varied demographic cross-section and its busiest streets; the best time to navigate it is on a weekday morning. Camera-toting out-of-towners waiting for the cable car brush shoulders with street-corner evangelists; kids on skateboards whizz past horse-mounted cops; everyone seems to be carrying a bag from The Gap. Within a short walk of Union Square (where much of Francis Ford Coppola's movie *The Conversation* was shot) are the **San Francisco Shopping Center**, a nine-storey shopping mall including Nordstrom and other clothing stores, boutiques, shoe shops and a graceful exterior escalator; the upscale **Crocker Galleria** shopping complex; the ubiquitous retailer **Macy's**; toy shop **FAO Schwartz**; and enough clothing stores – from Banana Republic and Urban Outfitters to Tiffany, Hermès and Chanel – to satisfy even the most hardened shopaholic.

If you tire of consuming, **Union Square** itself, named after the Union rallies that were held there during the American Civil War, affords a nice enough place from which to watch passers-by. Scheduled for a redesign in the next few years, the square features a 27m (90ft) granite monument at its centre commemorating Admiral Dewey's victory over the Spanish Navy in 1898 during the Spanish-American War.

Several interesting art galleries can be found nearby, including the **Erika Meyerovich Gallery** (on Grant Avenue), with its permanent collection of pieces by Picasso, Chagall, Warhol and Matisse, and the **Joseph Dee Camera Museum** (above Brooks Camera shop on Kearny Street). Not far away, between Stockton Street and Grant Avenue, lies **Maiden Lane**. Once one of San Francisco's most dangerous and seedy alleyways (famous for having the cheapest prostitutes), the cul-de-sac has been transformed into an exclusive shopping street, the centrepiece of which is the exquisite **Circle Gallery** at No. 140, designed by Frank Lloyd Wright in 1949.

In addition, you'll find a huge choice of restaurants in the area; some – like **Farallon** on Post Street – are prohibitively expensive while others serve low-grade counter fare. There are some exceptions, however: **Café de la Presse** (352 Grant Avenue) has a broad selection of international magazines and newspapers to browse through, and is a perfect place to sit outside on a sunny morning and watch passers-by. Bustling **Café Claude**, tucked away in an alley (Claude Lane, near Union Square), feels like a Parisian sidewalk café, with chairs and tables outside and live jazz on certain evenings. For more good restaurants, head a few blocks west on Geary Boulevard towards the theatre district.

It would be hard to miss the **Powell Street turnaround**, where a long line of tourists waits to board each cable car. If you want to take a ride, do what the locals do: walk up the hill a block or two and board a car en route. At the end of the day pay a visit to **Club 36**, located on the 36th floor inside the Grand Hyatt Hotel on Union Square. A jazz venue with fabulous city views, it has been called one of 'the best places to kiss in California'.

Local buildings of particular interest include the **Humboldt Savings Bank Building** (783 Market Street). Under construction when the 1906 earthquake hit, work on it had to be started all over again; now newly restored, it is a beautiful example of one of San Francisco's earliest skyscrapers. It would be hard to miss the **Phelan Building**, built in 1908 by Mayor James Phelan as part of his famous reconstruction programme: it is San Francisco's largest 'flatiron' building (so-called because of its triangular shape) and takes up most of the block on Market Street between Third and Fourth Streets.

The Financial District

The Financial District, which comprises the triangle bounded by Market Street from Kearny Street to the Embarcadero and north to Jackson Street, has marked the commercial centre of San Francisco for over a century. Nowadays it is ruled by the **Transamerica Pyramid** on Montgomery Street, the city's tallest inhabited structure which looms 260m (853ft) above the area's earliest buildings. One of the most interesting structures is the **Merchant's Exchange** (465 California Street), rebuilt in 1906 after the Great Fire and home to an impressive collection of William Coulter seascapes. For a unique glimpse of the city's architectural creativity, notice how the high-rise at **456 Montgomery** straddles two turn-of-the-century banks: the Italian-American and the Anton Borel, both built in 1908.

Wannabe financial wizards can practise their skills on computer games that simulate the stock market inside the **Federal Reserve Bank Building** (101 Market Street). To catch the fever of the Gold Rush days, visit the **Wells Fargo History Museum** (420 Montgomery Street). Mementos of the Wild West include paintings, photographs, gold nuggets and a stage coach.

The neighbourhood also has some non-financial landmarks, including the **Transamerica Redwood Park**, next to the Transamerica Pyramid, notable for its free jazz and blues concerts, and the **Pacific Heritage Museum** (608 Commercial Street, also free), which traces the city's artistic, cultural and financial links to the Far East. On the region's southern border, the **American Indian Contemporary Arts Gallery**, at 685 Market Street, has a gift shop upstairs.

There are many excellent restaurants in the area. Particularly noteworthy are the austere **Rubicon** (558 Sacramento) – owned in part by Robert de Niro, Robin Williams and Francis Ford Coppola – and the magnificent **Tommy Toy's Cuisine Chinoise** (655 Montgomery), opposite the Transamerica Pyramid. Consistently voted the best Chinese restaurant in the city, Tommy Toy's is as famous for excellent service (a convoy of elegantly dressed waiters delivers every course) as for its signature menu, which is so popular that it that hasn't changed in ten years.

Geographically within the bounds of the Financial District, the area known as **Jackson Square Historical District** is a block of low-rise brick buildings dating from the 1850s which marked the city's original shoreline in the late nineteenth century. It also housed one of the city's most notorious red-light districts. In the 1930s Jackson Square became popular among artists and writers, including John Steinbeck and William Saroyan, who used to drink at the Black Cat Café (no longer in existence), and socialist artist Diego Rivera who had a studio on Gold Street. Now home to many advertising agencies and design studios, the area retains an artistic feel.

Two interesting establishments popular with after-work drinkers are the **Cypress Club** (500 Jackson Street), where a bizarre, 1940s-inspired interior might make you wonder if your appetisers have been spiked with psilocybin, and **Bix** (56 Gold Street), which tinkles with live jazz most evenings and enjoys a reputation for brilliant martinis.

Civic Center

An area in transition following some major seismic upgrades, Civic Center (the triangular region bounded by Gough, Market and Turk Streets) features as its centrepiece the splendid **City Hall**, designed by Coit Tower architect Arthur Brown – and currently closed to visitors until its retrofitted re-opening in 1999. To the west lie the magnificent **War Memorial Opera House** and **Louise M Davies Symphony Hall**; east across the plaza lies the former Main Library, planned to become the new home of the Asian Art Museum, the sparkling new **Main Library** and **United Nations Plaza** beyond; to the south lies **Bill Graham Civic Auditorium**; to the north several state and federal buildings. Civic Center marks the city's governmental nucleus. On Wednesday and Sunday mornings, UN Plaza hosts a local **Farmers' Market**.

For shopping and entertainment in the area, head north on Van Ness to **Opera Plaza** (at McAllister) where you'll find one of the city's best bookshops: **A Clean Well-Lighted Place For Books** features a great selection and authors' readings every week. Next door at **Max's Opera Café**, you can request operatic turns from your waiter or waitress. **Stars** restaurant (555 Golden Gate Avenue) is the place for celebrity spotting; if it's too pricey for you, the **California Culinary Academy**, on Polk and Turk Streets, serves bargain meals prepared by tomorrow's chefs.

The neighbourhood also houses two excellent sources for Northern California history: the **San Francisco History Room** occupies the top floor of the Main Library, and has several changing exhibits, an archive of a quarter of a million photographs and knowledgeable, friendly staff. The **Society of California Pioneers** at 456 McAllister Street (whose members are descendants of the state's first settlers) contains additional archives. Make an appointment on 861 5278.

The Tenderloin

The downtown area roughly bordered by Larkin, Mason, O'Farrell and Market Streets is San Francisco's red-light district. During the daytime, Cambodian grandmothers in sarongs scour the vegetable markets, while their grandchildren blend in among the homeless and crack dealers. At night, transgendered divas take to the streets, as do the hookers, male and female; aromas of Asian and Indian cooking mix with the sweet smells of cheap perfume. In the hours after dark, it's sensible to know where you're going in the Tenderloin: take a cab if necessary. But while much is made of the Tenderloin's potential for danger, there are many reasons to explore this fascinating neighbourhood, which is one of the most politically organised and ethnically diverse in the city.

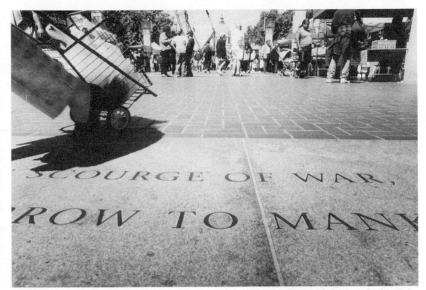

UN Plaza, *Civic Center site of a twice weekly Farmers' Market.*

Jazz and blues venue **The Blue Lamp** (561 Geary Street) is one reason, as is **The Edinburgh Castle** (950 Geary), a Scottish pub that serves fish and chips wrapped in newspaper. Also look up **Backflip** (601 Eddy Street), which shares ground with the **Phoenix Hotel**, the preferred lodging for rock stars playing at the nearby **Warfield Theater** (982 Market Street). **Biscuits and Blues** on Mason Street (for blues) and the **Mason Street Wine Bar** (for jazz) are also worth checking out. If you're up late, **The Grub Stake** on Pine and Polk Streets serves greasy-spoon fare until 4am, where exotic dancers from the local nude revues, transvestite singers and transsexual prostitutes mingle with tourists and clubbers.

Lots of great public art can be found in this neighbourhood. The **Children's Tenderloin Recreation Center** (570 Ellis Street, between Leavenworth and Hyde Streets) offers an amazing walk-through of children's works, as does the courtyard of the Phoenix Hotel. Also, don't miss the murals on the walls and inside the **Glide Memorial United Methodist Church** (330 Ellis Street), which serves food to around 3,000 homeless a day and where the famously enthusiastic Reverend Cecil Williams preaches on Sundays.

San Francisco's theatre district is located at the eastern edge of the Tenderloin. Within a few blocks are – among others – the **Theater on the Square** (on Post Street), the recently renovated **American Conservatory Theater** (on Geary), and the **Golden Gate Theater** (on Taylor).

Chinatown & North Beach

Hemmed in by the gleaming towers of the Financial District to the east and the affluent hotels of Nob Hill to the west, **Chinatown** is one of the oldest ethnic neighbourhoods in America. Before the discovery of gold in the Sierra foothills, there were only a few hundred people living here. Today, it's home to over 8,500 residents and forms part of the largest Asian community outside Asia. **North Beach**, San Francisco's predominantly Italian neighbourhood, is most famous for being home to the Beat poets in the 1950s and 1960s. Bordered by Bay, Washington, Montgomery and Leavenworth Streets, nowadays the area is an odd mixture of Italian, bohemian, touristy and sleazy, with strip joints and clubs doing business alongside some of the city's best restaurants and coffee shops. These enclaves are surrounded by the city's three most famous hills: Russian Hill, Telegraph Hill and Nob Hill.

Chinatown

The influx of Cantonese began in the late 1840s, fuelled by the dream of striking it rich and the need to escape the Opium Wars and famine at home, and later by the prospect of work on America's transcontinental railway. The area the Chinese had settled was completely destroyed by the 1906

全 世 界 最 平 乾 洗

男女 西裝一套（三件）	4	60
男女 西裝一套（二件）	3	60
要 西裝上衣（一件）	1	80
要 西褲一條	1	80
... 一件	2	20
... 一件	2	10

earthquake and fire, yet, despite attempts by city politicians to confiscate what had become premium land, the community managed to rebuild. The new Chinatown was as cramped as the old, and today the crowded streets are thronged with tourists and shoppers lured by the scent of herbal shops, Chinese food markets and hundreds of restaurants offering regional Chinese food.

A few blocks from Union Square on Bush Street, the dragon-topped **Chinatown Gateway** – a gift, in 1970, from Taiwan – opens onto **Grant Avenue**. Once called Dupont Street and a notorious thoroughfare of gambling and opium dens, it was patrolled by *tongs*, the secret groups formed in the late 1870s and 1880s to combat racial attacks, but which quickly developed into mafia-style gangs fighting to control the gambling and prostitution rackets. Today the street is Chinatown's official main drag, clogged with souvenir shops peddling tacky T-shirts, sweatshirts, cameras, Chinese art, ceramics and toys.

Several blocks north along Grant Avenue (and one block east) is **Portsmouth Square**, the historical centre and pulse of Chinatown. Bounded by Washington Street to the north and Clay to the south, the square has been unprepossessingly rebuilt over an underground car park. It was here that the small village of Yerba Buena was first claimed for the United States (from Mexico) in 1846, and where Sam Brannan, owner of the city's first newspaper, the *California Star*, announced the discovery of gold two years later. The surrounding streets were the first to be settled by the

Chinese in the 1840s and 1850s. Around 7am each morning locals gather in the square to practice tai chi and, later, Chinese men congregate on the east side to play hotly contested games of Russian poker or Chinese chess. Robert Louis Stevenson spent some time in San Francisco in 1879, and a monument on the north-west side of the square – the galleon *Hispaniola* – stands in his honour.

Across the square, on the third floor of the Holiday Inn at 750 Kearny Street, is the **Chinese Culture Center**, linked to Portsmouth Square by a concrete footbridge. The Center puts on art exhibitions throughout the year, sponsors cultural events and stocks a useful collection of books in its gift shop. Two blocks south, at 650 Commercial Street, the **Chinese Historical Society Museum** traces the history of the Chinese people in America in pictures and documents, and also houses the original – handwritten – Chinatown telephone directory.

It's worth exploring the surrounding network of side streets and alleyways. In the days when Chinatown was confined to a five-block area, you didn't need a map to get around – a good nose was enough. The street now called **Wentworth Alley**, off Washington Street, was known as 'Salted Fish Alley', and was the place to buy fresh and preserved fish. Refrigerators were a rarity in the cramped conditions where several families had

Step off the well-trodden tourist path and explore the side streets and alleyways of **Chinatown** *(above and opposite).*

to share one tiny kitchen, and fish was salted and 'sun-dried' on the rooftops. Eggs were preserved in brine for 40 days or more.

Walk back along Washington Street, and follow the scent of the **Golden Gate Fortune Cookie Factory** (56 Ross Alley) to watch the cookies being made by hand. On the south side of Washington Street is 'Fifteen Cent Street', named after the price of a haircut in the 1930s, and officially called **Waverly Place**. It's a wide, picturesque street that stretches between Washington and Sacramento Streets, parallel to Grant and Stockton. On the fourth floor of brightly painted 125 Washington is the **Tien Hau Temple**, dedicated to the Queen of the Heavens and Goddess of the Seven Seas. Opening times vary, but if you're lucky you'll be able to peep into the incense-filled sanctuary.

The **Bank of Canton** (743 Washington Street), almost directly across the street from Waverly Place, is one of the most photographed buildings in the area. The *California Star*'s offices originally occupied the site, but the present pagoda-like creation was built for the Chinatown Telephone Exchange.

The small alley to the west of Ross Alley, off Washington Street, is called **Old Chinatown Lane**. Once known as the 'Street of Gamblers', it was where **Donaldina Cameron**, the determined New Zealander who devoted her life to saving young Chinese girls from slavery and prostitution, once lived. **Cameron House** at 920 Sacramento Street – a youth centre that also offers social services to immigrants in Chinatown – is her legacy to the neighbourhood.

Chinese herbalists are one of the neighbourhood's pleasures. There's a string of them on Jackson and Clay Streets, with entire walls filled with hundreds of drawers containing various herbs, purchased not just to cure ills but also to maintain good health. Look in at the famous **Li Po** bar (916 Grant Avenue), decorated with Asian kitsch and one of San Francisco's more outlandish spots. At 949 Grant Avenue is the **Ten Ren Tea Shop**, the largest in San Francisco, where you can choose from 40 different types of Chinese tea.

To the west of Grant Avenue, running the length of Chinatown, is **Stockton Street**, where the locals shop. It is lined with Chinese fish markets, supermarkets, grocery stores, windows displaying roast pigs, and dim sum restaurants. If you're in a hurry, duck into one of the many takeaway restaurants to pick up an order of chow mein or a cha sil bow (steamed barbecued pork bun).

North Beach

Despite being a popular tourist attraction as much for its Beat heritage as for its thriving Italian cafés and restaurants, North Beach retains a sense of authenticity. Most of the people on the streets and in the cafés and bars live and work in the area, among them Francis Ford Coppola, who has an office in Columbus Tower – the curious green building on the corner of Columbus Avenue and Kearny Street.

A quick tour of Columbus Avenue and the nearby streets will unearth North Beach's treasures: **Tosca Café** (242 Columbus) has opera on the jukebox; **City Lights** bookstore (261 Columbus) is still owned by Beat poet Lawrence Ferlinghetti and is open until midnight every day. Once frequented by literary drunks Jack Kerouac and Dylan Thomas, **Vesuvio** (255 Columbus) still has a booth upstairs set aside for lady psychiatrists. Up the street, the Italian pottery store **Biordi Imports** (412 Columbus) purveys one-of-a-kind painted dinnerware and vases; as its name implies, **Quantity Post Cards** (1441 Grant Avenue) sells thousands of vintage card designs, and the nearby **Tattoo Art Museum** (841 Columbus) shows off a gallery of skin art.

Two hotels sum up the different sides of North Beach. The aptly named **Hotel Bohème** (444 Columbus Avenue) celebrates its Beat heritage with framed photographs of bohemian North Beach scenes from the 1950s and 1960s, while the *pension*-like **San Remo Hotel**, a pretty Italianate Victorian (2337 Mason Street), is more suitable if you want to soak up the area's Italian ambiance.

The neighbourhood's array of excellent coffee shops is truly dazzling. Particular landmarks include **Caffè Trieste** at Vallejo Street and Grant Avenue – the oldest coffee shop in San Francisco, where Coppola is supposed to have discussed the script of *The Godfather* with Mario Puzo, and where there are mini concerts on Saturday afternoons. Also try **Caffè Roma** (414 Columbus), where the coffee is roasted on the premises and John Lee Hooker is an occasional customer. **Mario's Bohemian Cigar Store** (566 Columbus), sells delicious focaccia sandwiches and great cappuccinos but no cigars.

You can't go wrong wandering through this neighbourhood. Pretty **Washington Square** is a lovely place to sit and watch people walk their dogs, play Frisbee or practise juggling, overlooked by the **Church of Sts Peter and Paul**, where Marilyn Monroe and Joe DiMaggio had their wedding photos taken (since both were divorcees, they got married at City Hall). Nearby Grant Avenue is packed with idiosyncratic shops, including **Figoni Hardware** (1351 Grant), run by Mel Figoni since 1924. It is the only place in San Francisco to sell bocce balls, a game which is still played at the North Beach Playground, two blocks north-east of Washington Square.

Continuing along Grant Avenue, **Prudente** (at Union Street) is the oldest butcher in the city and a good place to get exotic picnic ingredients such as own-cured cheeses and homemade sausages. There are also several good music bars on the street, including **Grant and Green Blues Club** (at Green Street) and **The Gathering Café**, (1326

Two North Beach landmarks: Lawrence Ferlinghetti's **City Lights** *bookshop* (top) *and* **Tosca Café**, *one of the city's oldest.*

Grant), the street's newest free venue for live jazz. Don't miss the rustic Spanish restaurant **La Bodega** (1337 Grant Avenue); the food is average but the flamenco dancing great.

There are so many Italian restaurants in the area, it almost seems unfair to highlight any in particular. However, **Enrico's** (504 Broadway) has good quality live jazz and a heated outdoor section set back from the street – perfect for people-watching. The hot new spot is **Rose Pistola** (532 Columbus), an upscale bistro that's packed every night. If you want to pretend you're really in Italy, eat at the **Bocce Café** at 478 Green Street. The food is plain Italian but it's cheap, and on sunny days or one of San Francisco's rare warm evenings, the garden at the back is a Tuscan-like haven dripping with bougainvillea, asparagus ferns and fig trees.

Russian Hill

Russian Hill, the quiet, residential neighbourhood roughly bordered by Van Ness Avenue, Broadway, Powell and Chestnut Streets, is most famous for having the 'crookedest' (and surely most photographed) street in the world, **Lombard Street**. Named after a group of Russian sailors thought to have been buried here, Russian Hill is also home to the **San Francisco Art Institute** (800 Chestnut), which houses a wonderful Diego Rivera mural.

Take a stroll up Vallejo Street to **Ina Coolbrith Park** at Taylor Street and have a secluded picnic; if you arrive early, you'll catch the Chinese elders practising tai chi. Walk back down via the **Vallejo Street Stairway**, designed by local architect Willis Polk and surrounded on each side by landscaped gardens. Landmark addresses include **29 Russell Street**, where Jack Kerouac lived with Neal and Carolyn Cassady in the 1950s, and the octagon-shaped house at **1067 Green Street**, one of the oldest dwellings in San Francisco.

One of the best views of the city can be seen from the **Vallejo Crest** at Vallejo and Jones Streets. If you turn right and continue across Green Street, you'll get to **Macondray Lane** – immortalised as Barbary Lane in Armistead Maupin's 'Tales of the City' series. And at 1088 Green Street is a two-storey **Fire Station** built in 1907, which incorporates a museum on the ground floor.

Polk Street, from Sacramento to Greenwich Streets, is a busy little area with a number of bars, shops and restaurants worth checking out. **The Real Food Deli** (2164 Polk Street) has a phenomenal selection of salads – perfect for a picnic in a nearby park. **Shanghai Kelly's** (2064 Polk) is a popular bar with locals who want a quiet beer. The biggest straight pick-up joint in San Francisco is undoubtedly **Johnny Love's** at 1500

Broadway where the 'bridge and tunnel' crowd is raucous, rowdy and randy.

The so-called **Polk Gulch** area (Polk Street from Sacramento Street to around Chestnut Street) used to be quite downmarket. The Tenderloin (east) edge is still trolled by transvestite prostitutes, but the Gulch is far from dangerous and there are some wonderful shops, gay bars, restaurants and bookstores to investigate. In early July the **Blues and Art on Polk** street fair brings the crowds out in droves.

Telegraph Hill

Telegraph Hill covers the area bordered by Grant Avenue, Green, Bay and Sansome Streets. Its main claim to fame is that it is home to **Coit Tower** (at the top of Filbert Street), which contains some magnificent murals by protégés of Diego Rivera and provides spectacular vistas of the city and Bay. Just down from Coit Tower, the **Julius' Castle** restaurant is small and intimate, with overpriced food but views that rival those of any tower block. From here you can descend via the steep wooden **Filbert Steps**, which run down from Montgomery to Sansome Streets; if you walk them at night, the blooms from the surrounding gardens smell gorgeous. At the bottom, head for **Levi Plaza**, where you can follow a path through a fountain designed by Lawrence Halprin. In the modern Levi offices, some of the first jeans ever bolted and stitched by Levi Strauss for the Forty-Niners back in the Gold Rush days are on display. (The factory, which you can tour, is in an unsalubrious block at 250 Valencia near 13th Street in the Mission. Phone 565 9153 for an appointment.)

Nob Hill

Named after the wealthy 'nabobs' who built their mansions in the area, Nob Hill was once described by Robert Louis Stevenson as 'the hill of palaces'. Bordered by Pacific Avenue, Bush, Larkin and Stockton Streets, it remains one of San Francisco's smartest (and highest) neighbourhoods with beautiful views over the city and many of its grandest hotels.

If you're suffering from hill overkill, take the California line cable car which runs up from the bottom of Market Street. In the midst of the area's crusty refinement are two kitsch gems – both located in the basement of the otherwise smart **Fairmont Hotel** on California and Mason Streets. In the **Tonga Room** cocktail bar, indoor

*The **Filbert Steps** climb Telegraph Hill. For more on city stairways, see page 58.*

tropical rainstorms occur every few minutes and a live band plays from a raft in the middle of a huge pool. Follow up your mai tai with dinner at the **Bella Voce** restaurant, where the waiting staff are dressed like extras from a Gilbert and Sullivan opera and take regular breaks to sing. Whatever you think of the music, the food is excellent. Round the evening off with a nightcap across the street at the **Mark Hopkins Inter-Continental Hotel**, where the famous **Top of the Mark** bar has fabulous views over the city.

Across California Street from the classy **Masonic Auditorium** (1111 California) sits **Grace Cathedral** (1051 Taylor Street). A beautiful mock-Gothic concrete structure modelled on Notre Dame in Paris, the church is well worth visiting for its concert performances which range from choral to jazz; a specially commissioned piece by Duke Ellington was performed here in 1965. Grace also houses the **Labyrinth Walk** – a meditative path on a carpet copied from the one laid in the floor of the cathedral at Chartres. There is a free guided tour at 1pm daily, or you can take the tour on your own any time between 7am and 6pm.

SoMa & the Mission

The area south of Market Street is known as **SoMa**, which, like New York's SoHo, was for many years a neglected area occupied by warehouses and sweatshops. The current moniker was first adopted to help overcome the district's sketchy reputation, and it worked: SoMa is now an emerging centre for multimedia businesses, the visual arts and all-night parties. To the south and west lies the buzzing **Mission** district, the city's oldest neighbourhood and one of its most lively.

SoMa

Today, much of SoMa (formerly known as South-of-the-Slot) has been transformed into a trendy and artistic area. It is home to two huge arts centres, a world-class convention hall, reconditioned towers with loft spaces that double as residences and offices, and a new waterfront plaza made possible by the removal of an earthquake-damaged freeway. SoMa changes rapidly from block to block and provides scores of interesting nooks worth exploring.

The **San Francisco Museum of Modern Art** (**SFMOMA**) marks ground zero for the city's modern art scene. The $60 million Mario Botta design – a work of art itself – stands a block from the **Moscone Convention Center** (747 Howard Street), the hive of exhibition halls named after former mayor George Moscone that draws so many from the national and international business community. At the time of writing, a wing of the Moscone was still under construction.

Across the street at Third and Howard Streets, the **Yerba Buena Center for the Arts**, set in the $87 million Yerba Buena Gardens arts complex, features several permanent exhibitions as well as touring shows. At 250 Fourth Street, facing the YBC and SFMOMA from the west, is the unmissable **Ansel Adams Center for Photography**.

But there's more to this area than large-scale civic buildings. If you prefer to seek out the raw, experimental and up-and-coming players in the arts, several small studios and independent galleries, some no bigger than a one-person flat, have sprung up like mushrooms in the alleys and above the retail spaces near the more established venues. Look out for the bi-monthly *Gallery Guide* available at SFMOMA, the Moscone Convention Center and a number of local cafés. Galleries worth investigating include **Blasthaus** (217 Second Street), the **Capp Street Project** (525 Second Street), **Gallery on the Rim** (333 Third Street) and **Refusalon** (20 Hawthorne).

If you're hungry in SoMa, you're in luck: in addition to dozens of cafés, one of the city's best restaurants, **Lulu** (816 Folsom Street) beckons nearby, as does the Basque-owned **Fringale** (570 Fourth Street) and President Clinton's choice, **Hawthorne Lane** (22 Hawthorne).

South Park & South Beach

A pioneer residential development designed by a Brit during the Gold Rush, South Park is now a pastoral haven from the three-lane boulevards just outside its oval surrounds. In the years following World War II, the neighbourhood became an African-American enclave and – as in too many US cities – this fact coincided with a drop-off in city services. If the authorities overlooked its value, however, South Park's potential was not lost on the private sector, which began renovating the garages, workshops and houses in the area in the early 1980s. The developers have lately been rewarded handsomely for their efforts.

Investors saw South Park initially as a perfect spot for urbane dining. First to open was the **South Park Café** (108 South Park Avenue). Encouraged by its success, its owners opened **Ristorante Ecco** (101 South Park), specialising in northern Italian food. Other lively venues such as **Caffè Centro** (102 South Park) and **Pepito's Parrilla** (24 South Park) weren't far behind.

The more recent and headline-grabbing element of the South Park story, however, is the multimedia explosion. The area marks the centre of the so-called 'Multimedia Gulch'. Though there isn't much of a gulch, the name has stuck and come to represent the area and the multimedia industry as a whole, just as Madison Avenue stands for the advertising world or Hollywood for the movies. Many of the customers jamming South Park's cafés and picnic tables are employed by telecommunications firms, multimedia

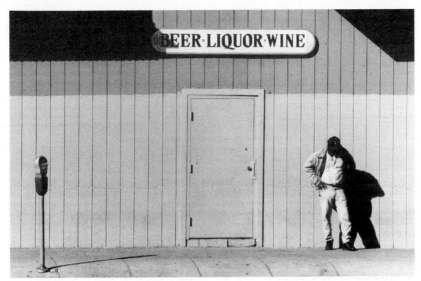

The **Mission** district: the city's oldest neighbourhood.

developers or other media, such as *Wired* and *PC World* magazines. This is the place to see the starry-eyed youth behind America's latest cultural fantasy/profit motive.

If this all proves too much, just around the corner from South Park are several unpretentious saloons serving straightforward fare, such as the fish sandwiches at **Butterfield's** (202 Townsend Street). Shoppers can browse in the discount outlets along Third Street. The **660 Center** has an impressive array of them and the **Isda & Co Outlet** (29 South Park Avenue) specialises in designer women's clothing, discounted by up to 70 per cent.

An additional area of activity within SoMa lies along the front of the Bay, a region known as **South Beach**. Among the waterfront attractions are the **Gordon Biersch** brewpub (2 Harrison Street), **Town's End Bakery** (2 Townsend Street) and the five-star **Boulevard** (1 Mission Street). The **Rincon Annex** at the corner of Mission and Spear Streets is a huge residential tower and shopping mall which contains one of San Francisco's coolest fountains, a 26m (85ft) high atrium with a cascade of water.

11th & Folsom Streets

SoMa after dark is definitely no place to go walking – the blocks are long and not particularly safe at night. But flag a cab down and don't be daunted: several corners are axes for multiple businesses. The conjunction of 11th and Folsom Streets is the area for the hottest clubs, and also

packed with restaurants. Start at the corner with the **Paradise Lounge** (1501 Folsom Street), then work your way through **20 Tank Brewery** (316 11th Street), **Slim's** (333 11th Street), the **DNA Lounge** (375 11th Street) and **Eleven** (374 11th Street), which are all on the same block. Just around the corner looms the **Holy Cow** (1531 Folsom Street), the hot new **V/sf** club (278 11th Street) and **Hamburger Mary's** (1582 Folsom Street). For a laundry stop and a cappuccino, drop into **Brainwash** (1122 Folsom Street), a full-service bar, café and laundromat.

From here, a number of offbeat attractions are within five minutes' walk. Check out the stretch of sidewalk in front of the **San Francisco Studios** (375 Seventh Street) where several large- and small-screen celebrities – comedians Whoopi Goldberg and Bobcat Goldthwait, as well as James Doohan (Scotty) and George Takei (Sulu) of the original *Star Trek* team – have made impressions of their hands. At the **Old Mint Museum** (88 Fifth Street) you can see where American bank notes were first printed in San Francisco.

For gift-buying, the **Wine Club** (953 Harrison Street) offers an exceptional selection of vintages and varietals and the notorious **Cake Gallery** (290 Ninth Street) specialises in genitalia gateaux.

The Mission

The city's oldest neighbourhood is the embodiment of change in San Francisco. Inhabited by the Spanish early in the city's 'civilised' history, the district has seen influxes of Irish, German, Italian, Latin and, most recently, Asian immigrants, all of whom brush shoulders today with the 'New Bohemians' who populate the region's cafés, bars and live music venues. The Mission is like no other area: the weather is warmer, the streets more crowded – even the smells are different: a mix of chilli peppers, garlic and onion, tomatoes, coriander and seared meat.

The first port of call for a steady influx of newcomers waiting to enter the American mainstream, the Mission's history is one of tolerance. It is home to a dazzling array of political and spiritual art: there are more than 200 murals in the district, painted on the walls of banks, schools and restaurants, many celebrating the struggles and achievements of its Latino residents. The *barrio* invites exploration beyond the charming Mission Dolores, the only stop on the tourist bus routes.

But the Mission is also afflicted with the ills of modern urban life. It has more than its share of prostitutes, drug addicts and gangs, so take the precautions you would in any city, while remembering that for decades the newspaper and television headlines have overstated the area's rough edges while ignoring its hidden treasures.

16th Street to Dolores Street

The stretch of 16th Street between Mission and Dolores Streets constitutes three short blocks, but it's packed with goodies. You pass crowded restaurants dispensing everything from French crêpes (**Ti Couz**, 3108 16th Street) to Spanish tapas and sangria (**Picaro**, 3120 16th Street). At Rondel Alley, just past the cool **Skylark** pub (3039 16th Street), **Pancho Villa** is one of the district's most visited taquerias, where the machine-gun rat-tat-tat of cleavers bouncing on butcher blocks is matched with the smell of seared onions. The **Casa Lucas La Hacienda** produce store at Valencia Street, with its fresh Latin groceries, is also worth exploration. Across the street, the **Roxie Cinema** (3117 16th Street) screens an eclectic playbill of avant-garde films.

A left at Dolores Street will take you to San Francisco's oldest building, the 200 year-old **Mission Dolores**, founded when a zealous *conquistador* planted a simple white cross on the edge of what was once a lake. The church and its peaceful flower garden and ornate cemetery remain, offering a quiet insight into the region's history. The names on the tombstones in the cemetery courtyard are the same as those of many of the city's streets.

Two blocks south is **Dolores Park**, worthy for the view of San Francisco and the Bay from the apex at 20th and Church Streets, and for the mélange of people and dogs who frequent the park. At the same intersection, notice the small, **bronze-painted fire plug**, which in 1906 provided

firefighters with the only working water source after the 1906 earthquake. The little hydrant did its job, keeping the flames away from homes in the Noe Valley district. A block and a half east on 18th Street, the **Women's Building** houses a refuge, recreation centre and theatre workshop. The building itself is a major work of beauty: local women artists have adorned it with the newest and grandest of the Mission's murals, a larger-than-life retelling of woman's history in the New World, topped with a portrait of Guatemalan Nobel Laureate Rigoberta Menchu.

Mission Street

The Mission Street corridor is the neighbourhood's economic lifeline, a river of commercialism catering to the area's middle-to-low-income residents with cheque-cashing operations, banks and shops crammed with cheap clothes, kitchen appliances, second-hand goods and groceries. It also offers some of the best people-watching in the city. Watch out for local notables such as the **Red Man** and the **White Lady**, two neighbourhood residents who for years have strolled the district's streets, their skin painted a flaming red and pallid white, respectively.

Despite Mission Street's overt commercialism, there are some unusual sights. You can explore **Ritmo Latina** (2401 Mission), with its huge selection of Latin music, or the **Cigarettes Cheaper** (2304 Mission) and **Mission Smoke Shop** (2063 Mission), outlets that cater to a stubborn population of tobacco aficionados resisting the Californian disapproval of smoking. Inside the **Bank of America** (2701 Mission), another powerful mural depicts the area's history.

Near 24th Street, the **Kings Bakery Café** (2846 Mission) offers a living example of how different cultures have met and melded in this neighbourhood: the trilingual Korean owner sells Mexican pastries to a stream of Anglo, Asian and Central American customers. **La Traviata** (2854 Mission), an upmarket Italian restaurant once favoured by visiting opera singers, offers a cosy, quiet retreat from the crowds. And **Cesar's Latin Palace** (3140 Mission) is the place to dance to Latin sounds until the sun comes up.

24th Street & Silicon Alley

24th Street is the Mission district at its diverse, traditional best. Like the neighbourhood's other main streets, 24th is lined with murals: at **South Van Ness Avenue**, an illustration of Mexican-American rockstar Carlos Santana is surrounded by plumed participants in the Mission's annual carnival. **Balmy Alley** portrays the roots of residents' countries' political history with a constantly changing gallery of outdoor paintings. Further down 24th Street, on the north wall of **St Peter's Catholic**

Church, a mural describes the catastrophic meeting of the Old and New Worlds from the perspective of Mayan scholars. At the intersection with Bryant Street, you'll find **Galeria de la Raza**, where ever-changing exhibitions by local artists draw visitors from around the country. The adjoining **Studio 24** supports the gallery by selling contemporary and traditional Latin American crafts.

For the hungry, 24th Street offers a variety of tastes from different Latin American countries: the Caribbean-spiced **El Nuevo Frutilandia** (near Folsom Street); **El Farolito** (at Alabama), which serves simple but good Mexican food; **La Palma** (at Bryant), which sells the only authentic, handmade corn tortillas in the district, and **Pollo Supremo** (at Harrison), whose fruit-juice-and-garlic-marinated chicken draws Financial District business types and local families alike. Another local favourite is the **St Francis Fountain and Candy Store** (2801 24th Street), birthplace of the city's beloved 49ers football team.

Near the intersection of 18th and Bryant, a tiny media community has sprung up. Dubbed 'Silicon Alley' by the locals, the conglomerate includes local public station KQED-TV, the new ZDTV Network, the *San Francisco Bay Guardian*, and a host of tiny multimedia start-ups – animation studios, publishers and pioneers in online electronic commerce – enjoying the neighbourhood's still-reasonable rents. The social hubs for this 'hood-within-a-'hood seems to be the **Slow Club** (2501 Mariposa Street) for drinks and the sunny **Universal Café** (2814 19th) for lunch and dinner.

Valencia Street

On Valencia, you can measure your walk by checking out the two **Muddy Waters** cafés, set nearly a mile apart on 24th and 17th streets. In between, the curious will find off-beat bookshops like **La Casa de Libros/Books on Wings** (near 20th Street), hip novelty shops such as the **Yahoo Herban Ecology** store (near 19th Street) and the long-standing women's sex shop **Good Vibrations** (at 23rd Street). The **Botanica Yoruba** (at 21st Street) sells traditional Caribbean religious items.

Near 19th Street is the colourful **Daljeets** clothing and accessories store (541 Valencia); a block away, **Leather Tongue Video** (714 Valencia) does brisk business; and a greasy spoon called the **Burger Joint** (807 Valencia) is disguised as a 1950s' hangout with brightly coloured leather booths and stools. Across the street, **The Marsh** (1062 Valencia), a popular, postage stamp-sized theatre, draws regular crowds.

This mix of shops is perhaps an economic response to the nightly arrival of insatiable San Franciscans in search of good restaurants. Just try to get a table at **Esperpento's** Spanish hideaway (3290 22nd Street), or the eclectic **Rooster** next door (1101 Valencia). Upmarket **Val 21** (995 Valencia) is always packed, as is the expensive **Flying Saucer**, a block west at 1000 Guerrero Street. Even the bars serve good food: **La Rondalla** (901 Valencia) is a favourite for its margaritas, Christmas lights and *mariachi*

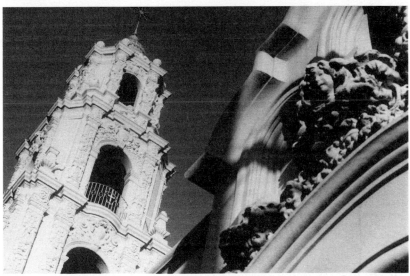

*The **Mission Dolores** basilica, built at the beginning of this century.*

performances, while **Timo's** (842 Valencia) offers Spanish tapas and seafood plates.

Finally, take a detour up **Liberty Street** to ogle the row of Victorian houses, including some pre-1906 earthquake survivors, and check out the former Jewish synagogue, on 19th and Lapidge Streets, next to a recreation centre splashed with a surrealist mural.

Potrero Hill

Like the nearby Mission district, Potrero Hill is nearly always sunny, even when the rest of the city is shrouded in fog. Bordered by Potrero Avenue, Army Street, 17th Street and the docks, it is a predominantly residential area, but there is still plenty for the traveller to do and see.

Have an alfresco lunch at **Sally's** or **Rustico** (both at 300 DeHaro) – mini-oases in the virtual wasteland of their surroundings. Take a tour at the **Anchor Brewing Company** (1705 Mariposa Street, book at least two weeks in advance), to sample some of California's best brews.

Farleys café (1315 18th) is a favourite dessert hangout, as is **Klein's Delicatessen** (510 Connecticut) for succulent sandwiches. Just a few blocks away is the **Esprit** outlet store (499 Illinois Street) for marked-down designs. Across Esprit's parking lot, **42 Degrees** is an excellent spot for lunch or a reviving cup of coffee after a hard morning's shopping. The **Bottom of the Hill** (1233 17th Street) has good local live bands and an outdoor patio where barbecues are held on Sunday afternoons.

The Haight & the Castro

The Haight-Ashbury

Only the fabulous Edwardian architecture remains as evidence of the Haight's original incarnation as a late nineteenth-century weekend resort where people came to play in the park or take the steam train to Ocean Beach, and the wealthy stayed in weekend homes or at the Stanyan Park Hotel. But if the Victorian era gave the Haight its building design, 1967's Summer of Love provided its ideology, which, 30 years' later, the neighbourhood has yet to live down. Nowadays, the young panhandlers who jokingly ask for 'spare change for drugs and alcohol?' are following the ethos of the 1960s when many of the shops gave away clothes and food and several restaurants went bust because they let so many people eat without paying.

To 1960s popstar aficionados (as well as those who smoke marijuana) the historical value of this neighbourhood is high. The **Grateful Dead** lived at 710 Ashbury Street; **Janis Joplin** at 122 Lyon Street, and **Jefferson Airplane** at 2400 Fulton Street. The address of the 'Red House' referred to in the Jimi Hendrix song is now the **Ashbury Tobacco Center** at 1524 Haight Street. Less appealing landmarks include **Charlie Manson's** mid-1960s house at 636 Cole Street. Wandering the length of Haight Street from Stanyan Street (where the entrance to Golden Gate Park is a homeless hangout) to around Central Avenue will give you a true feel for the area.

To stay in the thick of things you can't do better than **The Red Victorian** hotel (1665 Haight). The rooms are decorated in hippy style and everyone has breakfast together in the morning. Or get a huge breakfast at the **Pork Store Café** (1451 Haight), then work it off rollerblading in the park – you can rent blades from **Skates on Haight** (1818 Haight). In the evening, you can watch an independent movie at the **Red Vic** cinema (1727 Haight), which has church pew seating (with cushions) and serves homemade snacks and popcorn in big wooden bowls.

Up the street, **Kan Zaman** (1793 Haight) and **Zona Rosa** (1797 Haight) offer (respectively) good Mexican and Middle Eastern foods. **Cha Cha Cha** (1801 Haight) is the place to go for an authentic Brazilian/Northern California ambiance; it's cheap, always packed and the sangria is excellent – guaranteed to break the ice on even the chilliest first date. **The Booksmith** (1644 Haight) is an excellent bookstore that also sells international newspapers and magazines. Check their listings to see which authors are due to give readings.

The Haight is a rare mix of black and white, rich and poor, young and old. In line with its gentrification, the neighbourhood has its celebrities: Danny Glover has moved into the **Spreckels Mansion**, on Buena Vista Avenue West, next door to Bobby McFerrin's house. (There are two Spreckels Mansions in San Francisco; writer Danielle Steel lives in the grander one in Pacific Heights.) If you don't want to miss a thing, take local girl Rachel Heller's Haight-Ashbury Flower Power Walking Tour (221 8442).

Lower Haight

The Lower Haight is the name given to the area at the once-seedier eastern end of Haight Street. Here the tattooed skateboarding crowd mixes with street vendors selling junk from rugs on the pavement. The demolition of nearby project housing indicates an almost certain gentrification for the neighbourhood. It's a young and hip area, with

A couple of Haight Street habitués.

neighbourhood. It's a young and hip area, with myriad gems to be found.

On Haight Street itself, don't miss the **Mad Dog in the Fog** pub (530 Haight), where you can buy British as well as American beer, eat bangers and mash and shepherd's pie and play darts with the locals. At 557 Haight is the self-consciously hip bar **Noc Noc**, just down the street from **Used Rubber USA** (597 Haight), a unique shop selling goods made from old tyres. The best breakfast in town can be scored at **Kate's Kitchen** (471 Haight), though plan to queue at the weekend – aren't you glad you bought that magazine at **Naked Eye News and Video** (533 Haight)? Across the street, one of the city's best dancing venues is **Nickie's Barbecue** (460 Haight); small and intimate, the club always plays great music.

At the bottom of Fillmore Street, turn left at the Muni tracks and then right onto Church Street; the **Safeway** to your left is known as the gay pick-up equivalent of the (straight) Marina Boulevard Safeway. Just across the street, **Art's Coffee Shop** (138 Church) is the place to go for delicious soul food and jolly service; and **Chow** (215 Church) serves superb, cheap Italian fare. Turn left onto Market Street to get to **The Mint Karaoke Lounge** (1942 Market) where some of the best – and some of the worst – amateurs in town do their thing nightly.

Cole Valley

Cole Valley covers the small area bordered by Cole and Waller Street and Parnassus and Hill Point Avenues – an easy walk from the Haight. On the way up Cole Street, keep an eye out for the local character who sits on the steps outside his house wearing a Viking helmet or a huge golden crown, chatting with passers-by.

This area is mainly known for its cafés and bars. Pick up a magazine or newspaper at the **Val-Grin** drugstore and then pop next door to **Spinelli's** (919 Cole Street) to read it over a cup of coffee (there are so many coffee shops in San Francisco, it's a wonder they all stay in business). If you're hungry, the **Tassajara Bakery** (on the corner of Cole and Parnassus Streets) sells homemade bread and pastries that are out of this world.

The tiny, stylish **Zazie Café** (941 Cole Street) is open for breakfast, lunch and dinner. Two crêperies – **Crêpes on Cole** and **The Crêpery** – almost opposite each other on the corner of Carl and Cole Streets, are always busy. At the same junction, **The Kezar Bar and Restaurant** (900 Cole) is a friendly local bar that also does food. If you're feeling more elegant, the **Eos Restaurant and Wine Bar** (901 Cole) offers sophisticated dining in a bright, airy setting.

If you want some peace and quiet, walk south up Stanyan Street and turn left on Belgrave

Avenue to reach **Tank Hill**. This secluded area of grass and rocks is nearly always empty and offers a very romantic view of San Francisco at night; on the way up keep your eyes open for raccoons exploring the rubbish bins. During the day, the **UCSF Hospital** on Parnassus Avenue holds free lunch-time lectures on diverse health-related subjects; phone 584-4416 for more information.

The Castro

Bordered by 20th, Market, Diamond and Church Streets, the Castro was once the city's Catholic centre. Originally a Mexican ranch, the land was broken into lots and sold off in the 1880s to mainly working-class Irish families. Rumour has it that the opening of **Twin Peaks** (at Castro and Market Streets), the area's first gay bar, caused a mass exodus of Catholics; subsequently, the cheap but beautiful housing was bought and fixed up by those who gradually established the area as the capital of gay San Francisco – if not the whole US.

The Castro is one of San Francisco's busiest neighbourhoods. The people are friendly, open and relaxed and you are almost guaranteed to start a conversation in any one of the coffee shops in the area. **The Café** (2367 Market Street) is one of the few lesbian pick-up bars; the rest are predominantly male-oriented. The neighbourhood's geographical marker is the huge neon sign of the beautiful **Castro Theater** (at Castro and Market), where movies are preceded by entertaining renditions on a Wurlitzer organ, which eventually lowers below the floor to the whoops and cheers of the audience. The main thoroughfare is **Castro Street**, between Market and 20th Streets.

There are plenty of interesting shops and restaurants on Castro. Pop into **Cliff's Variety** (479 Castro), which sells fabrics, gifts, interesting toys and general hardware; it gets packed around Hallowe'en when everyone flocks in to buy costume accessories. Just a few doors away, **A Different Light** (489 Castro) sells books and magazines by, for and about gays and lesbians. Take a walk up 18th Street to find even more shops: one of the most unusual is **Southwest Tradewinds** on 18th and Sanchez Streets, which sells jewellery, pottery, Native American artifacts, Himalayan antiques, rugs, clothing and unusual cacti. In the other direction, don't miss **Firewood Café's** tasty roasted chicken (4248 18th Street).

On Market Street heading towards downtown, **The Names Project** (2362 Market) serves as a memorial museum to all those who have died of Aids. It exhibits panels from the Aids quilt, each square of which was created in memory of a lost friend or family member. At 2335 Market, **Crystal Way** sells New Age books, crystals and incense and offers tarot and psychic readings.

Among the many outdoor cafés and restaurants along Market Street, **La Mediterranée** (on the corner of Market and Noe Streets) serves delicious Middle Eastern food and is always busy – especially in the evenings. Just across the street, the garden at **Café Flore** is a good people-watching spot where the food is cheap but good.

Carry on down Market Street to find one of the best used clothes stores in town: at **Crossroads Trading Co** (2231 Market) you can pick up second-hand Levi's for $12 or a suede jacket for only $22. Just before Church Street, **Café Du Nord** is popular with twenty- and thirtysomething heterosexuals. Go there for salsa dancing lessons and to hear bands play several nights a week. Almost next door, **Centrium Furnishings** (2166 Market) sells furniture, lighting and decorative arts from the 1930s to the 1970s. Make a detour to **Romantasy** across the street (2191 Market), which purveys a racy selection of erotic toys, gifts and cards.

Noe Valley

Noe Valley, the area roughly bordered by 20th, Dolores, 30th and Douglass Streets, was, like nearby Castro, once populated by Irish families. Still a predominantly residential area, nowadays it is peopled by young couples pushing strollers and yuppies who flock to the area because the architecture is splendid and it's so quiet and sunny.

Activity in Noe Valley is centred around **24th Street**, which has an excellent selection of clothes shops, book and magazine stores and cafés.

Starting at the top of the hill, at Douglass Street, the **Firefly** restaurant serves enormous portions in intimate, romantic surroundings. Heading east down the hill, **Déjà Vu** (4156 24th Street) sells second-hand wedding dresses, vintage clothing, American pottery and dinnerware, as well as small pieces of furniture. **The San Francisco Mystery Bookstore** on the corner of Diamond and 24th Streets is a tiny gem selling new and second-hand mystery books and magazines. **Star Magic** (4026 24th Street) is a must for 'space age' gifts; it sells everything from telescopes to globe-shaped pencil sharpeners.

Continuing along 24th Street, **Just For Fun** (3982 24th) sells stick-on tattoos, jewellery, toys and other gifts. Stop off at **Spinelli's** (3966 24th) for a cup of coffee and a seat outside if it's not too windy. Across the street, **Chocolate Covered** sells just that – chocolate guitars, animals and telephones and chocolate-coated organic strawberries. The sushi at **Hamano**, at 24th and Castro Streets, is excellent. Nearby **Peek-a-boutique** (1306 Castro Street) sells second-hand children's clothes, including Osh Kosh overalls at less than half the price they'd be in the UK.

The latest gem to appear in the area is **Lovejoy's Antiques and Tea Room** (1195 Church Street), where you can have a traditional English high tea and then buy the cup and saucer you drank it from, as well as the chair you sat in and the paintings on the wall. **La Sirena Botanica** (1478 Church Street) supplies magical herbs, incense and spiritual goods to neighbourhood witches.

Noe Valley *is quiet, sunny and mostly residential.*

Twin Peaks

Twin Peaks are the two hills (275m/903ft and 278m/913ft, respectively) that overlook the Castro and Cole Valley neighbourhoods. The slightly taller hill is always swarming with tourists during the day, but it's still a nice place to sit on a windy day or evening. The other peak, only a short walk away, is always deserted (perhaps because it has no parking space), though the view from the top is just as beautiful. Further south, *Dirty Harry* fans will recognise **Mount Davidson**. At 286m (938ft), it is the highest spot in San Francisco; originally named Blue Mountain in 1852 by city surveyor George Davidson, it was subsequently renamed after him. It is topped by a distinctive 31m (103ft) white concrete cross, the future site of an Armenian Memorial.

The Waterfront

The Presidio

With a long and colourful history, the Presidio is a huge, 1,400-acre green area that is currently experiencing the laborious process of turning from an army base into a National Park. It stretches from the western tip of the Marina around the Bay to the Golden Gate Bridge, and has forests, hiking trails, streams and some excellent views of Golden Gate Bridge and the ocean. The entrance in Pacific Heights (on Presidio Boulevard and Jackson Street) leads you through fairytale woods to another entrance at Lombard and Lyon Streets in the Marina district. Points of interest include the **Presidio Army Museum** on Funston Avenue, the creepy **Pet Cemetery** on McDowell Avenue, and the **California Palace of the Legion of Honor** in Lincoln Park, to the west of the Presidio, most famous for its Rodin collection. **Baker Beach** on the west side of the Presidio is the city's nearest nude beach, but swimming is discouraged because of the currents. Better still, watch the surfers under the Golden Gate Bridge from historic **Fort Point**. During **Fleet Week** in October, there's no better vantage point to watch the Blue Angels' air show – the pilots fly *under* the Golden Gate Bridge – than from the **National Cemetery** on Lincoln Boulevard.

The Marina

The Marina district, between Fort Mason and the Presidio, is known to San Franciscans as the neighbourhood of yuppie singles. Unashamedly heterosexual, the local bars are full of young and trendy, bare-midriffed, twentysomethings drinking juices or coffee and making eye contact – even the local **Safeway** at 15 Marina Boulevard is a famous pick-up joint. Built on the rubble of the 1906 earthquake, the Marina was the worst hit of San Francisco's neighbourhoods in the 1989 Loma Prieta quake. Nearly a decade later, some evidence of the disaster – new pavements and several suspiciously new-looking buildings – remains.

There are some interesting bars, restaurants and shops, particularly along the main drag, Chestnut Street. Don't miss **Pasta Pomodoro** (2027 Chestnut Street) for great Italian fast-food, nor eco-conscious **EarthSake**, a clothing and home furnishings shop at 2076 Chestnut. Lombard Street, between Fillmore and Pierce Streets, has little to recommend it except for the bar **Blues** (2125 Lombard), which showcases the best local bands.

Locals go to fly kites, jog or picnic in **Marina Green**, which offers grand views of the Golden Gate Bridge and San Francisco Bay. At the end of the yacht harbour jetty, the amazing **Wave Organ**, a bizarre structure of underwater pipes, produces 'music' with the changing currents. Behind the **Palace of Fine Arts** at the end of Lyon Street is the marvellous **Exploratorium** science museum. The Palace itself is a neo-classical temple constructed for the 1915 Panama-Pacific Exposition and now an attractive picnic area where locals take their children to feed the ducks in the pond.

From the Palace it's a few blocks south to **Cow Hollow**, a one-time dairy pasture turned popular yuppie shopping area. The crowd here are slightly older and more established than in the rest of the Marina, which is reflected in the relative chicness of the bars, shops and restaurants along **Union Street**, between Broderick and Fillmore Streets, housed mainly in tastefully renovated Victorians.

Fort Mason & the Northern Waterfront

The Northern Waterfront unofficially describes the area that runs west of Fisherman's Wharf towards the Marina; it also encompasses the **Fort Mason Center** arts complex. Here you can eat at **Greens**, the best vegetarian restaurant in the city; listen to folk music at the **San Francisco Music Center**, which attracts artists from all over the country, or take in a performance at the innovative **Magic Theater**. The centre also houses a number of museums and art societies, including the San Francisco Craft and Folk Art Museum, the

For great views of the Golden Gate Bridge, stroll along China Beach, past the Presidio at the end of Seacliff Avenue.

Mexican Museum, the Museo Italo-American, the African-American Historical and Cultural Society and the National Poetry Association.

Don't leave the area without making a small detour to 600 Embarcadero to sample the delights of the **Delancey Street Restaurant**, which is part of the huge Delancey Street rehabilitation organisation and is staffed and run by reformed ex-cons.

Fisherman's Wharf

Except as a departure point for day trips by ferry to **Alcatraz Island**, Fisherman's Wharf doesn't have a great deal to recommend it, unless you're a fan of tacky, over-priced souvenirs and streets chock-a-block with tourists. If tat is your thing, however, you won't want to miss the **Wax Museum**, **Ripley's Believe It Or Not! Museum** (both on Jefferson Street) and **Pier 39**, a 45-acre amusement arcade/shopping complex where you can get anything from fast food and souvenir T-shirts to giant chocolate teddy bears (**Chocolate Heaven** sells 1,200 different chocolate items). Otherwise, do yourself a favour and restrict your Wharf experience to watching the barking seals that populate the harbour (both fun and free).

Other free activities include a trip to the **National Maritime Museum** in Aquatic Park, the interior of which has been done up to resemble an Art Deco ocean liner. If your cash is burning a hole in your pocket, **Cost Plus** on Taylor and North Point Streets is a huge warehouse selling everything from exotic food and drink to rugs, jewellery and furniture. At night avoid the area immediately surrounding the nearby housing projects on Bay and Taylor Streets, when you stand a reasonable chance of being mugged.

Ghirardelli Square, once home to the San Francisco chocolate factory, now houses yet another complex of shops and restaurants. Sort through your swag in the central plaza accompanied by the soothing trickle of the lovely Mermaid Fountain designed by local artist Ruth Asawa. Another reminder of the area's former life is **The Cannery** (2801 Leavenworth Street). Built in 1909 as a fruit-canning factory, it is now a twee shopping mall along the lines of London's Covent Garden, complete with street performers. The Cannery also houses **Cobb's Comedy Club**, which showcases some of the top comedians in the country; on open mike night, you might even witness the career-baby steps of the next Robin Williams. Finally, **Alioto's** restaurant at the end of Taylor Street, near Jefferson Street – around since 1938 – is one of the best seafood restaurants in town. A bonus is its spectacular view of the Golden Gate Bridge.

The Embarcadero

Before the Bay and Golden Gate Bridges were built in the 1930s, the Embarcadero, which stretches along the waterfront from Market Street in both directions from the Bay Bridge, used to be the landing point for upwards of 50,000 daily commuters from Marin and the East Bay. Subsequently overshadowed by an ugly freeway, the area went from being one of San Francisco's busiest places to one of its emptiest. Considerably improved after the 1989 earthquake damaged the freeway beyond repair, the newly old-again vicinity is now light and airy, stretching from **Fisherman's Wharf** all the way to **South Beach**. A perfect place for a long walk on a balmy autumn evening, the Embarcadero remains pleasantly uncrowded except for the area immediately surrounding the looming presence of the **Embarcadero Center** – a huge complex of hotels, offices, restaurants and shops that spans eight city blocks.

Another notable Embarcadero landmark is the 1896 **Ferry Building**, the design of which was inspired by the bell tower of Seville Cathedral, and under which the ferry commuters from Marin still disembark. It is also the venue for the popular **Ferry Plaza Farmers' Market**, held every Saturday morning. Take a picnic and, if it's not too windy, join the local office workers on the waterfront promenade and watch the incoming ships.

Central Neighbourhoods

Pacific Heights

Pacific Heights, north of California Street and west of the Presidio, is San Francisco's high society neighbourhood, as is evident from the wide, mansion-lined streets. Socialites Gordon and Ann Getty have a house here, as do rockstar Linda Rondstadt, San Jose Sharks owner George Gund and romantic novelist Danielle Steel, who lives in the **Spreckels Mansion**, which spans the entire block between Jackson, Gough, Washington and Octavia Streets.

It's possible to spend hours here, just wandering the streets marvelling at the opulence. Look out for the **Octagon House** (2645 Gough Street), built for a health fad and now restored to its 1861 splendour, and the 28-room 1886 **Haas-Lilienthal House** (2007 Franklin Street); both are open to the public. A walk down any lane or avenue offers glimpses of beauty and magnificence, though **Broadway** between Divisadero Street and the Presidio affords some of the best. A stroll through either **Alta Plaza** or **Lafayette Park** supplies a

The unmissable **Ferry Plaza Farmers' Market**, *held every Saturday.*

great excuse to ogle the surrounding homes and chat with the dog-walking locals and their children.

Upper Fillmore Street between Jackson and California Streets is the neighbourhood's central shopping hub, with plenty of excellent shops and smart restaurants. **Vivande Porta Via** (2125 Fillmore) used to be cookery queen Elizabeth David's favourite restaurant for lunch in San Francisco – quite a recommendation, when you consider that she had over 3,500 others to choose from. Further south, **Oritalia** (1915 Fillmore) specialises in a magical mixture of Asian and Italian cuisine. The quirky **Pizza Inferno** (1800 Fillmore) is a good place for a quick bite. For designer furniture, decorating accessories and gifts, check out **Fillamento** (2185 Fillmore), though their marvellous selection is notoriously overpriced. At Clay Street, the **Clay Theater** screens first-run art and foreign films.

Further west, the antiques and clothes shops on Sacramento Street between Presidio Avenue and Spruce Street are comparatively expensive, but some bargains can be had at **Good Buys** (3464 Sacramento Street), a fabulous second-hand clothes store where you might find a Chanel bag or suit for less than half the original price. Considering the area it serves, the **Vogue Cinema** (at Presidio Street) is surprisingly flea-bitten, but often shows good double bills. If you want to lodge in the area, the Victorian **Mansion Hotel** (2220 Sacramento Street) is genuinely eccentric, with life-sized dummies of people lounging in the hallway chairs and a pianola that plays by itself in one of many antique-filled sitting rooms.

Japantown

Tiny Japantown used to comprise a much larger area covering about 40 blocks, but the Japanese immigrants who settled here were forced to move after the bombing of Pearl Harbour. Many were interned – and treated abominably. In 1968, in a vague spirit of reparation, San Francisco's urban planners created the **Japan Center**, a huge shopping, dining and entertainment complex, which takes up three blocks between Post Street and Geary Boulevard and one block of Buchanan Street. The area feels a little hollow, but the businesses are thriving.

To immerse yourself (literally) in the Japanese experience, indulge in a relaxing massage at **Kabuki Hot Spring** (1750 Geary Boulevard), a traditional Japanese bathhouse with communal pools, saunas and steam rooms. Spend a restful half hour or so in the **Buddhist Church of San Francisco** on Pine Street, or just sit in the Peace Plaza garden, overlooked by the five-tiered, concrete **Peace Pagoda**, which was given to the community by Japan. In April, the region's **Cherry Blossom Festival** marks a month-long celebration of

Japanese culture, with flower-arranging demonstrations, martial arts displays, traditional dance performances and a parade on the last day.

Any one of the area's restaurants are excellent for Japanese noodles and sushi. The inexpensive **Sanppo** (1702 Post Street) serves delicious bowls of udon and soba noodles, as does **Mifune** inside the Japan Center. For a sublime culinary experience, purse willing, go to the **Yoyo Tsumami Bistro** on Post Street, an upmarket Japanese tapas restaurant. You can always work off dinner at **Japantown Bowl** on Post Street, at Webster.

Also on Post Street, the eight-screen **Kabuki 8** cinema complex is the venue for most of the events and films shown during the annual San Francisco International Film Festival in April and May, and for the latest movies during the rest of the year. Like many of the city's cinemas, the Kabuki has cheaper tickets at certain times of day; phone 931 9800 for more information.

The Western Addition

The Western Addition (referred to by some as 'Midtown') is the city's largest neighbourhood, an area roughly bordered by California, Fell and Divisadero Streets and Masonic Avenue. Once predominantly African-American, the area was home to the original jazz clubs and the heart of black culture in the city. Some elements of this era prevail – the soul food and barbecue restaurants on Divisadero, the bookshops in the Lower Fillmore – and reflect a time that's been slowly replaced by demographical change. The region combines a mixture of cultures, young and old, families and single residents.

The area is now primarily residential, with street corner businesses and a gorgeous park: **Alamo Square** on Steiner Street features the most photographed row of Victorians in the city. **The University of San Francisco** sits perched on its western edge; the 'panhandle' of Golden Gate Park marks its southern; wide, ugly Geary Boulevard, the city's main east-west arterial, bisects it. For lodging, the **Chateau Tivoli** B&B (1057 Steiner Street) has been restored to its former Victorian splendour and is filled with enough four poster beds and *objets d'art* to keep Christies in business for years.

At the lower end of Fillmore Street by Geary Boulevard, check out the new **Boom Boom Room**, a blues club open in the former digs of Jacks Bar, where partner John Lee Hooker has been known to turn up for impromptu gigs. The nearby **Fillmore Auditorium**, which booked the likes of Jimi Hendrix and The Doors in the 1960s, continues to feature upcoming new acts as its headliners. **Marcus Books** (1712 Fillmore Street) is a specialist African and African-American bookshop. Several excellent second-hand clothing stores lie north of

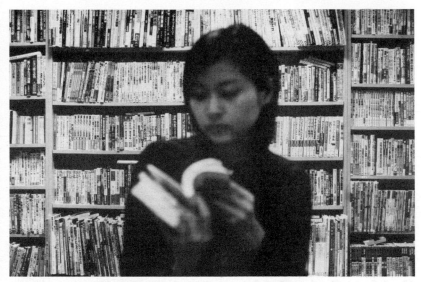

Japantown – *for the complete Japanese experience.*

here. For a magical Sunday experience head for the **First Union Baptist Church** on Webster Street and Golden Gate Avenue (for real gospel singing) or the uniquely San Franciscan **Church of John Coltrane** at 351 Divisadero. For Sunday dinner, you can't beat **Powell's Place** (511 Hayes) for tender fried chicken and mashed potatoes.

Hayes Valley

North of Market Street and west of the Civic Center, San Francisco's most exciting, fastest developing – and uncharacteristically flat – neighbourhood used to be one of its least salubrious, in spite of its close proximity to the Davies Symphony Hall and War Memorial Opera House. Few came to Hayes Valley except to visit the prostitutes and drug dealers who did business under cover of an ugly raised freeway. But when damage from the 1989 earthquake brought down the viaduct and, more recently, government agencies dismantled the project housing development up the hill, the area started to gentrify.

Today, the area is one of contrasts: older establishments such as the 20 year-old **Sharp Brothers** (525 Hayes Street), an unruly mound of junk where you can still unearth under-priced treasures, do business alongside the stores owned and run by the talented young fashion and furniture designers who have taken over the area. Block parties are held four times a year when shops serve wine and hold fashion shows, bands play, fire-eaters perform and the streets are packed with revellers.

Shops worth a special mention are **Zeitgeist Timepieces** (437B Hayes Street) for vintage watches; **Bella Donna** (539 Hayes) for wonderful clothes and unusual fabrics; and **Worldware** (336 Hayes), which sells furniture and body-pampering accoutrements. The **African Outlet** (524 Octavia Street) sells African art; here, too, you can get your body decorated with henna. **Richard Hildert** (330 Hayes) deals in new books, but is probably the best source in the US for valuable, second-hand and out-of-print editions on interior design. Just across from Hildert's, the **San Francisco Women Artists' Gallery** (370 Hayes) grew out of the all-women Sketch Club of the 1880s and continues to showcase the work of women artists in the Bay Area. Finally, **Star Classics** (425 Hayes) stocks a huge selection of classical CDs.

The area's restaurants are similarly diverse. If you like tarot with your tea, get down to **Mad Magda's Russian Tea Room** (579 Hayes Street). The intimate **Momi Toby's Revolution Café** (528 Laguna Street), is the perfect place to relax and read the newspaper over a latte or a light meal and has excellent live music in the evenings. The best food in the area is at the **Hayes Street Grill** (320 Hayes) or the always delightful **Caffe Delle Stelle** (395 Hayes). Down the road, **Marlena's** bar (Hayes at Octavia Street) is at its best on a Friday night when the pool table is turned into a stage on which transvestites lip-synch their favourite songs. And don't miss the extremely stylish **Suppenküche** restaurant (601 Hayes), which is run along the lines of a German *wirtshaus*.

At 66 Page Street, between Franklin and Gough, the oldest Harley Davidson dealership in town, **Dudley Perkins Co**, has been selling noisy bikes since 1914. **Bell'occhio** (8 Brady Street) is worth the minor detour for European toiletries, antique ribbons and jewellery, as is the clothes shop next door, **Salon de Thé**. In the other direction, the **San Francisco Performing Arts Library and Museum** (399 Grove Street) has a huge collection of performing arts memorabilia.

There are also several large, hard-to-miss, antique shops on the section of Market Street that leads you towards Hayes Valley proper. Make time to stop for breakfast or lunch at **Zuni Café** (1658 Market). Just across the street, check out **New Deal** (1632 Market) for one-off, new and used furniture and *objets d'art*, before cutting through tiny Rose Street to Gough Street and then turning right for more treasures. This really is San Francisco's nearest equivalent to New York's SoHo, chock-a-block with wonderful shops and restaurants. Don't miss **Flax** (1699 Market) for incredible art supplies, nor the monthly-changing menu at **Carta** (1772 Market).

Golden Gate Park & the West

Golden Gate Park, which stretches from Stanyan Street to the Pacific in the area between Fulton Street and Lincoln Way, is extraordinarily diverse. Its 1,013 acres include manicured gardens, wild areas, fairytale woodlands, illegal homeless encampments, rollerblading paths, bike trails, lakes, rose gardens, chess tables, a playground and a first-class natural history museum. Knowing that its construction didn't begin until the late 1870s, it almost impossible to walk through the park without marvelling at the imaginations of its creators, civil engineer William Hammond Hall and park supervisor John McLaren, who worked here from 1887 until 1943.

The park's long, narrow shape makes for quite a trek from end to end, so you might want to rent a bicycle (from **Park Cyclery** at 1749 Waller Street) or rollerblades (from **Golden Gate Park Skate and Bike** at 3038 Fulton Street) to speed your time betweeen sights. In any case, **John F Kennedy Drive** will take you the distance and yield the best viewing points.

Start at the east end, outside the ornate **Conservatory of Flowers**, where tourists from all nations disembark from buses to view the manicured grounds. At **Stow Lake,** the largest lake in the park, you can rent a paddle boat or rowing boat. Further west, the **Golden Gate Park Stables** at 36th Avenue offers horse riding lessons. **Spreckels Lake** is a haven for model

yacht racers, while the **Buffalo Paddock** always has a small herd of bison conveniently clustered near its fence for easy viewing. At the western edge of the park, the **Wilhelmina Tulip Garden**, surrounds the windmill next to 48th Avenue – both gifts to the city from a Dutch queen.

Off John F Kennedy Drive, the **Japanese Tea Garden** is an oasis of peace with a little bridge, flowering trees, a huge bronze Buddha and an outdoor tearoom with waitresses in kimonos; entry is free on the first Wednesday of the month. Botanical enthusiasts will love the **Strybing Arboretum**, planted with 6,000 species of plants, trees and shrubs from different countries, while literary gardeners should head for the **Shakespeare Garden**, which is stocked with plants mentioned in the Bard's plays and poetry. Kids of all ages will delight in a ride on the beautifully restored **carousel**, next to the children's playground just off Kezar Drive.

The park is home to many events throughout the year: **Opera in the Park**, **Shakespeare in the Park** and **Comedy Celebration Day** are late summer treats when locals bring a picnic for an afternoon of performances. More often than not, there's a music festival going on; one of the most popular is **Reggae in the Park**, held during the beautiful weather that arrives in early autumn.

Along Music Concourse Drive, don't miss the **California Academy of Sciences**, which houses a number of scientific exhibitions, including the Natural History Museum, Morrison Planetarium and Steinhart Aquarium. The latter includes a beautiful living coral reef, and the popular Fish Roundabout where a huge and populous fish tank encircles the room. Currently, the **MH de Young Memorial Museum**, which houses art from the Americas, and the **Asian Art Museum**, which has the largest collection of Asian art outside Asia, are open. Within the next several years however, the Asian will move to Civic Center and the de Young to an as-yet-undetermined location downtown. For a map of the park, *see page 54* **Sightseeing**.

Richmond

Richmond borders the northern edge of Golden Gate Park, from Arguello Boulevard to the ocean and from Fulton Street to the Presidio. Once a sandy wasteland, the region became a viable residential area following the 1906 construction of the Geary Boulevard tramway. Settled by Russian and Eastern European Jews after World War I, it's now a mixed neighbourhood, dominated by Russian, Irish and, increasingly, Chinese immigrants.

Clement Street, from Fourth to 20th Avenues, is the district's main commercial centre and viewed by many as the city's 'real' Chinatown. Huge shops sell cheap kitchenware and enamel crockery; acupuncture clinics and small Chinese medicine shops can be found on every block. Hundreds of Asian restaurants are here too: notable ones include **The Fountain Court** (354 Clement, at Fifth Avenue); **Minh's Garden** (208 Clement), where you can get a meal for under $5; the more upmarket Vietnamese **Le Soleil**, on the next block; and the vegetarian **Red Crane** (115 Clement, at 12th Avenue).

Non-Asian delights include the **Blue Danube** 1960s-style coffee house (306 Clement) and **Haig's Delicacies** (642 Clement), which sells British food, Middle Eastern goods and a fabulous selection of Indian spices. Further west, **Bill's Place** (2315 Clement) is a local diner with a back garden, which serves hamburgers named after local celebrities (the Carol Doda, in honour of the woman who introduced topless dancing to the city, features two hamburgers each topped with an olive, served side by side).

Across the street, the **Family Sauna Shop** (2308 Clement) has been providing saunas and beauty treatments since 1975. Almost next door, the **Buddhist Temple** is a relaxing haven from the street. Finally, **Green Apple Books** (506 Clement) is indisputably the neighbourhood's favourite shop for new and second-hand books.

At the Ocean Beach end of the Richmond, **Sutro Heights Park** is a tiny idyll, virtually empty except for a few Russians walking dogs or playing chess. By the park entrance at Geary Boulevard, a statue of the goddess Diana is often decorated with flowers by local pagans. In the nearby walled garden you can enjoy a secluded picnic and marvel at the spectacular panoramic view of the ocean – fog permitting. Walk down to Point Lobos Avenue and stop off for a milkshake at **Louis'** (902 Point Lobos Avenue), which offers truckstop-style food and a view just as good as the one from nearby, touristy **Cliff House** (1090 Point Lobos Avenue). Tobacco magnate Adolph Sutro built the first Cliff House in the 1860s; after a fire in 1894, he replaced it with a Victorian turreted palace. When this burned down, it was replaced by the present architectural muddle.

Behind the Cliff House, check out the antique arcade machines at the **Musée Mécanique**, view the Seal Rocks from the nineteenth-century **Camera Obscura** (on a clear day, you can see the Farallon Islands, 48 kilometres/30 miles out to sea) and then walk down to the ruins of **Sutro Baths** to the north. Built by Sutro in 1896, these were once the world's biggest swimming baths with seven heated pools under a magnificent glass roof, all sadly destroyed by fire in 1966. To the right of the baths is a long cave. A spooky walk through this opens onto the side of the cliffs where the sea crashes against the rocks; don't attempt it at high tide, however, when the cave fills up and you could get trapped. Instead, you can walk the three-mile windswept **Coastal Trail** from the Cliff House to the **Golden Gate Bridge**.

Don't leave the Richmond without visiting the **Columbarium** (1 Loraine Court, off Anza Street), open from 10am-1pm daily. This beautiful Victorian building and miniature 'museum' of funeral architecture is set in two acres of gardens and the only cemetery for cremated remains in the city. Admire the lovely stained glass windows and magnificent tiled floor. Afterwards, if you're hungry, nearby **Ton Kyang** (3148 Geary Boulevard) serves some of the best Chinese food in town.

Sunset

Sunset is a large and mainly residential neighbourhood stretching along the southern length of Golden Gate Park to the ocean and south to Rivera Street. Like the Richmond district, it can be foggy between June and September; on clear days, however, there are spectacular sunsets over the ocean.

Start your tour on **Irving Street**: the main shopping area stretches from Fifth to Tenth Avenues. Indulge in a refreshing concoction from **Jamba Juice** (1300 Ninth Avenue), one of a new chain of fresh juice bars. **Ninth Avenue Books** (1348 Irving Street) sells new and second-hand books, while **Le Video** (1239 Ninth Avenue) is probably the best video store in San Francisco, with a broad selection of films from mainstream to the downright obscure. Anyone with photo ID, a credit card and a San Francisco address is welcome to rent one.

The neighbourhood is a haven for restaurants, including seafood specialist **PJ's Oysterbed** (737 Irving Street); **Ebisu** (1283 Ninth Avenue), which serves some of San Francisco's best sushi; **Yaya** (1220 Ninth), where you can taste 'the food of Mesopotamia', and **Raw** (1224 Ninth), which offers entirely vegetarian, uncooked meals. Asian-flavoured **House** (1269 Ninth) and all-American **Avenue 9** (1243 Ninth) are relative new-comers. Among the area's coffee shops are **The Beanery** on the corner of Irving and Seventh and the **Java Place** on Ninth and Judah. For a cheap breakfast, you can't do better than **Art's Café** (on Irving and Eighth).

At the northern end of Sunset, **Ocean Beach**, the city's biggest beach, is good for a blustery walk and for watching surfers. Take a break at the **Java Beach** café (at Judah and 47th), where the coffee is famously good. The best restaurant in the immediate vicinity is the Vietnamese **Thanh Long** (4101 Judah Street), famous for its garlic crab.

To the south-west of Sunset, the **San Francisco Zoo** is small but exotic with a scary insect house and a special children's section where kids can feed domestic farm animals. Further east, **Stern Grove** (at 19th Avenue and Sloat Boulevard) is a 63-acre oasis of eucalyptus, redwood and fir trees, popular in the summer when San Franciscans brave the fog to attend the free Sunday afternoon jazz and classical concerts. **Stonestown Galleria** shopping mall, on 19th Avenue at Winston Drive, a few blocks north of **San Francisco State University**, satisfies most consumers in the area.

Consumer SF

Accommodation

Lodging logistics for the City by the Bay.

As one of the most popular tourist destinations in the world, San Francisco goes the distance to cater to every type of visitor – from penny-pinching hostel-goers and 1960s throwbacks to wealthy jet setters and gender-benders. But, even though it boasts more than 50,000 rooms available nightly, it's not unusual to find the town sold out during high season and convention weekends, so make sure you secure your accommodation well in advance.

Most hotels are packed into the ultra-touristy downtown Union Square/Nob Hill area, handy for shopping, cable cars, Chinatown, North Beach, SoMa and some of the city's best restaurants. Though downtown is definitely the most happening place to stay, its drawbacks include expensive parking rates and separation from the 'real' San Francisco where most residents live and play. If you do want to explore other neighbourhoods, the city is condensed enough to make it easy to get anywhere else from downtown by cab or public transport.

For basic accommodation – double bed, private bathroom, phone and TV– within the city, expect to pay $80-$120 a night during peak season (May-October). This doesn't include a 12 per cent room tax, telephone surcharges and nightly parking fees, which range from free to about $25.

When making a hotel reservation, have your credit card handy and be prepared to pay for at least one night in advance, though this isn't always necessary. Your reservation will be held until about 6pm, unless you've told the hotel you'll be arriving late; otherwise, you may lose your room.

Cash, credit cards and US dollar travellers' cheques are the preferred methods of payment, and most hotels will ask for an imprint of your credit card upon arrival for 'incidental expenses' and to prevent walk-outs. Service from the staff at most moderate to expensive hotels in San Francisco is usually superb, but don't think for a minute that they're doing it purely out of the kindness of their hearts, so tip accordingly.

All 1-800 numbers can be dialled free within the US (and at international rates from outside); however, some hotels add a surcharge for use of their phones, whatever number you call. For a list of websites providing accommodation information and booking services, *see page 252* **Directory**. For a list of gay and lesbian hotels in the city, *see chapter* **Gay & Lesbian San Francisco**. For long-term rented accommodation, *see page 263* **Directory**.

Best for ...

... romantic grandeur **Archbishop's Mansion** *p111*
... small-scale charm **Bed and Breakfast Inn** *p115*
... contemporary cool **Commodore International** *p113*
... families **Holiday Lodge** *p116*
... location **Hotel Bohème** *p111*
... grandiosity **Hotel Monaco** *p113*
... heavenly views **Mandarin Oriental** *p105*
... business **Nob Hill Lamborne** *p111*
... the funky factor **The Phoenix** *p113*
... hippy living in the Haight **Red Victorian** *p113*
... the wow factor **Ritz-Carlton** *p105*
... budget bargains **San Remo** *p116*
... the swimming pool **Sheraton Palace** *p111*
... fat cats **Sherman House** *p105*

Top Dollar

Campton Place Hotel

340 Stockton Street, CA 94108, at Post Street (1-800 235 4300/781 5555/fax 955 5536/reserve@compton. com). Bus 2, 3, 4/cable car Powell-Hyde or Powell-Mason. **Rates** *single/double* $230-$345; *suites* $450-$750. **Credit** AmEx, DC, MC, $TC, V. **Map G3**
After a hefty $18 million retro-fit back in 1981, the former Drake-Wiltshire Hotel re-opened as the Campton Place and has attracted a very discreet (and wealthy) following ever since. A nifty use of mirrors in the lobby and the 117 rooms helps to disguise the hotel's surprisingly small size, although some guests may still wonder what their money is paying for. The services, however, are exceptional, and include valet-assisted packing and unpacking, French laundry service and 24-hour room, concierge, maid and valet service. Two additional enticements are the central location (on the corner of Union Square) and the highly rated Campton Place Restaurant. **Hotel services** *Air-conditioning. Babysitting. Bar. Concierge. Conference facilities. Currency exchange. Disabled: access; rooms for disabled. Fax. Laundry. No-smoking rooms. Parking. Restaurant. Roof garden.* **Room services** *Hair-dryer. Mini-bar. Radio. Room service (24-hour). Safe. VCR.*

Clift Hotel

495 Geary Street, CA 94102, at Taylor Street (1-800 652 5438/775 4700/fax (reservations) 931 7417/fax (guests) 441 4621). Bus 2, 3, 4, 30, 38, 45/cable car Powell-Hyde or Powell-Mason. **Rates** *single/double* $245-$295; *suites* $350-$645. **Credit** AmEx, DC, JCB, MC, $TC, V. **Map G4**

After its $24 million facelift, the **Hotel Monaco** *offers lavish lodging on a grand scale. See page 113.*

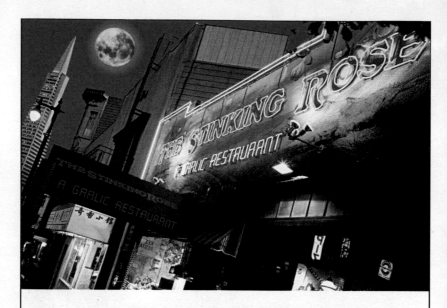

The Stinking Rose Restaurant

Follow your nose to The Stinking Rose®: A Garlic Restaurant,
where you'll find one of San Francisco's
most unique and entertaining dining experiences...

325 Columbus Avenue
415/PU-1-ROSE

Since Ian Schrager, king of hip hotels, acquired this 326-room property, everyone's anxious to see what will happen. But two things are certain: Philippe Starck will design it – and it will be the hottest hotel in town. Located in the city's Theatre district, two blocks from Union Square, the Clift is renowned for its pampering staff, palatial lobby and romantic Redwood Room. The décor still leans toward old-fashioned, with high ceilings, elaborate mouldings and Georgian reproductions, but renovations should be finished by the end of 1998. Services include twice-daily maid service, and pets are allowed (as many as you like for an additional $40 plus food). **Hotel services** *Babysitting. Business services. Concierge. Conference facilities. Currency exchange. Disabled: access. Fax. Gift shop. Gym. Laundry. Limousine service. No-smoking rooms. Parking.* **Room services** *Fax machine and modem jack. Hair-dryer. Mini-bar. Radio. Refrigerator. Room service (24-hour). Safe.*

Mandarin Oriental

222 Sansome Street, CA 94104, between Pine and California Streets (1-800 622 0404/885 0999/fax 433 0289). Bus 1, 12, 42/cable car California. **Rates** *single/double $305-$495; suites $775-$1,600.* **Credit** AmEx, DC, Disc, JCB, MC, TC, V. **Map H3**
Few hotels in the world can boast such an extraordinary view as the Mandarin Oriental. Its lobby is on the ground floor of the 48-storey First Interstate Building and all its 158 rooms and suites are up on the top 11 floors. The view is phenomenal, particularly when the fog settles below you – it's like being in heaven. In keeping with the Asian décor, rooms contain a sparse selection of blond-wood furnishings and Asian artwork, and rumour has it that the staff-to-guest ratio is 1:1. Adjoining the lobby is the hotel's renowned restaurant, Silks, considered one of the best in the country. **Hotel services** *Air conditioning. Babysitting. Bar. Concierge. Conference facilities. Disabled: access; rooms for disabled. Fax. Gym. No-smoking rooms. Parking. Restaurant. Safe.* **Room services** *Fax/modem jack on request. Hair-dryer. Mini-bar. Radio. Refrigerator. Room service (24-hour). Video library.*

Ritz-Carlton

600 Stockton Street, CA 94108, at California Street (1-800 241 3333/296 7465/fax 986 1268). Bus 1, 30, 45/cable car California, Powell-Hyde or Powell-Mason. **Rates** *rooms $335-$450; suites $525-$575, executive suites $3,000-$3,500.* **Credit** AmEx, DC, Disc, JCB, MC, TC, V. **Map G3**
There are several fine hotels at the top of Nob Hill – such as the Huntington, the Fairmont and the Mark Hopkins – but it's this relative newcomer that's getting all the attention, and deservedly so. After a four-year, multi-million dollar renovation, the 336-room Ritz-Carlton opened its doors in 1991 and has continued to wow its guests ever since. Amenities include an indoor spa with swimming pool, whirlpool and sauna; a fully-equipped training room; the award-winning Dining Room restaurant; and an armada of valets and ushers to assist your every need. The rooms, all recently renovated, are a bit of a let-down compared to the fancy façade and lobby, but are quite comfortable and come with all the luxury items you would expect from the Ritz. **Hotel services** *Air-conditioning. Babysitting. Bar. Business services. Concierge. Conference facilities. Disabled: access; rooms for disabled. Fax. Garden. Gym. Laundry. Limousine service. No-smoking rooms. Parking. Restaurants. Swimming pool.* **Room services** *Hair-dryer. Mini-bar. Radio. Refrigerator. Room service (24-hour). Safe.*

Sherman House

2160 Green Street, CA 94123, between Webster and Fillmore Streets (1-800 424 5777/563 3600/fax 563 1882). Bus 22, 41, 45. **Rates** *rooms $210-$425; suites $625-$775.* **Credit** AmEx, DC, MC, $TC, V. **Map E3**
This stately, four-storey, Victorian mansion had its ups and downs over the years until the present owners dumped a small fortune into a four-year restoration project. Now its 14 rooms – each furnished in Jacobean, German Biedermeier or French Second Empire style with fireplaces, tapestries and brocaded bed hangings – are good enough for the likes of Shirley MacLaine, Ted Kennedy and Bill Cosby, which means if you have an equally fat bank account you, too, can afford to stay here. **Hotel services** *Babysitting. Business services. Concierge. Fax. Garden. Laundry. Limousine service. Parking. Restaurant. Safe.* **Room services** *Computer. Fax/modem jack. Hair-dryer. Radio. Room service (24-hour). VCR.*

Still Sumptuous

The Maxwell

386 Geary Street, CA 94102, at Mason Street (1-800 821 5343/986 2000/fax 397 2447). Bus 2, 3, 4, 30, 38, 45/cable car Powell-Hyde or Powell-Mason. **Rates** *rooms $135-$165; junior suites $180-$195; suites $250-$675; additional person $10.* **Credit** AmEx, DC, Disc, MC, TC, V. **Map G4**
Call it chic boutique or masterfully moody, but whatever you do, don't liken this hot new hotel to its aged, quirky predecessor, the Rafael. After re-opening in 1997, the only feature to survive this 12-storey, 153-room hotel's metamorphosis is its excellent location (one block from Union Square). Now rooms blend rich colours, patterns and eclectic extras to create a theatrical and vaguely Deco look, complete with Edward Hopper and Lautrec reproductions. The adjoining Gracie's Restaurant is open until 2am. **Hotel services** *Air conditioning. Bar. Café. Business services. Concierge. Conference facilities. Disabled: access. Fax. Laundry. No-smoking rooms. Parking. Restaurant. Safe.* **Room services** *Fax/modem jack. Hair-dryer. Radio. Voicemail.*

The Prescott

545 Post Street, CA 94102, at Taylor Street (1-800 283 7322/563 0303/fax 563 6831). Bus 2, 3, 4/cable car Powell-Hyde or Powell-Mason. **Rates** *rooms $225-$255; suites $275-$295.* **Credit** AmEx, DC, Disc, JCB, MC, $TC, V.* **Map G3/4**
There was a time when guests would check into the Prescott solely to get preferential seating at the adjoining Postrio restaurant (*see chapter* **Restaurants & Cafés**). While Postrio has lost some of its divine status (although it's still very popular), the Prescott remains one of San Francisco's finer small hotels. The 165 rooms, including 30 suites and a penthouse – a lavish affair complete with rooftop jacuzzi, grand piano and twin fireplaces – are decorated with custom-made cherrywood furnishings, silk wallpaper and wonderfully cushy beds. Highly recommended is the Club Level, a private floor where the deal includes free drinks, hors-d'oeuvres, continental breakfast and a host of other amenities. The Prescott is well located, too, with Union Square a short walk away. **Hotel services** *Air-conditioning. Bar. Conference facilities. Disabled: access; rooms for disabled. Fax. Interpreting service. Laundry. Limousine service. No-smoking rooms. Parking. Restaurant. Safe.* **Room services** *Fax machine and modem jack. Hair-dryer. Mini-bar. Radio. Refrigerator. Room service (6am-midnight daily).*

Savoy Hotel

580 Geary Street, CA 94102, between Jones and Taylor Streets (1-800 227 4223/441 2700/fax 441 2700). Bus 38/cable car Powell-Hyde or Powell-Mason. **Rates** *rooms $115-$200.* **Credit** AmEx, DC, Disc, JCB, MC, $TC, V. **Map G4**
Imported French furnishings, lovely curtains, billowy feather beds and continental breakfast served in the brasserie add

Hip hotels

*Step inside the **Commodore** for some of the coolest décor in town. See page 113.*

With so many places to explore in the city, the majority of time spent in your hotel will probably be in sleeping. But if you want a scene along with your room, consider one of the following.

Every hotel Ian Schrager touches becomes the ultra-hip spot in town (LA's Mondrian, NY's Paramount and Royalton, Miami's Delano). When he's done with the recently purchased, historical **Clift**, it promises to host celebrities and a swinging nightlife, as well as Philippe Starck décor. The **Phoenix**'s shady location (in the notoriously seedy Tenderloin district), oval pool and fun-kitsch décor has long attracted the incognito rock 'n' roll crowd. And its ever-so-hip bar/lounge/ restaurant, Backflip, brings in an eclectic and festive local crowd.

The fame of the **Prescott** may reflect its quality rooms and service, but its affiliation with the adjoining, perennially popular Postrio restaurant makes the experience complete. Head to the bar to mingle with the upper-class singles set, savour a quintessential California pizza or take advantage of the hotel's preferential seating arrangement and go for the full-blown dining experience.

You need only step outside the lobby to get to one of the coolest bars in town if you're staying at the **Commodore International Hotel.**

At the adjoining cocktail lounge, the Red Room, the scene is retro-red, but the fashion is definitely bohemian-black.

Matching its top-rated service and style, the dining room at the **Ritz-Carlton** in Nob Hill serves one of the best and most coveted dinners in town. Here you can over-indulge in some of the finest San Francisco cuisine, head to the cigar lounge for a few puffs and a *digestif*, then retreat to your ultra-exclusive digs without ever leaving the hotel.

*The hip crowd at the **Phoenix**. Page 113.*

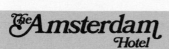

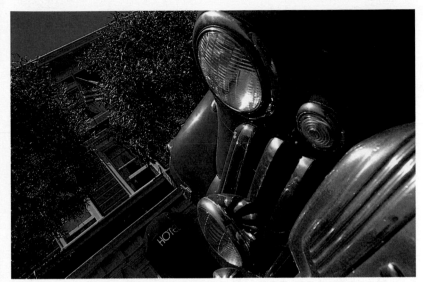

*The **San Remo** is one of the city's best bargains. See page 116.*

to the sophistication of the 83 small rooms that make up this hotel. Built in 1913 for the Panama-Pacific Exposition and resurrected in a profusion of black marble and mahogany, the Savoy is centrally located in the Theatre district, a few blocks from Union Square, but near enough to the sleazy Tenderloin to keep its prices low. Well worth considering if you're looking for a moderately priced hotel.

Hotel services *Bar. Business services. Concierge. Conference facilities. Disabled: access; rooms for disabled. Fax. Laundry. No-smoking rooms. Parking. Restaurant. Safe.* **Room services** *Hair-dryer. Mini-bar. Radio. Room service (6.30-11am, 5-10pm, daily).*

Tuscan Inn

425 Northpoint Street, CA 94133, at Mason Street (1-800 648 4626/561 1100/fax 561 1199). Bus 42, 49/cable car Powell-Mason. **Rates** *rooms $138-$178; suites $198-$218.* **Credit** AmEx, DC, Disc, MC, $TC, V. **Map G1**

This may be part of the Best Western motel chain but it's still a classy hotel. It's hard to find fault with the 220-room Tuscan Inn, located in the bowels of Fisherman's Wharf: the rooms are handsome, spacious and comfortable; the staff are exceedingly helpful and the adjoining Café Pescatore – a gleaming Italian trattoria – is a good bet for breakfast, lunch or dinner. If you tire of the touristy Wharf, escape is on hand: the Inn is a block away from the cable car turnaround.

Hotel services *Air-conditioning. Babysitting. Bar. Concierge. Conference facilities. Courtyard. Disabled: access; rooms for disabled. Fax. Laundry. Limousine service. No-smoking rooms. Parking. Restaurant. Safe.* **Room services** *Hair-dryer. Mini-bar. Radio. Refrigerator. Room service (7am-10pm daily). VCR.*

The Chain Gang

For a round-up of hotel chains, including top-end places catering for the business crowd as well as motels and budget options, *see page 111.*

Grand Hyatt

345 Stockton Street, CA 94108, between Post and Sutter Streets (1-800 233 1234/398 1234/fax 391 1780). Bus 2, 3, 4, 30, 45/cable car Powell-Hyde or Powell-Mason. **Rates** *rooms $189-$280; suites $450-$1,500.* **Credit** AmEx, DC, Disc, JCB, MC, $TC, V. **Map G3**

The 693-room Grand Hyatt offers just about everything the business or pleasure traveller would expect from a four-star hotel. Its location – at the north-east corner of Union Square – couldn't be better, and the view from most of the 36 floors is spectacular. Room décor is rather corporate, but additional perks include use of the spacious health club, a car service to the Financial district, a fully equipped business centre and surprisingly good food at the handsome Plaza Restaurant. A drink in the top-floor, panoramic Club 36 is unmissable at sunset.

Hotel services *Air-conditioning. Babysitting. Bar. Beauty salon. Business services. Concierge. Conference facilities. Currency exchange. Disabled: access; rooms for disabled. Fax. Gym. Interpreting service. Laundry. No-smoking rooms. Parking. Restaurant. Safe.* **Room services** *Fax/modem jack. Hair-dryer. Mini-bar. Radio. Refrigerator. Room service (6am-midnight daily).*

Marriott Hotel

55 Fourth Street, CA 94103, between Market and Mission Streets (1-800 228 9290/896 1600/fax 1-408 567 0391). BART Powell Street/Muni Metro F, J, K, L, M, N/bus 5, 6, 7, 9, 21, 30, 31, 45, 66, 71. **Rates** *single/double $265-$285.* **Credit** AmEx, DC, Disc, JCB, MC, $TC, V. **Map G/H4**

Completed in 1989, when a storm of controversy blew up over its design (critics likened it to a giant jukebox or parking meter), the 39-storey Marriott is undoubtedly striking, with its numerous arches of tinted glass and steel. One almost expects to see Batman astride the roof. The 1,498 rooms, however, are more down to earth, with huge beds, large bathrooms and wonderful views of the city and Bay (ask for a room overlooking Yerba Buena Gardens). Free unlimited use of the on-site health club, indoor pool and jacuzzi make the Marriott worth considering.

Hotel services *Air-conditioning. Bars. Business services. Concierge. Conference facilities. Currency exchange (up to $100). Disabled: access; rooms for disabled. Gym. Laundry. No-smoking rooms. Parking. Safe. Swimming pool. Restaurant.* Room services *Hair-dryer. Mini-bar. Radio. Room service.*

Sheraton Palace Hotel

2 New Montgomery Street, CA 94105, at Market Street (1-800 325 3535/392 8600/fax 543 0671). BART Montgomery/Muni Metro J, K, L, M, N. Rates *single $300-$310; double $320-$330; suites $800-$2,900.* Credit AmEx, DC, Disc, JCB, MC, $TC, V. Map H4
It took 27 months and a cool $170 million to restore the Palace Hotel to its original grandeur, but in return the Sheraton can boast one of the most breathtaking dining rooms in the world. The spectacular Garden Court has 80,000 panes of stained glass, and the hotel's glass-domed swimming pool is by far the finest in the city. By comparison, the 551 rooms are rather modest, though spacious enough, with rich wooden furniture and marble-clad bathrooms.
Hotel services *Air-conditioning. Babysitting. Bar. Business services. Conference facilities. Currency exchange (up to $100). Disabled: access; rooms for disabled. Fax. Gym. Laundry. Limousine service. No-smoking rooms. Parking. Swimming pool. Restaurant.* Room services *Fax/modem jack. Hair-dryer. Radio. Refrigerator. Room service (24-hour). Safe.*

Romantic

Archbishop's Mansion

1000 Fulton Street, CA 94117, at Steiner Street (1-800 543 5820/563 7872). Bus 5, 22. Rates *rooms $129-$199; suites $215-$385.* Credit AmEx, DC, MC, $TC, V. Map E5
The Archbishop's Mansion is one of the most opulent small hotels in San Francisco. What's more, despite the ostentation – elaborate chandeliers, gorgeous antiques, canopied beds – the staff are genuinely friendly. Indulge in splendour in one of the Mansion's 15 wildly elegant rooms, which include the Don Giovanni suite (with hand-carved, cherub-

*The very splendid **Archbishop's Mansion.***

encrusted four-poster bed, two fireplaces and a seven-headed shower). Built in 1904 for the Archbishop of San Francisco – and a fortunate survivor of the earthquake two years later – the Mansion manages to combine romance, history and luxury into a surprisingly affordable package. *De rigueur* for honeymooners.
Hotel services *Babysitting. Concierge. Conference facilities. Continental breakfast. Fax. Laundry. Limousine service. No smoking. Parking. Safe.* Room services *Hair-dryer. Radio. Room service (8am-11pm Mon-Fri, 24-hour Sat, Sun). VCR.*

Hotel Bohème

444 Columbus Avenue, CA 94133, between Vallejo and Green Streets (433 9111/fax 362 6292/www. hotelboheme.com). Bus 15, 30, 41, 45/cable car Powell-Mason. Rates *single/double $125.* Credit AmEx, DC, Disc, JCB, MC, V. Map G2
Small, suave and artistic. If you hate corporate incubators such as the Hyatt and Marriott, you'll love the Bohème, where art, poetry and hospitality collide in a particularly engaging combination. Conveniently located on Columbus Avenue, the aorta of North Beach, the 15-room hotel is surrounded by dozens of small cafés and boutiques and within walking distance of Chinatown and Fisherman's Wharf. Light sleepers should request a room that doesn't face Columbus Avenue. All rooms are no-smoking.
Hotel services *Concierge. Fax. No smoking. Safe.* Room services *Fax/modem jack. Hair-dryer. Radio.*

Hotel Majestic

1500 Sutter Street, CA 94109, at Gough Street (1-800 869 8966/441 1100/fax 673 7331). Bus 2, 3, 4, 38, 42, 47, 49. Rates *single/double $135-$175; suites from $295.* Credit AmEx, DC, Disc, MC, $TC, V. Map F4
The Majestic has long been regarded as one of San Francisco's most romantic hotels. Built in 1902, it was one of the city's first grand hotels, and the owners have obviously spent a fortune keeping it that way. Each of the 57 newly redecorated rooms and nine suites has a canopied four-poster bed with quilts, a host of English and French Empire antiques and matching furniture. Many rooms also have fireplaces. The adjoining Café Majestic has a drippingly romantic setting and good seasonal dishes. After dinner, adjourn to the mahogany bar for a cognac.
Hotel services *Air-conditioning. Babysitting. Bar. Concierge. Conference facilities. Disabled: access; rooms for disabled. Fax. Laundry. No-smoking rooms. Parking. Restaurant. Safe.* Room services *Fax/modem jack. Hair-dryer. Radio. Room service (24-hour). Voicemail.*

Only in California

Nob Hill Lamborne

725 Pine Street, CA 94108, between Powell and Stockton Streets (1-800-274 8466/433 2287/fax 433 0975). Bus 1, 2, 3, 4, 30, 45/cable car Powell-Hyde or Powell-Mason. Rates *rooms $145-$225.* Credit AmEx, DC, Disc, JCB, MC, $TC, V. Map G3
Billed as an 'urban spa' catering to the executive traveller, the 20-room Lamborne has found its niche as a health haven for well-paid business executives. Mints on the pillow? Hardly! The extras here include beta-carotene tablets and aromatherapy gels, as well as your own personal fax machine, voicemail, modem and Internet access and laptop computer if required. Heck, even the Ritz-Carlton around the corner sends its guests here when it's overbooked.
Hotel services *Babysitting. Beauty salon. Business facilities. Concierge. Conference facilities. Continental breakfast. Fax. Laundry. Limousine service. No smoking. Parking. Safe. Spa.* Room services *Fax machine and modem jack. Hair-dryer. Kitchenette. Mini-bar. Radio. Room service (11am-11pm daily). VCR. Voicemail.*

Old Faithful Geyser
of California at Calistoga

One of the World's
Three Old Faithfuls
Open 9 am • 365 days a year
Picnic area

As featured in
NATIONAL GEOGRAPHIC

1299 Tubbs Lane • Calistoga • CA • 94515
707-942-6463

White Swan Inn

845 Bush Street, CA 94108, between Taylor and Mason Streets (1-800 999 9570/775 1755/fax 775 5717). Bus 2, 3, 4, 76/cable car Powell-Hyde or Powell-Mason. **Rates** *rooms* $145-$160; *suites* $195-$250. **Credit** AmEx, Disc, MC, $TC, V. **Map G3**

If you like the sort of boutique hotel that is decorated with teddy bears and serves platters of fresh-baked cookies, read on. The 26-room White Swan Inn likes to think of itself as a cosy English inn, right down to the 'English' wallpaper and prints, working fireplaces and fresh flower arrangements in each room. Afternoon is, of course, tea time, served in a large parlour decorated with old teapots and yet more teddy bears. The entire hotel is as twee as can be and not to everyone's taste, but for its location near Union Square its competitively priced.

Hotel services *Babysitting. Breakfast. Business services. Concierge. Conference facilities. Fax. Garden. Laundry. No smoking. Parking. Safe.* **Room services** *Hair-dryer. Radio. Refrigerator.*

Hip Hotels

Commodore International Hotel

825 Sutter Street, CA 94109, at Jones Street (923 6800/1-800 338 6848/fax 923 6804). Bus 2, 3, 4, 27, 76. **Rates** *single/double* $89-$139 (reduced rates off-season) **Credit** AmEx, DC, Disc, MC, $TC, V. **Map G3**

Are you cool? Are you contemporary? Are you wearing black? If the answer is yes, then you're Commodore material. From the company that raised the legendary Phoenix Hotel from its ashes comes the most far-out, curvaceous and unquestionably cool hotel to hit the San Francisco scene since the Triton. Billed as an 'urban adventure' hotel, the Commodore has young and chic staff who know all the tips for touring the far side of San Francisco, and will even take you there by van or on foot. Of the 113 spacious rooms – all with large walk-in closets and bathtubs – request one of the 'post-modern deco' rooms with custom furnishings fashioned by local artists. Hang out in the Red Room cocktail bar.

Hotel services *Babysitting. Bar. Business services. Coffee shop. Concierge. Conference facilities. Fax. Laundry. No-smoking rooms. Safe.*

Hotel Monaco

501 Geary Street, CA 94102, at Taylor Street (292 0100/1-800 214 4220/fax 292 0149). Bus 38. **Rates** *rooms* $195-$245; *suites* $270-$495. **Credit** AmEx, DC, Disc, JCB, MC, $TC, V. **Map G4**

Few hotels offer the romantic and larger-than-life ambience of the Monaco. The remodelled Union Square district Beaux Arts building, built in 1910, re-opened in June 1995 after a $24-million facelift. Everything about the Monaco is big: from the hand-painted ceiling domes and grandiose common areas juxtaposing antique knick-knacks with local contemporary art, to the 201 rooms with canopy-draped beds surrounded by a jumble of vibrant patterns. If you tire of gawping at the details, wander next door to the Grand Café restaurant and get a load of the fantastic 1920s and 1930s décor accented by more local art – including a three storey-high bunny sculpture. Each room has two telephones.

Hotel services *Air-conditioning. Bar. Business services. Conference facilities. Disabled: access; rooms for disabled. Fax. Laundry. Limousine service. No-smoking rooms. Parking. Restaurant. Safe. Spa.* **Room services** *Fax machine and modem jack. Hair-dryer. Kitchenette. Mini-bar. Radio. Refrigerator. Room service (6am-11pm daily). Voicemail.*

Hotel Triton

342 Grant Avenue, CA 94108, at Bush Street (394 0500/1-800 433 6611). Bus 2, 3, 4, 30, 45/cable car Powell-Hyde or Powell-Mason. **Rates** *rooms* $149-$250; *suites*

$229-$379. **Credit** AmEx, DC, Disc, JCB, MC, $TC, V. **Map G3**

Everything about the Hotel Triton screams hip, from the glimmering dervish chairs in the lobby to the bellmen's eclectic uniforms. Designed by a team of Bay Area artisans, the 140-room hotel is a visual smorgasbord of stylish eccentricities including mythological murals, inverted-pyramid podiums and gilded floor-to-ceiling pillars. Add a prime location (steps away from the entrance to Chinatown) and the adjoining Café de la Presse, a small 'European' coffee house, and you have San Francisco's version of a hotel straight out of *Alice in Wonderland.*

Hotel services *Air-conditioning. Babysitting. Café. Concierge. Conference facilities. Disabled: access. Fax. Gym. Interpreting service. Laundry. No-smoking rooms. Parking. Safe.* **Room services** *Hair-dryer. Mini-bar. Radio. Refrigerator. Room service (7am-10.30pm daily).*

The Phoenix

601 Eddy Street, CA 94109, at Larkin Street (1-800 248 9466/776 1380/fax 885 3109). Bus 19. **Rates** *rooms* $89-$109; *suites* $139-$159 $99. **Credit** AmEx, DC, Disc, JCB, MC, $TC, V. **Map F4**

What do Ziggy Marley, Johnny Depp, John F Kennedy Jr, and Pearl Jam have in common? They've all stayed at the funky Phoenix, one of San Francisco's hippest hostelries, located, oddly enough, in one of the city's worst neighbourhoods. Forty-four bungalow-style rooms equipped with bamboo furniture and tropical plants help to create that oasis atmosphere, particularly when guests bask by the pool on a sunny day. The adjoining Backflip restaurant and cocktail lounge provides funky food and music to help everyone get together and feel alright.

Hotel services *Babysitting. Bar. Concierge. Conference facilities. Continental breakfast. Disabled: access. Fax. Laundry. Limousine service. Parking (free). Swimming pool. Restaurant. Safe.* **Room services** *Hair-dryer. Radio. VCR.*

The Red Victorian

1665 Haight Street, CA 94117, at Cole Street (864 1978/fax 863 3293). Muni Metro N/bus 33, 37. **Rates** *rooms* $86-$200. **Credit** AmEx, MC, $TC, V. **Map C6**

Nothing comes as close to offering the quintessential Haight-Ashbury experience as a night at the Red Vic. Haight Street's only hotel offers 18 wildly decorated rooms (14 with shared bathroom), each with its own thematic twist – you could stay

More chains

Business/Luxury
Hilton 1-800 445 8067
Holiday Inn 1-800 405 4329
Hyatt 1-800 233 1233
Ritz 1-800 241 3333
Sheraton 1-800 325 3535
Westin 1-800 228 3000
Mid-range
Best Western 1-800 528 1234
Howard Johnson 1-800 654 2000
Budget
Comfort Inn 1-800 228 5150
Cow Hollow Motor Inn 921 5800
Days Inn 1-800 222 3297
MOTEL6 1-800 466 8356
Ramada Inn 1-800 272 6232
SUPER8 1-800 800 8000
Travelodge 1-800 255 3050

in the rainbow-coloured Flower Child room or the tie-dyed Summer of Love double. A continental breakfast is included in the room price, as is free use of the meditation room. Highly recommended for hippy-loving souls. Note that rooms do not have TVs.
Hotel services *Continental breakfast. Conference facilities. Fax. No smoking.*

Home Away From Home

Edward II Inn & Pub
3155 Scott Street, CA 94123, at Lombard Street (1-800 473 4666/922 3000). Bus 28, 43, 76. **Rates** *rooms with shared bath $74; rooms with private bath $94; suites $165-$225.* **Credit** AmEx, MC, $TC, V. **Map D2**
A self-styled 'English Country' inn. Its Lombard Street location is a little over-congested with traffic, but nearby Chestnut and Union Streets offer some of the best shopping and dining in the city. You can choose from fancy suites with whirlpool baths or the more basic rooms with shared baths. Tea is served at 3pm daily, sherry at 5pm, and breakfast is included in the room price.
Hotel services *Bar. Continental breakfast. Fax. No smoking. Parking. Safe.* **Room services** *Radio.*

Washington Square Inn
1660 Stockton Street, CA 94133, at Filbert Street (1-800 388 0220/981 4220/fax 397 7242). Bus 39, 41, 45/cable car Powell-Mason. **Rates** *rooms $120-$185.* **Credit** AmEx, DC, Disc, JCB, $TC, V. **Map G2**
You can't ask for a better hotel location in San Francisco – across from Washington Square in the heart of North Beach and within walking distance from Chinatown. The smoke-free, 15-room hotel has a European flavour, and each room is decorated with French and English antiques. The overall feeling is of casual, quiet elegance. A continental breakfast and afternoon tea complete with finger sandwiches is included in the room price. All rooms have bathrooms ensuite.
Hotel services *Business services. Concierge. Continental breakfast. Disabled: access. Laundry. No smoking. Parking. Safe.* **Room services** *Hair-dryer. Radio. Room service (7.30am-9pm daily). VCR.*

Bed & Breakfast

Bed and Breakfast Inn
4 Charlton Court, CA 94123, at Union Street (921 9784/ fax 921 0544/info@1stb-bsf.com). Bus 41, 45. **Rates** *rooms with shared bath $75-$100; rooms with private bath, telephone & TV $135-$150; penthouses $210-$300.* **Credit** $TC. **Map E2**
The Bed and Breakfast Inn is a real charmer. A forerunner of the B&B craze, this small, no-smoking, 13-room inn is awash with fresh flowers, antiques and the sort of personal touches that create the American version of an old English hostelry. Tucked into a tiny cul-de-sac off Union Street, the inn consists of three immaculate Victorian houses and one exquisite garden – a good place to enjoy breakfast on sunny mornings. It's in a great location, too, with some of the city's best shopping and dining steps away. Only the ensuite rooms have a telephone and TV.
Hotel services *Communal TV room. Concierge. Garden. No smoking. Parking. Safe.* **Room services** *Fax/modem jack. Hair-dryer. Radio. Room service (8am-9.30pm daily).*

Critics may have compared the **Marriott Hotel** *to a parking meter, but you can live the high life there. See page 109.*

Jackson Court
2198 Jackson Street, CA 94115, at Buchanan Street (929 7670/fax 929 1405). Bus 12, 24. **Rates** *rooms $139-$195.* **Credit** AmEx, MC, $TC, V. **Map E3**
Not many people know about Jackson Court, a nineteenth-century brownstone mansion that has been converted into a superb ten-room bed-and-breakfast inn. Located on a quiet residential stretch of Pacific Heights – one of San Francisco's more prestigious neighbourhoods – the inn is as quiet as a church and as elegant as, well, a mansion. All rooms have private showers, antiques and contemporary furnishings – and surprisingly reasonable rates. If you don't mind walking five or six blocks (or getting a cab), there are some wonderful shops and restaurants on Union Street.
Hotel services *Fax. No smoking.* **Room services** *Radio.*

Practical

The Andrews ⌐ 7 0 0 l 4 4 5 5 6 3 6 8 ⊓ ⊓
624 Post Street, CA 94109, between Jones and Taylor Streets (1-800 926 3739/563 6877/fax 928 6919). Bus 2, 3, 4, 76. **Rates** *rooms $89-$119; suites $129.* **Credit** AmEx, DC, JCB, MC, $TC, V. **Map G3/4**
Finding a decent hotel room within two blocks of Union Square for under $100 is as hard as finding a taxi when you need one. The seven-storey Andrews Hotel offers 48 small-but-comfortable rooms, each decorated in a pleasant pastel and floral theme with an ensuite bathroom and the usual TV, radio and telephone amenities. A bonus is the free continental breakfast. The adjoining Fino restaurant is highly recommended for its moderately priced Italian food.
Hotel services *Air-conditioning. Babysitting. Bar. Conference facilities. Continental breakfast. Fax.*

Find value for money at **The Andrews**.

Laundry. No smoking. Restaurant. **Room services**
Hair-dryer. Kitchenette. Mini-bar. Radio. Refrigerator.

Holiday Lodge

1901 Van Ness Avenue, CA 94109, between Jackson and Washington Streets (1-800 367 8504/776 4469/fax 474 7046/sftrips1@ix.netcom.com). Bus 12. **Rates** *rooms $99-$119; suites $135-$165.* **Credit** AmEx, DC, Disc, JCB, MC, $TC, V.* **Map F3**
This weathered motor lodge looks out of place among San Francisco's boutique and high-rise hotels, but it serves a useful – and affordable – purpose. The large garden courtyard and heated swimming pool are perfect for children (all that's missing is the pink flamingo), while the room rates will please most parents. Despite the funky façade, the 77 rooms (all ensuite) are clean and modern. Free parking and a central, though traffic-heavy, location are further bonuses.
Hotel services *Babysitting. Concierge. Conference facilities. Disabled: access. Fax. Laundry. Limited parking (free). No-smoking rooms. Swimming pool. Safe.*

The New Abigail

246 McAllister Street, CA 94102, between Hyde and Larkin Streets (1 800-243 6510/861 9728/fax 861 5848). BART Civic Center/Muni Metro F, J, K, L, M, N/bus 5, 19. **Rates** *rooms $89; suites $149.* **Credit** AmEx, DC, Disc, JCB, MC, $TC, V.* **Map F/G4**
Another so-called 'European' hotel, due in part to the European antiques, down quilts and turn-of-the-century English lithographs and paintings adorning each room. Located in Civic Center, within walking distance of the Opera House and Symphony Hall but an otherwise insalubrious area, the 66-room Abigail is a good bet for visitors looking for a clean, comfortable room at a reasonable price. The weekly and monthly rates are a bargain. The Millennium restaurant offers organic vegetarian food.
Hotel services *Concierge. Continental breakfast. Fax. Laundry. No-smoking rooms. Restaurant. Safe.*
Room services *Radio.*

Budget

Adelaide Inn

5 Isadora Duncan Court, CA 94102, off Taylor Street between Post and Geary Streets (441 2261/fax 441 0161). Bus 2, 3, 4, 38. **Rates** *room with shared bath $52-$58.* **Credit** AmEx, MC, V.* **Map G4**
Because American tourists tend to avoid less conventional budget options for predictable (and usually boring) motel accommodation, it's mostly European tourists who reap the benefits of this old-fashioned pensione tucked into a quiet downtown cul-de-sac. All three levels are bright, cheerful and adorned with the sort of unintentionally funky furniture that reminds you just how old this place is. If you don't mind sharing a bathroom and sleeping on a spongy mattress, this place is cheap and cheerful.
Hotel services *Fridge. Pay phone.*
Room services *TV.*

Grant Plaza Hotel   No Single

465 Grant Avenue, CA 94108, at Pine Street (1-800 472 6899/434 3883/fax 434 3886). Bus 1, 30, 45/cable car California or Powell-Hyde. **Rates** *single $49; double/twin $59; double $89.* **Credit** AmEx, DC, JCB, MC, V.* **Map G3**
As long as you don't have a car – the Grant Plaza is located smack-bang in Chinatown – you'd be hard pressed to find a better deal anywhere in the city. As little as $49 buys you a night in an immaculately clean (albeit small) room complete with contemporary furnishings, private bath, colour TV and even a phone. If you split one of the larger rooms four ways then you'll pay less than hostel rates – definitely a bargain (request one of the newer rooms).
Hotel services *Disabled: access. Safe.*

Golden Gate Hotel

775 Bush Street, CA 94108, between Powell and Mason Streets (1-800 835 1118/392 3702/fax 392 6202). Bus 2, 3, 4, 30, 45, 76/cable car California, Powell-Mason or Powell-Hyde. **Rates** *rooms with shared bath $65; rooms with private bath $99.* **Credit** AmEx, DC, MC, $TC, V.* **Map G3**
The 25-room Golden Gate Hotel is one of San Francisco's best small hotels, particularly given the more-than-reasonable prices. It's a family-run establishment, so expect to be fussed over by John and Renate Kenaston, the affable innkeepers who value obvious pride in their clean, cute establishment. Rooms have antique, turn-of-the century furnishings and fresh flowers. Request one with a claw-foot tub if you enjoy a good soak. You'll like the location, too: two blocks from Union Square and the crest of Nob Hill, with cable car stops at the corner for easy access to Fisherman's Wharf and Chinatown.
Hotel services *Afternoon tea. Concierge. Continental breakfast. No-smoking rooms. Parking. Safe.*

Motel Capri

2015 Greenwich Street, CA 94123, at Buchanan Street (346 4667/fax 346 3256). Bus 28, 43, 76. **Rates** *single $58; double $70; suites $90-$148.* **Credit** AmEx, DC, Disc, JCB, MC, $TC, V.* **Map E2**
Low-maintenance travellers who need little more than a quiet, inexpensive room will enjoy staying at the funky old Capri. Here the décor is anything but up-to-date (rather, it's unintentionally 1970s retro) but you'll find that the 46 rooms are squeaky clean and the beds comfortable. Added bonuses are free parking (a valuable commodity in the crowded Marina district) and its location, a few blocks from the Chestnut and Union Streets action. The suites have a kitchenette with refrigerator.
Hotel services *Concierge. Fax. No-smoking rooms. Parking (free). Safe.*

Marina Inn

3110 Octavia Street, CA 94123, at Lombard Street (1-800 274 1420/928 1000/fax 928 5909). Bus 28, 43, 76, 40. **Rates** *double $65-$115.* **Credit** AmEx, MC, V.* **Map E2**
Though this 1924 four-storey Victorian is located on one of the busiest streets in San Francisco, the rooms are surprisingly quiet and stylishly furnished with pinewood fittings, a four-poster bed, pretty wallpaper and soothing tones of yellow, green and rose. There are even top-dollar touches such as new remote-control televisions, full bathtubs with showers, and a nightly turndown service with chocolates on your pillow. Rates include continental breakfast and afternoon sherry and the shops and restaurants of the Marina district are within easy walking distance.

San Remo

2337 Mason Street, CA 94133, at Chestnut Street (1-800 352 7366/776 8688/fax 776 2811). Bus 15, 30, 39/cable car Powell-Mason. **Rates** *single $50-$60; double $60-$70; penthouse $100.* **Credit** AmEx, DC, JCB, MC, $TC, V.* **Map G2**
Originally a boarding house for dock workers displaced in the Great Fire of 1906, this meticulously restored three-storey Italianate Victorian is one of San Francisco's best hotel bargains. Though the rooms are small and the baths (showers, actually) shared, you will not find finer accommodation at this price anywhere in the city. The spotless bathrooms are practically a work of art, and all the 60 rooms have brass or cast-iron beds, wicker furniture and antique armoires. Ask for a room on the upper floor facing Mason Street if you can, or if the penthouse is free, book it – you'll never want to leave.
Hotel services *Conference facilities. Fax. Laundry. Restaurant (breakfast only). Parking. Safe.* **Room services** *Hair-dryer.*

Youth Hostels

Globe Hostel/Inter-Club

*10 Hallam Place, CA 94103, off Folsom Street between
Seventh and Eighth Streets (431 0540/fax 431 3286).
BART Civic Center/bus 12, 19, 27, 42.* **Rates** *single* $17;
double $40. **Credit** $TC. **Map G5**

Although the South of Market district can be shady at times,
there's no closer location to the area's many hopping bars
and clubs. Open around the clock, the hostel's 33 rooms have
five beds per room and – hallelujah! – each room has a private bath. No reservations are taken during peak season, but
there are no curfews or chores either. No visitors after 11pm.
Hotel services *Café. Communal lounge. Fax. Free
coffee. Free safe deposit boxes. Laundry. No-smoking
rooms. Pay phones (hallway 626 0385/stairway 626
0396). Pool table. Sun deck (closed after dusk). TV.*

Globetrotter's Inn

*225 Ellis Street, CA 94102, at Mason Street (346
5786/fax 346 5786). BART Powell Street/Muni Metro F,
J, K, L, M, N/bus 5, 6, 7, 21, 27, 31, 66, 77.* **Rates** *bed*
$12; *private room* $24. **Credit** $TC. **Map G4**

Located a stone's throw from Union Square, the two-storey
Globetrotter has 30 beds and shared baths. It's open 24 hours
a day and you get free linen, tea and coffee. Some rooms have
a refrigerator and TV. It shouldn't be your first choice, but
you can't beat the location or the price.
Hotel services *Fax. Kitchen. Laundry. No-smoking
areas. Pay phone. TV. VCR.*

Hostel at Union Square (AYH)

*312 Mason Street, CA 94102, between Geary and
O'Farrell Streets (788 5604/fax 788 3023). BART
Powell Street/Muni Metro F, J, K, L, M, N/bus 27, 38.*
Rates *members* $16; *non-members* $18; *under-18s with
parent* $7. **Credit** MC, $TC, V. **Map G4**

Make your reservation at least five weeks in advance during the high season (June to September) to stay at this downtown 230-bed hostel. Guests sleep in small two- to five-person
rooms, with their own lock and key (the four- and five-person rooms also have their own bathroom). AYH membership
is required, but you can buy it on the spot. There are always

beds for walk-ins on a first come, first served basis, but
remember to bring ID or you'll be turned away at the door.
The hostel is no smoking, but there is a smoking room.
Hotel services *Dining room. Disabled: access. Free
linen. Free nightly movies. Library. Lockers. Microwave.
No smoking. Pay phones. Refrigerator. TV.*

Hostel International Fort Mason (AYH)

*Fort Mason Building, 240 Fort Mason, CA 94123 (771
7277/fax 771 1468). Bus 28, 42, 47, 49.* **Rates** $16. **Credit**
MC, $TC, V. **Map E1**

Many San Franciscans would kill for the Bay view from here.
One of the most desirable locations in the city is available
for under $20 per night – and you don't even have to be an
AYH member (though you do have to book at least 24 hours
in advance). The hostel's dorm-style accommodation sleeps
155 souls in rooms fitting three to four people. Enjoy the fire-
place, pool table, dining room, coffee bar and the rarest of
San Francisco amenities – free parking. There's no curfew,
either, but alcohol is not allowed.
Hotel services *Disabled: access; rooms for disabled.
Kitchen. Laundry. Lockers. Parking (free). Pay phones.
No-smoking rooms.*

Accommodation Agencies

A number of reputable companies will find you a
hotel; the best is **San Francisco Reservations**
(227 1500/1-800 677 1500/www.hotelres.com). At
no cost to you, they'll find a hotel, motel or B&B
in your price range, and even negotiate a discounted rate. Alternatively, try **Bed & Breakfast
California** (696 1690); **Bed & Breakfast
International** 696 1690/fax 696 1699/info@
bbintl.com/www.bbintl.com), **California Reservations** (1-800 576 0003/252 1107), which offers
up to 50% off hotel's usual prices, or the **Central
Reservation Services** (1-800 548 3311/1-407 339
4116/www.reservation-services.com), ideal for
travellers on a budget.

*Enjoy one of the best – and cheapest – locations in the city at the **Fort Mason** hostel.*

Restaurants
& Cafés

There are more foodies in San Francisco than you can shake a shiitake at – and an establishment to suit every one of them.

San Francisco is one of the best cities in the world for eating well. A number of factors contribute to this: the diversity of cooking influences and ingredients derived from a largely immigrant population; the rich local agricultural base and the city's proximity to the ocean, which make high quality, fresh produce and pristine seafood available to restaurateurs all year round; the city's proximity to the wine regions of Napa, Sonoma, and Santa Cruz; and a healthy competition among chefs. For San Franciscans, fine food is more than just sustenance – it's one of the main reasons they live in the city.

The Bay Area became a foodie mecca in the 1970s, when California cuisine was born – infusing local organic and seasonal ingredients and traditional recipes with cross-cultural influences. Almost every chef or restaurateur in San Francisco has worked for Alice Waters of Chez Panisse in

Berkeley, the birthplace of California cuisine. Or for Jeremiah Tower, the Harvard educated architect turned chef/owner of Stars. Or for Wolfgang Puck, the Los Angeles-based, Austrian chef whose culinary empire of restaurants and food products generated nearly 23 million dollars in 1996.

But good food isn't just to be found in high-priced restaurants. Great ethnic cooking can be found in any number of smaller eateries – from savoury taquerias in the Mission, Italian bakeries in North Beach, the stunning array of Thai, Chinese, Vietnamese, and Korean restaurants that line the streets of the Sunset district, or the in-and-out noodle shops of Japantown. Whatever you choose, you'll be amazed by the number and variety of restaurants in San Francisco.

For a list of the city's ever-popular supper clubs – where you can combine good food with live music – *see chapter* **Nightlife**.

Enter the watery world of **Farallon**. *See page 119.*

The average prices listed below are for a three course meal without alcohol.

Restaurants

Around Union Square

Farallon
540 Post Street, between Mason and Powell Streets (956 6969). Bus 2, 3, 4, 76/cable car Powell-Hyde or Powell-Mason. **Lunch served** 11.30am-2.30pm, **dinner served** 5.30-10.30pm, Mon-Sat. **Average** lunch $38, dinner $55. **Credit** AmEx, DC, Disc, MC, V. **Map G3**
One of the city's newest – and most expensive – restaurants, Farallon is named after the islands visible (on a clear day) from the Golden Gate Bridge. The watery theme is carried through in the design, right down to the jelly fish light fixtures. Housed in the original Elks Lodge, the restaurant tunnels out into a vast, atmospheric, vaulted dining room. Fishy appetisers include three kinds of caviar as well as fresh crab with urchin sauce; to follow try ginger-steamed wild salmon or seared sea scallops. Finish off with 'small endings', a lucky dip of miniature chocolate and nougat treats. The wine and *digestif* list is ocean-sized.
Disabled: toilet.

Fleur de Lys
777 Sutter Street, between Jones and Taylor Streets (673 7779). Bus 2, 3, 4, 27, 76. **Dinner served** 6-9.30pm Mon-Thur; 5.30-10.30pm Fri, Sat. **Average** $90. **Credit** AmEx, DC, JCB, MC, V. **Map G3**
Hubert Keller is an extraordinary chef with a vast culinary repertoire, and his rich, red-hued restaurant is lush and extraordinarily expensive. But the quality of the French food and the splendid wine list go a long way towards helping you forget you've spent a fortune on them. Service is attentive without being overbearing. Splash out on the prix-fixe, five-course tasting menu – a real treat.

Don't miss

Betelnut p134
Great Chinese food… on Union Street?
Café de la Presse p138
As Parisian as you'll find in San Francisco.
Caffè Centro p140
The nucleus of Multimedia Gulch.
Carta p134
A different regional menu monthly.
Farallon p119
When the boss is buying.
Gold Mountain p125
Little English, lots of great dim sum.
Mario's Bohemian Cigar Store p139
An unmissable North Beach stalwart.
Raw p137
For delectable, uncooked cuisine.
Thirsty Bear p127
For tapas and microbrewed beer.
Tomassos p123
A queue for their pizza is no surprise.

Postrio
545 Post Street, between Taylor and Mason Streets (776 7825). Bus 2, 3, 4, 76/cable car Powell-Hyde or Powell-Mason. **Breakfast served** 7-10am, **lunch served** 11.30am-2pm, Mon-Fri. **Dinner served** 5.30-10.30pm Mon-Wed, Sun; 5.30-10.30pm Thur-Sat. **Brunch served** 9am-2pm Sat, Sun. **Average** lunch $25, dinner $55. **Credit** AmEx, DC, Disc, JCB, MC, V. **Map G3**
Celebrity chef Wolfgang Puck's entry into the competitive Northern California restaurant market has been a success since day one; the chefs have changed here but Puck is still co-owner. Make your entrance down the dramatic staircase

Scala's Bistro *on Union Square. See page 121.*

Restaurants by cuisine

Afghani The Helmand p123.
American 2223 Market p131; Fog City Diner p133; Hamburger Mary's p126; Harris' p126; Pluto's p132; Rumpus p121; Sam's Grill p122; World Wrapps p132.
Asian Betelnut p134; Eos Restaurant & Wine Bar p130; Long Life p133; Pickled Ginger p127.
Californian Bay Wolf p136; Boulevard p127; Chez Panisse p136; Farallon p119; Firefly p132; Flying Saucer p128; The Globe p121; Hawthorne Lane p126; The House Restaurant p136; The Moa Room p128; Moose's p123; Oliveto p136; Plump Jack Cafe p134; Postrio p119; Rubicon p122; Socca p136; Stars p123; Townhouse Bar & Grill p136; Universal Café p130; Zuni Café p135.
Cajun Elite Café p134.
Caribbean Cha Cha Cha p130.
Chinese Alice's p131; Gold Mountain p125; House of Nanking p125; Imperial Tea Court p125; Lichee Garden p125; Mayflower p136; Pearl City p125; R&G Lounge p125; Ton Kiang p136; Yuet Lee p125; Wu Kong p128.
Cuban/Puerto Rican El Nuevo Frutilandia p128.
French Alain Rondelli p135; Fleur de Lys p119; Fringale p126; La Folie p125; Pastis p134; Rivoli p136; South Park Café p127; Ti Couz Crêperie p130.
German Suppenküche p135.
Indian Maharani p123.
Italian & Cal-Ital Alioto's p132; Antica Trattoria p125; Catté Macaroni p121; Capps Corner p123;

Cypress Club p121; Enrico's p123; Il Fornaio p133; Laghi p136; LuLu p126; L'Osteria del Forno p123; Pane e Vino p134; Pasta Pomodoro p132; Rose Pistola p123; Scala's Bistro p121; Vivande Porta Via p134; Zinzino p132.
Italian-Asian Oritalia p134.
Japanese Ebisu p136; Isobune Sushi p133; Isuzu p133; Kabuto p135; Mifune p133; Sanppo p133; Yoshida Ya p134.
Korean Brothers Restaurant p135; Seoul Garden p133.
Lebanese Byblos p132.
Mexican Café Marimba p132; La Rondalla p128; Pozole p130; Roosevelt Tamale Bar p130; Taqueria Cancun p130.
Pizza Pauline's Pizza p130; Tomassos p123; Vicolo Pizzeria p123.
Peruvian Fina Estampa p128.
Seafood Franciscan Restaurant p133; Hayes Street Grill p122; PJ's Oyster Bed p137; Plouf p122; Swan Oyster Depot p126; Tadich Grill p122.
Spanish Thirsty Bear p127; Zarzuela p125.
Thai Khan Toke p135; Neecha Thai Cuisine p133; Thep Phanom p130.
Vegetarian Greens p132; Raw p137.
Vietnamese Golden Turtle p125; The Slanted Door p130.
World Carta p134.

into the (invariably packed) restaurant below and tuck into Fusion food along the lines of Chinese-style duck with mango sauce, fried quail with a pineapple glaze or stir-fried garlic chicken served in radicchio cups. Desserts are extraordinary. The bar is a scene in its own right. *Disabled: toilet.*

Rumpus

1 Tillman Place, off Grant Avenue, between Sutter and Post Streets (421 2300). BART Montgomery/Muni Metro F, J, K, L, M, N/bus 2, 3, 4, 30, 45, 76/cable car Powell-Hyde or Powell-Mason. **Lunch served** 11.30am-2.45pm Mon-Sat. **Dinner served** 5.30-10.30pm daily. **Average** lunch $12, dinner $40. **Credit** AmEx, DC, MC, V. **Map G/H3**
Tucked into an alley off Union Square, Rumpus is a good place for a pre-theatre dinner or a break from shopping. The chef is British, but he gained most of his experience in LA and the menu is generally Californian. But the mashed potatoes are some of the best around, and there are bangers to go with it if you want them.

Scala's Bistro

432 Powell Street, between Post and Sutter Streets (395 8555). Bus 2, 3, 4, 76/cable car Powell-Hyde or Powell-Mason. **Breakfast served** 7-10.30am Mon-Fri; 8-10.30am Sat, Sun. **Lunch served** 11.30am-2pm, **dinner served** 5.15pm-midnight, daily. **Average** $12-$20. **Credit** AmEx, DC, MC, V. **Map G3**
This bustling bistro is frequented by tourists staying in Union Square (it's part of the Sir Francis Drake Hotel) and locals who come for the reasonably-priced Italian food. Salads always feature the freshest produce in season, and the sweetbreads, when available, are worth every calorie. Seared salmon is a signature dish, as is the mushroom taglierini. For dessert, try the 'Bostini' cream pie – another house speciality.

Financial District

Caffè Macaroni

59 Columbus Avenue, at Jackson Street (956 9737). Bus 12, 15, 41. **Lunch served** 11.30am-2.30pm Mon-Fri. **Dinner served** 5.30-10pm Mon-Sat. **Average** lunch $12, dinner $20. **No credit cards.** **Map H3**
This tiny and romantic restaurant has lots of character, charming and loud Italian waiters, dried pasta that adorns the ceiling, and authentic Italian dishes. Book ahead.

Cypress Club

500 Jackson Street, between Montgomery Street and Columbus Avenue (296 8555). Bus 12, 15, 42, 76. **Dinner served** 5.30-10.30pm Mon-Thur, Sun; 5.30-10.30pm Fri, Sat. **Average** $50. **Credit** AmEx, MC, V. **Map H3**
Set in a fantasy setting, with plump banquettes, curvaceous pillars and draped fabrics, the Cypress Club's food is similarly magical. Try the ravioli of smoked duck and leeks, or (really) curry and sesame dusted veal with a foie gras yogurt sauce. Desserts come as a suitably grand finale – perhaps chocolate coconut terrine or crème brûlée. The bar is stocked with bourbons, single-malts and all manner of spirits. *Disabled: toilet.*

The Globe

290 Pacific Avenue, at Battery Street (391 4132). Bus 12, 42, 76, 83. **Lunch served** 11.30am-3pm Mon-Fri. **Dinner served** 6pm-1am Mon-Sat. **Average** lunch $15, dinner $25. **Credit** AmEx, DC, MC, V. **Map H2**
Chef Joseph Monzare is a New Yorker and protégé of LA's Wolfgang Puck, which explains both the Globe's late-opening hours and its penchant for California cuisine. Standards

such as wood-oven pizzas and grilled salmon with buttery pasta and watercress are transformed by the freshness of their ingredients and the skill of a chef who knows how to put them to good use. The Globe is open until 1am, a rarity in early-to-bed San Francisco.

Plouf
40 Belden Lane, between Bush, Pine, Kearny and Montgomery Streets (986 6491). Bus 2, 3, 4, 15. **Lunch served** 11.30am-2.30pm Mon-Fri. **Dinner served** 5.30-10pm Mon-Thur; 5.30-10.30pm Fri, Sat. **Average** lunch $17, dinner $30. **Credit** AmEx, Disc, MC, V. **Map H3**
'Plouf' is French onomatopoeia for the sound of a pebble dropping into water, and all dishes at this restaurant come from the water. Mussels are served at least ten different ways, including the popular standard with parsley and garlic. Fish dishes are excellently prepared: try the grilled tuna niçoise salad with baby greens. The sleek restaurant also has outdoor seating, making it popular for business lunches on sunny days.
Disabled: toilet.

Rubicon
558 Sacramento Street, between Sansome and Montgomery Streets (434 4100). BART Montgomery/ Muni Metro F, J, K, L, M, N/bus 1, 12, 15, 41. **Lunch served** 11.30am-2pm Mon-Fri. **Dinner served** 5.30-10pm Mon-Sat. **Average** lunch $30, dinner $50. **Credit** AmEx, DC, MC, V. **Map H3**
Despite backing from Robin Williams, Francis Ford Coppola and New York chef Drew Nieporent, Rubicon has none of the pzzazz you might expect. It does, however, have excellent California cuisine and a superb wine list assembled by one of the top sommeliers in the country. There are two tasting menus ($59 for six courses; $79 with wine) as well as the more affordable main menu.
Disabled: toilet.

Sam's Grill
374 Bush Street, between Montgomery and Kearny Streets (421 0594). BART Montgomery/Muni Metro F, J, K, L, M, N/bus 3, 4, 15. **Meals served** 11am-9pm Mon-Fri. **Average** $30. **Credit** AmEx, DC, MC, V. **Map H3**
Established in 1867, Sam's – all wood-panelling and worn lino – is a monument to the old days of leisurely three-martini lunches. The waiters are older and more sincere than elsewhere and the dishes are traditional but none the worse for it – there's no designer lettuce here. Fried zucchini, creamed spinach and fish (any way you'd like it) all hit the spot. By contrast, the wine list is current and Californian.

Tadich Grill
240 California Street, between Battery and Front Streets (391 1849). BART Embarcadero/Muni Metro F, J, K, L, M, N/bus 1, 12, 41, 42/cable car California. **Meals served** 11am-9.30pm Mon-Fri; 11.30am-9.30pm Sat. **Average** $25. **Credit** MC, V. **Map H3**
Since 1849, the Tadich Grill has been revered as the quintessential San Francisco restaurant. There are private wooden booths, plenty of counter seating and professional staff, many of whom have worked here for decades. This is the place to come for high-quality seafood: thick clam chowder, cioppino (San Francisco's answer to bouillabaisse), calamari or swordfish steaks, prawns sautéed in Chardonnay or fresh salmon in lobster sauce. Sourdough is the bread of choice, and desserts are simple yet satisfying.
Disabled: toilet.

Civic Center

Hayes Street Grill
320 Hayes Street, between Franklin and Gough Streets (863 5545). BART Van Ness/Muni Metro F, J, K, L, M, N/bus 21, 42, 49. **Lunch served** 11.30-2pm Mon-Fri. **Dinner served** 5-9pm Mon-Thur; 5-10.30pm Fri;

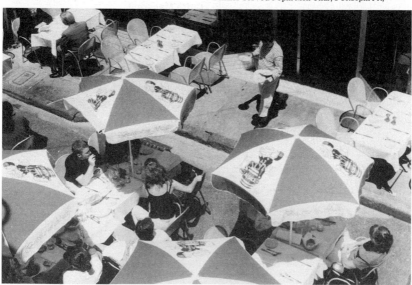

*For sunny sidewalk lunches, try **Plouf**.*

5.30-10.30pm Sat; 5-8.30pm Sun. **Average** lunch $18, dinner $35. **Credit** AmEx, DC, Disc, MC, V. **Map F5**
After nearly two decades, this restaurant is still one of the best places for fish in San Francisco. The menu changes daily, offering a choice of different sauces and grilled fish with which to match them. The room is simply decorated, and the walls are covered with black and white photos of musicians, reminders that the Opera and Symphony perform nearby.
Disabled: toilet.

Maharani
1122 Post Street, between Polk Street and Van Ness Avenue (775 1988). **Lunch served** 11.30am-2.30pm daily. **Dinner served** 5-10pm Mon-Thur; 5-10.30pm Fri-Sun. **Average** lunch $9, dinner $20-$37. **Credit** AmEx, DC, JCB, MC, V. **Map F4**
This North Indian restaurant has a healthy emphasis, with reduced amounts of oil and salt in many of its dishes. House specialities include fabulous breads and vegetarian main courses.
Disabled: toilet.

Stars
555 Golden Gate Avenue, between Van Ness Avenue and Polk Street (861 7827). **Bus** 19, 42, 47, 49. **Lunch served** noon-2pm Mon-Fri. **Dinner served** 6-10pm daily. **Late supper served** 11pm Mon-Thur, Sun; 11.30pm Fri, Sat. **Average** lunch $23, dinner $45. **Credit** AmEx, DC, MC, V. **Map F4**
During the height of California cuisine's popularity in the 1980s, this bustling brasserie, made famous by celebrity chef Jeremiah Tower, reigned supreme. Now the hubbub has died down somewhat, but Stars is still the place where San Francisco's élite come to see and be seen. Portions are large and prices high (although you can eat well and more affordably at the extra-long bar) and feature the best of American food, from burgers, hot dogs and chowders to crisp duck confit with white beans or spicy lamb with zucchini couscous. The desserts are some of the best in town. Booking is essential.
Disabled: toilet.

Vicolo Pizzeria
201 Ivy Street, at Franklin Street (863 2382). **BART** Van Ness/Muni Metro F, J, K, L, M, N/bus 21, 42, 17, 49. **Lunch served** 11.30am-2pm, **dinner served** 5 9.30pm, Mon-Fri. **Meals served** noon-10.30pm Sat; noon-9.30pm Sun. **Average** $12. **Credit** MC, V. **Map F5**
Vicolo's gourmet pizza crusts are thick and made of cornmeal, and the toppings range from roasted garlic and gorgonzola to standards such as mushroom. Salads are fresh and desserts above average. Tucked away in an alley between Hayes and Grove Streets, the place is hard to find, but handy for a pre-theatre meal when you do locate it.
Disabled: toilet.

North Beach

Capps Corner
1600 Powell Street, at Green Street (989 2589). **Bus** 15, 30, 41, 45/cable car Powell-Mason. **Lunch served** 11.30am-2.30pm Mon-Fri. **Dinner served** 4.30-10.30pm daily. **Average** lunch $9, dinner $17. **Credit** AmEx, Disc, MC, V. **Map G2**
Located next door to the longest-running theatrical spoof in San Francisco, *Beach Blanket Babylon*, Capps is a great Italian dive filled with baseball memorabilia and American kitsch. The hearty Italian food is basic, but the location and prices come as compensation.

Enrico's
504 Broadway, at Kearny Street (982 6223). **Bus** 12, 15, 30, 41, 83. **Lunch served** 11.30am-5pm Mon-Sat; 11.30am-4pm Sun. **Dinner served** 5-11pm Mon-Thur; 5pm-midnight Fri, Sat; 4-11pm Sun. **Average** lunch $12, dinner $22. **Credit** AmEx, MC, V. **Map G2**
Nestled in between Broadway strip joints, Enrico's remains as perennially popular as it was before it underwent renovation. Outdoor seating is possible all year-round (thanks to heat lamps), and there's excellent live jazz, a full bar and first-rate food. Wood-fired pizzas with toppings like sausage or porcini, a range of tapas and the roast lamb are unfailingly good. It's also great for people-watching.
Disabled: toilet.

The Helmand
430 Broadway, between Kearny and Montgomery Streets (362 0641). **Bus** 12, 15, 30, 41, 83. **Dinner served** 5.30-10pm Mon-Thur, Sun; 5.30-11pm Fri, Sat. **Average** $20. **Credit** AmEx, MC, V. **Map G/H2**
The Helmand consistently appears on lists of recommended eateries, partly because the city has so few Afghani restaurants, but also because the food is inexpensive and deliciously aromatic. The cooking is influenced by India, Asia and the Middle East; marinades and fragrant spices give each dish its own character. Pumpkin ravioli with a leek sauce, when available, is exquisite.

Moose's
1652 Stockton Street, between Union and Filbert Streets (989 7800). **Bus** 15, 30, 39, 41, 45, 83. **Lunch served** 11.30am-2.30pm Mon-Sat. **Dinner served** 5.30-10pm Mon-Thur; 5.30-11pm Fri, Sat; 5-10pm Sun. **Average** lunch $25, dinner $60. **Credit** AmEx, Disc, DC, MC, V. **Map G2**
Long-time restaurateurs Ed and Mary Etta Moose seem to know how to create environments that are uniquely San Franciscan. A full bar, an open kitchen serving fairly consistent California cuisine and an extensive wine list are the draws here. Regardless of changes in menu or chef, the Mooseburger persists. Moose's also serves brunch at the weekend.
Disabled: toilet.

L'Osteria del Forno
519 Columbus Avenue, between Green and Union Streets (982 1124). **Bus** 15, 30, 41, 45, 83. **Meals served** 11.30am-10pm Mon, Wed, Thur; 11.30am-11.30pm Fri, Sat. **Average** $20. **No credit cards**. **Map G2**
Some great food can be had at this tiny hole-in-the-wall. An imaginative and ever-changing menu features thin-crusted pizzas and pastas, and if you're lucky, focaccia and pork braised in milk, a Tuscan and North Beach favourite. The wine list is short and Italian.

Rose Pistola
532 Columbus Avenue, between Green and Union Streets (399 0499). **Bus** 15, 30, 39, 41, 45, 83. **Lunch served** 11.30am-5.30pm daily. **Dinner served** 5.30-10.30pm Mon-Thur, Sun; 5.30-11.30pm Fri, Sat. **Late-night menu** 10.30pm-midnight Mon-Thur; 11.30pm-1am Fri, Sat. **Average** lunch $15, dinner $27. **Credit** AmEx, DC, MC, V. **Map G2**
Named after a longtime North Beach resident, Rose Pistola's cuisine is predominantly from Liguria in the north of Italy. Grilled dishes are the stars at this large, open-plan and buzzing restaurant – chef Reed Hearon is in the celebrity league and so attracts fans from far and wide. The wine list is exhaustive, with an emphasis on California and Italy.
Disabled: toilet.

Tomassos
1042 Kearny Street, at Broadway (398 9696). **Bus** 12, 15, 30, 41, 45, 83. **Dinner served** 5-11pm Tue-Sat; 4-10pm Sun. **Average** $25. **Credit** AmEx, DC, MC, V. **Map G2**

MODERN PAINTERS

Major British and American writers contribute to the U.K.'s most controversial art magazine:

- JULIAN BARNES

- WILLIAM BOYD

- A.S.BYATT

- PATRICK HERON

- HILTON KRAMER

- JED PERL

- JOHN RICHARDSON

- PETER SCHJELDAHL

- RICHARD WOLLHEIM

Britain's best-selling quarterly journal to the fine arts.

Best of Chinatown

Gold Mountain

644 Broadway, between Columbus Avenue and Stockton Street (296 7733). Bus 12, 15, 30, 41, 83. **Lunch served** 10.30am-3pm, **dinner served** 5-9.30pm, daily. **Average** £12. **Credit** MC, V. **Map G2**
You'll get no help with the menu and it may be impossible to communicate with the mostly non-English speaking staff, but hail the dim sum carts and just enjoy the adventure.

House of Nanking

919 Kearny Street, between Jackson Street and Columbus Avenue (421 1429). Bus 12, 15, 41, 83. **Meals served** 11am-10pm Mon-Fri; noon-10pm Sat; 4-10pm Sun. **Average** $12. **No credit cards. Map G2**
There's always a queue, because the place is the size of a walk-in closet and prices are cheap. The food is mediocre unless you choose the more imaginative dishes which are inspired by whatever the chef buys in each day.
Disabled: toilet.

Imperial Tea Court

1411 Powell Street, between Broadway and Vallejo Street (788 6080). Bus 12, 83/cable car Powell-Mason. **Open** 11am-6.30pm daily. **Average** $5. **Credit** AmEx, DC, MC, V. **Map G2**
This is not a restaurant but a teahouse, and definitely a respite from the bustle of Chinatown. Take a break and sip some exotic teas like Silver Needle or chrysanthemum.

Lichee Garden

1416 Powell Street, between Broadway and Vallejo Street (397 2290). Bus 12, 83/cable car Powell-Mason. **Meals served** 7.30am-9.30pm daily. **Average** $12. **Credit** MC, V. **Map G2**

There's a reason many Chinese celebrate birthdays and anniversaries at Lichee Garden: ingredients are of the highest quality and prices are incredibly low.
Disabled: toilet.

Pearl City

641 Jackson Street, between Kearny Street and Grant Avenue (398 8383). Bus 12, 15, 30, 45, 83. **Meals served** 8am-10pm Mon-Thur; 8am-11pm Fri, Sat. **Average** $10. **Credit** AmEx, MC, V. **Map G3**
It's a challenge if you don't speak Chinese, but you'll be rewarded with some of the best dim sum in San Francisco. Gets very busy at weekends.
Disabled: toilet.

R&G Lounge

631 Kearny Street, between Sacramento and Clay Streets (982 7877). Bus 1, 15. **Meals served** 11am-9.30pm daily. **Average** $9. **Credit** AmEx, MC, V. **Map H3**
An excellent choice for seafood. Choose your lobster, prawns or fish from the tank, then sit down to a feast that won't break your budget.

Yuet Lee

1300 Stockton Street, at Broadway (982 6020). Bus 12, 15, 30, 83. **Meals served** 11am-3am Mon, Wed-Sun. **Average** $15. **No credit cards. Map G2**
Chefs and restaurant folk are often spotted at this tiny, bright green Chinese place, probably because the seafood is excellent and its available until 3am. Also worth trying are the roasted squab with fresh cilantro and lemon, and the Eight Precious Noodle Soup, made with eight different kinds of meat. Cash only.
Branch: 3601 26th Street, at Valencia Street (550 8998).

The cave-like dining room is filled with appetising aromas and a buzz from the hordes of people who frequent this well-known North Beach haunt. The wood-oven pizzas and calzones are extremely popular, as is the house red which is served in ceramic pitchers. You can't reserve a table, so you may have to wait for one.

Russian Hill

Antica Trattoria

2400 Polk Street, at Union Street (928 5797). Bus 19, 41, 45, 76. **Dinner served** 5.30-10pm Mon-Thur, Sun; 5.30-10.30pm Fri, Sat. **Average** $25. **Credit** DC, MC, V. **Map F2**
While Italian restaurants are a dime a dozen in San Francisco, this one stands out. It is Italian-owned, the surroundings are sophisticated yet casual and the food is great: dishes like sliced fennel with blood oranges and red onions, polenta with wild mushrooms, grilled pork tenderloin with pancetta and gorgonzola are bargain-priced (no entrée costs more than $14).
Disabled: toilet.

Golden Turtle

2211 Van Ness Avenue, between Broadway and Vallejo Street (441 4419). Bus 12, 42, 47, 49, 76, 83. **Dinner served** 5-11pm Tue-Sun. **Average** $20. **Credit** AmEx, DC, MC, V. **Map F3**
Authentic Vietnamese food in comfortable surroundings make this a nicer-than-average place for ethnic food.

Standard Vietnamese fare such as five-spiced chicken, spring rolls and sliced beef marinated in lemongrass rise above average here.
Disabled: toilet.
Branch: 305 Fifth Avenue, between Geary Boulevard and Clement Street (321 5285).

La Folie

2316 Polk Street, between Union and Green Streets (776 5577). Bus 19, 41, 45, 47, 49, 76. **Dinner served** 5.30-10pm Mon-Sat. **Average** $75. **Credit** AmEx, DC, Disc, JCB, MC, V. **Map F2**
Chef Roland Passot presides over this delightful Californian-French eaterie on Russian Hill. The Provençal décor and attentive staff add to its charm. Prices are steep, but the cooking is exquisite and refined. Especially noteworthy is the five-course discovery menu ($59.50), which allows you to sample Passot's creativity. The extensive wine list is under the aegis of Passot's brother, Georges.
Disabled: toilet.

Zarzuela

2000 Hyde Street, at Union Street (346 0800). Bus 41, 45/cable car Powell-Hyde. **Meals served** noon-10.30pm Mon-Thur; noon-11pm Fri, Sat. **Average** $20. **Credit** Disc, MC, V. **Map F2**
Take a cab or walk over Russian Hill so you don't arrive too stressed for dinner here (parking is impossible). Zarzuella features authentic Spanish cuisine in a cosy restaurant filled with posters of bull fights and maps of

Spain. The special tapas are always a treat, but old stand-bys such as grilled eggplant filled with goat's cheese, sautéd shrimps in garlic and olive oil, and fried potatoes with garlic and sherry vinegar never disappoint. No bookings accepted.
Disabled: toilet.

Polk Gulch

Harris'
2100 Van Ness Avenue, at Pacific Avenue (673 1888).
Bus 42, 47, 49. **Dinner served** 6-10pm Mon-Fri;
5-10.30pm Sat, Sun. **Average** $40. **Credit** AmEx, DC,
Disc, JCB, MC, V. **Map F3**
Harris' offers old-style dining: start with a strong cocktail, sink into your booth, then proceed with a Caesar salad made at your table, steak and a baked potato with all the trimmings and, of course, a hefty dessert. Beef – for which the place is famous – is dry-aged for 21 days and proudly displayed from a refrigerator window facing the street. The lobster isn't bad either.
Disabled: toilet.

Swan Oyster Depot
1517 Polk Street, between California and Sacramento Streets (673 1101). Bus 1, 19, 42, 47, 49, 76/cable car California. **Meals served** 8am-5.30pm Mon-Sat.
Average $12. **Map F3**
Half fish market and half counter-service hole-in-the-wall, Swan has served San Franciscans seafood since 1912. The best time of year to visit is between May and November, when the local Dungeness crab is in season. Classic clam chowder, the smoked salmon plate and Blue Point oysters are specialities of the house.

SoMa

Fringale
570 Fourth Street, between Bryant and Brannan Streets (543 0573). Bus 15, 30, 42, 45, 76. **Lunch served** 11.30am-3pm Mon-Fri. **Dinner served** 5.30-10.30pm Mon-Sat. **Average** lunch $15, dinner $30. **Credit** AmEx, MC, V. **Map H4/5**
Literally translated, the restaurant's name means the urge to eat. And since the restaurant is tiny, the food first-rate and the prices incredibly reasonable, booking is almost mandatory. Basque chef Gerald Hirigoyen, who also runs Pastis (*see p114*), is particularly skilled with duck and fish, but began his career as a pastry chef. Seating here is shoulder-to-shoulder and the atmosphere laid-back.
Disabled: toilet.

Hamburger Mary's
1582 Folsom Street, at 12th Street (626 1985). Bus 9, 12, 42. **Meals served** 11.30am-12.15am Mon-Thur; 11.30am-1.15am Fri; 10am-1.15am Sat; 10am-12.15am Sun. **Average** $15. **Credit** AmEx, Disc, MC, V.
Map G5
The food doesn't hit the high spots it used to, but this place, now almost 20 years old, is fabulous in its junky and eclectic décor. Numerous burger offerings give out-of-towners the impression that Americans live up to their meat-eating reputation. After the clubs close, the place gets packed.
Disabled: toilet.

Hawthorne Lane
22 Hawthorne Street, between Second and Third Streets (777 9779). Bus 12, 15, 30, 45, 76. **Lunch served** 11.30am-2pm Mon-Fri. **Dinner served** 5.30-10pm Mon-Thur, Sun; 5.30-10.30pm Fri, Sat. **Average** lunch $20, dinner $38. **Credit** MC, V. **Map H4**
With such diverse clientele as President Clinton and

members of U2, this $3 million restaurant is the creation of Wolfgang Puck protégés David and Anne Gingrass, chefs from Postrio. The food is outstanding, creative and ultra fresh – the cold lobster spring rolls with mint in rice paper are so light you could eat a double order. The restaurant is spacious and the wine list impressive; desserts are divine. If you want to indulge, this is the place, especially at dinner when the people-watching is just as appetising as the food.
Disabled: toilet.

LuLu
816 Folsom Street, between Fourth and Fifth Streets (495 5775). Bus 12, 27, 45, 76. **Lunch served** 11.30am-2.30pm Tue-Sun. **Dinner served** 5.30-10.30pm Mon-Thur, Sun; 5pm-midnight Fri, Sat. **Average** lunch $20, dinner $33. **Credit** AmEx, DC, JCB, MC, V.
Map H4
This warehouse space, serving Mediterranean food, is usually filled to capacity. The huge open kitchen, monster floral arrangements and sea of seats make LuLu a fun place for eating, but difficult for conversation. Grilled dishes are excellent as are the signature mussels served on a hot iron skillet, wood-fired pizzas, garlic mashed potatoes and vegetables also cooked in the wood oven. Dishes come served on large platters and sharing is encouraged. Reserve a table in advance, or wait your chances in the buzzing bar.
Disabled: toilet.

Beach Chalet

Overlooking the Pacific Ocean at the western edge of the city, the Beach Chalet is a recently reborn San Francisco treasure. Originally opened in 1925, the stately 'Board of Park Commissioner's Pavilion' (as it was then called) stands just a few hundred yards from the beautiful tulip garden in the shadow of the windmill in Golden Gate Park. Designed by local architect Willis Polk, the building housed a fine restaurant and changing rooms for flapper-era sunworshippers headed for Ocean Beach.

Eleven years later, the Beach Chalet was chosen as the site for one of the city's most magnificent displays of murals. Painted in 1936 by Lucien Labaudt, a French-born artist and dress designer who emigrated to San Francisco in 1910, the murals depict San Francisco life during the Depression. Baker Beach, the Embarcadero, Fisherman's Wharf, Chinatown – vistas from the city's history unfold from every wall. Labaudt painted familiar faces into his pieces: local socialites, politicians, businessmen and even his wife appear within the frescoes; elaborate carvings and mosaics were also added as part of the design.

In the 1940s, the Beach Chalet was recommissioned for use by the Army Corps of Engineers and later became a meeting hall, bar and – in 1981, the same year it closed for lack of funding – a national landmark.

Thirsty Bear

661 Howard Street, between Second and Third Streets (974 0905). Bus 9, 12, 15, 30, 45, 76. **Lunch served** 11.30am-2.30pm Mon-Sat. **Tapas served** 2.30-10.30pm Mon-Thur, Sun; 2.30-11pm Fri, Sat. **Average** lunch $18, dinner $30. **Credit** AmEx, DC, MC, V. **Map H4**
Though many come to the Thirsty Bear for its microbrewed beers, the food is fantastic too. Sample a series of Spanish tapas – mushrooms and garlic with grilled bread, white beans and fennel sausage, spicy potatoes. Upstairs houses two pool tables and another bar.
Disabled: toilet.

South Park & South Beach

Boulevard

1 Mission Street, at Steuart Street (543 6084). BART Embarcadero/Muni Metro F, J, K, L, M, N/bus 1, 2, 6, 7, 9, 14, 21, 31, 32, 66, 71. **Lunch served** 11.30am-2pm Mon-Fri. **Dinner served** 5.30-10pm Mon-Wed, Sun; 5.30-10.30pm Thur-Sat. **Average** lunch $25, dinner $50. **Credit** AmEx, DC, Disc, MC, V. **Map J3**
The draws here are the spectacular setting, enhanced by a view of the Bay Bridge, and the dynamic combination of designer Pat Kuleto and self-taught chef Nancy Oakes. Oakes' stacked, elaborate dishes (such as sautéd Sonoma foie gras served on corn bread with a wild blackberry sauce and mâche) make local suppliers proud. Signature entrées at

dinner include honey-cured pork loin and grilled American lamb chops, and wood-roasted dishes are another forte. Service is casual although the prices are not: try the bar at lunch-time as a cheaper option.

Pickled Ginger

100 Brannan Street, at Embarcadero (977 1230). Bus 32, 42. **Lunch served** 11.30am-2pm Mon-Fri. **Dinner served** 5-10pm Mon-Thur, Sun; 5-11pm Fri, Sat. **Average** lunch $14, dinner $19. **Credit** AmEx, DC, MC, V. **Map J4**
Dishes at this East-West eatery don't exactly blend the two cultures, although their marriage is successful in the Asian tortellini stuffed with pork, the scallops and spinach with roasted pepper sauce, and the fettucine with rock shrimp, scallops, shiitake mushrooms and cilantro (coriander) pesto.
Disabled: toilet.

South Park Café

108 South Park Avenue, between Second, Third, Bryant and Brannan Streets (495 7275). Bus 15, 30, 42, 76. **Breakfast served** 7.30-11am, **lunch served** 11.30am-2.30pm, **light lunch served** 2.30-6pm, Mon-Fri. **Dinner served** 6-10pm Mon-Sat. **Average** lunch $15, dinner $35. **Credit** AmEx, MC, V. **Map H/J4**
Located in the heart of 'multimedia gulch', this long-standing and popular bistro overlooking South Park is as first-rate as ever. The food is French: pistou (a bean soup with masses of

But an aggressive business plan supported by preservationists determined to save its murals resulted in the Beach Chalet's phoenix-like re-opening on New Year's Eve 1996. Its frescoes restored to their original state, the main floor of the Chalet now serves as a visitor's centre for Golden Gate Park.

Upstairs, the Beach Chalet Brewery and Restaurant is a hip dining room with a simple menu of burgers and pastas, as well as dishes like the delicious couscous with lamb sausages, a variety of salads, and good desserts. There's a choice of several house-brewed beers, including the hand-pumped Pacific Porter. If you're waiting for a table at the busy bar, you'll be issued you with a beeper so you can be paged when your table is ready – giving you time to nip downstairs for another look at the murals.

Though its prices may have changed somewhat (the 1925 menu offered sirloin steak for 25¢), the Beach Chalet is a resurrected San Francisco jewel.

Beach Chalet Brewery & Restaurant

1000 Great American Highway, between Fulton Street and Lincoln Avenue (restaurant 386 8439/visitor centre 751 2766). Bus 5, 18.
Restaurant **Brunch served** 10am-3pm Sun.
Meals served 11.30am-10pm Mon-Thur; 5.30pm-11pm Fri, Sat. **Average** $15. **Credit** MC, V.
Visitor centre **Open** 9am-6pm daily.

The **Flying Saucer** – out of this world.

basil) is good, as is the boudin noir with apples. Desserts are classics: crème brûlée and the best profiteroles in town.
Disabled: toilet.

Wu Kong Restaurant
One Rincon Center, Spear Street, between Folsom and Harrion Streets (957 9300). BART Embarcadero/ Muni Metro F, J, K, L, M, N/bus 1, 2, 6, 7, 9, 14, 21, 31, 32, 66, 71. **Lunch served** 11am-2.30pm, **dinner served** 5.30-9.30pm, daily. **Average** lunch $13, dinner $30. **Credit** AmEx, DC, JCB, MC, V.
Map J3
Wu Kong, with its white linen tablecloths and black lacquered furniture, provides a respite from the numerous fast-food eateries in the Rincon Center, an office building that also houses a post office. Food is clean-cut: try the crystal shrimp, which is peeled, boiled and served with pak choi in a lightly thickened chicken broth. The Shanghai or Cantonese dim sum is delivered to your table on foot, not by cart.
Disabled: toilet.

The Mission

El Nuevo Frutilandia
3077 24th Street, between Folsom Street and Treat Avenue (648 2958). BART 24th Street/bus 12, 48, 67. **Lunch served** 11.30am-3pm Tue-Fri. **Dinner served** 5-9pm Tue-Thur; 5-10pm Fri. **Meals served** noon-10pm Sat; noon-9pm Sun. **Average** lunch $8, dinner $12. **Credit** MC, V.
Castro/Mission Map Z2
Specialising in Cuban and Puerto Rican fare, this tiny, noisy eaterie offers up appetisers such as dumplings stuffed with chicken, meat-filled plantains and yucca fritters, as well as 'higado a la Fruitlandia', a succulent dish of calf's liver cooked with green peppers and onions in a spicy sauce. Vegetarian dishes include yucca with garlic, black beans and rice. Most of the mains can also be ordered as tapas or small plates.

Fina Estampa
2374 Mission Street, between 19th and 20th Streets (824 4437). Bus 14, 33, 49. **Lunch served** 11.30am-3.30pm, dinner served 5-9pm, Tue-Thur. **Meals served** 11am-9pm Fri-Sun. **Average** lunch $7, dinner $10. **Castro/ Mission Map Y1**
Outstanding and wide-ranging Peruvian food is served in this nondescript space. There's seafood, chillies, meat and potatoes, grilled chicken, Peruvian beer and Spanish wines. **Branch:** 1100 Van Ness Avenue, at Geary Street (440 6343).

Flying Saucer
1000 Guerrero Street, at 22nd Street (641 9955). BART 24th Street/bus 14, 26, 49. **Dinner served** 6-9.30pm Tue-Fri; 5.30-9.30pm Sat. **Average** $40. **Credit** AmEx, MC, V. **Castro/Mission Map Y2**
As the décor and name suggest, Flying Saucer is out of this world. Plates are creatively and gorgeously presented and the menu reflects a well-travelled chef who offers dishes such as prawn and shiitake potstickers or roast rack of lamb with a ratatouille and basil confit. Portions are huge and the wine list excellent, especially considering the menu's surprising food combinations.

La Rondalla
901 Valencia Street, at 20th Street (647 7474). Bus 14, 26, 49. **Meals served** 11.30am-3.30am Tue-Sun. **Average** $10. **No credit cards. Castro/Mission Map Y1**
It's Christmas all year round at this Mexican dive with its tree lights, stuffed birds and other outlandish decorations. Mariachi musicians drown out your conversation and margaritas drown out your taste buds – not a bad thing, since the food is mediocre. Try the asado – thin, barely grilled steak smothered with fresh onions, potatoes and tomatoes before the noise level reaches deafening point.

The Moa Room
1007 Guerrero Street, at 22nd Street (282 1007). Bus 26, 48. **Dinner served** 5.30-10pm Mon-Thur, Sun; 5.30-11pm Fri, Sat. **Average** $30. **Credit** AmEx, Disc, MC, V. **Castro/Mission Map Y2**

A Vietnamese restaurant with Californian flair – the **Slanted Door**. *See page 130.*

The chef and the name come from New Zealand (moa is a bird), but the produce and flowers showcased at this tiny new restaurant come from the owner's ranch in Calistoga. The menu features dishes such as duck confit spring rolls served with a tamarind dipping sauce, or sand dabs en papillote (baked in parchment paper). *Disabled: toilet.*

Pancho Villa Taqueria

3071 16th Street, between Mission and Valencia Streets (864 8840). BART 16th Street/bus 14, 22, 26, 49, 53. **Open** 10am-midnight daily. **Average** $6. **Credit** AmEx, MC, V. **Map F6**
You'll get some of the best – and fattest – burritos in the Mission here; the fruit drinks change daily and are also great. Try the horchata (a sweetened rice drink), or the new red snapper burrito with a dash of lime. Noisy and packed at lunch-time – and open late. *Disabled: toilet.*

Pauline's Pizza

260 Valencia Street, at Brosnan Street, between Duboce Avenue and 14th Street (552 2050). Muni Metro F/ bus 26. **Dinner served** 5-10pm Tue-Sun. **Average** $11. **Credit** MC, V. **Map F6**
Pauline's specialises in inventive, thin-crusted pizza made with top-quality products. Sausages are made on the premises, and some of the produce comes from the owner's organic garden, including edible flowers, sorrel, kiwis, green beens and boysenberries. The yellow, saloon-type building next door is the original headquarters of Levi Strauss (*see chapter* **Museum & Galleries**).

Roosevelt Tamale Bar

2817 24th Street, at Bryant Street (550 9213). Bus 27, 48. **Meals served** 10.30am-9.40pm Tue-Sat; 11.30am-8.40pm Sun. **Average** $7. **No credit cards.** **Castro/Mission Map Z2**
Since 1922, this establishment has been cranking out huge servings of pork or chicken tamales. They also make their own mole sauces. *Disabled: toilet.*

The Slanted Door

584 Valencia Street, at 17th Street (861 8032). BART 16th Street/bus 22, 26, 53. **Lunch served** 11.30am-3pm, **dinner served** 5.30-10pm, Tue-Sun. **Average** lunch $15, dinner $23. **Credit** MC, V. **Map F6**
This Vietnamese restaurant has the flair of a top class California-cuisinerie, a unique wine list and desserts that range from chocolate cake to exotic fruit sorbets. The crispy imperial rolls are greaseless and addictive. Other favourites are the green papaya salad, sea bass (served only in the evening) and the spicy seafood curry. The all-American waiting staff combined with the all-Vietnamese kitchen staff make for a unique restaurant in the predominantly Latino Mission district.

Taqueria Cancun

2288 Mission Street, between 22nd and 23rd Streets (252 9560). BART 24th Street/bus 14, 49. **Meals served** 10am-12.30am daily. **Average** $5. **No credit cards. Castro/Mission Map Y2**
The burritos are outstanding and this spot is open until 3am most nights, though they stop serving food long before that. It's such a favourite hole-in-the-wall that we hate to divulge the secret. *Disabled: toilet.*

Ti Couz Crêperie

3108 16th Street, between Guerrero and Valencia Streets (252 7373). BART 16th Street/bus 14, 22, 26, 33, 49, 53. **Meals served** 11am-11pm Mon-Fri; 10am-11pm Sat; 10am-10pm Sun. **Average** $20. **Credit** MC, V. **Map F6**

Ti Couz's crêpes are made with buckwheat flour and served as in Normandy – in savoury and sweet versions. Fillings include ratatouille, cheese, almond butter or chocolate, and the onion soup's great too. You'll have to queue for a seat, and once you've eaten (don't forget to save room for dessert) it's not a place to linger. *Disabled: toilet.*

Universal Cafe

2814 19th Street, between Bryant and Florida Streets (821 4608). Bus 12, 27. **Brunch served** 9am-2.30pm Sat, Sun. **Lunch served** 11.30am-2.30pm Tue-Fri. **Dinner served** 6-10pm Tue-Sun. **Average** lunch $8, dinner $18. **Credit** AmEx, DC, MC, V. **Castro/Mission Map Z1**
The look of this neighbourhood café is semi-industrial and the place has links with two other hip SoMa spots, the South Park Café (*see p127*) and Ristorante Ecco (101 South Park; 495 3291). Universal's menu includes pizzas and various forms of focaccia sandwiches at lunch. In the evening, try the filling steak with gorgonzola mashed potatoes, or the less substantial chicken liver pâté on grilled toast served with fresh greens. At the weekend, linger over banana French toast with strawberries for brunch at a table outside in the sun. *Disabled: toilet.*

The Haight

Cha Cha Cha

1801 Haight Street, at Shrader Street (386 5758). Muni Metro N/bus 6, 7, 33, 43, 66, 71. **Lunch served** 11.30am-4pm daily. **Dinner served** 5-11 pm Mon-Thur, Sun; 5-11.30pm Fri, Sat. **Average** lunch $15, dinner $20. **Credit** MC, V. **Map C6**
This spicy hotspot churns out huge, reasonably priced plates of Caribbean tapas: calamari, deep-fried new potatoes, fried plantains, black beans, yellow rice, Cajun-style fish dishes and refreshing sangria to go with them. Although the quality can be inconsistent and the queue ridiculously long, the ambience and the company make this a festive place worth trying. *Disabled: toilet.*

Eos Restaurant & Wine Bar

901 Cole Street, at Carl Street (566 3063). Muni Metro N/bus 37, 43. **Dinner served** 5.30-11pm Mon-Sat; 5-11pm Sun. **Average** $33. **Credit** AmEx, MC, V. **Map C6**
This sleek, architecturally designed restaurant presents the best of East-West fusion by the classically trained chef/ owner Arnold Wong. Dishes such as Caesar salad with a ginger accent, and lamb marinated in a Thai curry sauce are complemented by one of the most extensive wine lists in the Bay Area. The same menu is served in the small wine bar next door. *Disabled: toilet.*

Thep Phanom

900 Waller Street, at Fillmore Street (431 2526). Bus 6, 7, 22, 66, 71. **Meals served** 5.30-10.30pm daily. **Average** $8. **Credit** AmEx, DC, Disc, MC, V. **Map E5**
The Thai food at Thep Phanom is as spicy as the neighbourhood. The angel wings – fried chicken wings stuffed with glass noodles – are universally popular.

The Castro

See also chapter **Gay & Lesbian San Francisco**.

Pozole

2337 Market Street, between Castro and Noe Streets (626 2666). Muni Metro F, K, L, M/bus 24, 33, 35, 37. **Meals served** 4-11pm Mon-Thur; noon-midnight Fri-Sun. **Average** $8. **No credit cards. Map E6**

Colourful surroundings and inexpensive meals make this Mexican restaurant popular. Try Cuban quesadillas stuffed with roast garlic, peppers and mushrooms or Oaxacan tamales with mole sauce, fried bananas, black beans and rice. There are also Caribbean and South American dishes.

2223 Market

2223 Market Street, between Noe and Sanchez Streets (431 0692). Muni Metro F, K, L, M/bus 24, 37. **Dinner served** 5.30-10pm Mon-Thur, Sun; 5.30-11pm Fri, Sat. **Brunch served** 10am-2pm Sat, Sun. **Average** brunch $15, dinner $24. **Credit** AmEx, DC, MC, V. **Map E6**
After opening without an official name, restaurateur John Cunin didn't want to jinx his success by changing anything

– so he didn't add one. The all-American menu includes huge pork chops with red pepper stuffing or pan-roasted chicken with garlic mashed potatoes and fried onion rings. Desserts are of the same divine ilk.

Noe Valley

Alice's

1599 Sanchez Street, at 29th Street (282 8999). Muni Metro J/bus 24, 26. **Lunch served** 11am-3pm Mon-Sat; noon-3pm Sun. **Dinner served** 3-9pm Mon-Thur, Sun; 3-10pm Fri, Sat. **Average** lunch $5, dinner $10. **Credit** MC, V.

Best breakfasts

Bay Watch

2150 Lombard Street, between Fillmore and Steiner Streets (775 9673). Bus 22, 28, 43, 76. **Meals served** 7am-2.30pm daily. **Credit** AmEx, DC, MC, V. **Map E2**
It looks like a budget hotel from the outside and seating is fast-food in design, but breakfast here is deluxe. Omelettes and pancakes are the best items on the menu. You can order one pancake if you wish: a good idea, since they're huge. Service is quick and the supply of coffee endless. *Disabled: toilet.*

Doidge's

2217 Union Street, between Fillmore and Steiner Streets (921 2149). Bus 22, 41, 45. **Meals served** 8am-1.45pm Mon-Fri; 8am-2.45pm Sat, Sun. **Credit** MC, V. **Map E2**
If possible, make a reservation. We know it sounds crazy for breakfast, but this unpretentious café is understandably popular. The plethora of breakfast offerings ranges from omelettes, thick bacon, French toast with fresh fruit to eggs Florentine.

Ella's

500 Presidio Avenue, at California Street (441 5669). Bus 1, 3, 4, 43. **Brunch served** 9am-2pm Sat, Sun. **Breakfast served** 7-11am, **lunch served** 11.30-5pm, **dinner served** 5-9pm, Mon-Fri. **Credit** AmEx, MC, V. **Map D4**
Breakfasts here are stellar but the wait – inevitable given the place's small size and immense popularity – is ridiculous. People come for the turkey hash alone. Ella's is closed for a few weeks in late summer.

Kate's Kitchen

471 Haight Street, between Fillmore and Webster Streets (626 3984). Bus 6, 7, 22, 66, 71. **Meals served** 9am-2.45pm Mon; 8am-2.45pm Tue-Fri; 9am-3.45pm Sat, Sun. **No credit cards. Map E5**
Customers at Kate's range from yuppie and healthy types getting a good breakfast before a hike, to altogether less salubrious customers who hang out in the Lower Haight. All the usual breakfast specials are offered: we recommend the huge banana walnut pancakes and the excellent BLTs. *Disabled: toilet.*

Miss Millie's

4123 24th Street, between Diamond and Castro Streets, (285 5598). Bus 24, 35, 48. **Breakfast served** 7.30am-11.30am, **lunch served** 11.30am-2.30pm, **Dinner served** 6-10pm Wed-Sat. **Brunch served** 9am-2pm Sat, Sun. **Credit** MC, V. **Castro/Mission Map X2**

Mel's Diner, *for milkshakes and meatloaf.*

The secret is to arrive around 12.30pm and avoid the long queue for the large and flavour-packed breakfasts here. Lemon ricotta pancakes come with a generous slather of blueberries, baguette-made French toast with bananas, and omelettes are served with a side of roasted root vegetables, plus coffee and more coffee. There are coveted seats on the small patio outside. Lunch and dinners involves similarly hearty American fare at reasonable prices.

Mel's Diner

2165 Lombard Street, between Steiner and Fillmore Streets (921 3039). Bus 22, 41, 45. **Meals served** 6am-3am Mon-Thur; 24 hours Fri, Sat; 6am-3am Sun. **No credit cards. Map G2**
The diner made famous by the movie *American Graffiti* is famous for its breakfasts today. You won't wait long and the offerings are plentiful: eggs every which way, pancakes, oatmeal and fruit – even steak. People also come for milkshakes, meat loaf, turkey and mashed potatoes. A great place for kids, but touristy.
Branch: 3355 Geary Boulevard, between Parker and Stanyan Streets (387 2244).
Disabled: toilet.

Sears Fine Foods

439 Powell Street, between Sutter and Post Streets (986 1160). Bus 2, 3, 4, 38, 76/cable car Powell-Hyde or Powell-Mason. **Meals served** 6.30-3pm daily. **No credit cards. Map G3**
Once you've found that coveted parking spot and braved the Union Square crowds, try the little pancakes at Sears – they're justly famous. *Disabled: toilet.*

Don't miss this new Chinese-Californian restaurant in Noe Valley, offering a very happy marriage of the best of both cusines. It may be off the beaten track but it's worth the trek. Book if you can because the locals will wait literally hours to eat the innovative mango chicken, the ever-popular asparagus salmon in black bean sauce or the delicate orange beef. The prices are good, too.
Disabled: toilet.

Firefly
4288 24th Street, between Diamond and Douglass Streets (821 7652). Bus 35, 48. **Dinner served** 5.30-10pm daily. **Average** $25. **Credit** AmEx, MC, V. **Castro/Mission Map X2**
The purée of eggplant and garlic served with bread gives you the first hint of the imaginative food to come at this neighbourhood restaurant. Firefly's menu features everything from potstickers, acorn squash latkes with apple sauce and salmon rolls, to the chef's mother's beef brisket with gravy and mashed potatoes. Dishes take on a new twist with the change of seasonal ingredients and there are several vegetarian offerings.
Disabled: toilet.

The Marina

Byblos
1910 Lombard Street, at Buchanan Street (292 5672). Bus 22, 41, 45. **Dinner served** 5-11pm daily. **Average** $9-$17. **Credit** MC, V. **Map E2**
One of the few Lebanese restaurants in San Francisco; even the wine list has a few selections from the Lebanon. Pull together a group of at least six and you can order a special spit-roasted lamb; otherwise, stick to the mezes (there are more than 20 of them) – small plates ranging from pickled vegetables, dolmas and lambs' tongues to fresh yogurt.

Café Marimba
2317 Chestnut Street, between Divisadero and Scott Streets (776 1506). Bus 28, 30, 43, 76. **Meals served** 5.30-10pm Mon; 11.30am-10pm Tue-Thur; 11.30am-11pm Fri; 10.30am-2pm Sat, Sun. **Brunch served** 2-11.30pm Sat; noon-11pm Sun. **Average** $20. **Credit** AmEx, MC, V. **Map D2**
Enjoy Mexican food from Oaxaca and fabulous drinks in one of the most brilliantly colourful restaurants in the city. Try the spicy octopus as an appetiser or main course. Chicken enchiladas with a choice of mole sauces are a nice rendition, as is the chile rellenos with mushrooms, zucchini and cheese in tomato sauce. Noisy and cordial, Marimba also stocks various tequilas – perfect for the blood orange margaritas that are served with weekend brunch.
Disabled: toilet.

Pasta Pomodoro
2027 Chestnut Street, at Fillmore Street (474 3400). Bus 22, 30, 43. **Meals served** 11am-11pm Mon-Sat; noon-11pm Sun. **Average** $8. **No credit cards. Map E2**
If only Pasta Pomodoro could set the standard for all fast-food places: the food is cheap and fast and ingredients generally fresh. Fifteen kinds of pastas include one with roast chicken, sun-dried tomatoes, cream and mushrooms, and a spaghetti fruitti di mare with calamari, mussels and scallops. Sandwiches made with focaccia are priced under $7. It's always packed.
Branches: 2304 Market Street, at Castro Street (558 8123); 655 Union Street, at Columbus Avenue (399 0300); 816 Irving Street, between Ninth and Tenth Avenues (566 0900).

Pluto's
3258 Scott Street, between Lombard and Chestnut Streets (775 8867). Bus 22, 28, 30, 43, 76. **Meals served** 11.30am-10pm Mon-Thur, Sun; 11.30am-11.30pm Fri, Sat. **Breakfast served** 9.30am-11.30am Sat, Sun. **Average** lunch $7, dinner $14. **Credit** MC, V. **Map D2**
It's chaotic figuring out how to order and pay for your food in this place, especially if you're hungry. You have to get in the appropriate queue for salads, main courses and side dishes. Once you have been served, however, the food is mouthwatering: garlicky mushrooms, mashed potatoes, grilled marinated steak, chicken or turkey sausages and great homemade desserts. Eat outside if you like people-watching.
Branch: 627 Irving Street, between Seventh and Eighth Avenues (753 8867).

World Wrapps
2257 Chestnut Street, between Scott and Pierce Streets (563 9727). Bus 22, 28, 30, 43, 76. **Meals served** 11am-11pm daily. **Average** $5. **Credit** MC, V. **Map D2**
'Wraps' are rolled-up bundles similar to Mexican burritos, although here they're filled with ingredients from all over the world. This takeaway place serves them filled with grilled Thai chicken and peanut sauce, salmon with mango and rice and other unusual variations, in spinach or flour tortillas. Wraps are cheap and filling enough for a complete meal; they're the best thing to hit San Francisco since the Italians imported coffee. Complete your meal with a smoothie.
Branch: 2227 Polk Street, between Green and Vallejo Streets (931 9727).
Disabled: toilet.

Zinzino
2355 Chestnut Street, between Scott and Divisadero Streets (346 6623). Bus 28, 30, 43, 76. **Dinner served** 6-9.30pm Mon; 6-10pm Tue-Thur; 5.30-11pm Fri, Sat; 4-9.30pm Sun. **Average** $17. **Credit** AmEx, MC, V. **Map D2**
Only a block from Lombard Street, with its numerous hotels, this long restaurant serves Italian food with Californian flair. Eat at the counter in front of the open kitchen or on the outdoor heated patio. Try the lobster with potatoes and caviar; steak is also a winner.
Disabled: toilet.

Fort Mason

Greens
Building A, Fort Mason Center, Marina Boulevard at Buchanan Street (771 6222). Bus 28. **Brunch served** 10am-2pm Sun. **Lunch served** 11.30am-2pm Tue-Fri; 11.30am-2.30pm Sat. **Dinner served** 5.30-9pm Mon-Fri; 6-9pm Sat. **Average** lunch $20, dinner $35. **Credit** DC, MC, V. **Map E1**
With an incredible view of the Golden Gate Bridge and an award-winning vegetarian menu, Greens, despite its dated burlwood interior and Prozac-laden service, keeps its reputation sterling. Fresh produce and an extensive wine list complement mesquite-grilled vegetables or wood-fired pizzas topped with wild mushrooms. Pastas, flans and salads are likewise veggie-laden. Greens makes a good stopping-off place between Fisherman's Wharf and the Fort Mason Center; take advantage of their takeaway counter for sandwiches and soups if you don't want to brave the queue.

Fisherman's Wharf

Alioto's
8 Fisherman's Wharf, at Taylor Street (673 0183). Bus 32, 39, 42/cable car Powell-Mason. **Lunch served** 11am-4pm, **dinner served** 4-11pm, daily. **Average** lunch $14, dinner $25. **Credit** AmEx, DC, Disc, MC, V.

Best of Japantown

Isobune Sushi
Restaurant Mall, Kinetsu Building, 1737 Post Street at Webster Street (563 1030). Bus 2, 3, 4, 28, 32. **Meals served** 11.30am-10pm daily. **Average** $15. **Credit** JCB, MC, V. **Map E4**
Located in Japantown across the walkway from Mifune, this restaurant is a fun place for sushi. Orders are delivered on wooden boats, which circle in a waterway around a long oval sushi bar. When your ship comes in, take the little plates from the boats. You'll be charged for the size and number of plates you take.

Isuzu
1581 Webster Street, at Post Street (922 2290). Bus 2, 3, 4, 22, 38. **Lunch served** 11.30am-2pm Mon-Fri. **Dinner served** 5-10pm Mon-Fri; noon-10pm Sat; 4-10pm Sun. **Average** lunch $7, dinner $12. **Credit** DC, MC, V. **Map E4**
Sushi and tempura and much more, dished up in an atmosphere that really is Japanese family-style. Ask the helpful staff for their recommendations.
Disabled: toilet.

Mifune
Japan Center, 1737 Post Street, between Webster and Buchanan Streets (922 0337). Bus 2, 3, 4, 22, 38. **Meals served** 11am-9pm daily. **Average** $7. **Credit** AmEx, DC, Disc, JCB, MC, V. **Map E4**
Noodles prepared in at least 30 different ways come quickly, inexpensively and deliciously to your table. A good place to take kids and also great for vegetarians who can get their protein from seaweed, egg or miso.

Neecha Thai Cuisine
2100 Sutter Street, at Steiner Street (922 9419). Bus 2, 3, 4, 22, 38. **Lunch served** 11am-3pm Mon-Fri. **Dinner served** 5-10pm daily. **Average** lunch $6, dinner $12. **Credit** AmEx, MC, V. **Map E4**
A Thai interloper in Japantown, the highlights of this neighbourhood restaurant are good salads, appetisers and noodle dishes at remarkably low prices.
Disabled: toilet.

Sanppo
1702 Post Street, opposite Japan Center, at Buchanan Street (346 3486). Bus 2, 3, 4, 22, 38. **Meals served** 11.30am-10pm Mon-Thur; 11.30am-10.30pm Fri, Sat; 11.30am-9.30pm Sun. **Average** lunch $7, dinner $10. **Credit** MC, V. **Map E4**
For over 20 years, this small, casual restaurant has been turning out consistently good, rustic food – soups, lightly battered tempuras, fresh fish and East-West salads – all at the right price.

Seoul Garden
22 Peace Plaza, Japantown (563 7664). Bus 2, 3, 4, 22, 38. **Meals served** 10.30am-10.30pm daily. **Average** $12. **Credit** AmEx, DC, MC, V. **Map E4**
Grill the marinated beef at your table and try all the little dishes that typically make up Korean cuisine. A good place to remember when all the Japanese restaurants in Japantown are packed.
Disabled: toilet.

Owned by a prominent San Francisco family, Alioto's has an amazing view of the Bay, if you're prepared to fight your way through the crowds of Fisherman's Wharf to get to it. The kitchen turns out fine – but expensive – seafood prepared any way you want and there are Sicilian specialities for those who don't want to eat seafood. The wine list is outstanding.

Franciscan Restaurant
Pier 43½, Embarcadero (362 7733). Bus 15, 32, 39, 42/ cable car Powell-Mason. **Lunch served** 11.30am-4pm daily. **Dinner served** 4-10pm Mon-Thur, Sun; 4-10.30pm Fri, Sat. **Average** lunch $30, dinner $45. **Credit** AmEx, DC, MC, V. **Map G1**
The décor has been renovated and the menu updated, but the Franciscan's requisite dishes – classic Dungeness crab with lemon mayonnaise, cioppino, prawns, sea scallops, clams and fresh fish – have remained to please the tourists. Every seat in the house has an expansive view of either North Beach or the Bay, while the café downstairs has outdoor seating. Your best bet in this touristy area.
Disabled: toilet.

The Embarcadero

Fog City Diner
1300 Battery Street, at Embarcadero (982 2000). Bus 32, 42. **Meals served** 11.30am-11.30pm Mon-Thur, Sun; noon-11.30pm Fri, Sat. **Average** $25. **Credit** DC, Disc, MC, V. **Map H2**
Business boomed when Visa decided to include this all-American/Californian retro diner in a commercial. Best bets are the small plates – Hong Kong noodle salad, three small crab cakes, mu shu pork burritos, or the salmon BLT – and desserts. While the main courses tend to be more globally influenced, desserts are typically American (try the root beer float). Go for lunch.
Disabled: toilet.

Il Fornaio
Levi Plaza, 1265 Battery Street, at Union Street (986 0100). Bus 12, 42, 76. **Breakfast served** 7.30-10.30am, **lunch served** 11.30am-3.30pm, Mon-Sat. **Dinner served** 5.30-11pm Mon-Thur, Sun; 5.30pm-midnight Fri, Sat. **Brunch served** 9am-2pm Sun. **Average** lunch $23, dinner $45. **Credit** AmEx, DC, MC, V. **Map H2**
Fornaio means baker in Italian and the ciabatta here is award-winning. But while the breads are sold in gourmet groceries throughout the state, it's the excellent and reasonably-priced Italian cooking that's the draw at this branch of a successful Californian chain. There are homemade pastas, creamy polenta and just about anything roasted – chicken, veal chops, steak. It's popular with local ad agency types.
Disabled: toilet.

Long Life
139 Steuart Street, between Mission and Howard Streets (281 3818). BART Embarcadero/Muni Metro F, J, K, L, M, N/bus 1, 2, 6, 7, 9, 14, 21, 31, 32, 66, 71. **Lunch served** 11.30am-5pm Mon-Thur, Sun; 5-11pm Fri, Sat. **Average** lunch $9, dinner $12. **Credit** MC, V. **Map J3**
This is an anglicised version of the noodle shops that nourish all of Asia. Noodle salads, soups, jooks (porridge), rice

dishes, fried noodles and popiahs (wraps) fill the menu, and also appear in dishes such as pad Thai, Shanghai-style crispy spring rolls with barbecue pork and cabbage, and Ghengis buns – one of the token dishes from China. A seat at the bar gives you a view of the chefs in action. Unlike in Asia, however, most dishes will set you back around $10. *Disabled: toilet.*

Pastis

1015 Battery Street, between Union and Green Streets (391 2555). Bus 42. **Lunch served** 11.30am-3pm Mon-Fri. **Dinner served** 5.30-10.30pm Mon-Sat. **Average** lunch $25, dinner $50. **Credit** AmEx, MC, V. **Map H2**
While the aniseed-flavoured pastis is found all over France, the food at chef Gerald Hirigoyen's place is from his native Basque country. Favourites are bouillabaisse with a hint of saffron, the artichoke, tomato and fennel salad, and grilled chicken with a caramelised orange sauce. Desserts, such as the purple basil ice-cream, are creative and delicious. *Disabled: toilet.*

Pacific Heights

Betelnut

2030 Union Street, between Webster and Buchanan Streets (929 8855). Bus 22, 41, 45. **Meals served** 11.30am-11pm Mon-Thur, Sun; 11am-midnight Fri, Sat. **Average** $20. **Credit** DC, MC, V. **Map E2**
With all the authentic Chinese restaurants San Francisco has to offer, it's a bit of a surprise that the formula of 'Asian' cooking – paired here with beer, wine and Californian influences – is such a success. This place is packed with the young, single professionals who live in the neighbourhood, so booking ahead is a good idea. Once you're in, try the pork and shrimp dumplings or glazed pork ribs with Thai basil and garlic sauce. *Disabled: toilet.*

Elite Cafe

2049 Fillmore Street, at California Street (346 8668). Bus 1, 3, 22. **Lunch served** 11am-2.30pm Sat. **Dinner served** 5-11pm daily. **Brunch served** 10am-3pm Sun. **Average** brunch/lunch $12, dinner $25. **Credit** AmEx, DC, Disc, MC, V. **Map E3**
One of the few Cajun-inspired restaurants in the city, the Elite offers real gumbo, a stew made with celery, carrots, onions, sausage and crawdads from New Orleans. All the dishes have a pronounced Louisiana accent, except the sourdough bread and those from the oyster bar. There's a great Cajun brunch as well, complete with most un-Cajun Bloody Marys. *Disabled: toilet.*

Oritalia

1915 Fillmore Street, between Pine and Bush Streets (346 1333). Bus 1, 3, 22, 24. **Meals served** 5-10.30pm Mon-Thur, Sun; 5-11pm Fri, Sat. **Average** $30. **Credit** AmEx, DC, MC, V. **Map E4**
Oritalia features flavours from the Orient and Italy – hence its name. Poached chicken is turned into a healthy spring roll with avocado and a tamarind peanut sauce; boneless quails with potato and gorgonzola gratin share menu space with tuna tartare marinated in soy sauce served with wasabi and Asian pears atop a rice cake. The food helps you forget the dose of attitude you encounter when you walk through the door. *Disabled: toilet.*

Plump Jack Cafe

3127 Fillmore Street, between Greenwich and Filbert Streets (563 4755). Bus 22, 28, 41, 43, 45, 76. **Lunch served** 11.30am-2pm Mon-Fri. **Dinner served** 5.30-10.30pm Mon-Sat. **Average** lunch $35, dinner $50. **Credit** AmEx, MC, V. **Map E2**
When this tiny restaurant opened in the 'Bermuda Triangle'

(a zone of singles bars), it was a glorious sight to see the limos of old money pouring into the place. Owner Gavin Newsome is a local society brat-turned-Supervisor, his partner the son of railroad magnate Gordon Getty, and his eaterie a centrepiece for outstanding California-French cuisine incorporating the season's freshest ingredients. An inexpensive wine list indicates the restaurant's affiliation with Plump Jack Wines down the street. Chef Maria Helm understands the neighbourhood and the clientele, but doesn't sacrifice her standards, preparing dishes from burgers to thyme-roasted rabbit with shallots, morels and braised greens. Service is exceptional. *Disabled: toilet.*

Pane e Vino

3011 Steiner Street, at Union Street (346 2111). Bus 22, 41, 45. **Lunch served** 11.30am-2.30pm Mon-Sat. **Dinner served** 5-10pm Mon-Thur, Sun; 5-10.30pm Fri, Sat. **Average** lunch $20, dinner $30. **Credit** AmEx, MC, V. **Map E2/3**
This small Italian trattoria, filled with friendly waiters and a Pacific Heights clientele, has good, authentic food. Lightly sauced pasta dishes are excellent, especially the fusilli with eggplant and sausage, as are other simple dishes like the striped bass grilled with fennel. The wine list is mostly Italian. Booking is advised. *Disabled: toilet.*

Vivande Porta Via

2125 Fillmore Street, between Sacramento and California Streets (346 4430). Bus 1, 3, 22, 24. **Lunch served** 11.30am-5pm, **dinner served** 5-10pm, daily. **Average** lunch $12, dinner $30. **Credit** AmEx, DC, Disc, JCB, MC, V. **Map E3**
From the outside, Vivande looks like as if it sells cookbooks and Italian plates. Inside, however, a long deli counter filled with takeaway items encloses a tightly packed dining area. Renowned chef Carlo Middione serves authentic Italian grub with a Sicilian accent. Make sure you leave room for his luscious, light desserts. On your way out, you can stock up on fundamentals like balsamic vinegar and olive oil. *Disabled: toilet.*

Yoshida Ya

2909 Webster Street, at Union Street (346 3431). Bus 22, 41, 45. **Lunch served** 11.30am-2pm Mon-Fri. **Dinner served** 5-10.30pm Mon-Thur, Sun; 5-11pm Fri, Sat. **Average** lunch $9, dinner $22. **Credit** AmEx, Disc, DC, JCB, MC, V. **Map E2**
This quiet restaurant has some of the best Japanese food in San Francisco. An extensive sushi list complements teriyakis and yakatoris, and a coastal touch prevails in the California roll with crab and avocado and the salmon teriyaki. There's a tatami room upstairs for the full, authentic experience. *Disabled: toilet.*

Hayes Valley

Carta

1772 Market Street, at Gough Street (863 3516). Muni Metro F, J, K, L, M, N/bus 6, 7, 66, 71. **Brunch served** 10am-3pm Sun. **Lunch served** noon-3pm Tue-Fri. **Dinner served** 5.30-11pm Tue-Sun. **Average** lunch $9, dinner $20. **Credit** AmEx, DC, MC, V. **Map F5**
Every month, this small but airy restaurant features a different cuisine from around the world. A focus on the Pacific Islands offers a shrimp and coconut ceviche from Guam, and gado gado, the Indonesian vegetable dish topped with peanut sauce. From the American heartland, there are cornmeal-dusted onion rings, pan-fried red trout with bacon and mint, or three-cheese macaroni. Phone to find out what region they're currently featuring.

Suppenküche

601 Hayes Street, at Laguna Street (252 9289). Bus 21.
Dinner served 5-10pm daily. **Brunch served** 10am-3pm Sat, Sun. **Average** brunch $9, dinner $33. **Credit** AmEx, MC, V. **Map F5**
A respite from California cuisine, dishes here are authentically German – spätzle, schnitzels and dense, dark breads. The fresh Californian ingredients can seduce a person into a love affair with sauerkraut, and then commit to a relationship with sweetbreads, hearty salads and homemade soups. There are beers from Germany, served in tall steins, and seating is on benches at bare pine tables.

Zuni Café

1658 Market Street, between Franklin and Gough Streets (552 2522). Muni Metro F, J, K, L, M, N/bus 6, 22, 47, 49, 66, 71. **Lunch served** 11.30am-3pm, **late lunch served** 3-6pm, **dinner served** 6pm-midnight, Tue-Sun. **Average** lunch $25, dinner $35. **Credit** AmEx, MC, V. **Map F5**
A quintessential San Francisco experience, Zuni serves Cal-Ital food round the clock in bustling surroundings. The choice of dishes is minimal but the freshest ingredients imaginable make them memorable. For some, sourdough bread and oysters served on an iced platter is enough; others can investigate the more substantial dishes cooked in a wood-fired oven. The plate-glass windows overlooking Market Street make the place great for watching the world go by.
Disabled: toilet.

Richmond

Alain Rondelli

126 Clement Street, between Second and Third Avenues (387 0408). Bus 1, 2, 4, 33, 38. **Dinner served** 5.30-10pm Tue-Thur, Sun; 5.30 10.30pm Fri, Sat. **Average** $40. **Credit** MC, V. **Map B4**
This small restaurant has an immense following, so booking in advance is always advised. Elegant surroundings complement the beautifully presented and deliciously

prepared French cuisine. Witty renditions include the egg and caviar combo – a homemade onion bagel topped with an egg, sauce Soubise and Ossetra caviar. Tasting menus ($52, $72, $92) are available in the early evening.
Disabled: toilet.

Brothers Restaurant

4128 Geary Boulevard, between Fifth and Sixth Avenues (387 7991). Bus 38. **Meals served** 11am-3am daily. **Average** $15. **Credit** MC, V. **Map B4**
It seems like all the Korean restaurants in San Francisco are owned by Brothers, and even Koreans can't agree which one is better. They all look the same, but this one serves better food than most. Order the bulgogi (marinated beef), chap chae (vermicelli with beef, spinach and mushrooms) or bi bim bop (vegetables, a fried egg and beef on rice; there's also a vegetarian version). Don't miss the kimchee – pickled cabbage in a light, hot pepper sauce, served in one of the many small dishes that come with the main courses.
Disabled: toilet.

Kabuto

5116 Geary Boulevard, between 15th and 16th Avenues (752 5652). Bus 28, 38. **Dinner served** 5.30-11pm Tue-Sat. **Average** $25. **Credit** MC, V. **Map A4**
San Francisco restaurateurs have been spotted at this tiny sushi place, so you know the fish must be fresh. There's always a wait, especially for a seat at the bar, where the chefs put on a show.

Khan Toke

5937 Geary Boulevard, between 23rd and 24th Avenues (668 6654). Bus 29, 31, 38. **Dinner served** 5-10pm daily. **Average** $6-$11. **Credit** AmEx, MC, V.
Remove your shoes and take a seat on the floor (on a chair with a padded back support) in one of the larger Thai restaurants in the city. Fiery and colourful curries and excellent noodle dishes are accompanied by a good selection of Sauvignon Blancs and Gewürztraminers.
Disabled: toilet.

Suppenküche – *for superb schnitzels and sauerkraut.*

Bay Area dining

If you're heading out of the city, there are some first-class restaurants to enjoy in the East Bay, among them the famous **Chez Panisse** in Berkeley, where chef/owner Alice Waters created 'California cuisine' back in the 1970s. It is still the Bay Area mecca for food-lovers; the main dining room downstairs serves an pricey prix-fixe menu but you can eat similar food for less in the first-floor café. Ingredients are of the very best, and the excellent wine list is French and Californian. Expect to pay $50 for dinner in the restaurant.

Chef Paul Bertoli, formerly of Chez Pannise, has brought its savvy and reputation to his first-floor Mediterranean restaurant, **Oliveto**. Dinner costs around $35 a head; lunch is cheaper. Also in Berkeley, **Rivoli** is a small, French-inspired restaurant run by talented chef Wendy Brucker. Menu favourites include the starter of fried mushrooms with a dipping sauce and the oven-braised lamb shanks (when available). It's only open for dinner and costs about $30 a head.

In Oakland, the 21 year-old **Bay Wolf** serves Mediterranean food using the freshest produce available. Try the pan-fried soft-shell crabs served with roasted new potatoes, string beans and a streak of crème fraîche, followed by crème brûlée refreshed with a dose of mint. Lunch costs about $15, dinner double that.

Once a saloon, the lovingly restored **Townhouse Bar & Grill** in Emeryville has an eclectic Californian menu and the best outdoor dining (and weather, to boot) in the East Bay. Fish specials, served with garlic mashed potatoes and green beans, are simply delicious. The garlic fries are famous and addictive.

Bay Wolf 3853 Piedmont Avenue, opposite Rio Vista Avenue, Oakland (1-510 655 6004). BART Rockridge.
Chez Panisse 1517 Shattuck Avenue, at Cedar Street, Berkeley (1-510 548 5525). BART Berkeley.
Oliveto 5655 College Avenue, at Shafter Avenue, Berkeley (1-510 547 5356). BART Rockridge.
Rivoli 1539 Solano Avenue, at Neilson and Peralta Street, Berkeley (1-510 526 2542). BART Berkeley or El Cerrito, then AC Transit bus 67.
Townhouse Bar & Grill 5862 Doyle Street, at Powell Street, Emeryville (1-510 652 6151). BART Ashby, then AC Transit bus 6.

Laghi

1801 Clement Street, at 19th Avenue (386 6266). Bus 1, 2, 38. **Dinner served** 5-9.30pm Tue-Sun. **Average** $25. **Credit** AmEx, DC, MC, V.
Map A4
This is authentic, rustic Italian cooking, like you'd find in a trattoria in Emilia Romagna, the remote region from which Laghi's food comes. Run by a husband-and-wife team, it's a tiny neighbourhood restaurant which offers a brief and Italian-flavoured wine list, homemade pasta (cornmeal, calamari ink and eggless) with rich sauces, some unusual dishes such as poussin with grappa and good basics such as lamb or risotto with sausage.

Mayflower

6255 Geary Boulevard, at 27th Avenue (387 8338). Bus 28, 38. **Lunch served** 11am-2.30pm Mon-Fri; 10am-2.30pm Sat, Sun. **Dinner served** 5-9.30pm daily. **Average** $18. **Credit** MC, V.
This family Cantonese restaurant is consistently good. Seafood is a speciality, but they never disappoint with the clay pot dishes, roast chicken or duck. The best time to go is after 8pm when the hordes of families have left.
Disabled: toilet.

Socca

5800 Geary Boulevard, at 22nd Avenue (379 6720). Bus 31, 38. **Dinner served** 5.30-9.30pm Mon-Thur; 5.30-10pm Fri, Sat. **Average** $30. **Credit** AmEx, Disc, V.
In a neighbourhood dominated by Russian delis and Chinese restaurants, Socca's Mediterranean slant seems out of place. But the clean food, fresh produce, well-rounded wine list and reasonable prices are the draw: the $19 prix-fixe dinner might include duck confit, grilled quail salad with grapefruit and a balsamic glaze, or warm niçoise vegetable cake with a white bean and fennel salad.

Ton Kiang

5821 Geary Boulevard, between 22nd and 23rd Avenues (387 8273). Bus 29, 38. **Meals served** 10.30am-10pm Mon-Fri; 10am-10.30pm Sat, Sun. **Average** lunch $10, dinner $16. **Credit** AmEx, MC, V.
This restaurant serves hakka, Chinese gypsy cuisine, as well as some of the best dim sum outside Chinatown. Carts roll by your table laden with dumplings filled with vegetables, duck and chicken. Our favourites are chive, pork or shrimp. The branch doesn't serve dim sum, although the food is still top-notch. Try the salt-baked chicken served with a paste made of ground garlic and ginger.
Branch: 3148 Geary Boulevard, at Spruce Street (752 4440). *Disabled: toilet.*

Sunset

Ebisu

1283 Ninth Avenue, between Irving Street and Lincoln Way (566 1770). Muni Metro N/bus 6, 44, 66. **Lunch served** 11.30am-2pm, **dinner served** 5-10pm, Mon-Wed. **Meals served** 11.30am-midnight Thur-Sat; 11.30am-10pm Sun. **Average** lunch $12, dinner $18. **Credit** AmEx, DC, MC, V. **Map B6**
Considered by many locals to be the best sushi bar in town – some say the best outside Japan. As soon as you arrive, register your name on the list and have a beer while you wait for a seat. You'll soon be whooping it up with the sushi chefs as they astound you with their skill. Try the ama ebi (raw prawn): if you don't fancy the crunchy heads, try the salmon, tuna or cooked eel instead.

The House Restaurant

1269 Ninth Avenue, between Irving Street and Lincoln Way (682 3898). Muni Metro N/bus 6, 44, 66. **Lunch served** 11.30am-3pm Tue-Sun. **Dinner served** 5.30-

10pm Tue-Thur, Sun; 5.30-11pm Fri, Sat. **Average** lunch $12, dinner $25. **Credit** MC, V. **Map B6**
Chef Larry Tse is a graduate of the California Culinary Academy and runs two Houses showcasing exemplary fusion food at fantastic prices. Buttermilk calamari with chives is served with a side order of bean sprout salad; soft-shell crab comes tempura style; sea bass with a miso soy sauce is accompanied by mashed potatoes. Desserts run the gamut from exotic sorbets to flourless chocolate cake.
Disabled: toilet.
Branch: 1230 Grant Street, at Columbus Avenue (986 8612).

PJ's Oyster Bed
737 Irving Street, between Eighth and Ninth Avenues (566 7775). Muni Metro N/bus 6, 4, 66. **Lunch served** 11.30am-2.30pm, **tapas served** 2.30-5pm, daily. **Dinner served** 5-10pm Mon-Thur, Sun; 5-11pm Fri, Sat. **Average** lunch $9, dinner $15. **Credit** MC, V. **Map B6**
A noisy, friendly neighbourhood oyster bar, PJ's dishes out some of the best and most authentic Cajun food in San Francisco. Seafood selections are displayed on ice. Portions are generous and the restaurant is always packed. If you're looking for dinner on a budget, enjoy a bowl of clam chowder and a salad.
Disabled: toilet.

Raw
1224 Ninth Avenue, at Lincoln Way (665 6519). Muni Metro N/bus 44, 71. **Meals served** 11am-10pm Mon-Thur; 11am-11pm Fri, Sat; 11am-9pm Sun. **Average** $8. **Credit** AmEx, MC, V. **Map B6**
Ambient music, lots of plants and mellow folks with plenty of body piercing fill the blue room at Raw, where everything is vegetarian and nothing – that's *nothing* – is cooked. A 'burrito' is a purple cabbage leaf coated with pine nut spread, packed with crunchy vegetables and wild rice (which has been soaked for 30 days); carrot cake is made from pulp. There is 'sushi' and ice-sundaes, too. It's not for the timid, but Raw is an unmissable eaterie in a city of foodies.

Cafés

To spend time in San Francisco is to become at least partially café-nated: the city once known for having a pub on nearly every corner now sports myriad coffee houses selling a chalkboard menu of cheap eats and strong java, all served with a dash of ambience. Some cafés feature poetry readings and locally curated art; others provide the business crowd with a quick bite and a place to catch up on the financial section of the newspaper. Most establishments are of the mom-and-pop variety, tiny businesses that cater to the tastes of their neighbourhood and its residents. But more and more, unfortunately, the mighty Starbucks chain is taking over established businesses and erecting its own ubiquitous green-and-white signs. Together with Peet's Coffee & Tea, the Spinelli Coffee Company (both home-grown favourites) and downtown commuter coffee shops like Oh La! La! and Pasqua, these chains account for more than 100 outlets throughout the city.

Most of the city's cafés are fashioned as places to relax, where you can command a table for the duration of a chapter or the time it takes to reacquaint yourself with an old friend. A few, however – particularly those in the Financial District – are designed for executive lunches. If a crowd of people is staring you down during lunch hour, consider finishing your meal, uprooting yourself and returning later. In the evening hours, many coffee houses also offer beer and wine and, occasionally, a happy hour.

A French café at the gateway to Chinatown: **Café de la Presse***. See page 138.*

Armani Café

1 Grant Avenue, between O'Farrell and Market Streets (677 9010). BART Montgomery, Powell Streets/Muni Metro F, J, K, L, M, N/bus 5, 6, 7, 21, 30, 31, 38, 45, 66, 71. **Open** 10am-7pm Mon-Fri; 11am-6pm Sat; noon-6pm Sun. **Credit** AmEx, DC, Disc, JCB, MC, V. **Map G/H4**

The food is as stylishly Italian as the expensive Giorgio Armani clothes that are sold upstairs – though, thankfully, not in the same price range. There are pastas, risottos, salads and sandwiches, served for lunch only. Another plus is the outdoor seating, although the high surrounding buildings keep you in perpetual shade. *Disabled: toilet.*

Café Bastille

22 Belden Lane, between Montgomery and Kearny, Pine and Bush Streets (986 5673). Bus 2, 3, 4, 15/cable car California. **Open** 11am-10.30pm Mon-Sat. **Credit** AmEx, MC, V. **Map H3**

Francophiles and homesick Parisians flock here for pastis, steak frites, pâté with cornichons, croque monsieur (or madame) or just for the feel of an authentic café. Bastille has indoor and outdoor seating, and the staff are as genuine as the food. Belden Lane is also the venue for the city's annual Bastille Day party in July, which spills out into the nearby Financial District.

Café Claude

7 Claude Lane, between Sutter and Bush Streets, Kearny Street and Grant Avenue (392 3505). BART Montgomery Street/Muni Metro F, J, K, L, M, N/bus 2, 3, 4, 15, 30, 45, 76. **Open** 10am-9.30pm Mon-Fri; 10am-10pm Sat. **Credit** AmEx, Disc, JCB, MC, V. **Map H3**

If this place feels like an authentic Parisian bistro, that's because it is. Owner Stephen Decker bought out Le Barbizon café in France and shipped it over into this space. With dishes such as cassoulet, sandwiches, soups and mousse au chocolat – voilà – you could be in Paris. *Disabled: toilet.*

Café de la Presse

352 Grant Avenue, at Bush Street (398 2680). Bus 2, 3, 4, 15, 30, 45, 76. **Open** 7am-11pm daily. **Credit** AmEx, DC, Disc, MC, V. **Map G3**

Prices for coffee and bistro fare are slightly on the high side, but this café is authentically French. There's a variety of

Cybercafés

According to Pac Bell's recent stats, around 40 per cent of all e-mail sent and received in the world comes from or ends up in the Bay Area. You'd think 40 per cent of the world's caffeine was consumed here, too, considering the sheer volume of coffee shops and the bewildering variety of forms the drug is delivered in. So it's no surprise to find cybercafés providing the opportunity for a double fix. There are even cafés with coin-operated CafeNet terminals, which take a little time to work out but do allow general Internet access, while most Kinko's copy shops are online (*see page 260* **Office Services**), and there are also internet 'kiosks' at San Francisco International Airport and 3Com Park stadium.

A useful resource for the electronically aware traveller, *Cybercafes* ($9.95) lists more than 370 cybercafés around the world; it's available from bookshops throughout the US. Tap into the company's website at www.traveltales.com for free, web-based email and a constantly updated database of cybercafés.

The CoffeeNet

774 Harrison Street, between Third and Fourth Streets (4957447/roastmaster@coffeenet.net/www.coffeenet.net). Bus 30. **Open** 7am-6pm Mon, Tue; 7am-9pm Wed; 7am-11pm Thur-Sat; 10am-6pm Sun. **Rates** free with minimum food purchase. **Credit** Disc, MC, V. **Map H4**

Purple surfaces, modern art and a wall of intent faces greet you on entering from the little alley known as Lapulapu, off Harrison in the heart of SoMa. There are nine terminals, outside tables and the salads and sandwiches are more than decent. Staff are chirpy and eager to help.

Cyberworld Cafe

528 Folsom Street, between First and Second Streets (278669/cwordcafe@aol.com/www.cyberworldsf.com). Bus 15, 42. **Open** 6am-midnight Mon-Fri; 8am-midnight Sat; 9am-6pm Sun. **Rates** $5 per ½ hour, $10 per hour. **Credit** AmEx, MC, V. **Map H4**

Futuristic-looking Cyberworld is huge, with 10 terminals and all kinds of amenities for the fully fledged surfer: you can scan in your latest holiday snaps and send them home or video-conference with the folks in the office so you can actually see their faces when you tell them you're never coming back. The grub's pretty fancy and staff are knowledgeable.

Internet Alfredo

790A Brannan Street, at Seventh Street (437 3140/ alfredo@ina.com/www.ina.com). Bus 12, 19, 27, 42. **Open** 24 hours daily. **Rates** $2.75 per ½ hour, $7.50 per hour. **Credit** AmEx, MC, V. **Map H5**

With an impressive 18 computers and 24-hour service, online access at this quirky, first-floor cybercafé is efficient and easy. The entertainment's pretty good, too – Alfredo himself, complete with dickie-bow, hosted and commentated on the first live-on-the-web broadcast of a female kick-boxing match, and cyber drag queens regularly cavort on the café's central sofa.

Seattle Street Coffee

456 Geary Street, between Mason and Taylor Streets (415 922566/bro@traveltales.com/www.batnet.com/ q-media/sscpage.html). Muni Metro F, J, K, L, M, N/bus 38, 76/cable car Powell-Hyde or Powell-Mason. **Open** 6am-7pm Mon; 6am-midnight Tue-Fri; 7am-midnight Sat; 7am-7pm Sun. **Rates** $4 per ½ hour, $8 per hour. **No credit cards. Map G4**

This café has only one terminal and you need to know your stuff because the staff aren't all cyber-literate, but it's conveniently located a block and a half from Union Square. Walk all the way to the back to find the screen and to the counter to find fantastic coffee and hearty snacks.

foreign newspapers and magazines to read, outdoor seating, postcards – and plenty of attitude. Celebs filming in San Francisco (and there are many) tend to find their way here, as do fashion industry mavens staying at the swanky hotel next door. Once you've recharged your batteries, the entrance to Chinatown is directly across the street.
Disabled: toilet.

Civic Center

Caffe Delle Stelle

395 Hayes Street, at Gough Street (252 1110). Bus 21, 42, 47. Open 11.30am-3pm, 5.30pm-10.30pm, Mon-Sat. **Credit** AmEx, DC, MC, V. **Map F5**
With the recent closing of Ivy's across the street, Caffe Delle Stelle has grown even more popular with Hayes Valley merchants and those headed for the opera and symphony. Set in a high-visibility streetcorner lot, Stelle offers rustic Italian fare that ranges from homemade pastas (try the pumpkin manicotti) to braised meat, stews, and fine soups. Reasonable wines by the glass and creamy tiramisu round out the hand-written menu. Service can be variable, but the staff counter their lethargy with plenty of Mediterranean charm.

Get online at the **Cyberworld Cafe**.

Saigon Sandwich Café

560 Larkin Street, at Eddy Street (474 5698). Bus 19, 31. **Open** 7am-4.45pm daily. **No credit cards. Map F4**
At this friendly café just north of Civic Center, baguettes are filled with five-spice chicken or roast pork and topped with an exotic sauce of chilli, cilantro (coriander) and a sweet and sour blend.

North Beach & Russian Hill

Art Institute Café

800 Chestnut Street, at Jones Street (749 4567). Bus 30/ cable car Powell-Mason. **Open** *early Sept-mid May* 8am-9pm Mon-Thur; 8am-5pm Fri; 9am-2pm Sat; *end May-Aug* 9am-2pm Mon-Fri. **No credit cards.** **Map F2**
The advantages of this place are multiple: a view of the Bay, shows of students' work-in-progress, the Diego Rivera mural on the way in – and it's rarely busy. For your money, you'll get medium-quality but filling food (this is a student café, after all), plenty of strong coffee and interesting talk about art. The opening hours are restricted during the summer.
Disabled: toilet.

Caffè Freddy's

901 Columbus Avenue, at Lombard Street (922 0151). Bus 15, 30, 39/cable car Powell-Mason. **Open** 11.30am-9.30pm Tue; 11.30am-10pm Wed-Fri; 10am-10pm Sat; 10am-9pm Sun. **Credit** AmEx, MC, V. **Map G2**
Conveniently located on the Powell-Mason cable car line, this spot serves cheap, creative pizzas, salads and sandwiches.
Disabled: toilet.

Caffè Greco

423 Columbus Avenue, between Green and Vallejo Streets (397 6261). Bus 15, 30, 39, 41, 45. **Open** 7am-midnight daily. **No credit cards. Map G2**
Despite the plethora of surrounding cafés, Caffè Greco stands out, its large sliding windows beckoning you to rest your weary feet, sip a cappuccino or indulge in some creamy tiramisu. If you want something more substantial, try the focaccia sandwiches or Italian antipasti. The crowd is mixed – Grecos, Italianos, Americanos – and the coffee consistently good.

Caffè Trieste

601 Vallejo Street, at Grant Avenue (392 6739). Bus 12, 15, 30, 41, 45, 83. **Open** 6.30am-11pm Mon-Thur, Sun; 6.30am-midnight Fri, Sat. **No credit cards.** **Map G2**
A North Beach holdover from the Beat era, this was the espresso bar of choice for Jack Kerouac and Allen Ginsberg – it's within walking distance of the famous City Lights bookstore. The dark walls are plastered with photos of opera singers and other famous Trieste regulars. There are muffins, pastries and sandwiches to eat and the lattes are wonderfully potent.
Disabled: toilet.

Mario's Bohemian Cigar Store

566 Columbus Avenue, at Union Street (362 0536). Bus 15, 30, 39, 41, 45/cable car Powell-Mason. **Open** 10am-midnight Mon-Sat; 10am-11pm Sun. **No credit cards. Map G2**
If you can get a seat, this corner-store café is a great place for a break during the day. Located across Union Street from Washington Square Park, Mario's offers a light menu of sandwiches made with focaccia (this is Italian North Beach, after all), salad, coffee, pizzas and beer. Keep an eye out for Francis Ford Coppola, who's rumoured to frequent the place during the week. Despite the name, cigars are banned.
Branch: 2209 Polk Street, between Vallejo and Green Streets (776 8226).

No cigars, but plenty of bohemians at **Mario's**. See page 139.

Savoy Tivoli

*1434 Grant Avenue, between Union and Green Streets
(362 7023). Bus 15, 30, 39, 41, 45.* **Open** 5pm-2am
Mon-Sat. **No credit cards. Map G2**
Nearly every twentysomething goes through a brief Savoy
Tivoli phase when they first hit town: it's *the* place to pick
up (or get picked up by) the (straight) person of your choice.
A continental-style, open-air café, it's also a great place to
drink imported beers and shoot pool. Not surprisingly, it's a
bun-fight on weekend nights.

Steps of Rome

*348 Columbus Avenue, between Green and Vallejo
Streets (397 0435). Bus 12, 15, 30, 41, 45, 83/
cable car Powell-Mason.* **Open** 8am-2am Mon-Thur, Sun;
8am-3am Fri, Sat. **No credit cards.**
Map G2
The huge windows are usually open, providing the best seats
in North Beach for people-watching. Ideal for a caffeine break
and a quick bite, or best of all, some dessert.
Disabled: toilet.

SoMa & the Mission

Brainwash

*1122 Folsom Street, between Seventh and Eighth
Streets (café 861 3663/laundromat 431 9274).
Bus 12, 27, 42.* **Open** 7.30am-midnight Mon-Thur,
Sun; 7.30am-1am Fri, Sat. **Credit** AmEx, DC, MC, V.
Map G5
A San Franciscan institution, this is the city's original
laundrette-cum-café. The simple menu ranges from soups,
salads and burgers to sandwiches and specials, all well
done. There's also beer, wine and coffee, all served in a
funky and friendly environment that's equal parts SoMa
industrial chic and post-apocalyptic amusement park. If
you're heading for the Folsom Street Fair (*see chapter* **San
Francisco by Season**), you won't find a better seat than
at Brainwash.

Café Istanbul

*525 Valencia Street, between 16th and 17th Streets (863
8854). Bus 26.* **Open** 11am-11pm Mon-Thur, Sun; 11am-
midnight Fri, Sat. **No credit cards. Map F6**
A charming Mission café right around the corner from the
Roxie cinema, Istanbul serves incredibly strong Turkish coffee. There's even a belly dancer who performs at the weekends.

Caffè Centro

*102 South Park, between Bryant and Brannan, Second
and Third Streets (882 1500). Bus 15, 30, 42, 76.*
Open 7.30am-7pm Mon-Fri; 9am-4pm Sat. **Credit** (over
$10) AmEx, MC, V. **Map H/J4**
This South Park café has large windows that open out on to
the heart of the city's so-called 'multimedia gulch'. The food
is straightforward and gratifying: focaccia sandwiches, fresh
salads with fancy lettuces, great pastries, plus coffee, tea and
a good selection of bottled juices. There is outside seating
and some nice shops nearby for window-shopping.

Caffè Museo

*151 Third Street, between Mission and Howard Streets
(357 4500). Bus 9, 12, 15, 30, 45, 76.* **Open** 10am-6pm
daily. **Credit** AmEx, DC, MC, V. **Map H4**
You don't have to visit the beautiful San Francisco Museum
of Modern Art to enjoy this café, though it does make the day
complete. Order from counter and grab a table near the huge
plate-glass windows. Food is standard café fare, but the chic
surroundings (and that stunning art book you've just purchased at the museum gift shop next door) will distract your
attention. *See also chapter* **Museums & Galleries**.
Disabled: toilet.

Radio Valencia

1199 Valencia Street, at 23rd Street (826 1199). Bus 26.
Open 5pm-midnight Mon, Tue; noon-midnight Wed-Sun.
Credit MC, V. **Castro/Mission Map Y2**
This is a great place to go if you want to linger over a cup of
coffee, hear good music and eat healthy food. Valencia has
an arty atmosphere and stays open late, seven days a week.
Disabled: toilet.

The Haight-Ashbury & the Castro

Café Echo

1409 Haight Street, at Masonic Avenue (863 2443).
Bus 6, 7, 37, 43, 66, 71. **Open** 7am-11pm daily.
No credit cards. Map D5
Talk about location: wedged between the X-Large store and Reckless Records at the epicentre of the Haight, Café Echo is one of surprisingly few cafés in the hippie and shopping enclave, but it's a good one. A big sandwich list, smoothies, drinks and specials are available from a huge chalked -up menu; fresh bagels and pastries lie under glass. The big, airy room is lined with a changing selection of local art, with quiet music, bright halogen lighting and copper-topped tables.

Cafe Flore

2298 Market Street, at Noe Street (621 8579).
Muni Metro F, K, L, M/bus 24, 35, 37.
Open 7.30am-11.30pm Mon-Thur, Sun; 7.30am-midnight Fri, Sat. **No credit cards. Map E6**
Some come to cruise and some come to watch other people cruise: a longtime Castro landmark, Cafe Flore is a great place for a cup of coffee, light snacks (the food is nothing extraordinary), sightseeing or people-watching. Its best feature is the coveted and protected outdoor patio, which is always packed.

Jammin' Java

701 Cole Street, at Waller Street (668 5282).
Muni Metro N/bus 6, 7, 37, 43. **Open** 7am-11pm daily. **No credit cards.**
Map C6
Located a block off Haight Street, this popular café offers a respite from the noisier locals in the neighbourhood, its comfortable hi-tech décor a mix of grungey and groovy. There are poetry readings, assorted newspapers to read and want ads on the bulletin board. Quiet during the day, it gets packed at night.
Branch: 1398 Judah Street, at Ninth Avenue (566 5282).

Noe Valley

Chloe's Café

1399 Church Street, at 26th Street (648 4116). Muni Metro J. **Open** 8am-3pm Mon-Fri; 8am-4pm Sat, Sun. **No credit cards.**
Chloe's serves great brunch on Saturdays and Sundays and is always packed. It's popular with women and local Noe Valley residents.

The Embarcadero

Cafe de Stijl

1 Union Street, at Front Street (291 0808). Bus 32, 42. **Open** 7am-5pm Mon-Wed; 7am-11pm Thur, Fri; 7am-3.30pm Sat. **No credit cards.**
Map G2
Easy parking, sidewalk seating and hearty food make this a great place for coffee, a quick bite or a lingering afternoon in the sun. Many dishes have a Middle Eastern accent – such as the chicken sandwich with tahini sauce, the Middle Eastern platter complete with kibbeh (ground lamb patty), baba ganoush (aubergine purée) and tabouleh (bulghur with mint, tomatoes and cucumbers) – but there are also 'Californian' offerings such as Caesar salad, Italian turkey sandwich with pesto and roasted peppers, and various pastries.
Disabled: toilet.

Pacific Heights & the Western Addition

Café Abir

1300 Fulton Street, at Divisadero Street (567 7654). Bus 5, 24. **Open** 6am-12.30am daily. **Credit** MC, V. **Map D5**
With an in-house international newsstand, great music, friendly staff and a wide variety of cheap nibbles, Café Abir is perfect student hang-out. From here you can walk to Golden Gate Park, Alamo Square, USF or the Haight. After sinking into a comfortable chair to soak up the sun, you might end up staying all day. Dogs outnumber locals at the weekend.

Food Inc

2800 California Street, at Divisadero Street (928 3728).
Bus 1, 4, 24. **Open** 9am-9pm Mon-Sat; 9am-3pm Sun.
Credit AmEx, MC, V. **Map D3/4**
The service is inconsistent, but the food is generally good at this relative newcomer. For breakfast, the waffles with fruit are a real winner. For lunch or dinner the small pizzas, sandwiches, salads, and a changing list of pastas and specials are worth investigating. Eat inside or out.

The Marina

Bugatti's Espresso Cafe

3001 Webster Street, at Filbert Street (922 4888).
Bus 22, 41, 45. **Open** 7am-6pm Mon-Fri; 7.30am-6pm Sat, Sun. **Credit** MC, V. **Map E2**
This café is in a residential area but it's just a few blocks from Union Street, one of San Francisco's best streets for strolling or shopping. Bugatti's serves real Italian coffee alongside a brief café menu. There's outdoor seating, where you can take advantage of the area's perpetually pleasant weather.

The Grove Cafe

2250 Chestnut Street, at Avila Street (474 4843).
Bus 28, 30, 43, 76. **Open** 8am-11pm Mon-Thur, Sun; 8am-midnight Fri, Sat. **Credit** AmEx, MC, V. **Map D2**
It looks like a fraternity house filled with sweatshirt-sporting alma mater, but the Grove is the most happening spot in the Marina, late into the night. The feel is of a Vermont cabin, and there are board games if you choose to loiter. The coffee, sandwiches, salads and pastries are decent. There's also beer and wine and plenty of hearty company.

Rose's Cafe

2298 Union Street, at Steiner Street (775 2200). Bus 22, 41, 45. **Open** 7am-10pm Mon-Thur; 7am-11pm Fri; 8am-11pm Sat; 8am-10pm Sun. **Credit** AmEx, MC, V. **Map E2/3**
After a day of strolling and shopping on Union Street, end up at this attractive and sunny café – a mini-version of celebrity chef Reed Hearon's Italian restaurant Rose Pistola in North Beach (*see p123*). Fortunately, the prices (especially for the quality of food) are easy on the wallet. There are focaccia sandwiches, salads with balsamic vinaigrette, pizzas and more substantial dinner specials. Try the tuna sandwich, made with fresh yellow fin.

Sunset

Java Beach Cafe

1396 La Playa Boulevard, at Judah Street (665 5282).
Muni Metro N/bus 18. **Open** 6am-11pm Mon-Fri; 7am-11pm Sat, Sun. **No credit cards.**
Java Beach is a hangout for surfers, cyclists and passers-by on their way to the oceanfront. With a basic sandwich and pastry menu, it's both funky and civilised and – because of its wetsuit-wearing clientele – unlike most other cafés in San Francisco.

Bars

Drink deep from a thirst-quenching range of lounges, dives, brewpubs, neighbourhood hangouts or swanky cocktail bars.

Tirelessly working to maintain its reputation as a cosmopolitan city, San Francisco beckons with an impressive repertoire of watering holes. These fall into several rough categories: there are pubs and brewpubs (named for their onsite brewing) which feature a wide range of beers on tap and generally a limited menu; upscale dives, which gain points among the locals for character and longevity, though their ambience is often more important than the service, drinks or food; the omnipresent sports bar for the football, baseball or basketball fan (some San Franciscans would consider it sacrilege to miss a 49ers game); and finally, there are the historical treasures that harken back to San Francisco's more decadent era and are often attached to a fine restaurant.

A recent – and popular – addition to their ranks is the martini bar (*see page 144*), which has re-emerged as the joint of choice among the well-dressed swing and lounge set, a visible social group who can be spotted taking a respite from jitterbugging to enjoy a cigarette and a stiff drink.

Some nightclubs, such as **Club 181** in the Tenderloin and **Liquid** in the Mission (*see chapter* **Nightlife**), have thriving bar scenes as well as packed dancefloors (and there are yet more watering holes listed in *chapter* **Gay & Lesbian San Francisco**). Many of those places listed in the **Restaurants & Cafés** chapter have a bar area where you can down a cocktail before or after your meal.

Don't miss

Backflip p143
When you're feeling blue.
The Embers p147
Dark and deliciously downscale.
Lilo Lounge p146
Tiki drinks at the top of Potrero Hill.
Persian Aub ZamZam p144
Great martinis for the chosen few.
Red Room p142
When you're feeling red.
Redwood Room p142
Comfortable and classy.
Skylark p146
A touch of class in the heart of new bohemia.
Twenty Tank Brewery p146
Top notch hops in a humming 'hood.

Around Union Square

Garden Court
Sheraton Palace Hotel, 639 Market Street, at New Montgomery Street (392 8600). BART Montgomery Street/Muni Metro F, J, K, L, M, N/bus 2, 3, 4, 5, 31, 66, 71. **Open** 11.30am-2am daily. **Credit** AmEx, DC, MC, V. **Map H3**
The other Art Deco bar that gives the Redwood Room (*see below*) a run for its money, the Garden Court was built after the 1906 earthquake. It's a living history of post-Gold Rush prosperity with its glass-domed roof and dozens of crystal chandeliers.

Red Room
827 Sutter Street, between Jones and Leavenworth Streets (346 7666). Bus 2, 3, 4, 27. **Open** 5pm-2am daily. **Credit** AmEx, MC, V. **Map G3**
Voted one of San Francisco's favourites, the Red Room has a prohibitively long queue most nights to prove it. Once you're seated at the bar, you'll find the name right on the money: blacklights make the martinis glow and the handsome clientele look even better. The glamour factor extends to the bartenders, dressed in black. For the adventurous Union square who's not afraid to head for the edge.

Redwood Room
The Clift Hotel, 495 Geary Street, at Taylor Street (775 4700). Bus 27, 38. **Open** 11am-1am Mon-Thur, Sun; 11am-2am Fri, Sat. **Credit** AmEx, DC, Disc, JCB, MC, V. **Map G4**
While others may emulate old-school class, this lounge is the genuine article: a high-ceilinged 1930s Art Deco hotel lounge with city atmosphere and the scent of a long and colourful history. True to its moniker, the room's mantelpieces are carved from a single piece of redwood, the mascot of Northern California flora. Aside from some classic jazz played on the grand piano, you won't have to compete with much other noise to enjoy a quiet conversation. *Disabled: toilet.*

Top of the Mark
Mark Hopkins Hotel, 1 Nob Hill at California and Mason Streets (392 3434). Cable car Mason-Powell or California. **Open** 3pm-12.30am Mon-Sat; 4.30pm-12.30am Sun. **Admission** after 8.30pm $6 Mon-Thur, Sun; $10 Fri, Sat. **Credit** AmEx, DC, Disc, JCB, MC, V. **Map G3**
This exclusive bar was the first rooftop cocktail lounge to offer a panoramic view of the city when it opened in 1939. At the top of Nob Hill, one of San Francisco's wealthiest neighbourhoods, the Top of the Mark is still considered exclusive. If you can part with $6 to get in after 8.30pm, it's definitely worth it for the extravagant view.

Civic Center & the Tenderloin

Beer Ness
1624 California Street, at Polk Street (474 6968). Bus 1, 19, 42, 47/cable car California. **Open** 2pm-2am daily. **Credit** AmEx, MC, V. **Map F3**

Out of town

If you're heading out of the city, you'll find some great bars to while away a few hours. Two favourite student hangouts in the East Bay are **Blake's** (*see chapter* **Music**) and **Jupiter**. One of the hippest record stores in Berkeley, Mod Lang, holds occasional appearances by rock musicians at Jupiter, and Berkeley band Papa's Culture plays weekly gigs.

North of the Golden Gate Bridge, the family-friendly **Marin Brewing Company**, set inside Larkspur's ultra-civilised shopping centre, has burgers, pizza, veggie food and a patio – and the beers win medals by the bucketful. In nearby Mill Valley, **Sweetwater** is the quintessential Californian hangout, with six microbrews and a full cocktail bar. Marin County is home to many well-known rock stars and the club has developed a reputation as the venue for 'secret' shows, by everyone from Pearl Jam to Bob Weir's band Rat Dog Revue.

If you're heading south from the city down Highway 1 (SR 1), stop in at the **Moss Beach Distillery**, an old, renovated Victorian in the town of Moss Beach, overlooking the Pacific Ocean. Most Bay Area residents have heard of the Distillery because of its resident ghosts: the TV show *Unsolved Mysteries* reported that at least one, perhaps three, apparitions live here, and employees will confirm it. If you get spooked, take a walk in the nearby Marine Reserve to bring you back to earth.

Jupiter *2181 Shattuck Avenue, Berkeley (1-510 843 8277). BART Berkeley.*
Marin Brewing Company *1809 Larkspur Landing, Larkspur (332 6600). Golden Gate Transit ferry to Larkspur.*
Moss Beach Distillery *Beachway, at Ocean Boulevard, 7 miles north of Half Moon Bay (728 5595). SR 1 south.*
Sweetwater *153 Throckmorton Avenue, Mill Valley (388 2820). US 101 north.*

Although the living-room vibe you get from the couches and fireplace might seem to signal a relaxed atmosphere, twentysomethings with an appetite for loud music dominate here. The young Hollywood set spend hours playing pool and gyrating to alt-rock sounds. Winona Ryder has been spotted dancing with her friends from Green Day.

Backflip

601 Eddy Street, at Larkin Street (771 3547). Bus 19, 31.
Open 5pm-2am daily. **Credit** AmEx, MC, V. **Map F4**
Backflip could double as Aqua Man's space-age, underwater bachelor pad. Crazy, sexy and blue, the décor is by Fun Display designers Craig Walters and Charles Doll, who were also the sartorial minds behind the Red Room (*see p142*). One wall shimmers with blue lighting, creating the illusion of sunshine reflecting from the surface above; a faux window is actually a wall of water. Down the hall from the main room and the round bar sit rows of cabanas and a strip of mirrors that lead to a dining room, where tapas and appetisers are served. In the back is a lounge room covered in white shag carpeting. With a setting this cool, who cares that the drinks aren't quite strong enough?

Hayes & Vine

377 Hayes Street, between Franklin and Gough Streets (626 5301). Bus 21, 42, 47, 49. **Open** 5pm-midnight Mon-Thur; 5pm-1am Fri, Sat. **Credit** MC, V. **Map F5**
This upscale room caters to symphony patrons as well as the well-heeled merchants and shoppers in Hayes Valley – lesbian, gay, straight or otherwise. Enjoy a glass of wine or champagne from a lengthy list (500 by the bottle, 21 by the glass) and complement it with pâté, cheeses, caviar or biscotti. It's a classy place. A word of warning, however: the panhandlers in this neighbourhood are relatively harmless, but be wary if you're leaving the bar late at night.

North Beach & Russian Hill

Hi-Ball Lounge

473 Broadway, between Kearny and Montgomery Streets (397 9464). Bus 15, 30, 41, 83. **Open** 7pm-2am Mon-Thur, Sat, Sun; 5pm-2am Fri. **Credit** MC, V. **Map H3**
Heaven for swingers who give the phrase 'to cut a rug' new depth, the Hi-Ball is a rediscovered San Francisco legend stuck between strip joints. Hep cats and urban professionals pack the narrow bar and postage stamp-sized dancefloor. When the swing band is hot, the better dancers will form what's known as 'Cat's Corner' and take turns whipping the place into a frenzy. Affordable dance lessons are held twice a week.

San Francisco Brewing Co

155 Columbus Avenue, at Pacific Avenue (434 3344/www.sfbrewing.com). Bus 12, 15, 41, 83.
Open 11.30am-1am Mon-Fri; noon-1.30am Sat, Sun.
Credit AmEx, Disc, MC, V. **Map G2**
Housed in a gorgeous turn-of-the-century saloon (once the hub of Barbary Coast nightlife), this brewpub, at the southeastern tip of North Beach, offers six draught home-brews and live music four nights a week. If you ask, staff will give you a tour of the brewery.

Spec's

12 Jack Kerouac Alley, at Broadway (421 4112). Bus 15, 41, 83. **Open** 4.30pm-2am Mon-Fri; 5pm-2am Sat, Sun.
No credit cards. Map G2
Spec's stands as the quintessential old-school San Francisco bar – smoky and noisy, packed with a variety of drinkers of all ages and consummately friendly employees. You'll hear live music at the weekends and witness an occasional heated discussion – political or literary – among friends, but you'll get the sense that Spec's will remain unchanged. From time to time, William Saroyan's San Francisco play *The Time of Your Life* gets staged here, and aptly so.

Tosca

242 Columbus Avenue, at Broadway (986 9651).
Bus 15, 30, 41, 83. **Open** 5pm-1.45am daily.
No credit cards. Map G2
San Francisco nightspots seldom boast a high concentration of celebrities (even when the celebs are in attendance, they generally get ignored). Tosca is the exception. Its old-fashioned, classy ambiance regularly draws a star-studded crowd: Bono, Mayor Willie Brown Jr, Francis Ford Coppola, Tom Waits and Sam Shepard have all been spotted among Tosca's red vinyl booths and high brass lamps. It's one of the city's oldest bars.
Disabled: toilet.

Shaken, not stirred

Martini and piano bar, **Martuni's**.

The city's cocktail scene has shifted of late, with an influx of swing dance aficionados and their well-heeled friends now giving the microbrew-pubs and cigar bars some healthy competition. Many of the joints they frequent existed long before martini-sipping was trendy; others have sprung up as a result of the craze. Vodka seems to be the poison of choice, but nearly anything can appear in a martini glass these days – try the Cosmopolitan, made with cranberry juice; the Lemon Drop, distant cousin to the Kamikaze; or the Raspberrry Drop, a recent innovation, made with raspberry liqueur. Still, nothing beats a healthy gin martini, served with a twist or spicy olive – local history in a glass. Waiter!

Bix
56 Gold Street, between Montgomery and Sansome Streets (433 6300). Bus 15, 30, 41. **Open** 11.30am-2am Mon-Fri; 5pm-2am Sat, Sun. **Credit** AmEx, DC, Disc, MC, V. **Map H2**
Combining the glamour of Harlem's 1930s Cotton Club and the splendour of a dining room on a first-class cruise liner, Bix is a bar where you might propose marriage or a business deal over a vodka martini. A jazz pianist and a singer in an evening gown provide the source music for this cinematic fantasy. With its three-storey ceilings, secretive locale on Gold Street and stunning supper-club menu, Bix is the kind of place where James Bond would take one of his double-agent lady friends, for more than just a little information. *Disabled: toilet.*

Club Deluxe
1511 Haight Street, at Ashbury Street (552 6949). Bus 6, 7, 33, 37, 43, 66, 71. **Open** 4pm-2am Mon-Fri; 3pm-2am Sat; 2pm-2am Sun. **No credit cards. Map D5/6**
Decked out with a deco motif, this classic retro bar hops, particularly at weekends, when the patrons are also dressed to the nines in sharp vintage garb. Weekdays finds it a little less serious about style (although they are always serious about their martinis and Bloody Marys). On some nights, small combos perform on a tiny stage in the east room while swing dancers take over the dancefloor. On others, the spotlit centre pedestal is occupied by the bar's owner, Jay, who does a turn as a 1930s-style crooner. Sit at a chrome stool looking on to Haight Street or belly up to the bar.

Elysium
Andora Hotel, 2434 Mission Street, between 20th and 21st Streets (282 2447). Bus 14. **Open** 5pm-2am Mon-Sat; 6pm-1am Sun. **Credit** MC, V. **Castro/Mission Map Y2**
The Elysium is decorated like a palace straight out of the *Arabian Nights*. Swingers and snappily dressed couples sip from wedge-shaped glasses as they relax in plush armchairs or gaze into the indoor fish pond. The crowd murmurs between the low sounds of Curtis Mayfield on the jukebox and the pleasant clink of glasses. A retro-chic gem.

Martuni's
4 Valencia Street, at Market Street (241 0205). Muni Metro F, J K, L, M/bus 26. **Open** 2pm-2am daily. **Credit** MC, V. **Map F5**
The back room is where it's really happening at this nouveau martini and piano bar. The piano player and his musical entourage keep the tipsy crowd swaying in their seats, while friendly, slightly harried waiters bearing trays of drinks weave through the crowd. What with the drag queens and single, middle-aged women, the tableau of humanity here is straight out of a film – John Cassavetes would have loved it.

Orbit Room
1900 Market Street, at Laguna Street (252 9525). Muni Metro F, J/bus 37. **Open** 7.30am-1am Mon-Thur, Sun; 7.30am-2am Fri, Sat. **No credit cards. Map F5**
With its hammered tin ceiling and cool fixtures, the Orbit feels timeless; a humming, friendly, neighbourhood hangout with a great jukebox and stoic, efficient bartenders. The Vespa set usually commands the outdoor tables, but there's plenty of room inside. If you don't fancy a martini, try a Lemon Drop – a lemon vodka-and-triple sec substitute served in a chilled, sugared glass. In the morning, when your hangover subsides, you can return for a top-notch espresso and a selection of pastries and bagels served during the day.

Persian Aub ZamZam
1633 Haight Street, between Clayton and Belvedere Streets (861 2545). Bus 6, 7, 33, 37, 43 66, 71. **Open** hours vary. **No credit cards. Map C6**
This place allegedly serves the best martini in the city, though few have had the honour of trying one: proprietor Bruno, a gentleman with a reputation for idiosyncratic treatment of his customers and for keeping completely random hours, tends to thwart your efforts. You may be lucky enough to catch the bar open only to be faced with the greater challenge of charming the owner into bringing out a tray of his legendary libations. He's a purist: order vodka here (or beer) and you'll find yourself out on the street.

Slow Club
2501 Mariposa Street, at Hampshire Street (241 9390). Bus 9, 27, 33. **Open** 11am-3pm Mon; 11am-11pm Tue-Fri; 6pm-midnight Sat. **Credit** MC, V. **Castro/Mission Map Z1**
Located on the border between the Mission and Potrero Hill, this converted garage sports an industrial design and plenty of business people – MSNBC, KQED (the city's public television station) and the *Bay Guardian* are all close by. The Slow is known mostly for its great meals, but also serves up mean martinis and margaritas at the back bar. While away the hours listening to early Miles Davis.

Bix: *the archetypal martini bar.*

Cafe Mars

798 Brannan Street, at Seventh Street (621 6277).
Bus 9, 42. **Open** 4pm-2am Mon-Fri; 5pm-2am Sat.
Credit AmEx, MC, V. **Map H5**
A bit of a pick-up scene this – and while the potstickers are
good, Mars isn't an overly popular bar in which to spend a
whole evening. The hip-hop tunes tend to be too loud for
conversation and while the out-of-town 'bridge-and-tunnel'
contingent is minimal, the stylish set seems to be just passing through.

Caribbean Zone

55 Natoma Street, between First and Second Streets
(541 9465). Bus 12, 15. **Open** 11.30am-2am Mon-Fri;
5pm-2am Sat. **Credit** AmEx, MC, V. **Map H4**
The corrugated tin walls of this bar under the freeway make
the Zone look like a dance hall in a Kingston shanty town.
Smack in the middle of a business district, it's in fact more
of a place where professionals let off steam ordering the
house cocktails and tropical drinks during happy hour. As
we went to press, the owners were due to re-open the defunct
DV8 nightclub next door as a retro-themed supper club,
called The Stork.

Gordon Biersch

2 Harrison Street, at Steuart Street and the
Embarcadero (243 8246). Bus, 1, 32, 41.
Open 11.30am-11pm Mon, Tue, Sun; 11am-midnight
Wed, Thur; 11.30am-1am Fri, Sat. **Credit** AmEx, DC,
MC, V. **Map J3**
When it first opened, Gordon Biersch was all the rage with
the downtown crowd, who crammed the minimalist brewpub after business hours with the hopes of getting laid. The
highly-charged atmosphere has died down a bit, and that's
a good thing. Now you can enjoy quality in-house beers, a
delectable bar menu (available until 10pm) and an unimpeded view of the Bay without worrying about the marital
status of the person next to you. Here's to conversation and
a good hamburger.

Twenty Tank Brewery

316 11th Street, between Harrison and Folsom Streets
(255 9455). Bus 12, 42. **Open** 11.30am-1.30am daily.
Credit AmEx, MC, V. **Map G5**
A noisy landmark among the wealth of nightlife options at
11th and Folsom (*see page 85* **SF By Neighbourhood**),
Twenty Tank is the kind of place that feels like home after
one visit. Stocked with more beers than any of the city's other
brewpubs, it offers a decent jukebox, shuffleboard, big tables
for large parties, a massive upstairs area, sandwiches, soups
and table service during dinner hours. The vegetarian chilli
is excellent; likewise, most of the menu. The home-brews?
The best in town.

The Attic

3336 24th Street, at Mission Street (643 3376). BART
24th Street/bus 14, 48, 76. **Open** 5pm-2am Mon-Fri, Sun;
6pm-2am Sat. **Credit** MC, V. **Castro/Mission Map Y2**
The Attic's black walls and ceiling are decorated with cast-
offs that usually end up in dark storage areas – an old tri-
cycle, boxing gloves, a rocking horse. Locals come to wind
down over a glass of wine or a pint of Anchor steam beer.
The presence of a mirror ball hints of the occasional wild
night when local DJs spin a gamut of rockin' beats.

Lilo Lounge

1469 18th Street, at Connecticut Street (643 5678).
Bus 22, 53. **Open** 5pm-12.30am Mon-Wed, Sun; 5pm-
2am Thur-Sat. **Credit** MC, V. **Map H6**
Billed as a tropical oasis in hip Potrero Hill, this lively bar has
a miniature Easter Island head watching over the proceedings
– which can get ribald pretty quick. Order the $18 Scorpion –
a concoction designed for four drinkers or one brave soldier,
which includes a 'volcano' of 151 rum – and you'll be hailing
a cab sooner than later. Thai appetisers are served in the bar.

The Rite Spot

2099 Folsom Street, at 17th Street (552 6066). Bus 12,
22, 33. **Open** 4pm-2am Mon-Thur; 2pm-2am Fri; 7pm-
2am Sat; 8pm-2am Sun. **No credit cards. Map G6**
The Rite Spot has a jazz pianist playing in the corner while
locals throw back pints of hefeweissen and assorted spirits.
With swinging doors marking the entrance and jukes that
range from old country and western to new wave, the place
has a noirish feel on a foggy night. A humble setting made
respectable by candlelight and white tablecloths, it's usually
fairly quiet, except when Friday night happy hour fills the bar.

Skylark

3089 16th Street, at Valencia Street (621 9294). BART
16th Street/bus 22, 26, 53. **Open** 4pm-2am Mon-Fri;
7pm-2am Sat, Sun. **No credit cards. Map F6**
The Skylark drives the final nail in the coffin of the grunge
bar. The sharp-dressed, fresh-eyed crowd packed in this
club are the folks who might have been drinking further
along 16th Street at notorious dive The Albion last year.
Friendly barkeeps make a mean margarita, which perfectly accompanies the Mexican food you can bring in from the
neighbourhood taquerias.

Midtown

582 Haight Street, between Steiner and Fillmore Streets
(558 8019). Bus 6, 7, 22, 66, 71. **Open** noon-2am daily.
No credit cards. Map E5

Booze & the law

All bars are subject to California's alcohol
laws: you have to be over 21 to buy and consume the stuff (take ID even if you look older),
and it can be sold between the hours of 6am
and 2am. Last orders vary between 1.15am
and 1.30am and, technically, staff are obliged
to confiscate unconsumed alcoholic drinks
after 2am.

Smokers searching for a place to light up will
be hard pressed in San Francisco: local ordi-
nances have forbidden smokers from indulging
indoors at cafés and restaurants. Bars, however, remain exempt from the health-conscious legislation of the city's Board of Supervisors – a
final refuge where one can guiltily enjoy both
liquor and tobacco.

Without a doubt, the Midtown is geared towards the beer and whisky crowd. Leather gals and guys with a penchant for Ozzy Osbourne and Alice in Chains come here for a few games of pool and a shot of Jaegermeister. While you wait for a game – a certainty if you arrive after 9pm – settle into one of the diner-style semi-circular booths.

Noc Noc
557 Haight Street, between Fillmore and Steiner Streets (861 5811). Bus 6, 7, 22, 66, 71. **Open** 5pm-2am daily. **No credit cards**. **Map E5**
An institution, and worth a trip just to check out the décor. The bar, stools and pillowed alcoves carved out of synthetic rock turn drinkers into happy troglodytes inside a dark post-modern cave. The great deals on saki and pints at happy hour make this a favourite dive.

Toronado
547 Haight Street, at Fillmore Street (863 2276). Bus 6, 7, 22, 66, 71. **Open** 11.30am-2am daily. **No credit cards**. **Map E5**
A well-stocked pub that's friendly to non-drinkers, the Toronado offers pints of home-brewed root beer and great hot ciders (both leaded and unleaded) as well as non-alcoholic beers on tap. The scene is a mix of roughnecks and young professional regulars who often show up for 'Simpsons Night', held on Sundays.

The Castro

Expansion Bar
2124 Market Street, at Church Street (863 4041). Muni Metro F, J, K, L, M/bus 22, 37. **Open** 10am-2am daily. **No credit cards**. **Map E6**
Just about the biggest 49er fans in the city own this no-frills saloon, a sports bar in the middle of a sports town. With TVs at each end of the room, it's a place for serious fans. On Saturday nights, the young city dwellers who don't want to fight the crowds at swankier joints can find the elbow room to settle in for a few games of pool or pinball.

Lucky 13
2140 Market Street, at Church Street (487 1313). Muni Metro F, J, K, L, M/bus 22, 37 **Open** 4pm-2am Mon Fri; 2pm-2am Sat, Sun. **No credit cards**. **Map E6**
'Umleitung' (detour) reads the arrow pointing to the entrance, and inside you're sure to find a gaggle of San Francisco bicycle messengers on a pitstop drinking pints of beer or cider. The dark décor and smoky atmosphere creates a grotto aura, and the patrons are on the young and hip side. *Disabled: toilet.*

Mecca
2029 Market Street, at Duboce Avenue (621 7000). Muni Metro F, J, K, L, M, N/bus 22. **Open** 5pm-1am daily. **Credit** AmEx, DC, Disc, JCB, MC, V. **Map E/F6**
Armani's best customers hold holy congregation at Mecca. Inside frosted-glass front doors, the urban warehouse look is melded successfully with baroque red velvet and chiffon drapery. A floor-to-ceiling marble column in the centre of the bar is encircled with glass trays holding dozens of grappa bottles. If this is your first trip to Mecca, the lounge area is an excellent place to get used to the finery. Once you've tried one of the $6.50 martinis, you'll understand why everyone's face seems to gleam here. *See also* **Supper Clubs** *in chapter* **Nightlife**.

The Marina & Pacific Heights

Harry's on Fillmore
2020 Fillmore Street, between Pine and California Streets (921 1000). Bus 1, 3, 22. **Open** 4pm-2am daily. **Credit** AmEx, MC, V. **Map E3**

Local socialite Harry Denton opened this bar years ago as his fledgling pub; the place became hugely popular and catapulted the ex-bartender into legendary status. It features a gorgeous walnut bar and live music several nights a week. The crowd is a mix of Pacific Heights locals, yuppies and regulars.

Horseshoe Tavern
2024 Chestnut Street, at Fillmore Street (346 1430). Bus 22, 30. **Open** 10am-2am daily. **No credit cards**. **Map E2**
More of a neighbourhood hangout than a roadside attraction, the Tavern is a friendly locals' bar for Marina residents with a penchant for pool and a strong taste for sports. It also shows vintage sports events on cable TV.

Paragon Bar & Grill
3251 Scott Street, between Chestnut and Lombard Streets (922 2456). Bus 28, 30, 43. **Open** 4pm-2am daily. **Credit** AmEx, MC, V. **Map D2**
The Paragon suffers from a dual personality. On any big-game night, you'll find sports fans camped out in front of the big screen TV, but on other nights, DJs and live bands provide musical entertainment and seem to chase off the jocks. The classy walnut long bar serves quality brews on tap, while the dining room at the back features fresh California cuisine. Unlike most Marina bars, it is (thankfully) not overloud nor a pick-up joint.

Richmond & Sunset

Cliff House
1090 Point Lobos Avenue, at the Great Highway (386 3330). Bus 18, 38. **Open** 11am-2am daily. **Credit** AmEx, MC, V.
If you like the company of the composite tourist with shutterbug tendencies and a penchant for sweet drinks, then you'll love the Cliff House. The beer on tap is Bud, there are no locals in sight and the waitresses (who don't expect to see any of their customers again) don't bother to be friendly. Still, it's a great place to come for a view of the Pacific and for the adjacent Musée Mécanique.

The Embers
627 Irving Street, between Seventh and Eighth Avenues (731 8270). Bus 6, 43, 44, 66. **Open** noon-2am daily. **No credit cards**. **Map B6**
One of the great dives of all time, The Embers is like the pub your blue-collar great-uncle loved in his working days before the war – and it hasn't changed since. Gruff bartenders, sleazy Naughahyde seats, walls that you wish could talk. Order a Fuzzy Navel and all you're likely to receive is a puzzled look.

Sinead's
3565 Geary Boulevard, at Stanyan Street (386 2600). Bus 38. **Open** 5pm-1.30am Mon-Sat; 10am-1.30am Sun. **Credit** AmEx, MC, V. **Map C4**
This upscale establishment, with its tasteful lighting and a curved, copper-plated bar, marks a new breed of outer-avenues pub. Because the city's Irish population tends to drink at the smaller, funkier neighbourhood bars or the Kezar Club (770 Stanyan Street; 386 9292) across town, the only real brogue you're likely to overhear is from the bartenders, who pour the Guinness with varying degrees of finesse.

Trad'r Sam's
6150 Geary Boulevard, at 26th Street (221 0773). Bus 29, 38. **Open** 10am-2am daily. **No credit cards**.
An unabashedly traditional tiki bar, where undergraduates bring their thirst for the kind of cocktails that can only be described as dangerous. Planters Punch, Mai Tais, Singapore Slings – there's a guaranteed hangover lurking beneath the cheesy umbrellas spinning in Sam's drinks. At the weekend, the place is as crowded as a bee hive and buzzing even louder.

Shopping & Services

Where to spend, spend, spend...

Although San Francisco has its fair share of department stores and malls, filled with the chain stores that are fast eliminating regional differences throughout the US, San Franciscans head for the neighbourhoods – each with its own character and charm – for the most rewarding shopping. Each is filled with an abundance of goodies and quirky one-off boutiques unique to each area. The following is a list of shopping districts to get you started, but there is much more within each area. Opening hours vary depending on the type of business: most shops are open from 10am to 7pm Monday to Friday, until 6pm on Saturdays and from noon until 5pm on Sundays; department stores often stay open until 9pm during the week.

Shopping Areas

Hayes Valley, a scant three blocks of Hayes Street between Laguna and Civic Center, is the most interesting and forward-looking shopping area at the moment. Each store has a different ambience and going from place to place makes the senses reel: there are trendy shoe shops, up-and-coming local designer boutiques, eclectic art galleries – all with top quality goods. Once a month there is a block party during which the shops stay open late and bars spill their punters out onto the streets. The area is rapidly expending and a number of funky antique shops have recently opened on Market Street and Gough Street.

Union Square is the premier shopping destination for the conservative consumer. Lined with department stores, this is where to find the likes of Tiffany's and Gucci. The surrounding area is packed with everything from chic boutiques to rip-off tacky tourist shops. Occasionally you might find an up-and-coming local designer's wares hidden away on Claude Lane, or a shoe shop that looks as if it should be in Hayes Valley.

Bordering Union Square, **Chinatown** is thronged with locals on their daily expeditions to the innumerable vegetable and fish markets. **Grant Avenue** is a haven for knick-knacks, medicinal herbs, export porcelain, silks, pearls and jade; here too are the restaurants, food shops and souvenir shops crowded with tourists.

Italian-American **North Beach** has the best pasta and cappuccino in the city. The smell of fresh focaccia wafts from the many restaurants and cafés. Among the shops is a diverse mix of bookstores and small clothing boutiques.

You can find Japanese language books and periodicals in the **Japan Center**, along with serene shops specialising in incense, miniature teapots for the tea ceremony, Japanese house-wares, artifacts and the Kabuki Hot Springs Japanese bath house. Great noodle and sushi restaurants abound.

Chestnut Street is the center of the Marina district's day- and nightlife. Upscale shops full of housewares, sporting goods, clothing and gifts cater to the young, health-conscious crowd that inhabit this neighbourhood. **Union Street**, four blocks south of Chestnut in Cow Hollow, is a mix of chic boutiques pitched at beautiful yuppies. Unlike Chestnut and Union, **Fillmore Street**, located in Pacific Heights has a mixture of expensive boutiques and second-hand clothing shops full of designer labels tossed aside by Pacific Heights society.

Thirty years after its heyday, **Haight Street** still pays homage to a famous past. If you're after used clothes, music, tattoos, body-piercing, tie-dye t-shirts, DMs, incense, or pot-smoking paraphernalia, then this is where you'll find it. The Haight

Tax & duty

Most shops accept travellers' cheques, but don't forget that local sales tax (currently 8.5 per cent) will be added to the price marked on anything you buy. You can avoid paying local sales tax if you live out of state and arrange for the shop to ship your purchase for you; or you can arrange shipment yourself via the US mail or a courier service *(see page 259* **Directory**). If you are taking goods out of the country, remember that you will be liable to pay duty and tax on goods worth more than a certain amount (£145 in the UK).

epitomises the Gen-X slacker lifestyle. *See* **San Francisco by Neighbourhood** for more on these and the surrounding areas.

Bookshops are found in every neighbourhood, but the highest concentration of both new and second-hand books is found on Valencia Street in the **Mission**. The stores here reflect the ethnic diversity of the area, with markets selling Mexican and South and Central American produce. You'll find an incredible selection of used furniture, as well as the best taquerias and burrito joints in town.

The **Castro** caters to trendy urban fashion-conscious residents, and most of the shopping is on Castro Street and along Market Street. Kidswear and less expensive imported goods can be found just over the hill to the south in low-key **Noe Valley**. A number of retail outlets for bargain-hunters can be found in the warehouse district South of Market, or **SoMa**.

Department Stores

Gump's
135 Post Street, between Grant Avenue and Kearny Street (984 9439). BART Montgomery Street/Muni Metro F, J, K, L, M, N/bus 2, 3, 4, 15. **Open** 10am-6pm Mon-Sat. **Credit** AmEx, MC, V. **Map H3**
Presided over by a large golden Buddha on the ground floor, the treasure chest of Old San Francisco advertises its wares as 'rare, unique and imaginative'. It's true. Gump's sells gorgeous items for the home, precious oriental wares and pearls, pearls, pearls.

Macy's
Union Square (397 3333). BART Montgomery Street/ Muni Metro F, J, K, L, M, N/bus 2, 3, 4, 38, 45, 76/cable car Powell-Mason or Powell-Hyde. **Open** 10am-8pm Mon-Sat; 11am-7pm Sun. **Credit** AmEx, JCB, MC, V. **Map G3**
Having recently taken over the former I Magnin building, Macy's now reigns as the giant of Union Square. It stocks everything under the sun under its several roofs, with prices from moderate to high. The menswear department is excellent.

Neiman Marcus
150 Stockton Street, at Geary Street (362 3900). BART Montgomery Street/Muni Metro F, J, K, L, M, N/bus 2, 3, 4, 38, 45, 76/cable car Powell-Mason or Powell-Hyde. **Open** 10am-8pm Mon, Thur, Fri; 10am-6pm Tue, Wed; 10am-7pm Sat; noon-6pm Sun. **Credit** AmEx. **Map G3/4**
Sometimes parodied as 'Needless Markup' by its detractors, this Dallas-based chain offers top-of-the-line designer clothing and a particularly well-stocked cosmetics department, including Chanel and the new Trish McEvoy line.

Nordstrom
San Francisco Shopping Center, 865 Market Street, at Fifth Street (243 8500). BART Powell Street/Muni Metro F, J, K, L, M, N/bus 6, 7, 27, 31, 66, 71/cable car Powell-Mason or Powell-Hyde. **Open** 9.30am-9pm Mon-Sat; 10am-7pm Sun. **Credit** AmEx, JCB, MC, V. **Map G4**
From its perch atop the San Francisco Center, Nordstrom continues to grow in popularity, not least because of its reputation for extremely helpful customer service. Sensible business clothing and a large shoe department are its stock in trade and it's also known for live piano music played on the baby grand in each of its stores. There are good women's leather jackets, an excellent selection of suits and loads of hats. The Personal Touch service offers a customised fashion service; ring for an appointment.

The golden Buddha of **Gump's**.

Saks Fifth Avenue
384 Post Street, at Union Square (986 4300). Muni Metro F, J, K, L, M, N/bus 2, 3, 4, 38, 45, 76/cable car Powell-Mason or Powell-Hyde. **Open** 10am-6.30pm Mon-Wed; 10am-8pm Thur, Fri; 10am-7pm Sat; noon-6pm Sun. **Credit** AmEx, Disc, MC, V. **Map G3**
A small branch of the New York store, Saks stocks more conservative designer clothing than Neiman Marcus, but has a good lingerie department and knowledgeable salespeople.

Shopping Centres

The Cannery
2801 Leavenworth Street, between Beach and Jefferson Streets (771 3112). Bus 19, 30, 32, 42/cable car Powell-Hyde or Powell-Mason. **Open** *summer* 10am-8.30pm Mon-Sat; 11am-6pm Sun; *winter* 10am-6pm daily. **Map F1**
Formerly the site of the Del Monte fruit-canning factory, this large open space is a favourite spot for buskers. Its upper levels are a warren of not particularly interesting stores. More of the same can be found at **The Anchorage** across the street, between Leavenworth and Jones Streets.

Crocker Galleria
50 Post Street, at Kearny Street (393 1505). BART Montgomery Street/Muni Metro F, J, K, L, M, N/bus 2, 4, 5, 15, 30, 38/cable car Powell-Mason. **Open** 10am-6pm Mon-Fri; 10am-5pm Sat. **Map H3**
San Francisco's most exclusive shopping centre houses European and American designers and the standard mix of brands, blended with individually owned and operated shops and a nice assortment of restaurants and cafés.

Embarcadero Center
Battery, Drum, Sacramento and Clay Streets (772 0500). BART Embarcadero/Muni Metro F, J, K, L, M, N/bus 1, 2, 7, 8, 9, 14, 21, 31, 38, 41, 42, 71/cable car California.

Open 10am-7pm Mon-Fri; 11am-6pm Sat; noon-5pm Sun.
Map H3
This shopping centre – purported to be the first of its kind
in the US – is divided into four buildings, housed on the first
and second floors of downtown office towers. Stores include
Banana Republic, The Limited, Pottery Barn, Nine West and
Liz Claiborne. Check out the delightful Embarcadero Cinema
after you're done shopping.

Fisherman's Wharf
*Jefferson Street, between Hyde and Powell Streets. Bus 15,
32, 30, 39, 42/cable car Powell-Hyde or Powell-Mason.*
Open times vary. **Map F1**
This area caters solely for tourists, so unless you're into innumerable T-shirt stalls and unscrupulous electronic shops,
steer clear.

Ghirardelli Square
*North Point, Beach, Larkin and Polk Streets (775 5500).
Bus 19, 30, 32, 42/cable car Powell-Hyde.* **Open** 10am-
9pm Mon-Sat; 10am-6pm Sun. **Map F1/2**
Home of the institutional Ghirardelli chocolate factory where
you can watch the stuff being made and consume it as you
wander through the variety of one-off, mostly souvenir-
inspired shops.

Pier 39
*Beach Street and Embarcadero (981 8030) Bus 15, 32,
42/cable car Powell-Mason.* **Open** 10.30am-
9.30pm Mon-Wed; 10.30am-10pm Thur-Sat; 10.30am-
8.30pm Sun. **Map G1**
Offers more individually owned stores. Noisy seals and wonderful views of the Bay are a bonus. Opening hours vary
with the season.

San Francisco Shopping Center
*865 Market Street, at Fifth Street (495 5656). BART
Powell Street/Muni Metro F, J, K, L, M, N/bus 6, 7, 27,
31, 66, 71/cable car Powell-Mason or Powell-Hyde.*
Open 9.30am-8pm Mon-Sat; 10am-7pm Sun. **Map G4**
Nordstrom (*see p149*) is the anchor store at the SF Shopping
Center. Most of the other shops are standard chains, includ-
ing the Body Shop, Ann Taylor, Express, J Crew, Williams
Sonoma and Z-Gallerie. Kids love the circular escalators.

Stonestown Galleria
*Winston Drive, at 19th Avenue (759 2626). Muni Metro
M/bus 17, 18, 28, 29.* **Open** 10am-9pm Mon-Sat; 11am-
6pm Sun.
Sandwiched between Nordstrom and Macy's, this outlying
shopping centre is where Sunset residents shop for those all-
too-familiar name brands.

Antiques

Butterfield & Butterfield
*220 San Bruno Avenue, at 16th Street (861 7500). Bus
9, 19, 22, 33, 53.* **Open** *office* 8.30am-5pm Mon-Fri.
No credit cards. Map G6
A San Francisco institution since 1865, B&B appraises all
collectables, but is best known for its year-round auctions
of furniture, art, antiques, silver, rugs, jewellery and wine.
Previews are held at weekends. Check across the street at
Butterfield West for lower-priced estate auctions, held
twice weekly.

Arts & Crafts

The African Outlet
*524 Octavia Street, between Hayes and Grove Streets
(864 3576). Bus 21.* **Open** 10am-7pm daily. **Credit**
AmEx, MC, V. **Map F5**

Hundreds of treasures for you and your home: brilliantly
coloured fabrics, beautiful jewellery and authentic African
clothes for men, women, and children.

The Americas
*1977 Union Street, between Buchannan and Laguna
Streets (921 4600). Bus 41, 45.* **Open** 10.30am-6pm
Mon-Sat; 11am-5pm Sun. **Credit** AmEx, Disc, MC, V.
Map E2
A delightful shop specialising in folk and tribal art from
North and South America.

Art Options
*372 Hayes Street, between Franklin and Gough Streets
(252 8334). Bus 21.* **Open** 11am-6pm Tue-Sat.
Credit MC, V. **Map F5**
Situated in the arty neighbourhood of Hayes Valley, this is
one of a number of galleries that displays up-and-coming
artists' sculptures, paintings and jewellery.

Canton Bazaar
*616 Grant Avenue, between California and Sacramento
Streets (362 5750). Bus 1, 15/cable car California.*
Open 10am-10pm daily. **Credit** AmEx, MC, V.
Map G3
Cloisonné enamelwork, carved jade, rose Canton chinaware,
hand embroidery, jewellery and antiques are all imported
from mainland China and sold here.

Global Exchange Fair Trade Craft Center
*3900 24th Street, at Sanchez Street (648 8068). Muni
Metro J/bus 24, 48.* **Open** 11am-7pm daily. **Credit**
AmEx, MC, V. **Castro/Mission Map X2**
Imported crafts from Mexico and Guatemala include woven,
embroidered and crocheted shoulder bags; pot holders; tiny
gifts for children; *retablo* paintings on tin and animal hides;
and carved creatures from Oaxaca. Profits go to support a
local crafts co-operative.

Three Eighty One
*381 Guerrero Street, at 16th Street (621 3830)
Muni Metro J/bus 22, 26.* **Open** noon-6pm Mon-Thur,
Sun; 11am-7pm Fri, Sat. **Credit** AmEx, MC, V.
Map F6
Kitsch doesn't even come close to describing this won-
derful *tienda*, packed with knick-knacks and religious
trinkets.

Tibet Shop
*1807 Polk Street, at Washington Street (982 0326).
Bus 1, 19, 27.* **Open** 10am-6pm Mon-Sat; 1-5pm Sun.
Credit AmEx, MC, V. **Map F3**
Bells, incense, singing bowls, carved skulls, prayer beads;
lapis lazuli, turquoise, silver and coral necklaces; clothing
and crafts of Tibet, including everything you need for the
practice of Tibetan Buddhism, can be found here. The
shop, in the heart of Polk Gulch, is run by a disciple of the
Dalai Lama.

A Touch of Asia
*1784 Union Street, between Octavia and Gough Streets
(474 3115). Bus 41, 45.* **Open** 11am-5pm Mon-Sat; noon-
5pm Sun. **Credit** AmEx, MC, V. **Map E2**
Specialises in Kyoto *tansus* chests, moderately priced. Some
antiques and reproductions.

Zonal
568 Hayes Street, at Laguna Street (255 9307). Bus 21.
Open 11am-6pm Tue-Sun. **Credit** AmEx, MC, V.
Map F5
Found objects, architectural details, furniture and more –
everything in this shop looks as though it was dug up from
being buried for years.

Art Supplies

See also page 161 **Gifts & Stationery.**

Flax
1699 Market Street, at Valencia Street (552 2355). Muni Metro F, J, K, L, M, N/bus 6, 7, 26, 66, 71. **Open** 9.30am-6pm Mon-Sat. **Credit** AmEx, MC, V. **Map F5**
Considered by San Franciscans the premier place for art supplies, Flax offers everything your heart desires in stationery, pens, paper, inks, paint, brushes, gift wrap and handmade speciality papers. Known for its snobby staff and stunning selections.

Kozo Bookbinding
1969 Union Street, at Buchanan Street (351 2114). Bus 41, 45. **Open** 10am-6pm daily. **Credit** AmEx, MC, V. **Map E2**
Elegant store offering ornate, handmade paper, beautiful silk-screen wall hangings and books of stationery. Also has a bookbinding service.

Pearl
969 Market Street, between Fifth and Sixth Streets (357 1400). BART Powell Street/Muni Metro F, J, K, L, M, N/ bus 6, 7, 27, 31, 66, 71/cable car Powell-Mason or Powell-Hyde. **Open** 9am-7pm Mon-Sat; 10am-6pm Sun. **Credit** AmEx, Disc, MC, V. **Map G4**
This mecca of art and craft supplies fills three floors. Feed your fetish for stationery here – prices are very reasonable.

Bookshops

San Francisco is a great literary town, a joy for the writers and readers who live in it. Almost every neighbourhood has its own bookshop, many of them specialist. Sadly, however, the survival of small, independent bookshops in the Bay Area – as elsewhere – is under threat from the giant chains.

Aardvark
227 Church Street, at Market Street (552 6733). Muni Metro F, J, K, L, M/bus 22, 37. **Open** 10.30am-10.30pm Mon-Sat; 9.30am-9pm Sun. **Credit** MC, V. **Map E6**
Located between the Castro and Hayes Valley, Aardvark overflows with cooking, literary, sci-fi and mystery books.

The Booksmith
1644 Haight Street, between Clayton and Cole Streets (863 8688). Muni Metro N/bus 6, 7, 43, 66, 71. **Open** 10am-9pm Mon-Sat; 10am-6pm Sun. **Credit** AmEx, Disc, MC, V. **Map C6**
A good, all-purpose bookstore in the Haight.

Borders Books and Music
Union Square, at corner of Powell and Post Streets (399 1633). BART Powell Street/Muni Metro F, J, K, L, M, N/ bus 2, 3, 4, 76/cable car Powell-Mason or Powell-Hyde. **Open** 9am-11pm Mon-Wed; 9am-midnight Thur-Sat; 9am-9pm Sun. **Credit** AmEx, MC, V. **Map G3**
Situated downtown and open late, this three-floor giant has much to recommend it. There's a good café to hang out in and a huge selection of magazines. Like its fellow chain-stores, Borders discounts current bestsellers.

Browser Books
2195 Fillmore Street, at Sacramento Street (567 8027). Bus 1, 3, 22. **Open** 10am-10pm Mon-Sat; 9am-10pm Sun. **Credit** MC, V. **Map E3**
The devoted staff, late hours and cosy armchairs cater to the many loyal customers.

City Lights
261 Columbus Avenue, between Broadway and Pacific Avenue (362 8193). Bus 12, 15, 41, 83. **Open** 10am-midnight daily. **Credit** AmEx, MC, V. **Map G2**
Founded by poet Lawrence Ferlinghetti, this historic bookshop is one of the places where the Beat movement began. The stock is strong on literature, and it's still a great spot for reading or writing poetry. *See also chapter* **Literary San Francisco.**

A Clean Well-Lighted Place for Books
Opera Plaza, 601 Van Ness Avenue, between Golden Gate Avenue and Turk Street (441 6670). Bus 42, 47, 49. **Open** 10am-11pm Mon-Thur, Sun; 10am-midnight Fri, Sat. **Credit** AmEx, MC, V. **Map F4**
This centrally located, general interest bookstore hosts frequent and popular readings and author events.

A Different Light
489 Castro Street, at 18th Street (431 0891). Muni Metro F, K, L, M/bus 8, 24, 33, 35. **Open** 10am-midnight daily. **Credit** AmEx, Disc, MC, V. **Castro/Mission Map X1**
A thorough selection of books by and about the gay community. Come here for gay, lesbian and transgender literature.

Fields Book Store
1419 Polk Street, between Pine and California Streets (673 2027). Bus 1, 19, 42, 47, 49, 76/cable car California. **Open** 11am-6pm Tue-Sat. **Credit** MC, V. **Map F3**
Fields specialises in books on metaphysics and spirituality.

Get Lost
1825 Market Street, at Guerrero Street (437 0529). Muni Metro F, K, L,M/bus 6, 7, 66, 71. **Open** 10am-7pm Mon-Fri; 10am-6pm Sat; noon-5pm Sun. **Credit** AmEx, DC, MC, V. **Map F5**
Specialises in travel guides, with more than 6,000 titles, plus maps, travel accessories, slide shows and readings.

Great Expectations
1512 Haight Street, at Ashbury Street (863 5515). Bus 6, 7, 43, 66, 71. **Open** 10am-8pm daily. **Credit** AmEx, Disc, MC, V. **Map D5/6**
Where to find hip reading material, underground comics, rockstar biographies, and cult classics such as Charles Bukowski's *Love is a Dog from Hell.* Stocks as many T-shirts as books.

Green Apple Books
506 Clement Street, at Sixth Avenue (387 2272). Bus 2, 38, 44. **Open** 9.30am-11pm Mon-Thur, Sun; 9.30am-midnight Fri, Sat. **Credit** MC, V. **Map B4**
San Franciscans are great believers in 'good vibes,' and this store has the some of the best. With helpful staff and a wonderful mix of new and second-hand books, it's highly recommended for the dedicated browser who doesn't mind disarray.

Marcus Book Stores
1712 Fillmore Street, between Post and Sutter Streets (346 4222). Bus 2, 3, 4, 22. **Open** 10am-7pm Mon-Sat; noon-5pm Sun. **Credit** MC, V. **Map E4**
Marcus specialises in books by African and African-American writers and on related topics.

Modern Times Bookstore
888 Valencia Street, between 19th and 20th Streets (282 9246). Bus 26. **Open** 11am-9pm Mon-Sat; 11am-6pm Sun. **Credit** AmEx, MC, V. **Castro/Mission Map Y1**
Originally a source of left-wing political tracts, Modern Times is now a community centre for the Mission district. It sells new and used books and is excellent browsing territory, as well as a venue for political readings and forums.

Get stuck into some poetry at **City Lights**. *See page 152.*

Sierra Club Bookstore

Fourth Floor, 85 Second Street, at Mission Street (997 5600/1 800 935 1056). BART Montgomery Street/Muni Metro F, J, K, L, M, N/bus 2, 5, 6, 7, 9, 21, 31, 66, 71, 76. **Open** 10am-5.30pm Mon-Fri; 10am-5pm Sat. **Credit** MC, V. **Map H3**

An extensive range of books about the environment and ecological resources, plus a complete selection of hiking trails and maps. You can also find listings for upcoming meetings and green events.

Cameras & Electronics

The geographical proximity of Silicon Valley means that new computer technologies are available in the Bay Area three or four months before they're seen in other parts of the world. What's more, laptop or notebook computers in the US often cost half European prices.

Whatever you buy, make sure that your item will work in the country in which you want to use it. TVs in the US and Japan use the NTSC system while those in the UK and most of Europe use the PAL system; so American TVs, VCRs, camcorders, laser discs and videotapes will only work in the UK if you have a NTSC-compatible VCR. However, the American-made cartridge-based video games (such as Super Nintendo) are playable, provided you have a converter. Check the item has a built-in voltage selector: transformers and voltage converters are available, but are bulky and fairly costly.

Deal with reputable merchants. Many of the downtown stores that advertise cheap cameras and electronics are fly-by-night: if a deal seems too good to be true, it probably is. Most locals buy their consumer electronics at **Good Guys** (1400 Van Ness Avenue, at Bush Street; 775 9323) or **Circuit City** (1200 Van Ness Avenue, at Post Street; 441 1300). Both sell everything at guaranteed low prices, will install car stereo equipment while you wait, and deliver larger items. Pick up a catalogue to compare prices. *See page 148* for information on tax and duty.

Adolph Gasser

181 Second Street, between Mission and Howard Streets (495 3852). Bus 12, 14, 26, 76. **Open** 9am-6pm Mon-Sat. **Credit** AmEx, MC, V. **Map H4**

This justly famous photographic store has the largest inventory of photo and video equipment in Northern California. It stocks SLR cameras by Canon and Nikon, priced far cheaper than in the UK; all sorts of lenses; point-and-shoot cameras; and, according to one staff member, 'every kind of photographic doohickey you can imagine'.

Discount Camera

33 Kearny Street, between Post and Market Streets (392 1100). BART Montgomery Street/Muni Metro F, J, K, L, M, N/bus 2, 3, 4, 7, 8, 9, 15. **Open** 8.30am-6.30pm Mon-Sat; 9.30am-6pm Sun. **Credit** AmEx, Disc, MC, V. **Map H3**

Concierges at major downtown hotels direct their guests here in the hope that they'll avoid the unscrupulous tourist traps that dot Powell Street by the cable car turnaround. Discount carries a full line of all major brands and stocks PAL system camcorders.

International Electronics

1163 Mission Street, between Seventh and Eighth Streets (626 6382). BART Civic Center/Muni Metro F, J, K, L, M, N/bus 19, 26. **Open** 10am-6pm Mon-Sat. **Credit** AmEx, Disc, MC, V. **Map G5**

Sells Walkmans, portable CD players, mini-stereos that work in the UK and voltage converters and transformers for computers: transformers range from $49 up to $399. It also specialises in kitchen appliances.

Whole Earth Access

401 Bayshore Boulevard, between Oakdale and Cortland Avenues (285 5244). Bus 9, 23, 24. **Open** 10am-7pm Mon-Fri; 10am-6pm Sat, Sun. **Credit** Disc, MC, V.
The computer department is small, but the sales and technical support people are well versed in what's currently available and can order almost any model you desire, although not all will be equipped with universal voltage. Whole Earth doesn't ship outside the US.

Film Processing

There are hundreds of one-hour photo shops that count on you to part with big bucks for instant developing, but if you're not impatient, the best bargains are at **Safeway** supermarkets and **Walgreens** drugstores, which offer overnight processing at amazingly low rates. Make the daily deadline (around 11am) to guarantee next-day service. Check the *Yellow Pages* for branches.

Fox Photo 1-Hour Labs

455 Powell Street, between Sutter and Post Streets (421 8033). BART Powell Street/Muni Metro F, J, K, L, M, N/bus 30, 45/cable car Powell-Hyde or Powell-Mason. **Open** 8am-7pm Mon-Fri; 9am-5pm Sat; 10am-4pm Sun. **Credit** AmEx, MC, V. **Map G3**
A chain offering one-hour service on all colour print film and same-day turnaround on slides, enlargements and other services. Cameras and photo frames are also sold, but aren't cheap. Check the *Yellow Pages* for branches.

Duty-free Shops

88 Grant Avenue, at Geary Street (296 3620). BART Powell Street/Muni Metro F, J, K, L, M, N/bus 30, 38, 45. **Open** 10am-8pm daily. **Credit** AmEx, DC, JCB, MC, V. **Map G3/4**
Duty-free shops sell cosmetics, perfume, clothing, liquor, tobacco, food, some small electronic items and a tiny selection of cameras. At the airport branch, you will have to show your airline ticket to the sales staff; at the downtown store, they will check your ticket and give you a shopping pass. Whatever items you purchase will be waiting for you at the boarding gate of your return flight home.
Branch: San Francisco International Airport (244 8754).

Earthsake

1 Embarcadero, between Battery and Front Streets (956 4555) BART Embarcadero/Muni Metro F, J, K, L, M, N/bus 1, 12, 41, 42. **Open** 10am-7pm Mon-Sat; noon-5pm Sun. **Credit** AmEx, Disc, MC, V. **Map H2**
Everything is eco-friendly or recycled: from reconstituted cars and little welded animals to furniture and clothing.
Branch: 2076 Chestnut Street, at Steiner Street (441 2896).

Used Rubber USA

597 Haight Street, at Steiner Street (626 7855). Bus 6, 7, 22, 66, 71. **Open** noon-6pm daily. **Credit** AmEx, Disc, MC, V. **Map E5**
Sells clothing made from recycled rubber, as well as products and clothing made from hemp.

Worldware

336 Hayes Street, between Franklin and Gough Streets (487 9030). Bus 21. **Open** 11am-6pm Mon-Fri; noon-6pm Sat, Sun. **Credit** AmEx, MC, V. **Map F5**
Eco-friendly clothing, bedding, cosmetics and baby clothes.

Though the fashion scene in San Francisco doesn't compare with New York, London and Paris, the city is still fashion-conscious: it's just that people don't wear their labels on their sleeves. The fashion on the street is as distinct as the neighbourhoods are different: button-downs in the Marina; grunge in the Haight; loafers in Pacific Heights; funky in the Mission; businessy downtown; clubby in the Castro. In general, anything goes. For more fashion, *see page 149* **Department Stores**.

Ambiance

1458 Haight Street, between Ashbury and Masonic Streets (552 5095). Bus 6, 7, 66, 71. **Open** 11am-8pm Mon-Fri; 11am-7pm Sat, Sun; *winter* 11am-7pm daily. **Credit** AmEx, MC, V. **Map D5**
Sells an enormous selection of dresses, with all the appropriate accessories, blending vintage and modern – hats, bags and jewellery. There's a good mix of sizes and styles, although items are pretty pricey.

Banana Republic

256 Grant Avenue, at Sutter Street (788 3087). BART Montgomery Street/Muni Metro F, J, K, L, M, N/bus 2, 3, 4, 15, 30, 45, 76. **Open** 9.30am-8pm Mon-Sat; 11am-7pm Sun. **Credit** AmEx, Disc, MC, V. **Map G3**
Young classic clothes that will last, for men and women. Understated well-cut suits for the urban professional and upmarket Gap-style weekend wear. Check the *Yellow Pages* for branches.

Bella Donna

539 Hayes Street, between Laguna and Octavia Streets (861 7182). Bus 21. **Open** 11am-7pm Tue-Sat; 11am-5pm Sun. **Credit** AmEx, MC, V. **Map F5**
Contemporary, handmade clothing for the Bay Area. Straw hats by Laurel Fenenga complement linen garden party dresses. There are hand-dyed cotton stockings, antique buttons, hand-knit women's sweaters and a nice bridal department, too.

Betsey Johnson

2031 Fillmore Street, between California and Pine Streets (567 2726). Bus 1, 2, 3, 4, 22. **Open** 11am-7pm Mon-Sat; noon-6pm Sun. **Credit** AmEx, MC, V. **Map E3**
What Mary Quant was to England, Betsey Johnson is to the US. Young, clingy, pretty and outrageous clothes for women, displayed in a campy, Art Deco, neon-lit environment.
Branch: 160 Geary Street, between Stockton and Grant Streets (398 2516).

CP Shades

1861 Union Street, between Laguna and Octavia Streets (292 3588). Bus 41, 45. **Open** 11am-7pm Mon-Sat; noon-6pm Sun. **Credit** AmEx, MC, V. **Map E2**
Loose, comfortable, washable and co-ordinated separates in rich colours for all seasons and every occasion. These clothes are addictive! Keep an eye out for the sales, when prices drop as much as 50%.

Diesel

101 Post Street, at Kearny Street (982 7077). Transport Muni Metro F, J, K, L, M, N/2, 15, 30, 45 bus.

Betsey Johnson. *See page 155.*

Open 10am-8pm Mon-Fri; 10am-7pm Sat; noon-6pm Sun.
Credit AmEx, MC, V. **Map H3**
Nineties clothing meets 1970s décor in this latest addition to
the city. Three floors of the latest, hippest Italian clothing
for both men and women, and even some very stylish children's clothing too. If the prices get too overweening for you,
take a load off on the Doogle-like shaggy sofa and watch the
beautiful people spend their money.

Emporio Armani

*1 Grant Avenue, at Market Street (677 9400/café 677
9010). BART Montgomery or Powell Streets/Muni Metro
F, J, K, L, M, N/bus 5, 6, 7, 9, 21, 38, 66, 71.*
Open 10am-7pm Mon-Fri; 10am-6pm Sat; noon-6pm Sun.
Credit AmEx, DC, JCB, MC, V. **Map H4**
Top-of-the-line androgynous clothing for men and women
by America's designer of choice. Step into the café for a
pricey cappuccino experience.

The Gap

*890 Market Street, at Powell Street (788 5909). BART
Powell Street/Muni Metro F, J, K, L, M, N/bus 5, 6, 7, 9,
21, 30, 45, 66, 71/cable car Powell-Mason or Powell-
Hyde.* Open 9.30am-8pm Mon-Sat; 10am-6pm Sun.
Credit AmEx, DC, JCB, MC, V. **Map G4**
American style on the cheap. Jeans, T-shirts, all-purpose
sportswear for men, women and children come at moderate
prices. Check the *Yellow Pages* for your nearest branch.

Joshua Simon

*3915 24th Street, at Sanchez Street (821 1068). Muni
Metro J/bus 24, 48.* Open 10.30am-6.30pm Mon-Fri;
10am-6.30pm Sat; 11am-6pm Sun. **Credit** AmEx, MC, V.
Castro/Mission Map X2
Loose-fitting women's clothing in natural fibres, featuring
unusual woven waistcoats and romantic-looking dresses.
Block-printed cottons and linens in muted colours from New
Mexico and Indonesia.

Mac

*5 Claude Lane, off Bush Street at Kearny Street (837
0615). Bus, 2, 3, 4, 15, 76.* Open 11am-7pm Mon-Sat;
noon-5pm Sun. **Credit** AmEx, MC, V. **Map H3**
Trendy menswear and shoes, including Hush Puppies in
lime green, grape purple and vivid puce suede. The branch
is for women.
Branch: 1543 Grant Street, at Union Street (837 1604).

Martha Egan

*1127 Folsom Street, between Seventh and Eighth Streets
(252 1072). Bus 12.* Open 10am-4pm Mon, Tue, Sat;
10am-6pm Wed-Fri. **Credit** AmEx, MC, V. **Map G5**
This up-and-coming designer has her own studio and shop
in SoMa, among the clubs. Moderately priced women's
clothes, with vintage styling but contemporary cuts.

Métier

*355 Sutter Street, between Stockton Street and Grant
Avenue (989 5395). BART Montgomery Street/
Muni Metro F, J, K, L, M, N/bus 2, 3, 4, 30, 45, 76.*
Open 10.30am-6.30pm Mon-Sat; noon-5pm Sun.
Credit AmEx, MC, V. **Map G3**
Women's clothing in luxurious fabrics by Peter Cohen,
Harriet Selwyn, Lat Naylor and others.

Na Na

*2276 Market Street, at Noe Street (861 6262). Muni
Metro F, K, L, M/bus 37.* Open 11am-8pm Mon-Thur;
11am-8.30pm Fri, Sat; 11am-7pm Sun. **Credit** AmEx,
Disc, MC, V. **Map E6**
With chains in Los Angeles and New York, Na Na offers up-
to-the-minute cheap city shoes, fashion and accessories for
Gen X-ers. Leather, rubber, latex – you name it.

New West

*2 South Park, at Second Street (882 4929). Bus 15, 30,
42, 45, 76.* Open 10am-5pm Mon-Sat; noon-5pm Sun.
Credit AmEx, MC, V. **Map J4**
If you can't afford Armani but like the look, this designers'
sale house is the place to stop. It's in the SoMa outlet district,
within walking distance of other outlets. Prepare to rifle
through, and you should come up with a big-name second.

Nomads

*556 Hayes Street, between Laguna and Octavia Streets
(864 5692). Bus 21.* Open 11am-7pm daily. **Credit**
AmEx, MC, V. **Map F5**
Contemporary menswear in natural fabrics. The cuts are
very simple, stylish and wearable.

Old Navy

*Potrero Center, between Byrant Street and Potrero
Avenue (255 1276). Bus 9, 22, 27, 33, 53.*
Open 9.30am-9.30pm Mon-Sat; 10am-6pm Sun.
Credit AmEx, Disc, MC, V. **Map G5**
For that clean-cut, all-American look at substantial savings,
check out Old Navy's stylish clothes for men, women and
children. You won't go broke looking cool.

Rolo

*450 Castro Street, between Market and 18th Streets
(626 7171). Muni Metro F, K, L, M/bus 24, 35, 37.*
Open 10am-9pm Mon-Sat; 10.30am-7.30pm Sun.
Credit AmEx, DC, JCB, MC, V. **Map E6**
Groovy threads for urban clubgoers. Each store caters to a
slightly different crowd: this branch features T-shirts, jeans and
men's shoes; Market Street has flamboyant menswear; Howard
Street has stylish womenswear, sale goods and shoes; Stockton
has women's clothes and a mix of the other stores' goods.
Branches: 2351 Market Street, between Noe and Castro
Streets (431 4545); 1301 Howard Street, at Ninth Street
(861 1999); 25 Stockton Street, between Ellis and O'Farrell
Streets (989 7656).

American Rag – *for the best in vintage gear. See page 158.*

Urban Outfitters

80 Powell Street, at Market Street (989 1515). BART Powell Street/Muni Metro F, J, K, L, M, N/bus 5, 6, 7, 9, 21, 31, 66, 71/cable car Powell-Hyde or Powell-Mason. **Open** 10am-10pm Mon-Sat; 10am-9pm Sun. **Credit** AmEx, DC, MC, V. **Map G4**

This loud, obnoxious store features an eclectic blend of new and used clothing to satisfy the raver; from baggy cords and synthetic Hawaii shirts for men to baby Ts and fake fur jackets for women. UO also carries cool items for the home: lamps, candles, bedspreads, picture frames and much more.

Discount Fashion

There are several fashion discount outlets based in SoMa, around Third and Townsend Streets. Within a four-block radius to the west and north, dozens of small outlet shops cater to every taste imaginable. When you get tired, you can stop off at the **South Park Café** for refreshments (*see chapter* **Restaurants & Cafés**).

Esprit Factory Outlet

499 Illinois Street, at 16th Street (957 2540). Bus 15, 22, 48. **Open** 10am-8pm Mon-Fri; 10am-7pm Sat; 11am-5pm Sun. **Credit** AmEx, Disc, MC, V. **Map J6**

Young, hip, women's clothes at substantial savings: 30-70% off department store prices. For that fantastic bargain, head for the back.

Isda and Company Outlet

29 South Park, between Second, Third, Bryant and Brannan Streets (247 0930 ext 110). Bus 15, 30, 42, 76. **Open** 10am-5.30pm Mon-Sat. **Credit** MC, V. **Map H/J4**

Spare, simple, small-scale designs for women, discounted by as much as 70%.

Loehmann's

222 Sutter Street, at Kearny Street (982 3215). BART Montgomery Street/Muni Metro F, J, K, L, M, N/bus 2, 3, 4, 15, 76. **Open** 9am-8pm Mon-Fri; 10.30am-7pm Sat; 11am-6pm Sun. **Credit** MC, V. **Map H3**

New York women who never, ever pay full price swear by this designer discount department store.

Vivon

424 Sutter Street, between Stockton and Powell Streets (781 2666). Bus 2, 3, 4, 30, 45, 76/cable car Powell-Mason or Powell-Hyde. **Open** 10am-7pm Mon-Sat; noon-5pm Sun. **Credit** AmEx, DC, JCB, MC, V. **Map G3**

Imported menswear at wholesale prices. Multicoloured Coogi sweaters, in computer-generated designs, are roughly half-price, at around $150.

Vintage & Second-hand Clothes

The best place to look is **Haight Street** or the **Mission**, where vintage clothing abounds and you're sure to find that dependable polyester shirt or basic black dress. Check out the smaller shops first; they tend to be less picked over. Check your bag in, sharpen your elbows, and join the fray.

American Rag

1305 Van Ness Avenue, between Bush and Sutter Streets (474 5214). Bus 47, 49, 76. **Open** 10am-9pm Mon-Sat; noon-7pm Sun. **Credit** AmEx, MC, V. **Map F3/4**

Ultra-hip vintage clothing in excellent condition and taste, mixed in with designer labels. Arguably the best place in the city for shoes, but definitely not for the bargain hunter.

Buffalo Exchange

1555 Haight Street, between Clayton and Ashbury Streets (431 7733). Bus 6, 7, 43, 66, 71. **Open** 11am-7pm Mon-Sat; noon-6pm Sun. **Credit** AmEx, MC, V. **Map D6**

Don't know what to do with that Christmas sweater that's been sitting in your wardrobe? Trade it in at this well-known second-hand recycler, one of the best thrift stores in the city. Not necessarily cutting-edge stuff, but consistently cheap. **Branch:** 1800 Polk Street, at Washington Street (346 5726).

Crossroads Trading Company

2231 Market Street, between Sanchez and Noe Streets (626 8989). Muni Metro K, L, M, N/bus 24, 33, 35, 37. **Open** 11am-7pm Mon-Thur; 11am-8pm Fri, Sat; noon-6pm Sun. **Credit** MC, V. **Map E6**

The Market branch houses mostly 1980s wear, while the Fillmore shop is better for jeans, dresses and classic vintage wear. Trade in your unwantables here, too. **Branch:** 1901 Fillmore Street, at Bush Street (775 8885).

560 Hayes Vintage Boutique

560 Hayes Street, between Laguna and Octavia Streets (861 7993). Bus 21. **Open** noon-7pm daily. **Credit** AmEx, MC, V. **Map F5**

If you're planning to go swing dancing, here's where you'll find that outfit. You'll also find racks of stylish trousers, jackets, coats and shoes.

Wasteland

1660 Haight Street, at Belvedere Street (863 3150). Bus 6, 7, 43, 66, 71. **Open** 11am-7pm daily. **Credit** AmEx, JCB, MC, V. **Map C6**

Trendy and outrageous second-hand clothing, possibly the most popular in the city and perhaps the most pricey. A good source of vintage costume jewellery and gowns.

Children's Clothes

See also page 149 **Department Stores** *and page 156* **The Gap** *and* **Old Navy**.

Kids Only

1608 Haight Street, at Clayton Street (552 5445). Bus 6, 7, 33, 37, 43, 66, 77. **Open** 10am-6pm Mon-Sat; 11am-5pm Sun. **Credit** AmEx, Disc, JCB, MC, V. **Map C6**

Fun clothes in funky colours – even tie-dye for kids. Let your child pick out something.

Mudpie

1694 Union Street, at Gough Street (771 9262). Bus 41, 45. **Open** 10am-6pm Mon-Sat; 11am-5pm Sun. **Credit** AmEx, MC, V. **Map E2**

An utterly charming shop for clothes and toys, full of unique, handmade and pricey gifts for privileged tots. **Branch:** 2220 Chestnut Street, between Pierce and Scott Streets (474 8395).

Peek-A-Boutique

1306 Castro Street, at 24th Street (641 6192). Bus 24, 48. **Open** 10.30am-6pm Mon-Sat; noon-5pm Sun. **Credit** MC, V. **Castro/Mission Map X2**

The place to come for second-hand children's clothing.

Fashion Accessories

Leather Goods & Luggage

The Coach Store

190 Post Street, at Grant Avenue (392 1772). BART Montgomery Street/Muni Metro F, J, K, L, M, N/bus 2, 3, 4, 15, 30, 38, 45, 76. **Open** 10am-7pm Mon-Wed; 9.30am-7pm Thur, Fri; 9.30am-6.30pm Sat; noon-5.30pm Sun.

Credit AmEx, JCB, MC, V. **Map G/H3**
The place to buy those Coach handbags and wallets chosen by all-American legends. The most recent collection is stylish and modern, and you can even buy a matching leather mobile-phone holder. Not cheap.

Edward's Luggage

3 Embarcadero Center, at Sacramento and Drumm Streets (981 7047). BART Embarcadero/Muni Metro F, J, K, L, M, N/bus 1, 12, 41, 42. **Open** 10am-7pm Mon-Fri; 10am-6pm Sat; noon-5pm Sun. **Credit** AmEx, DC, Disc, MC, V. **Map H3**
Offers everything you need for travelling and much more. Also an excellent source for desk planners.

Johnson Leather Corp

1833 Polk Street, between Jackson and Washington Streets (775 7392). Bus 12, 27, 30, 42, 47, 49, 83. **Open** 10.30am-6.30pm Mon-Sat; noon-5pm, Sun. **Credit** AmEx, DC, Disc, JCB, MC, V. **Map F3**
Both a factory and a shop, which means you can get good buys on lambskin unisex jackets and have alterations done while you wait.

North Beach Leather

190 Geary Street, at Stockton Street (362 8300). BART Powell Street/Muni Metro F, J, K, L, M, N/ bus 2, 3, 4, 30, 38, 45. **Open** 10am-7pm Mon-Sat; noon-5pm Sun. **Credit** AmEx, DC, Disc, JCB, MC, V. **Map G4**
The walls are covered with photos of celebrities wearing multi-coloured jackets and tight-fitting dresses in NBL's signature styles.

Tannery West

SF Shopping Center, 865 Market Street, at Fifth Street (495 5656). BART Powell Street/Muni Metro F, J, K, L, M, N/bus 6, 7, 27, 31, 66, 71/cable car Powell-Mason or Powell-Hyde. **Open** 9.30am-8pm Mon-Sat; 11am-6pm Sun. **Credit** AmEx, Disc, MC, V. **Map G4**
Leather here comes in fancy beaded and fringed styles. Your classic black motorcycle jacket, in better than usual quality, costs $150-$200.

Lingerie

See also page 149 **Department Stores**

Victoria's Secret

1 Embarcadero Center, at Sacramento and Drumm Streets (433 9473). BART Embarcadero/Muni Metro F, J, K, L, M, N/bus 1, 12, 41, 42. **Open** 10am-7pm Mon-Fri; 10am-6pm Sat; noon-5pm Sun. **Credit** AmEx, Disc, MC, V. **Map H3**
This standard mall chain has seen off all other competition in the area and the company's soft-porn catalogues haven't hurt sales, either. A boudoir of less practical underwear. There are branches all over town: check the *Yellow Pages* for your nearest.

Luggage Repair

The Luggage Center

828 Mission Street, between Fourth and Fifth Streets (543 3771). BART Powell Street/Muni Metro F, J, K, L, M, N/bus 14, 26, 45. **Open** 9.30am-6pm Mon-Sat; 11.30am-5pm Sun. **Credit** AmEx, MC, V. **Map G/H4**
Luggage professionals will either repair your busted bag or guarantee you a bargain price on a new one. Check out the great deals on last year's models. For shoe repairs, *see page 160*.

Shoes

Bulo

437A Hayes Street, at Gough Street (864 3244). Bus 21. **Open** 11.30am-6.30pm Mon-Sat; noon-6pm Sun. **Credit** AmEx, Disc, MC, V. **Map F5**
Imported Italian and English shoes in the latest styles. Excellent sales rack, but overpriced Patrick Cox.

Daljeets

1744 Haight Street, at Cole Street (752 5610). Muni Metro L/bus 6, 7, 33, 37, 43, 66, 71. **Open** 11am-7pm daily. **Credit** AmEx, Disc, MC, V. **Map C6**
This is where to find Doc Marten's, that basic British shoe.

Frank More

285 Geary Street, at Powell Street (421 1635). Bus 2, 3, 4, 38, 76/cable car Powell-Mason or Powell-Hyde. **Open** 9.30am-6.30pm Mon-Wed; 9.30am-7pm Thur, Fri; 9.30am-6pm Sat; 11.30am-5.30pm Sun. **Credit** AmEx, DC, JCB, MC, V. **Map G4**
Elite Italian men's shoes by Bruno Magli, as worn by the city's notorious son, OJ.

Gimme Shoes

416 Hayes Street, at Gough Street (864 0691). Bus 21. **Open** 11am 6.30pm Mon-Sat; noon-6pm Sun. **Credit** AmEx, Disc, MC, V. **Map F5**
European designer shoes for men and women. Also stocks hard-to-find trainers by Adidas and other more elusive manufacturers. **Branch**: 2358 Fillmore Street, at Washington Street (441 3040).

Kenneth Cole

2078 Union Street, at Webster Street (346 2161). Bus 41, 45. **Open** 10am-8pm Mon-Sat; 11am-6pm Sun. **Credit** AmEx, MC, V. **Map E2**
'Soles of the City': stylish shoes and accessories for men and women.

Become a martyr to fashion at **Bulo.**

Shoe Biz

*1446 Haight Street, between Ashbury and Masonic
Streets (864 0990). Bus 6, 7, 33, 37, 43, 66, 77.*
Open 11am-7pm daily. **Credit** AmEx, MC, V. **Map D5**
High-quality shoes at fantastic discounts. You name it, they
have it: platforms, stilettos, glitter, sequins – the latest in
European styles to satisfy any raver.

Shoe Repair

Anthony's Shoe Service

*30 Geary Street, between Grant Avenue and Kearny
Street (781 1338). BART Montgomery Street/Muni
Metro F, J, K, L, M, N/bus 2 to 7, 15, 21, 30, 31, 38, 45,
66, 71.* **Open** 8am-5.30pm Mon-Fri; 9am-5pm Sat.
Credit DC, Disc, JCB, MC, V. **Map H3**
A recommended cobbler, and convenient to downtown. You
name it, they mend it – they'll even put the taps on your
tap shoes.

Elite Shoe Repair

*1614 Haight Street, at Clayton Street (863 3260).
Bus 6, 7, 33, 37, 43, 66, 71.* **Open** 9.30am-6pm Mon-Sat.
No credit cards. Map C6
This Haight-Ashbury establishment comes highly recom-
mended by shoe gurus at the trendy Bulo shop (*see p159*).

Florists

Ixia

*2331 Market Street, between Castro and Noe Streets
(431 3134). Muni Metro F, K, L, M, N/bus 8, 24, 35, 37.*
Open 9am-6.30pm Mon-Fri; 11am-6pm Sat. **Credit**
AmEx, MC, V. **Map E6**
You should at least window shop at this Castro merchant –
the likes of the living plant and flower sculptures have never
been seen. Displays change weekly.

Pappas at the Plaza

*1255 Battery Street, at Filbert Street (434 1313).
Bus 32, 42.* **Open** 8.30am-5.30pm Mon-Fri. **Credit**
AmEx, DC, Disc, MC, V. **Map H2**
This tiny shop magically builds bouquets into structural
masterpieces. While the flowers are sure to dazzle the recip-
ient, they may also stun your wallet.

Podesta Baldocchi

*508 Fourth Street, at Byrant Street (434 1313). Bus 15,
30, 45, 76.* **Open** 8am-6pm Mon-Fri; 8am-4pm Sat.
Credit AmEx, DC, Disc, MC, V. **Map H4**
Everyone's favourite local source for floral arrangements and
live plants. With 130 years in business under its belt, you can
expect exceptional arrangements. Pricey, but worth it.

Food & Drink

Bakeries

Boudin Sourdough Bakery & Café

*2890 Taylor Street, at Jefferson Street (776 1849).
Bus 32, 39, 42/cable car Powell-Mason.* **Open** *summer*
7.30am-8pm Mon-Thur; 7.30am-10pm Fri, Sat; 7.30am-
9pm Sun. **Credit** AmEx, MC, V. **Map F1**
Stop in for a fresh loaf of San Francisco's famous sourdough
bread or delicious hot soup served in a bread bowl. Boudin
will deliver all over the world: check the *Yellow Pages* for the
branch nearest to you. In winter, the shop closes earlier.

Cake Gallery

290 Ninth Street, at Folsom Street (861 2253). Bus 9, 12.
Open 9am-6pm Mon-Sat. **Credit** AmEx, Disc, MC, V.
Map G5

There's nothing these cake artists can't do with their custom
shaped and designed edible masterpieces: from panda bears
and enormous chocolate penises to edible likenesses of
famous people. Stop by and thumb through their provocative portfolio.

Dianda Italian American Pastry

*2883 Mission Street, at 24th Street (647 5469).
BART 24th Street/bus 14, 48, 49.* **Open** 6am-6.30pm
Mon-Sat; 6am-5pm Sun. **No credit cards. Castro/
Mission Map Z2**
Delight your taste buds with cream-filled Italian cakes and
pastries. Eat in or take away.

Just Desserts

*3 Embarcadero Center, at Sacramento and Davis Streets
(421 1609). BART Embarcadero/Muni Metro F, J, K, L,
M, N/bus 1, 12, 41, 42.* **Open** 6.30am-7pm Mon-Fri;
10am-5pm Sat; 10am-5pm Sun. **Credit** MC, V.
Map H3
A good bet for last-minute birthday cakes, this bakery and
café makes some of the best chocolate gâteaux and poppy-
seed cakes in town.
Branches: 248 Church Street, between 15th and Market
Streets (626 5742); 3735 Buchanan Street, at Marina
Boulevard (922 8675); 836 Irving Street, at Tenth Avenue
(681 1277); 1000 Cole Street, at Parnassus Avenue (664
8947); Plaza Foods, 1750 Fulton Street, at Masonic
Avenue (441 2207).

La Victoria

*2937 Alabama Street, at 24th Street (550 9292). Bus 12,
27, 48.* **Open** 7am-10pm daily. **No credit cards.
Castro/Mission Map Z2**
A real Mexican bakery in the heart of the Mission district.

Stella Pastry & Caffe

*446 Columbus Avenue, between Green and Vallejo
Streets (986 2914). Bus 15, 41.* **Open** *summer* 7.30am-
10pm daily; *winter* 7.30am-6pm daily. **Credit** MC, V.
Map G2
Famous for its St Honoré cake, a gooey rum-soaked delight.
You can sit and enjoy your pastry with a cup of coffee.

Tassajara Bread Bakery

*1000 Cole Street, at Parnassus Avenue (664 8947).
Muni Metro J/bus 6, 37, 43.* **Open** 7am-9pm Mon-Thur;
7am-10pm Fri, Sat; 8am-9pm Sun. **Credit** MC, V.
Map C6
This neighbourhood favourite continues to bake the fresh-
est breads, cakes and pastries. It was recently taken over by
Just Desserts (*see above*).

Beer & Wine

Jug Shop

*1567 Pacific Avenue, at Polk Street (885 2922). Bus 12,
19, 27, 83.* **Open** 9am-9pm Mon-Sat; 9.30am-7pm Sun.
Credit MC, V. **Map F3**
The friendly, knowledgeable staff are always on hand to
help you make your selection from a variety of French,
Australian, Italian, Spanish and Chilean wines. There are
scheduled tastings from visiting vineyards, and for large parties the staff will deliver cases of wine and kegs of beer.

Napa Valley Winery Exchange

*415 Taylor Street, between Geary and O'Farrell Streets
(1-800 653 9463/771 2887). Bus 2, 3, 4, 27, 38, 76.*
Open 10am-7pm Mon-Sat. **Credit** AmEx, JCB, MC, V.
Map G4
Specialising in California wines, including unusual and hard-
to-find bottlings, this shop has over 500 wines in stock and
will ship anywhere in the world.

The Wine Club

953 Harrison Street, between Fifth and Sixth Streets (512 9086). Bus 30, 37, 42, 45, 76. **Open** 9am-7pm Mon-Sat; 11am-6pm Sun. **Credit** MC, V. **Map H5**
The Wine Club offers some of the greatest bargains around, with prices starting at $4.99. The club's knowledgeable staff will guide you through the 1,200 options and you can taste your choices. The club stocks an ever-changing selection of Californian, French and Italian wines.

Gourmet Groceries

Casa Lucas Market

2934 24th Street, between Alabama and Florida Streets (826 4334). BART 24th Street/bus 48, 67. **Open** 7am-7.30pm daily. **Credit** AmEx, Disc, MC, V. **Castro/Mission Map Z2**
Produce, groceries and spices used in Mexican cooking, with imported Latin tinned goods and numerous types of chillis.

Haig's Delicacies

642 Clement Street, between Seventh and Eighth Avenues (752 6283). Bus 1, 2, 4, 38, 44. **Open** 9.30am-6.30pm Mon-Fri; 9am-6pm Sat. **Credit** Disc, MC, V. **Map B4**
Haig's sells British foodstuffs, Middle Eastern goods, Indian spices and all manner of exotic flavourings.

Molinari Delicatessen

373 Columbus Avenue, at Vallejo Street (421 2337). Bus 15, 41. **Open** 8am-6pm Mon-Fri; 7.30am-5.30pm Sat. **Credit** MC, V. **Map G2**
Molinari was dishing out home-made pasta and *pesto alla genovese* long before yuppies ever heard of the stuff, and it's still going strong.

Rainbow Grocery

1745 Folsom Street, at 13th Street (863 0621). Bus 9, 12, 22, 27, 33. **Open** 9am-9pm Mon-Sat; 10am-9pm Sun. **Credit** Disc, MC, V. **Map G5**
One of the most reasonably priced gourmet markets around, Rainbow offers natural foods that have been organically grown. You won't find anything frozen. Cookware, tableware and essential oils and vitamins are also available. Check out the bulletin board for items for sale, sub-lets and meditation and healing workshops.

Real Foods

2164 Polk Street, at Vallejo Street (775 2805). Bus 12, 19, 27, 42, 47, 49, 76, 83. **Open** 7am-8pm daily. **Credit** MC, V. **Map F2/3**
This San Francisco health food chain carries a beautiful selection of organic produce and vegetables, as well as gourmet oils and vinegars and fresh pre-packaged foods. The Fillmore and Polk branches have a gourmet deli – ideal for stocking up for a picnic. The staff are not always the most helpful, but persevere; it's worth it.
Branches: 1023 Stanyon Street, at Carl Street (564 2800); 3939 24th Street, at Noe Street (282 9500); 3060 Fillmore Street, at Filbert Street (567 1540).

Trader Joe's

555 Ninth Street, between Bryant and Brannan Streets (863 1292). Bus 19, 27, 42. **Open** 9am-9pm daily. **Credit** Disc, MC, V. **Map F3**
You'll find delicious organic goods, healthy fast food and the least expensive but best tasting selection of wine and beer in the city. Packed at the weekend.

Whole Foods

1765 California Street, at Franklin Street (674 0500). Bus 1, 12, 42, 47, 49. **Open** 9am-10pm daily. **Credit** AmEx, Disc, MC, V. **Map F3**
The newest gourmet shop to hit San Francisco and it's already quite a scene. There is a bakery, a deli and separate markets for meat, cheese and fish. The salad bar is to die for.

Food Delivery

Many of the smaller restaurants in the city offer free delivery services, so it's worth checking those near your hotel. A tip of 15 per cent is customary. *See also chapter* **Restaurants & Cafés**.

Dine One One

(928 3278). **Open** 10.30am-11pm Mon-Fri; 11am-10pm Sat, Sun. **Credit** AmEx, DC, MC, V.
This upmarket restaurant delivery service brings dishes from more than 75 restaurants to your doorstep. Open daily for lunch and dinner, serving any silver-walleted soul within the city limits.

Waiters on Wheels

425 Divisadero Street, at Oak Street (252 1470). Bus 6, 7, 66, 71. **Open** 11am-11pm daily. **Credit** AmEx, DC, Disc, MC, V. **Map D/E5**
Like Dine One One, this service delivers restaurant fare to your home – for a price. Choose from 50 restaurants, serving anything from American to Thai cuisine and nearly everything in between; phone for a menu listing.

Tea & Coffee

Caffè Trieste sells coffee beans blended and roasted to your specification, as well as coffee-making equipment, as do the chains **Peet's Coffee & Tea**, the **Spinelli Coffee Company** and the increasingly omnipresent **Starbucks** Check the *Yellow Pages* for your nearest branches. *See also chapters* **Restaurants & Cafés** *and* **Bars**.

Graffeo Coffee Roasting Company

735 Columbus Avenue, at Filbert Street (986 2429/1-800 222 6250). Bus 15, 30, 41/Powell-Mason cable car. **Open** 9am-6pm Mon-Fri; 9am-5pm Sat. **No credit cards**. **Map G2**
A longstanding North Beach shop – practically a San Franciscan institution.

Ten Ren Tea Company of San Francisco

949 Grant Avenue, between Washington and Jackson Streets (362 0656). Bus 1, 15, 30, 45/cable car California. **Open** 9am-9pm daily. **Credit** ($10 minimum) AmEx, MC, V. **Map G3**
Stocks about 40 different types of Chinese tea, from the leaves recommended for an ordinary cuppa to the expensive infusions kept for special occasions. Taste before you buy.

Gifts & Stationery

See also pages 151-152 **Arts & Crafts** *and* **Art Supplies**.

The Balloon Lady

1263 Howard Street, between Eighth and Ninth Streets (864 3737). Bus 12, 19, 47. **Open** 8.30am-5.30pm Mon-Sat; 10am-2pm Sun. **Credit** AmEx, Disc, MC, V.
Amazingly creative balloon bouquets and structures are created out of 100% biodegradable latex. Prices range from $29.95-$59.95, with delivery by a tuxedo-clad man.

The Cinema Shop

606 Geary Street, at Jones Street (885 6785). Bus 2, 3, 4, 27, 38, 76. **Open** 11am-5pm Mon-Sat. **Credit** AmEx, MC, V. **Map G4**
Feed your film fetish with printed and photographic memorabilia from 1848 to the present, including original movie marquee posters, stills and lobby cards.

Cost Plus Imports

2552 Taylor Street, at North Point Street (928 6200).
Bus 32, 39, 42. **Open** 9am-9pm daily. **Credit** AmEx,
Disc, MC, V. **Map G1**
With a constantly changing mix of over 20,000 products
from more than 40 countries – including exotic collectables
such as statues and masks, dinner and glassware, gourmet
foodstuffs, clothing and accessories, baskets and kitchenware – Cost Plus is a San Francisco landmark. A great place
to buy unusual and inexpensive gifts.

Quantity Postcards

1441 Grant Avenue, between Union and Green Streets
(986 8866). Bus 15, 30, 39, 41. **Open** 11am-11pm Mon-
Thur, Sun; 11am-12.30am, Fri, Sat. **Credit** AmEx, MC, V.
Map G2
An incredible selection of new and vintage postcards, including quaint Victorian flowery tributes and domestic scenes
from the 1950s, as well as tinted landscapes of faraway
places. Also a good selection of Frank Kozik's music posters.
Check out the earthquake machine.
Branches: 507 Columbus Street, at Green Street (788
1112); 1427 Haight Street, at Masonic Street (255 1199).

Virginia Breier

3091 Sacramento Street, at Baker Street (929 7173).
Bus 1, 3, 43. **Open** 11am-6pm Mon-Sat. **Credit** MC, V.
Map D3
A folk art gallery, specialising in the works of local artists.
A good place for one-of-a-kind gifts. *See also chapter*
Museums & Galleries.

Glass

Compositions

317 Sutter Street, between Grant Avenue and Stockton
Street (693 9111). Bus 2, 3, 4, 30, 45, 76. **Open** 10am-
6pm Mon-Sat. **Credit** AmEx, DC, MC, V. **Map G3**
A gallery of blown-glass art.

de Vera

384 Hayes Street, at Gough Street (861 8480). Muni
Metro J, K, L, M, N/bus 21 42 47, 49. **Open** noon-6pm
Tue-Sat. **Credit** AmEx, MC, V. **Map F5**
Federico de Vera sells contemporary, 1950s and 1960s Italian
and Swedish glass from this Hayes Valley shop.
Branches: 29 Maiden Lane, between Grant Avenue and
Kearny Street (788 0828); 580 Sutter Street, between
Mason and Powell Streets (558 8865).

Health & Beauty

Chinese Herbalist

Vinh Khang Herbs & Gensengs

512 Clement Street, between Sixth and Seventh Avenues
(752 8336). Bus 1, 2, 4, 38, 44. **Open** 9.30am-7pm Mon-
Wed, Fri-Sun; noon-7pm Thur. **No credit cards.** **Map B4**
Chinese herbalism is one of the hottest trends in alternative
medicine and this shop is open seven days a week to cater
for the city's ills. Inspect the splendid array of roots and
remedies as herbal specialists mix up a customised concoction of ancient remedies.

Cosmetics & Beauty Products

Body Shop

SF Shopping Center, 865 Market Street, at Fifth Street
(281 3760). BART Powell Street/Muni Metro F, J, K,
L, M, N/bus 6, 7, 27, 31, 66, 71/cable car Powell-
Mason or Powell-Hyde. **Open** 9.30am-8pm Mon-Sat;
11am-6pm Sun. **Credit** AmEx, Disc, MC, V.
Map G4
Of the more than 250 Body Shop stores nationwide, there are
40-odd in the Golden State alone, offering the now familiar
skin and hair care products. Aside from the scented slew of
moisturising creams, soaps and scrubs, the company's
would-be eco principles keep them in the public's favour.

Experience an uncanny sensation – and then write home about it. **Quantity Postcards**.

Branches: 2106 Chestnut Street, between Fillmore and Steiner Streets (202 0112); 16 California Street, at Drumm Street (397 7455); 506 Castro Street, at 18th Street (431 8860); 100 Powell Street, at Ellis Street (399 1802).

Mac Cosmetics

1833 Union Street, between Laguna and Octavia Streets (771 6113). Bus 41, 45. **Open** 11am-8pm Mon-Fri; 10am-7pm Sat; 11am-6pm Sun. **Credit** AmEx, MC, V. **Map E2**

Not to be confused with the clothing store, this gigantic, well-lit shop carries the vamp-look cosmetics formerly available only in top department stores.

Hair Salons

Architects and Heroes

580 Bush Street, between Grant Avenue and Stockton Street (391 8833). Bus 2, 3, 4, 30. 45, 76. **Open** 9am-6pm Tue-Sat. **Credit** MC, V. **Map G3**

There are plenty of $10 cuts available at small hairdressers throughout the city, but if you want a hair experience, book in advance for a cut with one of this salon's professionals. The pre-cut shampoo is more like a luxurious head massage (and will probably lull you to sleep). If you don't have lots of cash, ask for a trainee: even the novices here are top-notch. **Branch**: 2239 Fillmore Street, between Sacramento and Clay Streets (921 8383).

Cowboys & Angels

Suite 400, 207 Powell Street, at O'Farrell Street (362 8516). BART Powell Street/Muni Metro F, J, K, L, M, N/bus 6, 7, 27, 31, 66, 71/cable car Powell-Mason or Powell-Hyde. **Open** 9am-6pm Tue-Sat; 11am-7pm Thur. **Credit** MC, V. **Map G4**

You won't see any rich old ladies getting shampoos and sets here. This trendy young salon also boasta a rotating art exhibition. Cuts range from $35 to $65.

Novella-Aveda Concept Salon & Day Spa

2238 Union Street, between Fillmore and Webster Streets (673 1929). Bus 22, 41, 45. **Open** 11.30am-9pm Mon; 9am-9pm Tue-Fri; 9am-7pm Sat, Sun. **Credit** AmEx, MC, V. **Map E2**

Recharge your batteries and luxuriate in Aveda products – this salon is truly a sanctuary. Cuts range from $45 to $65; body treatments are expensive, but worth it.

Manicures & Pedicures

As in most big cities, there are hundreds of small boutiques in San Francisco offering manicures, pedicures and waxes (consult the *Yellow Pages* for a full list). Expect to pay $8-$12 for a manicure and $10-$15 for a pedicure. Salon prices are substantially higher, but if it's pampering you're after, they're your best bet.

77 Maiden Lane Salon & Spa

77 Maiden Lane, second floor, between Grant Avenue and Kearny Street (391 7777). Bus 12, 15, 30, 30X, 41, 45. **Open** 9am-7pm Mon-Wed, Fri, Sat; 9am-8pm Thur; 10am-5pm Sun. **Credit** MC, V. **Map H3**

If you've got $40 to spare, treat yourself to the hour-long heavenly pedicure here and you'll have a new spring in your step. Recently renovated and expanded, this full-service salon runs the pampering gamut, including massage, makeovers, hair styling and facials. It's not the cheapest place in town, but the services come highly recommended.

Tattoos & body piercing

What the hell – you're in San Francisco.

Body Manipulations

3234 16th Street, between Guerrero and Dolores Streets (621 0408). Bus 6, 7, 22, 66, 71. **Open** noon-7pm daily. **Credit** MC, V. **Map F6**

With a great new location, Body Manipulations specialises in custom body piercing, scarring, branding and just about anything else that can be done to the human figure (except tattooing). Check out the catalogues – you can pierce just about anything these days.

Gauntlet

2377 Market Street, at Castro Street (431 3133). Muni Metro F, K, L, M/bus 8, 24. **Open** noon-7pm Mon-Wed, Fri, Sat; noon-9pm Thur; 1-6pm Sun. **Credit** AmEx, MC, V. **Map E6**

Body manipulating isn't new fashion to these experts, who have been piercing everything from noses to labia for over 20 years. If you're into it, this is the place to get yourself a new hole or two. This branch is in the heart of the Castro – there are others in Los Angeles, New York, Paris and Chicago.

Lyle Tuttle Tattooing

841 Columbus Avenue, at Greenwich Street (775 4991). Bus 15, 30/cable car Powell-Mason. **Open** noon-9pm Mon-Thur; noon-10pm Fri, Sat; noon-8pm Sun. **Credit** MC, V. **Map G2**

Lyle Tuttle is one of the most respected tattoo artists in the world, and for those in the know, this parlour (*pictured below*) is an essential stop-off point. It's best to make an appointment. For the adjoining museum, *see chapter* **Museums & Galleries**.

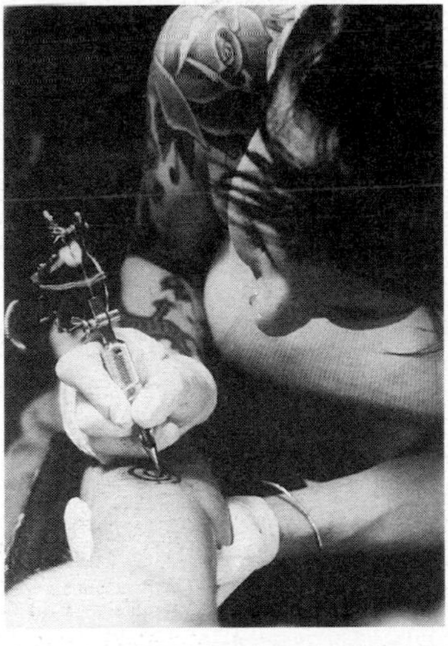

Zeitgeist – *for resuscitated Rolexes. See page 165.*

High Tech Nails
*2007 Divisadero Street, at California Street (928 0324).
Bus 1, 24.* **Open** *9am-7pm Mon-Sat; 10am-6pm Sun.*
Credit MC, V. **Map D3/4**
This Pacific Heights salon is a favourite among locals. The
busy staff are always warm and friendly and welcome walk-
ins. Bring your own polish or choose from an array of
colours, from classic reds to trendy baby blues.

Spas, Saunas & Bath Houses
See also chapter **Trips Out of Town**.

Family Sauna
*2308 Clement Street, at 24th Avenue (221 2208).
Bus 1, 2, 29, 38.* **Open** *noon-10pm daily.* **Credit** MC, V.
Everyone has good things to say about this mellow neighbourhood retreat offering dry-heat Finnish saunas, two therapeutic whirlpool spas (the redwood tub retains heat better
but the fibreglass option has more leg room), massage,
facials and waxing. Unlike most of the city's spas, there's no
pretension here – nor high prices – only a casual, clean, and
comfortable environment where all types of San Franciscans
come to cleanse their body and mind in a private hot tub.

Kabuki Hot Springs
*Japan Center, 1750 Geary Boulevard, at Fillmore Street
(922 6002). Bus 22, 38.* **Open** *10am-10pm Mon-Fri;
9am-10pm Sat, Sun.* **Admission** day pass without
massage $10; day pass with 25-minute massage $35;
baths, steam and 55-minute massage $60. **Credit** AmEx,
MC, V. **Map E4**
A traditional Japanese bath house, complete with deep
ceramic communal tubs, a steam room, sit-down showers,
saunas and even a restful *tatami* room. Shiatsu massages are
given from 2pm to 9.30pm Mon-Thur, and are by appointment only. Women-only days are Wednesday, Friday and
Sunday; it's men-only the rest of the week. Spend an hour here
and you'll come out feeling fantastic, revived and pampered.

Osento
*955 Valencia Street, at 21st Street (282 6333). BART
24th Street/bus 14, 26, 49.* **Open** *1pm-1am daily; last
admission midnight.* **Admission** $9-$13. **No credit
cards. Castro/Mission Map Y2**
A bath house for women only. Walk in to the peaceful surroundings, leave your clothes in a locker, shower off and
relax in the whirlpool. Take a dip in the cold plunge, and
then choose between the wet and dry saunas. An outdoor
deck offers the chance to cool down or enjoy the weather on
a sunny day. Massages are available by appointment.

Spa Nordstrom
*SF Shopping Center, 865 Market Street, at Fifth Street
(977 5102). BART Powell Street/Muni Metro F, J, K,
L, M, N/bus 6, 7, 27, 31, 66, 71/cable car Powell-
Mason or Powell-Hyde.* **Open** *9am-7pm Mon-Sat;
10.15am-5.45pm Sun.* **Credit** AmEx, JCB, MC, V.
Map G4
When you're struggling for air in the middle of hundreds of
shoppers at this downtown shopping centre, you'd never
know that rejuvenation is just a few floors away. Yet the
minute you collapse through the door of this spa, you leave
the hectic retail pace behind. Soak your shopping-tired feet
in a warm tub before going to a private room to indulge in
one of many restorative services, ranging from aromatherapy, massage and skin care spa packages, to an eyebrow or
bikini wax. Save the manicure for the small – and cheaper –
independents.

Household

Also worth checking out is the ancient, chaotic but
well-stocked hardware store, **Workingman's
Headquarters,** at 2871 Mission Street, between
24th and 25th Streets (282 2403).

Centrium Furnishings

2166 Market Street, between Church and Sanchez Streets (863 4195). Muni Metro F, J, K, L, M. **Open** noon-6pm Tue-Sat; 1-5pm Sun. **Credit** AmEx, MC, V. **Map E6**
Furniture, lighting and decorative arts from the 1930s to the 1970s.

Crate & Barrel

125 Grant Avenue, at Geary Street (986 4000). Bus 2, 3, 4, 38, 76. **Open** 10am-7pm Mon-Fri; 10am-6pm Sat; 11am-5pm Sun. **Credit** AmEx, Disc, MC, V. **Map G/H3**
With its simple, clean-lined, functional designs for the home, C&B is your best bet for reasonably priced household items. The service is friendly and the seasonal sales are excellent.

Fillamento

2185 Fillmore Street, at Sacramento Street (931 2224). Bus 1, 3, 22. **Open** 10am-6pm Mon-Sat; noon-5pm Sun. **Credit** AmEx, DC, Disc, JCB, MC, V. **Map E3**
Elegant dishes, stylish glassware, distinctive lamps and avant-garde home furnishings: this is truly the hippest place for furnishings in town, though service is not always on hand.

Pottery Barn

2100 Chestnut Street, at Steiner Street (441 178). Bus 22, 28, 43, 76. **Open** 10am-9pm Mon-Fri; 10am-8pm Sat; 11am-6pm Sun. **Credit** AmEx, Disc, MC, V. **Map D2**
Find the latest in upscale basics: glassware, linens, dishware, lamps, candles, cushions and picture frames. You name it, they stock it – and prices are moderate. The staff are always very helpful, especially at this branch which sells larger furniture items.
Branches: 1 Embarcadero Center, at Battery and Sacramento Streets (788 6810); Stonestown Galleria, Winston Drive (731 1863).

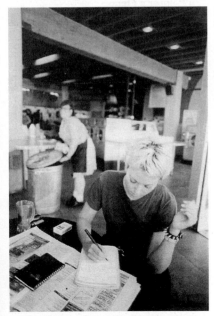

Café-cum-laundrette, **Brainwash.**

Jewellery & Watches

See also page 149 **Department Stores.**

Jerusalem Shop

313 Noe Street, at Market Street (626 7906). Muni Metro F, K, L, M/bus 24, 37. **Open** 10am-10pm Mon-Fri; 10am-9pm Sat; 11am-7pm Sun. **Credit** AmEx, DC, Disc, MC, V. **Map E6**
This women's clothing and jewellery shop has been lauded as the best in town for hand-crafted jewellery. The selection is wide ranging, with an emphasis on silver.

Lang

323 Sutter Street, between Stockton Street and Grant Avenue (982 2213). BART Montgomery Street/Muni Metro F, J, K, L, M, N/bus 2, 3, 4, 76. **Open** 10am-5pm Mon-Sat. **Credit** AmEx, DC, JCB, MC, V. **Map G3**
Stocks an extensive selection of antique and estate jewellery and lots of old silver.

Magical Trinket

524 Hayes Street, at Laguna Street (626 0764). Bus 21. **Open** 11am-7pm Tue-Sat; noon-5pm Sun. **Credit** AmEx, Disc, MC, V. **Map F5**
An extensive array of beads and baubles for jewellery making. The staff are very helpful in offering suggestions and even offer bead-making workshops; call for a schedule.

Zeitgeist

437B Hayes Street, at Gough Street (864 0185). BART Van Ness/Muni Metro F, J, K, L, M, N. **Open** noon-6pm Tue-Sun. **Credit** MC, V. **Map F5**
The place to come for second-hand watches, including Philippe Patek and Rolex.

Laundrettes & Dry Cleaners

Brainwash

1122 Folsom Street, between Seventh and Eighth Streets (café 861 3663/laundromat 431 9274). Bus 12, 27, 42. **Open** 7.30am-midnight Mon-Thur, Sun; 7.30am-1am Fri, Sat. **Credit** AmEx, DC, MC, V. **Map G5**
San Francisco's first and only café/laundromat has been a trendy neighbourhood gathering spot since it opened. Rock out with the latest CDs and live music at the weekend, and have an espresso, a glass of wine or some pasta while you throw your clothes into a machine or have them dry cleaned.

Locust Cleaners

3585 Sacramento Street, between Locust and Laurel Streets (346 9271). Bus 1, 3, 4. **Open** 7.30am-6pm Mon-Fri; 8.30am-5pm Sat. **No Credit** cards. **Map C3/4**
Locust may not be as convenient (or as cheap) as the downtown one-day cleaning operations, but if you want quality alterations, then bring your garments here.

Meaders Cleaners

1475 Sansome Street, at Lombard Street (781 8200). Bus 42. **Open** 7am-7pm Mon-Fri; 8.30am-5pm Sat. **Credit** MC, V. **Map H2**
In the washing and scrubbing business since 1912, Meaders Cleaners offers a reliable dry cleaning and cleaning service. Phone for your nearest branch.

Mother Earth Cleaners

4721 Geary Street, at 12th Avenue (751 2822). Bus 38. **Open** 7am-6pm Mon-Fri; 9am-5pm Sat. **Credit** AmEx, Disc, MC, V. **Map A4**
This local dry cleaner uses only environmentally safe products, so your freshly cleaned, politically-correct clothes come back with that horrid toxic smell. Pick-up and delivery services.

Musical Instruments

Drum World
5016 Mission Street, at Geneva Avenue (334 7559).
Bus 9AX, 14, 15, 29, 43. **Open** 10am-6pm Mon-Sat;
11am-4pm Sun. **Credit** AmEx, Disc, MC, V.
Zildjian cymbals and small percussion instruments.

Haight-Ashbury Music Center
1540 Haight Street, at Ashbury Street (863 7327).
Bus 6, 7, 43, 66, 71. **Open** 11am-7pm Mon-Fri; 10am-6pm
Sat; noon-6pm Sun. **Credit** AmEx, DC, Disc, JCB, MC, V.
Map D5/6
A stop-off point for musicians of all sorts, but a particular
favourite with local and out-of-town rock and rollers. The
shop sells new and second-hand instruments, sheet music,
amps and has notices about bands looking for new
members.

Real Guitars
15 Lafayette Street, off Mission Street (552 3310).
BART Van Ness Avenue/Muni Metro J, K, L, M, N/bus
9, 42, 47. **Open** 11am-6pm Mon-Sat. **Credit** MC, V.
Map F5
Sells used and vintage guitars, including Martin, Gibson
and Gretsch.

Stereo Equipment

Bang & Olufsen
345 Powell Street, at Post Street (274 3320). Bus 2, 3, 4,
76/cable car Powell-Mason or Powell-Hyde. **Open** 9am-
7pm Mon-Wed; 9am-8pm Thur-Sat; 10am-6pm Sun.
Credit AmEx, DC, JCB, MC, V. **Map G3**
State-of-the-art stereo and audio equipment by appointment
to Danish royalty.

New Age, Religion & Magic

Botanica Yoruba
998 Valencia Street, at 21st Street (826 4967). BART
24th Street/bus 14, 26, 49. **Open** 10am-6pm Mon-Fri;
10am-6.30pm Sat; noon-5pm Sun. **Credit** MC, V.
Castro/Mission Map Y2
Candles, potions, powders, oils, herbs, statues of saints –
everything you need for the practice of Santeria, the African-
Cuban religion practiced in some Latin countries.

Enchanted Crystal
1895 Union Street, at Laguna Street (885 1335).
Bus 41, 45. **Open** 10am-6pm Mon-Sat; noon-5pm Sun.
Credit AmEx, Disc, JCB, MC, V. **Map E2**
Crystals of every description: geodes, pendants, jewels. Lots
of little fairies and magical things.

Psychic Eye Bookshop
301 Fell Street, at Gough Street (863 9997).
Muni Metro F, N, M/bus 6, 7, 42. **Open** 10am-10pm
Mon-Sat, 11am-7pm Sun. **Credit** AmEx, Disc, MC, V.
Map F5
This is the newest and grandest pooh-bah of alternative religion shops: a leader in new age, self-help, philosophy and
the occult, Psychic Eye will satisfy every non-traditional
spiritual need you have. On-site tarot readings, CDs and
tapes, incense, musical instruments, bottles and stones,
cards, books, jewellery – the place is addictive.

Red Rose Gallerie
2251 Chestnut Street, at Scott Street (776 6871).
Bus 28, 30, 43, 76. **Open** 11am-9pm daily. **Credit**
AmEx, Disc, MC, V. **Map D2**
For that Zen state of mind, this shop is an oasis of Eastern-
inspired spiritual products, to heal the mind, body, and soul.
There is also a catalogue of products available; call 1-800 374
5505 for details.

Opticians

City Optix
2154 Chestnut Street, between Pierce and Steiner Streets
(921 1188). Bus 22, 28, 43, 76. **Open** 10am-6pm Mon-
Sat; noon-5pm Sun. **Credit** AmEx, MC, V. **Map D2**
Sometimes shopping for new frames in this comprehensive
store can feel like a group project – customers advise each
other on their look and the staff are helpful. You might come
out a new person.

Eyedare
3199 16th Street, at Guerrero Street (241 0240).
Bus 22, 26, 53. **Open** 11am-7pm Mon-Thur; 10am-6pm
Fri, Sat. **Credit** AmEx, Disc, JCB, MC, V. **Map F6**
The latest designs: Magli, Gaultier, Ferre. The staff will give
you their honest opinion and not simply a sales spiel.

Picture Framing

The Great Frame Up
2358 Market Street, between Noe and Castro Streets
(863 7144). Muni Metro F, K, L, M/bus 24, 35, 37.
Open 10am-9pm Mon-Fri; 10am-6pm Sat; noon-5pm Sun.
Credit AmEx, MC, V. **Map E6**
A budget option is to frame your own pictures: the friendly
staff at these chains will take you through the process.
Branch: 1530 Union Street, at Van Ness Avenue
(771 5800).

The Painter's Place
355 Hayes Street, between Franklin and Gough Streets
(431 9827). Muni Metro F, J, K, L, M, N/bus 21, 42, 47,
49. **Open** 10am-4pm Mon, Sat; 10am-6pm Tue-Fri.
Credit AmEx, Disc, MC, V. **Map F5**
The place to visit when you just can't wait to get your
favourite print or artwork behind glass.

Records, Tapes & CDs

Occupying the old Rock & Bowl space, the huge
new **Amoeba** (1855 Haight, at Stanyan; 750 9368)
opened as we went to press.

Aquarius Records
1055 Valencia Street, at 21st Street (674 2272). Bus 14,
26, 49. **Open** 10am-9pm Mon-Thur, Sun; 10am-10pm Fri,
Sat. **Credit** MC, V. **Castro/Mission Map Y2**
Now in new larger premises in the Mission district, this San
Franciscan institution stocks some of the best alternative
and underground music in the city. Look no further: you're
guaranteed to find that vinyl you've been searching for.

Reckless Records
1401 Haight Street, at Masonic Street (431 3434).
Muni Metro L/bus 37. **Open** 10am-10pm Mon-Sat; 10am-
9pm Sun. **Credit** AmEx, Disc, JCB, MC, V. **Map D5**
A reliable source for second-hand CDs, vinyl and tapes: indie,
hip-hop and soul.

Reggae Run-Ins Village Store
505 Divisadero Street, at Fell Street (922 2442).
Bus 21, 24. **Open** 11am-7pm Mon-Sat; noon-6pm Sun.
Credit AmEx, MC, V. **Map D/E5**
If reggae is your jive, this is your hive. Records, tapes, videos,
a juice bar, Jamaican food and much more.

Out of town

Shopping further afield can have its advantages: you'll be able to escape the crowds and get to see much more of the Bay Area.

In the East Bay, besides the boutiques and antique shops that abound on Piedmont Avenue in Rockridge, Berkeley's **Telegraph Avenue** is a street with every kind of store imaginable. For new books, stop in and browse the shelves of **Cody's Bookstore** (2454 Telegraph Avenue, at Haste Street; 1-510 845 7852). For rare or used tomes, try **Moe's Books** (2476 Telegraph; 1-510 849 2087). If you're a music fan, **Amoeba Music** (2455 Telegraph; 1-510 549 1125) and **Rasputin's** (2350 Telegraph; 1-510 848 9004) are the Bay Area's quintessential record shops. At weekends, the stands on Telegraph sell locally made arts and crafts, tie-dyed clothing and handmade silver jewellery.

Berkeley has its fair share of outlet shopping. Clothing outlets include **Mishi** (801 Delaware Street; 1-510 525 1075) for down-to-earth women's clothing, and **Weaver's Outlet** (2570 Bancroft Way; 1-510 540 5901) for casual cotton clothes by the barrel. For household items, check out **Crate & Barrel Outlet** (1785 Fourth Street; 1-510 528 5500) or the weekend-only **Smith & Hawken Outlet Store** (1330 Tenth Street; 1-510 525 2944) for gardening supplies. And you can't call yourself a second-hand junkie until you've been to **Urban Ore** (1333 Sixth Street; 1-510 559 4450).

If you're heading north, the **Napa Factory Outlets** (1-707 226 9876), located about one hour north of San Francisco (SR 29), exit First Street), are definitely worth a visit. Some 45 leading designers offer discounts of 25-65 per cent. Stores include Ann Taylor, Esprit and Liz Clairborne for women, Nine West shoes and Tommy Hilfiger for men and women. Twenty minutes north of Napa on SR 29, you'll find a further selection of stores at **St Helena Premier Outlets** (1-707 226 9876), including Brooks Brothers menswear, London Fog coats, Joan & David shoes, Donna Karen for men and women and Coach for leather goods.

The Peninsula and South Bay are mostly suburban residential areas with the same strip malls carrying the same name brands. But if it's bargains you're after, seek and you shall find. San Jose's **Capitol Flea Market** (3630 Hillcap Avenue; 1-408 225 5800) and **The Flea Market Inc** (1590 Berryessa Road, between Lundy and Commercial Streets; 1-408 453 1110) are great places for bargain pickings. More factory outlets are located in **Gilroy**, about 75 minutes south of San Francisco on US 101. The shops are mainly the same as in the northern outlets; however, they do have more shoes, such as Timberland, Bass, Nike, Reebok and Fila.

Ritmo Latino
2401 Mission Street, at 20th Street (824 8556). BART 24th Street/bus 15, 49. **Open** 10am-9.30pm Mon-Thur, Sat; 10am-10.30pm Fri, Sun. **Credit** Disc, MC, V. **Castro/Mission Map Y1**
The place for Latin music: ranchera, mariachi, salsa, Tex-Mex, merengue and more. Equipped with listening stations.

Star Classics
425 Hayes Street, at Gough Street (552 1110). Muni Metro J, K, L, M, N/bus 21, 42, 47, 49. **Open** 10am-8pm Mon-Fri; 11am-8pm Sat; noon-7pm Sun. **Credit** AmEx, MC, V. **Map F5**
The classical music specialists. For more, *see chapter* **Music**.

Streetlight Records
3979 24th Street, between Sanchez and Noe Streets (282 3550). Bus 48. **Open** 10am-10pm Mon-Sat; 10.30am-8.30pm Sun. **Credit** AmEx, Disc, MC, V. **Castro/Mission Map X2**
For the used and the rare, bargain prices and a helpful staff. Money back guaranteed.
Branch: 2350 Market Street, at Castro Street (282 8000).

Tower Records
2525 Jones Street, at Columbus Avenue (885 0500). Bus 15, 41/cable car Powell-Mason. **Open** 9am-midnight daily. **Credit** AmEx, Disc, MC, V. **Map F2**
The giant music store on Columbus Avenue is still the locals' favourite spot for browsing and buying and it's open late. The branch on Third Street sells back-catalogue albums at great discounts.
Branches: 2280 Market Street, between Noe and 16th Streets (621 0588); Stonestown Galleria, Winston Drive (681 2001); 660 Third Street, at Brannan Street (957 9660).

Virgin Megastore
2 Stockton Street, at Market Street (397 4525). BART Powell Street/Muni Metro F, J, K, L, M, N/bus 6, 7, 8, 9, 21, 30, 45, 66. **Open** 9am-11pm Mon-Thur; 9am-midnight, Fri, Sat; 10am-10pm Sun. **Credit** AmEx, Disc, MC, V. **Map G4**
One of the largest music and entertainment stores in North America. You can sample a CD from 60 listening stations, listen to the store's own DJ or sit upstairs in the café. Richard Branson knows how to look after his American audiences.

Smoking

Pipe Dreams
1376 Haight Street, at Masonic Street (431 3553). Bus 6, 7, 43, 66, 71. **Open** 10am-7.50pm Mon-Sat; 11am-6.50pm Sun. **Credit** AmEx, Disc, MC, V. **Map D5**
A Haight shop that will take you back to the days when the area was known as the 'Hashbury'. It offers the full monty in smoking paraphernalia, T-shirts and psychedelic sundries.

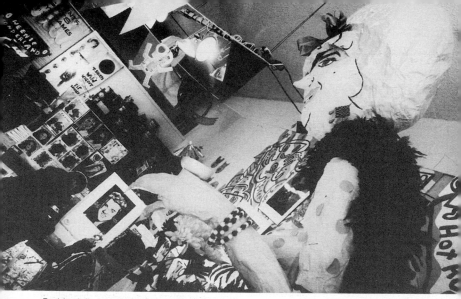

Barbie dolls are thin on the ground at the **Scairy Hairy Toy Company**. *See page 169.*

Don't ask for a 'bong' but for a water pipe, and remember that the shop can only sell to those who intend, or at least seem to intend, to use their products with legal substances.

Speciality Shops

Britex Fabrics

146 Geary Street, between Stockton Street and Grant Avenue (392 2910). Bus 30, 38, 45/cable car Powell-Mason or Powell-Hyde. **Open** 9.30am-6pm Mon-Wed, Sat; 9.30am-7pm Thur, Fri. **Credit** AmEx, MC, V. **Map G3/4**
Four floors of fashion and home textiles, including an awesome collection of buttons.

Greenwich Yarn

2073 Greenwich Street, between Webster and Buchanan Streets (567 2535). Bus 22, 41, 45. **Open** 10am-6pm Mon, Tue, Thur-Sat; 1-5pm Sun. **Credit** MC, V. **Map E2**
Travelling knitters take note of this well-stocked shop full of patterns, yarn and helpful advice.

Haight-Ashbury T-shirts

1500 Haight Street, at Ashbury Street (863 4639). Bus 6, 7, 43, 66, 71. **Open** *summer* 10am-9pm daily; *winter* 10am-8pm daily. **Credit** AmEx, Disc, MC, V. **Map D5/6**
Everything you ever dreamed of in a music scene, hip cartoon or rock show commemorative shirt. This shop is covered from floor to ceiling in tie-dyes, Garcia collectables, Beatles mania, Haight-Ashbury 94117 (90210 rip-offs) and much more.

SF Rock Posters & Collectables

1851 Powell Street, between Greenwich and Filbert Streets (956 6749). Bus 15, 39. **Open** 10am-6pm Mon-Sat. **Credit** AmEx, MC, V. **Map G2**
Handbills, tickets, original art and posters galore.

Uncle Mama

2075 Market Street, between 14th and Church Streets (626 1953) Muni Metro F, J, K, L, M, N/bus 22.

Open noon-7pm Mon, Wed, Fri; 4-7pm Tue, Thur; noon-5.30pm Sun. **Credit** MC, V. **Map E6**
With Patsy and Eddy blaring from leopard skin TVs in the shop window, Uncle Mama is the quintessential in Americana memorabilia. Customers take a trip down memory lane as they seek out Oscar Meyer Wiener whistles, Pillsbury Boy and Girlfriend salt and pepper shakers, Charlie's Angel's lunch boxes and pop-rocks.

Sex Accessories

See also **Good Vibrations** *and* **Stormy Leather** *in chapter* **Gay & Lesbian San Francisco**.

Image Leather

2199 Market Street, at Sanchez Street (621 7551). Muni Metro F, J, K, L, M/bus 8, 22. **Open** 9am-10pm Mon-Sat; 11am-7pm Sun. **Credit** AmEx, Disc, MC, V. **Map E6**
Whips, chains, harnesses, nipple rings, corsets, masks and all that kinky jazz.

Ticket Agencies

BASS

(1-510 762 2277/1-800 225 2277 outside California). **Open** 8.30am-9pm daily. **Credit** AmEx, MC, V.
If you need a ticket, the Bay Area Seating Service can probably sell it to you, either over the phone (be armed with your credit card) or at one of its many outlets throughout the city. Find your nearest outlet via the phone message.

TIX Bay Area

Union Square, on Stockton Street (433 7827). BART Powell Street/Muni Metro F, J, K, L, M, N/bus 2, 3, 4, 30, 45, 76/cable car Powell-Hyde or Powell-Mason. **Open** 11am-6pm Tue-Thur; 11am-7pm Fri, Sat. **Credit** (full-price tickets only) MC, V. **Map G3**
TIX Bay Area is San Francisco's only outlet for half-price tickets on selected theatre, dance, opera and performance events. Standard price tickets are available, too. You pay a service charge.

Toys

See also page 151 **Arts & Crafts** *and page 161* **Gifts & Stationery**. For other toy shops, including **FAO Schwarz**, *see chapter* **Children**.

Main Line
1928 Fillmore Street, at Pine Street (563 4438). Bus 1, 3, 22. **Open** 10am-7pm Mon-Wed; 10am-8pm Thur, Fri; 10am-6pm Sat; 11am-6pm Sun. **Credit** AmEx, Disc, JCB, MC, V. **Map E4**
Looking for a gift for someone who appears to have everything? This shop has more kitsch than you can count – a must for any self-respecting coffee table owner.

Scairy Hairy Toy Company
3804 17th Street, at Sanchez Street (864 6543). Muni Metro F, J/bus 33. **Open** 11am-7pm Thur-Sun. **Credit** Disc, MC, V. **Map E6**
This weird and wacky shop personifies the twisted side of San Francisco. You can be the proud owner of a Lil' Miss PMS doll, a Hang'in Weenie windsock, a collection of Beatnick Island finger puppets, or a cat's meow T-shirt.

Star Magic Space Age Gifts
4026 24th Street, at Castro Street (641 8626). Bus 24, 48. **Open** 10am-8pm Mon; 10am-7pm Tue-Thur; 10am-8.30pm Fri, Sat; 11am-7pm Sun. **Credit** MC, V. **Castro/Mission Map X2**

New Age meets Space Age at Star Magic: toys for grown-ups as well as children.

Video Rental

Leather Tongue
714 Valencia Street, at 18th Street (552 2900). Bus 14, 26, 33, 49. **Open** noon-11pm Mon-Thur, Sun; noon-midnight Fri, Sat. **Credit** MC, V. **Map F6**
An extensive collection of videos by independent and local filmmakers, many sold on the sidewalk at weekends.

Le Video
1231 and 1239 Ninth Avenue, between Lincoln Way and Irving Street (566 3606). Muni Metro N/bus 44, 71. **Open** 10am-11pm daily. **Credit** AmEx, MC, V. **Map B6**
The occult, the obscure: if it's on video, you'll find it here. Peruse more than 31,000 titles ranging from good ol' American pop films to New Age, cult or Japanese animation. The staff are exceptionally knowledgeable.

Naked Eye News and Video
533 Haight Street, between Fillmore and Steiner Streets (864 2985). Bus 6, 7, 22, 66, 71. **Open** 10am-10pm Mon-Thur; 10am-11pm Fri, Sat; 11am-10pm Sun. **Credit** AmEx, MC, V. **Map E5**
Cult videos, alternative comics, trading cards, local 'zines: what more could you ask for under one roof?

Shopping the Haight

From denim jeans and religious artifacts to body piercings, incense and funky furniture, you can find just about anything to buy on Haight Street. The Haight has gone through many stages since its heyday back in the 1960s, and many shops still carry remnants from times past. Upper Haight is more gentrified: among the clothes shops that line the streets between Masonic and Stanyan Streets you'll find the **Mascara Club** (1408 Haight Street; 863 2837), a Mexican folk art store that sells colourful oilcloths, Frida Kahlo paper dolls, tin toys, and enough images of Jesus and the Virgin of Guadalupe to keep collectors happy for years.

Turn the corner onto Ashbury Street and walk a block to **Touch Stone** (1601A Page Street; 621 2782), where knowledgeable staff will enlighten you on the benefits of oils, rocks, minerals, healing stones and other spiritual and metaphysical tools. In contrast to throbbing Haight Street, this peaceful shop is an oasis; it's also the only full service jewellery store in the Haight. **Positively Haight** (1400 Haight Street; 252 8747), on the corner of Masonic, sells trinkets from yesteryear, including a large selection of Grateful Dead patches. On the next block, **Gargoyle Beads** (1324 Haight; 552 4727) sells – just as its name implies – gargoyle-like knick-

knacks and other fetish objects, such as candles, herbs, stationery and gothic jewellery.

It's about a ten-minute walk to the Lower Haight (between Divisadero and Webster Streets – hop on any bus travelling east for a quick trip), a region that has picked up where the 1960s and 1970s left off. On the corner of Pierce Street, you'll find **Costumes on the Haigh**t (735 Haight Street; 621 1356), which has one of the best assortments of outfits in the city, to buy and hire. After all, you can never have too many feather boas or Cleopatra wigs. It also sells cool vintage clothes – more 1980s polyester than 1960s tie-dye.

A great resource for excellent deals on used clothing is **Bulletproof** (5892 Haight Street; 626 3481) where you can buy stylish duds at $7 a pound. What a steal! For cutting-edge hemp wear, check out **Labyrinth Phassions** (463 Haight; 552 3082) whose funky clothing in flamboyant colours for both men and women takes this versatile fibre to the extreme. Finally, stop in at **Groove Merchant Records** (687 Haight) and chat to the enthusiastic staff about the latest acid jazz, world beat or dance music. Retro or futuro, you'll definitely be turned onto something new by the time you leave the Haight.

To get to the Haight from downtown, take bus 6, 7, 66, 71 or 73.

Entertainment

Children

For the big kid in all of us; or for the ones you brought with you.

If you thought San Francisco was for grown-ups only, you're in for a pleasant surprise. It's a child-friendly place where under-fives travel free on public transport, many hotels provide babysitting and kids get a great fuss made of them in the Latino and Asian neighbourhoods.

If you're looking for fun excursions with children, start by walking (or driving) down Lombard Street, the 'Crookedest Street in the World', riding a cable car and taking the lift up the Coit Tower. The Bay Area – and northern California in general – is also a terrific place for kids interested in animals and marine mammals, especially sea lions, whales, otters and seals. As well as trying out the suggestions listed below, read the pink Datebook section of the Sunday *San Francisco Chronicle* and check the listings under Children's Events.

For more ideas, *see also chapters* **Sightseeing**, **Sport & Fitness** *and* **Trips Out of Town**.

Animals, Circuses & Carousels

For an enjoyable family outing, there's plenty going on at the **San Francisco Zoo**, as 1.2 million visitors per year attest. Travelling further afield,

the **Oakland Zoo** (1-510 632 9523) is also worth visiting. Travelling circuses come to San Francisco all year round – watch out for the beautiful French-Canadian **Cirque du Soleil** every second summer – leaving swarms of fans in their wake. The **New Pickle Circus** (544 9344) is the friendly local group, which usually performs in San Francisco in December and sometimes has other performances in the Bay Area; look out for their advertisements or phone them to find out their schedule. **Make-A-Circus** (242 1414), based at Fort Mason, performs in the Bay Area during the summer. San Francisco is also a great place for carousels: there's one in the Zoo, one in Golden Gate Park and a two-storey Venetian Carousel on Pier 39.

The Jungle, Fun and Adventure

555 Ninth Street, between Bryant and Brannan Streets (552 4386). Bus 19, 27, 42. **Open** 10am-8pm Mon-Thur, Sun; 10am-9pm Fri; 9am-9pm Sat. **Admission** *unlimited play until 5pm* $3.95-$5.95 Mon-Fri; *after 5pm* $2.95 Mon-Thur, $3.95 Fri; *2 hours play* $3.95-$6.95 Sat, Sun. **Credit** MC, V. **Map G5**
An indoor play centre for children from six months to 12 years old, aimed at helping out weary shoppers. There's a tangled macaroni maze of colourful tubes to slide and crawl

*Get in touch with your inner sheep at the **San Francisco Zoo**. See page 173.*

Perfect for small children: the **Randall Museum**. *See page 174.*

through, netting to climb and tanks full of coloured balls. Grab a cappuccino in the Parents Only room while the employees look after your kids.

San Francisco School of Circus Arts
755 Frederick Street, at Arguello Boulevard (759 8123). Muni Metro N/bus 6, 43, 66, 71. **Open** summer camps late June-early Aug. **Credit** MC, V. **Map C6**
There are clown classes for 5-12s throughout the year and week-long summer camps for 7-15 year-olds (9am-3pm, Mon-Fri) where they learn acrobatics, juggling, stilt-walking and clowning. A one-week course costs about $150.

San Francisco Zoo
Sloat Boulevard, near 45th Avenue (753 7080). Muni Metro L/bus 18, 23. **Open** *Main Zoo* 10am-5pm daily; *Children's Zoo* 11am-4pm Mon-Fri; 10.30am-4.30pm Sat, Sun. **Admission** $7; $1.50-$3.50 concessions; free first Wed of the month. **Credit** AmEx, MC, V.
With more than 1,000 different species of mammals and birds, there's a lot to see here. Koala Crossing (it's one of the few zoos in the US that has koalas), Musk Ox Meadows, Gorilla World (inhabited by two young and five adult gorillas), Tuxedo Junction for penguins and Wolf Woods all beckon. Recent zoo babies include lion cubs and baby rhinos. Children-oriented features are feeding times at 2pm daily (3pm for the penguins); the Zebra Zephyr train; a wonderfully creepy Insect Zoo; and a great choice of creatures to touch in the Petting Zoo ($1 admission), with some 'show and tell' information on pet care. Ask about the 'ZooFest for Kids', a night-time tour featuring mimes, puppeteers and live music.

Steinhart Aquarium
Golden Gate Park, inside the Academy of Sciences (750 7145). Muni Metro N/bus 5, 21, 44, 71. **Open** *summer* 9am-6pm daily; *winter* 9am-5pm daily. **Admission** $8.50; $2-$5.50 concessions. **Credit** AmEx, MC, V. **Map B6**

Kids love the dark confines of this aquarium, which holds more than 14,000 different sea creatures – some of them incredibly weird – from all over the globe. Check out the grumpy eels, the fluorescent-gilled sailfish and the harmless-looking piranhas that glide past the windows. The recently remodelled Fish Roundabout is a delightfully disorienting spiral with schools of finned creatures zig-zagging in one direction or another; try to arrive at feeding time for the most active panorama. There's a tidepool where kids can touch a variety of slimy creatures and, of course, a parcel of goofy penguins. The place gets crowded and claustrophobic at the weekend, so go during the week.

Babysitting/Childcare

American Child Care Service
(285 2300). **Credit** AmEx, MC, V.
An upmarket child care agency serving the downtown hotels, which will also take children on excursions to the Zoo, Exploratorium and other places. Rates are $11.50 per hour for up to three kids, minimum four hours.

Bay Area Childcare Agency
(991 7474). **No credit cards**.
In business for 50 years, this agency serves all the major hotels, screens sitters very carefully and won't employ anyone under the age of 30. The rates are $9 per hour plus transport (minimum four hours), which probably means $30-$40 for a child-free evening.

Historical Sites

Alcatraz Island
See chapter **Sightseeing** *for listings.*
The world-famous maximum-security prison remains one tourist attraction locals grudgingly admit is pretty fascinating. Kids will love 'The Rock' for its gritty ambiance and the

undercurrent of malevolency that the island still embodies. Rangers lead walking tours of the grounds, and the multi-lingual audio cellblock tour, narrated by former prisoners and played though headphones, is well worth the addition-al $3.25 per person. Dress warmly – The Rock can be as chilly as it is chilling.

USS Pampanito
Pier 45, Embarcadero (441 5819). Bus 15, 30, 32, 39, 42/cable car Powell-Hyde, Powell-Mason. **Open** *summer* 9am-8pm daily; *winter* 9am-6pm daily. **Admission** $5; $3 concessions. **No credit cards. Map F1**

You're in for a surprise at the **Exploratorium.**

The Pampanito is the only remaining fleet submarine from World War II that you can thoroughly explore. It's an eye-opener to what it was like to spend the war years underwater in such cramped quarters.

<h2>Libraries</h2>

Many local library branches offer regular story hours and 'lap readings', during which young chil-dren can sit on the knees of a local lady and hear a tale. Especially recommended are the multi-lingual Mission (695 5090) and Chinatown (274 0275) branches.

San Francisco Main Library
See chapter **Sightseeing** *for listings.*
San Francisco's gorgeous new Main Library boasts half an entire floor for children, with a circular storytelling room and more than a dozen computer terminals; videos, audio tapes and books in 40 languages; a children's multimedia and electronic discovery computer unit; a fairytale and folk collection; a 'creative centre' for live performances and crafts; and a Teenagers' Drop-In section. Children's art exhibits change periodically.

<h2>Museums</h2>

There's no shortage of museums in San Francisco, but those listed below are particularly good for children, with plenty of hands-on exhibits. The **Cable Car Barn Museum**, **Cartoon Art Museum** and **National Maritime Museum** are also worth a visit; for details of these and other spaces, *see chapter* **Museums & Galleries.**

Exploratorium
See chapter **Museums & Galleries** *for listings.*
If you and your kids are looking for something uniquely San Franciscan, put the Exploratorium at the top of your list. This science museum is perfect for kids since every-thing is designed to be touched. With over 700 hands-on experiments, your family can learn about sensory percep-tions, weather, botany, mechanics, health issues and the physics of sound and light. The favourite attraction is the Tactile Dome, a geodesic hemisphere of total blackness where you fumble around in the dark touching different objects. It's so popular that it attracts noisy crowds, so book in advance. The gift shop is full of educational and inter-esting scientific toys.

Museum of the City of San Francisco
Third floor, The Cannery, 2801 Leavenworth Street, at Beach Street (928 0289). Bus 19, 30, 32, 42/cable car Powell-Hyde. **Open** 10am-4pm Wed-Sun. **Admission** free. **Map F1**
Features include a special earthquake display, a huge Goddess of Liberty head from the pre-1906 quake City Hall and regular storytelling sessions. Curator Gladys Hansen is on hand to show you her great-aunt's sewing machine, which was saved from the flames of the Great Fire, and to tell you tales about the survivors.

Randall Museum
199 Museum Way, at southern tip of Masonic Avenue (554 9600). Bus 37. **Open** 10am-5pm Tue-Sat. **Admission** free. **Map D/E6**
This small, friendly museum is scenically located above the city in Corona Heights Park, and has a petting zoo with

Out of town

Bay Area Discovery Museum
557 McReynolds Road, Fort Baker, near north end of Golden Gate Bridge, Sausalito (487 4398). Golden Gate Transit bus 63 (Sat, Sun)/north on US 101 to Alexander Avenue exit, then follow signs. **Open** *summer* 10am-5pm Tue-Sun; *winter* 9am-4pm Tue-Thur; 10am-5pm Fri-Sun. **Admission** $7; $6 concessions. **No credit cards.**

This collection of historic army barracks has been carefully and imaginatively transformed into a place aimed at 1-10 year-olds, and includes an art room where toddlers learn how to paint and model and a series of distorting mirrors and light shows. You'll also find a pleasant café and outside picnic tables.

Lawrence Hall of Science
Centennial Drive, near Grizzly Park Boulevard, Berkeley (1-510 642 5132). BART to Berkeley, then AC Transit bus 8, 65. **Open** 10am-5pm daily. **Admission** $6; $2-$4 concessions. **Credit** Disc, MC, V.

This fascinating science museum in Berkeley offers a replica of the Challenger spacecraft's nose cone, a Wizard's Lab and a huge DNA model to scramble over. Check out the giant telescope, too.

Marine Mammal Center
Marin Headlands, Golden Gate National Recreation Area, Sausalito (289 7325/shop 289 7355).

Bus 76/north off US 101. **Open** 10am-4pm daily. **Admission** free, donations welcome. **Credit** MC, V.

There are now two marine mammal centres, one on Pier 39 (289 7325/shop 289 7373), just above where the sea lions congregate. Kids can see a sea lion skin and skeleton, learn about marine mammals and try out interactive computer activities. Just across the Golden Gate Bridge, the Sausalito centre is a sanctuary where sick or injured seals and sea lions are fed and nursed back to health by young volunteers.

Paramount's Great America
Great America Parkway, Santa Clara (1-408 988 1776). BART Fremont, then County Transit bus to Santa Clara. **Open** *Mar-June* 10am-9pm Sat, Sun; *June-Aug* 10am-9pm Mon-Thur, Sun; 10am-11pm Fri, Sat; *Aug-Oct* 10am-8pm Sat, Sun. **Admission** $29.99; $16.50-$18.99 concessions. **Credit** AmEx, MC, V.

About 65km (40 miles) south of the city in Santa Clara, Great America is the closest amusement park to San Francisco. Check out the Nickelodeon Splat City Slime Zone, The Drop Zone, which is the equivalent of throwing yourself off a skyscraper (but only lasts a few seconds), and the latest ride, Xtreme Skyflier, which simulates skydiving. There are also gentler jaunts and a carousel for smaller kids plus countless booths with soft toys as prizes. Admission includes all rides.

lambs, raccoons, hawks and a lovely pair of San Francisco garter snakes. There are art workshops and an elaborate model railway that enthusiasts run occasionally. Perfect for small children.

Park Amusements

As well as the attractions of **Golden Gate Park**, you can go cycling in the **Presidio** or take a picnic and watch the kite-flyers on **Marina Green**. The **Musée Mécanique** in the Cliff House is also worth a visit (*see chapter* **Museums & Galleries**). At the **Seal Rocks**, below the Cliff House, and at nearby **Point Lobos**, seals gather day and night: the ones with little ears are California seals; the shiny graceful ones are Harbour seals.

Golden Gate Park
See chapter **Sightseeing** *for listings.*
If you've got just one day, spend it in the rolling green acres of Golden Gate Park. It's full of more organised fun – roller-skating, horseriding, boating, hothouse palm forests and museums. Older kids can visit the **California Academy of Sciences** (*see chapter* **Museums & Galleries**), which houses the Steinhart Aquarium (*above*), and Morrison Planetarium. If you produce your Muni ticket, you get $1 off the admission price. Experience the SafeQuake, visit African natural history dioramas and visit the Discovery Room for Children, with its hands-on nature exhibits. There's also an alligator pit, hundreds of reptiles in cages and a decent cafeteria in the basement. The planetarium has shows

such as Star Death and the Birth of Black Holes and there's rock music for teenagers in the evening at the Laserium.

At the eastern corner of the park, opposite Kezar Stadium, you'll find an old-fashioned carousel, a tree house and swings in the Children's Playground, with summertime Punch and Judy shows. At Stow Lake you can hire rowing boats, paddle boats and bicycles. Near the west end of the park, opposite Spreckels Lake at JFK Drive, is the Golden Gate Park Riding Academy (668 7360), which offers pony trails through the park for kids. There are also windmills, a buffalo herd and the beautiful Japanese Tea Garden (admission $1-$2.50), where you can have a pick-me-up jasmine tea by the goldfish ponds after a hard day's play.

Shops

Chinatown is ideal for children, with its baskets full of small toys and trinkets on display on the pavements. The **San Francisco Center** and **Embarcadero Center** also do well by kids; for these and children's clothes shops, *see chapter* **Shopping & Services**.

Basic Brown Bear
444 De Haro Street, at Mariposa Street (626 0781). Bus 19. **Open** 10am-5pm Mon-Sat; noon-5pm Sun. **Credit** AmEx, Disc, MC, V.
There are stuffed bears galore and free tours (at 1pm daily plus an extra 11am tour on Saturday) of this teddy bear factory.

Chinatown Kite Shop
717 Grant Avenue, at Sacramento Street (989 5182). Bus 1, 15, 30, 45. **Open** 10.30am-9pm daily. **Credit** AmEx, Disc, MC, V. **Map G3**

Stocks hundreds of different kites, for flying or decoration. Other kite shops in the city include **Air Time of San Francisco** (759 1177) for stunt kites, **Kite Flite** (956 3181) in the touristy Pier 39 arcade, and, in the East Bay, **Highline Kites** (1-510 525 2755).

FAO Schwarz
48 Stockton Street, at O'Farrell Street (394 8700). BART Powell Street/Muni Metro F, J, K, L, M, N/bus 5, 6, 7, 21, 30, 31, 38, 45, 66, 71/cable car Powell-Mason or Powell-Hyde. **Open** 10am-7pm Mon-Sat; 11am-6pm Sun. **Credit** AmEx, DC, Disc, MC, V. **Map G4**
Everything from Davy Crockett hats to rocking horses can be bought in the mother of all toy shops.

Imaginarium
Laurel Shopping Center, 3535 California Street, between Locust and Spruce Streets (387 9885). Bus 1, 4. **Open** 10am-6pm Mon-Sat; noon-5pm Sun. **Credit** AmEx, Disc, MC, V. **Map C4**
A very hands-on and child-friendly toy shop.

Toys R Us
2675 Geary Boulevard, at Masonic Avenue (931 8896). Bus 38, 43. **Open** 9.30am-9.30pm Mon-Sat; 9.30am-7pm Sun. **Credit** AmEx, Disc, MC, V. **Map D4**
The biggest toy stores in the US, TRUs are everywhere. This one is the most centrally located in the city. Shop till you drop – your kids certainly won't. The entrance is on O'Farrell Street.

The Waterfront & Islands

The waterfront isn't all overpriced kitsch. At **Pier 39** you can see – and hear – a pride of gallumphing great sea lions, and there are street performers here and at **Fisherman's Wharf**, **The Cannery** and **The Anchorage** (*see chapter* **Shopping & Services**).

Trips to the islands in the Bay are a great diversion. Visit the prison on **Alcatraz** (*see page 173*) or take bicycles to **Angel Island**, the largest island in the Bay, and cycle around the old barracks at Camp Reynolds (you can also hire bikes on the island). In December, take a boat to look for whales around the **Farallon Islands**.

For more information on Angel Island, *see chapters* **Sightseeing** *and* **Trips Out of Town**; for bicycle hire and whale watching, *see chapter* **Sport & Fitness**.

Hyde Street Pier
Jefferson Street, at the west end of Fisherman's Wharf (556 2904). Bus 19, 30, 32, 42/cable car Powell-Hyde. **Open** *summer* 10am-6pm daily; *winter* 9. 30am-5pm daily. **Admission** $4; $2 concessions; free first Tue of the month. **No credit cards. Map F1**
This is somewhere that adults will enjoy as much as kids. Several ships are docked along the pier, including the *Balclutha*, a three-masted square-rigger built in 1886. Next door is the *CA Thayer*, a schooner built in 1895, and on the other side, the *Eureka*, a paddle-wheel ferryboat used by commuters across the Bay in the 1920s. There's also the *Hercules*, the US's last operable steam-powered tug boat.

Jeremiah O'Brien Liberty Ship
Pier 39, Embarcadero (441 3101). Bus 32, 42. **Open** *office* 9am-5pm Mon-Fri; *ship* 9am-3pm Mon-Fri; 9am-4pm Sat, Sun. **Admission** $5; $1-$3 concessions. **No credit cards. Map G1**

Come rain or shine

Foggy days
Visit the **California Academy of Sciences**, which houses the Steinhart Aquarium, Morrison Planetarium and the Natural History Museum. Or resort to bribery at **FAO Schwarz**, the mother of all toy shops. Sink back in a seat and watch a sunnier version of the city in the screen-shattering 70mm **'San Francisco – The Movie'** at the Citybank Cinemax Theatre on Pier 39 (956 3456).

Blue skies
Take a ferry across the Bay – to **Alcatraz Island**, **Angel Island** or **Sausalito**. Or take the train to **Santa Cruz** and ride the rollercoaster on the Beach Boardwalk (*see chapter* **Trips Out of Town**). Hire a rowing boat on Stow Lake in **Golden Gate Park** or join the throng and hire some rollerblades (*see chapter* **Sport & Fitness**). Head for the waterfront and explore the ships at the **Hyde Street Pier**.

You can explore this ship's engine room, officers' bunkrooms and a three-inch 50-calibre gun, and operate the foghorn. It's located on the south side of the Ferry Building.

Treasure Island Museum
Building 1, Treasure Island (652 2772). Bus T Transbay Terminal. **Open** phone for details.
Currently moving into civilian hands and undergoing major renovation, this naval museum (formerly the National Marine Corps and Coast Guard Museum) re-opens in April 1998. Themes will include the building of the bridges and a history of the Navy and Marine Corps.

Underwater World
Pier 39, Embarcadero (623 5300). Bus 32, 42. **Open** 9am-9pm daily. **Admission** $12.95; $6.50-$9.95 concessions. **Credit cards** AmEx, Disc, MC, V. **Map K2**
The latest addition to San Francisco's aquatic theme parks, Underwater World gives you a 'dive r's-eye view' of the Bay through clear plastic underwater tunnels. Though admission prices are a bit steep, it's still a great place to spy on crabs and sharks, stare in wonderment at the benign-looking jellyfish and watch the slow, gentle combat of giant octopuses. Like any tourist attraction, this place gets mobbed at the weekends and around midday, so get there early.

Film

San Francisco has always played a starring role on celluloid; these days it also boasts its fair share of resident directors.

The City by the Bay is best known for its prolific and award-winning avant-garde and documentary film-makers. From Terry Zwiegoff, who made 1994's *Crumb*, and Iara Lee, director of *Synthetic Pleasures* in 1996, to Rob Epstein and Jeffrey Friedman, who won an Academy Award for both *The Life and Times of Harvey Milk* and *Common Threads* (the story of the Names Project Aids quilt), the city is home to the better-known film makers in that genre.

San Francisco is also a favourite location, and several mainstream directors have settled in the Bay Area (notably Francis Ford Coppola and George Lucas, whose Marin-based LucasFilm studio is noted for its special effects abilities). It's claimed that – except for one small town in Kentucky that's home to a film-making foundation – San Francisco has more film-makers per capita than any other city in the world.

San Francisco State University, Stanford University, the San Francisco Art Institute and City College have thriving film-making programmes, each encouraging and developing new and established film and video artists (*see page 264* **Where to Study**). In addition, two San Francisco institutions – the Film Arts Foundation (*see page 178*) and the Bay Area Video Coalition (861 3282) – provide services and continuing education and networking for film-makers and videographers in the area. Phone the San Francisco Film Commission (recorded information 554 4004) to find out casting and production details of current films being made in the Bay Area, or check their website (www.filmdependent.com.ssfests.html).

THE CINEMAS

San Franciscans also have a sizeable appetite for foreign and art house movies, and the city contains more than a few cinemas that specialise in screening those films. The Landmark theatre chain is one: it includes the **Lumière** (1572 California Street, between Polk and Larkin Streets), **Bridge** (3010 Geary Boulevard, at Blake Street), **Opera Plaza** (601 Van Ness Avenue, between Turk Street and Golden Gate Avenue), **Clay** (2261 Fillmore Street, at Clay), and **Embarcadero Center Cinemas** (1 Embarcadero Center, on Battery between Sacramento and Clay Streets). You can get information on all five cinemas from one telephone number: 352 0810. Landmark

The **Embarcadero Center Cinemas**.

cinemas will often pick up audience favourites from one of the frequent San Francisco film festivals. The **San Francisco Cinematheque** (*see page 180*) provides a prime venue for avant-garde screenings.

Many of the city's mainstream movie houses are well-appointed, with comfortable seating and state-of-the-art sound systems. Notable among these are the **Kabuki 8 Cinema** (1181 Post Street, at Fillmore Street; 931 9800), the **Galaxy** (1285 Sutter Street, at Van Ness Avenue; 474 8700), the **Regency I** (1320 Van Ness Avenue, at Sutter; 673 7142), and the **Regency II** around the corner (1268 Sutter Street, at Van Ness; 776 2071). And don't worry if you see a queue snaking through the car park at the **United Artists Coronet** (3575 Geary Boulevard, at Arguello Boulevard; recorded info 752 4400/direct line 752 4403) – more people can fit in this cinema than you'd have thought possible.

It's always worth checking festival programming when you're in town, since you might be able to catch a talk by a director or several of the actors before or after a show. And if you're after a film-going 'experience', head for one of the old movie palaces, such as the **Regency** (*see page 177*), or the **Castro Theater** (*see page 180*), where an organist seated at the mighty Wurlitzer entertains the audience before the weekend showings.

TICKETS & INFORMATION

Advance tickets for some cinemas and festivals are available by credit card from **Movie Phone** (777 3456); there's a $1 service charge per ticket. Otherwise, you should purchase tickets from festival organisers or at the cinema box offices. Check the newspapers for listings and film times at all of the theatres (the *San Francisco Examiner*, *San Francisco Chronicle* and *Bay Guardian* have up-to-date listings and reviews), and expect opening nights to be popular.

Film Festivals

That the Bay Area appreciates film is obvious: almost every month of the year there's a festival of some sort taking place, many of them drawing directors from around the world. The works of local moviemaking and video artists feature prominently in every San Francisco festival, where pieces can vary from extremely high quality to dire. Some events are tiny and roving, among them the **Low Res Festival** (567 9052) and the **Short Attention Span Film & Video Festival** (*see page 179* **Artists Television Access**) as well as the **Cin(E)-Poetry Festival** (776 6602). For the increasingly popular **Spike & Mike** festival, *see page 181.*

¡Festival Cine Latino!

Information (553 8135). **Venues** Yerba Buena Gardens; Victoria Theater, 2961 16th Street, at Mission Street (863 7576). **Date** Sept.
Although it's relatively young in comparison with other Bay Area sprees, Cine Acción's festival has quickly come into its own as the premier showcase for films from South and Central America, Mexico and those by US Latino filmmakers – works that are surprisingly under-distributed in the US. The festival includes films, videos and appearances by the film-makers.

Film Arts Foundation Festival

Information (552 8760). **Venues** Castro Theater; The Roxie; UC Theater, Berkeley. **Date** first week of Nov.
This six-day festival provides the essential venue for a real snapshot of film-making in Northern California. All programming is drawn from Bay Area independent work, and features documentary, experimental and traditional narrative pieces.

Jewish Film Festival

Information (621 0556/www.sfjff.org/). **Venues** Castro Theater; UC Theater, Berkeley. **Date** late July-early Aug.
This festival, launched in 1981, is intended to showcase contemporary films from around the world on Jewish subjects

The mother of all car chases from the movie 'Bullitt' – filmed on location in San Francisco.

and to strengthen awareness of Jewish secular culture. Most of the programming is contemporary, but it does also include some retrospective and archival work.

SF International Asian-American Film Festival

Information (252 4800/www.sirius.com/~naata/exhibit/ sfiaaff97/). **Venues** Kabuki 8 Cinema; Castro Theater. **Date** March.

Some 15 years old, the AAFF features film by and/or about Asian Pacific people, their culture and experience. Recent hits have included a sneak preview of *The Wedding Banquet*, and Steven Okasaki's award winning *Days of Waiting*, about the imprisonment of Japanese Americans during World War II. An eight-day event, the festival draws huge audiences.

SF International Film Festival

Information (929 5000/SF Film Society 931 3456/www.sfiff.org). **Venues** Kabuki 8 Cinema; other cinemas around town. **Date** mid April-early May.

Produced by the San Francisco Film Society, this 42 year-old festival galvanises the city (over 75,000 tickets are sold). Over the course of a few weeks, the society presents multiple screenings of more than 200 films and videos, from dozens of countries and in dozens of languages, and it's usually hard to find a loser in the bunch. A variety of glitterati attend – US director Jim Jarmusch, Czech animator Jan Svankmajer and Hong Kong actress Maggie Chueng showed up recently. Most films are screened at the Kabuki 8 Cinema in Japantown, with related screenings at other venues around town. Tickets go on sale, in advance, at the Kabuki a few weeks before the festival opens.

SF International Lesbian & Gay Film Festival

Information (703 8650/www.frameline.org). **Venues** Castro, Victoria and Roxie Theatres. **Date** last two weeks of June; ends with Freedom Day parade.

Opening night at the Lesbian & Gay Film Festival, which celebrated its 20th anniversary in 1996, has become the kick-off for San Francisco's month-long celebration of Gay Pride. Recent years have seen a rise in gay-themed films produced in Hollywood and the festival often premieres such mainstream fare. The rest of the programming runs the gamut from high-quality independent shorts and full-length features, to avant-garde film with a queer sensibility, to high- and low-quality shorts from new and old film-makers alike. Sponsored by Frameline, the event is the world's oldest and largest of its kind. A programme is available a month in advance from bookshops and cafés and in the *Bay Guardian*.

Classic, New & Experimental

Alliance Française

1345 Bush Street, between Polk and Larkin Streets (775 7755). Bus 2, 3, 4, 19, 76. **Admission** free members; $5 non-members. **Credit** MC, V. **Map F3**

You can watch French films twice a week, on Tuesday evenings and Saturday afternoons.

Artists' Television Access

992 Valencia Street, at 21st Street (824 3890). BART 24th Street/bus 14, 26, 49. **Open** 10am-10pm daily. **Admission** from $5. **No credit cards. Castro/Mission Map Y2**

Artists Television Access often has experimental and unusual programming, usually from Thursday to Saturday. It supported the first Short Attention Span Film & Video Festival in 1992 – a two-hour programme of *very* short shorts (each offering is under two minutes); more information on the festival can be found at www.creative.net/~weather.

Out of town

If you're headed out of town for a movie, your best bet is to check the cinema listings in Oakland or Berkeley. The East Bay has a superb selection of film resources and festivals, as well as some of the best cinemas in the Bay Area.

In Berkeley, the programme at the **UC Theater** (2036 University Avenue, at Shattuck Avenue; 1-510 843 3456) is always worth investigating; it also screens *The Rocky Horror Picture Show* every Saturday night during the school year. The **Pacific Film Archive**, located in the same complex as the University Art Museum (2626 Bancroft Way, between Bowditch and College Streets; 1-510 642 5249/1124/www. bampfa.berkeley.edu), keeps the reels rolling almost every evening with classic films and a program of Bay Area-based independent documentaries. Finally, **The Paramount** in Oakland (2025 Broadway, between 20th and 21st Streets; 1-510 465 6400) is a wonderful, cavernous theatre in which to see a rep film or an old classic.

Bay Area Women's Film Festival

Information (554 6244). **Venue** UC Theater, Berkeley. **Date** March.

Programmers at this young festival aim to introduce the work of first-time women directors, show new work by experienced directors and help to build an international women's film-making community. In the past, the festival has included retrospectives, including, recently, most of the films by Academy Award-winning Antipodean director Jane Campion.

Black Filmworks Festival of Film and Video

Information (1-510 465 0804). **Venues** The Paramount; Laney College; Oakland Museum (all in Oakland). **Date** Sept.

Presented by the Black Filmmakers Hall of Fame, this fest features films by, for and about the African and African American experience. The festival has included tributes to US director Spike Lee and the late Marlon Riggs, whose groundbreaking experimental documentary *Tongues Untied* explored the experiences of African American gay men.

Mill Valley Film Festival & Videofest

Information (383 5256/www.finc.org). **Venues** Sequoia Twin Theaters and the Masonic Hall, both in Mill Valley. **Date** Oct.

US and international independent films and videos are the focus of this Marin County festival, which screens dozens of feature films. It also includes a six-day 'Videofest', interactive media exhibitions, seminars, special events and children's programmes, among other projects.

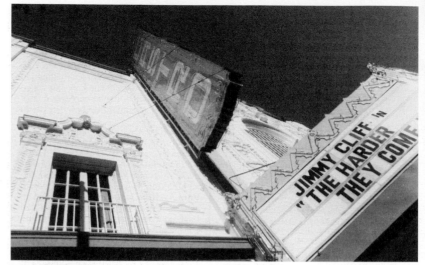

*The **Castro Theater**: for camp classics and the mighty Wurlitzer.*

Center for the Arts at Yerba Buena Gardens
See chapter **Museums & Galleries** *for listings.*
Located on the second floor of the arts building, Yerba Buena's 96-seat media screening room is often used for contemporary and experimental offerings connected with the exhibitions in the Center's galleries.

Film Arts Foundation
Second floor, 346 Ninth Street, at Folsom Street (552 8760). BART Civic Center/Muni Metro F, J, K, L, M, N/bus 12, 19, 27, 42. **Admission** varies. **Map G5**
The Foundation screens works-in-progress (there's no regular schedule) and hosts lectures and classes by and for film-makers.

Goethe Institute
530 Bush Street, between Stockton Street and Grant Avenue (391 0370). Bus 30, 45. **Admission** free.
Map G3
Both contemporary and classic German films are screened at the Institute on Tuesdays and Thursdays.

Istituto Italiano di Cultura
425 Bush Street, between Kearny Street and Grant Avenue (788 7142). Bus 30, 45. **Admission** free.
Map G/H3
The Italian Institute shows both contemporary and classic Italian films. Screenings are at 6pm on Tuesdays.

San Francisco Cinematheque
Information (558 8129). Thursday night screenings at Center for the Arts at Yerba Buena Gardens (see above). Sunday night screenings at San Francisco Art Institute, 800 Chestnut Street, at Jones Street. BART Montgomery Street/Muni Metro F, J, K, L, M, N/bus 30. **Map F2**
Both **Admission** $7; $3.50 students. **No credit cards.**
Cinematheque is at the epicentre for avant-garde film in the Bay Area, offering programmes from late September until early June. It's a place to gather information and inspiration

and to see experimental works – from documentaries to features and animated films.

San Francisco Museum of Modern Art
See chapter **Museums & Galleries** *for listings.*
There's a large 278-seat theatre in the museum, which usually hosts screenings in the spring and autumn, often in conjunction with SFMOMA exhibitions.

Repertory

Castro Theater
429 Castro Street, off Market Street (621 6120). Muni Metro F, K, L, M/bus 24, 33, 35, 37. **Admission** $6.50.
No credit cards. Map E6
Go on a weekend night for the full Castro Theater experience. The popcorn-munching audience is entertained before the screening by an organist playing a battery of favourites on the Wurlitzer; lushly painted murals line the domed Art Deco ceilings. The film might be anything from an old Bette Davis picture (where everyone knows and recites the best lines) to a director's cut of *Blade Runner* or a world première by an independent queer film-maker. The Castro is a San Francisco moviegoing tradition like no other.

The Red Vic
1727 Haight Street, at Cole Street (668 3994). Bus 6, 7, 43, 61, 77. **Admission** $4.50-$6. **No credit cards.**
Map C6
Where else can you sprawl on an old sofa in the heart of the Haight, eat popcorn out of wooden bowls and watch revivals or a current funky flick with a wildly eclectic crowd?

The Roxie
3117 16th Street, at Valencia Street (863 1087). BART 16th Street/bus 22, 26, 53. **Admission** $6; $3 concessions. **No credit cards. Map F6**
Revivals of film noir classics, Fassbinder festivals and horror movies cover the range of the Roxie's roster. The seats are hard and the sound system is second-rate, but go for the atmosphere.

Spike & Mike

From Hitchcock's *Vertigo* and Coppola's *The Conversation* to *Mrs Doubtfire* and *So I Married an Axe Murderer*, cinemagoers think of San Francisco as an ideal setting for memorable movies. But for others, the city is a nucleus for animated arts: computer-generated, clay-sculpted, stop-acted or hand-drawn short flicks that range from sophisticated political commentary to lowbrow satire. Three major animation studios – Pixar, Skellington (maker of *James and the Giant Peach* and *The Nightmare before Christmas*) and LucasArts' Industrial Light and Magic – call the region home, as do countless animators and captive audiences who comprise the genre's fans. And the kings of the cartoon carnivals are Spike and Mike, whose biannual Festival of Animation has for more than two decades reigned supreme in Bay Area movie houses.

Craig 'Spike' Decker and Mike Gribble met in Southern California in 1974, when Decker was promoting rock 'n' roll bands, all-night horror-thons and special film screenings that featured opening shorts. Their first festival was held in 1977. In 1990, they began their now-popular Sick and Twisted series, screening off-colour animated pieces (a still from Neil Ishimine's *Smoking* is pictured below) for midnight audiences ironically dubbed more 'mature'.

The city seems the ideal environment for such offerings. As Spike says, 'San Francisco audiences stand out for their diversity – they definitely come out strong for the Sick and Twisted stuff.'

With screenings in April and November at the Roxie, Castro and Palace of Fine Arts cinemas in the city, and elsewhere in Berkeley, Larkspur and San Jose, both festivals have become springboards for local artists' success – Pixar producer John Lasseter (who stunned cinemagoers with his recent *Toy Story* films) got his start on a Spike and Mike fest; a work by San Francisco filmmaker Timothy Hittle was recently nominated for an Oscar. Spike describes San Francisco as 'a hotbed for animators', praising the work coming out of Pixar and Skellington as well as film-makers and directors such as T Reid Norton, Todd Kurtzman, David Thomas and Kat Miller.

Mike Gribble died in 1993, but his departure hasn't slowed Mellow Manor, Spike and Mike's promotion company, in the least. Most recently, the enterprise created the Entertainment Olympiad for the 1997 Warped Tour, another lollapalooza of alternative bands. The Festival of Animation continues apace, now showing in 40 cities in the US and Canada and due to emigrate to Australian and British soil in the next year or two. Watch out for the special San Francisco events, including the Sick and Twisted Christmas Special, the arrival of a cable TV series and trademark appearances by Scottie the Shredding Wonder Dog. Animaniacal connoisseurs with a queasy sense of humour, the Spike and Mike festival continues to convert more fans every year.

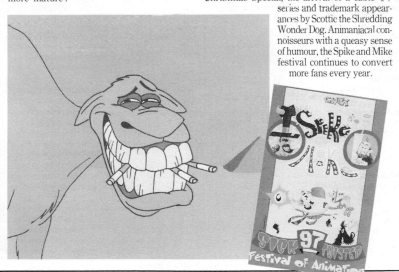

Gay & Lesbian San Francisco

You're here, you're queer – where do you go from here?

To understand just how gay San Francisco is, consider a civic attraction like the annual Folsom Street Fair, where formal wear means black leather and bondage gear. This September festival is packed with thousands of outrageous, kinky queers, but plenty of straight San Franciscans join in the fun, ambling past piercing booths like farmers at a county fair. The mayor, district attorney and sheriff all show up for photo-ops, draping their arms around leather-clad go-go boys in poses that would ruin politicians anywhere else. Drag queens and dominatrices stand in line for lemonade, while city officials distribute condoms to the crowds. As a popular T-shirt sold at the Fair reads: 'I think we're not in Kansas anymore!'

Not all San Francisco's gay scene is so flamboyant. The city also offers a welcome refuge for gay people from all over the world in search of lives, not lifestyles. There's a place for everyone: you can connect with lesbian moms at PTA meetings or make new gay friends at church suppers just as easily as you can flirt at a trendy club. You'll find a guide to all kinds of community activities – from a support group for deaf Latina lesbians to a prom for queer teens – in free gay papers like the *Bay Times* and *Bay Area Reporter*. When you read the mainstream press and see a headline like 'Straight White Man Appointed to Board of Supervisors', you'll realise how thoroughly lesbian and gay culture has been integrated into San Francisco's civic life.

CELEBRATING HISTORY

San Francisco's gay pride and vitality are rooted in a long history of struggle for equality, rights and freedom. The 1978 assassination of Harvey Milk, the first openly gay elected official in the country, was a turning point for local gay politics, and is remembered each year with a passionate march from the Castro to City Hall. The

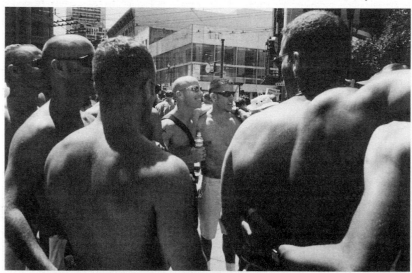

The city's best-attended street bash: **Freedom Day Parade**.

Bernal Heights – *a new gay mecca.*

Aids Candlelight March is another annual event that brings the community together, and every day visitors and residents can visit the Names Project (*see page 185*), where the Aids Memorial Quilt began.

San Francisco holds its Freedom Day Parade every June, commemorating the 1969 Stonewall Riots in New York and the beginning of the modern American gay liberation movement. The city's best-attended street parade, it's a pageant where gays, straights and plenty of liberal out-of-town onlookers celebrate regional diversity. For a more reflective look at San Francisco's gay past and present, travellers might explore the Gay and Lesbian Center at the new Main Library, or join a walking tour – one organised by the Northern California Lesbian and Gay Historical Society (777 5455); or Trevor Hailey's 'Cruisin' the Castro' tour (*see chapter* **Sightseeing**).

For details of annual gay events, *see chapter* **San Francisco by Season**.

NEIGHBOURHOODS

The **Castro** flaunts its reputation as the centre of the known queer universe, and even a brief stroll through its busy streets gives a sense of the riches gay San Francisco has to offer. Start at the magnificently restored **Castro Theater**, home each June to the International Lesbian and Gay Film Festival, and enjoy live music from the vintage Wurlitzer organ before a movie. Down the block you'll find **Cliff's Variety** (479 Castro Street; 431 5365), the fabulously eclectic hardware store

whose campy window displays are a show in themselves. If you're ready to climb some hills, you can discover fragrant, hidden gardens and view the Castro's beautiful Victorian homes; if you're more interested in the current scene, stop by bookstore **A Different Light** and chat with the friendly clerks. Make sure you wind up on the patio of **Café Flore** (the see-and-be-seen spot locals dub 'Café Hairdo') sipping a latte as the fog rolls in.

Gay life in San Francisco also extends far beyond the Castro to lesser-known but equally interesting neighbourhoods. **Polk Street** is poorer, rougher and draggier: check out its amazing transgender divas at bars like **The Motherlode**. SoMa (home of the Folsom Street Fair) offers bars, trendy restaurants and gay dance clubs full of hot, muscled men.

The Valencia Street corridor, in the **Mission district**, is more low-key, and houses a number of lesbian and gay businesses. A perennial favourite is Osento, a women-only spa where you can melt in the hot tub or a eucalyptus-scented sauna, then lie outside on the deck under the stars. You should also discover the charms of **Bernal Heights**, a quietly romantic neighbourhood way off the tourist maps that's become a mecca for gay homeowners. Walk up its winding streets past cottages covered in flowering vines to the top of Bernal Hill. On a sunny day you'll be rewarded with a spectacular Bay view – and beautiful Bernal lesbians walking their dogs.

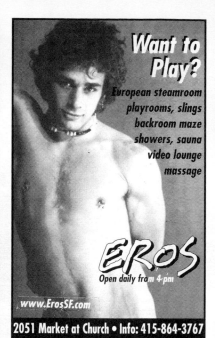

But don't stop there: any neighbourhood you explore will yield more examples of lesbian and gay contributions to the city's character. San Francisco is one place where queers aren't exaggerating when they proclaim, 'We're everywhere!'

INFORMATION

The best sources for up-to-the-minute information on new clubs, shows, films, events and general gay news are the free newspapers, which can be found in almost every café or in boxes on street corners. Look for the *Bay Times*, the *San Francisco Sentinel*, *Odyssey*, *SF Weekly* and the *San Francisco Bay Guardian*. **The Names Project** (2362 Market Street, between Castro and Noe Streets; 863 1966) has a visitor's centre and next-door shop benefiting the Aids Memorial Quilt, which is made up of more than 41,000 panels, each commemorating one person who has died from Aids. For Aids helplines and gay counselling and medical services, *see page 261*.

Boys

Accommodation

It's not as necessary in San Francisco as in some cities to make sure that your lodgings are gay-friendly, because most hoteliers are either welcoming or indifferent. (for lodging, *see chapter* **Accommodation**. Some establishments, however, cater specifically to gay clients:

Alamo Square Inn

719 Scott Street, CA 94117, at Fulton Street (922 2055/fax 931 1304/wcorn@alamoinn.com/www.alamoinn.com). Bus 5, 24. **Rates** *single* $85-$125; *suite* $195-$295. **Credit** AmEx, MC, V. **Map E5**
One of the most charming and comfortable guesthouses in the city, located across from the famous row of painted Victorians on Alamo Square. All rooms are no-smoking, breakfast is included and there is free parking – at a premium in this neighbourhood.

Beck's Motor Lodge

2222 Market Street, CA 94114 , at 15th Street (621 8212/fax 421 0435). Muni Metro F, K, L, M/bus 37. **Rates** *single* $86; *double* $91-$110. **Credit** AmEx, DC, Disc, MC, V. **Map E6**
Your typical American motel, down to the hideous carpets and glasses sealed in plastic, but with relatively cheap rates and very near the centre of the Castro scene, hence its popularity. A word of warning: the management frowns on cruising from the balconies overlooking the parking lot, so behave yourself. There are some no-smoking rooms, free parking and the rates are cheaper in winter.

Black Stallion Inn

635 Castro Street, CA 94114, between 19th and 20th Streets (863 0131/fax 863 0165). Muni Metro K, L, M/bus 37. **Rates** *single* from $80; *double* from $95; *Wolf Den room* $95-$110. **Credit** AmEx, Disc, MC, V. **Castro/Mission Map X1**
This black-painted Victorian, located in the groin of the Castro, deems itself 'San Francisco's only leather/Levi/Western bed-and-breakfast'. Eight minimalist rooms, a

communal lounge with TV and VCR and a dining room make up the two-storey B&B. The ground floor is a uniquely Castro 'social club' where you can chat until the small hours or just watch the action. Services include breakfast, limited parking, fax and voicemail. Ask for a *Time Out* discount (10%).

Gough Hayes Hotel

417 Gough Street, CA 94102, at Hayes Street (431 9131). Bus 21. **Rates** *single* $55 per night; *double* $65 per night, $155-$165 per week. **Credit** MC, V. **Map F5**
On the edge of Hayes Valley and near to the Opera House and Symphony Hall, this is a pleasant, gay-run little pension. A friendly bar is downstairs; car parking is available nearby for $3.50 per day.

Inn on Castro

321 Castro Street, CA 94114, at Market Street (861 0321). Muni Metro F, K, L, M/bus 24, 35, 37. **Rates** *single* $85; *double* $95; *suite* $135-$160. **Credit** AmEx, MC, V. **Map E6**
This beautifully restored Edwardian building has served as San Francisco's premier gay and lesbian hotel for nearly two decades. It has eight rooms, each with a private bath, original modern art and elaborate flower arrangements. The highlight of the stay is the full breakfast, including homemade muffins and piles of fresh fruit. The hotel is non smoking, (though it's allowed on the back patio), and there are rooms for disabled visitors. Treat yourself like a queen.

24 Henry

24 Henry Street, CA 94114, between Sanchez and Noe Streets (1-800 900 5686/864 5686/fax 864 0406). Muni Metro F, K, L, M/bus 24, 37. **Rates** *single* $55-$80; *double* $65-$90; *apartment suite* from $95. **Credit** AmEx, MC, V. **Map E6**
Geared toward gay vacationers but welcoming everyone, 24 Henry offers traditional San Francisco charm in the heart of the Castro at a very reasonable rate. Each of the five guest rooms within the Victorian has a private phone line with voicemail and a shared or private bath.

Willows Inn

710 14th Street, CA 94114, between Sanchez and Church Streets (431 4770/fax 431 5295). Muni Metro F, K, L, M/bus 22, 37. **Rates** *single* $74-$92; *double* $82-$100; *suite* $110-$130. **Credit** AmEx, MC, V. **Map E6**
The Willows offers 11 nice rooms in a 1904 Edwardian building, breakfast in bed and a location just outside the craziness of the Castro. All rooms have shared bath facilities and there's limited off-street parking ($8 per night).

Bars

See also chapter **Bars**.

Alta Plaza

2301 Fillmore Street, at Clay Street (922 1444). Bus 1, 3, 12, 22, 24. **Open** *bar* 4pm-2am Mon-Sat; 10am-2pm, 5.30pm-10pm, Sun; *restaurant* 5.30-10pm Mon-Thur; 5.30-11pm Fri, Sat; 10am-3pm Sun. **Credit** AmEx, DC, Disc, MC, V. **Map E3**
From the suited lawyers and doctors to the well-groomed staff, the Alta Plaza is the classiest gay bar in town. Several years ago, new owners tried to make it appeal to a straight clientele – and failed miserably. It's back in its prime again, appealing to queer clients in an ultra-yuppie Pacific Heights location. There's a good restaurant upstairs.

Badlands

4121 18th Street, at Castro Street (626 9320). Muni Metro F, K, L, M/bus 24, 33, 35, 37. **Open** 11.30am-2am daily. **No credit cards. Castro/Mission Map X1**
One of those bars that is popular for no apparent reason.

Usually packed with a varied crowd playing pinball, pool, or just cruising. Not a place to visit if you're particular about smoke – the air gets awfully thick on weekend nights. After the Eagle breaks up on Sunday nights, follow the crowd here.

Detour

2348 Market Street, at Castro Street (861 6053). Muni Metro F, K, L, M/bus 24, 35, 37. **Open** 2pm-2am daily. **No credit cards. Map E6**
High-decibel music, chainlink fence and angst-ridden Gen-X boys with piercings galore – this is a place to look rougher than you feel and get away with it. Pool and pinball are sidelines to ferocious cruising.

Esta Noche

3079 16th Street, at Mission Street (861 5757). BART 16th Street/bus 14, 22, 26, 49, 53. **Open** 1pm-2am Mon-Thur, Sun; 1pm-3am Fri, Sat. **No credit cards. Map F6**
Unpretentious and easily overlooked, Esta Noche is one of the city's hottest Latin bars – particularly on Friday nights when it hosts an evening of Latino striptease.

Giraffe Video Lounge

1131 Polk Street, at Post Street (474 1702). Bus 2, 3, 4, 19, 76. **Open** 8am-2am daily. **No credit cards. Map F4**
Perhaps the most popular of the Polk Street bars, the Giraffe is low-key and friendly – a good place for pool or pinball. Rather dead during the week, but hopping at the weekend.

Hole in the Wall

289 Eighth Street, between Howard and Folsom Streets (431 4695). Bus 12, 19. **Open** noon-2am Tue-Thur; 6am-2am Fri-Sun. **No credit cards. Map G5**
Rapidly becoming one of the most popular hangouts of the Gen-X queers who are turning their backs on the clone scene of the Castro. Drop in to compare tattoos with hot boys in torn clothing – a real San Francisco experience.

The Lion Pub

2062 Divisadero Street, at Sacramento Street (567 6565). Bus 1, 24. **Open** 3pm-2am daily. **No credit cards. Map D3**
Largely frequented by the sweatered professionals of surrounding Pacific Heights, the Lion also catches some of the younger crowd on their way to the clubs. It's an odd combination of Victorian chic and Gen-X soundtrack, and the clients range in age from minors to seniors. Friendly bartenders and a good happy hour.

Lone Star Saloon

1354 Harrison Street, between Ninth and Tenth Streets (863 9999). Bus 19, 27, 42. **Open** noon-2am Mon-Fri; 9am-2am Sat, Sun. **No credit cards. Map G5**
As the name indicates, a western/leather bar, with a big following and an important centre for San Francisco's leather scene. Serious looks, serious scene and some serious fun.

The Metro

3600 16th Street, at Market Street (703 9750). Muni Metro K, L, M/bus 37. **Open** 2.30pm-2am Mon-Fri; 1pm-2am Sat, Sun. **Credit** ($15 minimum) MC, V. **Map E6**
Perched above the busy intersection at 16th and Market in the Castro, the Metro's balcony is a great place to have a drink and watch the boys heading out for the night. It has friendly bartenders, great margaritas and a karaoke machine. The place can get very crowded on weekend nights – the weekday happy hour is more sedate. The attached Chinese restaurant is also worth a try.

The Midnight Sun

4067 18th Street, between Castro and Noe Streets (861 4186). Muni Metro F, K, L, M/bus 33, 35. **Open** noon-2am daily. **No credit cards. Castro/Mission Map X1**
A popular video bar and a good cruising spot. Generally

packed for the after-work happy hour (two-for-the-price-of-one cocktails, 3-7pm, weekdays), and crammed full at the weekends. Frequented by a fairly young crowd that enjoys chanting along with favourite movie or TV clips.

The Mint

1942 Market Street, between Laguna and Buchanan Streets (626 4726). Bus 26. **Open** 11am-2am daily. **No credit cards. Map F5/6**
The Mint's main attraction is its karaoke – watch the musical theatre queens come out of the woodwork. It's rather a hit-or-miss spot as it can be unbearably slow on some evenings, though it's well worth a visit when it's hopping.

Moby Dick's

4049 18th Street, at Hartford Street (no phone). Muni Metro F, K, L, M/bus 24, 33, 35. **Open** noon-2am daily. **No credit cards. Castro/Mission Map X1**
A cross between a neighbourhood pub and a gay bar, Moby Dick's is most popular with pool players (although there's only one table) and pinball addicts (four machines in the back). Big windows make street cruising easy.

The Motherlode

1002 Post Street, at Larkin Street (928 6006). Bus 2, 3, 4, 19. **Open** 6am-2am daily. **No credit cards. Map F4**
The Polk Street corridor isn't known for particularly high-class gay bars, but there's no denying the underbelly appeal of The Motherlode. Hang at the bar and watch San Francisco's liveliest – some say scariest – transgender divas do their thing. Impromptu karaoke performances mix with a friendly (if screechy) scene, punctuated with glitter, high heels and lots of wigs. Parking is lousy and the neighbourhood dicey at night, so it's best to travel by cab.

QT

1312 Polk Street, at Bush Street (885 1114). Bus 2, 3, 4, 19, 42, 47, 49, 76. **Open** noon-2am daily. **No credit cards. Map F3**
Another Polk bar worth a look, and like its neighbours, slow during the week and packed at the weekend. Growing in popularity with the young Gen-X crowd.

The San Francisco Eagle

398 12th Street, at Harrison Street (626 0880). Bus 9, 12, 42. **Open** 4pm-2am Mon-Fri; 2pm-2am Sat; 1pm-2am Sun. **No credit cards. Map G5**
The row of motorcycles always parked out front signifies that the Eagle is the centre of San Francisco's leather community. The Sunday afternoon beer bash is near-legendary for its consumption and blatant cruising. Dress to the cat-o'-nines and check it out.

Restaurants & Cafés

San Francisco doesn't have 'gay restaurants' *per se*: gay and lesbian diners are welcome everywhere. That said, most queer diners congregate in the Castro, Hayes Valley, Bernal Heights and SoMa neighbourhoods, because they live nearby, and are less likely to be visible than in the Marina, Pacific Heights or North Beach. Many cafés offer a limited menu of sandwiches and soups, but it's also common to have a beer in one venue, dinner in another, and dessert at another down the street. Quick-turning, reasonably priced bistros like **Pasta Pomodoro** (*see chapter* **Restaurants & Cafés**) and the **Firewood Café** (*see page 188*) are becoming hugely popular among gay diners.

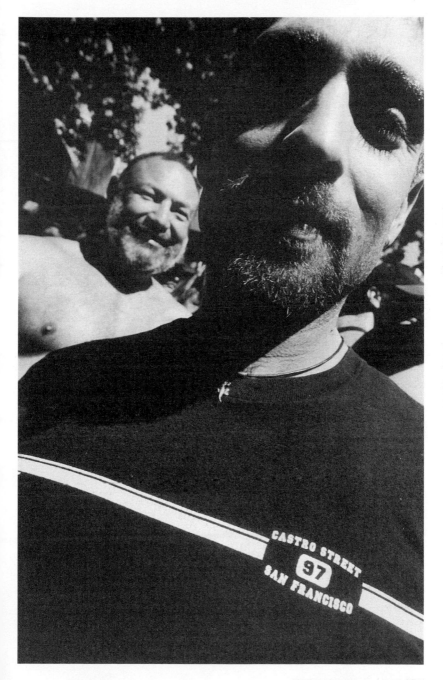

Or try **Pozole** (*see chapter* **Restaurants & Cafés**), where the boys who work there and the wild décor tend to overshadow the food.

Bagdad Café

2295 Market Street, at Noe Street (621 4434). Muni Metro F, K, L, M/bus 22, 35, 37. **Open** 24-hours daily. **Average** $6-$13. **No credit cards. Map E6**
Diner-type food and generous portions can be found here (try the Desert Fries). Perfect for a late-night snack after a hard evening in the bars.

Café Flore

2298 Market Street, at Noe Street (621 8579). Muni Metro F, K, L, M/bus 22, 35, 37. **Open** 7.30-11.30pm Mon-Thur, Sun; 7.30pm-midnight Fri, Sat. **Average** $8-$18. **No credit cards. Map E6**
The one San Francisco café where the patrons spend more time studying one another than their books. Always popular and always crowded, Flore and its garden is the see-and-be-seen centre of the Castro. The food is good and the coffee excellent. Get a table outside for maximum viewing potential.

Firewood Café

4248 18th Street, between Castro and Diamond Streets (252 0999). Muni Metro F, K, L, M/bus 24, 35, 37. **Open** 11am-11pm Mon-Thur, Sun; 11am-midnight Fri, Sat. **Average** $10. **Credit** MC, V. **Castro/Mission Map X1**
This hip, high-ceilinged bistro has a queue out of the door most nights – but don't let that stop you from joining in it: you'll order before you sit down from a large overhead menu, then get seated just before your food arrives. The roasted chickens are moist and succulent and the individual-sized pizzas consistently delicious. Head down the street for coffee and dessert so someone else in line can have your table.

Hot 'N' Hunky

4039 18th Street, between Hartford and Noe Streets (621 6365). Muni Metro F, K, L, M/bus 33, 35. **Open** 11am-midnight Mon-Thur, Sun; 11am-1am Fri, Sat. **Average** $5. **No credit cards. Castro/Mission Map X1**

An exception to the normal ho-hum Castro dining, the Hot 'N' Hunky burger joint is a perennial favourite. Ignore the 1980s décor and sink your teeth into one of the best burgers in town – this is a place for carnivores to revel in their bloodlust. **Hot 'N' Chunky** (1946 Market Street, at Duboce Avenue; 621 3622), which used to have the same owners, is also worth a look.

Mad Magda's Russia Tea Room

579 Hayes Street, at Laguna Street (864 7654). Bus 21. **Open** 8am-9pm Mon-Tue; 8am-midnight Wed-Fri; 9am-midnight Sat; 9am-7pm Sun. **Average** $7. **No credit cards. Map F5**
A uniquely San Franciscan spot – all the artsy funk of Hayes Valley with a queer, in-your-face twist. Go for Russian pastries and tea in the garden or have your Tarot read by the psychic by the door. A perfect cap to an afternoon's browsing in the surrounding shops and galleries, Magda's also hosts a range of evening 'events', many of which defy description; call for details.

Muddy Waters

260 Church Street, between Market and 15th Streets (621 2233). Muni Metro F, K, L, M/bus 22, 27. **Open** 6.30am-11pm Mon-Thur; 6.30am-midnight Fri; 7am-midnight Sat; 7am-11pm Sun. **No credit cards. Map E6**
A café that takes its name from its unusually strong coffee – they will gladly water it down for the faint of heart. Expect lots of students and people reading the free newspapers, as well as interesting rotating exhibitions by local artists.
Disabled: toilets.

Patio Café

531 Castro Street, between 18th and 19th Streets (621 4640). Muni Metro F, K, L, M/bus 24, 35. **Open** 8am-10.30pm Mon-Fri; 8am-11pm Sat, Sun. **Average** $7. **Credit** AmEx, MC, V. **Castro/Mission Map X1**
The most popular brunch spot in the area, so be prepared to

A lull before the crowds descend on the popular **Firewood Café**.

queue. Seating is in a greenhouse-like structure off the street, a soothing place to recover from a hangover. It's tricky to find the entrance; look for the corridor behind the shops.

Sparky's
242 Church Street, at Market Street (626 8666). Muni Metro F, K, L, M/bus 22, 35. **Open** 24-hours daily. **Average** $6. **Credit** AmEx, DC, Disc, MC, V.
Open 24 hours and particularly popular late at night. If you're craving hash browns at 4am, this is the place. There's a large menu and relatively low prices. The food is lousy, but at 4am after a night of drinking and dancing, who cares?

Clubs

Dancing is a San Franciscan passion and the club scene is always on the move as new clubs appear and old ones fade away. The places listed below are likely to be around for some time to come, but it is wise to check first: pick up a copy of *Odyssey*, the club scene magazine to find out the latest on what's in and who's wearing what to go where. For the long-running S&M fetish club **Bondage-a-Go-Go** – and others – *see chapter* **Nightlife**.

The Box
715 Harrison Street, between Third and Fourth Streets (206 1652). Bus 15, 30, 45, 76. **Open** 10pm-4am Thur. **Admission** $7. **No credit cards. Map H4**
This San Francisco institution marks the domain of legendary DJ Mistress Page Hodel. The Box is all things to all people and prides itself on making everyone welcome – diversity is the watchword. Plan to dance and sweat until you drop.

The Café
2367 Market Street, at Castro Street (861 3846). Bus 35, 37. **Open** 12.30pm-2am daily. **No credit cards. Map E6**
Once the neglected Café San Marcos and bitchily dubbed the 'lesbian airport lounge', the Café is now the most popular dance club in the Castro. It has two bars, a dance floor and a patio as well as pool and pinball – plus some of the hottest young things (male and female) in town. Expect to queue on Friday and Saturdays, and wear something lightweight (and revealing): the temperature soars as the night gets going.

Club Universe
177 Townsend Street, at Third Street (985 5241/www. 177townsend.com). Bus 30, 42, 45, 76. **Open** 9.30pm-7am Sat. **No credit cards. Map J4/5**
A big warehouse-type club with an emphasis on house sounds, which operates on Saturday nights only. Popular with gay and straight clubbers, it's a good place to go with a mixed group of people. Check *Odyssey* for each week's 'environment'.

El Rio
3158 Mission Street, at Cesar Chavez Street (282 3325). Bus 12, 14, 27, 49. **Open** 3pm-midnight Mon; 3pm-2am Tue-Sun. **No credit cards.**
A mixed club featuring international and Latino music. Good fun, but try to get there before 9pm – the line can be one of the longest and slowest. The Sunday afternoon summer salsa garden parties are famous, with superb live music and the best-looking lesbian crowd in the city. *See also chapter* **Music: Rock, Jazz & Blues**.

The End-Up
Corner of Sixth Street, at Harrison Street (487 6277). Bus 27, 42. **Open** 10.30pm-4am Thur; 9pm-3pm Fri, Sat; 5pm-2am Sun. **No credit cards. Map H5**
If Saturday night has turned into Sunday morning and you're still going strong, the party continues at The End-Up,

starting at 6am. There's a great dance floor in a large space, and the Sunday 'tea dance' (better even than their 'Fag Friday') is always popular. If you don't go, you can't say you've really seen gay San Francisco.

Pleasuredome
177 Townsend Street, at Third Street (985 5256). Bus 30, 42, 45, 76. **Open** 9pm-6am Sun. **No credit cards. Map J4/5**
The longest-running gay club in the city and still going strong. More bare pectoral muscles than you can shake a stick at – if you've been faithful in your gym attendance, here's the pay-off. Sunday nights only.

Rawhide II
280 Seventh Street, at Folsom Street (621 1197). Bus 12. **Open** 4pm-2am Mon-Thur; noon-2am Fri-Sun. **Credit** MC, V. **Map G5**
A truly authentic country and western bar full of – almost – authentic cowboys and cowgirls. There are $2 western dance lessons in the early evenings (makes for a good date).

The Stud
399 Ninth Street, at Harrison Street (863 6623). Bus 19, 27, 42. **Open** 5pm-2am daily. **No credit cards. Map G5**
A San Francisco institution, buried in SoMa (take a cab both ways), the Stud has one of the most varied crowds: from college students out for an exploratory evening to hardcore muscle boys posing in the corners. Sunday night is 1980s retro, but Wednesday night is the customary time to drop in.

Entertainment

If the men don't provide sufficient diversion, gay San Francisco offers other equally theatrical alternatives. You'll be told to see *Beach Blanket Babylon* (do it) and probably the drag show at Finocchio's (don't – it's really aimed at awestruck Midwestern tourists), but check out the venues listed below as well. *See also chapters* **Film** *and* **Theatre & Dance**.

Castro Theater
429 Castro Street, off Market Street (621 6120). Muni Metro F, K, L, M/bus 24, 33, 35, 37. **No credit cards. Map E6**
A queen of a movie palace, the recently renovated Castro Theater – and the mighty Wurlitzer organ that plays before all its features – is one of the city's finest repertory cinemas. It truly comes alive for the great gay and camp classics: until you've seen *Mommie Dearest, Valley of the Dolls* or *All About Eve* in a queer-packed theatre with full audience participation, you haven't really lived. Call for titles and times, or drop by the theatre to pick up a three-month schedule.

Josie's Juice Bar and Cabaret
3583 16th Street, between Market and Pond Streets (861 7933). Muni Metro F, K, L, M/bus 37. **Open** *café* 9am-7.15pm daily; *cabaret* 7.15-10pm Mon-Thur, Sun; 7.15-11.30pm Fri, Sat. **Admission** $5-$12. **No credit cards. Map E6**
The best place in town to catch gay comics, one-man and one-woman shows or performance pieces. The house is small – 130 seats – so get tickets in advance. The garden at the back is also a favourite weekend brunch spot. *See also chapter* **Nightlife**.

Theatre Rhinoceros
2926 16th Street, between Mission Street and South Van Ness Avenue (861 5079). BART 16th Street/bus 14, 22, 33, 49, 53. **Performances start** 8pm or 8.30pm Tue-Sun. **Admission** about $15. **Credit** MC, V. **Map F6**

Many other venues offer queer plays, but Theatre Rhino is the city's only truly gay theatre. A wide variety of shows are performed, many of them original plays. Check the listings in any of the free weeklies for what's on during your stay.

Shops

See also chapter **Shopping & Services**.

Does Your Mother Know

4079 18th Street, between Castro and Noe Streets (864 3160). Bus 24, 33, 35. **Open** 9.30am-10pm Mon-Thur; 9.30am-11pm Fri, Sat; 10am-9pm Sun. **Credit** AmEx, DC, JCB, MC, V. **Castro/Mission Map X1**

The Castro has plenty of places to buy greetings cards but DYMK, around the corner from the area's main drag, remains the favourite with many. Plus magazines, books and gifts.

Headlines

557 Castro Street, between 18th and 19th Streets (626 8061). Bus 24, 33, 35. **Open** 10am-9pm Mon-Thur; 10am-10pm Fri, Sat; 11am-8pm Sun. **Credit** AmEx, DC, JCB, MC, V. **Castro/Mission Map X1**

A housewares/gift/clothing store that is sure to satisfy your queer capitalist cravings. From fridge magnets to cards, jeans, underwear, condoms and sex toys, you'll find myriad gifts for your favourite queen. The staff are friendly, the selection awesome, the prices low. The women's version, two doors down (549 Castro Street; 252 1280), has more clothing than kitsch.

Worn Out West

528 Castro Street, between 18th and 19th Streets (431 6020). Bus 24, 33, 35. **Open** 11am-6pm Mon, Tue, Sat; 11am-9pm Wed, Fri; 11am-7pm Thur; noon-6pm Sun. **Credit** DC, JCB, MC, V. **Castro/Mission Map X1**

WOW appears at first sight to be a second-hand Western clothing store, but they've got lots of new duds, too, plus sexier paraphernalia and fashion accessories. If you're craving for full leather, a California State Patrol officer's uniform or just a great-fitting cowboy hat, this is the place.

Bookshops

Almost any good San Francisco bookshop – of which there are droves – has a good gay and lesbian section, both new and second-hand. The best by far is **A Different Light** (489 Castro Street, at 18th Street; 431 0891), the SF branch of the national gay chain. If it doesn't stock what you're looking for, it probably isn't available. Around the corner is **Books Inc** (2275 Market Street, at 16th Street; 864-6777) and **Jaguar Adult Books** (4057 18th Street, at Hartford Street; 863 4777), which offers a wide selection of the 'other' gay literature: porn mags and books.

Working Out

The fitness craze has hit San Francisco as much as any other city and the question is no longer 'Do you work out?' but 'Where?' The city abounds in gyms, but some are more gay-friendly than others. Below are some of the most popular, which also offer day or short-term passes. *See also chapter* **Sport & Fitness**.

City Athletic Club

2500 Market Street, at 17th Street (552 6680). Muni Metro F, K, L, M/bus 35, 37. **Open** 6am-10pm daily. **Admission** $10 per day; $25 per week. **Credit** AmEx, DC, Disc, MC, V. **Men only.** Map E6.

Market Street Gym

2301 Market Street, at Noe Street (626 4488). Muni Metro F, K, L, M/bus 37. **Open** 6am-10pm Mon-Fri; 8am-8pm Sat, Sun. **Admission** $10 per day; $38 per week. **Credit** AmEx, MC, V. **Mixed.** Map E6

Muscle System

2275 Market Street, between Sanchez and Noe Streets (863 4700). Bus 37. **Open** 5.30am-10pm Mon-Fri; 8am-8pm Sat, Sun. **Admission** $8 per day; $27 per week. **Credit** MC, V. **Men only.** Map E6

Branch: 364 Hayes Street, between Franklin and Gough Streets (863 4701).

Girls

Although women patronise the Castro and Hayes Valley bars, cafés and restaurants, the more affordable Mission area – particularly Valencia Street from 16th to 22nd Streets – provides a scene for many lesbians, especially younger ones. The district is roughly bordered by Red Dora's Bearded Lady café, the women-run, sex toy emporium Good Vibrations and Osento women's bathhouse.

Socialising in the 1990s is organised more around cultural events than bars or parties. Check the local papers once you've arrived in the city for the most up-to-date information on what's on. The *Bay Times* contains the most complete calendar for lesbian events and, it is said, the most lively lesbian personal ads in the US. Newspapers and guides with lesbian listings can be found at the Women's Building, as well as on the streets and in the shops in the Castro and western Mission districts.

INFORMATION

The **Women's Building** (3543 18th Street, between Valencia and Guerrero Streets; 431 1180) is home to various women's organisations and also a central place for newspapers, bulletin board postings, events and information. The rich colours of the mural that covers the outside of the building have made the centre a landmark. For helplines, counselling and medical services, *see page 261.*

Accommodation

Phone either of these places in advance to reserve a room and get their address. *See also page 185* **Beck's Motor Lodge** *and chapter* **Accommodation**.

House O' Chicks Guesthouse

(861 9849). **Rates** *single* $75 per night, $450 per week; *double* $85 per night, $550 per week. **Credit** AmEx, MC, V.

off-peak hours women frequent the bar's low-key pool tables. On weekend nights you'll often find a mixed clientele watching a good jazz or blues band.

Club Q
177 Townsend Street, at Third Street (974 6020).
Bus 15, 30, 42, 45, 76. **Open** 9pm-3am, first Friday of each month. **No credit cards. Map J4/5**
If you're in town while it's happening, be sure and catch one of the longest-running women's clubs in San Francisco. Club Q features fun music, girls galore and a hard-dancing, culturally varied crowd.

The CoCo Club
139 Eighth Street, between Mission and Howard Streets (626 2337). Bus 12, 14, 19, 26. **Open** 8pm-2am Wed-Sun. **No credit cards. Map G5**
The hottest new lesbian venue features a sweaty dance club on Fridays, live music on Saturdays and showcases of local bands on Sundays, all in an intimate setting with a low cover charge. There are happy hour specials during the week.

Lexington Club
3464 19th Street, at Lexington Street, between Mission and Valencia (863 2052). Bus 26, 33. **Open** 3pm-2am daily. **No credit cards. Castro/Mission Map Y1**
This funky street-level hideaway just might be San Francisco's sole lesbian-only bar, replacing Amelia's (RIP) in the Mission. Cosy, inviting booths and dim lights set the scene, with women of all kinds smoking, talking and cruising. There's also a great jukebox (The Cure to Johnny Cash).

Wild Side West
424 Cortland Avenue, at Wool Street (647 3099). Muni Metro J/bus 14 or 9, then 24. **Open** 1pm-2am daily. **No credit cards.**
This place has been around forever (although it used to be located in North Beach), and the story goes that Janis Joplin would hang out and pick up girls at the very same wooden bar that now graces its Bernal Heights location. The walls are a shifting art installation and the clientele mixed. There's also a fabulous jukebox of classics – you can count on hearing Joplin, Patsy Cline and, of course, Lou Reed's *Walk on the Wild Side*.

Bondage-a-Go-Go *at the Trocadero Transfer.*

Two rooms in this seven-room flat are available for female visitors to the city. It caters to a mostly European clientele, and features a continental breakfast and shared bath. Not a stuffy B&B – there are notes and scrapbooks compiled by past guests, as well as guidebooks and current lesbian listings for around the city.

Nancy's Bed
(239 5692). **Rates** $25-$35. **No credit cards.**
There are two rooms available in this private home, which is close to the Castro area and public transport.

Bars & Clubs

Once the main gathering point for lesbians, **The Café** (*see page 189*) remains a favourite; it has also become very popular with gay men at the weekends. The **CoCo Club** (*see below*) has good live music and a café upstairs, and **The End-Up**, a long-standing gay men's bar (*page 189*), is home to G-Spot on Saturday nights. For a drink in classy surroundings, try **Hayes & Vine** (*see chapter* **Restaurants & Cafés**). And **El Rio** shouldn't be missed as the ultimate San Francisco Sunday experience (*page 189*). *See also chapters* **Bars** *and* **Nightlife**.

Blondie's Bar & No Grill
540 Valencia Street, between 16th and 17th Streets (864 2419). BART 16th Street/bus 22, 26, 53.
Open 2pm-2am daily. **No credit cards. Map F6**
On Tuesdays and Sundays, Blondie's is filled with hip young women ready to dance, cruise and watch each other. During

Cafés & Restaurants

If you're looking to join the lesbian scene, you might start with a walk along Valencia Street between 16th and 22nd Streets, where any of a number of restaurants and cafés are filled with lesbians of all shapes and sizes. The cafés around Bernal Hill will probably serve nearly as well, and if you've got a dog to walk you'll have an even better excuse to chat. We've listed some of the highlights of the lesbian scene – lipstick and dyke – below. For the popular **Café Flore**, among other gay and lesbian hangouts, *see page 188. See also chapters* **Bars** *and* **Restaurants & Cafés**.

Da Flora
701 Columbus Avenue, at Filbert Street (981-4664). Bus 15, 30, 41/cable car Powell-Mason. **Open** 6-10pm Tue-Sun. **Average** $20. **Credit** MC, V. **Map G2**
This delightful *osteria* is a first for San Francisco: a decent, lesbian- and gay-friendly Italian restaurant in North Beach. The place is tiny, with kitschy décor and excellent food. Try the baccala on fresh polenta, the sardines with balsamic onions, or any number of fresh, seasonal pasta dishes cooked to order. There's great vegetarian fare, too. Flora, a gregarious dyke who's also a movie star (ask her!), runs the place and will make you feel welcome.

Just For You

1453 18th Street, at Connecticut Street (647 3033).
Bus 22, 53. **Open** 7am-2.30pm Mon-Fri; 8.30am-5pm Sat,
Sun. **Average** $5. **No credit cards.**
It's a bit off the beaten track, but worth the trip. This tiny
dyke-run restaurant serves a hearty New Orleans-style
breakfast and lunch with superb grits and great pancakes.
Most of the seating is at the counter overlooking the cook-
ing area, where muscled women prepare your delicious meal.

Red Dora's Bearded Lady

485 14th Street, at Guerrero Street (626 2805). Muni
Metro F, K, L, M/26 bus. **Open** 7am-7pm Mon-Fri; 9am-
7pm Sat, Sun. **No credit cards. Map F6**
The Bearded Lady is a café by day and, often, a performance
space by night. The walls are hung with work by lesbian
artists, and at the counter you can order anything from
espresso to pesto eggs and breakfast cereal favourites.

Entertainment

For the **Theatre Rhinoceros**, a theatre devoted
exclusively to lesbian and gay plays, and **Josie's
Juice Bar and Cabaret** (*the* place to see up-and-
coming lesbian and gay comics) *see page 189. See
also chapter* **Theatre & Dance.**

Brava! for Women in the Arts

Theatre Center, 2789 24th Street, between York and
Hampshire Streets (Brava! office 641 7657). Bus 9, 27,
48. **Open** *office* 10am-6pm Mon-Fri. **Performances**
start 7-8pm. **Admission** $8-$20. **Credit** MC, V.
Castro/Mission Map Z2
The results of women's performance and writing workshops are featured in this small theatre space. Brava! has

Eponymous chef/proprietress **Flora**. *P191.*

encouraged the work of women playwrights and writers
for years, and although it can be hit or miss, you may get
a sneak preview of great work to come.

LunaSea

Room 216C, 2940 16th Street, between Capp Street and
South Van Ness Avenue (863 2989). BART 16th Street/
bus 33, 53. **Performances start** 8pm. **Admission**
$8-$15. **No credit cards. Map F6**
Here you'll find experimental and sometimes cutting-edge
work by local lesbian performance artists and writers, as
well as a supportive, interested and creative audience. Shows
are usually every Friday and Saturday.

Health & Fitness

For details of spas and retreats, as well as the
popular women-only **Osento** bath house, *see*
chapter **Shopping & Services;** for general sports
facilities, *see chapter* **Sport & Fitness.**

The Women's Training Center

2164 Market Street, between Church and Sanchez Streets
(864 6835). Muni Metro F, K, L, M/bus 37. **Open** 6am-
9.30pm Mon-Fri; 8am-6pm Sat; 10am-5pm Sun.
Admission $10 day pass; $40 two-week guest pass.
No credit cards. Map E6
Work out travel kinks at this women-only (and largely lesbian) gym. A pass includes free weights, basic aerobic
equipment, dry sauna, showers and lockers.

Shopping

See also chapter **Shopping & Services.**

Good Vibrations

1210 Valencia Street, at 23rd Street (550 7399). Bus
26. **Open** 11am-7pm daily. **Credit** AmEx, Disc, MC,
V. **Castro/Mission Map Y2**
You've seen the ads in nearly every progressive publication
in the world; now it's time to check out Good Vibrations for
yourself. Good Vibes, as this women's erotica store is known,
features a vibrator museum, all sorts of sex toys and a video
collection, and sponsors readings and sexual workshops.

Modern Times Bookstore

888 Valencia Street, between 19th and 20th Streets (282
9246). Bus 26. **Open** 11am-8pm Mon-Thur; 11am-9pm
Fri, Sat; 11am-6pm Sun. **Credit** AmEx, MC, V.
Castro/Mission Map Y1
A collectively-owned progressive bookstore with an excellent women's and lesbian section, featuring writers from all
over the world. A very friendly place to stop in and say hello.

Scarlett Sage Herb Company

1173 Valencia Street, between 22nd and 23rd Streets
(821 0997). BART 24th Street/bus 14, 26, 49.
Open 11am-6.30pm Mon-Sat; noon-5pm Sun.
Credit AmEx, MC, V. **Castro/Mission Map Y2**
Drop in to experience the comfortable and soothing atmosphere of this lesbian-run store. Wares include organic bulk
herbs, herbal extracts, flower essences, bodycare products
and a wide selection of books on herbs and homeopathy.

Stormy Leather

1158 Howard Street, between Seventh and Eighth Streets
(626 6783). Bus 12. **Open** noon-7pm Mon-Sat; 2-6pm
Sun. **Credit** AmEx, Disc, MC, V. **Map G5**
A woman-owned leather, fetish and sexual fantasy shop with
everything from leather and latex bustiers to finely crafted
whips and paddles. Staff are friendly and helpful.

Media

San Francisco's laissez-faire attitude extends towards its media.

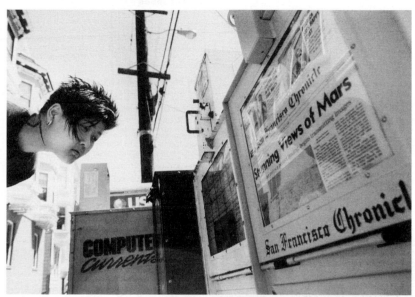

Media in San Francisco is about friendly competition. The city has twin newspapers and arts weeklies, myriad TV and radio stations and battling Internet publications. Yet unlike, say, New York, rivals are rarely cut-throat. Few media businesses are willing to take the risk of outspending or outperforming their competitor. The result is that the city has yet to see a five-star newspaper, a fully realised entertainment tabloid or – God forbid – an exceptional television station.

Media coverage apparently functions not only to report and reflect what's going on, but to confirm the local audience's belief that they're living the zaniest, most trendsetting, most exceptional lives ever. Mass media is essential to the collective psyche. While the city hosts a number of innovative magazines, TV programmes and web resources, it seems to view media's role as something just short of what it could be. The city appears content to navel-gaze, to convince itself that, just as its weather is pleasant and its populace conciliatory and easygoing, so should its media be.

Newspapers & Magazines

Dailies

San Francisco Chronicle

The *Chronicle* (50¢) is the region's largest circulation paper; complaining about how bad it is has become something of a cliché. But the paper thrives in the suburbs, where its emphasis on 'quality of life' over hard news and business is welcome – if a bit of a panacea. The paper hosts a number of good columnists – Jon Carroll, Ruthe Stein, Scott Ostler – though no one has yet filled the oxfords of the late Herb Caen, the city's best-known newspaperman, who died in 1997 (*see p196*). The Chron's regional news, sports, business and entertainment sections are adequate. National, and international news, however, are sorely lacking.

San Francisco Examiner

The city's afternoon paper (25¢) is no competition to the *Chronicle*, though its Style section is worthwhile and its business coverage seems to be improving. The two papers have a joint operating agreement, but the *Examiner* has wilted and become a financial liability to both partners. Like the Chron, most of its non-local news comes from wire services or is reprinted from the *New York Times* or *Los Angeles Times*.

Sunday Examiner/Chronicle

On Sundays, the Chron combines with the Examiner to produce the fat *San Francisco Examiner and Chronicle* ($1.50). It contains a Datebook supplement, or what locals call the 'pink' section – a tabloid entertainment and arts section published on pink paper, which includes listings, concert reviews, capsule movie reviews and suchlike. For visitors, the Pink is probably the single most valuable section of any local newspaper.

Other Daily Papers

The regional edition of the *New York Times* ($1) or national edition of the *Los Angeles Times* ($1) are your best bet for good news reporting. If you can, pick up a copy of the *San Jose Mercury News* (35¢), the region's best paper for news, business and sports. An entity that's trying to break the Chron/Ex's stranglehold on the city's readership, the Merc also maintains a superb website at www.sjmercury.com. Otherwise, the *Wall Street Journal* ($1) has an excellent news brief on the front page and some of the best feature writing in the country – though its Op-Ed page is dominated by reactionary and tiresome conservatives who blame the country's ills on the 1960s. The vapid *USA Today* (50¢) serves only in a pinch – you'll soon learn why it's handed out free in hotels.

Weeklies

San Francisco Bay Guardian

Like the daily papers, two free weekly arts tabloids battle for supremacy in San Francisco. The *SF Bay Guardian* is a fat, lively rag that mixes an unapologetically liberal political stance with dedication to a full range of arts listings. It's definitely the better of the two weeklies. Executive editor Ron Curran grabs greedy utilities, and just about anyone else who's thrusting or hypocritical by the short and curlies, regularly pissing off the more conservative local establishment by exposing cronyism, graft, fraud or double standards. Many writers cover their beats with pith and wit, from alternative political writers to the latest punk-rock journalists. The paper's 'Lit' book review is a great read; likewise, its yearly fiction contest. Everybody loves the *Guardian*, but it could benefit from some real competition: sometimes the paper's editorial groove feels spookily like a rut. Look for it distributed every Wednesday at myriad free newspaper boxes and cafés throughout the city.

SF Weekly

The second fiddle of arts weeklies has suffered greatly at the hands of New Times, the Phoenix, AZ-based corporation that bought it a few years ago. Its stories have grown thin, its tone embittered, its content patchy, its writers haggard. Still, when the *Weekly* hits, it hits hard, and its easy-to-read listings section is up to par with the Guardian's. Most importantly, 'Savage Love,' its syndicated sex column, is far more humorous and outrageous than the yawn-inducing 'Ask Isadora' in the SFBG. The Weekly also comes out on Wednesday and is free.

Gay & Lesbian Papers

There is a host of free papers targeted at gay and lesbian readers, including the *Bay Times* (a tabloid), *BAR* (Bay Area Reporter) and *Icon*. Available from coffee shops and bookstores in the Castro and New Bohemia (the Mission), almost all carry listings of events for gay audiences as well as personal ads and social and political commentary. Other queer publications produced in San Francisco include *Curve* for lesbians and the X-rated *Taste of Latex*.

Monthlies

In San Francisco, magazines are like screenplays are in Los Angeles – everyone's working on one. Though a couple of favourites – *Mondo 2000* and *Might* – have recently perished, some actually make it to production and even make a splash, such as the monthly *Wired*. As we went to press, a num-ber of new magazines were enduring precariously. They include *Speak* ($4.50), a 'fictionmusicfashion-film' quarterly that's artful and interesting; *Juxtapoz* ($3.95), a lowbrow 'art through chaos' journal; *Red Herring* ($4.95), a smart business-and-technology monthly; and *The Web* ($3.95), the only surviving slick dedicated to content on the World Wide Web.

Mother Jones

The bi-monthly *Mother Jones* ($3.95) has changed format and masthead quite a lot in the past few years, but it still pounds out the heartbeat of the liberal agenda with its left-lurching stance. *MoJo* regularly takes on the Christian Coalition, the Republican Party and any of a number of anti-environmental groups; its writing, while not as combative as it once was, is fresh and compelling.

San Francisco Focus

Published by the largest public television station in the Bay Area, *San Francisco Focus* ($2.95) is sent to KQED subscribers and is also available at some newsstands. It features interviews with regional personalities and reportage on such Northern California issues as the environment; its recent redesign also includes several pages of recommended events for the month. But don't for a minute think of it as the city's *New Yorker* ($2.50): unfortunately, *Focus* is light on content.

Wired

With its neon design and self-righteous editorial stance, *Wired* ($4.95) represents the most visible magazine success from San Francisco since *Rolling Stone*. To those who don't play video games, surf the Net or imagine that working with computers ushers them into a new reality, the monthly can prove bewildering, but as an emblem of the digital revolution it has no match. Recently the magazine underwent a design change and editorial shift; time will tell whether these will affect *Wired*'s recent trajectory from a culture magazine into one intended solely for rich cyberlibertarian businessmen. Let's hope so.

Foreign-language Publications

San Francisco hosts more than 70 resident nationalities, almost all of whom have an own-language paper serving their respective community's local needs and desire for news from 'home'. The *Tenderloin Times*, for instance, is a weekly paper published in Cambodian, Vietnamese, Cantonese and English. On Valencia Street, in the predominantly Latin-American Mission district, the following bookshops sell Spanish-language newspapers and *libros en Español*: **Modern Times Bookstore** (888 Valencia Street; 282 9246), **Dog Eared Books**, (1173 Valencia; 282 1901), and **Books On Wings** (La Casa del Libro, 973 Valencia; 285 1145). On the same street you can also find the **Arabic Book Center** (791 Valencia; 864 1585). Chinatown is also the place for news from Asia, and the magnificent **Books on Japan** (1581 Webster Street in Japantown; 567 7625) stocks Japanese language publications. Italians can pick up the latest installment of *Diabolik* at **Cavalli Italian Bookstore** (1441 Stockton Street; 421 4219); and the **European Book Company** (925 Larkin Street; 474 0626) stocks various language publications from the continent.

Outlets

San Francisco is a town long on specialists and short on generalists. Still, there are a few locations that endeavour to give readers a single destination for all their periodical needs. The very well-read **Harold's International Newsstand** at 524 Geary Boulevard, between Jones and Taylor Streets (441 2665) offers as complete a selection as you'll find in the city; **Farley's** at 1315 18th Street, between Texas and Missouri Streets (648 1545), is a decent café with magazines; and **Juicy News** at 2453 Fillmore Street, between Jackson and Washington Streets (441 3051), is a deceptively small shop given the number of titles it carries.

Those on the hunt for art and poetry publications should try **City Lights Bookstore** (*see chapter* **Shopping & Services**). Collectors will want to visit **The Magazine** at 920 Larkin Street, between Geary Boulevard and Post Street (441 7737), a store that sells vintage publications. Those wishing to see a great selection of 'zines (self- and desktop-published volumes often written with a very personal perspective) should visit **Naked Eye News & Video** (533 Haight Street; 864 2985), or, for an excellent selection of gay and lesbian publications, try **A Different Light** (*see chapter* **Gay & Lesbian San Francisco**).

Tower Records at Market and Noe Streets (621 0588) and Columbus and Bay Avenues (885 0500)

*Decent coffee and the papers at **Farley's**.*

can be counted on for the latest pop culture and music rags. Homesick Euros needn't miss a beat at **Café de la Presse** (352 Grant Avenue), an ultra-modern Parisian-style café, which has an espresso bar and sells all the major European dailies and glossies (*see chapter* **Restaurants & Cafés**).

Television

Those unaccustomed to American television should be prepared for a blaring deluge of advertisements and a surprising lack of resistance to it from regular viewers. The fact, for instance, that programming in the US is driven by advertising has moved from the evident to the obvious, the result being that few give this troubling relationship a second thought. What's more, many of television's greatest talents are employed part- or full-time by advertisers to direct or star in their spots. Consequently, for pure entertainment value, advertisements often outshine programming.

The best printed resource for what's on the air remains the *TV Guide* (99¢). Daily newspapers have 24-hour TV listings, and a stapled booklet for the week is included in the combined Sunday *San Francisco Examiner and Chronicle*.

The Networks

The San Francisco Bay Area has affiliates of all three major networks: ABC (local station is **KGO**, found on channel 7), NBC (**KRON**, channel 4) and CBS (**KPIX**, channel 5). The long-lasting independent station, **KTVU** (channel 2) is now part of the Fox TV network. Reflecting their dependence on advertising, there is little difference, politically or ideologically, between these four networks – their primary concern is the size of their audience, not any social tendency within it. Their daily fare is almost identical, with variations on a theme.

The morning brings chatty news reports; mid-morning, the confessional and celebrity-driven talk shows begin, yielding to soap operas at midday. After lunch, the soaps wrap up and it's back to more talk shows. As early as 4pm you can catch national network news taped on the East Coast or broadcast live from its 7pm slot in New York and Washington. Early evenings are dominated by news programmes, game shows and re-runs of sitcoms. Melodramas and movies edited for commercial breaks dominate 'Prime Time' and then it's onto the late-night talk shows where celebrity hosts (David Letterman, Jay Leno, Conan O'Brien and others) interview stars, introduce hit-making bands and work for laughs.

CNN and a local independent station, **KOFY** (channel 20), broadcast news. Weekly highlights on the networks include *60 Minutes* (CBS, Sundays at 7pm) and the ever-popular *Saturday Night Live* (NBC, Saturdays at 12.30am). Most stations run programming around the clock, so American insomniacs are never without distraction.

Cable TV

To improve their choice of small-screen entertainment, many people in the Bay Area pay monthly fees for cable TV (and most hotels worth their nightly rates offer cable as a standard feature). In addition to the 24-hour music videos of **MTV** (on cable channel 48) and round-the-clock sport on **ESPN** (cable 34), cable provides access to a number of stations that specialise in news (**CNN**, cable 42), classic movies (**AMC**, cable 34; the **Movie Channel**, cable 1) or recently released movies (**HBO**, cable 8). Furthermore, some hit movies and sporting events are available on a pay-as-you-view basis. Some sports bars will pay these fees to attract customers. For Public Access television, check out **Bay TV** (cable 35), a station dedicated to local issues.

Public TV

The alternative to the relentless advertising of commercial stations is **PBS**, the Public Broadcasting Service, which has stations in San Francisco (**KQED**, on cable 9), San Jose (**KTEH**, channel 54, cable 19) and San Mateo (**KCSM**, channel 60, cable 21). These stations receive a meagre subsidy from the federal government and solicit funds from viewers. Criticised for being short on local programming, KQED has an unenviable reputation as one of the fattest of the subsidised stations, with much of the money going into executives' salaries. It broadcasts the *News Hour with Jim Lehrer* every weekday at 6pm. While PBS may be a respite from the advertised life, it trades off its 'prestige' reputation a touch too smugly. The system might appeal to homesick Brits pining for 'quality' TV or re-runs of ancient sitcoms but it hardly represents an authentic American TV-watching experience.

Mr San Francisco…

On 1 February 1997, the city lost one of its most established and visible symbols. Herb Caen, the San Francisco *Chronicle*'s longtime columnist, died of lung cancer at the age of 80. More than just a familiar face about town, Caen was a legend, a monument, one of the journalistic rocks on which the city stood. His column was as familiar to San Franciscans as the Golden Gate Bridge or Coit Tower, a tangible piece of the city's heritage and the most common accompaniment to residents' morning coffee. For 58 years, Caen had written about the city, loved it, kidded it, drank and eaten at its restaurants, enjoyed its sights, sounded the call for it to better itself. For 58 years, Caen had served as the city's voice.

Herb Caen's column appeared for years on the first page of the *Chronicle*'s second section, a thousand-word pillar that culled local news, gossipy tidbits, corny one-liners and – more often than not – a bit of flowery prose dedicated to San Francisco. Items were separated by ellipses, a form Caen referred to as 'three-dot journalism'. Any given column could offer copious praise (or cruel panning) of a new restaurant, an insider tip that might embarrass a local politician, a tender note about a passing friend, a dollop of self-deprecating humour or a pun bad enough to make your eyes water. He noted clever company names (a coffee shop called Has Beans) as well as overheard witticisms and the best bars to find 'Vitamin V' – his legendary Stolichnaya vodka martini. Six days a week he wrote his piece, refusing the onslaught of technology by banging his copy out on a series of now-immortalised Royal typewriters.

Caen was born in Sacramento, where he first wrote a column for his school newspaper. Later, in the company of William Saroyan and Ernest Hemingway, he served as a war correspondent and reporter in World War II, then returned to settle in the town he loved (he claimed to have been conceived in the city). He wrote originally for the *Chronicle*, was wooed away by the *Examiner*, then returned to the Chron (for a then-exorbitant salary of $38,000 a year) in 1958. For the next 39 years,

he stayed and wrote, coining key local phrases such as 'Baghdad-by-the-Bay' and 'beatnik'.

In all, Caen published more than 16,000 columns. In a typical year, he dropped 6,768 names and received 45,000 letters and 24,000 phone calls. In his obituary, the Chron noted that, if placed end to end, Caen's columns would stretch 5.6 miles – 'from the Ferry Building to the Golden Gate Bridge'. He also found time to pen 11 books and countless introductions to others. Though he never presumed to don the name himself, many in the city knew him as 'Mr San Francisco'. To the average resident who met him on the street, he was personable and easygoing.

In his 80th year, Caen crossed several milestones, getting married for a fourth time and winning a Pulitzer Prize. Until he was diagnosed with cancer, one could occasionally see him out on the town with his wife, enjoying meatloaf and mashed potatoes (his favourite dish) or sipping a Stoli at Enrico's before joining the house band on the drums. He loved jazz, good writing, a stiff cocktail and San Francisco – though not necessarily in that order.

And the city loved him: Herb Caen Day on 14 June 1996, drew more than 75,000 people to the Ferry Building in the middle of the day, a celebration at which the city renamed a stretch of the Embarcadero 'Herb Caen Way…' – the trademark three dots intact. Less than a year later, his funeral packed Grace Cathedral to the rafters with 4,000 adoring fans, an event broadcast via live television, radio and the Internet.

Caen wasn't a political man, though he opposed US participation in the Vietnam war (and wrote about it) and staunchly participated in his union (and wrote for its paper during newspaper strikes). Rather, he was a writer fully comfortable with speaking for the metropolis he loved, something he did with more confidence and grace than any single entity in the city's history. When awarding him the Pulitzer, judges cited his 'extraordinary contribution as a voice and a conscience of his city'. To those who lived for his daily column, he was nothing less.

Radio

San Francisco's constantly changing radio profile reflects several difficulties: that of attracting elusive listeners in a competitive market and of outsmarting weather and geography, which combine to undermine reliable radio signals. But don't think for a minute that San Francisco Bay Area radio isn't spectacular. The weaker, non-commercial stations lie to the left of the FM dial; the powerhouses with the loudest ads cluster on the right. AM is mostly reserved for talk and news shows with a few foreign-language, oldie and Christian stations peppering the mix. Between both FM and AM bands, however, the range of programming is nothing short of amazing – from right-wing talk show hosts to hour-long devotions to indigenous music, covering obscure jazz or the latest in hip-hop, college rock and urban soul.

News & Talk

For the latest news, **KGO** (810 AM), **KQED** (88.5 FM) and its competitor, **KALW** (91.7 FM), remain your best bets. Beyond that, Berkeley-based **KPFA** (94.1 FM) is also determined to give KQED a run for its money, and **KCBS** (740 AM), the local CBS affiliate, has likewise proved itself a station devoted to quality news (and priceless traffic reports, every eight minutes!). **KSFO** (740 AM), meanwhile, boasts reactionary talk radio programmes in the morning and broadcasts Oakland A's baseball games in the afternoon. **KNBR** (680 AM) is the voice for Giants' baseball games and the place to tune in later for well-informed sporting debate.

Classical

Advertised as a 'radio concert hall', **KDFC** (102.1 FM, 1220 AM), remains a bit on the stuffy side, interrupting its conservative classical repertoire to run hyperactive ads for cars, wine and singles clubs. As a result, many listeners have defected to **KKHI** (100.7 FM), where the programming is more diverse and the ads more mellow. KKHI hosts delightful Morning, Afternoon and Evening Concerts.

Jazz

Following the demise of KJAZ in 1995, San Francisco and the region have been hurting for a good jazz station. The adventurous **KCSM** (97.7 FM), a public radio station broadcast from a college in San Mateo, has taken up much of the slack, though its signal is relatively weak. Local **KKSF** (103.7 FM) bills itself as a 'soft jazz' station, but all too often sounds more like muzak than anything worth an extended listening – don't tune in while operating any heavy machinery.

Dance, Hip-Hop, Soul

Rarely can one find more energy than on **KMEL** (106 FM), the Bay Area's foremost station for pop and hip-hop. Formerly 'Wild 107,' **KYLD** (94.9 FM) is something of a contender and definitely gets partygoers in the mood on weekend nights. For something different, tune in to tiny **KPOO** (89.5 FM), where innovative hip-hop and hardcore rap alternate with cool blues shows on weekend nights and a Tuesday afternoon slot featuring four hours of the music of John Coltrane.

Rock & Pop

KFOG (104.5 FM) may have the most loyal following of any radio station on the West Coast. These adoring masses even have a name – Fog Heads. KFOG describes its programming as 'quality rock', and it does provide an above-average mix of classic rock with new material, much of it local. 'Live 105' **KITS** (105 FM) bills itself as 'the rock of the 90s', though the station seems to focus too often on bands that made it big in

the 1980s – U2 and Depeche Mode meet Nirvana and Alanis Morissette. **KOME** (98.5 FM) has staked out the newest and youngest rock/pop territory and is a hit with teenagers. **KRQR** (97.3 FM) leans towards heavy metal; **KSAN** (107.7) recently displaced 'Wild 107' and plays generic rock classics – more Steve Miller Band, anyone?

College & Community Radio Stations

Those in search of more eclectic listening should listen to **KALX** (90.7 FM), **KUSF** (90.3 FM), **KFJC** (89.7 FM) or **KPOO** (89.5 FM). These are the channels where you'll find diversity and innovative sounds, including acid jazz, Irish music, kids' shows, African and Latin music programmes and the latest trip-hop remix. The best aural blend in the region, the indie stations represent the diverse, non-commercial musical bouillabaisse for which San Francisco Bay Area is known.

Country & Western

Several country stations have popped up of late, most notably 'Young Country' **KYCY** (93.3 FM) and **KNEW** (910 AM). Between the two, they play a range from Garth Brooks and Wynona Judd to some of the genre's early innovators like Johnny Cash and Hank Williams.

Websites & Online Locations

Away from the broadcast and print media, the Internet offers a wide range of interesting information sites. The *San Francisco Bay Guardian* operates the best newspaper link to the Net from its site at www.sfbg.com, where you'll find the current issue as well as additional articles and columns. The *Chronicle* and *Examiner* share an online link, called the **SF Gate** (www.sfgate.com/), where you can search the archives of both papers and read the current edition.

The **WELL** (www.well.com), standing for Whole Earth 'Lectronic Link, was founded on April Fool's Day 1984 and was one of the first virtual communities to attract public use. It is an ideal source of information for exploring 'overground' San Francisco. **C|Net** (www.cnet.com/) is an indispensable source for what's happening in computers and multimedia. It combines a computer network, the largest original content on the World Wide Web and several television programmes – C|Net Central, the Web, and the New Edge – which air on the USA Network, the Sci-Fi Channel and on the local KPIX (channel 5).

Other San Francisco Internet sites include **HotWired** (www.hotwired.com/), the original online cultural resource; its biggest visual rival, **Salon** (www.salon1999.com/); **SF Station** (www.sfstation.com/), an arts hub and listings resource; and **CitySearch** (www.citysearch7.com/), another excellent source for arts listings. Finally, **Yahoo!** maintains a good regional site at www.sfbay.yahoo.com. Useful travel and hotel information can be found at the **San Francisco Hotel Reservations** (www.hotelres.com/) and **Bay Area Transit Information** (www.transit-info.org/). If you're seeking the latest earthquake info, go to http://quake.wr.usgs.gov. For a list of websites covering San Francisco and the Bay Area, *see page 252* **Directory**.

Music

A magical musical tour of the city, from symphonies in Civic Center, to surf music in the Mission.

To find out what's on when you're in town, check the Datebook section of the *San Francisco Chronicle* or the Style section of the *San Francisco Examiner*. The pink pages of the combined Sunday *San Francisco Chronicle and Examiner* and the free *Bay Guardian* or *SF Weekly* also include music listings. For rock listings, also check out the bi-weekly *BAM* and the weekly-updated, pre-recorded 'Alternative Music and Entertainment News' line on 221 2636, maintained by radio station KUSF. Keep an eye out for handouts and posters in cafés, record shops and bars.

An important thing to remember about clubs in San Francisco: with a few exceptions, no venue books one particular kind of music seven nights a week. While some are known strictly for jazz, most feature a palette of music as wide and diverse as the city itself. For details of the city's annual jazz and blues festivals and the music-orientated street fairs, *see chapter* **San Francisco by Season**. For supper clubs, which offer music, dancing and food in classy surroundings, *see chapter* **Nightlife**.

TICKETS

Where possible, buy tickets from the box offices of the major venues, and you won't have to pay the mark-up charged by **BASS** (1-510 762 2277). Cut price tickets are available each day at the **TIX Bay Area** kiosk in Union Square. For details of both, *see chapter* **Shopping & Services**. Most of the smaller clubs provide a recorded phone message with up-to-date information on where and when tickets go on sale – if they are sold in advance. The smallest clubs don't sell advance tickets at all, but instead collect a door charge or insist on a drink minimum.

Classical & Opera

San Francisco's reputation for classical music – especially contemporary music, early music and opera – has always been sterling, with more going on there today than in any other city on the West Coast. The recently renovated **War Memorial Opera House** has re-opened with a lavish splash, joining the **Davies Symphony Hall**, **Civic Auditorium** and **Herbst Theater** to form a four-part civic complex for all downtown musical events and attract audiences in ever-increasing numbers. The **San Francisco Symphony**

Orchestra, under the direction of Michael Tilson Thomas (*see opposite*), is world-renowned; its season runs between September and May. The multi-million dollar arts complex at **Yerba Buena Gardens** has also begun hosting musical events in an unconventional, low-budget attempt to become the Lincoln Center of the West.

NEW MUSIC

True to its counter-culture roots, San Francisco continues to encourage musical adventure, and is the base for many small, experimental musical outfits, like the globe-trotting **Kronos Quartet** or the internationally acclaimed *a cappella* choir **Chanticleer**, as well as countless choirs, from the SF Bach Choir, to the SF Gay Men's Chorus. Some of these groups are keen to commission new works by young composers, and the result can be anything from an opera about the 1989 earthquake by composer John Adams (*I Was Looking At The Ceiling... And Then I Saw The Sky*), to Lou Harrison's compositions for gamelan, played on homemade instruments.

To the great annoyance of the smaller musical outfits, however, it is the three major companies – the San Francisco Symphony, the Opera and the Ballet – that continue to get the lion's share of city grants for the arts, although with the demise of the National Endowment for the Arts they stand to lose much of their federal funding. Regardless, all three have an art-conscious array of wealthy benefactors, sponsors and 'angels' to top up their funds.

OPERA BUFFS

Above all, San Francisco has always been an opera town. The **San Francisco Opera** attracts frequent visits from big names like Placido Domingo and Luciano Pavarotti, Jessye Norman and Cecilia Bartoli. The opening Gala night, always held on the first Friday after Labor Day, is a glittering event attended by everyone from the Mayor to the latest reigning football champion. Free **Opera in the Park** follows the Gala on the first Sunday after Labor Day, and features the singers of the season in arias and duets performed in Golden Gate Park.

No slouch in any musical department, the city has a good selection of shops where you can buy music, recorded or published. At **Byron Hoyt** (431 8055), a venerable sheet music and instrument shop at the top of Lion House at 2525 16th Street,

Maestro!

In 1995, when Michael Tilson Thomas signed on with the San Francisco Symphony, you'd have thought Madison Avenue was choreographing the event. The promotion – more evocative of a Versace clothing ad or Hollywood movie campaign than a fanfare for the new conductor of the city's five-star orchestra – found Tilson's visage everywhere, staring up from direct mail brochures or down from billboard-sized posters lining record stores and public kiosks. The symphony guild was rightly enthusiastic about its then 51 year-old maestro, whose good looks proved an effective marketing tool. Thomas – or 'MTT', as he was grandly dubbed – was replacing Herbert Blomstedt, a reliable but thoroughly bland director who'd seen the symphony through ten seasons.

Raised in southern California as the son of poor Russian Jews, Tilson Thomas began his career as a pianist, studying with such masters as Igor Stravinsky, Karlheinz Stockhausen and Aaron Copland. At the age of 24, he was appointed assistant conductor (and later principal guest conductor) of the Boston Symphony Orchestra. He became music director of the Buffalo (NY) Philharmonic two years later, and was principal guest conductor of the Los Angeles Philharmonic from 1981 to 1985. The *wunderkind* also served as principal conductor of the London Symphony Orchestra from 1988, leading the LSO across Europe and momentarily swapping posts with Sir Colin Davis in 1995. Tilson Thomas' résumé is long and colourful, including premieres of great works, revivals of others, numerous awards for recordings – and a decades-old drug possession charge that raised international eyebrows at the time.

But MTT has brought more than a wide trophy shelf and a photogenic face to the San Francisco Symphony. A protégé of Leonard Bernstein, he has demonstrated his commitment to works by twentieth-century American composers, a preference that means classics by George Gershwin, oddities by John Cage and Harry Partch and innovations by Steve Reich will find an audience here; that Charles Ives and the Kronos Quartet stand alongside Mozart and the three B's – Beethoven, Bach and Brahms – in the canon. He is known for performing benefit concerts (for causes such as UNICEF and earthquake relief for Kobe) and for his affiliation with music education: he founded the New World Symphony, a national training orchestra, in Miami in 1988.

Locally, Tilson Thomas has pushed an already talented collection of musicians to take greater musical chances and reap greater benefits. The symphony's range of guest artists – Meredith Monk to former members of the Grateful Dead – is but one sign; successful performances in New York's Carnegie Hall and a pair of stunning international tours are another. Like Bernstein, this conductor is reportedly tough on members and not particularly cheerful or conversational, yet he has returned the group to the splendour for which it was once known – and done so in record time. More than anything, he's made it exciting to spend an evening at the symphony again. For that, the city can permit MTT some unabashed egoism and his promoters some orchestrated hype.

Out of town: classical

Zellerbach Hall on the US Berkeley campus is used by the **Berkeley Symphony** (1-510 841 2800), which attracts a roster of distinguished stars under music director Kent Nagano. It is also the venue for concerts, recitals and solo shows organised by **Cal Performances** (1-510 642 9988); **Berkeley Opera** (1-510 841 1903) also puts on about three productions a year here.

Other musical venues worth investigating include the **First Congregational Church** in Berkeley (1-510 848 3696), and the **Mormon Temple Auditorium** in Oakland where the Oakland Symphony and Chorus (1-510 428 3172) regularly perform. Travelling further afield, the **Mountain View Center for the Performing Arts** in Mountain View's Civic Center complex (phone 903 6000 for more information) is an ultra-modern and facility-laden venue.

Over the Golden Gate Bridge, the **West Marin Music Festival** (663 1075) concentrates on early and baroque music, 'loud band' and secular music. It takes place over two weekends in August at St Columba's off Sir Francis Drake Boulevard in Inverness, a delightful village near Point Reyes, and less than an hour by car north of the city.

you'll find a stunning view, solicitous and knowledgeable assistants, and copies of every possible score you could ever want, from Bach to Irving Berlin. It's also a good place for information about musical events in the city.

Of all the CD and tape stores in town, the **Tower Outlet** (660 Third Street, between Townsend and Brannan Streets; 957 9660) is a lucky dip of great bargains; Tower also runs a classical-only shop at Columbus and Bay Streets (441 4880). The **Wherehouse** (165 Kearney Street, at Sutter Street; 249 0871) has a wide range of opera recordings upstairs. **Star Classics** is a wonderful small shop in Hayes Valley devoted entirely to classical CDs and tapes and the huge **Virgin Megastore** also has a cheap selection of classical CDs (*see chapter* **Shopping & Services** for details). The **Opera House Gift Shop** stocks boxed opera sets and other musical paraphernalia, but it's only open during performances.

Civic Center Venues

For the **Bill Graham Civic Auditorium**, *see page 203*.

Herbst Theater

401 Van Ness Avenue, at McAllister Street (621 6600). BART Civic Center/Muni Metro F, J, K, L, M, N/bus 42, 47, 59. **Map F4**
The Art Deco Herbst Auditorium is the preferred performance space for the Kronos Quartet, when they are not performing at Theater Artaud (*see chapter* **Theatre & Dance**). It's a good size for solo recitals, talks and seminars, authors' readings and small-scale dance and ballet performances – though the acoustics are atrocious at the back. Herbst shares a roof with the **Green Room**, used by chamber ensembles and quartet recitals. The **San Francisco Chamber Symphony** is based here.

Louise M Davies Symphony Hall

Corner of Grove Street and Van Ness Avenue (431 5400). BART Civic Center/Muni Metro F, J, K, L, M, N. *Open box office 10am-6pm Mon-Fri; before a performance noon-6pm Sat, Sun.* **Credit** MC, V. **Map F5**
A circular, multi-tiered, glittering glass doughnut with good sightlines, the home base of the San Francisco Symphony Orchestra opened in 1980 – to disappointing aural effect. Renovated in the early 1990s, Davies now flaunts expensively improved, hear-every-pin-drop acoustics. Even from the top row of the back balcony you can hear everything, and see it all, too. Tickets start at $20, though there are concessions for the old, young and students, and other occasional discounts. The recent arrival of Californian-born conductor Michael Tilson Thomas, hot from the London Symphony Orchestra, has injected new adrenalin into the Symphony's hitherto rather tired repertoire; players and audience alike are thrilled at the change.

War Memorial Opera House

301 Van Ness Avenue, at Grove Street (864 3330). BART Civic Center/Muni Metro F, J, K, L, M, N/bus 21, 42, 47, 49. **Open** *box office 10am-6pm Mon-Sat.* **Credit** AmEx, MC, V. **Map F5**
When cracks appeared in the ceiling of the San Francisco Opera House after the 1989 earthquake, they marked the beginning of another chapter in the magnificent building's history, one that began with a performance of *Tosca* in 1932. Thankfully, that chapter has just ended. The Beaux Arts beauty, dedicated to soldiers who fought in World War I, re-opened for the Opera's 75th anniversary in 1997 with an $86.5 million retrofit and major makeover. No detail has been spared: new curtains hang from the stage, a new chandelier from the ceiling, newly gilded trim on the walls and ceiling, and there's a freshly upholstered seat beneath each patron. The auditorium retains its exquisite acoustics, best appreciated from the back of the uppermost circle. It was among the first in the world to introduce 'supertitles', the simultaneous translation above the proscenium that was so resisted elsewhere. The winter opera season runs from just after Labor Day (first Monday in September) until mid-January; the summer season is usually three weeks in June. Tickets range from $40 to $400. For advance information, phone the **San Francisco Opera Association** box office (864 3330).

Other Venues

Center for the Arts at Yerba Buena Gardens

See chapter **Museums & Galleries** *for listings.*
Yerba Buena contains the city's most graceful middle-sized

theatre, which so far has been used mostly for a brilliantly conceived avant-garde music programme. Though it belies an emphasis on San Francisco-based artists, it has of late stretched out to include various international performers – from Laurie Anderson to Trimpin, an electro-acoustic computer musician – in the realms of dance, music, spoken-word performance and a host of multimedia events. *See also chapter* **Theatre & Dance.**

Masonic Auditorium

1111 California Street at Taylor Street (776 4917). Cable Car California/bus 1.
Built in 1958 with a seating capacity of 3,100, the gorgeous white marble Masonic Auditorium is worth investigating during any visit to the city. A big, luxurious room with dark wood walls and excellent sightlines, the Masonic hosts a number of events – jazz festivals, author's readings, conferences and pop concerts by headliners from Gilberto Gil to Van Morrison. The recently-renovated Henry W. Coil Masonic Library Museum (open from 10am to 3pm Mon-Fri, admission free) houses historical artifacts culled from the fraternity's lodges throughout the world.

Palace of the Legion of Honor

Florence Gould Auditorium, Lincoln Park at Clement Street and 34th Avenue (750 3600). Bus 18, 38.
Now re-opened after seismic upgrading, this gloriously sited building near Land's End is making a comeback as a venue for Sunday organ and chamber concerts.

San Francisco Conservatory of Music

1201 Ortega Street, at 19th Avenue (759 3475/recorded information 759 3477) Bus 28, 28L. **Open** 9am-5pm Mon-Fri.
As the cradle for local singers and musicians, the Conservatory has a loyal following, a collective of students, faculty, patrons and those in the know that come for recitals by the **San Francisco Sinfonietta**, as well as other performances (usually free) given by music students.

Churches & Temples

Recitals and concerts – often free – are performed in many of San Francisco's churches. They include the **Old First Church** at 1751 Sacramento Street (474 1608, where Chanticleer often performs), the **Unitarian Church** on Franklin Street, and **Grace Cathedral** (*see chapter* **Sightseeing**). The **Temple Emanu-El** (2 Lake Street, near Arguello Boulevard; 751 2535), occasionally hosts the talented Pocket Opera chamber company, and the **Noe Valley Ministry** (1021 Sanchez Street, between 23rd and Elizabeth Streets; 282 2317) puts on a diverse array of concerts than range from baroque recitals to works by American composers such as Philip Glass or John Cage, plus a few singer-songwriters.

In addition, **Old St Mary's Cathedral**, San Francisco's first Catholic cathedral, is a regular venue for piano recitals and quartets, and has a Noontime Concert Series on Tuesdays and Thursdays (288 3861); **St Mary's Cathedral** is a great venue for organ recitals or performances by the San Francisco Bach Choir; and the **Mission Dolores Basilica** also sees performances by Chanticleer, among others. For listings, *see chapter* **Sightseeing**.

Festivals & Special Events

Check the Visitor Information Center's 24-hour information line (391 2001) for details on what's on while you're in town. Events to watch out for include the annual **Midsummer Mozart Festival** (954 0850), which celebrated its 25th birthday in 1998 under director George Cleve, with concerts at Berkeley's Congregational Church and in the Davies Symphony Hall. The **Early Music Society** has an annual concert series in May (528 1725) that concentrates on chamber music played on original instruments, and the **Philharmonic Baroque Orchestra** (392 4400) offers an annual baroque series. If you're in town for the **Black and White Ball** (864 6000), held every odd-numbered year in early May, you can take part in the city's biggest block party, a two-toned extravaganza that benefits the San Francisco Symphony. *See also chapter* **San Francisco by Season.**

Rock, Jazz & Blues

Unless you're travelling to New York, you'll find no finer city in the country for live music than San Francisco. Within its 46 square miles, dozens of venues and stages compete for your entertainment dollar, and hundreds more beckon from the surrounding Bay Area. Music aficionados – fans, critics, musicians themselves – have always made the scene, one that balances sounds stemming from challenging new acts with those offered by touring artists for whom the city remains a favourite stop. Many major headliners, who fill all types of top-40 lists and genres, call the San Francisco Bay Area home, among them Tracy Chapman, Metallica, Sammy Hagar, Counting Crows, Green Day and Bobby McFerrin. The city is also home to some of the freshest developments in innovative new music.

San Francisco's musical history is rich and diverse: Janis Joplin, Jimi Hendrix and Jefferson Airplane all played the **Fillmore Auditorium**, which re-opened in 1993 to re-establish itself as one of the prime venues for live music. The city's major concert promoter, Bill Graham Presents, began by producing Grateful Dead shows and now has a hand in nearly everything that comes to town. The Haight-Ashbury scene that exploded onto the national consciousness in the late 1960s and early 1970s seemed to let out its final gasp with the death of Grateful Dead lead guitarist Jerry Garcia in the summer of 1995.

But the music in the city has always been vibrant and ground-breaking. A rich jazz scene thrived in the Fillmore and Western Addition neighbourhoods in the 1950s – the African Orthodox Church of John Coltrane is still flourishing on Divisadero Street (*see page 57*

Sightseeing). Seminal hardcore band the Dead Kennedys put the city's punk parameters on the map in the early 1980s, the full aftershocks of which have yet to be felt. White neo-funk bands such as Primus began playing to small audiences in the late 1980s at venues like Nightbreak (now known as **Boomerang**); many went on to became multi-platinum stars. In the mid-1990s, acid jazz bloomed in clubs such as the **Up & Down** (*see chapter* **Nightlife**) and

Elbo Room, several of which remain show-places for the genre.

Today, the live music scene offers a broad mix, including improvisational jazz, swing, pop and punk, a steady stream of musicians who wheel their gear in and out of clubs like **Storyville**, **Kilowatt**, **Hotel Utah**, **Bottom of the Hill** and the **Great American Music Hall**. Testament to both the city's diverse population and its cosmopolitan aspirations, Cuban jazz and Brazilian-

Sounds & strange airs

You walk through a curtained doorway into what looks like a futuristic bomb shelter, an angular concrete room with high walls, a platform on one side and theatre seating. Dozens of dimmed lights appear to be hanging from the ceiling, then you realise they're speakers; that, in fact, the room is filled with speakers: protruding from the corners, mounted in the floor, rising in a column in the middle of the room. The lights dim to black.

You have entered Audium, a house-sized musical instrument built of 169 speakers, a unique performance space where sound assumes spatial, kinetic and communicative qualities. For the next 90 minutes, in pitch darkness, your ears will experience sensations they've never known: tactile, multi-dimensional, audio sculptures, paintings in noise, compositions that vary from airy soundscapes to claustrophobic aural nightmares. Cartoonish chirps of sound ping-pong madly around the room; atonal passages of synthesizer music transform into industrial static that presses you to your seat; just before the intermission, a virtual marching band crosses the room.

Started with an NEA grant in 1975, this nondescript space testifies to an unexplored direction for music and sound. 'I work from two fundamental concepts,' explains Stanley Shaff, Audium's co-designer and promoter, ticket-taker and sole performer. 'The idea that sound's motion can be an element of musical composition, and that the space itself is an essential part of the work.' Twice a week, he 'plays' the space for live audiences.

Audium's appeal is in its re-arrangement of primary senses. Deprived of sight, audience members find elements of smell, touch and memory heightened. 'Some people come expecting New Age – what I call wallpaper – music,' he says. 'Obviously, I'm taking a certain aesthetic that not everybody is interested in. I don't compromise: I'm not trying to appease or appeal to

anyone.' The programme ends as it begins, with ambient noises – chirping birds, running water, children's voices – while the lights come up.

'There's something dramatically different about giving sound pointed energy,' Shaff says. 'When you push and move music, you're introducing a whole new dynamic. Harmony, melody, rhythm – and now energy, or space. Audium challenges some basic assumptions about sound; it's kind of a musical threat. I see it as a giant arrow pointing in a multitude of directions.'

Audium
1616 Bush Street, at Franklin Street (771 1616). Bus 2, 3, 4, 42, 47, 49, 76. **Admission** $10. **Performance** 7.30pm Fri, Sat. **No credit cards.** **Map F3**

The **Bill Graham Civic Auditorium**.

inspired salsa artists regularly top the marquees at **El Rio**. In some venues, performances by local trip-hop DJs draw as many fans as those by bands.

Every year, the **Making Waves Festival**, which takes place on the summer solstice, transforms San Francisco into a giant performance space where bands play from two dozen outdoor stages scattered throughout the city: *see chapter* **San Francisco by Season** for details.

Major Venues

Bill Graham Civic Auditorium
99 Grove Street, between Polk and Larkin Streets (974 4000/267 6400). BART Civic Center/Muni Metro F, J, K, L, M, N/bus 9, 19, 21, 26. **Map F5**
San Francisco Opera was born in the 5,000-seat, broad-staged Civic Auditorium on 26 September 1923, when an adventurous young Neapolitan called Gaetano Merola took the podium to conduct *La Bohème* starring Queena Mario as Mimi, Giovanni Martinelli as Rudolfo and local girl Anna Young as Musetta. Since renamed after San Francisco's famous rock impresario, the Civic Auditorium handled productions during the renovation of the Opera House and now hosts a variety of affairs, from not-quite-stadium-sized rock shows to conferences, multimedia presentations and special events.

Cow Palace
Geneva Avenue, at Santos Street, Daly City (469 6065). Bus 9, 9X, 9AX, 9BX, 15/CalTrain Bayshore, then bus 15. **Open** *office* 10am-5.45pm Mon-Sat. **Admission** depends on event. **Credit** AmEx, Disc, MC, V.
The most revealing fact about the Cow Palace is that it serves as the venue for many other events, including monster truck derbies, International Hockey League games and even livestock auctions and rodeos. Not an intimate space for music,

it puts on concerts that are little better than stadium shows, but the parking lot is big, with plenty of room for pre-show tailgate parties. Book your ticket through BASS.

Fillmore Auditorium
1805 Geary Boulevard, at Fillmore Street (346 6000/ 24-hour hotline 346 0600). Bus 22, 38. **Open** *box office* 2 hours before show; 10am-4pm Sun. **Admission** depends on event. **Credit** AmEx, MC, V. **Map E4**
The Fillmore is a classic, a dance hall with a ballroom and mezzanine upstairs, a carpeted lounge and a long history of traditions including the pail of free apples by the front entrance and the many photographs that line its walls. One of the true institutions of the 1960s, it was here that the late promoter Bill Graham began building his music empire, purveying psychedelic rock to San Francisco and the world. Recently re-opened after retrofitting, it's still a great venue for live tunes, with plenty of room to shake it or to stand back and soak up the vibes. Book well in advance through BASS.

Greek Theater
Piedmont Avenue and Gayley Road, Berkeley (1-510 642 9988). BART Berkeley, then bus 52 or walk. **Open** *office* May-Sept 10am-5.30pm Mon-Fri; 10am-2pm Sat, Sun. **Admission** depends on event. **Credit** MC, V.
The Greek Theater is an open-air stone amphitheatre located just across the Bay at the edge of the UC Berkeley campus, with lawn and reserved seating. A night at the Greek means a gorgeous setting under the sunset and stars with excellent acoustics. When the Greek is packed for a show, it can be a bit hectic, but most of the crowd comes for love of the music, not the scene. Pop and jazz acts touring in the summer usually gig here.

Oakland-Alameda County (UMAX) Coliseum Complex
700 Coliseum Way, Oakland (1-510 639 7700). BART Coliseum. **Open** *office* 9am-5pm Mon-Sat. **Admission** depends on event. **Credit** AmEx, MC, V.

Home to the Golden State Warriors basketball team, the Oakland Coliseum (as it is most often called) is an indoor sports arena first and concert hall second – which may be all you need to know. It seats 15,000 or so and supergroups like U2, REM and Pearl Jam sell out massively unatmospheric shows here. If you're buying tickets in advance, have a look at a seating chart, or you stand the risk of ending up behind the bandstand. There are no phone sales, so book through BASS.

Warfield
982 Market Street, between Fifth and Sixth Streets (775 7722). BART Powell Street/Muni Metro F, J, K, L, M, N/bus 7, 27, 31, 66, 71. **Open** *box office half-hour before show.* **Admission** *depends on event.* **Credit** AmEx, MC, V. **Map G4**
A favourite venue for rock fans, the Warfield was built in 1922 and has an ornate interior that glitters. There are superb views from the balcony, three bars and some VIP booths at the back. With its high ceiling and massive public-address system, the Warfield feels like a box cavern and fills easily with a decent sound. High-energy acts here often prove the most memorable of a concert-goer's career. You can get tickets from box office at the Fillmore Auditorium (*see p203*) or book in advance through BASS.

Rock Clubs

Bottom of the Hill
1233 17th Street, at Missouri Street (box office 621 4455/advance tickets 1-510 601 8932). Bus 22, 53. **Open** *5.30pm-1am Tue-Thur, Sun; 5.30pm-2am Fri, Sat.* **Admission** $3-$8. **Credit** V. **Map H6**
Bottom of the Hill occupies the first floor of an old Victorian at the foot of Potrero Hill and sports one of the best neon signs ever crafted above its front door. A rebuilt stage (you can finally see!), great acoustics and quirky décor make it the favourite for small-time rock acts and their local fans; myriad rock posters by Frank Kozik and Coop and others line the walls. The main room can get a bit cramped, but there's a small patio at the back for cooling off. Sweating and a ringing in the ears are all part of the experience.

Boomerang
1840 Haight Street, at Stanyan Street (387 2996). Bus 6, 7, 66, 71. **Open** *1am-2am daily.* **Admission** *free-$6.* **No credit cards.** **Map C6**
With the closure of the I-Beam and Kennel Club (may they rest in peace) down the street, the Boomerang – formerly known as Nightbreak and before that, the Thirsty Swede – remains the last live music venue standing in the heart of the Haight. Long and narrow, it's a dive where you'll find local bands and occasional indie touring acts crowding the tiny stage tucked into the corner, where no one can really see them. You'll have no problem hearing them, though: bring ear protection.

Chameleon
853 Valencia Street, between 19th and 20th Streets (821 1891). Bus 26, 33. **Open** *10am-2pm daily.* **Admission** *free-$6.* **No credit cards.** **Castro/Mission Map Y1**
The Chameleon is something of an institution, a boxy club with awful acoustics and more cigarette smoke than you would have thought possible, which continues, year after year, to ply adventurous music. The usual local bands are to be found here, but more often the marquee features interesting artists heard only on edgy college radio stations. Surf music, lounge acts, occasional spoken-word yowlers – from dork rock to cool jazz and punk, the Chameleon has plenty to offer.

Great American Music Hall
859 O'Farrell Street, between Polk and Larkin Streets (885 0750). Bus 19, 38, 42, 47, 49. **Open** *office 10am-4pm Mon, Sun; noon-6pm Tue-Sat; until 9.30pm on day of show.* **Admission** $6-$20. **Credit** MC, V. **Map F4**
One of the oldest theatres still in operation, the Great American Music Hall presents an eclectic, virtuoso-studded playlist that includes stand-up comedy acts and touring musicians in equal measure. The remarkable interior of this local favourite is worth the trip alone: the hall was originally a bordello, and much of its lavish décor remains intact. Snag a coveted seat in the upper balcony if you arrive early enough: from there your bird's-eye view of the band and the crowd below are sure to be memorable.

Kilowatt
3160 16th Street, between Guerrero and Valencia Streets (861 2595). BART 16th Street/bus 22, 26, 53. **Open** *3pm-2am daily.* **Admission** *free-$7.* **No credit cards.** **Map F6**
The Haight district used to be the centre of town for live music but that's changed of late: the Mission and, more specifically, the Kilowatt, has emerged as a regular stop on the live music express. The Watt has a long bar down one side, a high stage across the back, great art hanging from the rafters and several pool tables on the floor. On show nights the place gets crowded as hell, but the decent bartenders keep an eye out for your order. The music ranges from goofy instrumental rock to college- and commercial-radio headliners, local bands and showcases of varying genres and durations. In other words, a good cross-section of what alternative San Francisco is listening to these days.

The **Great American Music Hall.**

Out of town: rock, jazz & blues

Two of the city's largest venues – The Greek Theater and Oakland UMAX Coliseum – are also outside the city limits (*see page 203* **Major Venues**).

Ashkenaz
1317 San Pablo Avenue, at Gilman Street, Berkeley (1-510 525 5054). BART El Cerrito Plaza, then bus 72, 73. **Open & admission** call for details. **No credit cards**.
Ashkenaz is non-institutionalised multiculturalism in action. Booking 'world beat', Afro-Cuban and reggae acts, and with timber rafters, it's like a Jamaican mountain lodge. Get sweaty on the dance floor with students, travellers and free-thinking locals and then cool off with a Red Stripe.

Blake's
2367 Telegraph Avenue, at Durant Avenue, Berkeley (1-510 848 0886). BART Berkeley, then bus 51, 64 or walk. **Open** 11am-2am Mon-Sat; 11am-10pm Sun. **Admission** $2-$8. **Credit** AmEx, MC, V.
Over 50 years old, Blake's remains a Berkeley institution, but its musical fare has changed considerably over the past few years from traditional blues to modern rock and acid jazz, with acoustic sets one night a week. Tuesday is Grateful Dead night, with a live band and DJ.

Kimball's East
5800 Shellmound Street, at Christie Street, Emeryville (1-510 658 2555). BART Ashby, then bus 7. **Open** *office* 11am-6pm Mon, Tue; 10am-10pm Wed-Sun; *doors open* 6.30pm daily. **Admission** average $20. **Credit** MC, V.
Odd as it may seem, Kimball's East has become more renowned in its time than its original in San Francisco.

Filling in the booking cracks left from mighty Yoshi's (*see below*), this club gives the audience a more close-up and personal experience with the musicians, many of whom are at the peak of their careers.

Shoreline Amphitheater
1 Amphitheater Parkway, Mountain View (967 4040). CalTrain Mountain View, then cab/drive south on US 101 to Mountain View, take Rengstorff Avenue, then Amphitheater Parkway. **Open** box office 10am-6pm Mon-Fri; 10am-2pm Sun. **Admission** depends on event. **Credit** MC, V.
A perfectly pleasant place to see a show, the Shoreline has reserved seating near the stage and a groomed lawn for the rest. It can handle large and unruly crowds, such as those that partied at Lollapalooza for the past few summers. Getting back to the city in the evening by public transport is difficult; go by car if you can.

Yoshi's
510 Embarcadero West, at Jack London Square (1-510 238 9200). BART Oakland City Center, then bus 58, 72L. **Open** *restaurant* lunch 11.30am-2pm Mon-Fri; noon-3pm Sat, Sun; dinner 5.30-9.30pm Mon-Thur, Sun; 5.30-10pm Fri, Sat; *club* 6pm-12.30am daily; shows at 8pm, 10pm. **Admission** $16-$22. **Credit** AmEx, DC, Disc, JCB, MC, V.
It doesn't get much sweeter than Yoshi's, the Bay Area's number one jazz club/sushi restaurant. Recently re opened, Yoshi's huge new venue offers the kind of refined setting that makes for a splendid occasion. Its separate dining room does a good business on the strength of its kitchen, but go there for the music – Yoshi's books the hottest touring talent every week and plays host to some of the best local musicians as well. Shows are often booked out, so phone first to check availability.

Maritime Hall
450 Harrison Street, between Fremont and First Streets (974 0634). Bus 42, 76. **Open** phone for schedule. **Admission** $7-$40. **Credit** MC, V. **Map J4**
One of the newest venues to open in the city, the Maritime reminds the music junkie of a monstrous rat maze or gymnasium converted to a theatre. Two huge stages are its central draw, but any obscure room (no matter how boxy and ill-qualified) can double as a stage. The club doesn't yet have a coherent booking theme, leaning more towards major rock and some retro acts. Now and then, you can catch an upcoming jazz great or a big reggae artist here. Prices are steep.

Paradise Lounge
1501 Folsom Street, at 11th Street (861 6906). Bus 9, 12, 42. **Open** 6pm-2am daily. **Admission** from $3. **Credit** MC, V. **Map G5**
The Paradise is something of a superstore nightclub, with as many as three stages active concurrently or in series during the course of an evening – although it's much more intimate than it sounds. With a few regulars and poetry slams on Sundays, the Paradise accounts for all musical tastes: local bands, touring acts, singer-songwriters and the occasional once-great who's still plucking or crooning. The pool tables and drink specials may not be your idea of paradise, but it's a safe bet you'll find something to like. The upstairs lounge, known as **Above Paradise**, is reserved for acoustic and folk music or spoken-word events. Amazingly, the Paradise has

recently added a *third* performance space to its empire, the **Transmission Theatre** – a slightly larger venue offering (you've guessed it) more local bands and DJ dancing.

Purple Onion
140 Columbus Avenue, between Pacific & Jackson Streets (398 8415). Bus 12, 15, 30, 41, 45, 83. **Open** 6pm-2am daily. **Admission** free-$5. **No credit cards. Map G2**
Located where North Beach slips into downtown, the down and dirty Purple Onion remains an anomaly: a mostly punk and local band club catering to the ultra-alternative crowd, but located in the heart of a neighbourhood that floods with out-of-towners at the weekend. Don't worry – cram your way inside, note the crotchety owner (famous for ostracising bands) holding court at the bar and rock out, dude...

Slim's
333 11th Street, between Folsom and Harrison Streets (522 0333). Bus 9, 42. **Open** phone for details. **Admission** $5-$25. **Credit** AmEx, MC, V. **Map G5**
Slim's employs one of the best booking agents in the business, who signs big names for limited, intimate engagements as well as a variety of artists that ensure the crowd is ethnically mixed and multi-generational. The sightlines are compromised by floor-to-ceiling pillars in the centre of the room, but, since music is often best heard and not seen, this is a minor drawback. A laid-back venue.

Blues Clubs

Biscuits and Blues

*401 Mason Street, at Geary Street (292 2583).
Bus 2, 3, 4, 38, 76/cable car Powell-Hyde or Powell-Mason.* **Open** 5pm-1am Mon-Fri; 6pm-1am Sat, Sun.
Admission $3-$10. **Credit** AmEx, DC, MC, V. **Map G4**
The blues club closest to Union Square has established a good reputation for quality music and award-winning Southern food. It books a blend of local favourites, acoustic players and roots groups, some of whom have achieved national fame. You'll be in the company of tourists and (when you leave the club late at night) a bevy of hookers, but the neighbourhood is relatively harmless and the music's great.

Blues

*2125 Lombard Street, at Fillmore Street (771 2583).
Bus 22, 28, 43, 76.* **Open** 8pm-1.30am daily.
Admission $5. **Credit** MC, V. **Map E2**
Blues books the kind of hard-driving roots groove that can leave you feeling whiplashed. This Marina district club is packed regularly with locals, especially on Sunday nights when New Orleans zydeco features on the bill.

Boom Boom Room

1601 Fillmore Street, at Geary Boulevard. Bus 2, 3, 4, 22, 38. **Open** 2pm-2am daily. **Admission** from $5.
No credit cards. Map E4
Located opposite the Fillmore Auditorium on one of the city's busier corners, the Boom Boom Room stands on the site of what was Jacks Bar, a San Francisco nightlife fixture for more than 50 years. The new club is presided over by blues legend John Lee Hooker, a regular performer at Jacks and a Bay Area resident. As we went to press, it was unclear what physical changes the new club would see, but given the rich musical histories of both the space and its new maître d' (as well as the growing rarity of blues clubs in the city), the Boom Boom seems guaranteed to be a hit.

Pier 23

Pier 23, Embarcadero, at Front Street (362 5125). Bus 32, 42. **Open** 4pm-2am Mon-Thur; 2pm-2am Fri-Sun.
Admission from $5. **Credit** AmEx, MC, V. **Map H2**
The closer you move towards the water in San Francisco, the less likely you are to find locals – ain't that a contradiction? At Pier 23, you're bound to uncover a few holdovers from the Financial District, but the bulk of the crowd hails from the suburbs. Blues bands blast a mix of covers and others; salsa bands blare on certain week nights. The crowd is white and straight and drinking heavily; you can bet they'll wake up the next morning at least an hour from the city.

Last Day Saloon

*406 Clement Street, at Fifth Avenue (387 6343).
Bus 2, 38, 44.* **Open** 4pm-2am Mon-Thur; 2pm-2am Fri-Sun. **Admission** $3-$6. **No credit cards. Map B4**
This longtime favourite venue in the heart of the Richmond district offers blues, rock and country bands in a smoky setting that's noisy and friendly. Utterly nondescript but for the TVs that transform the place into a sports bar on weekend afternoons, the Last Day is the only club in the neighbourhood to feature live music. It's packed with Irish, Russian, Chinese and American blues fans.

The Saloon

1232 Grant Avenue, at Vallejo Street and Columbus Avenue (989 7666). Bus 15, 30, 41, 45. **Open** noon-2am daily. **Admission** $3-$6 Fri, Sat. **No credit cards.**
Map G2
A blue-collar bar that showcases many of the city's best local roots musicians, the Saloon is a low-rent joint, a piece of North Beach that predates the upmarket eateries and hints

at the district that Tom Wolfe aptly described as 'slums with a view'. The interior is lit up like a pinball machine and you'll be able to hear the music from nearly a block away.

Jazz Clubs

See also supper clubs **Bruno's** *and* **Storyville** *in chapter* **Nightlife**.

Bimbo's 365 Club

*1025 Columbus Avenue, at Chestnut Street (474 0365).
Bus 30/cable car Powell-Mason.* **Open** phone for schedule. **Admission** depends on event. **No credit cards. Map G2**
Named after one of the club's original proprietors, Bimbo's is the perfect place to indulge in a time-travel delusion: set your clock for the 1940s, pull on your best swing dance duds and don your fedora. From the swanky bar in the south room to the cheesy tinsel curtain and latticework booths in the big room, the club hasn't changed a bit in nearly 50 years. It has a ballroom-sized dance floor, main stage and separate cocktail lounge; groups with a full, rich sound (big bands, reggae artists and so on) do best here. The club is only open when it's hosting a show, but they do so four or five nights a week.

El Rio

See chapter **Gay & Lesbian San Francisco** *for listings.*
You owe it to yourself to take part in a San Francisco tradition – head to El Rio early on a Sunday afternoon and squeeze past the shuffleboard and pool tables to the sunny garden at the rear, where you'll find the city's most diverse and friendly Latin jazz party. An outdoor barbecue, decent margaritas, the friendliest (primarily lesbian) crowd you can imagine and great live music greet you; you'll think you've gone to heaven – or at least to Rio – for the afternoon.

Elbo Room

647 Valencia Street, between 17th and 18th Streets (552 7788). BART 16th Street/bus 26, 33. **Open** 5pm-2am daily. **Admission** $5-10. **Credit** V, MC. **Map F6**
Too bad about this great club, which has been commandeered by yuppie out-of-towners who think they're slumming in the Mission. The Elbo was one of the incubators of acid jazz, performed in the smoky, open-raftered space upstairs by artists like the Mo'Fessionals and Charlie Hunter. Now the place feels like something you'd find in the Marina, with a range of live and dance shows and a predominantly male clientele who gulp microbrews and look to get laid. Sunday night's Dub Mission dance night is your best bet.

Hotel Utah

500 Fourth Street, at Bryant Street (421 8308). Bus 30, 45, 76. **Open** noon-2am daily. **Admission** free-$7.
No credit cards. Map H4
Amazingly, the club with the most-difficult-to-see stage continues to offer good music. From country to punk to a great night of improv jazz and myriad singer-songwriters, the Utah stands as a tribute to decades of successful live music in San Francisco. There's a great bar menu, too.

Rasselas

*2801 California Street, at Divisadero Street (567 5010).
Bus 1, 24.* **Open** 5pm-12.30am Mon-Thur, Sun; 5pm-1.30am Fri, Sat. **Admission** two-drink minimum.
Credit AmEx, MC, V. **Map D3/4**
This longtime venue operates next door to a good Ethiopian restaurant, where you can have a satisfying meal and move to the bar when the music starts. Some nights feature pickup bands culled from local musicians; on other nights, star headliners take the stage (John Handy is a regular player here). From free jazz to lounge-flavoured female vocalists, Rasselas's books plenty of great jazz acts.

Nightlife

Bop till you drop, learn the lambada, or eat to the beat in one of the city's many nightlife joints.

San Francisco offers a diverse nightlife menu – from mainstream to fetishistic, from pop to punk to political, clubs exist that account for everyone's tastes. As with any scene, it's the fledgling and underground spaces that cut the sharpest edge: one-off clubs, travelling performance spaces, edgy comedy venues.

Given both the visibility of gayness in San Francisco and the presence of at least a few highly evolved heterosexuals, there's a good amount of poly-sexual mixing. Clubs such as the **End Up** or **Josie's Juice Bar and Cabaret** are as likely to have a straight following, as a 'straight' club like **V/sf** or **Nikki's BBQ** is to have lesbian couples dancing. For most places, sexual orientation doesn't really matter.

INFORMATION

Your best source for current club listings is the *SF Bay Guardian, SF Weekly* or the Sunday *San Francisco Chronicle and Examiner*'s Datebook section – though the latter is less likely to follow the truly innovative scenes. For club information on the fly, try the recorded **Be-At Line** (626 4087), which lists daily details of where to be and when. Call after 2pm or you'll get the previous night's information. There are also several good websites – such as www.sfstation.com and www.citysearch7.com – with regularly updated listings.

Although many dance clubs stay open well past last orders, by law they cannot serve alcohol from 2-6am, nor to anyone under 21. With the closing of DV8 in 1997, the city lost one of its largest, most established under-18 clubs. Though the rumour is it will re-open as a 'fine dining' establishment, no word is definite yet (phone 777 1419 to find out). This leaves **715 Harrison** to fill in the gap as the city's only 'all-age' megaclub, where blacklight reflective hand stamps discriminate between those who can and can't drink booze. If you are under 21, check in advance whether you can get into a venue.

Admission prices for the clubs listed below vary depending on the night, but are usually between $5 and $15.

TRANSPORT

The Muni Metro Owl Service operates on the L & N lines from 12.30am until 5.30am. All other lines stop at 12.30am, and the major routes are covered instead by Owl Service buses, which run from 1am until 5am. BART runs roughly until midnight, although it's always best to check the time of the last train to your destination. *See page 256* **Directory** for a list of taxi companies.

Latin Clubs

See also page 212 **330 Ritch**.

Bahia Cabana Restaurant & Club
1600 Market Street, at Franklin Street (626 3306). BART Van Ness/Muni Metro F, J, K, L, M, N/bus 6, 7, 66, 71. **Open** *restaurant* 5-10pm daily; *club* 5pm-2am Mon-Fri; 2pm-2am Sat, Sun. **Credit** AmEx, Disc, MC, V. **Map F5**
There's salsa and samba most nights of the week plus lambada classes on Saturdays and African music on Fridays. Phone for the latest schedule of events.

Cesar's Latin Palace
3140 Mission Street, at Army Street (648 6611). BART 24th Street/Muni Metro J/bus 12, 14, 26, 27, 49, 67. **Open** usually Fri-Sun; phone for details. **No credit cards.**
The place to catch a big brass salsa band: look out for occasional performances by Tito Puente. With room for 1,000, Cesar's is indeed palatial.

Rhythm and Motion
1133 Mission Street, between Seventh and Eighth Streets (621 0643). BART Civic Center/Muni Metro F, J, K, L, M, N/bus 14, 19, 26. **Open** phone for details. **Map G5**
On some nights, this dance studio hosts the Bare Foot Boogie, with the music including classical, samba and hip-hop. It offers other dance classes throughout the week.

Dance Clubs

Any bar can hire a DJ to spin dance music, but there's a big difference between pub-clubs and true dance clubs in San Francisco. Suffice it to say that the listings that appear here are those places that encourage and emphasise the politics of dancing, as opposed to politics discussed over a beer. These clubs draw crowds that, as often as not, spend some time cultivating a look or pose for the evening; venues where it pays to know what's on the calendar for the evening or else face fashion-conscious agoraphobia; venues where you may well leave in a sweat or a stupor. As any true dance devotee will tell you, house music alone does not a club make.

Many live music venues offer DJ dancing on certain nights: the **Elbo Room**'s Dub Mission (*see page 206* **Music**) spins a mix of world music on Sundays;

or try Club NZinga at **El Rio** (*see page 189* **Gay & Lesbian San Francisco**) during the week.

The Arena

2260 Van Ness Avenue, at Vallejo Street (771 0123).
Bus 42, 47, 49, 76. **Open** 3pm-2am daily. **Credit** MC, V.
Map F3
Further north than most nightspots and located on the busy three-lane artery that is Van Ness Avenue, The Arena attracts Europhiles (or Eurotrash, if you're feeling less forgiving). The interior features rich colours and textures, which, in the right company, can feel less like a deliberate money-clip-and-Versace scene and more like a restaurant that erupted into a dance party. Dress code on Saturdays.

Big Heart City

836 Mission Street, between Fourth and Fifth Streets (777 0666). BART Powell Street/bus 12, 14, 27, 30, 45.
Open phone for details. **Credit** AmEx, MC, V. **Map G/H4**
This relative newcomer, recently purchased by the owners of the Sound Factory (*see p209*), wants you to think it's the hottest dance club in town. Occasionally, it is – on certain week nights when the bridge-and-tunnel crowd hasn't taken over. Big-name DJs spin house, acid jazz and trip-hop tunes in a long, narrow setting with an upper-floor balcony and bi-level dancefloor downstairs. Lots of attitude at the door – in this case, not necessarily an indication of how cool it is inside.

Cat's Grill and Alley

1190 Folsom Street, at Eighth Street (431 3332).
Bus 12, 19. **Open** 5pm-2am Mon-Thur; 7pm-2am Fri-Sun. **Credit** AmEx, MC, V. **Map G5**
Cat's Grill houses a variety of scenes, from goth to 1980s new wave to occasional ambient nights and, lately, has seen a series of electronic and trip-hop DJs. The space features a big bar with couches and tables up front, and a large self-contained dance room with a bar in the back. Stay late if you want the real feel of the place.

Club 181

181 Eddy Street, at Taylor Street (673 8181). Muni Metro F, J, K, L, M, N/bus 27, 31. **Open** 9pm-2am Thur; 9pm-4am Fri, Sat. **Credit** AmEx, MC, V. **Map G4**
Club 181's moment as the lounge and dancefloor for the beautiful people may have elapsed, but stylish, mostly straight singles gather here to shoot pool, make alluring eye contact and dance to hip-hop and soul. A stage for live bands that doubles as a dancefloor is the focus of the front room, while in the back room an *Alice in Wonderland* theme presides. Two back-to-back bars keep the juices flowing.

Covered Wagon

911 Folsom Street, at Fifth Street (974 1585). Bus 12, 27. **Open** 4.30pm-2am Mon-Fri; 7.30pm-2am Sat.
No credit cards. Map H4
Two rooms and a bar that can feel cramped, the CW is no place to go if you can't stand to sweat. The interior and live music run towards grunge, and there's a different club each night of the week.

DNA Lounge

375 11th Street, at Harrison Street (626 1409). Bus 9, 12, 19, 42. **Open** 9am-2am Tue-Thur; 9pm-4am Fri, Sat.
No credit cards. Map G5
The DNA feels a bit like a dungeon inside, as though you hadn't walked in but fallen through a trap door. A main stage (open for show-offs when there isn't a band) is flanked by stairs that lead to a mezzanine with corner booths for drinking and necking. A solid, if not especially inspired choice for a night's entertainment.

Harry Denton's

161 Steuart Street, at Embarcadero (882 1333). BART Embarcadero/Muni Metro J, K, L, M, N/bus 2, 7, 9, 14,

111 Minna – *minute but fun.*

21, 31, 66, 72. **Open** 7am-midnight Mon-Sat; 8am-midnight Sun. **Credit** AmEx, Disc, MC, V. **Map J3**
Ostentatious Harry Denton's has a dress code and a two-figure admission charge at the weekends. For this, you can dance with mostly straight, middle-aged singles to a cover band (nightly except Sundays) playing Motown faves and squeeze through the crowd to the back dancefloor, where the waterfront is visible. It can be nightmarish, but, as most cabbies will tell you, if you can't get laid at Harry Denton's, you can't get laid.

Liquid

2925 16th Street, between South Van Ness Avenue and Mission Street (431 8889). BART 16th Street/bus 14, 22, 26, 53. **Open** 7pm-2am daily. **No credit cards.**
Map F6
Liquid is a late-night club for fans of turntable culture: while some bars have DJs occasionally spinning records, Liquid has a different one every night. Sometimes it's Latin music, sometimes house, sometimes a cut-up of several performers. The décor is pleasant, but the dancing is the focus and the dark blue lighting makes it difficult to see anyway.

Nikki's BBQ

460 Haight Street, between Webster and Fillmore Streets (621 6508). Bus 6, 7, 22, 66, 71. **Open** 9pm-2am daily.
No credit cards. Map E5
Nikki's is an intimate space, and although no one will hold it against you that you're a tourist, they'd just as soon you didn't tell all your travelling friends about it – it gets full enough as it is. The club is located on a block of Haight that sees its share of trouble, but the folks at Nikki's are mostly looking to dance their troubles away. The musical selection is fluid – lots of soul, funk, hip-hop, jungle – and the crowd predominantly straight.

111 Minna

111 Minna Street, at Second Street (974 1719).
Bus 5, 14, 15, 38. **Open** 1pm-2am Tue-Fri; 4pm-2am Sat.
No credit cards. Map H4
Currently the club to beat among intimate spaces, shoebox-sized 111 Minna is an art gallery by day and occasionally hosts musicians during the night hours. But it's best known for a series of dance nights: LoveWorks, Electroni-Cool and other frenetic mixes featuring the best beats and DJs in the Bay Area. Worth tracking down.

715 Harrison

715 Harrison Street, between Third and Fourth Streets (979 8686). Bus 15, 30, 45, 76. **Open** 9pm-2am daily.
No credit cards. Map H4
You won't find a local here on Friday and Saturday nights, when the place becomes a mecca for the underaged (18-21) who've driven up from the suburbs to command the club's three dancefloors. On Thursday nights, however, 715 hosts The Box, San Francisco's longest running gay dance night

(*see page 189* **Gay & Lesbian San Francisco**). Other nights are variable – it's best to come with middling expectations.

Sound Factory
525 Harrison Street, at First Street (243 9646). Bus 12, 42, 76. **Open** *9.30pm-6am Fri; 9.30pm-4am Sat.* **No credit cards. Map J4**
In a cavernous warehouse space, the Sound Factory boasts two floors and multiple rooms. It attracts late waves of new, mostly young partygoers coming in after they finish waiting tables or cocktailing. Like its twin in New York, the Sound Factory is as close to an institution as one can get for a dance club. Plenty of house, funk, the latest imports and pop. Admission is free until 10pm.

1015 Folsom
1015 Folsom Street, between Sixth and Seventh Streets (431 0700/recorded information 431 1200). Bus 12, 27, 42. **Open** *10pm-6am Thur, Fri; 10pm-9am Sat.* **No credit cards. Map G5**
Like the DNA Lounge (*see p208*), the 1015 (pronounced Ten Fifteen) is always a safe bet for several hours of dancing. With three rooms, each with its own vibe, you can move through space and time without changing venues. It also has a speakeasy downstairs where jazz trios provide a cool-down groove or where you might stumble upon a record or magazine release party. It's further east on Folsom Street than the more pedestrian-friendly clubland around 11th Street, so you'll probably want to flag down a cab.

Trocadero Transfer
520 Fourth Street, at Bryant Street (437 4446). Bus 27, 30, 42, 45, 76. **Open** *usually 9pm-2am Wed-Sat; phone for details.* **No credit cards. Map H4**
Home to the city's longest-running (and only weekly) S&M fetish club – Bondage-a-Go-Go, on Wednesday nights – and a big GothRock scene, the Troc has something going on at least four nights a week, almost always pushing the envelope of social decorum. Expect a crowd of wealthy participant-

observers investigating the fringe, some hardcore leather devotees and many modern primitives.

V/sf
278 11th Street, at Folsom Street (621 4863). Bus 9, 12, 42. **Open** *9pm-3am Mon-Thur; 9pm-4am Fri, Sat; 9pm-6am Sun.* **Credit** AmEx, MC, TC, V. **Map G5**
The recently envisioned V/sf occupies a space that's part of a long chapter in San Francisco club history. Formerly the Oasis and Club O among others, the space at 11th and Folsom has been completely redecorated, renovated and rejuvenated. Against an aural backdrop of house, techno, breakbeat and 1970s funk, the place now comes alive as the busiest big club in the city. Tuesday nights are excellent, and Shag, a Brit-night scene, livens up Thursdays. You'll always find something interesting going on here.

Comedy Clubs

An alternative to the nightclub scene is comedy clubs, where you can sip drinks and dare stand-up comedians to make you laugh. San Francisco has been the starting point – or at least a stop along the way – for many of the most prominent comedians in the US, notably film stars Whoopi Goldberg and Robin Williams, and television sitcom stars Ellen DeGeneres and Margaret Cho. The winner of the annual SF International Comedy Competition can be the comedian to watch in the coming year. For information about Comedy Celebration Day, an outdoor event held every August at Sharon Meadow in Golden Gate Park, *see chapter* **San Francisco by Season**.

With the recent closing of the Improv in Union Square, the city lost one of its biggest national

For some of the best stand-up comedy in town, head for **Josie's**. *See page 210.*

Swing time at **Cafe Du Nord**. *See page 211.*

draws for live stand-up. **Cobb's Comedy Club** and the **Punch Line** are taking up some slack, but the club's departure may indicate that San Francisco isn't as funny a city as it once thought it was. Several smaller venues host open mike nights – among them **Cafe International** (552 7390) in the Haight-Asbury on Wednesdays, **The Luggage Store** (255 5971) in the Financial District on Tuesdays, and **One World Café** (776 9358) in Western Addition on Fridays (plus stand-up on Wednesdays).

Cobb's Comedy Club

2801 Leavenworth Street, at Beach Street (928 4320). Bus 30, 32, 42. **Open** *from 8pm daily; phone for showtimes.* **Credit** *MC, V.* **Map F1**
Located in The Cannery shopping centre near Fisherman's Wharf, this long-standing restaurant and club is packed with tourists, but is still the second-best venue – after the Punch Line – to catch stand-up-and-coming headliners. The club holds comedy marathons on Mondays, and guests can usually enter most nights of the week with a 2-for-1 coupon clipped from local papers.

Josie's Cabaret and Juice Bar

See chapter **Gay & Lesbian San Francisco** *for listings.* The pulse of the city's comedy scene beats at Josie's in the heart of the Castro, a 130-seat space with some of the best and most interesting talent in the region. Josie's has honed its reputation as a gay club, and that's still true: but you'll see a variety of performances here by all kinds of comedians and comediennes – all of them worthwhile.

Mock Café

1070 Valencia Street, at 22nd Street (641 0235). BART 24th Street/bus 26. **Open** *phone for details.* **No credit cards.** **Castro/Mission Map Y2**

A small and uncluttered space, this new venue is the stepchild of the wonderful Marsh performance theatre (*see chapter* **Theatre & Dance**) next door. The Mock features a rotating line-up of political comedy and satire, a mix of local and better-known performers, plenty of female wordsmiths and an open mike night.

Punch Line

444 Battery Street, at Clay Street (397 7573). Bus 1, 12, 41, 42. **Open** *shows 9pm Tue-Thur, Sun; 9pm, 11pm Fri, Sat.* **Credit** *AmEx, MC, V.* **Map H3**
Tucked away on a rooftop garden with a great view of the city, the Punch Line is now the big gun of comedy in town. Major headliners play here, from Margaret Cho and Scott Silverman to Greg Proops and Warren Thomas. The club has one or two shows nightly, decent food, hard-working staff and lots of great laughs. Even the $5 showcases are excellent, usually spiced with an occasional well-known on top of the usual troop of local newcomers.

Supper Clubs

Among California's many gifts to the world is its unrelenting ability to set and then work to death the trend *du jour*. Tie-dye, smoothies… supper clubs. As civilised urban creatures seek comfort food and a little nightlife, supper clubs continue to thrive and San Francisco deserves much of the credit (and possibly the blame).

Back in their heyday, supper clubs were elegant, exciting nightspots. Imagine the grand dames of cocktail chatter – Bette Davis wrapped in mink, Dorothy Parker steeped in irony – amid warm and smoky rooms full of atmosphere and the sounds of a 15-piece orchestra. Be it 1927 or 1957, the phrase 'supper club' conjures up images of an idealised past, where a guy would take his date for dinner and dancing, and then live happily ever after. Roll credits.

These days, supper clubs fill an array of niches, from fine dining destination to singles stomping ground to tourist trap. Most of the supper clubs found in San Francisco fall into the sensible centre. You're apt to get a good meal, hear pretty good tunes, spend a little more money than you'd like to, but certainly feel you are, once and for all, steppin' out. So dust off that seersucker, press that little black dress and put on the ritz. You've some supper clubbing to do.

Bruno's
2389 Mission Street, between 19th and 20th Streets (550 7455). Bus 14, 49. **Open** 3pm-2am daily. **Credit** AmEx, MC, V. **Castro/Mission Map Y1**
First opened in the late 1930s, Bruno's was a dive, reborn after it was purchased by owners of the popular Flying Saucer and Cafe du Nord. With its round burgundy leatherette booths, dark wood panelling and flattering lighting, it remains a breath of fresh air in the world of supper clubs. The food is excellent (a small but elegant menu puts a high class spin on comfort food) and the tunes – from

Charles Brown to Clubfoot Orchestra and everyone in between – remain top-notch.

Cafe Du Nord
2170 Market Street, between Church and Sanchez Streets (861 5016). Muni Metro F, K, L, M/bus 22, 37. **Open** 6pm-2am Mon, Tue, Sun; 4pm-2am Wed-Sat. **Credit** AmEx, MC, V. **Map E6**
Du Nord offers something musically different every night, including salsa and swing dance lessons and an experimental lounge night in the middle of the week. Dinner is served from Wednesday to Saturday, but you'll want to stay for the music more than the cuisine. Blues bands, DJs, up-and-coming jazzists, lounge acts, Cuban combos, even comedy – all their acts perform in a comfortable, bi-level, intimate setting.

Coconut Grove
1415 Van Ness Avenue, between Pine and Bush Streets (776 1616). Bus 2, 3, 4, 19, 42, 47, 49. **Open** 5pm-2.30am daily. **Credit** AmEx, MC, V. **Map F3**
An overdone palm-tree atmosphere here results in Supper Clubland at Disney (with cigars). Big bands, big dishes and big, busty blondes who've spent a little too much time in the sun. The club remains the destination for out-of-towners more than locals: seating is staggered for the two nightly shows (7pm, 10.30pm) and those eating dinner must conform to a dress code – coat and tie and no jeans. Nonetheless, it's

Night owls

So you and your crew are leaving the club, piling into a cab to head to the after-hours underground rave you just got the tip on. Or you're sick of dancing and you just want to get a bite of healthy breakfast to ward off the hangover you're courting. Or you have a sudden urge to go bowling or settle an argument you're having over a game of pool. Whatever the scenario, you're in luck. Though San Francisco isn't New York or Paris (much to its chagrin) and many of the city's establishments close relatively early, night owls still have plenty of options when they're stumbling from the clubs with some money left in their pockets.

Numerous restaurants carry on serving past midnight, among them several diners, including **Video Café** (5700 Geary Boulevard, at 21st Avenue; 387 3999), **Orphan Andy's** (3991 17th Street, at Castro; 864 9795), **The Grubstake** (1525 Pine Street, at Polk Street; 673 8268) and the ever-famous **Bagdad Café** (2295 Market Street, at 16th Street; 621 4434). If you're hungry for a Chinese meal or some seafood, try **Yuet Lee** (1300 Stockton Street, at Columbus Avenue; 982 6020). For Middle Eastern fare, **Kan Zaman** (1793 Haight Street, at Cole; 751 9656) is open until 2am at the weekends. For authentic Mexican food, head for **La Rondalla** (901 Valencia Street, at 20th Street; 647 7474). And **Mr Pizza Man** (3146 24th Street, at

Shotwell Street; 641 0333) never closes its doors to late-night customers.

For early-hour dessert options, try **Bepples Pies** (1934 Union Street, at Laguna Street; 931 6225, or 2142 Chestnut Street, at Steiner; 931 6226) or the delectables at **Tart to Tart** (641 Irving Street, at Eighth Avenue; 753 0643). And you can always head to **All Star Donuts** (399 Fifth Street, at Harrison Street), the best of several doughnuteries open all night.

Several other businesses are open late to vie for your dusk-to-dawn dollar: **Hollywood Billiards** (61 Golden Gate Street, at Market; 252 9643) is open 24 hours – though it's in the heart of one of the city's least safe neighbourhoods at night – and **Great Entertainer** (975 Bryant Street, at Eighth Street; 861 8833) lets you shoot pool till 2am. If you have a craving to soak in a hot tub, head for **Grand Central Sauna and Hot Tub** (15 Fell Street, at Van Ness Avenue; 431 1370), where they'll also accommodate you until 2am. For the bowler, **Japantown Bowl** (*see chapter* **Sport & Fitness**) is open without pause, with reduced prices in the dead of night. Finally, the **Kabuki 8 Cinema** (*see chapter* **Film**) shows midnight movies at the weekend; if you want to rent them, head for **Into Video** (1439 Haight Street, at Ashbury; 864 2346), which offers a good selection and is open until 1am. Who needs sleep?

worth a trip for late-night kicks. Hang at the bar, catch the music, have a drink and a smile at the Supper Club of Last Resort. Not for those on a budget.

Eleven

374 11th Street, between Harrison and Folsom Streets (431 3337). Bus 9, 27, 42. **Open** 5.30pm-1.30am Mon-Sat. **Credit** AmEx, MC, V. **Map G5**
The SoMa crowd is looking good and letting you know about it, as its members munch down good Cal-Ital food and over-priced drinks. The stage is precariously perched above the austere dining room (some performers surely get vertigo) with a small alcove of upper-level seating. Sounds range from straight-up jazz to well-known trios and solo artists and the occasional rock and blues night. The best place in town to pretend you're a model or an agent without actually having to assume such a tiresome existence.

Essex

847 Montgomery Street, Jackson Square (397 5969). Bus 12, 83, 41. **Open** 5.30-10.30pm Tue-Thur; 5-11pm Fri, Sat. **Credit** AmEx, DC, JCB, MC, V. **Map H3**
Ernie's, the once-famed SF eatery made immortal in Hitchcock's *Vertigo* and with a wine cellar to make the French drool, has become Essex, a swinging singles multiplex à la North Beach. Luckily, it retains Ernie's classic look, though the feeling is now decidedly more hip. There's great food and drink, and a lot of men with wads of cash who seem to be rather loose with it when it comes to the ladies. This place is all about options, from the swinging R&B or jazz upstairs to the bump-and-grind dancefloor adjoining the first-floor bar to the Bacchus Cellar, a wine-cellar-cum-cigar-bar where you can play pool or take in a late-night game of chess.

Harry Denton's Starlite Room

Sir Francis Drake Hotel, 450 Powell Street, between Post and Sutter Streets (395 8595). Bus 2, 3, 4, 30, 45, 76/ cable car Powell-Hyde or Powell-Mason. **Open** 4.30pm-12.30am Mon; 4.30pm-1.30am Tue-Sat. **Credit** AmEx, MC, V. **Map G3**
Harry Denton and his places are a love 'em or leave 'em affair. This one has a stunning 21st-floor view over Union Square, lots of mirrors for askance eye contact, floral carpets and booths filled with social and financial climbers. The music is less innovative than more R&B covers: don't come if you can't stand 'Mustang Sally'. Denton is famous in San Francisco as a man who makes his bars a non-stop twenty- and thirtysomething party.

Julie Ring's Heart and Soul

1695 Polk Street, at Clay Street (673 7100). Bus 1, 19, 42, 47, 49, 76. **Open** 8pm-2am Mon, Sun; 5pm-2am Tue-Fri; 6pm-2am Sat. **Credit** AmEx, MC, V. **Map F3**
Julie's sports a small, intimate style, with an understated clubbiness at work that bodes well for those who prefer to dine with a modicum of peace. Evenings begin with a gentle tinkling of the ivories, followed by the main event at 8.30pm. The tunes tend to focus on swing-era and blues material. Cuisine is Californian with a touch of French Creole and there's a fine collection of whisky. For a crowd, go at the weekend; to talk all night without feeling rushed, grab a table upstairs early in the week. You can feel the history at Julie's Supper Club – the building once housed a kidnapped Patty Hearst and it blazed the path for the SF supper club revival. The big, beautiful bar serves big, beautiful drinks, while the kitchen is creatively tasty.

42 Degrees

235 16th Street, at Third Street (777 5558). Bus 15, 22, 48. **Lunch served** 11.30am-3pm Mon-Fri. **Dinner served** 6.30-11.30pm Wed-Sat. **Credit** MC, V. **Map J6**
Highly hip: an industrial setting, great Mediterranean food,

live jazz, outdoor seating and a scarcity of cabs after midnight. Try the celery and fig salad or salt cod brandade; alternatively curl up in one of the oversized booths and enjoy a glass of champagne and listen to the jazz trio.

Mecca

2029 Market Street, between 14th and Dolores Streets (621 7000). Muni Metro F, J, K, L, M/bus 24, 35, 37. **Dinner served** 6-11pm Mon-Wed, Sun; 6pm-midnight Thur-Sat. **Credit** AmEx, DC, MC, V. **Map E/F6**
The upper-Market hottie in town doesn't disappoint. Dig the silk and velvet curtains, high ceilings and classic round bar – ideal for navel-gazing the sophisticated-sloppy set. And throw in amazing Californian food that's easily digested as you take in the unobtrusive dinner jazz. Both the bar and restaurant are no-smoking. *See also* chapter **Bars**.

Sol Y Luna

475 Sacramento Street, between Battey and Sansome Streets (296 8696). BART Montgomery Street/Muni Metro F, J, K, L, M/bus 1, 12, 15, 41. **Open** 5pm-2am daily. **Lunch served** 11.30am-2.30pm Mon-Fri. **Dinner served** 5-10pm Mon-Thur; 5-11pm Fri, Sat. **Credit** AmEx, DC, MC, TC, V. **Map H3**
Think American bar in Europe, only in the Financial District. Witness the piles of hungry Euro-bears lining the walls waiting for the little bunnies to hop in. The music alternates between good Latin jazz and flamenco to thumping, dirty dancing. The food is a pleasant trip to tapas city.

Storyville

1751 Fulton Street, between Masonic and Central Streets (441 1751). Bus 5, 43. **Open** 5pm-2am Tue-Sat. **Credit** AmEx, MC, V. **Map D5**
Storyville's deep red walls and warm fireplace nod to something that's seriously missing in most of the city's jazz clubs: good, old-fashioned class. Located in a nondescript block across from a neighbourhood marketplace, this recent addition to San Francisco's nightlife might be its current best-kept secret. Storyville has a full bar, good Creole food, excellent service and jazz acts that range from headliners to nervous locals testing their pipes on open mike nights.

330 Ritch

330 Ritch Street, between Brannan and Townsend Streets (541 9574/522 9558). Bus 15, 30, 42, 45, 76. **Open** 6am-2am Wed-Sun. **Credit** AmEx, MC, V. **Map H/J4/5**
The inevitable and not altogether unfortunate result of the slackers growing up and discovering swing. A young crowd seems right at home amid the exposed brick and dark wood adorning this spacious yet intimate SoMa spot, which has an attractive bar and a dancefloor that means business. The Latin jazz crowd flock here on Saturdays, for Tu Pueblo – a night of live and spun salsa dancing (there's a dress code). Though the menu wins the 'Cheapest Supper Club Fare' award, remember: you get what you pay for.

Up & Down Club

1151 Folsom Street, between Seventh and Eighth Streets (626 2388). Bus 12, 19. **Open** 8pm-2am Mon-Thur; 7.30pm-2am Fri, Sat. **Credit** AmEx, MC, V. **Map G5**
As one of the centres of the early 1990s jazz renaissance in San Francisco, the Up & Down has built a reputation for quality tunes, hosting original bands with a sound that can hold your full attention. Long and narrow and at times hard to see, the club nonetheless packs in the fans at the weekend, and offers another groove (often house music) upstairs, so you can sample two scenes for the price of one. Model Christy Turlington and her sister are co-owners, but don't count on seeing her here. The kitchen serves nouveau cuisine early in the evening.

Sport & Fitness

Welcome to a city of fitness fanatics, where you can indulge in every sporting interest – the zanier the better.

Though big-money spectator sports such as baseball, football or ice hockey might not seem to have a place in the 'alternative' lifestyles of San Francisco, the Bay Area teems with sports fans. In fact, many aficionados revel in sport as if it were a guilty pleasure left over from the era before their Californian enlightenment. Of course, it doesn't hurt the enthusiasm of local fans that the San Francisco 49ers, have, in the past decade or so, proved to be one of the most polished and successful National Football League (NFL) teams in North America. They have won five Super Bowl championships in 14 seasons, and their gold and red colours hang in gas stations, convenience stores, bars and even upmarket boutiques.

Spectators also watch closely the collegiate athletic team of their choice – the Bears from the University of California at Berkeley have a great football team; the Stanford women's Cardinal basketball team is another local favourite. The Cal-Stanford 'big game' marks a huge rivalry and an annual football contest that sells lots of press. And the love of sport goes on: San Francisco voters recently elected themselves two new sports stadiums to be built sometime around the turn of the century (*see chapter* **San Francisco Today**).

INFORMATION

For local sports information, the Sporting Green section of the *San Francisco Chronicle* is a good place to start. It publishes a calendar with each of the pro team engagements as well as details of broadcasts. Both the *Chronicle* and *San Francisco Examiner* maintain a free sports information line (808 5000 ext 3) as does KRON-TV (837 5000 ext 1710). 'Sports talk' radio remains popular but is not an efficient source of information: KNBR (680 AM) can be counted on for hyperbole and the occasional bit of practical info.

Reflecting the nation's overriding passion for sport, newsstands are swamped with weekly and monthly publications; *Sports Illustrated* ($2.95) remains one of the nation's best-written sports magazines. On the web, The Gate's sporting section (found at http://www.sfgate.com/sports) is a good bet. Finally, for special events or printed schedules, visit the Visitor's Information Center (*see page 251* **Directory**).

For baseball, see page 214.

TICKETS

The sanest and thriftiest place to go for tickets is the box office of the team you want to see. This direct approach may save effort and, even if you do end up going to a ticket service or broker, will at least give you a better idea of prices. If you get referred to BASS (1-510 762 2277), which has several offices, desks in Tower Records and a telephone switchboard, expect to pay a service fee of $2.75 or more (*see page 168* **Shopping & Services**).

TICKET BROKERS

Money may not buy you love, but it can, on occasion, purchase a seat at a sold-out game. Find ticket brokers in the *Yellow Pages* under Ticket Sales – Entertainment & Sports. Ticket brokers buy and sell tickets, so if you're stuck with a valuable ticket you can't use you could sell it for some quick cash. Check with the **St Francis Theater**

Ticket Service (362 3500) inside the Westin St Francis hotel on Union Square. Better for sports, however, are **Mr Ticket** (1-800 424 7328/1-888 722 5737/292 7328), **Enter-tainment Ticketfinder** (756 1414) or **Premier Tickets** (346 7222).

SCALPERS (TOUTS)

Purchasing tickets via a scalper ought to be a last resort, although sometimes going to the stadium without a ticket and seeing what happens can add adventure to your plans. There are risks, of course – you might end up buying a fake ticket, purchasing admission for the following evening's game or ending up with a seat in the third deck where you need binoculars to see the action.

Auto Racing

Sears Point Raceway

At the intersection of SRs 37 and 121, Sonoma (1-707 938 8448). US 101 north to SR 37 exit, then 10 miles to SR 121. **Admission** $5-$55. **Credit** Disc, MC, V.
Sears Point hosts just about every kind of motorised race on land, from nostalgic cars to monster truck derbies. One loud slice of Americana.
Disabled: toilet.

Baseball

The Bay Area hosts two major-league baseball teams. As with many West Coast clubs, the San Francisco Giants and the Oakland A's have an East Coast history (in New York and Philadelphia, respectively) prior to their years here. But they're well-loved local franchises: the A's won three World Series in a row in the 1970s; the Giants in the 1990s have – for the time being, anyway – Barry Bonds, three-time winner of the Most Valuable Player award, on their roster. The two teams rarely play each other (Giants are in the National League and A's in the American): they were set to play one another in Game One of the World Series in 1989 when they were rudely interrupted by the Loma Prieta earthquake. The baseball season runs from April to October; tickets are usually available at the ballparks on the day of the game. You can also buy individual tickets through BASS's baseball line (1-510 762 2255).

Oakland A's

Oakland-Alameda County Coliseum Complex (A's 1-510 638 0500/Coliseum 1-510 639 7700). BART Coliseum. **Open** *A's office* 9am-6pm Mon-Fri; 10am-4pm Sat. **Admission** $4-$20.
Disabled: toilet.

San Francisco Giants

3Com Park, Giants Drive, at Gilman Avenue (467 8000). Special event Muni bus 47X at Van Ness Avenue and Market Street, 28X at Funston and California Streets. **Open** 8.30am-5.30pm Mon-Fri (and weekend if game is on). **Admission** $5.50-$20.
Except on the sunniest of afternoons, bring a warm jacket to 3Com (formerly Candlestick Park) or you may find yourself a wind-whipped icicle.
Disabled: toilet.

Basketball

From fast, trash-talking games in the panhandle of Golden Gate Park to college and professional squads, if you want to watch (or play) roundball while in town, you'll have plenty of company. The Warriors represent the Bay Area in the National Basketball Association (NBA) and play from November to May.

Golden State Warriors

Oakland-Alameda County Coliseum Complex (Warriors 1-510 986 2222/Coliseum 1-510 639 7700). BART Coliseum. **Open** 8.30am-5.30pm Mon-Fri. **Admission** $13.75-$220.
Disabled: toilet.

Football

Autumn Sundays in the Bay Area could leave one convinced that football is the new religion (or that a neutron had dropped on the streets). The Raiders' return to Oakland (for the 1995-96 season) brought the league's most notorious winners of yesteryear back into the fold while the 49ers continue as the National Football League's élite. The season runs from September to January. Getting tickets to football games is almost impossible.

Oakland Raiders

Oakland-Alameda County Coliseum Complex (1-510 639 7700). BART Coliseum. **Open** 9am-5pm Mon-Sat. **Admission** from $51.
Disabled: toilet.

San Francisco 49ers

3Com Park, Giants Drive, at Gilman Avenue (468 2249). Special event Muni bus: 47X at Van Ness Avenue and Market Street, 28X at Funston and California Streets. **Open** 9am-5pm Mon-Fri (and weekend if game is on). **Admission** $45.
You can buy tickets in person at the stadium (cash only) or by phone from BASS (1-510 762 2255) from the second-to-last week in July.
Disabled: toilet.

Horse Racing

Bay Meadows Racecourse

2600 S Delaware Street, San Mateo (574 7223). CalTrain to Bay Meadows or Hillsdale. **Open** phone for details. **Admission** $3-$15. **Credit** AmEx, MC, V.
Disabled: toilet.

Golden Gate Fields

1100 Eastshore Highway, Albany (1-510 559 7300). BART North Berkeley, then AC Transit shuttle bus on race days. **Open** phone for details. **Admission** $3-$17.50. **Credit** AmEx, MC, V.
Disabled: toilet.

Ice Hockey

Spectacularly fast-paced and, despite the National Hockey League's efforts, still known for its violence, ice hockey has found surprisingly broad support in the Bay Area. The San Jose Sharks may not be the most accomplished team in the National Hockey League, but they are one of the leading

Japantown Bowl – *open until the wee small hours. See page 216.*

merchandisers – their teal and black colours worn all over. And their fans are rabid: Sharks games come complete with music from *Jaws* and a signature cheer, the 'Shark bite'. The season runs from October to May.

San Jose Sharks

San Jose Arena, at W Santa Clara and Autumn Streets (tickets 1-800 888 2736/arena 1-408 287 9200). CalTrain to San Jose. **Open** 9.30am-5.30pm Mon-Fri; 9.30am-1pm Sat. **Admission** $15-$78. *Disabled: toilet.*

Active Sports

To claim that many prefer life in the San Francisco Bay Area because of its easy access to outdoor pleasures and adventures is an understatement, something along the lines of 'San Francisco sees its share of fog'. Like arcane healing arts and body piercings, participatory sports – the zanier the better – come with the territory.

Excellent running paths traverse the Marina, Golden Gate Park and the perimeter of Lake Merced; if you're into aerobics or cross-training, there's a health club on every corner. For gear sports, the city has many superb bike and skate shops as well as those that sell surfing, camping and rollerblading merchandise.

New bike paths and an auto-free Golden Gate Park on Sundays are further draws. Some aquatic sports are better served by other parts of the region: the best resources for kayaking and scuba diving can be found in nearby Bay Area cities (*see*

page 220); for skiing and snowboarding, of course, head to the Sierras (*see page 217 and chapter* **Trips Out of Town**).

When hiring equipment, photo ID or a credit card is usually necessary as a deposit.

GENERAL INFORMATION

As with spectator sports, the *San Francisco Chronicle* has listings and information on outdoor activities. On Thursdays it publishes an Outdoors mini-section within the daily Sporting Green pages. Also useful is *CitySports*, a free national magazine available in the lobby of many gyms and sports stores.

Boating & Sailing

If you sail a lot, chances are you'll find a mate, captain or boat you know in one of the several marinas around the Bay. For information on windsurfing and surfing *see pages 220-221*.

Sailing Education Adventures

Fort Mason, at Laguna and Buchanan Streets (775 8779). Bus 28. **Open** 8am-10pm daily. **No credit cards.** **Map E1**
This non-profit charity offers instruction for all levels of sailing skill and a summer sailing camp for kids.

Spinnaker Sailing

Pier 40, Embarcadero at First Street (543 7333). Bus 32, 42. **Open** 10am-8pm daily. **No credit cards.** **Map J4**
Spinnaker offers 7m to 24m (22ft to 80ft) boats, professional instruction and a great location off the Embarcadero.

Stow Lake Boathouse

Stow Lake, Golden Gate Park (752 0347). Bus 5, 28, 29, 71. **Open** *summer* 9am-5pm daily; *winter* 9am-4pm daily.
No credit cards.
On a clear day, pack a picnic, grab some company and head to Stow Lake in Golden Gate Park, where you can rent a paddleboat or rowing boat.

Bowling

Japantown Bowl

1790 Post Street, at Webster Street (921 6200). Bus 2, 3, 4, 22, 38. **Open** 9am-1am Mon-Thur, Sun; 24 hours Fri, Sat. **Rates** $1.50 shoe rental; $2.85-$3.25 per game. **Credit** MC, V. **Map E4**
After Park Bowl – the infamous 'Rock 'n Bowl' – closed in 1997, Japantown Bowl became the one and only place to bowl in the city. In the heart of Japantown, this 40-lane alley is always crowded, though less so at odd hours. Ask about the free three-hour parking if you've come by car.

Camping

Although Kirby Cove, a six-site campground tucked in the shadow of the Golden Gate Bridge, is available with far-in-advance reservations (call the National Parks department on 556 0560 – and good luck), you can't camp anywhere in the city unless you're homeless; even then it's illegal. You can load up on gear, however.

Dave Sullivan's Sport Shop

5323 Geary Boulevard, between 17th and 18th Avenues (751 7070). Bus 38, 38AX, 38BX. **Open** 8.30am-8pm Mon-Fri; 8.30am-6pm Sat; 9am-5pm Sun. **Credit** AmEx, Disc, MC, V. **Map A4**
A San Francisco institution: friendly, helpful service and great deals on camping and ski equipment rentals.

G&M Sales

1667 Market Street, at Gough Street (863 2855). Muni Metro F, J, K, L, M, N/bus 6, 7, 66, 71. **Open** 9.30am-6pm Mon-Wed, Fri; 9.30am-6pm Thur; 9am-5pm Sat; 11am-4pm Sun. **Credit** AmEx, Disc, MC, V. **Map F5**
A cornucopia of sporting paraphernalia for every rigorous outing you can think off, including backpacking, skiing and fishing.

Cycling

Just about anywhere you want to go in San Francisco you can go by bicycle (although you'll need mega-legs for the hills): for cycling tours *see page 60* **Sightseeing**; *see page 258* **Directory** for more on getting around town by bike. Day trips to Angel Island, over the Golden Gate Bridge to Marin or to Tilden Park in Oakland offer an excellent combination of exercise and sightseeing. Cycle route maps ($2.95) are available in most bike shops, and if you plan on seeing the Bay Area by bike, pick up Ray Hosler's *Bay Area Bike Rides* ($10.95). Legend has it that mountain biking originated on the slopes of Mount Tamalpais, an hour (by bike) north of San Francisco. For specific trail information about Mount Tam, call the Golden Gate National Recreation Area Visitor Center (331 1540) or the Pan Toll Ranger Station (388 2070).

Most local buses and trains have bowed to bike activists. You can take bikes (free) on BART (992 2278), except during commuter hours when they are banned. CalTrain (1-800 660 4287) has limited bike space in designated cars on a first-come-first-served basis. Some Muni buses should be able to handle bikes by the time you read this. Currently, however, the best way to travel with a bike on public transport is by ferry.

American Bicycle Rental

2715 Hyde Street, between North Point and Beach Streets (931 0234). Bus 30, 32, 42/cable car Powell-Hyde. **Open** 8am-10pm daily. **Rates** $5 per hour; $25 per day. **Credit** AmEx, Disc, JCB, MC, V. **Map F1**
From here you can cycle across the Golden Gate Bridge into Sausalito and then return by ferry near the store. Maps, helmet and lock are included in the price; bring a passport or credit card for a deposit. You can also rent scooters.

Park Cyclery

1749 Waller Street, at Stanyan Street (221 3777/ 751 7368). Muni Metro N/bus 6, 7, 33, 66, 71. **Open** 10am-6pm daily. **Rates** $5 per hour; $25 for 24 hours. **Credit** MC, V. **Map C6**
Conveniently located on the corner of Golden Gate Park.

Start To Finish

672 Stanyan Street, between Haight and Page Streets (750 4760). Bus 7, 33, 37, 43. **Open** 10am-7pm Mon-Fri; 10am-6pm Sat; 10am-5pm Sun. **Rates** $5 per hour; $25 for 24 hours. **Credit** AmEx, MC, V.
Map C6
San Francisco's biggest bike shop, next to Golden Gate Park, offers sales and rentals and a range of bikes for all budgets.

Take a hike

Hiking trails with rewarding views or paths that lead through redwood groves to the ocean await you just 30 minutes from downtown San Francisco. For a short, introductory hike, try the **Morning Sun Trail**, which climbs from a parking lot at the Spencer Avenue exit off US 101 north, just above the Golden Gate Bridge. You can look east over the Bay, Angel Island and the urban sprawl or west to the Pacific. A good day-long hike, a little further into Marin County, is the **Dipsea Trail**, which leads from Mill Valley to Stinson Beach. Reach Mill Valley on Golden Gate Transit bus 10. The **Bootjack Trail**, which leads to the summit of Mount Tamalpais, is also popular. Get trail information for Mount Tam from the Pan Toll Ranger Station (388 2070).

For more information about exploring San Francisco on foot, *see page 58* **Sightseeing** *and page 258* **Directory**. The city's hills will take care of nearly all your quadriceptic needs.

Valencia Cyclery
*1077 Valencia Street, between 21st and 22nd Streets
(550 6600). Bus 26.* **Open** *10am-6pm daily.*
Rates $5 per hour; $24 per day. **Credit** MC, V.
Castro/Mission Map Y2
Most bike shops are clustered around Golden Gate Park; the
Mission's best bike broker, however, rents or sells cycles for
more hilly topography.

Fitness Centres & Gyms

Just as San Franciscans savour their corner cafés
and bars, they love their corner gyms – every
neighbourhood seems to have one, offering the
usual weight rooms and fitness classes . For dance-
related movement classes, try Rhythm and Motion
(621 0643).

Embarcadero YMCA
*169 Steuart Street, at Mission Street (957 9622). BART
Embarcadero/Muni Metro F, J, K, L, M, N/bus 2, 6, 7, 9,
14, 21, 31, 32, 66, 71.* **Open** *5.30am-10pm Mon-Fri;
8am-8pm Sat; 9am-6pm Sun.* **Rates** day pass $12.
Credit MC, V. **Map J3**
One of several YMCAs in the city, the Embarcadero Y serves
downtown SF from a waterfront location. A day pass covers any one of 80 weekly aerobics classes, free weights,
Cybex and Nautilus machines, racquetball and basketball
courts and a 25m pool.

24 Hour Fitness Centers
*Seven locations throughout San Francisco (1-800 249
6756).* **Open** 24 hours in most locations; phone to check.
Rates day pass $15. **Credit** AmEx, MC, V.
Not exceptionally personal, 24 Hour Fitness gets the job
done, with cardiovascular and weight machines and free
weights. Most aerobics and fitness dance classes are held
around the workday schedule, so the best times to drop in
are early morning, lunchtime or early evening.

Golf Courses
Harding Park & Golf Course
*Harding Road and Skyline Boulevard (664 4690).
Bus 18, 88.* **Open** 6.30am-7pm daily. **Rates** $26 Mon-Fri;
$31 Sat, Sun. **No credit cards.**
City-owned and operated, Harding lies by Lake Merced and
has a shop and a small bar and café.

Golden Gate Park Course
*John F Kennedy Drive, at 47th Avenue, in Golden Gate
Park (751 8987). Bus 5, 18.* **Open** 6am-6pm Mon-Sat.
Rates $10 Mon-Fri; $13 Sat, Sun. **No credit cards.**
A nine-hole course sits at the west end of the park, with a
pro shop, café and cart rental.

Lincoln Park Golf Course
*34th Avenue and Clement Street (221 9911). Bus 2, 18,
38.* **Open** sunrise to sunset. **Rates** $9-$23 Mon-Fri; $10-
$27 Sat, Sun. **Credit** MC, V.
One of the most photographed courses in the States, with a
famous 17th hole view of the Golden Gate Bridge. Prices drop
as the light fades. There's also a practice area, putting green,
rental shop, pro shop, bar and refreshments.

Golf Instruction
Driving Obsession
*Suite 402, 310 Grant Avenue, between Bush and Sutter
Streets (397 4653). BART Montgomery Street/
Muni Metro F, J, K, L, M, N/bus 15, 30, 45.*

Getting piste

The ambitious skier can sometimes make a
day trip to the Sierras, but it's best to give
yourself at least a weekend. Leading ski
resorts around Lake Tahoe (about 3½ hours
from San Francisco by car) include **Alpine
Meadows** (1-800 441 4423/1-916 583 4232/
snow conditions recorded message
1-916 581 8374), **Heavenly Valley** (1-916
541 7544), **Kirkwood** (1-209 258 3000),
Northstar at Tahoe (1-916 562 1010) and
Squaw Valley (1-916 583 6985). **Mogul Ski
Club** (456 1000) can hook you up with other
skiers and provide the latest snow information. During the season (usually end of
November to early April), most ski shops will
have calendars of events and ads for package
deals. For more details, *see chapter* **Trips
Out of Town**.

Soma Ski & Sportz
*689 Third Street, at Townsend Street (777 2165).
Bus 15, 30, 32, 42, 45, 76.* **Open** *Nov-April* 10am-
7pm Mon-Wed; 10am-8pm Thur, Fri; 10am-6pm
Sat; 11am-5pm Sun; *May-Oct* 10am-6pm daily.
Credit AmEx, Disc, MC, V. **Map J5**
This SoMa outfit recently moved to a larger store,
allowing it to cater even better to all your on-the-slopes
needs. Besides the prerequisite downhill skis, poles,
boots and bindings, they've got snowboards, cross-
country equipment, clothing and car racks. They also
do repairs and tune-ups, their rental prices are competitive, staff are friendly and knowledgeable – and
they play great music in the store.

Open 8.30am-5.30pm Mon-Fri; 9am-5pm Sat; 10am-4pm
Sun. **Credit** AmEx, DC, Disc, JCB, MC, V.
Map G3
Individual and group golf instruction are available using
computers and digital video analysis. Initial one-hour lesson
and evaluation costs $110.

Mission Bay Golf Center
1200 Sixth Street, at Channel Street (431 7888). Bus 15.
Open 7am-11pm daily. **Credit** AmEx, JCB, MC, V.
Map H5
With a unique view of the freeway, East Bay and the South
San Francisco hills, Mission Bay offers a 300-yard, two-
tiered driving range, as well as a restaurant and discount
golf shop.

Horse Riding

Unless you're a mounted police officer, horse riding in San Francisco is limited to Golden Gate
Park. Within a 30- to 75-minute drive, however, the
options open up. Stables that hire horses and lead
tours include **Sea Horse Ranch and Friendly
Acres Ranch** (726 8550) near Half Moon Bay or
Chanslor Guest Ranch & Stables (1-707 875
3520) next to Bodega Bay.

Golden Gate Park Stables

John F Kennedy Drive, at 36th Avenue, in Golden Gate Park (668 7360). Bus 5. **Open** 8am-6pm daily.
Rates $45 private lesson; $25 trail ride.
Credit MC, V.
Golden Gate Park Stables offers everything from pony rides for small kids to advanced equestrian courses for experienced cowboys and girls.

Indoor Rock Climbing

Mission Cliffs

2295 Harrison Street, at 19th Street (550 0515). Bus 12, 22, 33. **Open** 6.30am-10pm Mon, Wed, Fri; 11am-10pm Tue, Thur; 10am-6pm Sat, Sun.
Rates $14 per day. **Credit** AmEx, Disc, MC, V.
Castro/Mission Map Z1
To enter Mission Cliffs is to penetrate a 3,800sq m (12,000sq ft) kingdom that melts the boundary of 'urban' and 'wilderness' and distills it into a highly polished jungle gym.

Inline Hockey

Street hockey has made a comeback with rollerblades, and a number of San Franciscans are rushing to place their knees and ankles in harm's (and fun's) way. You can often join in a game at the playground on the corner of Scott and North Point Streets. Rentals at Marina Skate & Snowboard (*see below* **Rollerblading**) include pads and a free lesson. Serious players will want to go to the Bladium, where any level of play is possible, morning, noon and night.

Bladium

1050 Third Street, at Berry Street (442 5060). Bus 15, 30, 42, 45. **Open** 8am-midnight daily. **Rate** $5 per person during 'open session'. **Credit** MC, V. **Map J5**
An indoor inline skating rink, Bladium houses several hockey leagues, a licensed juice bar, pro shop and rents all the gear you need for a drop-in game. There is a league on Wednesdays (noon-3pm).

Paragliding

Easier to learn than most flying methods, paragliding offers the chance to fly for minutes or hours with less than a day's instruction. Not to be confused with parasailing, paragliding involves no boat. The equipment itself weighs only 10lbs and can do just about anything a hang-glider does, except turn upside-down.

Air Time

3620 Wawona Street, at 47th Avenue (759 1177). Muni Metro L. **Open** 10am-2pm, 4-7pm, Mon, Thur, Sun; 10am-7pm, Fri, Sat. **Rates** $150-$160. **Credit** MC, V.
You couldn't ask for a better place to learn to paraglide or to take the five-day course to get Class 1 certification.

Pool & Billards

Pool tables are as common in bars as sofas are in living rooms, but the city also has several purpose-designed pool halls with attached bars.

Chalkers

1 Rincon Center, at Spear and Mission Streets (512 0450). BART Embarcadero/bus 14.
Open 11.30am-2am Mon-Fri; 2pm-2am Sat; 3-11pm Sun.
Rates $5-$14 per hour Mon-Thur, Sun; $7-$15 per hour Fri, Sat. **Credit** AmEx, MC, V. **Map J3**
With 30 cherrywood tables, a bar and restaurant, Chalkers occasionally invites trick-shot experts and pros to dazzle the lunch crowd. Families are allowed 2-7pm, at the weekend. If you prefer it busy, Friday is your night, when the after-work crowd stops in for happy hour.

South Beach Billiards

450 Brannan Street, between Second and Third Streets (495 5939). Bus 15, 30, 32, 42, 45, 76. **Open** noon-2am daily. **Rates** $3-$10 per hour. **Credit** AmEx, MC, V. **Map J4**
South Beach is the hipper of the two big billiards parlours. It has a non-smoking section, a tournament room, snooker tables and a bocci ball court down the centre. With 50 tables available, you won't have to wait long for one.

Racquetball

Koret Health & Recreation Center

Turk and Parker Streets (422 6820). Bus 31.
Open *to non-USF students* 6am-2pm Mon-Fri; 8am-2pm Sat, Sun. **Map C5**
This health club is part of the University of San Francisco but non-students can use the facilities until 2pm. There are six racquetball courts and a swimming pool and gym. The only catch is you have to bring you own racquet and ball.

Rollerblading

Formerly only for die-hard outdoor enthusiasts, rollerblading (aka inline skating) has crossed fully over into the mainstream. For the novice or veteran,

Join the rest of the city on wheels – in the park (opposite) *or along the oceanfront.*

skating in Golden Gate Park on a Sunday is hard to top: the beach at one end, plenty of sunny meadows and shady benches along the way and no auto traffic. A mix of rollerblading and break dancing provides entertainment near Sixth Street on John F Kennedy Drive.

Golden Gate Park Skate and Bike

3038 Fulton Street, at Sixth Avenue (668 1117). Bus 5, 21, 44. **Open** 10am-6pm Mon-Sat; 10am-7pm Sun. **Rates** $6 per hour; $24 for 24 hours. **Credit** MC, V. **Map B5**
Spending the day in the park? Stop here for rollerblades as well as bicycles, roller skates and safety gear.

Marina Skate & Snowboard

2271 Chestnut Street, at Scott Street (567 8400). Bus 22, 30. **Open** 11am-8pm Mon-Fri; 8am-8pm Sat; 10am-7pm Sun. **Rates** $5.50 per hour; $19 for 24 hours. **Credit** AmEx, MC, V. **Map D2**
Check out the young, single and beautiful at nearby Marina Green on skates rented from this shop, which also specialises in the latest snowboards and skate-rat attire. Free lessons (with skates) on Saturday mornings.

Nuvo

3108C Fillmore Street, between Filbert and Pixley Streets (771 6886). Bus 1, 2, 3, 4, 22. **Open** 11am-7pm Mon, Tue, Thur; 10am-6.30pm Wed; 10am-7pm Fri; 9am-7pm Sat; 9am-6pm Sun. **Rates** *Mon-Fri* $7 per hour, $10 two hours, $15 24 hours; *Sat, Sun* $7 per hour, $20 24 hours. **Credit** AmEx, MC, V. **Map E2**
Fees include protective gear (knee and elbow pads, helmet – get them).

Skates on Haight (SOH)

1818 Haight Street, at Stanyan Street (752 8375). Bus 6, 7, 71. **Open** 10am-6pm daily. **Rates** $5 per hour; $20 per day; $30 overnight. **Credit** AmEx, DC, Disc, JCB, MC, V. **Map C6**

Rent or buy inline skates, roller skates or snowboards at this outlet responsible for inspiring the worldwide skateboard craze back in the 1970s.

Rowing

Rowing of all kinds can be had in the Bay Area, from single sculls to whale boat racing. Scullers may want to have a go on the San Francisco Bay; call **Open Water Rowing** (332 1091), which also maintains a water conditions report at the same phone number.

Running

Many locals will tell you the best place to run, bike and rollerblade is the same – **Golden Gate Park** – but there's some disagreement on this. One of the most stunning places for a jog is the **Marina Green** (bus 22). A track encircles the esplanade itself, but a trail extends all the way to Fort Point, just before the Golden Gate Bridge. With the recent expansion of the Embarcadero, many runners prefer the stunning view of the Bay Bridge and piers.

The annual San Francisco Marathon is held in mid-July and the Bay to Breakers Foot Race, a 12km run from downtown to Ocean Beach, at the end of May (*see chapter* **San Francisco by Season**).

Skateboarding

No one needs to tell a skate rat where to go. If you're one, you'll find Justin Herman Plaza, a Safeway parking lot or any of a number of downtown concrete ramps on your own.

DLX

1831 Market Street, between Guerrero and Pearl Streets (626 5588). Muni Metro F, J/bus 8, 37.
Open noon-8pm Mon-Sat; noon-7pm Sun.
Credit MC, V. **Map F5**
The skateboard merchandiser formerly known as 'Deluxe' is the mother of them all. Make a pilgrimage to them for a complete line of clothes, boards, accessories and those annoying little stickers you see everywhere. Check out their irreverent window displays, too – one recently featured a hold-up in progress.

Squash

Bay Club

150 Greenwich Street, between Battery and Sansome Streets (433 2200). Bus 42/Bay Club shuttle from BART Embarcadero. **Open** 5.30am-11pm Mon-Fri; 7am-9pm Sat, Sun. **Rates** guest fee $15. **No credit cards.**
Map H2
Without turning away business, the Bay Club does try to make its well-to-do members feel exclusive. As such, they insist drop-in players either come with a member or demonstrate that they are a member of an IRSA-affiliated squash gym, club or organisation. For racquetball courts at the Embarcadero YMCA, *see page 217*.

Surfing

You have to be an experienced surfer to tackle the waves around San Francisco. Currents are strong, sharks occasional and temperatures icy – for most surfers, a wetsuit is a must. But whether you're a pro headed to Ocean Beach or Fort Point, or a newbie boogie-boarding the black sand beaches in Marin County, you'll need the appropriate gear.

Wise Surfboards

3149 Vicente Street, at 42nd Street (665 7745). Bus 18, 23. **Open** 9am-6pm Mon-Fri; 8am-5pm Sat, Sun. **Credit** AmEx, MC, V.
This is where the locals go – it's just a few blocks from Ocean Beach. Wise sells boards, wetsuits and accessories, and maintains a 24-hour information line – 665 9473 – for surf conditions. You'll probably run into Mermen, San Francisco's favourite psychedelic-surf band, who live just down the street.

Swimming

The ocean is usually too chilly and turbulent to swim in, so your best bet is a pool. For Olympic-sized swimming pools, try the **Embarcadero**

Out of town

The Bay Area and Pacific coastline offer a multitude of activities to lovers of water-based sports. Whether you're a devotee of boating, sailing, kayaking or scuba diving, there are numerous outfits nearby that hire equipment, provide lessons and organise trips.

In Berkeley, **Cal Adventures** hires out Coronado 15-footers for sporty sailing on the South Sailing Basin; to lease one without recognised certification, you must spend $60 to sail with an instructor who will confirm your ability. Also in Berkeley, **Cal Dive & Travel** arranges trips to Monterey Bay, where scuba divers will find the best diving on the California coast. They also run beginners' classes and hire out scuba equipment for about $60.

California Canoe & Kayak in Oakland is one of the best shops for hiring and buying kayaks and sea-going gear of all sorts. A sea canoe costs $20 for three hours, and lessons and day outings are available on the nearby Oakland Estuary.

On the Sausalito waterfront, **Sea Trek** has become something of an institution. They run summer camps and trips for kids, book expeditions to Alaska and Baja and join forces with environmentalists to preserve waterways as well as offering beginners several opportunities to explore the Bay by kayak, from guided tours ($50 for three hours) and lessons to moonlight paddles.

If you'd prefer an engine to propel you, head for nearby **Capt Case**, the only place that can get you on the Bay proper in a powerboat ($65-$90 per hour). The boats are Boston Whalers with outboards and require some experience. Alternatively, try human-powered waterbikes ($15 per hour) that spider along at under 10mph. If all this doesn't sound adventurous enough, **Escape Artists Tours**, down the coast at Half Moon Bay, arranges adventures for groups and individuals ranging from kayaking on the Bay to flying air-combat planes.

Cal Adventures *UC Aquatic Center, Berkeley Marina (1-510 642 4000). BART Berkeley, then bus 51.* **Open** 10am-6pm Mon-Fri.
Cal Dive & Travel *1750 Sixth Street, Berkeley (1-510 524 3248). BART North Berkeley.* **Open** 10am-6pm Mon-Fri; 10am-2pm Sat.
California Canoe & Kayak *409 Water Street, on Jack London Square at Franklin Street, Oakland (1-510 893 7833). BART 12th Street.* **Open** 10am-8pm Mon-Fri; 9am-8pm Sat; 9am-6pm Sun.
Capt Case Powerboat & Waterbike Rental *Schoonemaker Point Marina, Libertyship Way, Sausalito (331 0444). Bus Golden Gate Transit 10, 50.* **Open** 10am-6pm daily.
Escape Artist Tours *150 Tiller Court, Half Moon Bay (1-800 728 1384/726 7626/www.sfescapes.com).* **Open** 9am-9pm Mon-Sat.
Sea Trek *Schoonemaker Point Marina, Libertyship Way, Sausalito (488 1000/beach 332 4465). Bus Golden Gate Transit 10, 50.* **Open** 9.30am-5.30pm Mon-Fri; on the 'beach' *during season* 9am-5pm Tue-Sun; *winter* 9am-5pm Sat, Sun.

YMCA (*see page 220*), the **Bay Club** (*see page 217*) or the **Koret Center** (*see page 218*). Some health and fitness clubs also have swimming pools; call to enquire. The City of San Francisco maintains eight municipal pools, each with separate times for open swimming. The most central ones are at **Hamilton Recreation Center** at Geary Boulevard and Steiner Street (292 2001) and the **North Beach Pool** at Lombard and Mason Streets (274 0200); adult admission is $3. For your nearest, check the listings in the *White Pages* under City Government Offices: Recreation and Parks. For information on the best beaches in the city, *see page 55* **Sightseeing**.

Tennis

Indoor tennis in San Francisco is almost exclusively a members-only affair, but much of the best play is outdoors anyway. **Golden Gate Park** has several courts (at the Stanyan Street entrance) and **Dolores Park** in the Mission district is always busy. Both are open from sunrise to sunset, and are free.

Volleyball

More popular in Southern California, where beach volleyball has become a televised and well-attended spectator sport, volleyball is also played in San Francisco. Experienced players can look up the **SF Volleyball Association** (931 6385), which organises leagues. Otherwise, look for pick-up action at the north end of **Marina Green** on weekend mornings. Unfortunately the games held in Lindley Meadow in **Golden Gate Park** are rarely pick-up games, but rather family or corporate get-togethers.

Whale Watching

Whale watching can be as easy as taking a pair of binoculars to the shore and having a look. One recommended shore location is the tip of **Point Reyes**, an hour's drive north of San Francisco. For more landlocked views of passing whales, pick up *The Delicate Art of Whale Watching* ($10) in the Sierra Club Bookstore, 85 Second Street, at Mission Street (977 5600).

Oceanic Society Expeditions

Fort Mason Center (474 3385). Bus 22, 28, 42, 47, 49. **Open** 9am-5pm Mon-Fri. **Rates** $29-$65. **Credit** AmEx, MC, V. **Map E1**
Trips are a cut above most tourist excursions because the staff are experts in natural history and marine life. The full-day trip ($65) heads 42km (26 miles) west of the Golden Gate to the Farallon Islands, home of the largest sea bird rookery in the continental US; along the way, guides lead the search for humpback and gray whales, seals and sea lions.

Windsurfing (Sailboarding)

The Bay Area boasts no less than 32 launch sites for windsurfing, including Coyote Point, 3Com

(formerly Candlestick) Park and Crissy Field – the latter has been the site of several international competitions, among them windsurfing's World Cup.

SF School of Windsurfing

1 Harding Road, Lake Merced (753 3235). Muni Metro M, then bus 18/bus 18, 23, 29. **Open** 9am-noon daily. **Rates** two-day beginner's course $130. **Credit** MC, V.
Offers lessons at all levels; equipment is provided. The school rents gear (2-7pm Tue-Fri; 10am-7pm Sat, Sun) on Candlestick Beach near 3Com Park.

City Front Sailboards

2936 Lyon Street, between Lombard and Greenwich Streets (929 7873). Bus 28, 30, 41, 43, 45. **Open** 11am-7pm Mon-Fri; 10am-6pm Sat, Sun. **Rates** complete sailing rig $45. **Credit** AmEx, Disc, MC, V. **Map D2**
City Front is the 'pro' shop, the place to go if you're already good and have brought along your wetsuit and harness.

Yoga

Also try the **Yoga Society of San Francisco** (285 5537).

Yoga College of India

Second floor, 910 Columbus Avenue, at Lombard Street (346 5400). Bus 15, 39, 41/cable car Powell-Mason. **Open** *classes for visitors* 9am, 4.30pm, 6.15pm Mon; 7am, 9am, 4.30pm, 6.15pm Tue-Fri; 9am, 10.45am Sat, Sun. **Rates** $10 per class. **Credit** MC, V. **Map G2**
First-time attendees can take their second class free at the city's long-standing favourite yoga institute. Bring a towel.

Theatre & Dance

From the 'Phantom of the Opera' to outdoor mime festivals or one-off experimental events, San Francisco's performing arts scene pulls in the punters.

Although San Francisco's theatre and dance scene doesn't have the depth and flash of New York or Los Angeles, the city's tolerance for the experimental and the weird makes it possible – for better and for worse – to see truly original performances here. Experimentation is encouraged, even savoured, and cutting-edge work isn't instantly sucked up, commercially packaged and hyped the way it is in NY and LA.

Offbeat performers are allowed the space to hone their creative vision: Whoopi Goldberg and Robin Williams both cut their teeth on stand up comedy in San Francisco. Socially conscious artists also thrive: Tony Kushner, the Pulitzer Prize-winning playwright of the New York Broadway smash *Angels in America*, developed the play and premiered it at San Francisco's Eureka Theater. There's also room for lunatic fringe performers, like Mark Pauline of the rogue robot and munitions makers Survival Research Laboratories, to blow themselves apart in the name of art. Other nationally known playwrights and performers such as Anna Deavere Smith and Eric Bogosian have recharged their cultural batteries in the city.

Gender-bending and ethnically specific theatre performances find a receptive audience here, as befits the Bay Area's radical, multicultural artistic and political traditions. Silicon Valley's hackers and inventors have likewise had an impact: holograms perform alongside actors, and the alternation of computer Muzak and live musicians further breaks down barriers separating virtual and theatrical realities.

The city also caters for die-hard traditionalists. Visiting companies bring successful Broadway shows to the Golden Gate, Curran and Orpheum Theaters; smaller repertory companies like the Lamplighters may specialise in Gilbert and Sullivan. About 14 per cent of the city's sky-high hotel tax goes towards the arts, so get your money's worth and enjoy them while you're here.

If you're planning ahead, the Datebook section of the combined Sunday *San Francisco Examiner*

and Chronicle, the free weeklies and *SF Arts Monthly* carry up-to-date reviews and listings. On the Internet, San Francisco's CitySearch site (www.citysearch7. com) maintains current box office data. Prices range from as little as $5 for an experimental show to $50 or more for a Broadway extravaganza. The opening hours listed below are for the box office unless otherwise stated.

For **Theatre Rhinoceros, LunaSea** and additional listings, *see chapter* **Gay & Lesbian San Francisco**.

TICKETS

The theatres' own box offices are usually the cheapest bet for tickets (phone ahead for opening times, bearing in mind there's often a fee for telephone bookings). **TIX Bay Area**, the small kiosk on the Stockton Street side of Union Square (433 7827), sells half-price tickets for theatre, dance and opera events on the day of the show (cash only). TIX also sells full-price tickets in advance (for which you can pay by credit card). Ticket brokers **BASS** (1-510 762 2277/1-800 225 2277 from outside California) has outlets all over the city, but expect to pay a hefty surcharge; it has an arts booking line on 776 1999). You can also try **St Francis Theater Ticket Service** (362 3500), **Mr Ticket** (1-800 424 7328/1-888 722 5737/292 7328) or **City Box Office** (392 4400). You can also buy tickets for some venues online through www.ticketweb.com.

Mainstream

Three beautifully restored theatres bring Broadway and other large-scale commercial productions to the city for a 'Best of Broadway' series. The venues share an information line for box office hours and ticket details. You can get tickets through BASS and, for the Golden Gate and Orpheum theatres, from the central box office at the Orpheum. At the time of writing, Andrew Lloyd Webber's *Phantom of the Opera* had taken up near-permanent residency at the Curran.

Curran Theater

*445 Geary Street, between Mason and Taylor Streets
(551 2000). BART Powell Street/Muni Metro F, J, K, L,
M, N/bus 27, 38/cable car Powell-Hyde or Powell-Mason.*
Open 10am-6pm Mon; 10am-8.30pm Tue-Sat; noon-4pm
Sun. **Credit** AmEx, MC, V. **Map G4**

Golden Gate Theater

*1 Taylor Street, between Sixth and Market Streets (551
2000). BART Civic Center/Muni Metro F, J, K, L, M, N/
bus 5, 6, 7, 9, 21, 26, 66, 71.* **Open** box office at Orpheum
noon-6pm Mon-Sat. **Credit** AmEx, MC, V. **Map G4**

Orpheum

*1192 Market Street, at Hyde Street (551 2000). BART
Civic Center/Muni Metro F, J, K, L, M, N/bus 6, 5, 7, 9,
21, 31, 66, 71.* **Open** noon-6pm Mon-Sat. **Credit** AmEx,
MC, V. **Map G4/5**

Regional Theatres

ACT and Berkeley Repertory (*see page 226*) are
the Bay Area's two largest and most established
theatre companies; both mount a full season of
shows each year.

American Conservatory Theater (ACT)

*Geary Theater, 415 Geary Street, between Mason and
Taylor Streets (834 3200); box office at 405 Geary Street
(749 2228). BART Powell Street/Muni Metro F, J, K, L,
M, N/ bus 27, 38/cable car Powell-Hyde or Powell-Mason.*
Open noon-6pm Mon, Sun; noon-8pm Tue-Sat.
Credit AmEx, MC, V. **Map G4**
Theater ACT produces contemporary and traditional shows
with a varied programme throughout the season: recent ros-
ters have included productions of Tennessee Williams' *A
Streetcar Named Desire* and Charles Dickens' *A Christmas
Carol*. After several years of nomadic existence at a rotating
list of venues, the company recently celebrated its triumphant
return to the retrofitted and restored theatre near Union Square.

Mid-sized Theatres

Some of the slightly smaller theatre companies in
the Bay Area are the most interesting. The Magic,
Asian American and Lorraine Hansberry all
mount original productions, often by local artists.
And although Theater Artaud doesn't have a company in residence, this unique theatre-in-a-ware-
house marks ground zero for cutting-edge national
and international performances.

Asian American Theater Company

(440 5545). **Open** phone for details. **No credit cards**.
The AATC provides a venue for Asian- and Pacific Islander-
American playwrights and actors to perform premieres and
classic works in a variety of local spaces. The group pre-
sented the award-winning *Gravity Falls from Trees* at the
Magic Theater; other performances have been at the New
Langton venue (*see page 226*).

Eureka Theater Company

(243 9899). **Open** 1-5pm Mon-Fri. **No credit cards**.
The Eureka Theater Company, best known for helping Tony
Kushner develop the Pulitzer prize-winning and Emmy-
laden *Angels in America*, provides a venue for provocative
new works – and works new to the Bay Area. The innovative company was forced by financial constraints to close for
a while, but at the time of writing was considering a move

to a permanent new space, promising to revive its tradition
of encouraging new talent. Phone for details and the location
of Eureka's next production.

Lorraine Hansberry Theater

*620 Sutter Street, between Mason and Powell Streets
(474 8800). Bus 2, 3, 4, 30, 45, 76/cable car Powell-Hyde
or Powell-Mason.* **Open** noon-6pm Mon-Wed, Sun; noon-
8pm Thur-Sat. **Credit** AmEx, MC, V. **Map G3**
The Lorraine Hansberry presents plays by America's foremost black playwrights, such as Pulitzer prize-winners
Charles Fuller and August Wilson. It also stages adaptations
of works by Alice Walker and Toni Morrison, among others, and an occasional classical dramatic work.

Magic Theater

*Building D, Fort Mason Center, at Laguna and
Buchanan Streets (441 8822). Bus 28.* **Open** 1-7pm
Wed-Fri; 4-7pm Sat. **Credit** AmEx, MC, V. **Map E1**
For nearly 30 years, the Magic Theater has been dedicated
to developing new plays, many of which respond to topical
political and social events. For a time, the theatre premiered
a new work by Sam Shepard every year; today, regulars
include San Francisco playwright Claire Chafee.

Theater Artaud

*450 Florida Street, at 17th Street (box office 621
7797/administration 647 2200). Bus 27, 33, 53.*
Open phone for details. **Credit** MC, V. **Map G6**
Theater Artaud stages high-quality avant-garde theatre,
music and dance performances from around the world, the
US and even San Francisco. It's worth the trip for the space
alone, which is built into a renovated warehouse. Every summer, it sponsors a weekend-long dramatic marathon, featuring dozens of artists performing live, around the clock.

Festivals

San Francisco's theatre festivals offer something for everyone. Look out for free events
like the Golden Gate favourite, **Shakespeare in the Park** and the **California
Shakespeare Festival** (both held in
September), and Sundays in Stern Grove
(June-August), where the city's finest – including the San Francisco Opera and Ballet –
stage productions for afternoon picnickers.
The **Solo Mio Festival**, a feisty series of
high-quality solo performances, is a high
point of Bay Area theatre, as is the annual
Mime Troupe in the Park, when the San
Francisco Mime Troupe brings its unique
combination of humour and hard-hitting politics to various park locations around the Bay
Area. For more details on these events, *see
chapter* **San Francisco by Season**.

Finally, during the ten-day **Annual San
Francisco Fringe Festival** (*see page 224
Exit Theater*) in September, you can expect
anything from Oscar Wilde performances to
Betty Grable impersonations by local and visiting companies performing in various
venues around town.

Smaller Spaces

Dozens of smaller theatres and performance spaces dot San Francisco and the Bay Area. Some feature long-running productions with proven commercial appeal: check the **Cable Car Theater** (956 8497), **Mason Street Theater** (982 5463), **Theater on the Square** (433 9500), and **Marine's Memorial Theater** (771 6900), among others. Space for local experimental work and festival programming is provided by the **Bayfront** and **Cowell Theaters** (both at Fort Mason, 979 3010), **Brava! for Women in the Arts** (641 7657), while **Josie's Juice Bar and Cabaret** has done plenty to develop queer performance in the area (*see chapters* **Gay & Lesbian San Francisco** *and* **Nightlife**). The handful of theatres listed below all have interesting reputations.

Climate Theater

252 Ninth Street, between Folsom and Howard Streets (262 2169/Solo Mio Festival 626 6422/box office 392 4400). BART Civic Center/Muni Metro F, J, K, L, M, N. **Open** phone for details. **Credit** MC, V. **Map G5**
Home to the acclaimed Solo Mio Festival (*see chapter* **San Francisco by Season**), the Climate nurtures new work by solo performers who have gone on to achieve wider acclaim. It also produces the annual Festival Fantochio, a fantastical puppet event that is definitely not for children only.

Exit Theater

156 Eddy Street, between Mason and Taylor Streets (931 1094/festival information 673 3847). BART Powell Street/Muni Metro F, J, K, L, M, N/bus 27, 31. **Open** half-hour before show. **No credit cards**. **Map G4**
Organises the annual San Francisco Fringe Festival (www. sffringe.org), and otherwise offers a variety of works, from one-act plays to adaptations of the likes of Edward Albee.

450 Geary Studio Theater

450 Geary Street, between Mason and Taylor Streets (673 1172). Cable car Powell-Hyde or Powell-Mason. **Open** phone for details. **Credit** MC, V. **Map G4**
A small space devoted to new work, including children's plays, and some solo performances.

Stage Door Theater

420 Mason Street, at Geary Street (834 3200). Bus 2, 3, 4, 76. **Open** 10am-6pm Mon-Fri. **Credit** MC, V. **Map G4**
The Samaritan who sheltered the ACT during its homeless years, the Stage Door now continues to stage solid works that draw the second-tier of Union Square's theatre-going society.

Experimental & Performance Art

By its very nature, experimental and performance art is a hit-and-miss affair. But San Francisco and the Bay Area have produced more than its fair share of underground hits. Indeed, the region's theatrical reputation is fired by the raw creative energies generated in its alternative performance spaces.

Intersection for the Arts

446 Valencia Street, between 15th and 16th Streets (626 3311). BART 16th Street/Muni Metro F, J, K, L, M, N/bus 14, 22, 26, 49, 53. **Open** phone for details. **No credit cards. Map F6**
An alternative arts centre mixing theatre with poetry readings, community art shows and avant-garde music.

The San Francisco Ballet performs (from the top) 'Agon', 'El Grito', 'Swan Lake', 'In the Night' and (opposite) 'Othello'.

Out of town

Berkeley Repertory
2025 Addison Street, between Shattuck Avenue and Milvia Street (1-510 845 4700). BART Berkeley. **Open** noon-7pm daily. **Credit** MC, V.
This East Bay company divides productions between its main stage, where it presents five plays a year, and a 'Parallel Season' of experimental and developing work. The productions often reflect the diverse communities and traditions of the Bay Area and California as a whole, making it a great place to catch innovative and insightful work. Half-price tickets are available from the box office on the day of each performance.

Cal Performances
Zellerbach Hall, UC Berkeley campus (1-510 642 9988). BART Berkeley. **Open** 10am-5.30pm Mon-Fri; 10am-2pm Sat, Sun. **Credit** MC, V.
Hosted in conjunction with UC Berkeley at Zellerbach Hall on campus, this series draws the best national dance companies, from Bill T Jones/Arnie Zane and Merce Cunningham to Trisha Brown and June Watanabe, as well as traditional companies from countries such as Indonesia, Senegal and Cambodia, and the odd local company like Margaret Jenkins.

The Marsh
1062 Valencia Street, at 22nd Street (641 0235). BART 24th Street/bus 26. **Open** phone for details. **Credit** AmEx, MC, V.
A venue that bills itself as a 'breeding ground for new performance', The Marsh offers select playwrights and performers an open stage to try out whatever they like. It features mostly solo work (don't miss Josh Kornbluth's twisted soliloquies) and an occasional ensemble piece.

New Langton Arts
1246 Folsom Street, between Eighth and Ninth Streets (626 5416). Bus 12, 19, 27, 42. **Open** 10am-6pm Mon-Fri. **Credit** MC, V. **Map** G5
The centre makes space in its programme of experimental art shows for original presentations penned by regional arts grants winners. Expect political and social commentary, gender-bending art and performance.

The Lab
2948 16th Street, between Capp Street and South Van Ness Avenue (864 8855). BART 16th Street/bus 14, 22, 33, 49, 53. **Open** phone for details. **No credit cards**. **Map** F6
An experimental gallery featuring performance artists and visual works.

In a Class of Their Own

Beach Blanket Babylon
Club Fugazi, 678 Green Street, between Columbus Avenue and Powell Street (421 4222). Bus 15, 30, 41, 45. **Open** 10am-6pm Mon-Sat; noon-6pm Sun. **Credit** MC, V. **Map** G2
This long-running musical revue features a constantly changing array of characters drawn from US popular culture, local legend and the politics of the day. The slapstick humour places heavy emphasis on the formulaic and the visual. Even so, BBB is a San Francisco original.

George Coates Performance Works
110 McAllister Street, at Leavenworth Street (863 4130/administration 863 8520). BART Civic Center/Muni Metro F, J, K, L, M, N/bus 5. **Open** 11am-9pm Mon-Fri. **Credit** AmEx, V. **Map** G4
Techno wizard George Coates is a pioneer in 'virtual' theatre, working actors and musicians into dazzling computer-generated environments. Operating out of a pseudo-gothic chapel over whose walls and ceilings 'float' images of everything from the wilderness to Chartres Cathedral to outer space, Coates creates a theatrical *son et lumière*. The space commissions only one show a year, usually running from November to March, but hosts special events (from Spalding Grey to Chanticleer) throughout the year.

Dance

A number of dance companies thrive in San Francisco, among them the **Margaret Jenkins Dance Company**, **Lines Dance Company**, **Contraband** and Oakland's **Dance Brigade** (which produces *The Revolutionary Nutcracker Sweetie* each year). Watch out also for the African-American choreographers' series at Theater Artaud (*see page 223*).

Center for the Arts at Yerba Buena Gardens
*See chapter **Museums & Galleries** for listings.*
The beautiful state-of-the-art theatre at the city's newest arts complex presents theatre, dance and music performances, with an emphasis on San Francisco-based artists. Its mission is to encourage experimentation and debate.

Dancers Group Studio Theater
3221 22nd Street, at Mission Street (824 5044/www.dancersgroup.org). BART 24th Street/bus 14, 67. **Mission Map** Y2
Look for the annual Edge Festival in February and March, the Improvisational Dance Festival in June and occasional residencies by dance troupes such as Asian American Dance Performances and Jo Goode Performance Group.

New Performance Gallery
3153 17th Street, between South Van Ness Avenue and Folsom Street (box office 863 9834/administration 626 6745). BART 16th Street/bus 33. **Map** F6
Like Dancers Group, this larger space showcases the work of mostly local dancers and helps develop innovative modern dance performances.

San Francisco Ballet
War Memorial Opera House, 301 Van Ness Avenue, at Grove Street (865 2000). BART Civic Center/Muni Metro F, J, K, L, M, N/bus 21, 42, 47, 49. **Open** 10am-6pm Mon-Sat. **Credit** AmEx, MC, V. **Map** F5
Founded in 1933, the San Francisco Ballet is America's oldest professional ballet company. Following its traditional seasonal opening with the *Nutcracker Suite*, SFB features other works choreographed by George Balanchine and Jerome Robbins and its artistic director Helgi Tomasson, among others. One of its most successful shows in recent years was *Billboards*, an uncharacteristically modern ballet with a score by the artist formerly known as Prince.

SF Performances
Suite 710, 500 Sutter Street, between Mason and Powell Streets (398 6449). Bus 2, 3, 4, 30, 45, 76/cable car Powell-Hyde or Powell-Mason. **Open** 9am-5pm Mon-Fri.
The season runs at five venues from September to May. Much like Cal Performances (*see above*), the series brings national and international performers to the Bay Area.

Trips Out of Town

Trips Out of Town

A day on the beach or a walk in the mountains, a New Age healing session or a grungey blues band – you'll find them all within a stone's throw of San Francisco.

Bordered by the bay on two sides and the ocean on another, San Francisco is ideally situated for easy getaways. Within an hour's drive, ride or boat trip are beaches, islands, mountains and other distractions. From Marin County in the north, Berkeley and Oakland to the east, and San Jose down the peninsula, each area has its own unique identity. Further afield lie the dramatic slopes of the Sierra Nevada mountain range, the celebrated golf links of the Monterey Peninsula, the protected shoreline of Marin County and the wineries and spas of the North Bay.

All telephone numbers listed in this chapter are within the 415 area code unless otherwise stated. For information on car rental, *see page 257.*

TRANSPORT

Most destinations are within easy reach of San Francisco and can be covered as a day trip or overnight stay. However, many of these areas are ill-served by public transport. If you can't hire a car, try the Bay Area Rapid Transit (BART) rail service, which connects the city with the East Bay (via an underground tunnel) or Golden Gate Transit, which has a regular schedule of bus services to and from many Marin County destinations, as well as a less frequent service to Sonoma County. You can also use Greyhound buses, Amtrak (the nearest train station is in Oakland), a charter tour or one of the ferries that run frequently to the North Bay during the day. But if your budget permits, it's best to rent a car; after all, driving is the Californian way. For a map of the Bay Area and surrounding coast, *see page 278.*

Amtrak 1-800 872 7245
BART 992 2278
Golden Gate Transit 455 2000
CalTrain 1-800 660 4287
Greyhound 1-800 231 2222

Heading North

Marin County

Marin County is one of the richest counties in California, as well as one of the most laid-back. It has a unique combination of yuppie wealth and hippie ideals – a sense of the free-spirited good life fills the air. The county extends from the Golden Gate Bridge north, along the coast to **Bodega Bay** and inland to the wine country, and is full of spine-tingling views.

Crossing the **Golden Gate Bridge** is something everyone should do at least once in their life, but unless you're on foot or a bicycle, it's hard to stop and take in the spectacular view. From **Vista Point**, the first exit north of the bridge, the city seems almost close enough to touch.

North-west of the bridge, a couple of roads traverse the **Marin Headlands** (Visitor's Center telephone 331 1540). The hills here offer amazing views and the valleys are filled with wild flowers. The vistas are familar to most Americans from the innumerable automobile ads which use San

---

Best day trips

Angel Island: take a ferry and pack a picnic for the beach.
Tiburon: for a lazy day, hop on the ferry and have brunch at Sam's Anchor Café or dinner at Guaymas. Browse the shops along Ark Avenue afterwards.
Napa Valley: if you take the Napa Valley Wine Train you can see several wineyards in a day and taste to your heart's content.
Half Moon Bay: take the CalTrain and spend the day playing golf, horse riding, biking or hiking – or just vegging out on the beach.
Berkeley: it's a short hop by BART to Berkeley; spend the day exploring the other side of the Bay (*see chapter* **San Francisco by Neighbourhood**).

Visit the redwoods at **Muir Woods National Monument** *and be overawed by Mother Nature. See page 231.*

Francisco and the Golden Gate as a backdrop. World War II battlements can still be seen dotted about the hilltops.

Starting with these headlands, Marin County offers the best hiking and biking – mountain or otherwise – in the Bay Area. Thanks to state and federal legislation, a large percentage of the county is devoted to open space. The most famous parcel of land is **Point Reyes National Seashore** (information 663 1092), part of the vast **Golden Gate National Recreation Area** that extends north from San Francisco along most of the Marin coastline.

Marin lacks a real centre: **San Rafael** is its biggest town, but it's also the least interesting to visit, though it's worth making a short detour to see 'Big Pink', the grand **Marin Civic Center** designed by Frank Lloyd Wright. Here, from April to October, you'll find a farmers' market and live entertainment. For more information, call the **San Rafael Chamber of Commerce** (817 Mission Avenue; 454 4163). Head to **Mill Valley**, the quintessential Marin town, each autumn for the **Mill Valley Film Festival** (phone 383 5256 for more details).

Larkspur is less visited, even though it is at the end of the ferry line. Stop at the **Lark Creek Inn** (234 Magnolia Avenue; 924 7766), an understated, charming Victorian house that offers great home-made butterscotch pudding. Watersports equipment sales, rentals and lessons are available at **Sausalito Sailboards, Inc** (2233 Larkspur Landing Circle; 331 9463). Apart from the **Larkspur Landing** shopping centre and a first-rate pub, the **Marin Brewing Company** (*see chapter* **Bars**), the only other reason to come here is to visit someone in **San Quentin Prison** or to see the prison museum, located about three-quarters of a mile east along Sir Francis Drake Boulevard.

Angel Island & Sausalito

You can catch a ferry to **Angel Island**, the largest island in the San Francisco Bay. The **Visitors Center** (435 1915) documents the use of the island from the Civil War to World War II. There are a number of excellent trails and many great picnic spots where you can escape the crowds. On the island, the Angel Island Company rents mountain bikes for $9 an hour, $25 for a full day. *See chapter* **Sightseeing** for more details.

The southernmost Marin town of **Sausalito** may not be as quaint as its reputation claims, but it is undeniably picturesque, with a maze of tiny streets stretching from the shoreline up to US 101 far above. Charming bungalows, well-kept gardens and bougainvillea-covered fences characterise the area, one best appreciated on foot. Originally a fishing village, Sausalito is jam-packed with tourists during the summer, but

reclaims its waterfront in winter. A population of artists and writers help support the fair number of coffee shops, waterfront restaurants and galleries. Some live in the collection of houseboats a little north of town.

The commercial district of Sausalito largely straddles **Bridgeway**, though some diners and shoppers are lured to **Caledonia Street** one block inland. Along North Bridgeway, opposite Spring Street, is the turnoff for the **Bay Model Visitors Center** (*see chapter* **Museums & Galleries**), a scale model of the San Francisco and San Pablo Bays. Despite its chilly waters, Sausalito is a centre for bay kayaking and windsurfing. A tiny beach is the launching pad for such watersports. To get a sense of the old Sausalito, stop for a cocktail or meal at **Casa Madrona** (801 Bridgeway; 332 0502), a part-Victorian, part-modernised, luxurious inn that rambles down hill from Bulkley Street to downtown Sausalito.

For more information on Sausalito, contact the **Sausalito Visitors Center** on the fourth floor of the Village Fair Shopping Center, 777 Bridgeway (open Tue-Sun; 332 0505). Take the Alexander Avenue exit from US 101 north.

Tiburon

Across Richardson Bay is Tiburon, where a tiny old-fashioned downtown area brings daytrippers over on the ferry from San Francisco. If you're driving, park your car in any one of the parking lots on Tiburon Boulevard and continue the rest of the way on foot (if you're biking, the bike path brings you directly into town). There aren't a lot of tourist attractions; most people come to eat at the restaurants and take in the views. Sip a margarita and admire the vista from the patio at the Mexican restaurant **Guaymas** (5 Main Street; 435 6300). **Sam's Anchor Café** (27 Main Street; 435 4527) is excellent for Sunday brunch: sit out on the waterfront deck, order a Bloody Mary and watch the boats. The shops and galleries on **Ark Avenue** will definitely make a dent in your savings.

If you want to see the lie of the land from above, try an excursion with **San Francisco Seaplane Tours** (332 4843), a great way to get your bearings among the bridges, islands, peninsulas and waterfronts of the Bay Area. The company flies out to the coast, over the Golden Gate Bridge and along the San Francisco waterfront, a trip that's especially romantic at sunset.

Marin County is dissected from north to south by **US 101**, which runs virtually the length of California. It may be the most popular route for public transport, but it's boring. The other main road is the California State Highway, Hwy 1 (SR 1) – also known as the Coast Highway or Shoreline Highway – which leads out of Mill Valley, skirts the lower elevations of Mount Tamalpais and turns north at

Muir Beach. For the fully fledged trip over Mount Tam, take the **Panoramic Highway**, a beautiful two-lane spur with lots of hairpin bends leading through sun-dappled forests to the coast at Stinson Beach. From either Highway 1 or Panoramic, you can reach the turn-off to Marin's main attraction, **Muir Woods**. The Panoramic Highway leads past a number of trailheads, some of them near the **Mountain Home Inn** (810 Panoramic Highway, Mill Valley; 381-9000), a good stop for coffee, lunch or an overnight stay.

Mount Tamalpais & Muir Woods

Visible from as far away as Sonoma, **Mount Tamalpais** soars to nearly 800 metres (2,600 feet). Its dramatic rise is so steep it seems to be far taller. The 550-acre surrounding park contains some of the most majestic groves of redwoods in the world. It dominates and defines recreational life in southern and central Marin County. **Mount Tamalpais State Park** covers some 2,511 hectares (6,200 acres). The roads that snake over Mount Tamalpais are great for bicycling (the mountain bike was invented here), but unless you are a marathon athlete, don't expect to cover much ground. You can take bicycles on the ferries as well as on some of the buses run by Golden Gate Transit.

The coast redwoods growing at **Muir Woods** ($2 admission) are mostly between 500 and 800 years old and as tall as 72 metres (236 feet). The shade cast by these giant *sequoia sempervirens* creates excellent hiking on some 10 kilometres (six miles) of trails

(a short path is accessible to the disabled). **Redwood Creek** is lined with oak, madrone and buckeye trees, wild flowers (even in the winter), ferns and mushrooms. Deer, chipmunks and a variety of birds are frequently sighted in the sun-dappled spaces beneath the redwoods. Complete with gift shop and toilets, the visitors' centre at **Muir Woods National Monument** is open daily. Park rangers organise walks through the woods; call the ranger station (388 2595) for a schedule.

From Muir Woods, you can drive or bike to the coast and head on north from Muir Beach. The delightful Tudoresque **Pelican Inn** (Hwy 1, at Pacific Way; 383 6000) is a good place to re-fuel and could have been transplanted straight from Surrey. The pub's terrace and lawn make it an attractive lunch spot in good weather. Wash down a plate of fish and chips with a pint of British beer and ask about their overnight rates.

The Panoramic Highway rejoins Hwy 1 at **Stinson Beach**. Stinson is the closest you'll get to the Northern California version of the classic beach life popularised by surfers and sun worshippers. If you want to ride the waves, you can rent open-top kayaks at **Off the Beach Boats** (868 9445).

Just 5.3 kilometres (3.3 miles) north of the sole stoplight in Stinson Beach is the **Audubon Canyon Ranch** (4900 Hwy 1; 868 9244), a 405-hectare (1,000-acre) preserve on the shore of the Bolinas Lagoon. Headquartered in a nineteenth-century white frame house, Audubon Canyon Ranch houses environmental exhibits and a wonderful natural history bookshop located in an old

Whale watching at **Point Reyes Lighthouse**. *See page 232.*

milking barn at the back. The ranch is open at the weekends from mid-March until mid-July. Donations are welcome. The **Alice Kent Trail** leads a short way up to an observation point where telescopes are mounted for viewing the egrets and great blue herons that nest nearby.

Point Reyes

North of Stinson Beach at Olema is the turn-off for the **Point Reyes National Seashore**. This vast peninsula, now protected by federal law, is an unforgettable refuge with fresh sea winds, wild animals, sea mammals, incredible waterfowl, waterfalls, of unspoiled beaches, a highly variegated terrain and campsites. Call the **Visitors Center** (663 1092) for trail maps, camping permits, the latest weather information and tips on fishing, clamming and horse riding.

At Point Reyes, head west to **Drakes Beach**. About six miles north is **Point Reyes Lighthouse**, where there are a number of trails, including the popular **Chimney Rock**. The lighthouse sits at the top of the Point Reyes peninsula, and is the perfect spot for whale watching. If you want to bathe, bypass the beaches of this windswept coast and head along **Tomales Bay** on the eastern edge of the peninsula. Tiny beaches like **Heart's Desire** offer mild tides and water that's not *that* cold.

Outside Point Reyes, hikers flock to **Mount Wittenberg**, where miles of hiking and riding trails criss-cross the mountain, and chaparral, wildlife and fog are facts of life. There are excellent vantage points here and elsewhere for sighting migrating pacific grey whales off the coast during winter, as they pass on their round trip from Alaska to Baja California. A lighthouse stands on a dramatic promontory, and the **Miwok Indian Village** is nearby.

The 1,134-hectare (2,800-acre) **Samuel P Taylor State Park** (488 9897) has 60 campsites and 75 picnic sites, and is located less than three miles west of the town of **Lagunitas**. Book a campsite in advance through Destinet on 1-800 444 7275 (1-619 452 8787 from outside the US).

Getting There

By Car
Sausalito is 13km (8 miles) and **Muir Woods** 24km (15 miles) from San Francisco.

By Bus
Golden Gate Transit buses link the city to Marin County. For **Marin Headlands**, take Golden Gate Transit bus 2, which leaves from Pine and Battery Streets and from the Golden Gate Bridge Toll Plaza Mon-Fri; on Sundays you can take Muni bus 76 from Market and Montgomery Streets.

For **Sausalito**, Golden Gate Transit bus 10 leaves from the Transbay Terminal, Civic Center and the Toll Plaza (every half-hour Mon-Fri, every hour Sat, Sun).

There's no direct public transport to **Muir Woods**; you'll have to get on a tour or hire a car. Golden Gate Transit bus 63 takes you to trailheads during the weekend. It's a long bike ride to the coast, but if you go around the mountain, via Sir Francis Drake Boulevard, you'll see a lot of fabulous scenery. Bus 63 also stops at **Stinson Beach**, the **Bay Area Discovery Museum**, and **Audubon Canyon Ranch**.

To get to **Point Reyes**, take Golden Gate Transit bus 24, which leaves from Market and Mission Streets.

By Ferry
Golden Gate Transit ferries (923 2000) depart from the Embarcadero Ferry Building and travel north to **Sausalito** and **Larkspur** (on separate schedules) daily, with more trips on weekdays than at the weekend or on holidays. The Sausalito ferry takes about 30 minutes to cross the bay and is one of the best cheap thrills in the Bay Area. The lower deck is better in bad weather, but on most days you should ride on the top deck for unsurpassed views of the San Francisco waterfront, the Golden Gate Bridge and Alcatraz Island. The boat docks in downtown Sausalito, close to the shops and restaurants.

Blue & Gold Fleet Ferries (705 5555/recorded information 773 1188) runs ferries from Pier 41 near Fisherman's Wharf to **Sausalito** and **Angel Island** and from the Ferry Building on the Embarcadero to **Tiburon** and Vallejo, home of Marine World/Africa USA. The **Angel Island-Tiburon Ferry** (435 2131) runs a ferry from Tiburon to Angel Island ($6 return).

Wine Country

It's hard to believe that 'the Wine Country' (the Napa and Sonoma vineyards) is only an hour's drive or so north-east of San Francisco and can be visited in a day. Travelling there is almost like visiting another country. This region often makes for romantic weekend retreats, but avoid going in summer, when the temperatures soar and tourists come in droves, driving up accommodation prices. Off-season discounts are available in autumn and spring, when it is more peaceful.

Sonoma County

At 4,138 square kilometres (1,600 square miles), Sonoma County is larger than the entire state of Rhode Island, so touring it all can take days. The three major areas are the **Sonoma Valley**, which runs about 37 kilometres (23 miles) north from San Pablo Bay; the **Alexander Valley/Dry Creek** area east and north-west of Healdsburg; and the **Russian River Valley**, which stretches west from US 101 along the river towards the ocean. Unlike Napa, most of the wineries in Sonoma that offer free tastings are off the beaten track; be prepared to explore.

One of the principal attractions of a Sonoma wine tour – besides the wine itself – is driving along winding roads with sweetly rural views of vineyards and farms. The **SCWA – Sonoma County Wineries Association** (1-800 939 7666/1-707 586 3795) – is located near US 101 in Rohnert Park, one of the few towns with no wineries at all. The SCWA organises vineyard and winery demonstrations and daily tastings.

The Carneros district straddles southern Sonoma and Napa. Here you will find wineries such as the **Viansa Winery and Italian**

Deluxe dining

Bistro Don Giovanni
*4110 St Helena Highway, at Salvador Avenue, Napa
(1-707 224 3300).*
A lively Californian version of an Italian bistro serving
rustic dishes. Call ahead to ask for the table outside next
to the fireplace. About $30 a head for dinner.

Brix
*7377 St Helena Highway, off SR 29, Napa (1-707 944
2749).*
One of the hottest restaurants to open recently in the Napa
Valley. High ceilings with light pouring through expansive windows, and a menu that fuses East and West ($40
for dinner). Popular.

Catahoula Restaurant & Saloon
*1457 Lincoln Avenue, between Fairway and
Washington Street Calistoga (1-707 942 2275).*
Part Cajun, part Californian, but mostly American cook-
ing: try cornmeal fried catfish or Mardi Gras slaw.
Averages $35 for dinner. Closed on Tuesdays.

Domaine Chandon
*1 California Drive, Yountville (1-800 736 2892/1-707
944 2892).*
Classical French cooking, excellent wines (as you might
expect) and an expansive view of the Wine Country.
Expensive (over $60 for dinner), but worth it.

The French Laundry
*6640 Washington Street, at Creek Street, Yountville
(1-707 944 2380).*
An idyllic rustic setting and renowned French cuisine.
Like anything deluxe, it's expensive. Prix fix menus at
$44, $55 and $80.

The Greystone Restaurant at CIA
*2555 Main Street, at Pratt Street, St Helena (1-707
967 1010).*
The emphasis is more on the wine than on the food, but
who can blame them since the place is in the beautifully
restored Greystone winery. The tapas menu isn't bad.

Terra
*1345 Railroad Avenue, off Main Street, at Adam
Street, St Helena (1-707 963 8931).*
East-West cooking brought to the Wine Country by husband-and-wife team Hiro Sone and Lissa Doumani. One
of the best restaurants in the Napa Valley. Expect to pay
around $45 a head.

Tra Vigne
*1050 Charter Oak Avenue, at SR 29, St Helena (1-707
963 4444).*
Eat Cal-Ital food on the outside terrace with a fountain
trickling in the background. Like being on holiday in Italy.
Averages $28 for lunch, $35 in the evening.

Marketplace (25200 SR 121, Sonoma; 1-707 935
4700). A scion of one of the state's oldest wine families, Sam Sebastiani and his wife Vicki built a
Tuscan-style winery on a knoll facing the Sonoma
Valley. Their spacious tasting room also sells
Italian foodstuffs and the picnic tables outside,
beneath trellises, overlook the Sonoma Valley.

The town of **Sonoma** was founded in 1823 as
the Mission San Francisco Solano, the last and
northernmost of the Franciscan missions. It developed around a Mexican-style plaza and, in 1846,
was where the Bear Flag was raised to proclaim
the independent Republic of California (*see chapter* **History**). The plaza is now flanked by adobe
and Western-style false-fronted buildings, housing restaurants, bookshops, barbershops and plenty of places to grab picnic supplies, including a
cheese factory and a bakery. The square has lots
of shady trees and a dozen or so picnic tables. A
good stop for children is **Sonoma Train Town**
(1-707 938 3912), about a mile south of the plaza,
which offers a 20-minute ride on a miniature steam
train past scale models of buildings, a petting zoo
and a couple of waterfalls.

The **Sonoma Valley Visitors Bureau** (453
First Street East; 1-707 996 1090) distributes leaflets
on walking tours of the historic downtown area.
Among the landmarks are the whitewashed adobe
Sonoma Mission (1-707 938 9560, open 10am-5pm
daily) on West Spain and First Streets, which served

as a Mexican outpost in the seventeenth century.
Now restored, it houses a variety of relics. **Sonoma
State Historic Park** includes the Mission build-
ing as well as the Toscano Hotel and the Sonoma
Barracks where the troops under the control of
Mexican General Mariano G Vallejo were stationed.

The history of Sonoma is intertwined with that
of the Californian wine industry, which began here.
Hungarian count Agoston Haraszthy planted the
first European grapevines in Sonoma in the 1850s
at **Buena Vista Carneros Winery and Vineyards** (18000 Old Winery Road, Sonoma;
1-800 926 1266). The winery is open to the public.

Most vineyards offer complimentary tastings of
four different wines. Some charge for additional
samples or for older vintages. Of the 35 wineries in
the Sonoma Valley, several are near the Sonoma
Plaza. A great picnic choice is **Bartholomew Park
Winery** (1-707 935 9511), which has a museum and
a relief map dedicated to the appellation. The **Wine
Exchange of Sonoma** (452 First Street East; 1-800
938 1794) offers up to 15 Californian and European
wines (plus beers) for tasting daily.

The villages of **Kenwood** and **Glen Ellen** north
of Sonoma would be hard to find, were it not for the
presence of some of the best wineries. Jack London
– adventurer, farmer and one of the most prolific
authors of his day – made his home in Glen Ellen. A
mansion full of memories and the charred remains
of Wolf House make **Jack London Historic State**

Park (1-707 938 5216) one of the valley's top attractions (*see also chapter* **Literary San Francisco**). It's a nice place to stroll in the shade among oak and madrone trees. Near the entrance to the park, the **Sonoma Cattle Company** (1-707 996 8566) leads guided tours of the area on horseback.

One of the most popular stops in Kenwood is the **Kenwood Winery**, at SR 12 and Warm Springs Road, Kenwood (1-707 833 5891). The site's original barn, now the tasting room and shop, dates from the pre-Prohibition days of the early 1900s. This friendly, classic Sonoma winery is known for making wine with grapes grown on Jack London's former ranch.

The **Kenwood Inn** (10400 SR 12, Kenwood; 1-707 833 1293) is new and elegant, and has various spa services and a pool. For excellent value, try the **Sonoma Hotel** (on the Plaza at 110 West Spain Street and First Street West; 1-707 996 2996).

Napa County

Napa Valley wines are the number one attraction in this county, with food a close second. Besides sipping and dining, there's fishing and boating on remote **Lake Berryessa**, horse riding, bicycling, or riding the rails. The **Napa Valley Wine Train** (*see p237* **Getting Around**) runs daily lunch and dinner trips up and down the valley. The best way to get an overview is from a hot air balloon, a thrilling pre-dawn experience that demands several rolls of film and a mastery of any fear of heights. For a more down-to-earth look, several companies offer horse riding tours of the area.

Originally, Napa was populated by the Nappa Indian tribe; after Europeans had settled the area, Charles Krug introduced grapes into the valley in 1861. The 40-kilometre (25-mile) long **Napa Valley**, running almost parallel to the Sonoma Valley on the other side of the Mayacamas Mountains, is the heart of the Napa wine industry. SR 29 runs up the middle and is usually crowded because the largest wineries are found on it. Boutique wineries are mostly to be found on the **Silverado Trail**, or on one of the lanes that crisscross the valley, or along a winding road up one of the many hillsides.

For a complete listing of wineries, pick up a map at any one of the vineyards en route. The **Robert Mondavi Winery** (7801 St Helena Highway, Oakville; 1-800 666 3284) is a good bet for first-time wine tasters. Visit the historic German mansion of the **Beringer Wine Estates** (2000 Main Street, St Helena; 1-707 963 7115) or sample champagne at **Domaine Chandon** (1 California Drive, Yountville; 1-707 944 2280). It offers one of the best tours, with clear explanations of their fine sparkling wines, created using the *méthode champenoise*.

For information on places to stay in Napa, contact **Napa Valley Reservations Unlimited** (1-800 251 6272/1-707 252 1985): rooms get booked up quickly. A top-end hotel with many services and amenities is the **Auberge du Soleil** (180 Rutherford Hill Road, Rutherford; 1-707 963 1211), worth reserving for very special occasions. A contemporary B&B with fabulous views and moderate rates is the **Cross Roads Inn** (6380 Silverado Trail, Napa; 1-707 944 0646). But probably the best value in the valley is the **Vintage Inn** (6541 Washington Street, Yountville; 1-707-944-1112), which has great looking rooms and is located close to shops and restaurants.

For more information, call the **Napa Valley Conference and Visitors Bureau** (1-707 226 7459) or the **Napa Chamber of Commerce** (1-707 226 7455).

Calistoga & Healdsburg

More than any other town in the wine country, **Calistoga** looks Western: it's got saloons and a wide main street often festooned with banners promoting beer tastings or mustard festivals or other celebrations of the California good life. At the end of the avenue is a **glider port** (Calistoga Gliders, 1546 Lincoln Avenue; 1-707 942 5000) where gliders take off on sightseeing tours of the surrounding countryside. From the silent, winged craft, you can see much of the Napa Valley and the forested mountains that flank it.

Dioramas depicting nineteenth-century Calistoga life, along with photos and other artifacts, are displayed in the **Sharpsteen Museum** (1311 Washington Street; 1-707 942 5911). A mile north of town, on Tubbs Lane, **Old Faithful** geyser erupts about every 15 minutes. Water comes from an underground river and heats to around 177°C (350°F) before spewing high into the air. Another quirk of nature is the **Petrified Forest**, eight kilometres (five miles) west on Petrified Forest Road. Finally, the **Bale Grist Mill State Historic Park** on SR 29 near Calistoga is a good place to stop for a picnic.

Several wineries are located in and around Calistoga. People get a kick out of the tram ride up to **Sterling Vineyards** (1111 Dunaweal Lane, Calistoga; 1-707 942 3300). Famous for its Cabernet Sauvignon as well as its white wines, this hilltop winery has commanding views of the countryside and an excellent self-guided tour. **Château Montelena** (1429 Tubbs Lane, Calistoga; 1-707 942 5105) is an 1882 château overlooking a Chinese garden complete with lake, tea houses, bridges and an ancient Chinese junk. A charming example of a small, family-owned winery is the **Wermuth Winery** (3942 Silverado Trail, Calistoga; 1-707 942 5924).

Robert Louis Stevenson, who honeymooned near here, included some of his experiences in *The Silverado Squatters*. The **Robert Louis Stevenson State Park** (1-707 942 4575) is 11 kilometres (seven miles) north of Calistoga on SR 29. The **Silverado Museum** (1490 Library Lane, St

Helena; 1-707 963 3757) in nearby St Helena contains memorabilia of the author (*see also chapter* **Literary San Francisco**).

For accommodation, try **The Pink Mansion** (1415 Foothill Boulevard; 1-707 942 0558), an elegant restored mansion, offering in-house wine tastings. The **Mountain Home Ranch** (3400 Mountain Home Ranch Road; 1-707 942 6616) is a secluded resort, with all the amenities: swimming pools, tennis and volleyball courts, fishing and hiking trails.

For more information on Calistoga, contact the **Calistoga Chamber of Commerce** (1458 Lincoln Avenue, suite 4, Calistoga; 1-707 942 6333).

The town of **Healdsburg** is like a miniature Sonoma, with an unusual number of good restaurants and boutiques for its size, and an enviable location at the intersection of three wine valleys – Alexander, Dry Creek and Russian River. A much cooler wine growing region than Sonoma Valley, the **Russian River Valley**, which runs west towards the coast, is criss-crossed by several tiny roads, including Westside Road, which runs along the river for a distance through towns so small most don't even have stop signs. The largest, **Guerneville**, is popular for river rafting and as a summer resort for San Francisco's gay community.

The Russian River is also a good bet for fishing. There are bait shops in Guerneville and Healdsburg (you need a licence to fish in California, obtainable from most fishing and camping shops). On the coast, just north of the mouth of the Russian River and the town of Jenner, lies **Fort Ross State Historic Park** (1-707 847 3286), originally settled by Russian colonists in 1812. Open 10am-4.30pm daily, it has a visitors centre, an extensive park and beach access.

Vineyards to visit include sparkling wine and brandy maker **Korbel** (13250 River Road, Guerneville; 1-707 887 2294); where there is also a micro brewery, picnic grounds, a deli and rose gardens. Family-owned winery **Martinelli** in Windsor (3360 River Road; 1-800 346 1627/1-707 525 0570) has a gift shop and art gallery.

If you need somewhere to stay, try the **Camellia Inn** (211 North Street, Healdsburg; 1-707 433 8182). This Italianate Victorian inn near the heart of town is elegant but friendly, and the proprietor makes his own award-winning wines on the premises. Prices are moderate to expensive. For more information and a further list of places to stay in the area, contact the **Russian River Region Visitors Bureau** (1-800 253 8800/1-707 869 9212).

Mendocino County

Built on a wide bluff that juts out into the ocean, the picturesque town of **Mendocino** has the most dramatic views of any of the northern coastline. The quickest route is via the inland US 101 (about three hours from San Francisco), but the twisting coastal Hwy 1 with its small towns is more fun:

The rugged coastline near **Mendocino**.

take a detour to **Point Arena Lighthouse** for a spectacular view across the ocean.

The old-fashioned town of Mendocino is characterised by New England-style houses and clapboard churches. B&Bs and quaint inns have the monopoly on accommodation. **The Mendocino Hotel** (45080 Main Street; 1-707 937 0511/1-800 548 0513) is a luxury establishment. Filled with beautiful antiques, the **John Dougherty House** (571 Ukiah Street; 1-707 937 5266) looks as though it has been transplanted out of New England. Built in 1882, **The Mendocino Village Inn** (44860 Main Street; 1-707 937 0246) is more understated and very cosy.

Mendocino State Park (1-707 937 5397) is ideal for hiking, tide-pooling and whale watching. **Van Damme State Park** (1-707 937 4016) just south of Mendocino is covered with redwood trees, and popular for camping. There are several hiking trails through fern canyons and pygmy forests. **Russian Gulch State Park** (1-707 937 5804) just north of Mendocino, is famous for the **Devil's Punch Bowl**, a blowhole that sends the surf shooting skyward.

Travelling further away from San Francisco, California has plenty of other wine regions to explore. Amador County in the Sierra foothills (off SR 88) is home to some of the oldest vineyards in California (*see page 244* **The Gold Country** for the surrounding area). Further south along the

coast towards Los Angeles, Santa Barbara County – with the Santa Ynez and Santa Maria Valleys – also has its fair share of prominent wineries. For more information on this and trips in Southern California, consult the *Time Out Los Angeles Guide*.

Getting There

By Car
The Wine Country is roughly an hour by car (71km/44 miles) over the Golden Gate Bridge along **US 101**. Turn off at Ignacio on to **SR 37** and then take **SR 121** north. Once here, **SR 12** points you towards **Sonoma**, **SR 29** towards **Napa**. Though traffic can be hellish, particularly over the Golden Gate Bridge, travelling by road is the best way to get to the wine country.

To reach **Calistoga**, continue on **SR 29**, which turns into **SR 128**. To reach **Healdsburg** (119km/74 miles from San Francisco), stay on **US 101**.

To reach the town of **Mendocino** (233km/145 miles up the coast from San Francisco) take **US 101** north as far as Cloverdale, then take **SR 128** west, which joins up with **Hwy 1** at the coast.

By Bus
Golden Gate Transit operates buses as far north as Petaluma: bus 80 goes to Petaluma and bus 90 to Sonoma, (stopping at San Rafael on the way). Within the county, **Sonoma County Area Transit** and **The Vine**, Napa's bus service, provide local transport. Several San Francisco operators run Wine Country tours: for more information, contact the Visitor's Information Center in San Francisco or a local tourist office.

You can also take **BART** to El Cerrito, then Vallejo Transit bus 80 to Vallejo and then bus 10 to Napa. Phone the **Napa Valley Transit Authority** (1-707 255 7631) for more information. **Greyhound** runs daily buses from San Francisco to Napa. There are no buses to Healdsburg or Mendocino.

Getting Around

By Balloon
This is one of the best ways to see the wine country. Several companies offer packages, such as flights for two with champagne, or balloon, brunch and lodging at a local hotel and spa. In Sonoma, try **Sonoma Thunder** or **Wine Country Balloon Safaris** (in fact, the same company: 1-800 759 5638/1-707 829 7695/1-707 538 7359). In Napa, try the **Bonaventura Balloon Company** (1-800 359 6272) or **Balloon Aviation** (1-707 944 4400).

By Train
For a different kind of vineyard tour in the Sonoma Valley, try a horse-drawn carriage with **Wine Country Wagons** (1-707 833 1202) or the **Napa Valley Wine Train** (1-800 427 4124).

Heading South

Leaving San Francisco behind and heading south, you'll notice a change of scenery as well as a change of pace: from the bustling city to rolling hills full of artichokes, beautiful rugged beaches full of surfers and beach combers, and sleepy towns full of ramshackle barns and country stores.

A window on the world of nineteenth-century colonial life at **Fort Ross State Historic Park**. *See page 235.*

Half Moon Bay

Half Moon Bay, just off Hwy 1 and about 30 minutes from San Francisco, is a small, easygoing seaside town with a rural feel, famous for growing Hallowe'en pumpkins and Christmas trees. There are a couple of golf courses, riding stables, bike paths and beaches. Main Street is filled with bookstores, boutiques, health-food stores, flower gardens and antique shops. Stay at the **San Benito House** (356 Main Street; 1-650 726 3425), a hotel in a restored building in the heart of town. **The Cypress Inn** (407 Mirada Road; 1-650 726 6002) is a romantic hideaway, and each room has a fireplace and a private deck that overlooks the ocean.

Half Moon Bay is known as an agricultural region and worth exploring. May and June are the best months for foraging along the farm trails that dot the surrounding countryside. Worth a visit is the **San Georgio General Store**, just 13 kilometres (eight miles) south of Half Moon Bay on SR 84. This funky store has been serving the local farming community since 1889, selling everything you'll ever need from cast-iron pots and pans to second-hand books, antiques and music.

A string of beaches stretches down the coast between Half Moon Bay and Pescadero, including the popular **Half Moon Bay State Beach**. Probably the best of the lot is **San Gregorio State Beach**, a strip of white sand distinguished by sedimentary cliffs and a proximity to the nude beach further north. If you feel like taking horses out for a an hour-long trip along the coast, call **Sea Horse Ranch and Friendly Acres Ranch** (1828 Cabrillo/Hwy 1; 1-650 726 8550); they offer beach rides for all levels of ability.

For more information on **Half Moon Bay State Parks**, contact the district office (95 Kelly Avenue, Half Moon Bay; 1-650 726 8820) or the **Half Moon Bay Chamber of Commerce** (520 Kelly Avenue; 1-650 726 8380).

Just north of Half Moon Bay, **Princeton-by-the-Sea** is a lofty name for a tiny town and a great little harbour. It's a place for aimless ambling and perhaps lunch at a laid-back restaurant. **Barbara's Fishtrap** (281 Capistrano Road; 1-650 728 7049), by the harbour, has great local fish and seafood. The **Pillar Point Inn** (1-650 728 7377) opposite is a charming inn with snappy nautical décor and large breakfasts in a building overlooking the harbour.

A little further south, you can soak up the atmosphere of **Pescadero** at **Duarte's Tavern** (202 Stage Road; 1-650 879 0464), this little town's most celebrated saloon for over a century. The crab sandwiches have made them famous, and the bar is a friendly place for a drink. **Phipps Ranch** (2700 Pescadero Road; 1-650 879 0787) sells berries and other fruit and vegetables throughout the year, which can be eaten on the ranch at picnic tables or packed into your car.

*The coastal path between **Monterey** and **Pacific Grove**. See page 243.*

Getting There

By Car

Half Moon Bay and Princeton are about a 30-minute drive south of San Francisco on **Hwy 1**. Pescadero is another 15 minutes south, signposted off **Hwy 1**.

By Bus

SamTrans (1-800 660 4287) buses travel between Half Moon Bay, Pacifica and the Daly City BART Station, among other points.

Santa Cruz

Originally established as a mission and still recovering after extensive damage suffered from the Loma Prieta earthquake in 1989, this quintessentially quirky California beach town is known for being easygoing and politically progressive. The home of the University of California at Santa Cruz, it has a young population that keeps things lively, as well as plenty of longtime residents who are fiercely protective of the town's liberal heritage.

A hybrid of tacky and nostalgic (but mostly just tacky), the **Santa Cruz Beach Boardwalk** (400 Beach Street; 1-408 423 5590) offers 27 different rides, including bumper cars and tilt-a-whirls, a rambling arcade with games, shops and fast food joints. The Giant Dipper, a classic wooden roller coaster has been proclaimed a National Historic Landmark, along with the nearby 1911 carousel.

The town's popularity as a beach resort dates back to the mid-nineteenth century. The small **Surfing Museum** (1-408 429 3429), located on Lighthouse Point, contains old photographs and vintage boards that tell the story of the sport that has become an entrenched part of the Santa Cruz scene. **Steamer Lane** is right outside the lighthouse and is considered one of the best surfing spots in California. The boardwalk and **Coconut Grove Ballroom** (1-408 423 2053), remnants of the town's turn-of-the-century heyday, still come into their own at weekends, when a mixture of big bands and local rock and pop groups play.

Santa Cruz's **Pacific Garden Mall** is slowly recovering from the 1989 quake. All that remains of the **Mission de Exaltacion de la Santa Cruz** (1-408 425 5849), is the current replica, built in the 1930s, though the **Mission Adobe** (off Mission Plaza) is one of California's few original adobes. Built in 1929, the **Santa Cruz Museum of Natural History** (1-408 429 3773) contains information on the Ohlone Native Americans who originally populated the area.

For accommodation, the **Babbling Brook Inn** (1025 Laurel Street; 1-800 866 1131/1-408 427 2456) is a luxurious bed-and-breakfast set in wooded grounds in the heart of town. If you want a family atmosphere, stay at **Terrace Court** (125 Beach Street; 1-408 423 3031), where some of the rooms have kitchenettes. It's opposite the wharf. If you'd rather stay away from the bustle, the **Davenport**

*The stone church and tranquil gardens of **Carmel Mission**, built in 1797. See page 243.*

Cash Store Bed and Breakfast Inn (32 Davenport Avenue; 1-408 425 1818), has beautiful ocean views and access to the beach.

The redwood forests, perched on the hills surrounding Santa Cruz, are ideal for hiking and biking. Explore the **Big Basin State Park** (1-408 338 8860) and **Henry Cowell State Park** (1-408 335 4598). Just south of Santa Cruz, you can visit the **Forest of the Nisene Marks** (1-408 763 7063) to see the ruins of a Chinese labour camp, as well as the epicentre of the Loma Prieta earthquake.

There are two dozen wineries in the Santa Cruz area, without the crowds of Napa. **Bargetto Winery** (3535A North Main Street, Soquel; 1-408 475 2258) is casual and widely known for its fruit wines, including olallieberry and apricot. The staff are helpful and sell gourmet food to complement their selection. If you haven't filled up yet, head to **India Joze** (Art Center, 1001 Center Street; 1-408 427 3554) for delicious Middle Eastern and Indian cooking, and then onto the **Santa Cruz Coffee Roasting Company** (1330 Pacific Avenue; 1-408 459 0100) for a cup of joe. For more information on Santa Cruz, contact the **Santa Cruz County Conference and Visitors Council** (701 Front Street; 1-408 425 1234).

It's understandable that Santa Cruz and **Capitola** (which bills itself as the oldest Pacific seaside resort) have been overrun. Capitola boasts some good eateries, with very low prices: **Dharma's Natural Foods** (4250 Capitola Road; 1-408 462 1717) may be the oldest veggie restaurant in the US and **Mr Toot's Coffeehouse** (221 Esplanade; 1-408 475

3679) is an earthy hangout full of people slouching around on sofas listening to live jazz.

The village of **Aptos**, further down the coast, offers two of the best beaches in the region, **Rio del Mar** and **Seacliff**. It is also a good back-up choice for lodging on popular weekends such as the **Great Monterey Squid Festival** in late May: the cry of the wild calamari is a siren song for thousands of fans of this delectable treat, which is served in local restaurants during a long weekend of music and entertainment. On a similarly wild note, Aptos is also home to an endangered colony of long-toed salamanders. It also boasts the **World's Shortest Parade**, usually held on the weekend closest to 4 July.

Getting There

By Car

Santa Cruz is 119km (74 miles) south of San Francisco: about two hours' drive down **Hwy 1**. Capitola and Aptos are a few miles further south.

By Train

CalTrain leaves San Francisco from two stations (Fourth/King Streets and 22nd/Pennsylvania Streets) every half hour. Take the train to San Jose Amtrak station, from where a shuttle bus goes to Santa Cruz.

Monterey Peninsula

Jutting into the Pacific between the fun-loving town of Santa Cruz and the dramatic coastline of Big Sur, the Monterey Peninsula is one of the best attractions on the coast. Writers and artists, including

There's plenty to keep you amused on **Monterey State Beach**.

Spas & retreats

Spas and retreats have become the ultimate Californian experience, an everyday part of the therapeutic lifestyle: fix the body (goes the logic) and you fix the mind. So join 'em and you too can wallow in a hot tub or a mud bath – or simply wallow in self-satisfaction. For opening hours and directions, contact the individual resorts.

Calistoga got its name in the mid-1800s, when San Franciscan Sam Brannan created a resort near St Helena Mountain. Instead of proclaiming that the spa would be 'the Saratoga of California' (referring to the New York resort), Brannan quipped it would be 'the Calistoga of Sariforna'. The volcanic ash from neighbouring St Helena mountain is the magic ingredient in the mud baths that draw the health-conscious as well as the plain curious to Calistoga.

Dr Wilkinson's Hot Springs (1-707 942 4102/6257) is the grand-daddy of the mud bath spas. Old and comfortable, the place has an excellent reputation, drawing indulgent, self-pampering souls from all over the world who come for the ambiance, the reasonable rates and simply to mellow out.

There's a school of massage and an educational centre at **Harbin Hot Springs** (*pictured*) (1-800 622 2477/1-707 987 2477), a 470-hectare/ 1160-acre property located in the shadow of Mount Harbin in Lake County, but most people think of Harbin as a spa resort. Today it's is run by the Heart Consciousness Church, and you'll find a small theatre, organic vegetable gardens and a vegetarian restaurant here, as well as enough hiking trails to make your legs cry for mercy. Harbin is a good place to discard inhibitions about public nudity; it's *the* thing here, and while it's not mandatory, some people do begin to feel self-conscious in their clothes. There's a massage pavilion where you can get rubbed down in the great outdoors.

If you want a spa retreat but don't want a long drive or the high prices of Wine Country getaways, head to **Claremont Resort and Spa** (1-510 549 8566). In summer, when the city is blanketed in fog, this East Bay haven basks in sunshine and visitors soak up the rays alongside the enormous outdoor pool. Services include mud body wraps, glycolic acid treatments, waxing, a hair salon, tennis, swimming and fitness programmes.

Five kilometres (three miles) south of Julia Pfeiffer Burn Park in Big Sur is a sign on the right that directs you to the **Esalen Institute** (1-408 667 3000). A world-famous institution – which was at one time a whacked-out hippie colony – Esalen was one of the first places to introduce Gestalt theory in the late 1960s; today its self-help workshops are the draw. The Esalen's hot springs are only open to the public at 1am, and you'll need to make a reservation (1-408 667 3047). Experience late-night bathing (clothing optional), and you'll be hooked.

Simone de Beauvoir, Robinson Jeffers, Jack Kerouac and Henry Miller, have been drawn to the area for decades. The **Monterey Jazz Festival** (information 1-408 373 3366), held each September, and the **Monterey Bay Blues Festival** (information 1-408 394 2652), held at the end of June, draw the top names in jazz and blues. The area is perhaps best known for its spectacular golf courses, fishing and cycling.

The three major cities are Carmel, where Clint Eastwood completed a stint as mayor, Monterey, and Pacific Grove. **Carmel** is a love-it-or-hate-it sort of place. Secluded and populated by artists and craftspeople, it is also chock-full of mediocre (and expensive) shops. Much of it looks like a particularly picturesque film set, with perfect ginger-bread or fake adobe mansions discreetly tucked away in leafy groves leading down to the ocean. The beach is a fantastic white crescent of sand, but not suitable for swimming. **Ocean Avenue** is Carmel's main shopping street, with antique shops, art galleries, boutiques and a tea shop that's straight out of Disney's *Snow White and the Seven Dwarfs*. There are several good restaurants. **Carmel Mission** (3080 Rio Road; 1-408 624 3600), is a baroque stone church built in 1797, three museums, beautiful gardens and shouldn't be missed. For hikers and bikers, visit the **Mission Trail Park** just across the street. And then, of course, there's the sporty **Hog's Breath Inn** (San Carlos Street, between Fifth and Sixth; 1-408 625 1044) which is owned by Dirty Harry himself.

Just south of Carmel Highlands is one of the most beloved parks in California, **Point Lobos**. You can spend an entire morning or even a whole day exploring its nooks, crannies, beaches and awesome promontories.

The capital of Alta California during Spanish, Mexican and American governments, **Monterey** is one of the state's most historic cities. Popular spots include **Colton Hall**, where California's first constitution was written (in 1849) and the **Monterey State Historic Park** (1-408 649 7118), seven acres containing various artifacts relating to the area's architecture and history. **Jacks Regional Park** (1-408 647 7795), just 16 kilometres (ten miles) south, provides an escape from the tourists and traffic of downtown Monterey.

But the city's best attraction is undoubtedly the **Monterey Bay Aquarium** (886 Cannery Row; 1-408 648 4800, open 10am-6pm daily). Its gorgeous, labyrinthine display of undersea forests, marine life, tide pools and special exhibits are a treat. Even the gift shop deserves some serious browsing. If you

A long and winding road: head north along dramatic **Highway 1** *to find breathtaking coastal views.*

can, time your visit to coincide with one of the regularly scheduled feeding times of the sea otters. The aquarium is located on **Cannery Row**, a neighbourhood made famous by native son John Steinbeck. Today, alas, it's full of tacky shops and disappointing restaurants housed in canneries that were abandoned in the 1940s when the commercial sardine population was fished out.

Monterey is also a wine-producing region, known for its Chardonnay. Stop in at the **Bargetto Winery** (700 Cannery Row; 1-408 373 4053) and take a detour upstairs to the **Paul Masson Museum and Wine Tasting Room** (1-408 646 5446). **Monterey Wine Associates** (PO Box 1793, Monterey, CA 93942; 1-408 375 9400) provides a free map with information on 25 local wineries.

Just two miles west of Monterey is the much prettier small town of **Pacific Grove**, founded in 1875 as a camping retreat for the Methodist Church. Its best-known lodging site, the **Asilomar Conference Center** (800 Asilomar Boulevard; 1-408 372 8016), has an ascetic ambience that characterises the entire town. **Asilomar State Park** (1-408 372 4076) is a great venue for a picnic; for an evening romantic rendezvous, stop at **Lover's Point Beach**. Check out the butterfly tree at the **Pacific Grove Museum of Natural History** (1-408 648 3116). And as the sun sets, enjoy a to-die-for dessert at the **Old Bath House Restaurant** (620 Ocean View Boulevard; 1-408 375 5195) and take in the spectacular view. Another good bet is **Gernot's Victoria House Restaurant** (649 Lighthouse Avenue; 1-408 646 1477), wonderful but more expensive.

Pacific Grove makes a good base for exploring the surrounding coast. For lodging, try the **Gosby House** (643 Lighthouse Avenue; 1-408 375 1287) or the **Green Gables Inn** (104 Fifth Street; 1-408 375 2095), both cute B&Bs in great locations.

Pacific Grove's undeveloped shoreline, carpeted with native plants, is a wonderful place to stroll unhampered by throngs of frisbee players and picnicking families. **The Point Pinos Light Station** (1-408 648 3116), the oldest operating lighthouse on the coast, is one of dozens of older structures still in good repair. The **17-Mile Drive** from Pacific Grove through Pebble Beach takes you past some of the most famous and challenging golf courses in the country; but you have to pay for the privilege. Walk along the coastal path from Pacific Grove instead: the views are as good, and it's free. **Roy's at Pebble Beach** (The Inn at Spanish Bay, 2700 17 Mile Drive; 1-408 647 7423) is a good place to stop for a bite after 18 holes or a few hours behind the wheel.

For more information, contact the **Monterey Visitors Center** (401 Camino El Rey, at Del Monte Boulevard, open daily) or the **Pacific Grove Chamber of Commerce** (584 Central Avenue, Pacific Grove; 1-408 373 3304).

Getting There

By Car

Monterey is 214km (133 miles) – about 2¹⁄₂ hours by car – from San Francisco on **Hwy 1**.

By Train

Take **CalTrain** to San Jose Amtrak station, where a local bus connects with Monterey. **Amtrak** runs the Coast Starlight Train along the coast, stopping in San Jose, Salinas and Monterey.

By Bus

Greyhound buses connect San Francisco with Los Angeles, with regular services to Monterey via Salinas. Although there is local transit, this area is best explored by car.

Big Sur

The coastline from Carmel to San Simeon continues to prove a spectacular journey, and there are plenty of pull-outs along the rugged coast on Hwy 1 from which to take in the views.

The **Point Sur Lighthouse State Park** (1-408 625 4419), about 19 miles south of Carmel, is a historic lighthouse maintained by the Coast Guard and can only be visited as part of a tour. **Andrew Molera State Park** is a coastal sanctuary for seabirds. **Pfeiffer Big Sur State Park** (1-408 667 2315) is on the east side of Hwy 1, and is most popular for camping and hiking, especially in the summer. Pfeiffer Ridge and Pfeiffer Falls are worth checking out; Pine Ridge trailhead is also a favourite. The **Julia Pfeiffer Burns Park** (also 1-408 667 2315) offers camping and a large selection of hiking trails. The best trail is to the McWay Creek which pours 21 metres (70 feet) down to the ocean.

The town of **Big Sur** is about 25 miles south from Carmel; stop by the **Big Sur Station**, about half a mile south from Julia Pfeiffer park (1-408 667 2423), for information and maps on hikes and places to go. The solitude of Big Sur attracted writer Henry Miller to the region in the 1940s. He wrote of the land as a place where 'extremes meet in a region where one is always conscious of the weather, of space, of grandeur, of eloquent silence'. You can visit the **Henry Miller Memorial Library** (1-408 667 2574) located in the former home of artist Emil White. The **Coast Gallery** (1-408 667 2301), about three miles south, also has a collection of the author's lithographs.

Most people camp in this area, but the **Big Sur Lodge** (1-408 667 2171/www.bigsurlodge.com) is a rustic spot nearby, where many of the cottage-style rooms have kitchens and fireplaces; don't miss their fresh-baked pies. The **Deetjen Big Sur Inn** (1-408 667 2377) offers a hearty breakfast. **Nepenthe Restaurant** (1-408 667 2345) was once the haunt of Elizabeth Taylor and Richard Burton and still has views to die for (the food's not bad, either). The **Post Ranch Inn** (1-408 667 2200) and the **Ventana Inn** (1-408 667 2331) across the street compete for matching views and matching prices, so take your pick; you won't be disappointed. On Saturday nights, locals head to **River Inn** (1-408 667 2700) to listen to jazz and the **Big Sur Pub** (1-408 667 2355) sometimes hosts mariachi bands or guitarists.

For more information on Big Sur, call the **Big Sur Chamber of Commerce** (1-408 667 2100). For state park campground reservations, call **Desinet** (1-800 444 7275).

Heading East

The Gold Country

The Gold Rush of 1848-9 beckoned thousands of adventurers to seek their fortune. Most of the early pioneers came through Sutter's Point, which grew into **Sacramento**, California's state capital. It was the centre for the Pony Express and the western terminal for the transcontinental railroad, and much of the history is preserved in the city's many museums. East of Sacramento is the 350-square mile Gold Country itself, a stretch of quirky old mining towns, ideal for a driving trip.

The residents in the tiny gold rush town of **Downieville** like to hang out and chat, and chairs filled with locals passing the time of day line the sidewalk. The old gallows still stands next to the jail. Back in the old days, **Placerville** was known as Hangtown, and the town's staple oyster omlette is still known as the Hangtown Fry. Check out the **El Dorado County Historical Museum** (1-916 621 5865; open Thur-Sat 10am-4pm, noon-4pm Sun) and take a self-guided tour of the tunnels of the old **Goldbug Mine** (1-916 642 5232; for guided tours, call 1-916 642 5238).

James Marshall first discovered gold in **Coloma** in 1848. You can visit the **Gold Country Museum** and the **Bernhard Museum** (both 1-916 889 6500), origmnally built as a museum in 1851, located further north in **Auburn**. Among the most reasonably priced bed-and-breakfasts in the area is **Lincoln House** (191 Lincoln Way, Auburn; 1-916 885 8880).

The rolling countryside to the south is more refreshing, and the town of **Jackson** has a number of reasonable lodgings and is a good base for this stretch of a tour. Mark Twain penned his famous short story *The Celebrated Jumping Frog* in **Angels Camp**, and you can visit the cabin where he wrote it. To get a real feel for the Gold Country, head for **Columbia State Historic Park** in Columbia. Visit the **St Charles Saloon**, stay at the **Fallon Hotel** (1-209 532 1470) or the **City Hotel** (1-209 532 1479). You can hop a stagecoach, hire a horse from the **Columbia Stageline and Riding Stable** (1-209 532 0663) or take a trip with **Hidden Treasure Gold Mine Tours** (1-209 532 9693).

The town of **Sonora** is at the junction of SR 49 and SR 108, and is a little more populated than the other communities. Just south of Sonora the movie *High Noon* was filmed in **Jamestown**, which is the home of **Railtown 1897 Historic State Park** (1-209 984 3953).

A weekend guide in the Friday edition of the *Sonora Union-Democrat* in the south Gold Country and *The Nevada Country Voice* in the north offers information on local events. For details about the many music festivals in the area, call the **Tuolumne County Visitors Bureau** (55 West Stockton; 1-800 446 1333/1-209 533 4420).

Getting There

By Car

I-80 runs east-west through Sacramento, and I-5 runs north-south. You don't need a car in Sacramento, but exploring the Gold Country by car is the way to go. **SR 49** is the Gold Country backbone, with Placerville dividing the north from the south.

By Train

Amtrak serves Sacramento, but to explore the tiny towns spread out along route 49, you'll need to travel by car. Amtrak's Coast Starlight Train connects the area with San Francisco.

By Bus

Sacramento is the hub for **Greyhound** buses travelling throughout the state; the company serves most of the region, though its schedule to the Gold Country is infrequent.

Lake Tahoe

At the eastern border of California is **Lake Tahoe**, drawing millions of visitors each year to its natural beauty. No one knows how deep the lake actually is; locals call it Big Blue. Flanked by snow-capped peaks most of the year, the lake has become the Californian playground for skiing, waterskiing, fishing, hiking and legal gambling at a number of casinos that line the main drag in **Stateline**, just over the state border in Nevada (the state line cuts north-south through the centre of the lake).

The north end of the lake is a three-and-a-half hour drive from San Francisco (longer if there's heavy snow on I-80, in which case you'll need chains). The other route, via US 50 (which branches from I-80 at Sacramento), leads to the south shore, where hotels are usually packed, either with skiers or gamblers. From March to early November, it's easy to drive the 116-kilometre/72-mile perimeter of the lake (much of it is serviced by public transport). On the California side are attractions such as **Sugar Pine Point State Park** (1-916 525 7982), near **Meeks Bay**, and **Emerald Bay State Park** (1-916 541 3030), a little further south, which overlooks the bay of the same name.

There are plenty of beaches around the lake: **Sand Harbour**, **Zephyr Cove** and **Camp Richardson** are all on the water. Fed by snow and surrounded largely by mountains, Lake Tahoe is comfortable for swimming only in August and September, when the water has warmed slightly. One way to get out on the lake is to book a cruise on the *Tahoe Queen* paddlewheeler out of South Lake Tahoe (1-916 541 3364). Daily scenic cruises as well as dinner-dance cruises are available on this and several other tour boats. The **North Lake Tahoe Chamber of Commerce** (245 SR 28, Tahoe City; 1-916 581 6900) has information on guided tours and where to rent canoes and kayaks.

If you want to hit the slopes, **Squaw Valley** (1-916 583 6985), site of the 1960 Winter Olympics, and **Alpine Meadows** (1-800 441 4423/1-916 583 4232/snow conditions recorded message 1-916 581 8374) are two of the most popular ski areas in the west. Alpine is a bit more family-oriented, while Squaw is glitzier and has more exciting runs. Other ski areas include **Boreal** (1-916 426 3666) whose lower prices attract snowboarders; **Northstar at Tahoe** (1-916 562 1010), which offers excellent beginner slopes; and **Sugar Bowl** (1-916 587 1369), where there's a creaky old gondola that takes you to the base lodge. **The Ski Club Hotline** (1-510 827 4303) has information on Bay Area ski clubs. Ski rentals are available at the resorts, but if you're driving, its cheaper to rent your gear in San Francisco and avoid the queues. **Heavenly Valley**'s ski lifts operate for sightseeing in summer (1-916 541 7544).

The **Tahoe North Visitors and Convention Bureau** (1-800 824 6348) has information on where to stay in the north, from resorts to country inns, motels and condo referrals. You'll also find an abundance of cheap motels on the South Shore. Try **Camp Richardson** (2100 Jameson Beach Road, South Lake Tahoe; 1-800 544 1801/1-916 541 1801), whose lakefront cabins and hotel rooms appeal to an active young crowd, and where prices are fairly moderate. The **Kirkwood Ski and Summer Resort** (1-800 967 7500), 56 kilometres (35 miles south) of Lake Tahoe, is a family-oriented resort with many amenities and moderate prices. For more information, contact the **South Lake Tahoe Chamber of Commerce** (3066 Lake Tahoe Boulevard; 1-916 541 5255).

Truckee, an Old West town about 19 kilometres (12 miles) north of the lake, has board sidewalks and wood-frame shop fronts that make it look like a backdrop for a John Wayne film – if it wasn't for the tourist trade and growing number of bars and restaurants. **The Passage** at the **Truckee Hotel** (1007 Bridge Street; 1-916 587 7619) offers wonderful Californian food in a pretty, candlelit dining room. The inn itself offers quaint rooms at moderate prices. **The Squeeze Inn** (10060 Commercial Row; 1-916 587 9814) is a very popular local spot, and its omelette breakfasts are delicious.

Donner Memorial State Park (1-916 582 7894), a few miles west of Truckee off SR 80, is named after the Donner family, a pioneer party who perished trying to cross the pass in the winter of 1842. The visitor's centre has a short movie detailing their grisly fate (they ended up eating each other).

Getting There

By Car
It takes 3½ hours to reach Lake Tahoe from San Francisco, traffic permitting. To reach the north shore, follow **I-80** over the Bay Bridge, all the way to Truckee; then take **SR 89** to Tahoe City. To reach the south shore, take **I-80** as far as Sacramento and then turn off onto **US 50** to South Tahoe. For an update on road conditions, phone 557 3755.

By Air
Reno Canyon International Airport, 93km (58 miles) north-east of the lake, is served by several airlines. The **Tahoe Casino Express** (1-800 446 6128) offers daily scheduled transport to South Lake Tahoe.

By Train
There is an **Amtrak** station in Truckee (1-916 587 3822).

By Bus
Greyhound buses stop in Truckee, South Lake Tahoe and Reno (Nevada).

Getting Around

By Balloon
For a bird's-eye view of the area, a trip with **Mountain High Balloons** (locations in Truckee and Tahoe City; 1-888 462 2683/1-916 587 6922) takes you soaring over the Sierras in style, and includes a champagne celebration on landing.

Yosemite

It's enchanting, beguiling, intoxicating, stunning, breathtaking – the descriptions of **Yosemite** are as superlative as they are numerous. The National Park stretches for more than 3,108 square kilometres (1,200 square miles) of lush forests, alpine meadows, sheer granite cliffs, undisturbed wildlife, hiking trails and campsites. Touristy, 32 kilometre- (20-mile) long **Yosemite Valley** is packed with traffic, especially in the summer, but its views are indisputably spectacular. For non-valley sites, head for **Crane Flat** and **Tuolumne Meadows** (via SR 120), **Glacier Point** (near **Badger Pass**) and the **Hetch Hetchy Reservoir** (north of **Big Oak Flat**). They are most easily accessible from the hiking trials. If you can, avoid visiting in high summer. Spring finds the wildflowers in bloom and in winter the untamed majesty of the snow-capped peaks is awesome; many have been famously captured by photographer Ansel Adams – but remember that much of the park is inaccessible during the winter months.

Yosemite is all about views: as you drive into the valley, **El Capitan** is the first dramatic sight,

a sheer rock wall 914 metres (3,000 feet) above the valley. You'll get a bird's eye view from **Glacier Point** and a spectacular view of the Sierras from **Tunnel View**. **Mist Trail** is the most popular hiking trail: it's a five-kilometre (three-mile) round-trip to Vernal Falls and an 11-kilometre (seven-mile) round trip to Nevada Falls. Standing beneath the pounding water of Yosemite Falls is heart-stopping, and an ambitious hike is the round-trip to the top (just under seven miles) – **Yosemite Point**. The hike to Glacier Point is just as challenging, but you can also drive there.

For further information on lodging, camping supplies and grocery shops in Yosemite, contact the visitor centres in **Yosemite Valley** (1-209 372 0299; open daily 8.30am-3.30pm) and **Tuolumne Meadows** (1-209 372 0263; opening hours vary). If you're planning on hiking, you'll need a free wilderness permit, which can be picked up at either visitor centres. The **Park Information Service** (1-209 372 0265) can answer all questions about Yosemite. The **Yosemite Association Book-store** (1-209 379 2646) has maps, books and suggested hiking routes.

Getting There

By Car
There are three routes to Yosemite: **SR 41** from the south; **SR 140** from the west; and **SR 120** from the north-west. SR 120 (the Tioga Road) is the only road across the park and is closed in winter (usually Nov-May) due to snow. The recommended entrance to the park is SR 140: from San Francisco, take **SR I-580** east to **I-205**, and connect to **SR 120** and then **SR 140**. In winter, you'll need to have snow chains for your car; allow four hours in summer, five in winter. Once you reach Yosemite, kiosks and park rangers are stationed at each entrance. Gas is available all year round; if you need service, call the **Yosemite Village Garage** (1-209 372 1221).

By Bus
There is no direct public bus service to Yosemite from San Francisco. However, several companies run private tours, including **Gray Line Tours** (558 9400), which offers one-day ($130) and three-day tours and **Incredible Adventures** (1-800 777 8464/759 7071; $75 one-day, $169 three-day). **Greyhound** has buses to Merced, from where you can get a **Via Adventures** bus (1-209 722 0366) to Yosemite.

By Train
Amtrak leaves from San Francisco each morning to Merced and Fresno, from where you can catch a bus (*see above*).

Getting Around

By Car
SR 120 runs the entire east-west length 97km (60 miles) of the park, climbing up to 3,031m (9,945ft) at Tioga Pass (the highest automobile pass in California).

By Shuttle
Free shuttle buses operate throughout the year. The most popular is the **East Valley Loop**, which runs about every 10 minutes.

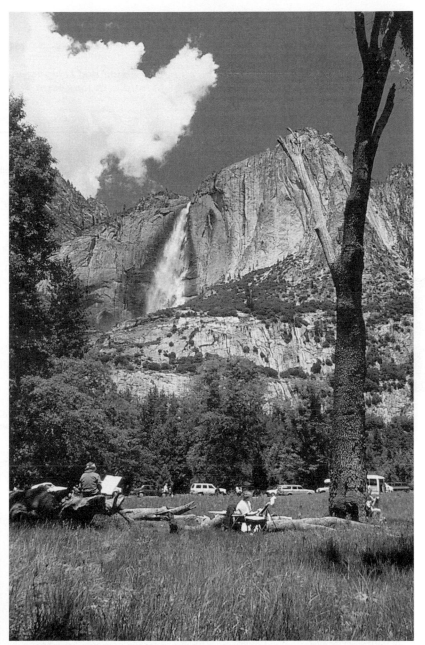

Awe-inspiring Yosemite: unmissable, though much of it is inaccessible during the winter.

Directory

How to cope with customs and the climate, tipping and telephones, plus useful names and addresses that will help with long-term survival in the city.

Essential Information

For information on abbreviations used in this guide, *see page vi* **About the Guide**.

If you're phoning from outside San Francisco, dial 1 then area code 415 before the numbers listed in this guide, unless otherwise stated. All 1-800 numbers can be called free of charge, although many hotels add a surcharge for use of their phones, whatever number you call.

Visas

Under the Visa Waiver Program, citizens of the UK, Japan, Australia, New Zealand and all West European countries (except for Portugal, Greece and the Vatican City) do not need a visa for stays in the United States of less than 90 days (business or pleasure) – as long as they have a passport that is valid for the full 90-day period and a return ticket. An open standby ticket is acceptable.

Canadians and Mexicans do not need visas but must have legal proof of their residency. All other travellers must have visas. Full information and visa application forms can be obtained from your nearest US embassy or consulate. In general, send in your application at least three weeks before you plan to travel. Visas required more urgently should be applied for via the travel agent booking your ticket.

For information on student visas, *see page 263* **Resources**.

US Embassy Visa Information Line

(Recorded information in the UK 0891 200 290).

Immigration & Customs

Standard immigration regulations apply to all visitors, which means you may have to wait (up to an hour) when you arrive at Immigration. During your flight, you will be handed an immigration form and a customs declaration form to be presented to an official when you land.

You will be expected to explain the nature of your visit. Expect close questioning if you are planning a long visit and don't have a return ticket or much money with you. You will usually be granted an entry permit to cover the length of your stay. Work permits are hard to get, and you are not permitted to work without one (*see page 263 for details*).

US Customs allow foreigners to bring in $100 worth of gifts ($400 for returning Americans) before paying duty. One carton of 200 cigarettes (or 100 cigars) and one litre of liquor (spirits) is allowed. No plants, fruit, meat or fresh produce can be taken through customs. For more detailed information, contact your nearest US embassy or consulate.

Any questions you could have about United States immigration policies or laws can be answered by calling the **Immigrant Assistance Line** (543 6767 Spanish/ English; open 9.30am-5pm Mon-Fri).

Emergencies

Ambulance, Fire Brigade or Police
Dial **911** (toll-free from any phone booth).

Pacific Gas and Electric Company (PG&E)
(Emergency service 1-800 743 5000/ information hotline 1-800 743 5002). **Open** 24 hours daily.

Poison Control Center
(1-800 523 2222). **Open** 24 hours daily.

Water Department City & County of San Francisco
(Emergency service 550 4911). **Open** 24 hours daily.

Insurance

It's advisable to take out comprehensive insurance cover before arriving: it's almost impossible to arrange in the US. Make sure that you have adequate health cover, since medical expenses can be high. *See page 261* **Health & Medical** for a list of San Francisco hospitals and emergency rooms.

Money

The US dollar ($) equals 100 cents (¢). Coins range from copper pennies (1¢) to silver nickels (5¢), dimes (10¢), quarters (25¢) and half dollars (50¢). Paper money (or bills) comes in denominations of $1, $5, $10, $20, $50 and $100, which are, confusingly, all the same size and colour. A few $2 bills and $1 coins are in circulation, but are rare. Small shops will rarely break a $50 or $100 bill.

Banks & Bureaux de Change

Most banks are open from 9am to 6pm Monday to Friday and a few are open on Saturday for limited hours. You need identification, such as a driver's licence with photo or a passport, to change travellers' cheques. Many banks do not exchange foreign currency, so it's a good idea to arrive with some US dollars. If you're scheduled to arrive in San Francisco after 6pm, change money at the airport or, if you have US dollars travellers' cheques, buy something in order to get some change. If you want to cash travellers' cheques at a shop, ask first – some require a minimum purchase. You can also obtain cash on a credit card account from certain banks; check with your credit card company before you leave, and be prepared to pay interest rates

that vary daily. Most banks and shops accept travellers' cheques in US dollars.

ATMs

San Francisco is brimming with Automated Teller Machines (ATMs or cashpoints). Most accept Visa, MasterCard and American Express, among others, if they have an affiliated PIN number. There is a usage fee, of course, although the convenience of cash-on-demand often makes it worth the price.

Phone the following numbers for ATM locations: **Cirrus** (1-800 424 7787); **Wells Fargo** (1-800 869 3557); **Plus System** (1-800 843 7587). If you don't remember your number or have somehow de-magnetised your card, most banks will dispense cash to card holders. Try **Wells Fargo** (765 4511), which offers advances at any of its branches.

Credit Cards

You are strongly advised to bring at least one major credit card or you will find yourself strangely handicapped in San Francisco. Credit cards are accepted (and often required) at nearly all hotels, car rental agencies and airlines, as well as most restaurants, shops and petrol stations.

The five major credit cards accepted in the US are **Visa**, **MasterCard**, **Discover**, **Diners Club** and **American Express**.

Lost or Stolen Credit Cards

American Express Card
(1-800 992 3404).

Diners Club
(1-800 234 6377).

Discover
(1-800 347 2683).

MasterCard
(1-800 826 2181).

JCB
(1-800 366 4522).

Visa
(1-800 336 8472).

Lost or Stolen Travellers' Cheques

American Express
(1-800 221 7282).

Visa
(1-800 227 6811).

Exchange Offices

American Express Travel Services
455 Market Street, at First Street (536 2600). BART Montgomery, Embarcadero/Muni Metro F, J, K, L, M, N/bus 2 to 7, 12, 15, 21, 31, 42, 66, 71, 76. **Open** 8.30am-5.30pm Mon-Fri; 9am-2pm Sat. **Map H3**
American Express will change money and travellers' cheques and offers, for AmEx card holders only, a poste restante service. Call for details of other branches within San Francisco.

Thomas Cook
75 Geary Street, between Grant Avenue and Kearny Street (1-800 287 7362). Muni Metro F, J, K, L, M, N/bus 2, 3, 4, 30, 45, 76. **Open** 9am-5pm Mon-Fri; 10am-4pm Sat. **Map H3**
A complete foreign exchange service is offered here, including money transfer by wire.
Branches (all 1-800 287 7362): Pier 39, Building M, Level 2, Unit M-10; Bank of America, 1 Powell Street, at Market Street.

Western Union
Phone 1-800 325 6000 to find your nearest branch.
The old standby for bailing cash-challenged travellers out of trouble. Expect to pay a whopping 10%-plus commission.

Postal Services

Most post offices are open from 9am-5.30pm, Monday to Friday, with limited hours on Saturday. Phone **1-800 275 8777** for information on your nearest branch and mailing facilities. Stamps can be bought at any post office and also at some hotel receptions and vending machines.

Poste Restante
(General Delivery)

Civic Center, 101 Hyde Street, San Francisco, CA 94142 (1-800 275 8777). BART Civic Center/Muni Metro J, K, L, M, N/bus 5, 9, 19, 42, 47. **Open** 10am-2pm Mon-Sat. **Map G4**

If you need to receive mail in San Francisco and you're not sure where you'll be staying, have it posted to the General Post Office at the above address. Mail is kept for 10 days from receipt and you must present some photo ID to retrieve it.

Western Union

(1-800 325 6000). **Open** 24 hours daily.

Telegrams are taken over the phone and charged to your phone bill (not available from pay phones). You can also get advice on how to get money wired to you and where to pick it up at one of a dozen San Francisco locations. You can wire money to anyone outside the state over the phone, using your Visa or MasterCard.

Disabled Access

Despite its challenging topography, San Francisco has made its mark as a highly accommodating city for disabled travellers. In fact, California is the national leader in providing the disabled with access to facilities and attractions. Privileges include unlimited free parking in designated (blue) parking stalls and free parking at most metered spaces (a visible blue and white disabled 'parking placard' is required), and special prices and arrangements for train, bus, air and sightseeing travel.

In addition, all public buildings within the city are accessible to wheelchairs and have wheelchair-accessible toilets; most city buses can 'kneel' to make access easier and have handgrips and spaces designed for wheelchair users; most city street corners have ramped kerbs, and most restaurants and hotels are either designed (or have been redesigned) to accommodate wheelchairs.

Of course, what a building is supposed to have and what it really has can be two different things, so the wheelchair-bound traveller's best bet is to contact the **Independent Living Resource Center** on 863 0581. For helplines for the disabled, *see page 260* **Disabled Information**.

Electricity

Throughout the United States, electricity voltage is 110-120V 60-cycle AC. Except for dual-voltage, flat-pin plug shavers, you will need to run any European appliances via an adaptor, available at airport shops, pharmacies and department stores.

Time & Dates

San Francisco is on **Pacific Standard Time**, which is three hours behind Eastern Standard Time (New York) and eight hours behind Greenwich Mean Time (Britain). Daylight Savings Time (which runs almost concurrent with British Summer Time) runs from the first Sunday in April to the last Sunday in October, when the clocks are rolled ahead one hour. Going from the west to east coast, Pacific Time is one hour behind Mountain Time (Arizona to Alberta), two hours behind Central Time (Texas to Manitoba) and three hours behind Eastern Time.

In the US, dates are written in the order of month, day, year: therefore 2.5.98 is the fifth of February, not the second of May.

Safety

Crime is a reality in all big cities, but San Franciscans generally feel secure in their town and follow one basic rule of thumb – use common sense. If an area doesn't feel safe to you, it probably isn't. Don't flaunt purses, shopping bags or cameras, avoid walking through dark streets and alleys and try not to look too much like a gullible tourist.

Areas where you should be particularly alert, especially at night, include the Tenderloin (around Civic Center); SoMa (especially around Sixth Street); Golden Gate Park; lower Haight Street (east of Fillmore Street); Mission Street from 13th to 22nd Streets; and in Hunter's Point, the neighbourhoods near 3Com (formerly Candlestick) Park. Many tourist areas are sprinkled with the city's

Liquor laws

California has strict drinking laws forbidding any bar, restaurant, nightclub or store from selling alcohol to minors (under-21s). Even if you look 30, bring ID with you (preferably a driver's licence with photo or passport) if you plan to drink – many nightclubs check ID as house policy. Minors are allowed in some clubs that serve alcohol, but it's a good idea to phone first to check.

A major *faux pas* is having any 'open container' in your car or any public area that isn't zoned for alcohol consumption. Cops will give you a ticket on the spot for walking down the street with a beer in your hand, or even having an empty beer can on the back seat of your car. You don't want to know what happens if you're busted driving drunk, so don't do it.

homeless (the Union Square shopping area, for example), who beg for change but for the most part are harmless.

If you are unlucky enough to be mugged, your best bet is to give your attacker whatever he wants (which is why you're carrying travellers' cheques and small amounts of cash, right?), then call the police from the nearest pay phone by dialling 911. Don't forget to get the reference number on the claim report for insurance purposes and travellers' cheques refunds. If you are the victim of a sexual assault and wish to make a report, call the police, who will escort you to an Emergency Room for a check-up. For helplines serving crime or rape victims, *see page 262* **Helplines & Agencies**.

see page 262

Smoking

Smokers are not particularly welcome in San Francisco, which has some of the stiffest anti-smoking laws in the US (and probably the world).

There is no smoking in lobbies, banks, public buildings, sports arenas, elevators, theatres, restaurants that don't have bars, offices, stores and any form of public transport. Many small hotels and bed-and-breakfast inns don't allow you to light up either (and, boy, do they get cross if you do).

Telephones

The phone system in San Francisco – and the entire US – is reliable and, at least for local calls, cheap. Americans love their phones, and thanks to the boom in cellular communication, are rarely seen without one stuck to their dashboard or stuffed into their pocket. Tourists, however, will have to rely mostly on public pay phones, which are scattered throughout the city, usually within a block of wherever you

Tourist information

Visitor's Information Center

Lower level of Hallidie Plaza, corner of Market and Powell Streets (391 2000). BART Powell Street/Muni Metro J, K, L, M, N/bus 6, 7, 8, 9, 21, 26, 27, 31, 66, 71. **Open** 9am-5.30pm Mon-Fri; 9am-3pm Sat; 10am-2pm Sun. **Map G4**
You won't find any parking here, but you will find tons of free maps, brochures, coupons and advice. For a 24-hour recorded message listing daily events and activities or to request free information about hotels, restaurants and shopping, call 391 2001. Or send a postcard with your address to PO Box 429097, San Francisco, CA 94102, USA.

San Francisco Convention and Visitors Bureau

Suite 900, 201 Third Street, at Howard Street (974 6900). BART Montgomery/Muni Metro J, K, L, M, N/bus 12, 15, 30, 45, 76. **Open** 8.30am-5pm Mon-Fri. **Map H4**
Free information on life's essentials: hotels, restaurants and shopping.

Out of Town

Marin County Convention and Visitors Bureau

Avenue of the Flags, at Civic Centre Drive, San Rafael (472 7470). **Open** 9am-5pm Mon-Fri.
Covering Muir Woods and Mount Tamalpais State Park, Sausalito, Tiburon and Angel Island.

Oakland Convention and Visitors Bureau

Suite 3214, 550 Tenth Street, at Broadway, Oakland (1-510 839 9000). **Open** 8.30am-5pm Mon-Fri.
The centre is aimed at convention-goers but also at tourists. Museums, historical attractions and local events are listed in a free guide.

San Jose Convention and Visitors Bureau

150 West San Carlos Street, between Almaden Avenue and Market Street, San Jose (1-408 283 8833). **Open** 8am-5.30pm Mon-Fri; 11am-5pm Sat, Sun.
Provides information about the South Bay and Silicon Valley, for tourists and business people alike.

Directory

happen to be. Pay phones only accept nickels, dimes and quarters, but check to see if you get a dialling tone before you start feeding them your change. Local calls cost 20¢, and the price rises as the distance between callers increases (an operator or recorded message will tell you how much to add).

Long-distance, particularly overseas calls, are best paid for by visiting the AT&T calling centre listed below or with a rechargeable, pre-paid phonecard ($6-$35) available from large stores like Walgreens, which give you a fixed amount of time anywhere in the US – or less time internationally. You can also

use your MasterCard with AT&T (1-800 225 5288) or MCI (1-800 269 2255).

Directories are divided into Yellow Pages (classified) and White Pages (business and residential) listings. These directories are available at most public phones and in hotels. If you can't find one, dial directory assistance (411, free from a phone booth, but not from a private phone) and ask for your listing by name.

Operator assistance dial 0.
Emergency (police, ambulance, fire) dial 911.
Local directory enquiries dial 411.
Long-distance directory enquiries dial 1 + area code + 555 1212 (calls are free from pay phones).

San Francisco online

A selection of sites on the World Wide Web that relate to San Francisco and the Bay Area. Just a reminder – the best way to see San Francisco *isn't* sitting inside, staring at an online computer screen. For more on multimedia, *see* chapter **Media**.

Bay Area Backcountry
http://www.kerygma.com/bab/bab.html
Places to hike and camp in the San Francisco Bay Area.
Bay Area Transit Information
http://server.berkeley.edu/Transit/index.html
Instant online access to transit information.
Bay Guardian
http://sfbg.com/
The *Bay Guardian*'s homepage, updated weekly.
Burning Man
http://www.burningman.com/
Online guide, history and photos of the world's wackiest festival.
Cinema Guide
http://www.movietimes.com
Bay Area movie times, with film clips, previews, photos.
City Culture Magazine
http://www.cityculture.com
City arts online publication.
Classified Flea Market
http://www.cfm.com/
Searchable database published on Wednesdays, covering the Bay Area.
Concerts
http://www.sfbayconcerts.com
What's on at which Bay Area venue.
Craft & Folk Art Museum
http://www.folkart.com/~latitude/museums/m_sfcfam.htm
Contemporary craft, 20th-century folk art and traditional ethnic art in the Fort Mason Center.
De Young Museum and Palace of the Legion of Honor
http://www.thinker.org/index.html
Two museums and an image base.
Earthquakes
http://quake.wr.usgs.gov/recenteqs/
Current San Francisco and Northern California quake information.
Escape Artist Tours Inc
http://www.best.com/~travel/sf-escapes/
Provocative tours of the city, Napa Valley, Lake Tahoe and

surrounding Bay Area.
Exploratorium
http://www.exploratorium.edu/
An unmissable site from the hands-on science museum.
Film & Video Festivals
http://www.filmdependent.com/ssfests.html
Comprehensive guide to celluloid festivals, small and large, in SF and the Bay Area.
General Info
http://sfbay.yahoo.com/
An excellent online source, including restaurants, classifieds, traffic reports and an events calendar.
http://www.citysearch7.com/
Exhaustive, well-researched, daily-updated guide to SF, plus links to other North American city guides.
http://www.transaction.net/sanfran/ult/index.html
Easy-to-use general guide, with an alternative bent.
Hostels
http://www.hostels.com/us.ca.sf.html
A complete list of hostels in San Francisco, with prices, addresses and phone numbers.
Hotel Reservations
http://www.hotelres.com/
Where to make your hotel reservations online.
Hotels
http://www.ipp.com/bay/hotels.html
Exhaustive list of SF and Bay Area accommodation.
JetPack Magazine
http://www.jetpack.com/
Online publication with counterblasts from the SF counter-culture.
Lesbian and Gay Freedom Day Parade
http://www.sfpride.org
Info on the annual festival plus gay/lesbian tourist links.
Mexican Museum
http://www.folkart.com/~latitude/museums/m_mexsf.htm
Art and cultural institution in the Fort Mason Center.
Museum of the City of San Francisco
http://www.sfmuseum.org/
A scrapbook of the city's past.
Q San Francisco Magazine
http://www.qsanfrancisco.com/
Gay and lesbian publication.
Randall Museum
http://www.wco.com/~dale/randall.html
A must for kids.

Rock & Roll Digital Gallery
http://www.hooked.net/julianne/index.html
San Francisco rock concert posters from the 1960s to the 1990s.
San Francisco Ballet
http://www.sfballet.org/
Forthcoming productions and ticket information.
San Francisco Bay Area Ski Connection
http://www.jaws.com/baski/home.html
Online guide to skiing in Northern California.
San Francisco Bicycle Coalition
http://reality.sgi.com/employees/jonim_csd/SFBC.home/
Bicycling in SF, discussions and membership details.
SF Gate
http://www.sfgate.com
The combined San Francisco newspapers, the *Chronicle* and *Examiner*.
San Francisco 49ers
http://www.nfl.com/49ers/
Strictly for fans.
San Francisco 49ers Tickets and Packages
http://www.best.com/~travel/sf-49ers/
Packages or game tickets for home games.
San Francisco Giants
http://www.sfgiants.com/homepage.html
The virtual dugout.
San Francisco Opera
http://www.sfopera.com/
Season schedule, history, tickets and lots of photos.
San Francisco Public Library
http://sfpl.lib.ca.us/
With many additional local resources.
San Francisco Symphony
http://www.sfsymphony.org/
Forthcoming concerts, ticket info and musicians' profiles.
Theater
http://www.sfstation.com/theatre/index.htm
SF Station arts and entertainment server includes an excellent theatre section.
Time Out
http://www.timeout.co.uk
What's on in San Francisco and other world cities.
Weather
http://www.sfmuseum.org/alm/wx.html
Including an hourly-updated weather map.

Toll-free numbers generally start with 1-800, while pricey pay-per-call lines (usually phone-sex numbers) start with 1-900, so don't mix up the two.

Area Codes

San Francisco and Marin 415.
The peninsula cities 650.
East Bay (including Oakland and Berkeley) 510.
San Jose 408.
Wine Country 707.

International Calls

Dial 011 + country code
Foreign codes include UK 44;
Australia 61; New Zealand 64.
If you need assistance with international calls, dial 102 880 or 1-800 225 5288.

Direct Dial Calls

If you are dialling outside your area code, dial 1 + area code + phone number, and an operator or recording will tell you how much money to add.

Collect Calls

For collect calls or when using a phone card, dial 0 + area code + phone number and listen for the operator or recorded instructions. If you are completely befuddled, just dial 0 and plead your case with the operator.

AT&T Global Communication Center

170 Columbus Avenue at Pacific Avenue (693 9520). Bus 12, 15, 41, 83. **Open** 9am-6pm daily. **Credit** AmEx, Disc, MC, V. **Map G2**

Tipping

Besides millions in revenues, visitors to San Francisco bring a reputation as bad tippers. This is partly due to the differing customs abroad, and partly to the fact that many locals in service industries make their money from gratuities, a fact which has raised expectations and heightened awareness about them. Do your part to subvert the bad tip paradigm: in general, you should tip bellhops and baggage handlers ($1-$2 a bag); cabbies, waiters and waitresses, coiffeurs, and food delivery people (15-20% of the total tab); valets ($2-$3); and counterpersons (from 25¢-$1, depending on the size of your order). Most sit-down restaurants will automatically add 15% to a table of six or more diners; check your bill. If you get good service, tip fairly; if you get snubbed, leave little and tip the management – with words.

Getting Around

In a nation where the car is king and trains are those things you wait for at railroad crossings, San Francisco is something of an anomaly: it is one of the few cities in the United States where having a car isn't a necessity. In fact, a car is often more of a hindrance, which is why most locals leave theirs parked for weeks at a time and commute on foot, by taxi or via the city's much maligned yet indisputably reliable public transport system – the San Francisco Municipal Railway, usually known as Muni.

The best plan for finding your way around the city's transport network is to purchase a Muni map (available at most bookshops and drugstores, or free from the Market Street **Visitor's Information Center**, *see page 251).* Next to hoofing it, buses are the cheapest and easiest way to get around.
The city's famous cable cars, which rumble along at about a mile every 10 minutes, are mostly for entertainment and taxis never seem to be around when you need one. Cycling around San Francisco is an option but – be warned – you'll need super-human legs to cope with some of the steep hills.
TravInfo (817 1717), is a very useful information line for all forms of transport in the Bay Area.

To & From the Airports

San Francisco International Airport

For more information about how to get to and from San Francisco Airport, phone 1-800 736 2008.

By Bus

There are three main options for getting to and from the airport. The cheapest method (and least convenient) is by SamTrans **7F** and **7B** buses, which run every 30 minutes from the airport's upper level to the Transbay Terminal at First and Mission Streets. Bus 7B runs from 5.43am to 1.16am, costs $1, takes an hour and has no luggage restrictions. Bus 7F runs from 6.03am to 12.07am, costs $2.50 and takes 30 minutes, but you're restricted to only one small carry-on bag. Phone 1-800 660 4287 for more information.
There are also two more complicated but cheap routes. From outside the North and South terminals, catch a **3X** to Colma or **3B** bus to Daly City stations ($1) and then take a BART train to downtown San Francisco. Or take the free **CalTrain** shuttle from the North and South terminals to Millbrae Station and then a 24-minute train ride ($1.75) to the CalTrain Depot on Fourth and Townsend Streets in the Mission district (not recommended alone at night).

By Shuttle

A definite step up from bussing it is travelling by shuttle. Rates range from $10 to $15 per person and many offer door-to-door service, including **Lorrie's Airport Service** (334 9000), **SuperShuttle** (558 8500), **Bay Shuttle** (564 3400), **American Airporter Shuttle** (546 6689/282 8700), **Quake City Airport Shuttle** (255 4899) and **SFO Airporter** (major hotel service only; 495 8404). Ask about discounted rates for two or more travellers. Most shuttles depart every 10-15 minutes from the upper level of the airport terminal at specially marked kerbs – follow the red signs saying 'Bayporter, Lorrie's and American' and look for the red-capped Lorrie's representative, who co-ordinates all the shuttle services until 11pm; after 11pm, your best bet is to head for the United exit area. Shuttles run throughout the night but are few and far between, so if your plane arrives in the small hours, you might be faced with an expensive taxi ride. For your return journey to the airport, book the shuttle at least 24 hours in advance.

By Taxi or Limousine

The most expensive – but most convenient – option for getting into town may be your only recourse if your plane lands in the wee small hours. Expect to pay about $40 plus tip for the 14-mile trip to the city; be sure to haggle for a flat rate. Taxis are found at the lower level of the terminal in an area marked with yellow columns.

For limousine service, use the toll-free white courtesy phones located in the terminal or phone **Limousine 2000** (877 0333).

Oakland International Airport

Getting to San Francisco from Oakland International is simple. Take the **Air-BART** shuttle ($2; you'll need exact change for the ticket machines) from the airport terminal (they run every 15 minutes from the central island outside terminals 1 and 2) to the Coliseum/ Oakland BART station, and then catch the next **BART** train to San Francisco ($2.75); for schedule information phone 992 2278.

Other options include a shared-ride shuttle service via **SuperShuttle** (phone 558 8500 for a reservation) or a very expensive taxi or limo ride.

San Jose International Airport

Though it's 60 miles to the South, San Jose is increasingly becoming the destination of choice for many Silicon Valley travellers. It's a tiny, efficient airport; too bad that it's more than an hour from San Francisco.

To get to the city from SJIA, take the Santa Clara Transit bus **10** – which runs every 20-30 minutes from 5.45am to 9.49pm and costs $1.10 – to the Santa Clara CalTrain station, then board **CalTrain** to San Francisco – which runs from

4.51am to 10.05pm, takes about 80 minutes and costs $4.25 at peak hours. Disembark at the end of the line, the Fourth & Townsend station (not recommended alone at night). For more information about CalTrain, call 1-800 660 4287.

Don't take a taxi or limo to San Francisco from San Jose unless you're a wealthy multimedia tycoon.

(see page 251).

Major International Airlines

For domestic and other international airlines, consult the *Yellow Pages*.

American Airlines
(1-800 433 7300)
British Airways
(1-800 247 9297)
Continental Airlines
(1-800 525 0280)
Delta Air Lines
(1-800 221 1212)
Northwest Airlines
(domestic 1-800 225 2525/ international 1-800 447 4747)
Southwest Airlines
(1-800 435 9792)
Trans World Airlines (TWA)
(domestic 1-800 221 2000/ international 1-800 892 4141)
USAirways (USAir)
(1-800 428 4322)
United Airlines
(1-800 241 6522)
Virgin Atlantic
(1-800 862 8621)

Cable cars

Brought back to life in 1984 at a cost of more than $60 million, San Francisco's beloved cable cars are without question the most enjoyable ride in town, as the lengthy queues at the circular turnarounds will attest. There are 44 cable cars in all, 27 of them used at peak times, travelling a steady 9.5mph on three lines: California, Powell-Mason and Powell-Hyde. (The Powell-Hyde line has the most thrills, the best scenery and, consequently, the most tourists; board a few stops up from the turnaround if you don't want to stand in line.) Lines run from 6am to 1am. If you don't have a Muni pass, buy a $2 non-transferable one-way ticket from the conductor as you board the car (children under five go free). Cable car stops are marked by pole-mounted signs displaying the cable car symbol; their routes are marked on all Muni bus maps. Hold on tightly, or you're likely to get thrown about as the car lurches around a corner and down a precipitous hill.

Public Transport Information

For information on Muni's schedules, passes and fares, phone **673 6864** (and expect to be put on hold), or seek out one of the numerous glass-enclosed bus shelters throughout the city, which will have a basic schedule of routes and times posted inside. Much handier is having your own Muni map. More esoteric transportation questions can be answered at the Visitor's Information Center (*see page 251*).

Travel Passes

If you plan to use Muni often, buy a one-day ($6), three-day ($10), or seven-day ($15) 'passport', which is valid on all Muni vehicles, including the pricey cable cars.

One-day passports can be purchased from cable car conductors; and three- or seven-day passports are available at the Visitor's Information Center; Maritime Market (3098 Polk Street, at Bay Street); Muni headquarters (949 Presidio Avenue, at Geary Boulevard); the Muni ticket booth/police kiosk at Powell and Market

Streets; the Muni ticket booth at Hyde and Beach Streets, the Bay Area TIX booth at Union Square, and various other locations. A Muni passport also entitles you to discounts at 23 of the city's major attractions. For more information and the location of passport vendors, phone 673 6864.

Buses

San Francisco's number one mode of public transport is Muni's homely fleet of orange and white buses. Spewing smog or sparks as they make their perpetually off-schedule rounds, at least they are relatively cheap and can get you within a block or two of just about anywhere you might want to go.

Fares

Fares are $1 for adults (18-64 yrs), 35¢ for kids, and travel is free for children under five. Exact change is required, and paper money is accepted. Place your change or bills in the automatic toll taker, and ask the driver for a free transfer, which is valid for two changes of vehicle in any direction within two hours.

Bus Stops

These are marked by one or more of the following: a large white rectangle painted on the street with a red kerb; a yellow marking on a telephone or light pole; a glass-walled bus shelter; a brown and orange sign listing the bus or buses that serve that route. Route numbers are posted on the front and rear of the bus (so you know which one you've just missed). On busy lines buses run every 5-10 minutes during peak hours. Between midnight and 5am a skeleton crew operates the Owl Service – nine lines on which buses run every 30 minutes.

Outside San Francisco

Bus services operating outside the city include:

AC Transit *(817 1717)*. Alameda and Contra Costa counties and transbay service between those counties and San Francisco.
Golden Gate Transit *(332 2600)*. Marin and Sonoma counties from Sausalito to Santa Rosa.
Greyhound Bus Line *(1-800 231 2222)*. Long-distance bus routes throughout the US.

SamTrans *(1-800 660 4287)*. San Mateo county with a service to downtown San Francisco and the Hayward BART station.

Muni Metro Streetcar

A cross between an electric bus and a cable car, the Muni Metro streetcar (tram) is used surprisingly rarely by tourists. Five lines (J, K, L, M and N) run underneath the downtown area and above ground in the outer neighbourhoods; the recently revived F line is made up of restored historic streetcars that run along Market Street. Heading from east to west on Market, Muni makes the same stops as BART, but past the Civic Center the routes branch off in different directions toward outlying districts such as the Mission, Castro and Sunset. Fares are the same as on the buses, and the same passports apply. Lines run between 5am and 10pm. For schedule information, phone 673 6864.

Bay Area Rapid Transit (BART)

Looking more like a ride at Disneyland than a form of public transport, BART is a $5-billion network of four interconnected high-speed rail lines that serve San Francisco, Daly City and the East Bay counties. It's one of the most modern, automated and efficient public transport systems in the world, run by computers at the Lake Merritt BART station in Oakland. Almost everything – trains, ticket dispensers, entry and exit gates, announcements – is automated. Passengers feed money into a vending machine, which dispenses a reusable ticket encoded with the dollar amount entered. When you reach your destination, the cost of the ride (measured by the distance travelled) is deducted from the ticket as you pass through the exit gate, so don't forget to

save your ticket! Any remaining value on the ticket can be used toward the next trip.

Though BART is of little use for getting around the city – it only stops at five locations within San Francisco – it's a great way for tourists to get an inexpensive tour of the Bay Area, as much of the rail is elevated above the streets. Special excursion-ride tickets allow passengers to ride all the lines for up to three hours, but they must enter and exit from the same station, and travelling during peak hours (7am-9am and 4pm-6pm weekdays) isn't recommended.

BART stations close at around midnight and open at 4am on weekdays, 6am on Saturday and 8am on Sunday. Fares range from $1.10 to $4.45. In downtown San Francisco, four boarding stations are located along Market Street; look out for the blue and white 'ba' signs and the escalators leading down into the station. You can take bicycles on BART free of charge, except between 6.30am and 9am, and 3.30pm and 6.30pm Mon-Fri, when they are banned. For more information, phone **992 2278** (1-510 839 2220 for the hearing-impaired).

CalTrain

This commuter line connects San Francisco with San Jose and ultimately Gilroy, 'the garlic capital of the world', passing through Burlingame, Redwood City, Palo Alto, Mountain View, Sunnyvale and other peninsula cities.
It's a famously punctual rail system that runs from 5am to midnight but few tourists bother to use it. One-way adult fares range from $1.25 to $6.25 ($4.50 from San Francisco to San Jose); senior, disabled, child and off-peak discounts are available, as is a 10-ride ticket at certain trains. Bicyclists can

Taxis & limos

Getting around San Francisco in a taxicab is an interesting experience. Because the city is so small, doing so is moderately cheap – fares average $7-$10, with a base fee of $1.70 and $1.50 for each additional mile. But the trick is hiring one. If you're downtown on a weekday afternoon, you'll have little problem flagging one from a street corner. If you're in an outlying or shabbier neighbourhood, however, or if it's dinnertime, or a holiday, or raining, or the commute is heavy that day, forget about it. There just aren't enough taxis to serve the city. This aberration is due to a quirky local law limiting the number of cab licences, or medallions. In a city with 25 per cent fewer parking spaces than it has cars in business districts, cabs could easily come to San Francisco's snarled transportation rescue – but they don't: repeated attempts to deregulate the medallion monopoly have been thwarted by the cab lobby.

A few hints on hiring the elusive beasts: if you're downtown, head for the big hotels, where most have a queue of cabs lurking nearby. If you're out to dinner or shopping, ask the business to call one for you. If you're in an outlying area, phone early and often to request one, and ask the dispatcher how long you'll have to wait. If you wait longer, phone again, or call another company, and don't apologise if (by the grace of the gods) two arrive simultaneously to pick you up – just hire the one that came when promised. The cabbie you eventually do pick will probably drive like a demon anyway. Major taxicab companies include: **Luxor** (282 4141), **Veteran's** (552 1300), **Yellow** (626 2345), **National** (648 4444), **De Soto** (673 1414) and **City Wide Dispatch** (920 0700).

Limousine services include **Robertson's** (775 6024), **Pure Luxury** (485 1764), and **Silver Cloud** (1-800 640 3851), which offers an eight-hour Wine Country special for up to six people for $375. Check the phone directories for more.

---

bring their bikes onto cars displaying yellow bike symbols, and stow them in lockers at the stations at either end of their trip. For more information, phone **1-800 660 4287** (508 6448 for the hearing impaired).

Ferries

The completion of the Golden Gate Bridge in 1937 marked the end of the ferry route between San Francisco and Marin – until 1970, when the ferry service resumed to take a load off commuter traffic. Used mainly by 'suits' during the peak commuting hours, the ferries double as wonderful and inexpensive excursions across the Bay and into Sausalito – the ferry docks just steps away from the town's shopping district – or Larkspur, where a footbridge leads you to a popular shopping mall and brew pub.

For more information, phone the **Golden Gate Transit Ferry Service** (332 6600), which serves Sausalito ($2.50 one way) and Larkspur ($4.25). **Blue & Gold** runs a service to Sausalito and various cruises to Alcatraz, Angel Island, a Sonoma-Napa Wine Tour and a Muir Woods Tour, all of which leave from Pier 41. Its commuter services to Alameda, Oakland (both $4 one-way), Tiburon ($5.50) and Vallejo ($7.50) leave from the Ferry Building at the foot of Market Street on the Embarcadero. Call **705 5555** for more details; during the summer, you should book in advance for the Alcatraz trip. *See also chapter* **Trips Out of Town**.

Driving

Renting a car to explore San Francisco is crazy. There's no place to park (and parking garages charge up to $12 per hour), locals honk and curse at you for slowing them down, the steep hills fry your nerves and clutch, and you're more than likely to get a parking ticket – the city's favourite source of revenue. The only reason for renting a car is to explore the Bay Area and beyond; otherwise, forget it.

If you must drive in the city, you should know a few things before you get behind the wheel. Unless otherwise posted, the speed limit within the city is 25mph (which every local ignores) and Californian law requires all occupants to wear seatbelts. Cable cars always have the right of way, and should be given a wide berth. When parking in residential neighbourhoods, do not block driveways even *slightly*, or you'll get fined and towed away. When parking on hills, you must set the hand brake and 'kerb' your front wheels (towards the kerb when facing downhill, away from the kerb when facing uphill) – or you'll get ticketed. You must always park in the direction of the traffic.

Parking spaces in San Francisco are as rare as they are tightly regulated; immediately after parking, the visitor should read the information on the meter, then read all the signs on his or her side of the block. One missed sign could lead to a towed car, in which case you'll have to take a taxi to the nearest police station to pay the fine ($100, plus the parking ticket), then take another taxi to the tow garage and pay more money for storage fees. Most parking meters accept quarters only.

But wait – there's more! Don't park at white painted kerbs, which indicate passenger drop-off zones; at blue, which are reserved for drivers or passengers with disabilities; at yellow, which are for loading and unloading commercial vehicles. Green kerbs signify parking for 10 minutes only. Parking in some red kerbs (particularly bus zones and in front of fire hydrants) can net you a $250 ticket, even if you're just sitting in your car. For long-term parking, car parks (public garages) are your best recourse in the downtown area, particularly if you're there for more than an hour.

Should you venture outside San Francisco across the Golden Gate or Bay Bridge, make sure you have enough cash to pay the toll on the return trip ($3 Golden Gate, $1 Bay).

Car Rental

When renting a car, you will need a credit card and a driver's licence. There are dozens of car rental companies within the city and at San Francisco International Airport, and it definitely pays to shop around. Before you rent, make sure your own auto insurance or credit card company covers you; otherwise, you might have to pay an

additional surcharge. Most car rental companies have minimum and maximum age requirements.

American Automobile Association (AAA)
150 Van Ness Avenue, between Fell and Hayes Streets, CA 94102 (565 2012/touring information 565 2711/ emergency service 1-800 222 4357). **Open** 8.30am-5pm Mon-Fri. **Map F5**
The fabulous Triple A provides excellent – and free – maps, guidebooks, specific travel routes (TripTiks) and towing services to members of the AAA or an affiliated organisation (such as the British AA or RAC).

Rental Companies
National companies usually offer the best deals and service. These include **Alamo** (1-800 327 9633); **Hertz** (1-800 654 3131); **Budget** (1-800 800 4000); **Thrifty** (1-800 527 0700); **Avis** (1-800 367 2277); **Enterprise** (1-800 831 2847); **Dollar** (1-800 325 8007); and **Rent-A-Wreck** (282 6293). Local car rental companies include **Ace** (771 7711); **Bay Area Rental** (621 8989); and **A-One** (771 3977).

Car Services

Automotive Repair Bureau
(1-800 952 5210).
Investigates complaints related to repair and smog inspection services. Part of the California Department of Consumer Affairs.

CalTrans Highway Information Service
(557 3755). **Open** 24 hours daily.
You must have a touchtone telephone to access this automated service, which gives out information on the latest highway conditions. If you don't, phone 1-916 445 1534 and listen to the recorded message.

Breakdown Services

AAA Emergency Road Service
(1-800 400 4222).
Open 24 hours daily.
Members (including members of affiliated clubs, such as the British AA) receive free towing and roadside service.

Golden Gate Towing Company
(826 8866). **Open** 24 hours daily.
If you don't have a motorclub card, telephone this company for roadside service. The company will also recommend repair shops.

Car Parks

Although there are some low-cost garages, prices increase dramatically for long-term parking. Phone in advance for rates ($5-$20 a day), check the posted prices before you park and inquire about discounted (or 'validated') rates and times. If you're parking during the day, keep an eye out for a few large city lots where you can plug a parking meter by the hour. Keep a pocketful of quarters handy for this. Here are some useful, late-opening parking garages.

Ellis-O'Farrell Garage
123 O'Farrell Street, between Powell and Stockton Streets (986 4800). **Open** 5.30am-1am Mon-Thur, Sun; 5.30am-2am Fri, Sat. **Map G4**

Embarcadero Center Parking
Between Battery, Drumm, Clay and Sacramento Streets, under Embarcadero Center (398 1878). **Open** 24 hours daily. **Map H3**
At certain hours, having your ticket 'validated' at an Embarcadero establishment will decrease the rate.

Fifth & Mission Yerba Buena Gardens Garage
833 Mission Street, between Fourth and Fifth Streets (982 8522). **Open** 24 hours daily. **Map G/H4**

Japan Center Garage
1660 Geary Boulevard, between Webster and Laguna Streets (567 4573). **Open** 6.30am-2.30am Mon-Thur, Sun; 24 hours Fri, Sat. **Map E4**

Lombard Garage
2055 Lombard Street, between Webster and Fillmore Streets (440 1984). **Open** 7am-midnight Mon, Sun; 7am-1am Tue-Wed; 7am-2.30am Thur; 7am-3am Fri, Sat. **Map E2**

New Mission Bartlett Garage
3255 21st Street, between Bartlett and Valencia Streets (821 6715). **Open** 6.30am-midnight Mon-Sat; 8.30am-midnight Sun. **Castro/Mission Map Y2**

Portsmouth Square Garage
733 Kearny Street, between Clay and Washington Streets (982 6353). **Open** 24 hours daily. **Map H3**

St Mary's Garage
433 Kearny Street, between Pine and California Streets (956 8106). **Open** 24 hours daily. **Map H3**

On foot

Few American cities can compare with San Francisco's stunning topography, and none can begin to offer comparable detail and beauty to those who choose to view it using the power of their own two feet. Amazing Victorian architecture, interesting faces, enticing smells, dozens of languages and dialects and unexpected pleasures round every corner, are treasures available only to the hearty souls with the hardy soles.

Though *à pied* isn't the fastest way to see the city, it's the most enjoyable and certainly the most complete. Not until you've peeped into a passing Pacific Heights window, hiked the twisting trails in the Presidio, slurped gelato while strolling through Washington Square park or window-shopped the *panaderias* of the Mission have you truly begun to experience the pleasure of pedestrian San Francisco.

The Sunday *San Francisco Examiner and Chronicle* pink-paged Datebook supplement lists more than 20 walking tour companies, whose themes range from strolling noshes and urban hikes to waterfront tours and Castro cruises. In a city with more than its share of frustrated drivers, surly cabbies and behind-schedule bus drivers, pedestrians – for the most part – walk unimpeded, often arriving sooner (and in better physical shape) than their petrol-consuming counterparts.

However, walking the streets of San Francisco does come with inherent risks: impatient drivers tend to separate those on foot between the quick and the dead; electric buses sneak up like silent, hulking ghosts; manic, tattooed bike messengers materialise out of the fog. People double-park in crosswalks. Red-light-running is epidemic. In the Financial District, pedestrian signals work independently of stoplights. Construction crews, house painters, window-washers, ill-mannered dogs – everyone wants to try to slow a pedestrian's progress.

Don't let them. Reborn after the earthquake and fire of 1906, San Francisco isn't the US's favourite tourist city for nothing, and if you want to savour the most detail and view it all from the best possible vantage point, lace up your walking shoes, pack some extra socks, and hit the pavement. The Church of John Coltrane, Balmy Alley murals, the gardens on Filbert Steps, the sidewalk plaque outside Harvey Milk's former camera shop – you'll miss them all if you're sitting in a vehicle. Seeing San Francisco on foot is the best-kept secret in the city. For details of walking – and other – tours, *see chapter* **Sightseeing**.

Sutter-Stockton Garage

444 Stockton Street, between Sutter and Bush Streets (982 8370). **Open** 24 hours daily. **Map G3**

Vallejo Street Garage

766 Vallejo Street, between Stockton and Powell Streets (989 4490). **Open** 7am-2am Mon-Sat; 9am-midnight Sun. **Map G2**

Union Square Garage

333 Post Street, enter on Geary Street between Stockton and Powell Streets (397 0631). **Open** 24 hours daily. **Map G3/4**

By Bicycle

The San Francisco Department of Parking and Traffic recently designated a grid of major bicycle routes that criss-cross the city, indicated by oval-shaped bike-and-bridge markers. North-south routes employ odd numbers; east-west routes even; full-colour signs indicate primary crosstown routes; neighbourhood routes appear in green and white. Look in the *Yellow Pages* ('Local Area Pages') for a route map or call **585 2453** for more details.

In addition, two scenic cycle routes – one from Golden Gate Park south to Lake Merced, the other from the southern end of Golden Gate Bridge north to Marin County – invite cyclists to share the road with the ubiquitous automobile.

Bicycles can be hired for around $25 per day or $125 per week. Always lock your bike when you're not riding it, or you'll be sacrificing your damage deposit for stolen goods. For a list of rental companies, *see chapter* **Sport & Fitness**.

By Motorcycle

What better way to see San Francisco than straddling a big fat hog? Easy riders should head for **Dubbelju Motorcycle Rentals** (271 Clara Street, between Fifth and Sixth Streets; 495 2774), which can set you up with a Harley ($111 one day) or BMW (from $92) of your choice, as long as you have a valid driver's licence, cash or credit card deposit (from $500 per day) and plenty of dollars burning a hole in your pocket. The **American Scooter and Cycle** company (2715 Hyde Street, between North Point and Beach Streets; 931 0234) is a bit more expensive but also rents out scooters from $45 per day; it's open from 9am until 10pm daily. If you're scooting, be especially aware of the dangers when driving near rails, paint stripes and wet pavements.

Resources

Business

For business-friendly hotels, *see chapter* **Accommodation**.

Convention Centres

Moscone Convention Center
Howard Street, between Third and Fourth Streets (974 4000). Bus 12, 15, 30, 45, 76. **Map H4**
The homely patriarch of the Yerba Buena Gardens complex, this 83,610sq m (900,000sq ft) exhibition centre nearly doubled its original working space after Moscone North was completed in 1992. Named after assassinated mayor George Moscone, it is the city's premier convention complex.

Courier Services

Local messenger and delivery services include the 24-hour Corporate Express (1-800 695 9732/536 0994), which promises under two-hour delivery to locations within the Bay Area; **Quicksilver Messenger Service** (495 4360), famous for its daring bikers; and **Aero Special Delivery** (1-800 443 8333), which specialises in statewide message and parcel delivery. The **Post Office** (1-800 222 1811) can deliver overnight to most US cities and, in some neighbourhoods, delivers express parcels on Sundays. Check the *Yellow Pages* for more companies.

DHL
(1-800 225 5345). **Open** 24-hours daily. **Credit** AmEx, DC, Disc, MC, V.
One of the most competitive delivery companies; ring for details and drop-off deadlines.

Federal Express
(24-hour 1-800 238 5355). **Open** 7am-9pm Mon-Sat. **Credit** AmEx, DC, MC, V.
One of the biggest courier services, FedEx has five downtown offices and distribution warehouses near the Moscone Convention Center and at both the San Francisco and Oakland airports. Phone for opening hours of pick-up places.

UPS
(24-hour 1-800 742 5877). **Open** 7.30am-8pm Mon-Fri. **Credit** (deliveries by air only) AmEx, MC, V.
Account holders can phone anytime during the business day for a pick-up; non-account holders must phone a day in advance.

Libraries

Law Library
401 Van Ness Avenue, at McAllister Street (554 6821). Bus 5, 42, 47, 49. **Open** 8.30am-5pm Mon-Fri. **Map F4**

Business facts

There are, arguably, only one or two other cities in the US that can match San Francisco's simultaneous qualifications as a world-class holiday and business destination. From recent MacWorld Conferences to the 50th Anniversary gala held for the United Nations, conventions annually draw 1.2 million participants to the city. Based on a 1993 survey, city Visitor and Convention Bureau officials say that seven million of San Francisco's 16 million yearly visitors perform at least a day or two for their bosses back home. Of that number, some 5.5 million are in town primarily for business meetings or conventions.

BAY AREA INDUSTRIES
The city and its greater Bay Area zone of influence are home to several of the country's biggest companies. Besides banking (the city is home to the Pacific Stock Exchange, a Federal Reserve Bank and the California State Banking Department, as well as Bank of America, Wells Fargo Bank and Charles Schwab & Co) the region's list of resident corporations covers industries such as telecommunications, bio-medical technology, law, shipping and clothes manufacturing.

High technology is also big business here. Silicon Valley, the name given to the stretch of the Bay Area from south of Redwood City to San Jose, is where the first working models of personal computers were developed some 25 years ago. Apple Computers, Sun Microsystems, Hewlett Packard, Intel and Advanced Micro Devices are all based in Silicon Valley. The city's revived South Park area has been nicknamed Multimedia Gulch because of the ever-growing number of small companies that fuse computers, graphics, information and art.

Open to the public for research, but only San Francisco-based lawyers can borrow books and materials.

Mechanics Institute's Library

57 Post Street, between Montgomery and Kearny Streets (421 1750). BART Montgomery/Muni Metro F, J, K, L, M, N/bus 2, 3, 4, 30, 45, 76. **Open** 9am-9pm Mon-Thur; 9am-6pm Fri; 10am-5pm Sat; 1pm-5pm Sun. **Admission** $10 research pass; $25 weekly pass. **Map H3**

This private, non profit-making organisation offers many of the same data sources as the Main Library, especially CD-ROM-based search tools, but in only a fraction of the space. Its true source of fame, however, lies in its chess room (421 2258; open 11am-10.50pm, Mon-Fri), which has long been considered one of the best places in town for a quiet game.

San Francisco Main Library

See chapter **Sightseeing** *for listings.* The Main Library offers access to annual reports from most major US and Bay Area corporations; Standard & Poors evaluations of publicly owned companies; the Dunn and Bradstreet Business Database; Securities and Exchange Commission data on US businesses; computerised private service and government-offered information on population and commercial demographics; US Census information; environmental compliance records; medical news and statistics. Phone **557 4488** for the Business Reference Section. Visitors can also gain access to the Lexis/Nexis service and its business databases.

You don't need a library card to do in-house research or read back-dated newspapers and magazines. The research desk's librarians are among the best trained in the business and information professionals – journalists, in particular – often seek their help.

Message Services

American Voice Mail

(1-800 347 2861). **Open** 5am-7pm Mon-Fri; 7am-4pm Sat. **Credit** (after first payment only) MC, V. Set up your own confidential voicemail service for unlimited phone messages, 24 hours a day.

Mail Boxes Etc USA

2269 Chestnut Street, between Scott and Pierce Streets (922 4500). Bus 28, 43, 76. **Open** 9am-6pm Mon-Fri; 10am-4pm Sat. **Credit** AmEx, DC, Disc, MC, V. **Map D2**

Services include passport photos, business cards, mailbox rental, mail forwarding, packing and shipping.

Office Services

Copy Central

425 California Street, between Sansome and Montgomery Streets (392 3373). Bus 1, 12, 15, 42, 83/cable car California. **Open** 8am-10pm Mon-Fri; 9am-2pm Sat. **Credit** AmEx, MC, V. **Map H3**

One of a dozen franchised shops specialising in photocopying, printing, fax and overnight mail delivery services. Copy Central is trying to compete with Kinko's and though they're not open 24 hours, they're nearly as successful. Many have attached computer centres. Staff are friendly and helpful.

Kinko's

201 Sacramento Street, at Davis Street (834 0240). BART Embarcadero/Muni Metro F, J, K, L, M, N/bus 1, 41. **Open** 24 hours daily. **Credit** AmEx, MC, V. **Map H3**

Kinko's numerous outlets are strategically located and offer an array of user-friendly business machines for temporary hire; phone 1-800 254 6567 for your nearest branch. Services include on-site use of computers, online facilities, typesetting, printing, photocopying, fax and overnight mail delivery and collection via Federal Express. Be prepared to queue.

Office Depot

855 Harrison Street, between Fourth and Fifth Streets (243 9959). Bus 27, 30, 42, 45, 76. **Open** 7am-8pm Mon-Fri; 9am-6pm Sat; 10am-6pm Sun. **Credit** AmEx, Disc, MC, V. **Map H4**

Photocopying, printing, desktop publishing, custom stamps, engraved signs, fax devices and every office product on the planet.

Consulates

For a complete list, consult the *Yellow Pages*, or phone directory assistance (411).

Australia *362 6160.*
Britain *981 3030.*
Canada *1-213 346 2700.*
Delegation of the European Commission to the United States (Washington DC) *1-202 862 9500.*
France *397 4330.*
Germany *775 1061.*
Republic of Ireland *392 4214.*
Italy *931 4924.*
The Netherlands *981 6454.*
New Zealand *399 1255.*

Consumer Information

Better Business Bureau

(243 9999).
Provides information on the reliability of a company or service and a list of companies with good business records. The Bureau also has referral listings for anything from plumbers to auto repair and is the place to call to file a complaint about a company.

California Attorney General's Office Public Inquiry Unit

(1-800 952 5225).
This office reviews consumer complaints. Call to make a complaint on consumer law enforcement or any other agency.

Disabled Information

See also page 250 **Disabled Access.**

Braille Institute

(1-800 272 4553). **Open** 9am-4pm Mon-Fri.
Volunteers at the institute connect anyone who has reading difficulties with services for the blind throughout the US.

Crisis Line for the Handicapped

(1-800 426 4263). **Open** 24 hours daily.
A talk line and referral service offering advice on topics ranging from transport to stress.

DIRECT LINK for the disABLED

(1-800 221 6827 ext 7130).
Open 8am-1pm Mon-Fri.
Information on disability-related needs and referrals to local, state and national resources.

Gay & Lesbian

Gay & Lesbian Medical Association

(255 4547). **Open** 9.30am-5.30pm Mon-Fri.
Over 1,800 gay, lesbian and bisexual physicians and medical students make up this professional organisation, which publishes guides, holds forums, advocates rights of gay and lesbian physicians and offers medical referrals.

Community United Against Violence

(333 4357). **Open** 24 hours daily.

A counselling group assisting gay and lesbian victims of domestic violence and hate crimes.

Lyon-Martin Women's Health Services

1748 Market Street, at Valencia Street, between Octavia and Gough Streets (565 7667). Muni Metro F, J, K, L, M, N. **Open** 8.30am-5pm Mon, Tue, Thur, Fri; 8.30am-7pm Wed. **Credit** MC, V. **Map F5**
Named after two of the founders of the modern lesbian movement in the US, the Lyon-Martin clinic offers affordable health care for women in a lesbian-friendly environment. Phone to make an appointment.

New Leaf

(626 7000). **Open** 9am-5pm Mon-Fri.
A counselling service for gay men, lesbians and bisexuals, dealing with issues ranging from substance abuse to HIV.

Parents, Families and Friends of Lesbians and Gays (P-FLAG)

(921 8850). **Open** 24-hour answerphone.
Helpline offering support for families and friends of gay and lesbian teens and adults.

See also **Helplines & Agencies** *below.*

Clinics

Haight Ashbury Free Clinic

558 Clayton Street, at Haight Street (487 5632). Muni Metro N/bus 6, 7, 33, 37, 43, 66, 71. **Open** 1-4pm, 6-8pm Mon-Wed; 1-4pm Thur; 1.5pm Fri; otherwise, 24-hour answerphone
Map C6
Free primary health care is provided to anyone who needs it. Speciality clinics include chiropody, chiropractics, pediatrics and HIV testing. You will need to make an appointment.

Planned Parenthood Clinics

815 Eddy Street, between Van Ness Avenue and Franklin Street (441 5454). Bus 19, 31, 42, 47, 49. **Open** 9am-6pm Mon, Wed, Fri; 9am-7pm Tue, Thur; 9am-1.30pm Sat. **Credit** MC, V. **Map F4**
The morning-after pill is $15. Contraception is charged on a sliding scale.
Branch: 222 Front Street, at California Street (765 6905).

Quan Yin Healing Arts Center

1748 Market Street, at Valencia Street (861 4964). Muni Metro F, J, K, L, M/bus 6, 7, 26, 66, 71. **Open** noon-6pm Mon, Tue, Thur, Fri; 11am-6pm Wed; 10am-2pm Sat. **Credit** MC, V. **Map F5**
This woman-owned centre is the best in town for acupuncture. Also herbal remedies, massage, reiki and yoga.

St Anthony Free Medical Clinic

107 Golden Gate Avenue, at Jones Street (241 8320). BART Civic Center/Muni Metro J, K, L, M, N. **Open** *drop-in clinic* 8.30am-11am Mon-Fri. **Map G4**
Free medical services for those with or without insurance. Arrive early.

Complaints

Physicians Complaint Unit

(1-800 633 2322).
Once a complaint is received by the unit, the process takes up to six months for it to be sent to the medical board for investigation.

Medical Society

(561 0853).
The Society investigates complaints from those who feel they've been overcharged for medical services.

Dentists

Dental Society Referral Service

(421 1435). **Open** 24 hours daily.
Referrals are made by the Society, based on geographic location and the services desired.

Drugstores (24-hour)

Walgreens Drugstore

3201 Divisadero Street, at Lombard Street (931 6417). Bus 28, 43. **Open** 24 hours daily. **Map D2**
Prescriptions and general drugstore purchases.
Branch: 498 Castro Street, at 18th Street (861 6276).

Emergency Rooms

You will have to pay for emergency treatment. Contact the emergency number on your travel insurance before seeking treatment and you will be directed to a hospital that will deal directly with your insurance company.
Emergency rooms are open 24-hours daily at:

Davies Medical Center

Castro Street, at Duboce Avenue (565 6060). Muni Metro N/bus 24. **Map E6**

San Francisco General Hospital

1001 Potrero Avenue, between 22nd and 23rd Streets (206 8111). Bus 9, 33, 48. **Castro/Mission Map Z2**

Saint Francis Memorial Hospital

900 Hyde Street, between Bush and Pine Streets (353 6300). Bus 1, 27/cable car California. **Map F3**

UCSF Medical Center

505 Parnassus Avenue, between Third and Hillway Avenues (476 1037). Muni Metro N/bus 6, 43, 66. **Map B/C6**

Medical Referrals

SF Medical Society Referral

(561 0853). **Open** 9am-5pm Mon-Fri. American Medical Association referrals.

AIDS/HIV

AIDS-HIV Nightline

(434 2437). **Open** 5pm-5am daily. Crisis hotline offering emotional support.

San Francisco AIDS Foundation Hotline

(863 2437/1-800 367 2437). **Open** 9am-9pm Mon-Fri; 11am-5pm Sat, Sun.
A multilingual hotline that offers the most up-to-date information related to the HIV virus, as well as advice on safe sex, taken from an enormous database of Californian services.

Alcohol/Drug Abuse

The **Haight Ashbury Free Clinic** (*see opposite* **Clinics**) runs a Drug Detox, Rehab and After Care Project, among other services.

Alcoholics Anonymous

(621 1326). **Open** 8.30am-5.30pm Mon-Fri.

Center for Substance Abuse Treatment

(1-800 662 4357). **Open** 9am-4pm Mon-Fri.

Directory

Earthquakes

It's highly unlikely that a major quake will strike during your stay, but for those who believe in being prepared, local lore has it the safest place to be during a quake is on the top of Nob Hill. Check the United States Geological Survey's website at http://quake.wr.usgs.gov/ for facts and figures, including hourly-updated maps of recent quakes in California and Nevada.

What to do during a quake

● If indoors, stay there. Keep away from windows. Get under a sturdy piece of furniture, such as a desk, or stand in a corner. If in a high-rise building, do not use elevators.
● If outdoors, get into an open area away from anything that might collapse, such as trees, buildings, bridges and power lines.
● If driving, pull over to the side of the road and stop. Avoid overpasses and power lines. Stay inside the vehicle until the shaking has stopped.
● After the earthquake, think before you act. Do not use lighters or candles or light a cigarette. Do not turn on lights or use any electrical appliances, including the telephone.

American Red Cross

(427 8000/www.crossnet.org/disaster/safety/earth.html). **Open** 8.30am-5pm Mon-Fri.
Where to find information on earthquake and disaster preparedness.

Drug Crisis Line

(362 3400/hearing-impaired 781 2224). **Open** 24 hours daily.
Call here if you need someone to talk you through a bad drug trip or want to know the effects of a particular drug, an overdose remedy or how to get into a treatment programme.

Narcotics Anonymous

(621 8600). **Open** 24 hours daily.

Child Abuse

Talk Line Child Abuse Prevention Center

(441 5437). **Open** 24 hours daily.
Trained volunteers counsel children suffering from abuse or parents involved in child abuse, and provide follow-up services.

Crime Victims

Victims of Crime Resource Center

(1-800 842 8467). **Open** 8am-6pm Mon-Fri; 24-hour answerphone Sat, Sun.
Advises victims of their rights and refers them to local resources.

Legal Help

Lawyers Committee for Civil Rights, Immigrant &

Refugee Rights Project

(543 9444).
Legal services are provided on a case-by-case basis for those seeking political asylum.

Lawyer Referral Service & Volunteer Legal Services Program

(764 1616).
Legal interviewers refer callers to experienced attorneys and attorney mediators for all legal problems, including criminal, business and immigration.

Psychiatric Emergency Services

San Francisco General Hospital

(206 8125). **Open** 24 hours daily.
Those suffering from a psychiatric breakdown or those looking for someone who has been taken by the police or paramedics for acting out of control should contact this hotline.

Rape

SF Rape Treatment Center

(821 3222). **Open** 24 hours daily.
Call here within 72 hours of a sex crime and nurses or social workers will provide counselling and guide

you through medical and legal procedures. Patients must be residents of San Francisco or victims of a crime occurring within the city.

Women Against Rape Crisis Hotline

(647 7273). **Open** 24 hours daily.
This is the place to find counselling, support and legal service for sexual assault victims and their partners.

Suicide

Suicide Prevention

(781 0500). **Open** 24 hours daily.
Trained community volunteers lend a sympathetic ear.

Left Luggage

Airport Travel Agency

(877 0422). **Open** 7am-11pm daily.
Located at the international terminal at San Francisco airport, this company will store anything from a carry-on piece of luggage to a bicycle. Prices range from $6 to $25 per item.

Lost Property

Property Control

850 Bryant Street, between Sixth and Seventh Streets (553 1377). Bus 27, 42. **Open** 8am-4.30pm Mon-Fri. **Map H5**
Make a police report and cross your fingers that you have Buddha's karma, because the likelihood of someone turning in a lost item to the cops is as good as winning the California lottery.

Public Transport

If you have left something on **Muni** transport, phone its lost-and-found office on 923 6168. For **BART**, phone 1-510 464 7090, for **AC Transit** 817 1717, **Golden Gate Transit** 923 2000 and **SamTrans** 1-800 660 4287.

Public Toilets/ Restrooms

These can be found in tourist areas such as Golden Gate Park and Fisherman's Wharf, and in shopping malls. Otherwise, don't hesitate to enter a restaurant or a bar and ask to use its facilities. In keeping with its cosmopolitan standing, San Francisco has installed 20 self-cleaning, French-designed,

Decaux lavatories throughout the high-traffic areas of the city. Keep an eye out for the forest-green commodes (they're plastered with high-profile advertising). Admission is 25¢ for 20 minutes; after that, you may be fined for indecent exposure, since the door opens automatically.

Religion

San Francisco is teeming with churches, whether Baptist or Buddhist, Jewish or Jehovah's Witness, Nazarene or New Age. For more places of worship, see the *Yellow Pages*.

Calvary Presbyterian
2515 Fillmore Street, at Jackson Street (346 3832). Bus 3, 12, 22, 24. **Map E3**

Congregation Emanu-el
2 Lake Street, at Arguello Boulevard (751 2535). Bus 1, 4, 33. **Map B/C4**

First Congregational Church
495 Post Street, at Mason Street (392 7461). Bus 2, 3, 4, 38, 76/cable car Powell-Hyde, Powell-Mason. **Map G3**

Glide Memorial United Methodist Church
330 Ellis Street, at Taylor Street (771 6300). BART Powell Street/Muni Metro F, J, K, L, M, N/bus 27, 31, 38. **Map G4**

Old St Mary's Cathedral
660 California Street, at Grant Avenue (288 3800). Bus 1, 15, 30, 45/cable car California. **Map G3**

St Mary's Cathedral
1111 Gough Street, at Geary Boulevard (567 2020). Bus 2, 3, 4, 38. **Map F4**

St Paul's Lutheran Church
930 Gough Street, between Turk and Eddy Streets (673 8088). Bus 31. **Map F4**

St Vincent de Paul
2320 Green Street, at Steiner Street (922 1010). Bus 22, 41, 45. **Map E3**

Vineyard Christian Fellowship
1098 Harrison Street, at Seventh Street (558 9900). Bus 42. **Map G5**

Zen Center
300 Page Street, at Laguna Street (863 3136). Bus 6, 7, 71. **Map F5**

Rented Accommodation

Look through the Sunday *Examiner/Chronicle* classifieds or the *Yellow Pages* for apartment or house rentals to get an idea of prices. *See also chapter* **Accommodation**.

American Property Exchange
(1-800 747 7784/447 2000/ampropex@aol.com/www.we-rent-sanfran.com). **Open** 9am-5pm Mon-Fri.
Luxury accommodation in condos and apartments (studios start at $2,000 a month), and long-term lets.

Metro Rent
(563 7368).
For a fee, you'll get daily updates (even by fax) on availability in the area and price range of your choice.

Roommate & Apartment Network
(441 2309).
Refers professionals and graduates to apartments, houses, flats, studios and shared rentals.

Safety

Bay Area Model Mugging
Mailing address *Suite 104, 629 Bair Island Road, Redwood City, CA 94063 (1-800 773 4448/366 3631/www.bamm.org).* **Open** *office* 9am-5pm Mon-Fri. **Credit** MC, V.
Model Mugging offers courses in which women learn effective

defence techniques, using full force against padded male 'attackers'. Classes are held in San Francisco, the East Bay and on the Peninsula; and there are sessions for teenagers and men, too.

Students
Visas & ID Cards

To study in the Bay Area (or anywhere else in the US), you must apply for either an **F-1 visa** (for exchange students) or a **J-1 visa** (for full-time students enrolled in a degree programme). Both are valid for the duration of your course and for a limited period afterwards. Most colleges have admissions offices that give advice and information on studying in the US, including visa requirements, fees and student accommodation.

Foreign students should have an **International Student Identity Card** (ISIC) as proof of student status. This can be brought from your local travel agent or student travel office. In San Francisco, an ISIC costs $19 at Council Travel (530 Bush Street, at Grant Avenue; 421 3473) or STA (51 Grant Avenue, between Market and Geary Streets; 391 8407) – you need

Work permits

It's difficult for foreigners to find legal work in the US. Some people get illegal 'under the table' jobs (in restaurants, bars, on building sites), which offer no security or benefits and are hard to come by. If you want to work legally, a US company must sponsor you for an **H-1 visa**, which enables you to work in the country for five years.

For the visa to be approved, your employer must convince the Immigration Department that no American is qualified to do the job as well as you.

Students, however, have a much easier time. Your student union should have information on US working holidays. For information on studying over the summer, contact the Council on International Education Exchange (CIEE), Work Exchanges Dept, 205 East 42nd Street, New York, NY10017, USA. *See also above* **Students**.

Where to study

The California higher education system operates as a hierarchy, starting with publicly funded community colleges and city colleges at the lower end of the scale, followed by California State Universities, which cater primarily to undergraduates and do not grant doctorates, and, at the top, the University of California establishments, which tend to be formal, research-oriented universities with rigorous entry requirements. There are also many private – and expensive – universities such as Stanford and USF (University of San Francisco).

In general, US universities are much more flexible about part-time studying than their European counterparts. Each university has a different definition of part-time requirements; check with the college you're interested in. Non English-speaking students might have to pass a TOEFL (Test of English as a Foreign Language) test, and most students have to show proof of financial support.

STUDENT ACTIVISM

University life in San Francisco and the Bay Area today reflects a wide mix of students, scenes and schools, and the central tenet seems to be that a once-searing liberal hotbed has cooled. In the 1960s during the Civil Rights protests, Berkeley was the site of the largest arrest in state history, an 800-student skirmish that resulted in the undergraduate occupation of Sproul Hall. Students at San Francisco State shut their own campus down protesting the war in Vietnam. Though flashes of this radical mentality have ignited during certain recent California events – the Rodney King verdict in 1992 and the debates over affirmative action-eradicating Proposition 209 in 1996 are two examples – students rarely get up in arms anymore. Instead, they're more concerned with procuring a degree that will pay them well, hanging out at the local cafés and clubs and looking cool.

The Colleges

Academy of Art College

79 New Montgomery Street, CA 94105, between Mission and Market Streets (274 2200/www. academyart.edu). BART Montgomery Street/Muni Metro F, J, K, L, M, N/ bus 2, 3, 4, 5, 9, 30, 66, 71, 76. **Map H3**
Foreign students flock to this visual arts college, with satellite campuses all over the city, offering practical graduate and post-graduate courses in fine arts, history and graphic design.

Art Institute of San Francisco

800 Chestnut Street, CA 94133, between Jones and Leavenworth Streets (1-800 345 7324/771 7020/www. sfai.edu). Bus 30, 42/cable car Powell-Hyde or Powell-Mason. **Map F2**
A hip and prestigious art school, offering the spectrum in fine arts including painting, film, photo, sculpture and new genres. Expensive but well-respected, SFAI has a good reputation for fostering one-on-one apprenticeships for its students. Its student exhibitions are legendary.

City College of San Francisco

50 Phelan Avenue, CA 94112, at Ocean Avenue (main switchboard 239 3000/international students 239 3837/www.ccsf.cc.ca.us). *Muni Metro J, K, M/bus 15, 29, 36, 43, 49.*
The largest community college in the US, City teaches more than 80 subjects on its eight campuses and 150 satellite sites. It's the most affordable place to study in

proof of studenthood, ID and a passport-size photo. Both also offer student discounts.

Accommodation

Unfortunately, cheap short-term accommodation is limited in San Francisco. Unless you're a student who has paid his/her tuition, you will find that on-campus accommodation is not available. It's even more difficult to find in Berkeley. However, both full- and part-time students at Berkeley can live in dorms or use the useful student housing information service (the Community Living Office, 1-510 642 3642) to find off-campus lodgings. Berkeley also offers summer visitor housing in its dorms from 1 June-11 August (call the conference office on 1-510 642 4444 for more information). *See also page 263 and chapter* **Accommodation**.

YMCA Golden Gate

220 Golden Gate Avenue, CA 94102, at Leavenworth Street (885 0460/fax 885 5439). BART Civic Center/Muni Metro F, J, K, L, M, N/bus 19, 31. **Rates** shared room $29.99; private room $39.99. **Credit** MC, V. **Map G4**
A YMCA open to men and women, though the grim Tenderloin environment may be enough to encourage you to look elsewhere.

Student Shopping

There is a multitude of ways for penniless students to spend their money in San

the city and a good choice for a foreign language or computer class over the summer.

Mills College
5000 MacArthur Boulevard, Oakland, CA 94613 (graduate admissions 1-800 876 4557/ undergraduate admissions 1-510 430 2135/www.mills.edu). BART Coliseum, then AC Transit bus 57, 58 to main entrance at Richards Gate/bus N from Transbay Terminal to Richards Gate.
A prestigious liberal women's college in Oakland, founded in 1852, Mills now admits men at graduate level. It offers excellent MFA courses in art and creative writing.

San Francisco Conservatory of Music
1201 Ortega Street, CA 94122, at 19th Avenue (564 8086/ www.sfcm.edu). Bus 28.
Full- and part-time students study music at this small, independent conservatory, known for its excellent faculty and high standards. Tuition costs about $16,500 per year and there is no on-campus housing. Musical proficiency is the most important criterion for being admitted.

San Francisco State University
1900 Holloway Avenue, CA 94132, at 19th Avenue (admissions 338 1113/www.sfsu.edu). Muni Metro M/bus 17, 18, 26, 28, 29.
Like all publicly funded California schools, SFSU is trying desperately to do more with less resources. It's the largest in the city, with 27,000 students, good for creative writing, business, ethnic studies and any number of engineering disciplines. But be patient: undergrad classes are always full and many potential students are turned away at the beginning of each semester. As a result, it can take five or six years to complete a degree.

Stanford University
Stanford, CA 94305-3005. CalTrain to Palo Alto, then free Marguerite shuttle to campus (graduate admissions 723 4291/undergraduate admissions 723 2091/www. stanford.edu).
A turn-of-the-century campus near Palo Alto, this private college is out of many students' league, with tuition, room and board costing about $31,500 a year. Academically highly competitive, Stanford is known for its business, law and medicine courses.

UC Berkeley
Office of Undergraduate Admissions, 110 Sproul Hall, UC Berkeley, CA 94720-5800 (graduate admissions 1-510 642 7404/undergraduate admissions 1-510 642 3175/international students 1-510 642 3246/ www. berkeley.edu). BART Berkeley, then walk up Center Street.
The oldest campus in the nine-campus University of California system, some 30,000 students attend Berkeley (called 'Cal' by locals), including 9,000 postgrads. Famous for law and engineering, Berkeley also runs a controversial nuclear research lab in Livermore, an East Bay suburb.

UC Berkeley Extension
English Language Programme, 55 Laguna Street, CA 94102, between Haight and Market Streets (course information and registration 1-510 642 4111/ www.unex. berkeley.edu:4243). Muni Metro F/bus 6, 7, 66, 71. **Map F5**
Berkeley Extension in San Francisco and other Bay Area cities offers night and weekend courses, which can be taken by working adults for college credits, but no degree courses. Plus an excellent array of spring, summer and autumn courses in such subjects as film, the Internet, writing and women's studies.

University of California, San Francisco
400 Parnassus Avenue, CA 94143, at Fourth Avenue (476 4394/ www.ucsf.edu). Muni Metro N/bus 6, 43, 66. **Map B6**
A Top-notch health and sciences university with schools of medicine, dentistry, pharmacy and nursing. UCSF also operates one of the best and least-expensive campuses in the city for good health care. Admission to the school is rigorous but not impossible.

University of San Francisco
2130 Fulton Street, CA 94117, at Masonic Avenue (admissions 422 6563/financial aid 422 6303/ www. usfca.edu). Bus 5, 31, 43. **Map C/D5**
One of 28 Jesuit universities and colleges in the US, with a pleasant campus near the Haight district and a liberal, humanistic ethos, USF has reputable business, communication arts and law programmes. Undergraduates and graduates account for some 4,000 each; foreign students make up 10% of the intake. Undergrad tuition costs $16,000 plus $7,220 to live on campus per year and international students must show proof of financial support.

Francisco. The best neighbourhoods for students include the Haight (upper and lower), the Mission and Polk. **Community Thrift** (623 Valencia Street, between 17th and 18th Streets; 861 4910) is a huge second-hand store, with clothes, books, electronics and kitchen equipment. Just down the street at **Clothes Contact** (473 Valencia Street, between 15th and 16th Streets; 621 3212), you can find vintage clothing sold by the pound.

San Francisco is also well endowed with bookshops selling new and second-hand titles. The mecca for second-hand bookshops is the Mission district: check out the **Adobe Bookstore** (3166 16th Street, between Valencia and Guerrero Streets; 864 3936), **Forest Books** (3080 16th Street, at Valencia Street; 863 2755) and **Dog-Eared Books** (1173 Valencia Street, between 22nd and 23rd Streets; 282 1901).

Record stores have a hard time making a go of it in the city, but try **Recycled** (1377 Haight Street; 626 4075) and the huge new **Amoeba** on the same street (1855 Haight Street; 831 1200). Smaller stores worth checking out include **Open Mind Music** (342 Divisadero Street, at Oak Street; 621 2244) and **Medium Rare** (2310 Market Street, at Noe Street; 255 7273). For more options, *see also chapter* **Shopping & Services**.

Further Reading

Fiction & Poetry

Francisco X Alarcon: *Body in Flames (Cuerpo en Llamas)*
Collection of poetry in English and Spanish from leading
Chicano/Latino literary activist.

Martha Baer: *As Francesca*
Dual identities and the allure of cybersex explored by the
local author in her brilliant début novel.

Ambrose Bierce: *Can Such Things Be?*
Tales of horror and the downright horrible.

Marci Blackman, Trebor Healey (eds): *Beyond
Definition: New Writing from Gay & Lesbian San Francisco*
Poetry and fiction from a cross-section of queer SF.

Po Bronson: *The First $20 Million is Always the Hardest*
Over-the-top high-tech novel from hot new local author.

Ethan Canin: *Emperor of the Air, The Palace Thief*
Two excellent collections from another local novelist.

Ann Charters (ed): *The Penguin Book of the Beats*
Excerpts from novels, short stories and songs.

Allen Ginsberg: *Howl and Other Poems*
The rant that caused all the fuss.

Dashiell Hammett: *The Maltese Falcon*
One of the greatest detective novels, set in a dark and
dangerous San Francisco.

Bret Harte: *Selected Stories and Sketches*
Adventurous tales from the gold-rush era.

Jack Kerouac: *On the Road, Desolation Angels,
The Dharma Bums, Some of the Dharma*
Drugs and sex in San Francisco and around the world,
from the most famous Beat of them all.

Ken Kesey: *One Flew Over the Cuckoo's Nest*
Tragic, heroic yet frequently comic story of the inmates
of a mental institution.

Maxine Hong Kingston: *The Woman Warrior*
Childhood and family history of a Chinese-American.

Jack London: *Tales of the Fish Patrol, John Barleycorn*
Early works, set in London's native San Francisco.

Armistead Maupin: *Tales of the City* (6 volumes)
Witty soap opera following the lives and loves of a group
of friends in the sexually liberated 1970s and sobering
post-AIDS 1980s.

Frank Norris: *McTeague*
Working class life and loss set in unromanticised
Barbary Coast days.

Thomas Pynchon: *The Crying of Lot 49, Vineland*
Funny, wild novels set in Northern California.

John Steinbeck: *East of Eden, The Grapes of Wrath*
Grim tales of California in the Depression.

Amy Tan: *The Joy Luck Club*
Exploration of the lives of several generations of Chinese,
and Chinese-American women.

Mark Twain: *The Celebrated Jumping Frog of
Calaveras County, From Scotland to Silverado, Roughing It*
Brilliant tales of San Francisco and early California.

Tom Wolfe: *The Electric Kool-Aid Acid Test,
The Pump House Gang*
Alternative life-styles in trippy, hippy, 1960s California.

Non-fiction

Walton Bean: *California: An Interpretive History*
Anecdotal account of California's sometimes shady past.

California Coastal Commission: *California Coastal
Access Guide*
Accessible guide to the coastal regions.

Carolyn Cassady: *Off the Road: My Years with
Cassady, Kerouac and Ginsberg*
Not the most enlightened of feminism, but an interesting
alternative examination of the Beats.

Joan Chatfield-Taylor: *San Francisco Opera:
The First 75 Years*
Richly-illustrated chronicle of the SFO's diverse history.

Randolph Delehanty: *The Ultimate Guide: San Francisco*
Meticulously researched compendium of 13 walking tours
through the city.

Joan Didion: *Slouching Towards Bethlehem,
The White Album*
Brilliant essays examining contemporary California.

Lawrence Ferlinghetti and Nancy J Peters:
Literary San Francisco
One of the better accounts of the literary circles that have
always been part of the city's history.

Robert Greenfield: *Dark Star: An Oral Biography of
Jerry Garcia*
The life and (high) times of the Grateful Dead's late
frontman.

James D Hart: *A Companion to California*
Hefty tome listing almost every category imaginable
from the origins of street names to literary history.

Don Herron: *The Literary World of San Francisco*
Vital and precise account of San Francisco's literary history.

Bert Katz: *16th Street: Faces in the Mission*
A photo collection of several Mission residents.

Oscar Lewis: *San Francisco: Mission to Metropolis*
Vintage photos and paintings, with a commentary on the
natural and urban environment.

Malcolm Margolin (ed): *The Way We Lived: California
Indian Stories, The Ohlone Way*
Accounts of the Bay Area's first inhabitants.

John Miller (ed): *San Francisco Stories: Great Writers
on the City.*
Includes contributions by Herb Caen, Anne Lamott, Amy
Tan, Ishmael Reed and many others.

Ray Mungo: *San Francisco Confidential*
A gossipy look at what goes on behind closed doors in
San Francisco.

Joel Selvin: *San Francisco: The Magical History Tour*
Guide to the sights and sounds of the city's pop music
history by the Chronicle's pop music critic.

Randy Shilts: *The Mayor of Castro Street*
On the rising political career of Harvery Milk and the
development of gay politics.

Sally Socolich: *Bargain Hunting in the Bay Area*
A must for shopaholics.

Gertrude Stein: *The Making of Americans*
Autobiographical work that includes an account of her
early childhood in Oakland.

Robert Louis Stevenson: *An Inland Voyage, The
Silverado Squatters*
Autobiographical narratives describing the journey from
rural Europe to western America.

Ronald Takaki: *Strangers from a Different Shore: A
History of Asian Americans*
A survey of immigration in North America.

Hunter S Thompson: *The Great Shark Hunt, Hell's
Angels*
Drug and alcohol-fuelled accounts of political campaigns,
popular culture and chain-whippings.

Sally & John Woodbridge: *San Francisco
Architecture*
The best of many books on the city's architecture.

Index

W

Y

Z

T

U

V

Advertisers' Index

Please refer to the relevant sections for
addresses/telephone numbers

Section sponsored by
AT&T

Maps

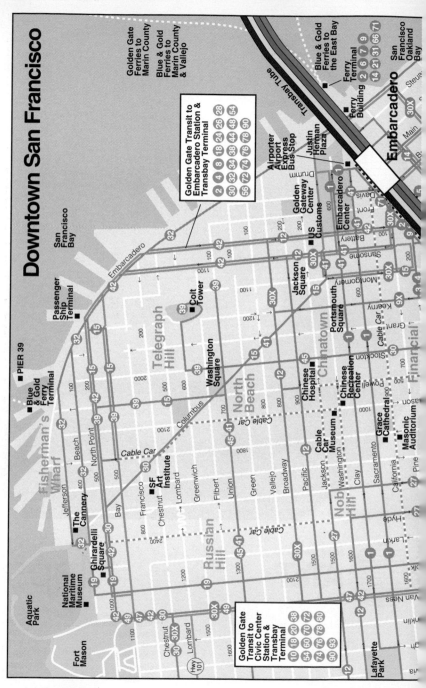

Downtown San Francisco

Golden Gate Ferries to Marin County

Blue & Gold Ferries to Marin County & Vallejo

Blue & Gold Ferries to the East Bay

Ferry Terminal

Ferry Building

San Francisco Oakland Bay

Embarcadero

Golden Gate Transit to Embarcadero Station & Transbay Terminal

Airporter Airport Express Bus Stop

Justin Herman Plaza

Transbay Tube

Golden Gateway Center

US Customs

Embarcadero Center

San Francisco Bay

Passenger Ship Terminal

Embarcadero

Jackson Square

Portsmouth Square

Coit Tower

Telegraph Hill

Washington Square

North Beach

Chinese Hospital

Chinatown

Chinese Recreation Center

Cable Car Museum

PIER 39

Blue & Gold Ferry Terminal

Fisherman's Wharf

Cable Car

SF Art Institute

Grace Cathedral

Masonic Auditorium

Nob Hill

Russian Hill

Cable Car

Ghirardelli Square

National Maritime Museum

Aquatic Park

Fort Mason

The Cannery

Golden Gate Transit to Civic Center Station & Transbay Terminal

Lafayette Park

Financial

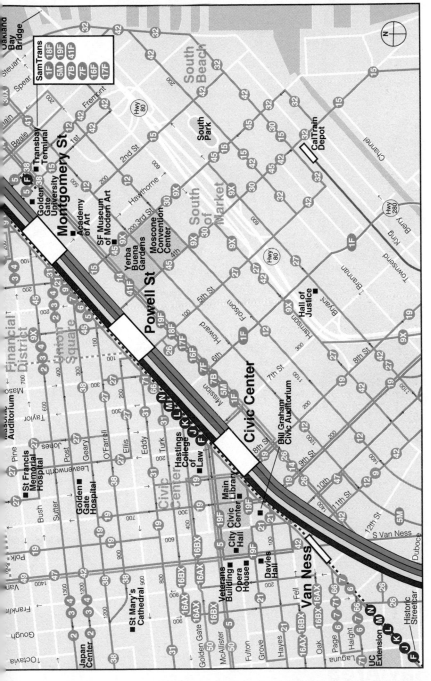

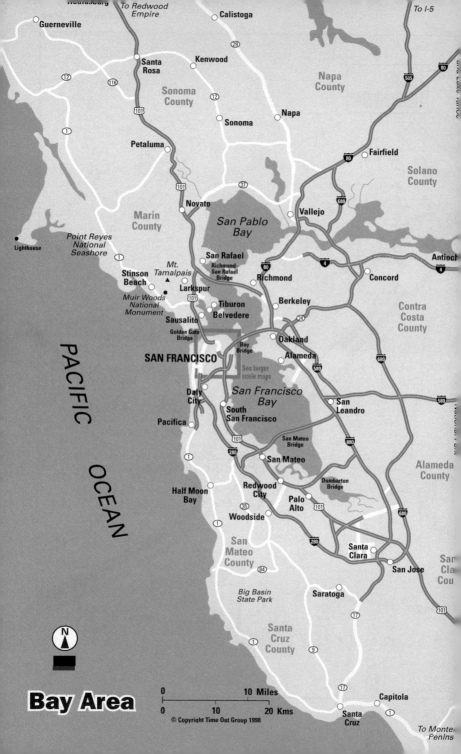

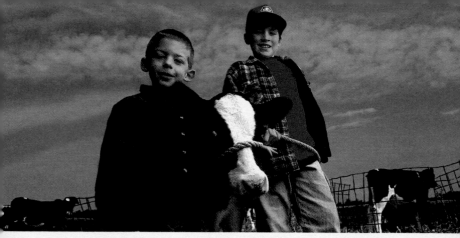

HOW TO GET FROM PEORIA TO PRETORIA.

© 1997 AT&T

AND 1 800 CALL ATT® GETS YOU
FROM THE U.S. TO THE WORLD.

It's all within your reach.

Street Index

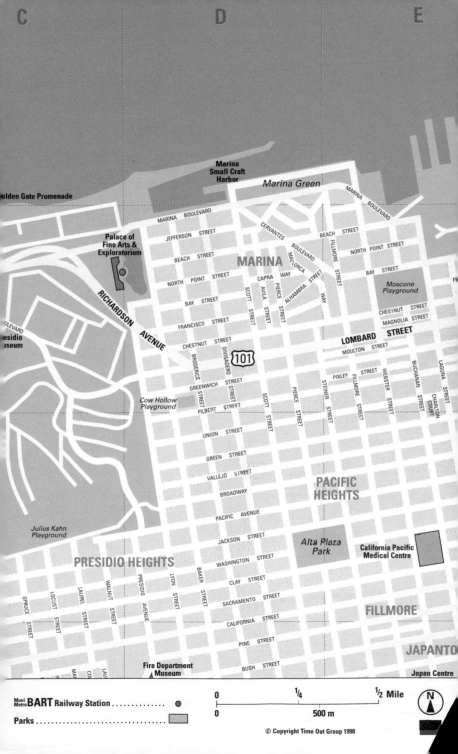

E F G

Municipal
Pier

Hyde Street
Pier

45

Fisherman's
Wharf

47

41

43

Pier
39

Aquatic
Park

JEFFERSON STREET

The
Cannery

The
Anchorage

BEACH STREET

Maritime
Museum

Cable
Car

FISHERMAN'S
WHARF

NORTH POINT STREET

Fort Mason
Center

BAY STREET

Cable
Car

North
Beach
Playground

Ghirardelli
Square

FRANCISCO STREET

CHESTNUT STREET

NORTH
BEACH

EVARD

NT STREET

BAY STREET

FRANCISCO STREET

Moscone
Playground

Lombard Street

LOMBARD STREET

GREENWICH STREET

COLUM

POWELL

STREET

CHESTNUT STREET

MAGNOLIA STREET

STREET

RUSSIAN
HILL

FILBERT STREET

GREENWICH STREET

MASON STREET

TAYLOR STREET

JONES STREET

LEAVENWORTH STREET

HYDE STREET

LARKIN STREET

POLK STREET

FRANKLIN STREET

GOUGH STREET

OCTAVIA STREET

LAGUNA STREET

BUCHANAN STREET

WEBSTER STREET

UNION STREET

GREEN STREET

VALLEJO STREET

Octagon House

CHARLTON COURT

Tunnel

PACIFIC AVENUE

JACKSON STREET

BROADWAY

Cable Car
Barn

WASHINGTON STREET

101

Haas-Lilienthal
House

CLAY STREET

NOB
HILL

SACRAMENTO STREET

Huntingdon
Park

Lafayette
Park

VAN NESS AVENUE

Cable
Car

CALIFORNIA STREET

Grace
Cathedral

nia Pacific
cal Centre

PINE STREET

BUSH STREET

AUSTIN STREET

FILMORE

SUTTER STREET

FERN STREET

POST STREET

HEMLOCK STREET

JAPANTOWN

CEDAR STREET

GEARY STREE

TENDERLOIN

O'FARRELL

Japan Centre

Peace
Plaza

Glide

A B C D E F G H J
1
2

Points of Interest . . . .

Neighbourhoods . . . . FILLMORE

Hospital or College . . . .

Visitor Information Center . . . . 🛈

H   J

1

San Francisco Bay

35 **Cruise Ship Terminal**

33

31

27

19

17

15

9

7

5

3

1

TELEGRAPH HILL

Coit Tower

GRANT AVENUE
ngton are
AVENUE

Washington Square

SANSOME STREET

BATTERY STREET

THE EMBARCADERO

KEARNY STREET

MONTGOMERY STREET

FRONT STREET

DAVIS STREET

BROADWAY

JACK KEROUAC ALLEY

GOLD ST

FINANCIAL DISTRICT

Jackson Square

CHINATOWN

Portsmouth Square

WAVERLY PLACE

Transamerica Pyramid

COMMERCIAL STREET

Wells Fargo Museum

Bank of California

Golden Gateway Center

Embarcadero Center

DRUMM STREET

Justin Herman Plaza

Ferry Building

BATTERY STREET

FRONT STREET

DAVIS STREET

Cable Car

Old St Mary's Cathedral

Bank of America

Merchant's Exchange

SANSOME STREET

Stock Exchange

Muni Metro BART Embarcadero

STEUART STREET

SPEAR STREET

San Francisco Oakland Bay Bridge

3

80

24

Chinatown Gateway

MONTGOMERY STREET

CLAUDE LANE

KEARNY STREET

MARKET STREET

MAIN STREET

BEALE STREET

26

Crocker Galleria

GRANT AVENUE

STOCKTON STREET

MAIDEN LANE

Union Square

POWELL STREET

Muni Metro BART Montgomery St

NEW MONTGOMERY STREET

MISSION STREET

MINNA STREET

2nd STREET

Transbay Terminal & Greyhound Bus Depot

1st STREET

FREMONT STREET

SPEAR STREET

28

30

32

Center for the Arts

HOWARD STREET

3rd

HAWT

Cable

Muni Metro **BART** Railway Station . . . . ●

Parks . . . .

0   ¼   ½ Mile

0   500 m

© Copyright **Time Out Group** 1998

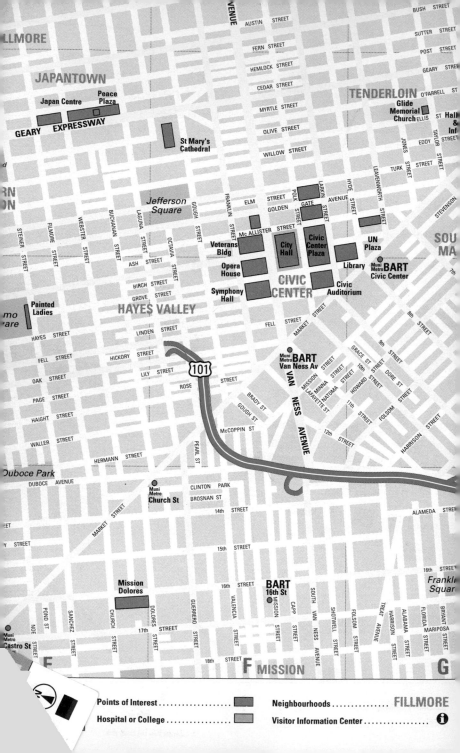

Union Square

Crocker Galleria

& Greyhound Bus Depot

BART Montgomery St

Cable Car

Plaza

Center for the Arts

Moscone Center North

Yerba Buena Gardens

SFMOMA

SF Shopping Center

BART Powell St

Moscone Center South

Old Mint

SOUTH BEACH

South Park

THE EMBARCADERO

4

South of Market Park

CalTrain Depot

China Basin

Mission Rock Terminal

5

Concourse Exhibition Center

Fashion Center

DIVISION STREET

280

Jackson Park

POTRERO HILL

H

101

Central Basin

6

J

BART Railway Station .... ●

Parks ....

0   ¼   ½ Mile

0   500 m

© Copyright Time Out Group 1998

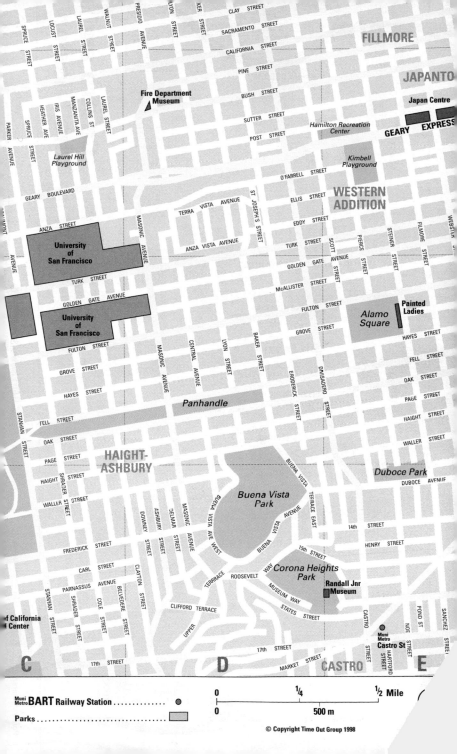

FILLMORE

JAPANTO

CLAY STREET
SACRAMENTO STREET
CALIFORNIA STREET
PINE STREET
BUSH STREET
SUTTER STREET
POST STREET
O'FARRELL STREET
ELLIS STREET
EDDY STREET
TURK STREET
GOLDEN GATE AVENUE
McALLISTER STREET
FULTON STREET
GROVE STREET
HAYES STREET
FELL STREET
OAK STREET
PAGE STREET
HAIGHT STREET
WALLER STREET

Japan Centre
GEARY   EXPRESS

Fire Department
Museum

Hamilton Recreation
Center

Kimbell
Playground

WESTERN
ADDITION

Laurel Hill
Playground

GEARY   BOULEVARD

TERRA   VISTA   AVENUE
ANZA   STREET
ANZA   VISTA   AVENUE

University
of
San Francisco

TURK   STREET

GOLDEN   GATE   AVENUE

University
of
San Francisco

FULTON   STREET

GROVE   STREET

HAYES   STREET

FELL   STREET

OAK   STREET

PAGE   STREET

HAIGHT   STREET

WALLER   STREET

Panhandle

Alamo
Square

Painted
Ladies

HAIGHT-
ASHBURY

Buena Vista
Park

Duboce Park
DUBOCE   AVENUE

14th   STREET

HENRY   STREET

Corona Heights
Park

Randall Jnr
Museum

15th   STREET

ROOSEVELT

CLIFFORD   TERRACE

MUSEUM   WAY

STATES   STREET

Muni
Metro
Castro St

17th   STREET

17th   STREET

MARKET   STREET

CASTRO

of California
Center

FREDERICK   STREET

CARL   STREET

PARNASSUS   AVENUE

C   D   E

MASONIC   AVENUE
CENTRAL   AVENUE
LYON   STREET
BAKER   STREET
FREDERICK   STREET
DIVISADERO
SCOTT   STREET
PIERCE   STREET
STEINER   STREET
FILMORE   STREET
WEBSTER
WALNUT   STREET
LAUREL   STREET
COLLINS   ST
MANZANITA AVE
IRIS   AVENUE
HEATHER   AVE
SPRUCE   STREET
LOCUST   STREET
LAUREL   STREET
PRESIDIO   AVENUE
LYON   STREET
KER   STREET
ST   JOSEPH'S   STREET
PARKER   AVENUE
SPRUCE   STREET
HEATHER   AVE
STANYAN   STREET
SHRADER   STREET
DOWNEY
ASHBURY
DELMAR
MASONIC   AVENUE
BUENA   VISTA   AVE   WEST
BUENA   VISTA   AVENUE
TERRACE   EAST
TERRRACE
CLAYTON   STREET
BELVEDERE   STREET
COLE   STREET
STANYAN   STREET
SHRADER   STREET
UPPER
CASTRO   STREET
POND   ST
NOE   STREET
HARTFORD   STREET
SANCHEZ
STREET

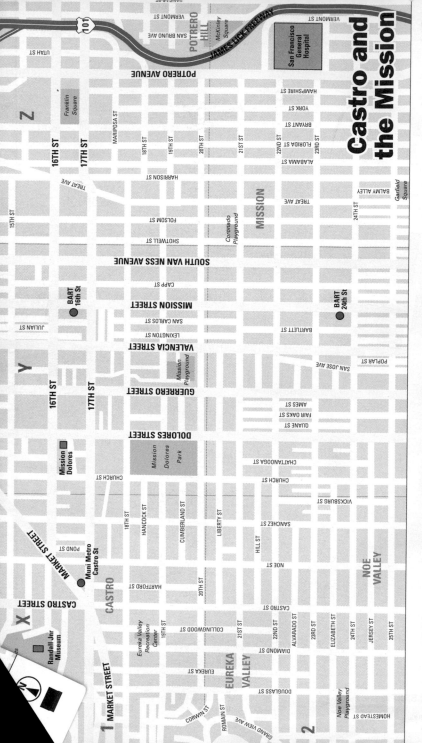

Castro and
the Mission

N

Points of Interest........ Neighbourhoods......... MISSION Muni Metro / BART Railway Station...... ●

0 ¼ ½ Mile

Map labels

101

UTAH ST

JAMES LICK FREEWAY
SAN BRUNO AVE
POTRERO HILL
McKinley Square
VERMONT ST
VERMONT ST

POTRERO AVENUE

Franklin Square

San Francisco General Hospital

HAMPSHIRE ST
YORK ST
BRYANT ST
FLORIDA ST
BRYANT ST
ALABAMA ST

MARIPOSA ST
18TH ST
19TH ST
20TH ST
21ST ST
22ND ST

16TH ST
17TH ST

N

TREAT AVE

HARRISON ST

15TH ST

TREAT AVE
24TH ST
Balmy Alley
Garfield Square

MISSION

FOLSOM ST

SHOTWELL ST

Coronado Playground

SOUTH VAN NESS AVENUE

CAPP ST

BART 16th St

JULIAN ST

MISSION STREET

SAN CARLOS ST
LEXINGTON ST

VALENCIA STREET

BART 24th St

BARTLETT ST

Y

16TH ST
17TH ST

GUERRERO STREET

Mission Playground

POPLAR ST

SAN JOSE AVE

DOLORES STREET

Mission Dolores

AMES ST
FAIR OAKS ST
DUANE ST

CHATTANOOGA ST

CHURCH ST

Mission Dolores Park

VICKSBURG ST

CHURCH ST

18TH ST
HANCOCK ST
CUMBERLAND ST
LIBERTY ST

SANCHEZ ST

HILL ST

NOE ST

POND ST
Muni Metro Castro St

MARKET STREET

X

CASTRO STREET

Randall Jnr Museum

CASTRO

Eureka Valley Recreation Center

HARTFORD ST

19TH ST
20TH ST
21ST ST
22ND ST
23RD ST

COLLINGWOOD ST
CASTRO ST
DIAMOND ST
EUREKA ST
DOUGLASS ST

EUREKA VALLEY

ALVARADO ST
ELIZABETH ST
24TH ST
JERSEY ST
25TH ST

NOE VALLEY

Noe Valley Playground

HOMESTEAD ST
GRAND VIEW AVE
ROMAIN ST
CORWIN ST

1 2

N